The Camden House History of German Literature

Volume 10:

*German Literature of the Twentieth Century:*
*From Aestheticism to Postmodernism*

# Camden House History of German Literature

# Volume 10

---

Forthcoming volumes in
The Camden House History of German Literature:

*Vol. 1: Early Germanic Literature and Culture*
Edited by William Whobrey, Yale University

*Vol. 2: German Literature of the Early Middle Ages*
Edited by Brian Murdoch, University of Stirling, UK

*Vol. 3: German Literature of the High Middle Ages*
Edited by Will Hasty, University of Florida

*Vol. 4: Early Modern German Literature*
Edited by Max Reinhart, University of Georgia

*Vol. 5: Literature of the German Enlightenment
and Sentimentality*
Edited by Barbara Becker-Cantarino, Ohio State University

*Vol. 6: Literature of the Sturm und Drang*
Edited by David Hill, University of Birmingham, UK

*Vol. 7: The Literature of Weimar Classicism*
Edited by Simon Richter, University of Pennsylvania

*Vol. 8: The Literature of German Romanticism*
Edited by Dennis Mahoney, University of Vermont

*Vol. 9: German Literature of the Nineteenth Century,
1830–1899*
Edited by Clayton Koelb and Eric Downing,
University of North Carolina

# German Literature of the Twentieth Century

## From Aestheticism to Postmodernism

Ingo R. Stoehr

CAMDEN HOUSE

First published 2001
by Camden House

Camden House is an imprint of Boydell & Brewer Inc.
PO Box 41026, Rochester, NY 14604–4126 USA
and of Boydell & Brewer Limited
PO Box 9, Woodbridge, Suffolk IP12 3DF, UK

ISBN: 1–57113–157–4

Library of Congress Cataloging-in-Publication Data

Stoehr, Ingo Roland.
    German literature of the twentieth century: from aestheticism to postmodernism / Ingo R. Stoehr.
        p. cm. — (Camden House history of German literature; v. 10)
    Includes bibliographical references and index.
    ISBN 1-57113-157-4 (alk. paper)
    1. German literature — 20th century — History and criticism.    I. Title.
II. Series.

PT401 .S76 2001
830.9'0091—dc21

                                                                            2001025717

A catalogue record for this title is available from the British Library.

# Contents

# Preface: Premises and Questions

ALL WRITING OF HISTORY is based on interpreting the past. Instead of presenting these interpretations as facts, any history should be flexible and should not just be open to but rather actively invite dialogue. This is even more relevant in the case of literature, for which the need for interpretation is obvious. To make the dialogue easier, all German quotations are given first in translation because the book has in mind as its audience those speakers of English who are novices to German literature (though not necessarily to literature in general). However, the discussion focuses on the original texts, not any published translations. Therefore, the German titles are given first and then the translation (unless it is self-evident as in *Kolik* for "colic"), and the characters' names (such as Jakob, not Jacob) are used according to the German text. All translations used in this book are mine.

Looking at literature from a broad historical perspective is justified if it helps formulate general observations that cannot be achieved through the search for the ultimate interpretation of a single work or of a single author's vision. Studying literary history makes sense if one assumes that literature provides an artistic connection between the inside world of the human mind and the outside world in which humans live. This premise is not unproblematic; however, if it is not true to some extent, then literature has nothing to say about the world in which we live, nothing to say about us as human beings, and ultimately is of little interest and of no consequence.

This premise makes it possible to ask precise questions: What does the connection between art and life look like? How does it work? Does it change over time? And if so, how? Of course, there are more questions, including the issue of the elusive function of literature itself: Why do people read literature — for pleasure, for education, for a challenge? The answers will remain speculative to some degree; however, I suggest that these questions can only be adequately addressed within a literary history.

The concept of literature as an artistic connection between mind and world identifies the space where literary meaning emerges. Literature always produces *imaginary worlds*. There is always a difference between the work of art, which is an imaginary world after all, and the real world. This difference is the basis of aesthetic enjoyment, which is, more specifically, a result of the production of meaning in the process of creating imaginary worlds. This process takes place in a complex interaction between the literary text, its author, and its reader. Each of these elements is historically determined in the realm of literature as a social institution. For modern literature, the reader is considered to be as creative as the writer, although in a different sense: since the reader can be said to *re*write a text, the author can similarly be assumed to *pre*-read that text. This would leave the writer with a redefined notion of his or her "authority" in terms of being a privileged reader. The process of reader participation means that the production of the new codes for unfolding the text's meaning needs to be primarily determined by aspects of the texts. Literary meaning has to be generated in a principled fashion to ensure that the imaginary world expresses a meaning commensurate with the text and not one expressive of an individual's view, regardless of the text.

Literature is literature because what it does is not done anywhere else: a literary work is established in terms of its own sphere, and other concerns (including those of religion, economics, or politics) stay out of the literary process. This view assumes a world that is defined by autonomy of individual spheres or, put in negative terms, lack of cohesion in the society as a whole. But this claim has to be modified because it misses the double character of literature as both autonomous and social fact. Nevertheless, since about 1800 the concept of autonomy has been important for literature. In fact, it provided the quintessential experience of German Romanticism: subject (the sense of liberation through autonomy) versus the world (the sense of lost totality through fragmentation). For Europe, the process of differentiation (into a system of autonomous spheres away from medieval totality) was considered complete around 1800, coinciding with the beginning of Romanticism. This makes Romanticism the first truly modern literary period.

It is helpful to distinguish between the goal of literature and its function. The goal, or primary parameter, of literature concerns the question of how language is capable of creating an imaginary world. This parameter is realized historically in different ways, and in the process literary language has evolved. Literature after 1800, step by step, loosened the link between the good and the beautiful versus the bad and the ugly; the goal of creating beauty still exists as an idea but is perceived in historical terms. This produces the final paradigmatic shift that is still operative today: the goal of literature is to present innovation, that is, a text attempts to be new. The dichotomy of *innovative* versus *not innovative* has been so important to literature that this aspect has even caused a crossover into another area of society: literary innovation has been legally encoded as copyright in the economic sphere.

The function of literature is aimed toward readers. Just as the primary parameter is concerned with literature itself — the creation of imaginary worlds — the function of literature follows directly as a secondary parameter, enabling the reader to understand the imaginary world. The function of literature is closely linked to the needs of the readers. Quite legitimately, many readers wish either to be entertained or to be instructed, and literature has to be interesting in the required sense in order to meet these expectations. To be interesting to the reader, literature can fulfill several functions; for example, the dual processes of entertaining and educating have also been long-established candidates for the function of literature, although more and more the educational aspect seems to have fallen by the wayside. In a socially differentiated world, literature can also provide a playing field for writers and readers to explore new ideas, precisely because it has no direct consequences in the practice of daily life. The resulting creation of counterworlds represents a tremendous potential of innovation and regeneration.

Literary history is a history of the development of literary language (in terms of the goal of literature), as well as of the development of literature in relation to the social whole and the development of the individual spheres (in terms of the function of literature). A brief look at various literary histories reveals that there are many approaches to classifying literature. This is an important issue because the underlying claim of each approach is that it renders a more accurate model (though never really more than just a model) of how literature evolved historically than the other approaches.

Metaphorically, I find it helpful to visualize the different literary movements. The map is an appropriate image for literature if one understands literary meaning in terms of creating imaginary worlds; a text would then be a kind of map to the imaginary world (and since we all read maps a little differently, this image would even account for different meanings).

Pragmatically, I deliberately use arbitrary time frames — typically decades (although the discussion is not narrowly confined). Using decades points to the fact that this model of literary history is a construct. Nevertheless, while history does not progress in steps of decades, there still seems to be some psychological validity to the concept. When people reminisce, they seem to exploit some form of shared concepts of the 1950s, 1960s, and so on.

Theoretically, I use the concept of movements (or modes) that are defined by dominants. The term *movement* implies that while a particular movement may be particularly strong at a given time, it does not exclude other movements from existing at the same time; the latter is something the term *period* seems to suggest. Furthermore, if a movement has faded into the cultural background, it does not prevent its principal modes (such as styles, devices, and themes) from still (or again) being practiced by individual writers. My classroom teaching has informed the orthographical conventions for movements, because students seem to appreciate the clarity of distinguishing between realism (as a style that even Romanticism may use) and Realism (the historical movement of nineteenth-century literature). The fact that some movements or modes are not capitalized, such as magic realism and postmodernism, reflects their "fuzzy" status in regard to German literature.

Crucial to the understanding of movements and modes is the concept of *dominant*, which is defined as "the focusing component of a work of art: it rules, determines, and transforms the remaining components." Therefore, a dominant "guarantees" a text's structural integrity. There are, however, many different, yet intertwined, dominants "depending upon the level, scope, and focus of the analysis" (McHale 6). First, the two dominants of representation — either the primary reference to the world or the self-referential focus on literary language itself — make it possible to look at the overall picture of literary history. Second, the Enlightenment favored scientific rationality, whose historical manifestations influenced literature which has tried either to emulate or to resist rationality. Third, the change from what McHale calls the epistemological to the ontological dominant helps explain the shift from Modernism to postmodernism. A typical Modernist text foregrounds epistemological questions, such as "How can I interpret this world of which I am a part?" In contrast, a postmodernist text foregrounds ontological questions, such as "Which world is this?" Fourth, since theme is a recurrent element of subject matter, thematic dominants are more specific than the representational, rational, and cognitive dominants. Yet they seem necessary for distinguishing between individual literary developments that are part of larger currents. It is also useful when it comes to the analysis of more-recent literature, for which standard approaches have not yet been developed. With these premises and questions in mind, we can approach German literature of the twentieth century.

**Part One**

# BEFORE 1945:

## MODERNISM AND MODERNISM DELAYED

# I
# *Inventing Master Maps: Modernism*

## Preliminary Thoughts on the Year 1900:
## Everyday Life and the Sciences

THE YEAR 1900 WAS THE MOMENT when new intellectual maps became necessary for reorientation: Becoming — "the mode of thinking that contemplates everything . . . as not merely changing, but as forever evolving into something new and different" (Baumer 20) — triumphed over Being — the "disposition to think about the world in terms of . . . stability" (34) and absolute ideas. Becoming was experienced, on various levels, as social, cultural, moral, and individual fragmentation. It was a daunting task to make a map of a world that was changing to the extent that the most basic categories, once absolute, became relative. Translated into the metaphor of mapmaking, this relativity would mean that either the compass is defective or that the magnetic pole has disappeared.

Everyday life changed as technological innovations and urbanization created a world that was distinctly different from nineteenth-century experience. The basic human concepts of time and space were fundamentally altered by inventions made at the end of the nineteenth century, such as the internal combustion engine (by Lenoir and Otto as early as in the 1860s, perfected in the 1880s and 1890s by engineers like Daimler, Benz, and Diesel), the cinematograph (by Lumière in 1894), wireless telegraphy (by Marconi in 1897), and the cathode-ray tube (by Braun in 1897). A "new sense of distance, created by technology and mediated by urbanism and imperialism" (Kern 240) thoroughly changed people's perception. With the telephone the impossible became possible: a person can, in a sense, be simultaneously in two places. The cinema became the quintessential modern art form because it "reproduced the mechanization, jerkiness, and rush of modern times" (117).

As a result, the understanding of the self and the world changed as the new world seemed to grow more and more uncertain. In psychology disillusioning changes took place. In his magnum opus, *Die Traumdeutung* (The Interpretation of Dreams, 1900), Sigmund Freud (1856–1939) emphasized the forces of the unconscious, thus assailing traditional ideas of identity and morality. In physics a picture of solid reality no longer seemed possible after a fundamental shift in the perception of time and space. Ernst Mach postulated that the unity of objects was a mere assumption in the flux of sensations that is understood as reality. In 1900 Max Planck proposed quantum theory, which recognizes that physical laws at the atomic level are statistical and not deterministic. In 1905 and 1915, respectively, Albert Einstein published his special and general theories of relativity, which described time and space as relative to the observer, asserted the equivalence of matter and energy, and unified time and space into a continuum. In 1927 Werner Heisenberg formulated his Uncertainty Principle, which postulated that it is impossible to accurately measure at the same time both the location and momentum of an electron.

Modernism emerged from what David Harvey calls the "tensions between internationalism and nationalism, between globalism and parochialist ethnocentrism, between universalism and class privileges" (24–25) at the beginning of the twentieth century. Modernism continued to resist or accept the political and social tensions from which it had emerged. Thus, it evolved in a dynamic of an aesthetization of politics and a politicization of aesthetics that finally, and ironically, led to its depoliticization after the Second World War.

## A Theory of Modernism

*Two paradigmatic attitudes*
The antimodern response of ignoring the experience of social fragmentation failed to address the realities of the modernist world. Coping with the world was the only way to find an appropriate map for it. There were, however, two choices one could make: either to resist it or to accept it. The first option, coping with but resisting fragmentation, implied that modern disorientation should be counteracted by finding reorientation — or, in the metaphor of the map, by finding a new compass — and reclaiming the totality that had been lost. The second option, accepting the loss of the center as an irreversible fact, implied that there was no way back to that center — in the metaphor of the map, the magnetic pole had disappeared. Such acceptance could lead to a full embrace of the modernist world.

The attitude expressed by the Austrian writer Hugo von Hofmannsthal (1874–1929) in his seminal fictitious letter of Lord Chandos, "Ein Brief" (A Letter, 1902), is paradigmatic of the dominant Modernist response: resistance to fragmentation. In contrast, the attitude expressed at about the same time by German sociologist Georg Simmel (1858–1918) in his study *Die Philosophie des Geldes* (The Philosophy of Money, 1900) is paradigmatic of the opposite view, that of accepting and embracing fragmentation as an irreversible fact.

*The first attitude:*
*the Modernist search*
*for the center*

At the core of Hofmannsthal's fictitious letter from Lord Chandos to Lord Bacon are the crisis in language and the loss of totality. Theoretically, the crisis in language can have two sources. On the one hand, language can precede reality to the extent that reality can never fulfill the expectations raised by language. On the other hand, as in the Chandos letter, reality can precede language. Hofmannsthal's letter writer believes that it is no longer possible for him to talk about reality because a new and stronger kind of language is required that he does not know.

The crisis in language was tied in with the loss of totality, something William Butler Yeats (1865–1939) expressed in "The Second Coming" (1924) with the phrase "the centre cannot hold." The topos of lost metaphysical security has been a central one in Western literature, beginning with Romanticism; but during the twentieth century this topos became symptomatic of an overwhelming experience of life as a continuous flux. Being in motion is Hofmannsthal's symbol for life; for him, motion embodies both the hope of finding one's destination and the fear that, once one stops being in motion, there will be only the sobering experience of alienation. Being in motion means, as he wrote in the story "Die Wege und die Begegnungen" (Paths and Encounters, 1913), that everything is possible. Here the attitude that fragmentation must be resisted finds its clearest expression.

The moment Lord Chandos experiences the rupture of language and reality, his crisis begins: he doubts his ability to speak coherently and meaningfully; as a consequence, he questions his own identity. Metaphors of sickness abound. Chandos calls his condition "an affliction of my mind" [eine Krankheit meines Geistes]. Five years later Hofmannsthal published "Die Briefe eines Zurückgekehrten" (The Letters of a Man Who Returned, 1907), which can be read as a continuation of the Chandos letter, because the same crisis in language is diagnosed in much the same way: as "a kind of quiet poisoning, a clandestine and creeping infection" [eine Art leiser Vergiftung, eine verborgene und schleichende Infektion]. Yet more openly than Lord Chandos, this letter writer is quite clear about the social origin of his sickness: it is an "evil of European origin" [Übel europäischer Natur].

Both fictitious letter writers yearn for what they experienced before they fell prey to feelings of fragmentation and alienation. Lord Chandos writes that he used to see the world as a totality, as if he were intoxicated: "spiritual and material world didn't seem to be in opposition to each other, neither did courtly and animal instincts, art and non-art, loneliness and community" [geistige und körperliche Welt schien mir keinen Gegensatz zu bilden, ebensowenig höfisches und tierisches Wesen, Kunst und Unkunst, Einsamkeit und Gesellschaft]. Now this totality eludes him, and he can no longer make things cohere in his mind: "Everything fell to pieces for me, and these pieces to pieces, and nothing could be brought together into one term" [Es zerfiel mir alles in Teile, die Teile wieder in Teile, und nichts mehr ließ sich mit einem Begriff umspannen]. While Lord Chandos stops perceiving himself as a subject, he still experiences some everyday things as objects in brief, yet intense, moments of mystical union: "a watering can, a harrow left on the field, a dog in the sun . . . all these things can become a vessel of revelation for me" [eine Gieskanne, eine auf dem Felde verlassene Egge, ein Hund in der Sonne . . . alles dies kann das Gefäß meiner Offenbarung werden]. The writer of the "Briefe eines Zurückgekehrten" stands even further outside the human community. A similarly random assembly of things becomes unreal for him, and thus the opportunity for revelation is lost. Instead, this letter writer's experience is radically nihilistic. For example, while looking at a tree, he can only see something that is not a tree, although it reminds him of one; at the same time he feels "such an indescribable horror of eternal nothing, of eternal nowhere, a breeze not of death but of nonlife, indescribable" [ein so unbeschreibliches Anwehen des ewigen Nichts, des ewigen Nirgends, ein Atem nicht des Todes, sondern des Nicht-Lebens, unbeschreiblich]. He reaches a turning point when he encounters a different kind of object: the artificial object. Confronted by Vincent Van Gogh's paintings and, in particular, by their colors, he feels through the "miracle of their existence" [Wunder ihres Daseins] a secret, "the essential, the indescribably fateful" [das Eigentliche, das unbeschreiblich Schicksalhafte]. Both fictitious letter writers describe a heightened sense of fragmentation, as well as their yearning to find a new totality and meaning. This is the dominant Modernist response: acknowledge the loss of the center that has made the world deficient, but keep searching for a center that will make the world whole again.

Lord Chandos's problem and his response to it constituted an extreme formulation of the Modernist awareness of an unprecedented fragmentation and complexity. Language was part of the predicament, because it was seen as ambiguous and, hence, as unreliable. Therefore, the Modernist search for a new center was not just a search for a new myth but also for a new language. As a result, literary texts from around 1900 onward were experienced as increasingly difficult to read; they communicated neither what readers already knew nor in a manner that readers were used to. The textual demands on the reader were justified by the Modernist belief that only complex art was capable of representing a complex world. The Chandos letter is a perfect example of the pessimism that pervaded the Modernist project of complex art: to communicate meaning in a world that is complex and has lost its center, a maximum of linguistic brilliance is necessary — but, ironically, it has to be uttered in the old language, which is not capable of expressing such meaning.

*The second attitude: embracing fragmentation*

Georg Simmel's *Philosophie des Geldes* presents a different response: it does not resist but embraces the way the world is. He shared the Modernist diagnosis of the world as being fragmented and assumed that modern human beings no longer had any relationship to the totality of being, except when they experienced emotions. But for Simmel the task was not to retrieve the lost center or search for a new one; rather, his task was to understand the fragmented world: "That our image of the world is thus 'suspended in mid-air' is quite all right, because that's just what our world itself is doing" [Daß unser Bild der Welt auf diese Weise "in der Luft schwebt," ist nur in der Ordnung, da ja unsere Welt selbst es tut]. This view led to significant differences in the two attitudes; for example, the process of motion, which, according to Hofmannsthal, destroyed human relationships in the dialectic of hope and alienation, became for Simmel the one factor that allowed him to create a sense of community for humanity in the present world. While the abstractness of modern times leads Hofmannsthal's letter writers to withdraw from society, Simmel considered society "the trans-singular entity that is, after all, not abstract" [das übersinguläre Gebilde, das doch nicht abstrakt ist].

Hofmannsthal approached Becoming with the hope of restoring Being, which implied that while one had to deal with the world as it was, one did not have to like it. In contrast, Simmel accepted Becoming in its own right, which meant that fragmentation was embraced and celebrated. Such an embrace was characteristic of only a few Modernist movements, most obviously in Dada, but it is typical of postmodernism. Both attitudes — resistance and acceptance, including critical acceptance and celebratory embrace — were legitimate Modernist responses to fragmentation and complexity, although the search for the center, resulting from the attitude of resistance, was the predominant response of Modernism.

*A definition of Modernist literature*

Modernist literature focused on its own medium, language, as the result of an increasing self-awareness of the artistic process. The development of Modernist literature was built on the writers' recognition of the world's complexity, which stemmed from an abundance of experiences that demanded to be formed into art. To express a complex world adequately in literary language, literature itself had to become complex. Modernist literature was a fusion of all the potentials that had previously been developed in separate movements in "an ebb and flow between a predominantly rational world-view (Neo-Classicism, Enlightenment, Realism) and alternate spasms of irrational or subjective endeavor (Baroque, *Sturm und Drang*, Romanticism)" (Bradbury and McFarlane 47). Complexity meant that Modernist literature remained defined by change and reacted to it by constantly changing itself in its quest for a new myth and a new language.

Around 1900 Modernist literature responded to the new perception of time and space by radically changing how language dealt with its own temporal and spatial constructs: it created a spatial art that, in turn, altered the sense of time by emphasizing synchronicity. The coherent plots of Realism, which unfolded one step at a time, had become *un*realistic in a world that was defined by multiplicity, synchronicity, and simultaneity. The Modernist spatial form used the text as its own space that was woven through and through with internal references; such self-reflexivity was both an expression of, and an answer to, Modernism's self-awareness of the problem that language had to deal with an abundance of experiences.

The charge that Modernist literature achieved its artistic refinement as a result of dehumanization exemplifies the need to distinguish between several "modernisms." First, Modernist art reacted to modernism, the condition of the reality of the early twentieth century, which it experienced as dehumanizing. A literature that expresses the inhumanity it sees in the world should not be assumed to be uncritically endorsing that inhumanity. Second, there are several strains of Modernist literature. Within the two fundamentally different Modernist attitudes toward complex reality — resistance and acceptance — the various movements of Modernism emerged: on the side of resistance, Aestheticism withdrew from reality and often appeared dark, pessimistic, and, indeed, dehumanized; on the side of acceptance, the Avant-Garde and Ironic Realism, though far from being homogenous movements, can be seen as tending toward reaffirmation of the value of being human and of political ideologies, such as democracy.

Modernist literature — consisting of Aestheticism, the Avant-Garde, and Ironic Realism — revolutionized literature. How far-reaching this revolution was can be seen by the attempts to find adequate terms for major Modernist achievements that redefined literature by crossing the boundaries between genres: the prose poem, epic theater, and the lyrical novel.

### Nietzsche's Continuing Presence

The year 1900 is significant in yet another respect: it is the year of the death of Friedrich Nietzsche (1844–1900), whose influence on German literature exploded in the twentieth century. His influence extended into other realms, and, by way of music and the cinema, it has even become part of American pop culture. Nietzsche's own favorite and indeed central work, *Also sprach Zarathustra* (Thus Spoke Zarathustra, 1883–1884), inspired Richard Strauss to write a tone poem with the same title in 1896, which was later used in movies. For instance, it is heard in three crucial scenes in Kubrick's *2001 — A Space Odyssey* (1968) and occupies a central place in the movie version of *Being There* (1979). In *Also sprach Zarathustra* Nietzsche introduced his concept of the *Übermensch* (superman or overman), and both films allude to this aspect of Nietzsche's philosophy.

It is less than clear, however, what this philosophy is, because many often-conflicting interpretations of his thoughts have been offered. But Nietzsche struck a chord with people when he strove to define new values. He did not destroy the old ones; rather, he was reacting to their demise. Furthermore, Nietzsche's qualities as a poet intersected with his qualities as a philosopher, and consequently, people were often swept away by his style and misunderstood his thoughts.

Most notorious is the appropriation of Nietzsche by National Socialism. It has been repeatedly pointed out that the Nazis exploited the popularity of the thinker by purging his writings of passages that contradicted Nazi interpretation. After all, Nietzsche abhorred the values that came to constitute the core beliefs of National Socialism, such as German nationalism and anti-Semitism. Indeed, Nietzsche maintained that the Aryan influence had destroyed the world, and, both in his works and his letters to his sister (who was married to a staunch anti-Semite), he rejected anti-Semitism.

*Perspectivism* Nevertheless, Nietzsche's work contains gaps and contradictions that laid the groundwork for misunderstanding. These gaps and contradictions presumably resulted from his use of perspectivism as his fundamental approach to philosophical issues. This view holds that it is impossible to consider all aspects of an issue; thus, perspectivistic thinking focuses on extreme aspects. This approach, which finds its corollary in Heisenberg's Uncertainty Principle in physics, makes Nietzsche's philosophy distinctly modern — but also vulnerable, especially to attacks by antimodern thinkers.

Like the typically Modernist attitude displayed in Hofmannsthal's Chandos letter, which contains both a modern element (no longer ignoring the world's fragmentation) and an antimodern one (a search for a new center), Nietzsche strove for a synthesis of Being and Becoming. He grudgingly accepted the new world of Becoming as the real one while still looking for Being. Since he found the synthesis in life itself, his philosophy is referred to as *Lebensphilosophie* (philosophy of life).

*Nihilism, or*
*God is dead*

The concept of life is the key to Nietzsche's experience of and solution to nihilism. At a practical level nihilism — the doctrine that nothing exists — does not mean that only nothingness exists; it means that absolute values no longer hold. In an age of absolute belief, such a loss of values could only be experienced in feelings of nothingness. When Nietzsche encountered nihilism, however, the medieval world of absolute belief had long vanished, and the concept of nihilism had been around at least since Romanticism. Nihilism was less a threat than a challenge, if, indeed, it was not a liberation.

For a world that had been dominated by Christianity, the loss of values can be summarized in the slogan "God is dead," which Nietzsche popularized. The death of God was a liberation for Nietzsche; to him, the old values represented oppression. Nietzsche perceived Christianity as the world's greatest perversion and as the opposite of life because he saw Christian morality as stifling human nature. In *Ecce Homo* (1903) Nietzsche explains that Christianity established the next world as the only important one in order to devalue this world, the term *soul* to despise the body and make it sick, and the concept of sin to create distrust of healthy human emotions. Such a morality negated life. Therefore, Nietzsche was proud to call himself "immoral" in the sense that he considered himself the first to have really understood Christian morality as the source of the world's corruption and, thus, to have gone beyond the concepts of good and evil.

*Will to power:*
*superman and*
*eternal recurrence*

Yet the problem was deeper, as Nietzsche pointed out: it did not suffice to ask from what humanity was liberated; it was crucial to ask for what purpose humanity was liberated. While he pronounced God dead, Nietzsche was aware that the function that God had served still had to be filled; this was the reason for his search of Being in a world that he understood in terms of Becoming. In *Also sprach Zarathustra* Nietzsche distinguishes three phases: that of the camel, which symbolizes the strong mind that willingly carries the burden of the old values and follows the old commandments; that of the lion, which resists the "thou shalt" of the old values and announces its fundamental freedom of "I will" but does not yet create new values — this was Nietzsche's own historical position; and that of the child, the phase where new values are created.

The creation of new values — "the transvaluation of all values" — requires a new kind of human being: the Nietzschean *Übermensch*. Contemporary people (only a few of whom are higher human beings such as Zarathustra) belong to a phase that needed to be overcome. The superman takes the place of God; however, he remains true to this earth, although his existence is thought of in spiritual rather than biological terms. The concept remained vague.

The second core concept of Nietzsche's philosophy, the eternal recurrence, stood, at first, in opposition to that of the superman — to the extent that Zarathustra is taken seriously ill when he understands the impact of this concept: history is but one huge circular motion, repeating its patterns over and over. This means that even the lowliest life forms will return again and again. This notion also rules out a straightforward, linear transition to the phase of the superman, who now appeared as an ahistorical concept of Becoming, as opposed to that of Being, which the eternity of repetition represented.

This, however, was exactly where the solution lay for Nietzsche. He lets his Zarathustra come to the insight that both core concepts, superman and eternal recurrence, are different manifestations of a single force: the will to power. Will to power is the force of life itself; it combines the linear motion of the superman and the circular motion of the eternal recurrence in a spiral — it progresses. Thus, even within the eternal recurrence, the will to power is humanity's power to know itself and to cope with the world's otherness. It is the basis of a still to be developed philosophy of the future — a philosophy that Nietzsche imagined as not needing absolute, definite solutions: it will be the philosophy of the "dangerous possibility" (gefährliches Vielleicht).

Based on the will to power, the new philosophy will provide the new morality beyond good and evil for a new Dionysian world. Opposed to the Apollonian spirit of order, rationality, and harmony, the Dionysian spirit embraces all irrational impulses. It would give rise to a world that is forever creating and destroying itself. This interaction of creation and destruction had a tremendous appeal for the arts, from Aestheticism to Expressionism and Dada.

Nietzsche's achievement was to understand and criticize a world without values. He understood that this situation required new values. But his discussion of these new values — judged in retrospect — suffered from two problems. First, many of Nietzsche's terms, such as *superman* and *will to power*, can be given meanings that are as diverse as their interpreters. Second, although his style of presentation seems concrete, Nietzsche's terms refer to abstract principles that govern the process of history and are — ironically — ahistorical. Still, the issues he tackled remained central throughout the twentieth century.

❦    ❦    ❦    ❦    ❦    ❦    ❦

# 1: The First Decade of the Twentieth Century: Aestheticism — Impressionism and Symbolism

## The Social Foundations:
### Germany as an Industrialized and Imperialistic Nation

WHILE GERMANY HAD FINALLY EVOLVED into a modern industrial nation by 1900, it still had an outdated political structure. After the German empire was established in 1870–1871, the smaller political units, although theoretically sovereign, were dominated by Prussia, whose king was also the German Kaiser, or emperor. Despite economic depressions between 1871 and 1890, the German population grew from forty-one million in 1871 to sixty-five million in 1914. During the 1890s the German economy started to boom; around 1900 full employment was reached; and in 1905 about one million workers from abroad, especially from Poland and Italy, were living permanently in Germany.

In spite of the booming economy, social questions became more and more pressing, because by 1900 about one third of the German population held jobs in the industrial sector, but the workers' share of the national income had declined by more than fifty percent between 1870 and 1890. The squalor in which the poor lived provides a good example: in Berlin alone about 30,000 living quarters qualified as over-crowded in 1900, which meant that six or more persons lived in one room or eleven or more lived in two rooms. Bismarck's legislation had been intended not only to address the social issues but also to keep workers from joining socialist movements by outlawing socialist endeavors in general and the Social Democratic Party (SPD) in particular. The legislation had not been effective in stopping the Social Democrats. As early as the 1907 elections the SPD became the strongest force in popular vote, receiving 3.25 million votes out of a total of 11.26 million, although district boundaries and run-off elections prevented the popular vote from translating into an appropriate representation in parliament.

The empire's new elite — the upper bourgeoisie joining forces with the German nobility — evolved in antagonism to the working class, and it weakened the lower middle class, which deferred to the upper classes. The new elite united both ideologically against the threat represented by the socialism of the working class and economically in pressuring the state to subsidize industry (owned predominantly by the bourgeoisie) and agriculture (owned predominantly by the aristocracy). The military played an important role in the alliance between the upper middle class and the aristocracy: in 1913 about thirty percent of the Prussian officers were aristocrats (a decline from about sixty-five percent around 1865); the military was largely independent of parliamentary control; it doubled in size between 1880 and 1913; and its budget grew by 360 percent during the same period — with money that, to a large extent, went to the upper middle class, who owned the factories that produced military goods. Furthermore, the military came to be considered the "school of the nation," inculcating not only basic values (for example, obedience, duty, diligence, and honor) but also anti-Semitic, antisocialist, and antidemocratic attitudes that were to become a dangerous mix for the history of Germany.

German politics took a turn toward isolation with several decisions that stemmed from Germany's late entrance into colonial imperialism. In the context of the depressions of the 1870s and early 1880s, the acquisition of economically and strategically irrelevant colonies can be seen as an ideological attempt to boost morale at home. An important consequence of Germany's becoming a colonial power was the unavoidable confrontation with British interests; therefore, in an attempt to find allies, Germany became more and more closely allied with Austria, whose multi-ethnic makeup was to become explosively unstable. In the 1906 international conference to solve the crisis over Morocco, Germany was isolated from all other countries except Austria. The same year, the British and French general staffs began regular consultations. In contrast to Germany, Austria's colonial ambitions were primarily directed toward neighboring states. In 1908, as a result of the instability of the Turkish empire, Austria annexed Bosnia and Herzegovina, a region that was considered a powder keg even then.

A central figure was Wilhelm II, German Kaiser from 1888 to 1918, who came, with his hollow rhetoric, to personify the callous superficiality of the ruling class and the nationalism and swashbuckling militarism of the age. Militarism under Wilhelm II was an even stronger influence, because his political guidance, which remained unpredictable and often showed his ignorance of political realities, gave the military an opportunity to establish itself as a major political player. In combination with the alliance between the upper middle class and the nobility, militarism was a great force in a society that was divided by class conflict.

This was the social reality from which Naturalism took its material in the 1890s and on which Aestheticism tried to turn its back around 1900. While Naturalism was primarily aligned with socialism, the Aestheticist response was both conservative (often in the sense of an aristocracy of the mind) and antibourgeois.

## The Literary Spectrum:
## Aestheticism and Non-Modernist Literature

Around 1900 the literary scene in Germany and Austria fragmented into a multitude of new movements, along with the continuation of earlier styles, such as Naturalism. The Modernist assumption that a complex world necessitated a complex art had as its corollary an artistic practice that itself was not monolithic yet still stemmed from a common project. During the first phase of Modernism this common project was defined by an aesthetic attitude, hence its name: Aestheticism. Individual styles were specific manifestations of the Aestheticist project, which, instead of referring to the outside world as realism did, stayed within the realm of literary language to create meaning.

While the Modernist movement produced the most innovative and, hence, the most important works for the development of literature, it was but one part of the broad literary spectrum during the first decade of the twentieth century. For Germany, in addition to *Arbeiterdichtung* (workers' literature) and *Neuklassik* (Neoclassicism), the two traditions that figured most prominently in non-Modernist literature were *Heimatkunst*, a reactionary brand of regionalism, and popular literature, called *Trivialliteratur* in German (the term *trivial* is indicative of the low esteem that popular literature usually enjoys among critics).

*Non-Modernist movements: a political project* The latter movements were not only non-Modernist, but some were downright antimodern, because they attempted to return to an idealized preindustrial world and ignored modern conditions. Essentially escapist, they focused (sometimes overtly, sometimes covertly) on their moral or political message and did little to advance literary language. Still, these movements represented the bulk of literary production and sales and thus allow inferences about the taste of the general public. They are also symptomatic of the politically and socially conservative climate in which the culture developed.

**Arbeiterdichtung** At first glance *Arbeiterdichtung*, literature created by workers themselves, does not seem to fit the conservative mold because of its socialist orientation. In the early phase of *Arbeiterdichtung* — around the turn of the century, just after the socialist worker's movement was legalized in Germany — the works were often unambiguously socialist in depicting workers living in squalor and being exploited at their jobs.

Bourgeois writers, including Arno Holz (1863–1929), Richard Dehmel (1863–1920), and the group "Werkleute auf Haus Nyland" (Workmen at Nyland House) around Joseph Winckler (1881–1966), also addressed this issue. Particularly important were the Naturalists, especially Gerhart Hauptmann (1862–1946) with his drama *Die Weber* (The Weavers, 1892), in view of the lack of a genuine socialist theater of agitation until later innovation by Erwin Piscator (1893–1966) and Bertolt Brecht (1898–1956).

Poets often rephrased slogans of class struggle and condemned war in no uncertain terms, as did Max Kegel (1850–1902) in his 1893 poem "Drei Worte des Wahns" (Three Words of Madness). The three words — *God, king*, and *fatherland* — are those in whose name war is fought. But the poem unmasks them as manipulative, hollow phrases and closes with an appeal to the proletariat not to be patriotic but to love humanity. Nevertheless, *Arbeiterdichter* are generally considered to have produced a "literature of indecision." On the one hand, they exposed the condition of the working class while, on the other hand, they saw beauty in technological accomplishments. Max Barthel (1893–1975), for example, praised the "halls of the train stations [as] much more beautiful than cathedrals" [Die Bahnhofshallen sind viel schöner als die Dome] in 1926. While *Arbeiterdichtung* has been defended as an authentic expression of the mixed feelings of the working class toward technological progress, it has also been accused of being bourgeois. It was less radical than the proletarian-revolutionary literature of Communist writers during the 1920s and 1930s. Yet the *Arbeiterdichter* typically were or had been workers.

Many *Arbeiterdichter* were later persecuted by the Nazis and left the country. Ironically, the five most important and popular *Arbeiterdichter* either died young (Gerrit Engelke, 1890–1918, who had affinities to Expressionism, and Alfons Petzold, 1882–1923), compromised with the Nazis after being imprisoned in a concentration camp (Karl Bröger, 1886–1944), or actively adopted the National Socialist ideology (Heinrich Lersch and Max Barthel). Heinrich Lersch (1889–1936) moved to the political right as a result of the rise in nationalist feelings caused by the outbreak of the First World War. In his poem "Soldatenabschied" (A Soldier's Farewell, 1914), Lersch came out in support of war, God, and fatherland to such an extent that it reads like a repudiation of Kegel's earlier antiwar poem. Each of the five stanzas in Lersch's poem culminates in the exclamation "Germany must live, even if we must die!" [Deutschland muß leben, und wenn wir sterben müssen!].

Neoclassicism centered around the years 1904 and
*Neoclassicism*      1905. Of its main representatives, Paul Ernst
(1866–1933), Samuel Lublinski (1868–1910), and
Wilhelm von Scholz (1874–1969), Ernst was the driving force. For
most writers, with the exception of Ernst, it was a short-lived and
anachronistic attempt — in spite of their rhetoric — to ignore the current state of the world and, by regressing to the ideals of classical antiquity, to regain a sense of religious morality based on a conservative
belief in a harmonious, closed, healthy, and organic society. This attempt opposed both Naturalism and Aestheticism, since these movements embraced modern urban life as their central theme. In this
opposition *Neuklassik* not only pursued escapist ideals but also used
dramatic forms that mostly repeated classical patterns and seemed
rather rigid.

In addition to classical topics, Ernst also dramatized the medieval
Nibelung material in two plays, *Brunhild* (1908) and *Chriemhild*
(1919), following the classical unities of place, time, and plot. In *Brunhild* King Gunther identifies himself and his sister Chriemhild as the
sources of evil. Hagen embodies the principle of loyalty — a loyalty to
the last man that was later extolled as *Nibelungentreue* that bonded the
German people to the *Führer*. Hagen, however, knows that the loyalty
binding him to Gunther will lead to evil. He says to Gunther: "And
since I swore loyalty, I must obey. / . . . If I weren't your man, I would
kill you, / you and Chriemhild. And all would be well" [Und weil ich
Treue schwur, muß ich gehorchen. / . . . / Wär ich dein Mann nicht:
dich wollt' ich ermorden, / Chriemhild und dich. Dann wär alles gut].
But the plot follows the traditional story of the Nibelungen, adding a
few aspects, such as Siegfried's dying thanks to Hagen for having killed
him, and, therefore, having relieved him from the guilt of having
tricked Brunhild into marriage with Gunther. The language remains
plain, as is demonstrated in the quote; thus, the linguistic level does not
approach the importance that Ernst saw in the subject matter.

This is also the context in which biography became significant for
literature. Both Ernst and Lublinski had at first considered themselves
Marxists and had been members of the SPD but then turned to conservative ideas. In his partly autobiographical novel *Der schmale Weg zum
Glück* (The Narrow Road to Happiness, 1904), Ernst re-created this
development. While there is a similarity to those writers of Arbeiterdichtung who were absorbed into National Socialism, Ernst's life and
the plot of his novel have a much stronger affinity to the lives of some
of the writers of *Heimatkunst* and to the plots of some of their novels,
where the hero is tempted by socialism in the city but overcomes this
temptation by finding his way back to God and fatherland and thus
finding his true place in the human community.

Literary regionalism itself was an international
**Heimatkunst** *and* phenomenon with, for example, local color writ-
*regionalism* ing in American literature. It encompassed critical, as well as escapist, tendencies. Critical
regionalism addressed social problems and did not glorify rural communities; representative of this approach in Germany were the satirical writings of Ludwig Thoma (1867–1921), although this author, too, increasingly tended toward nationalist thought. In contrast, *Heimatkunst* was an escapist regionalism that uncritically glorified the rural community as a value in its own right, as the place where good people achieve, after some conflict, a life in harmony with God and country, where "country" implied both nationalist and rural-agrarian sentiments. Because *Heimatkunst* lent itself to exploitation by National Socialist ideology, it was easily incorporated into the Nazi literary canon of *Blut und Boden* (blood-and-soil) literature.

Conservative and racist works, such as those by Paul Anton de Lagarde (pseudonym of Paul Bötticher, 1827–1891) and Julius Langbehn (1851–1907), provided the ideological foundation of *Heimatkunst*. The 1890s saw the first phase of *Heimatkunst*, of which Heinrich Sohnrey (1859–1948), Wilhelm von Polenz (1861–1903), and Peter Rosegger (1843–1918) were representatives. Writers of this phase attempted to portray a stabilization of the agrarian way of life that was drained by urbanization and its negative effects on agriculture. While the earthiness and love of country of this phase seemed less directly political, the works were political because of their anti-Semitism, anti-Communism, and lack of analysis of the actual source of the peasantry's squalor: the exploitation by rich aristocratic landowners.

The second phase of *Heimatkunst* began around 1900 with writers, such as Friedrich Lienhard (1865–1929) and Adolf Bartels (1862–1945), whose works retained the conservative values of love of country that had dominated during the first phase but led away from the earlier focus on rural and agrarian values, which became more and more openly unrealistic. As a result, the writers were better able to address the expectations of their readers, who came primarily from the petty bourgeoisie and not the peasantry. Germany's new participation in imperialist and colonialist endeavors opened up promising perspectives with which the petty bourgeoisie could identify. The dreams of national grandeur, however, depended on the country's industrial progress; therefore, the second phase of *Heimatkunst* valorized such progress. This shift in focus produced a paradox by embedding technology within an agrarian value system and by playing on the petty-bourgeois fear of both socialism and industrial capitalism.

The most influential works of this phase were written by Hermann Löns (1866–1914) and Gustav Frenssen (1863–1945). Löns's novel

*Der Wehrwolf* (1910) evokes a brutal and blood-drenched picture of the Thirty Years' War, during which the novel's hero organizes his fellow peasants to defend (hence the novel's title, where *Wehr* comes from "defense") and avenge themselves in a fight that justifies its means by its ends. The novel presented its justification of violent self-defense in the flattest of fake realism with no literary merit. Not only was it accepted by the Nazis in terms of their blood-and-soil ideology, but the Nazi militia that formed short-lived pockets of resistance even after the Second World War ended called themselves *Wehrwölfe*.

When Frenssen's *Jörn Uhl* was published in 1901, it was favorably compared to *Buddenbrooks*, by Thomas Mann (1875–1955), published the same year, as the "healthier" novel. Within a year of its publication Frenssen's novel had sold 130,000 copies; Mann's novel sold only 1,000 copies during the same period. Jörg Uhl overcomes failure and the loss of his farm, studies engineering, and becomes a success when he returns home to the village. The novel expresses two crucial messages. First, the world's problems are not social but moral in nature; thus, Jörn Uhl succeeds because of his humility and his faith. Second, his turning to technology is not a rejection of his basic work ethic; thus, he has not lost touch with his rural origins. The novel ends with the reaffirmation of Uhl's happiness because of these values.

The works of the second phase of *Heimatkunst* can easily be read as precursors of fascist literature; in particular, their embrace of technological progress in the guise of agrarian values prefigured National Socialist rhetoric. Some authors of *Heimatkunst* — above all, Bartels, who also published a notorious anti-Semitic literary history, and Frenssen — continued writing within the fascist fold during the Third Reich.

*Popular literature*

Works of *Trivialliteratur*, written for mass consumption, were wonderfully entertaining for a wide public; because of its often timeless quality, the escapist mode strikes a chord with a vast number of readers even today. *Trivialliteratur* intersects with those strains of writing that are also primarily concerned with the function of literature as entertainment, satisfying readers' expectations of being provided a release from the pressures of their daily lives. In the age of mass production this kind of literature became a commodity and later crossed over into other media.

As *Heimatkunst*, these novels provide outlets for those disenfranchised by urbanization and industrialization. Readers find true meaning in country, nature, God, and triumph over the bad guys. One of the most successful writers in this category was Ludwig Ganghofer (1853–1920), a personal friend and favorite author of Kaiser Wilhelm. Over thirty-two million copies of his works have been sold, and more than thirty television or film adaptations of his novels, usually set in an idealized world of the Alps, have appeared. As adventure novels, often set in exotic places, *Trivialliteratur* allows its readers to live out dreams of imperial greatness as they ride into foreign lands to do good and teach the inhabitants respect for Germans. Sales totaling more than fifty million copies have made Karl May (pseudonym of Karl Hohenthal, 1842–1912) the most successful writer in this category. Several of his novels were later turned into movies; annual theater festivals are put on in his honor, and he has remained a quintessential companion of generations of preadolescent male readers. As romance novels, *Trivialliteratur* provides wish fulfillment for the socially powerless by using stereotypical variations of the Cinderella plot in which the poor girl finds out that she is really a rich princess — or at least, against all odds, she gets the rich prince for her husband. There were many successful writers in this category, but the most successful was Hedwig Courths-Mahler (1867–1950), whose over two hundred novels have sold more than forty million copies and have been adapted for television (mainly in the 1970s).

In a final analysis, a distinction should be made between tendencies that are conservative or escapist and those that are genuinely prefascist or fascist. For example, Karl May's work is more complex than can be argued here; ambiguously, it also contains pacifistic and antibourgeois elements. Nevertheless, National Socialism exploited conservative values that had been part of German literature for some time and that were prevalent during the first decade of the twentieth century. If one considers both the political dimensions that pointed all the way to National Socialist exploitation of literature and the fact that the vast majority of literature produced in Germany (or in any other country, for that matter) was not Modernist, then the significance of Modernist literature becomes even more impressive.

*The early Modernist movement: Aestheticism*

European literature started paying close attention to the potential of language around the middle of the nineteenth century. The combination of giving priority to linguistic play, as opposed to representing the real world, and of stressing the independence of literature from moral, political, and other considerations led to the systematic formulation of an aesthetic project that began with Charles Baudelaire (1821–1867) in France and culminated from 1890 to 1910 throughout Europe — for instance, with Oscar Wilde (1856–1900) in England. This particular historical manifestation of the aesthetic project is referred to as *Aestheticism*.

*A theory of Aestheticism*

The participation of German-language literature in the international movement of Aestheticism was in full swing by 1900. Four characteristics of Aestheticism followed from its focus on language: rejection of realism, an antinature attitude, artificiality, and antimorality.

First, realism is rejected to focus on the play with language. Art for art's sake — "l'art pour l'art" in French — became the battle cry that expressed the basic premise of the Aestheticist project, which can be seen as the final consequence of Immanuel Kant's 1790 definition of art in terms of disinterestedness of pleasure. Even in its weakest form, the program of art for art's sake defended literature's autonomy against the intrusion of value judgments from other spheres, such as politics, religion, and ethics.

Second, the antinature attitude suggested that realism had been abandoned because it was misconceived from the beginning: art should not imitate life; rather, life should imitate art. The Aestheticist position assumed that art was more real than nature. In its weak form, this position implied that art was simply more interesting than nature, which was considered trivial. In its extreme form, the antinature attitude assumed that nature's existence depended on literary language. On the one hand, this could be a negative experience: where literary language failed to give substance to nature, nature did not exist, as the poem "Das Wort" (The Word, 1919), by Stefan George (1868–1933), claimed with resignation: "Thus I sadly learned to do without: / No thing exists where the word gives out" [So lernt ich traurig den verzicht: / Kein ding sei wo das wort gebricht]. On the other hand, the priority of language could celebrate the triumph of the human mind, as did the fourth sonnet in the second part of *Sonette an Orpheus* (1923), by Rainer Maria Rilke (1875–1926), in which linguistic existence leads to actual existence. The name, combined with the faith of the people, is sufficient to give reality to a mythical creature, the unicorn.

Third, assigning literature priority over nature led to artificiality. Nature and its realistic presentation had been rejected; now literature itself had to create new forms of existence, all of which would be, by definition, artificial. There were two options: to create an artificial and self-contained world or to create an artificial language. The dandy and the courtesan were considered prototypes of human beauty, but such beauty was aesthetically and artificially constructed and did not flow from nature. An artificial world had an artificial beauty, as in George's evocations of parks consisting solely of dead objects.

The other option, creating an artificial language, depended on the assumption that it was possible to create *poésie pure* — a work of language that referred exclusively to itself. The logical extremes were literary texts that consisted either partially or entirely of made-up words. In English literature, "Jabberwocky" in *Through the Looking-Glass* (1871), by Lewis Carroll (pseudonym of Charles Lutwidge Dodgson, 1832–1898), is a famous example. Christian Morgenstern (1871–1914) was widely popular for what is usually considered nonsense poetry, although it mocked the bourgeois claim that everything should have a clear order. His "Das große Lalula" (The Great Lalula, 1905) does not require translation because it is written entirely in a made-up language; the first stanza reads: "Kroklokwafzi? Sememi! / Seiokronto — prafriplo: / Bifzi bafzi; hulalemi: / quasti basti bo . . . / Lalu lalu lalu lalu la!"). Morgenstern's "Fisches Nachtgesang" (Night Song of a Fish, 1905) even abstracts from language altogether to represent the metric idea of a poem by arranging the notations for accented and unaccented syllables, line after line, so that their typographical appearance evokes the shape of a fish.

Fourth, antimorality was defined in relation to existing concepts of morality. For those who identified the beautiful with the good that they found in nature, placing a priority on artificiality was likely to be considered immoral. The antimoral attitude claimed that literature should operate freely, without restraint from any concerns that, though valid in their own spheres (such as religion, politics, or ethics), were simply not literary concerns. The next step was for literature to turn to what is commonly considered immoral: literature discovered morally perverted and ugly subject matter that would have been excluded from literary treatment before and, what is more, treated this subject matter without questioning it morally. The latter attitude, in particular, gave shock value to Modernism and, thus, the potential to spark public outrage and scandal — as did, for example, the depiction of sexuality in the dramas of Arthur Schnitzler (1862–1931).

What is striking about Aestheticism is a double paradox. Its claim of being independent from all other spheres created the first paradox: Aestheticist literature was always what it pretended not to be; for instance, it was political by resisting the political. This paradox led to another: while most writers of Aestheticism tended to be conservative in their personal politics, their writings often contained strongly subversive undercurrents.

*The Aestheticist styles*    Aestheticism encompasses various *isms* into which the literary scene exploded. Broad definitions of the *isms* often confound the styles so that they ultimately seem synonymous. In contrast, their narrow definitions often ignore the unifying Modernist project and create the equally false impression that these variations are unrelated movements that are only grouped together because they happen to share the same opposition to Naturalism. Any helpful definition needs to address the relationship between a specific movement of literary Modernism (here called *Aestheticism*) as the common basis and the styles (referred to here as Impressionism, Symbolism, decadence, and *Art Nouveau*) as individual manifestations of this common basis.

This approach has not only descriptive but also explanatory power. It explains the differentiation of the styles in terms of the literary devices and motifs that are generally characteristic of Aestheticism but are used with different emphases by the individual styles. It furthermore explains why the list of representative authors for one style largely overlaps with lists for other styles. These lists usually include Arthur Schnitzler, Hugo von Hofmannsthal, Rainer Maria Rilke, Stefan George, Peter Altenberg (pseudonym of Richard Engländer, 1859–1919), Eduard von Keyserling (1855–1918), Detlev von Liliencron (1844–1909), Richard Dehmel, Max Dauthendey (1867–1918), Thomas Mann, Heinrich Mann (1871–1950), Robert Musil (1880–1942), and Hermann Hesse (1877–1962). All of these authors participated in the broad project of Aestheticism; at different phases or in different individual works the same author might opt for different manifestations or combinations of manifestations of Aestheticism. Most of the names of the styles were either derived from or applied to art forms other than literature, especially to painting; this phenomenon serves to emphasize the common Modernist basis of the arts' responses to the modern world.

The term *Neuromantik* (neoromanticism) often appears in this context but needs to be used with special care. On the one hand, the term loosely refers to Modernist writers who were influenced by the Romantic tradition as it was mediated through French Symbolism; therefore, many aspects overlap with Symbolism and others with Impressionism and decadence, so it is more appropriate to use the more precise terms (or, alternatively, the term *Aestheticism*). On the other hand, there were authors — such as Hermann Stehr (1864–1940) in prose and Börries von Münchhausen (1874–1945), Lulu von Strauß und Torney (1873–1956), and Agnes Miegel (1879–1964) in poetry — who did not belong to Modernism: they used the Romantic tradition in a regressive attempt to ignore the modern world and were thus closer to *Heimatkunst*.

Impressionism assumed that the human mind is exposed to a continuous sensual perception of the forever-changing world. The major characteristic of this style was its attempt to capture the moment in motion. Impressionist texts shared with Impressionist paintings motifs that express the concept of flux, such as light, reflections, vibrations, water, and rivers (as water in motion). The image of flow was applied to the human mind as the *stream of consciousness* — the "continuous flow of thought and sensation in the human mind" (Lodge 42) — a term that was coined by William James (1842–1910). Writers attempt to reflect this stream in their texts, typically choosing between two techniques. First, interior monologue uses first-person discourse as if writer and reader were plugged into a character's actual flow of thoughts, which are rendered similar to normal speech by following the associative thought process and using the "natural" tense for whatever the thought is about. There is no signal, such as the inquit-tag ("she said," "he said," etc.), when the narrative shifts into interior monologue. Second, free indirect style (from the French *style indirect libre*) achieves directness by also leaving out the inquit-tag and by retaining deictic elements (such as "tomorrow," which would be changed to "the next day" in indirect speech), while it also uses some elements of indirect speech, such as third-person and past-tense forms, to represent the thoughts of a character. While free indirect style can be traced back to Jane Austen (1775–1817) in British prose and Gustave Flaubert (1821–1880) in French, it was not used in German literature until Naturalism. In contrast, interior monologue was a Modernist innovation, pioneered in German-language literature by Arthur Schnitzler.

Although literary Impressionism continued the Naturalist exactitude in observing details, its program of registering the impressions of the outside world on the senses, with the concomitant emphasis on subjectivity, ran counter to Naturalism. The resulting effect of diffusion, both in form (such as stream of consciousness) and atmosphere, was characteristically ambivalent: while it exhilarated in celebrating the nuances of the moment, it was melancholy because it is impossible for literature to capture motion without halting it. Favorite literary genres were lyric poetry and prose sketches. Peter Altenberg described his short prose texts, whose trademark is the pervasiveness of dashes, to be his experiences as condensed by his impressions: "They are extracts! Extracts of life. The life of a soul and an arbitrary day, dehydrated into two or three pages" [Es sind Extracte! Extracte des Lebens. Das Leben der Seele und des zufälligen Tages, in 2–3 Seiten eingedampft].

Symbolism also focused on the mind's sensual perception of the world; here, however, the mind seemed to be more in control, because it not only registered the incoming impressions of objects but was also actively involved in seeking (or, if necessary, creating) a second reality behind the objects. But the direction of the search was not clear, in marked contrast with the Romantic yearning, which can be seen as always directed toward home, as stated by the hero of the novel *Heinrich von Ofterdingen* (1802), by Novalis (pseudonym of Friedrich von Hardenberg, 1772–1801). This sense of a metaphysical home had been lost in the twentieth century. Now the mind interpreted objects as a "forest of symbols" [forêt de symbols] as the French poet Charles Baudelaire called it in his Symbolist signature poem "Correspondances" in *Les Fleurs du Mal* (The Flowers of Evil, 1857). Symbolism aimed to evoke the unsayable and secret truths that hide behind objects as these become perceptible from the nuances of each moment.

In the attempt to say the unsayable, Symbolism used tightly structured forms that exploited musical and metaphoric language; for instance, synesthesia was used to fuse the sense perceptions in order to point at the reality behind them. While Impressionism diffused reality into a series of sense impressions, Symbolism focused it by way of a "magic word" whose function was to lead to the secret truths. Some critics consider Stefan George the only Symbolist writer of the German language.

Decadence has the *fin de siècle* mood of ennui or *Weltschmerz* (world-sorrow) as its predominant component. This style went beyond pessimism and bordered on the pathological and morbid. Decadent authors expressed a keen awareness of social and, especially, cultural decay; unable to stop the decay, they actually seemed to celebrate it in a gesture of "perishing in style." The attitude was an elitist insult to contemporary bourgeois society and its values. Austrian writers were particularly representative of this mode, but so were Thomas and Heinrich Mann in the early phases of their careers. *Die Göttinnen* (The Goddesses, 1903), a trilogy of novels by Heinrich Mann, is considered a compendium of motifs of literary decadence.

*Jugendstil*, or *Art Nouveau*, is a term that originated in the visual arts and was borrowed to describe a similar attitude in literary works. The German term was derived from the title of the Munich weekly magazine *Jugend* (Youth), which was published from 1896 to 1940. The term *Jugendstil* is somewhat controversial in its application to literature because of its wide scope, extending from the fine arts to commercial art, and because of its connection with a wide spectrum of proposed social reforms, ranging from health to education, to be carried out in the name of youth. As a broad movement it swept Europe during the first decade of the twentieth century; therefore, it might be tempting to consider *Jugendstil* a more comprehensive phenomenon — *Jugendbewegung* (Youth Movement). It was the movement from which, for instance, the Boy and Girl Scouts emerged. The Youth Movement, however, was both too ambiguous (including modern and antimodern, progressive and reactionary tendencies) and, where it was modern, not comprehensive enough to subsume all Modernist endeavors.

Nevertheless, the Aestheticist response to the abundance of experience was common to all the styles discussed in this section. Similar to the dialectical relationship in which Impressionism and Symbolism can be seen as focusing on the fleeting moment to experience diffusion and to seek hidden truths, respectively, the styles of decadence and *Jugend-*

*stil* also represented different emphases on the same point of departure. Both grew out of the experience of social and cultural decline, especially in the cities; but while decadent literature emphasized morbidly beautiful life in the mood of decay, *Jugendstil* attempted to redefine beautiful life as that which is new (as opposed to the old, which is decaying) and truly alive (as opposed to morbid). Paradoxically, the precious and rarified aspect of *Jugendstil* overlapped with that of decadence.

*Jugendstil* in general refers to a largely ornamental representation of a stylized life in beauty and in the context of a nature that seemed less artificial than idealized; this nature, however, was quite devoid of real life, despite its often vibrant appearance. In literature, an exaggeration of Aestheticist language games could lead to a merely ornamental use of language, as in Hofmannsthal's poetic description of clouds ("Wolken," 1892): "Surging likenesses / Barely begun / Soar with fierceness / And are gone" [Wogende Bilder / Kaum noch begonnen / Wachsen sie wilder / Sind sie zerronnen]. Literary elements of *Jugendstil* included specific motifs, such as certain colors (red and white), characters ("femme fatale" or "femme enfant"), and metaphors (fountain). While George's poetry is Symbolist and at times decadent but at other times also ornamental, the layout of his books was truly *Jugendstil*: the typeface specifically developed for his poetry emphasized the preciously ornamental, and the illustrations by the *Jugendstil* artist Melchior Lechter (1865–1937) also exemplified the style.

## Viennese Foundations of a Nervous Art

Vienna became a center of literary Modernism around the turn of the century. As the capital of the double monarchy of Austria and Hungary, it was the focal point of a creative mix of old splendor and more-recent instability, with the latter hidden under the former's thin façade. Hermann Bahr (1863–1934) articulated the need for *Nervenkunst* (art of the nerves), which he considered a nervous romanticism or a mysticism of the nerves, as a response to the old system, as well as to the close attachment of literature to the sciences found in Naturalism and psychologism. Like Vienna's great iconoclast Karl Kraus (1874–1936), who declared this new movement dead in 1896, before its major works had been written, Bahr was ahead of his time when he published his definition of *Nervenkunst* in an article on overcoming Naturalism in 1891. Naturalism remained a force to be reckoned with for about another decade — especially where it developed a psychological focus; there were even close affinities to Aestheticism, for instance, with Gerhart Hauptmann and Johannes Schlaf (1862–1941). Yet the Naturalist movement had never been strong in Vienna, and the pervasive feeling of living in an era of decline of the Austrian empire found its appropriate expression in the emphasis on nerves in terms of symbols and dream images. This, in turn, led to the image of the nervous or even the neurotic as a condition of the creative process — a renewed version of the traditional image of the poet as an outsider and a genius.

One key to the new artists' self-understanding was the term *modern*, which they contrasted with the decaying world of their parents' generation. From this they derived a generally Aestheticist program and tried to live by its *fin de siècle* maxims, such as melancholy, pessimism, and dandyism. Known as *junges Wien* (Young Vienna), the group around Bahr included Leopold von Andrian (1875–1951), Richard Beer-Hofmann (1866–1945), and Peter Altenberg, as well as the two most significant Viennese writers of that era, Hugo von Hofmannsthal and Arthur Schnitzler. These authors' favorite place for displaying their antibourgeois, Bohemian lifestyle was the café, the *Kaffeehaus-Literat* becoming the Viennese version of the literary dandy. Peter Altenberg, for instance, briefly gave the Café Central as his address.

The new, modern attitude swept many areas, not just literature. In the Viennese fine arts a comparable movement was under way with the Secession. Even scientists pursued theories in the same direction; the most important was Sigmund Freud. Psychoanalysis, Freud's challenge to traditional culture, understood the unconscious as driven mainly by sexual desires, causing his theories to receive much attention in literary circles. Still, the relationship between the literary scene and psychoanalysis in Vienna was complex and ambiguous. Hofmannsthal did not think highly of Freud personally; nevertheless, he paid attention to psychoanalysis in his works, even to the extent that Hofmannsthal's versions of the classical Electra and Oedipus myths come across as dramatizations of aspects of psychoanalysis. These efforts, however, were mostly ignored, if not rejected, by Freud and his circle because of their belief that literature should not be derived from theory while, conversely, a theory could find support for its hypotheses in literature.

In contrast, Freud admired the work of Schnitzler, who did not take his notions primarily from Freud but, on the basis of his own training and experiences as a medical doctor, developed similar ideas himself and expressed them in his literary works — ideas so similar that Freud considered Schnitzler his literary doppelgänger. For this reason, ironically, Freud shied away from close contact with Schnitzler.

*Arthur Schnitzler* Schnitzler's literary work examined extreme conditions of the human psyche, stressing one popular theme of the time — sexuality — and combining innovative literary form and social criticism. Schnitzler's most important texts — the novella *Leutnant Gustl* (1900) and the play *Reigen* (Rondo, 1900) — were also his most notorious.

Social criticism was expressed by means of literary form; or, more precisely, Aestheticist means of presentation unmasked the artificiality of the fictional characters' world. *Leutnant Gustl* presented the first sustained interior monologue in German-language literature and revealed Gustl's military world of honor as hollow. According to this honor code, Gustl realizes, "I have to shoot myself dead because a baker called me a stupid boy" [ich muß mich totschießen, weil ein Bäkkermeister mich einen dummen Buben genannt hat]. Since he cannot restore his honor by challenging the baker to a duel (the baker's social position is considered to be unworthy of giving satisfaction), suicide appears to be the only way out, and Gustl resolves to kill himself at seven o'clock in the morning. The reader witnesses Gustl's presumably last hours as hours spent in idle, self-important thought without any depth and devoid of any values that tie Gustl to people (he has only superficial relationships and sexual exploits) or to God (he goes to a church because he feels that in his present situation this will not hurt). His bad conscience (or superego) lets him know that he has to kill himself even if the baker will not tell anyone; the important thing is that he, Gustl, knows. It becomes clear how shallow this resolve is when Gustl, having his presumably last breakfast in a café, learns from the waiter that the baker died of a stroke during the night. Now Gustl feels that he can go on with his life as usual and looks forward to his next duel the afternoon of the same day.

The story was first published in the Vienna *Neue Freie Presse* on December 25, 1900, and a military court revoked Schnitzler's status as an officer in the reserves on April 26, 1901, for defaming the Austrian military. While anti-Semitism most likely influenced the sentence, the antimilitary content expressed through interior monologue without a mediating narrator made the story so explosive. Thus, the exposition of Gustl's ridiculous code of honor achieved a degree of objectivity that was perceived as a scandalous attack on the military's code of honor.

The affinity of the stream-of-consciousness technique to psychoanalysis, especially to the method of free association, is as obvious as the main difference between them: the interior monologue is an art form and not a therapeutic discourse, because there is no therapist present and because the first-person narrator, in contrast to the patient, does not learn anything. Instead, the reader is supposed to learn by experiencing the aesthetic difference between literary creation and reality and by understanding the criticism voiced in the text. The combination of interior monologue with criticism in an analysis of an individual mind that is representative of its society set Schnitzler's use of interior monologue apart from its use merely to evoke an impressionistic mood by Edouard Dujardin (1861–1949), the French writer who is credited with having invented the form.

One of Schnitzler's main themes is social decay. As in *Leutnant Gustl*, it also dominates *Reigen*, which combines decay and sexuality into a picture of moral decadence. Schnitzler preferred one-act plays, and the ten scenes of *Reigen* can be understood as ten short one-act plays. One-act plays, though in existence since the mid-eighteenth century, became a favorite form of modern drama as a response to the crisis of classicist drama at the end of the nineteenth century. Classicist drama had attempted to focus the action on stage so that individual parts formed a unity created by the dialogue between the characters. When it was no longer felt that individual strands of action could be unified into a dramatic whole, the one-act play offered the option of focusing on one part that then assumed the function of the whole. Consequently, parts elevated to the form of the one-act play came to represent the unintelligible complexity of the whole that could no longer be encompassed by multiple-act classicist plays.

*Reigen* is a sexual version of a *danse macabre*: from one sexual encounter to the next, one of the two partners leaves and the other stays on stage for a new encounter with another partner until the rondo is completed in the tenth scene with the reappearance of the whore, who exited after the first scene. Erotic atmosphere and the parabolic and artificial character of the *danse macabre* lend a static quality to Schnitzler's play, which, therefore, seems to possess a certain degree of objectivity in the presentation of material that is usually considered to be antimoral — an objectivity that hides the criticism that is inherent in it. Thus the cycle, which was written in 1896 and 1897, met with substantial resistance, which resulted in another court case against Schnitzler and a protracted history of publication.

In *Reigen*, Schnitzler continued exploring erotic visions of the soul as he had done in earlier plays. For the printed version of Schnitzler's *Anatol* (1893), another play about the superficiality of sexuality, Hugo von Hofmannsthal wrote the preface under the pseudonym Loris, expressing the *fin de siècle* mood and summarizing the principle of Schnitzler's plays in a phrase: they are the "pretty formulas of bad things" [Böser Dinge hübsche Formel]. This phrase is perfectly descriptive: the "bad things," which represent moral decline in general, are clad in pretty Aestheticist formulas that play with the artificiality of life; profound insights were hidden right at the text's surface.

*Hugo von Hofmannsthal*   At heart, Hugo von Hofmannsthal always remained a lyrical poet whose thinking evolved in terms of the contrast between two conditions that he perceived, in mythological terms, as preexistence (a dreamlike state of premature insight detached from life) and existence (being fully part of authentic life). Formally, his writings often expressed this contrast in images of stasis and change. His later plays can be considered variations of his earlier lyrical dramas. Hofmannsthal's career can be divided into three stages. First, beginning at sixteen, he produced lyrical poetry and lyrical dramas in the *fin de siècle* individualistic mood of Aestheticism. Second, around 1900 he became increasingly aware of the limitations of the Aestheticist project, which culminated in his decision to turn from the private realm of poetry to a more social realm, or, in his own terms, from preexistence to existence. Third, with the production of various forms of texts for stage productions, from libretti to dramas, he attempted to write more concrete and socially relevant literature.

From the start Hofmannsthal's poems (at first published under the pseudonym Loris) displayed a high formal virtuosity. They were clearly influenced by European Aestheticism, and in 1891 he found his own Modernist voice. He approached *poésie pure*, where the sounds of a poem developed their own dynamic that was pushed forward by musical rhythm and sound patterns, such as consonance and alliteration, as in the evocation of clouds in 1892 as "surging likenesses." Yet this dynamic of motion did not become completely automatic but was held at bay by Hofmannsthal's attempt also to find meaning in the secrets of this dream world.

Since profound knowledge was considered to be hidden right at the surface of things, everything became a symbol, or a "fountain of parables" [Gleichnisbronnen]. The secret of the world (the title of the poem "Weltgeheimnis," 1894) found its expression in incomprehensible "magic words" [Zauberworte] that are to be understood in the context of Hofmannsthal's theory of preexistence and existence. Consequently, the aesthetic aspect dominated over the social; still, the contrast between art and social world was always present. On the one hand, Hofmannsthal asserts the independence of an artificial world; for example, prototypically in the poem "Welt und Ich" (World and I, 1893), the poet-speaker sends his song to Atlas to offer that he, the poet, will carry the burden of the world. In the event that Atlas might respond with incredulity, the poet instructs his song to ask Atlas: "How could his arms not bear the world, / Since he, my master, smilingly carries the world in his head?" [Wie ertrüg er sie im Arme nicht, / Mein Herr, da er sie lächelnd trägt im Haupt?].

On the other hand, Hofmannsthal's conservative politics seem to have made him aware of the social aspect to the extent that it found its way into his poetry; he answered the social questions in terms of Aestheticism. In 1900 a poem polemically reacted to the first workers' demonstrations marking May 1, the European Labor Day: "If the mob rages in the street, well, my child, let it shout. . . . Beautiful truth alone has life" [Tobt der Pöbel in den Gassen, ei, mein Kind, so lass ihn schrein . . . Schöne Wahrheit lebt allein]. This aloofness suggests that a poem, such as "Manche freilich" (Some, of course, 1895) — with its division between those who must die down below in the ship's belly and those who live next to the helm above — may not be an ambiguous poetic justification of social injustice. Rather, it may be an abstract, aesthetic celebration of the few versus the many in terms of the typical *fin de siècle* motifs, such as death and transitoriness, beauty and yearning; it may even be a poem about the social responsibility of the poet in connecting with life spheres that are only temporarily separate.

The striking result of this somewhat hidden, yet persistent, intrusion of the social on his poetry was that Hofmannsthal himself grew increasingly aware of the problematics of Aestheticism. More and more his affirmation of the mystic union rang hollow. Hofmannsthal was at his most explicit about possible doubts concerning the Aestheticist project in his prose texts, such as "Das Märchen der 672. Nacht" (The Tale of the 672nd Night, 1905) and the fictitious letters. How far the crisis in language expressed there reflected Hofmannsthal's own crisis is subject to speculation; some critics suggest that the rejection of Aestheticism in the Chandos letter was intended for Stefan George, who had tried to draw Hofmannsthal into his circle. Conversely, it has been argued that the Chandos letter merely expressed one possible poetological position among many that Hofmannsthal was exploring. After all, Lord Chandos writes that he still finds objects for a mystical union, although no longer in "the abstract words" [die abstrakten Worte] which have been decaying in his mouth like mold, or, literally, "like moldy fungi" [wie modrige Pilze].

By the same token, Hofmannsthal's abandonment of lyric poetry in favor of the more social literary form of the theater might be seen as only a minor shift in regard to the polarity of stasis versus change that runs through his entire oeuvre. Yet the form of the classicist drama itself had become problematic by the time Hofmannsthal turned to it. Classicist drama unfolded in the interpersonal realm by means of the dialogue. As a consequence of the general skepticism toward language, the possibilities for dialogue and, thus, the drama appeared to be limited. The form of the well-made play, or *Konversationsstück*, which had emerged during the second half of the nineteenth century, automatized dialogue as conversation at the witty, yet superficial, level of upper-class small talk in the attempt to disguise the state of crisis that the classicist drama had reached. This crisis was, ironically, similar to the crisis expressed in the Chandos letter.

Hofmannsthal wrote his first dramas at the same time as his poems; these dramas are often described as lyrical monologues. Yet he did attempt to move toward genuine dialogue, and the thematic change from these early plays to his last plays is considerable. The dramas of the first phase usually deal with *fin de siècle* themes, such as feelings of decline, decay, and morbidity. In contrast, Hofmannsthal's later career centered on social themes. He stepped the furthest into the social realm with plays he wrote in collaboration with the composer Richard Strauss, such as *Der Rosenkavalier* (1911), or set to music by Strauss after the play had been completed, such as *Elektra* (play, 1903; operatic version, 1909). With Max Reinhardt (pseudonym of Max Goldmann, 1873–1943) and others, Hofmannsthal founded the Salzburg Festival in 1920; *Jedermann* (1911), Hofmannsthal's adaptation of the medieval morality play *The Summoning of Everyman* (published 1509), became the festival's signature play. With the exception of these plays, his later dramatic work is little known.

The comedy *Der Schwierige* (The Difficult Man, 1921) repeats Hofmannsthal's skepticism regarding language in what is usually regarded to be the best well-made play in the German language, although it transcends that form by foregrounding what a well-made play was designed to hide: the precariousness of communication. Count Bühl, the main character, learns that communication is possible in true and unconditional love, and the play presents marriage as the social equivalent of such love. While affirming conventional values, the play re-established at least the hope for some magic word that at some point in the future — perhaps even in a yet unknown language alluded to in the Chandos letter — might re-create the totality that had been lost. Still in the tradition of Aestheticism because Hofmannsthal's humanism was so far removed from reality, this hope was even present in the first version of Hofmannsthal's last play, *Der Turm* (The Tower, published 1925) — an adaptation of *La vida es sueño* (Life Is a Dream, 1635), by Pedro Calderón de la Barca (1600–1681) — although the rebellion of the jailed son of the king fails.

## Lyrical Innovations

The year 1907 saw the two major lyrical publications of the twentieth century's first decade: Stefan George's perhaps most ambitious collection of poems, *Der Siebente Ring* (The Seventh Ring), and Rainer Maria Rilke's creation of the *Dinggedicht* (thing poem) in *Neue Gedichte* (New Poems), whose second volume, *Der neuen Gedichte anderer Teil* (New Poems: The Other Part), followed in 1908.

*Stefan George*

At the time of the publication of *Der siebente Ring*, Stefan George had established a controversial reputation as a poet who cultivated his image as a prophet and master surrounded by a small circle of friends and disciples. Some believed George to be an egocentric power-maniac in the way he dominated his circle, an attitude that was reflected in the pose of the prophet expressed in his poems and that was considered proto-fascist. For others, the narcissistic and hermetic quality of his poetry concealed George's homosexual tendencies. Regardless of such controversies — which do not diminish the quality of his texts — George embodied a radically new understanding of art in Germany, the attitude of art for art's sake, which he had encountered when he was introduced to the circle around the French Symbolist poet Stéphane Mallarmé (1842–1898) in 1889. George is usually credited with having brought the Symbolist style from France to Germany.

George's work was unified by his attempt to aestheticize existence. His poetry changed as his concept of the existence that was to be aestheticized evolved. George moved from his early creation of Aestheticist literature to his later wish to reform or even revolutionize life itself. The result was a mildly paradoxical dynamic of an elitist and esoteric practice for the few, on the one hand, and reformist or revolutionary intentions for the many, on the other — a dynamic that was reflected and mediated by a shift in focus from form to content that expressed George's Nietzschean hope for a new human being (the one leader or the select few) to lead the people (the many).

*Der siebente Ring* can be understood as demarcating a crucial phase in George's turn from self-referential literature toward life. George's poetic practice started out as quite removed from life. His first phase culminated in the collection of poems *Algabal* (1892) the same year in which George began his literary magazine, *Blätter für die Kunst* (published until 1919). In the preface to the magazine's first issue, George explained the Aesthetic project that he practiced in his poetry: "eine kunst für die kunst" [art for art's sake], based on the opinion that social reforms may be "beautiful" in their own right but have nothing to do with the sphere of literature. In the preface to the second issue of the second volume (1894), he described the formal aspects in more detail, including his observation concerning the precious character of rhyme, which required that once a particular rhyme had been used, it should not be used again.

The works of George's first phase played a significant role in the development of Modernist writing in Germany; although it was in the tradition of French Symbolism, George's poetry was quite new on the German literary scene. Following the French tradition in *Algabal,* George celebrated the option of an artificial existence within a self-contained dream world. Based on an actual notorious Roman emperor, Algabal provided unity to the collection of poems as an embodiment of the poet's ruler qualities. Rejecting realism, Algabal creates a subterranean world that is marked by complete artificiality: his "garden requires neither air nor warmth" [garten bedarf nicht luft und nicht wärme], because it is filled with lifeless artificial objects. In this sacred place Algabal wonders how he will be able to generate the "dark, great, black flower" [Dunkle grosse schwarze blume]. The black flower has been interpreted as the ultimate symbol of an artificiality that has the power to create a world of its own, set against life. George's Aestheticist project also exhibits antimorality in Algabal's emotional coldness when a servant's death provides the occasion for him to observe the play of the colors of red (the blood) and green (the floor), or when his reaction to his dear brother's dead body is calmly to "lift his purple train" [raffe leise nur die purpurschleppe] of his gown so that it will not get soiled — a reaction that aestheticizes death by embedding it in a stanza of exquisite poetic form using rhyme, rhythm, and consonance.

His early work firmly established George as a leading representative of Aestheticism in Germany. The poetry of George's second phase is collected in *Das Jahr der Seele* (The Year of the Soul, 1897). More personal than the previous poetry, it tries to depict the landscape of the soul as it unfolded in nature, which is still predominantly artificial like Algabal's garden and which functions as the background and the foil of the encounter of the soul with itself and with the loved one, who remains unattainable. From this symbolic exploration of the self, George's third phase took him to the expression of his understanding of his role of poet as prophet.

This development culminated in *Der siebente Ring*. The number seven becomes operative in various ways; especially important is the religious allusion to the seven days of creation, which takes on significance when combined with the arrangement of the poems into seven sections, because the central section celebrates George's new center: a new religion and its new god Maximin. The new god was prefigured by the angel as the messenger of beautiful life in *Der Teppich des Lebens* (The Tapestry of Life, 1899) and based on George's encounter with Maximilian Kronberger, who died in 1904, only sixteen years old, and whom George considered to be a poetic genius to the extent of being the incarnation of the divine. In the god Maximin, then, George found the center that had been lost in the modern world: Maximin became a symbol of the union of this world (the world of the objects) and the divine world (the secret world behind the things). The first poem to Maximin acknowledged George's subjectivity. While others might see Maximin as a child or a friend, "I see in you the god" [Ich seh in dir den Gott]. As a personal and irrational myth, this symbol remained vague, and even some of George's disciples disagreed with their master on his use of the symbol. The reason for this disagreement perhaps lay in the fact that George was moving to a stronger emphasis on the content, or even message, of his poems. Form became secondary to content; consequently, in some poems rhyme appears merely decorative, and in a few poems George abandoned end rhyme altogether.

As the circle of friends developed more and more into a cult with George as its leader, George seemed to expect aestheticized life to leave the realm of aesthetics and become one with actual life — with him as its prophet. In the sections "Zeitgedichte" (Poems of Time) and "Tafeln" (Plates), with which *Der siebente Ring* opens and closes, respectively, George criticizes the contemporary world in aesthetic terms of the opposition of the many versus the few. In the second poem, "Das Zeitgedicht," the source of the crisis of belief is identified as the people's willful ignorance of beautiful life: "You kept turning your heads until you could no longer see / The beautiful and great ones" [Ihr wandet so das Haupt bis ihr die Schönen / Die Grossen nicht mehr saht].

George's final two collections of poems, *Der Stern des Bundes* (The Star of the Union, 1914) and *Das neue Reich* (The New Empire, 1928), can be seen either as a continuation of the cultural criticism of his third phase or as a new phase. The latter approach would emphasize elements of the more political orientation of literature of the 1920s; for George, this meant a change in the tone of the poems and a shift in the cultural criticism that brought about a greater conceptual vagueness of stronger prophetic utterances, which remained primarily aimed at the circle of his disciples. The tone appeared to be more prosaic; in particular, the poems in *Der Stern des Bundes* did mainly without rhyme and displayed less rhythmical melody. And they directly expressed the diagnosis of the times: "He who lacks the law of the center / Will float, scattered, into space" [Fehlt ihm der mitte gesetz / Treibt er zerstiebend ins all]. The prophet's voice tells about "the sacred war" [der heilige krieg] that had become inevitable.

Because of its vagueness and basic conservative orientation, such prophecy was wide open to be co-opted by the Nazis, who found in George's texts not only what they considered general similarities in ideology but more specific affinities even at the level of word choices. In fact, in 1933, in their efforts to change German culture, the Nazis tried to persuade George to assume a leading position, as the president of the *Deutsche Dichterakademie*, but he withdrew to Switzerland, where he died the same year. George's ideas, however, represented a conservative core, which Stefan Breuer defines as aesthetic fundamentalism; as such, it had affinities to, but still remained separate from, nationalism and fascism.

*Rainer Maria Rilke*   W. B. Yeats, T. S. Eliot (1888–1965), and Rilke were the  foremost Modernist poets. Born in Prague, Rilke soon found his own themes and tone. His major theme was defined by his personal answer to the search for the center, which he attempted to give in terms of a fragile harmony between the world of tangible objects and that which is unsayable, a union of what is within and what is without. Rilke worked consistently on achieving this harmony; its emergence over the years determined the varying form and tone of Rilke's poetry. In his second phase, consisting of the three parts of *Das Stunden-Buch* (The Book of Hours, 1905, written in 1899, 1901, and 1903, respectively), Rilke used his formal virtuosity to express the mode of the search for the unsayable in terms of a subjective mysticism that was voiced through the persona of a fictitious Russian monk whose prayers or meditations the poems presented. Although there was the pose of the prophet with a mission, the mission remained to be defined; for example, the monk does not yet know whether he is going to be "a falcon, a storm / or a great song" [ein Falke, ein Sturm / oder ein großer Gesang]. By the same token, while influenced by Rilke's experience with religion in Russia on his trips to that country, the poems did not express traditional religious values; on the contrary, the monk voices concern about his death, because he fears that when he dies, his god will lose his meaning.

Although overlapping with *Stunden-Buch, Das Buch der Bilder* (The Book of Images, 1902) introduced the next phase, which culminated in the publication of the two volumes of *Neue Gedichte* in 1907 and 1908. This phase brought about a radical shift from subjectivity trying to approach objectivity: the *Dinggedicht* — usually traced back to poetic developments during the nineteenth century, such as poems by Conrad Ferdinand Meyer (1825–1898). Nevertheless, artistic objectification was only possible through an interaction of human subjectivity with the objects. This interaction, however, was no longer simply subjective but was based on a work ethic that Rilke developed during several months in 1905 and 1906, when he adapted the artistic process used by the French sculptor Auguste Rodin (1840–1917), for whom Rilke briefly worked as a secretary in Paris. In the intense engagement of the artist's subjectivity with the object, the object is transformed into a *Kunst-Ding* (art or artificial thing), which was, in Rilke's view — and in keeping with the Aestheticist position concerning artificiality — more than a mere object because the art thing was capable of eternity.

The apparent objectivity of the thing poem was an expression of encompassing that which is within and that which is without, and this union was the source of meaning in an otherwise chaotic and meaningless world. The essential goal was to objectify part of human experience (where the term *objects* encompasses things, animals, observation, even feelings) in such a way that objects were related to a totality. Meaning became possible at the point when that which was unsayable became, if not actually said, at least perceptible. The high tone of aesthetic earnestness and the traditionally rigid form of the sonnet clearly suggested that this was not just poetic play for Rilke but a serious answer to his search for the center.

The most accomplished thing poems, above all, "Der Panther" (The Panther) and "Archaischer Torso Apollos" (Archaic Torso of Apollo), demonstrated that the aesthetic process that changed a simple thing into an object of art isolated the object in order to point to a possible transcendent truth; in other words, the simple thing was transformed into a concrete manifestation of an abstract idea, somewhat similar to the concept of inscape, with which Gerard Manley Hopkins (1844–1899) worked. For instance, "Archaischer Torso Apollos" describes the torso, although missing its "unheard-of head" [unerhörtes Haupt], as radiant, because it seems to the observer, who does not voice his subjectivity in the poem, as though the torso still contains the center. In this poem the center is the source of sexuality and, thus, the source of life. Around the torso's center, therefore, the observer can reconstruct the lost totality and, thus, meaning.

Just as the observer has made the torso complete and meaningful again, he is challenged by the restored totality to make his own life complete and meaningful, too, in the startling shift of address at the end of the poem: "You must change your life" [Du mußt dein Leben ändern]. Despite all linguistic precision the enigma remains: Was the observer the poet himself, or is the reader included in the intense reconstruction of meaning? Either way, can the reconstructed meaning ever be anything more than a personal meaning? While Rilke's tone in the *Neue Gedichte* was varied — ranging from the high tone of objectivity to subtle irony — the manner in which the poems were created contained an incongruity, which resulted from Rilke's attempt to generate meaning by means of objectification (in art). At the same time, the real world suffered from a loss of meaning that originated in objectification where objects seemed to be more important than human beings, who, in turn, lost their sense of individuality. Rilke did not take this as a point of departure for political analysis; rather, in keeping with the basic project of Aestheticism, he responded in a highly individual fashion that, in addition, can be seen in the context of his highly individualistic life style; he was a wanderer, dependent on wealthy and admiring patrons. He shared the experience of alienation as an outsider but did not have to look at the real source. Instead, he sought eternal truths in his thing poems and his later poems. While these truths remained secret and ultimately unsayable and while they could be politically abused, the images that expressed these truths, such as the torso's imperative to change one's life, are still capable of speaking to a more general human condition.

In the best of Rilke's thing poems, it was that which was perceived as the world behind the objects that spoke. In spite of the poems' formal stability, which suggested objectivity, the poems were still subjective and vague. Though relegated to the background, the lyrical subject (either a poet-prophet persona or Rilke himself) shared the intense experience of working to accomplish harmony between the within and the without — this is the continued achievement of these poems.

The thing poems did not represent the reestablishment of the center; rather, they were a great poetic expression of the search for the center. Rilke himself was keenly aware of the shortcomings of his thing poems. He struggled — eventually with great success — to come to terms with this challenge for the remainder of his career as a writer, never abandoning the basic assumptions of Aestheticism. This struggle first led him into a productive crisis that defined his fourth phase of writing, primarily consisting of the novel *Die Aufzeichnungen des Malte Laurids Brigge* (The Notebook of Malte Laurids Brigge, 1910), several poems that expressed his awareness of the limitation of the *Dinggedichte* program, and writer's block which largely coincided with the First World War but which he did not overcome until 1922. Finally, during the last phase in his development as a poet, Rilke attained two major achievements: he finished the *Duineser Elegien* (Duino Elegies, 1923) and wrote *Die Sonette an Orpheus* (1923), two works that resolved Rilke's lifelong quest for meaning by celebrating poetry itself as the bridge between the visible and invisible realms.

## Modernist Redefinitions of Realism

From its beginning, Modernism redefined the realist approach by adopting the literary achievements of Realism — the literary movement that had dominated the second half of the nineteenth century — to the expressive needs of the twentieth century. Most important in narrative prose, this adaptation depended on an interaction with other Modernist modes, such as Aestheticism during the first decade of the twentieth century. Any Modernist approach to realism significantly deviated from nineteenth-century German Realism in at least the following three interrelated aspects.

First, the fundamental relationship to reality was different, because the experience of reality had changed; while nineteenth-century Realism largely tried to ignore the modern and increasingly complex world, the entire Modernist response to the world was based on the inability to ignore the world's complexity. Second, nineteenth-century Realism sought to offer its readers a unifying experience of beauty that was supposed to underlie reality; Modernism, however, whether it resisted or accepted the world's complexity, could no longer offer an unmediated experience of beauty. Third, the process of *Verklärung* (transfiguration) was at the core of nineteenth-century German Realism as an idealistic project of finding beauty in the world by distinguishing between what had beauty and what did not, and representing this beauty in literature in such a way that the readers could still recognize beauty as a representation of reality. Transfiguration now gave way to more than just a sense that such a distinction was impossible; instead, the Modernist experience of incongruity incorporated the ugly and was formally expressed through ambiguity and irony.

Consequently, for lack of a better term, one might refer to the Modernist redefinition of realism as "Ironic Realism." It went beyond nineteenth-century Realism because it reacted to the realist tradition in an almost paradoxical manner. The redefinition worked simultaneously in terms of a more exact representation of reality as mediated through Naturalism and in terms of a deformation of reality as influenced by the Modernist developments of Aestheticism (and later the Avant-Garde). The Modernist redefinition of realism was a self-conscious blend of realistic and nonrealistic modes.

*Emphasizing the realistic mode*    Thomas Mann and his brother Heinrich, whose partially antagonistic relationship was typical of two different approaches to writing, also exemplified the two major possibilities that existed for predominantly realistic narratives to be modern. On the one hand, Thomas Mann became the preeminent German novelist of the first half of the twentieth century — a fact reflected in his receiving the Nobel Prize for literature in 1929 — by adapting the realistic tradition by means of experimental writing. While this did not necessarily leave out the political dimension, he understood his conservatism as nonpolitical; even later, after he had become politically active against Nazism, his major novels were mythological and attempted to deal with his subject matter as something timeless, implying the political rather than directly stating it. On the other hand, Heinrich Mann was a consciously political writer early on; he typically extended the realistic mode to encompass the political by means of social satire that was directly critical of his time.

*Thomas Mann: Buddenbrooks*    Thomas Mann's work is structured in terms of dichotomies. He took the basic dichotomy of the artist as an outsider struggling against an antagonistic bourgeois society as it was handed down by the literary tradition of the German novel of education, or *Bildungs-* and *Entwicklungsroman*, represented in prototypical form in *Wilhelm Meisters Lehrjahre* (Wilhelm Meister's Apprenticeship, 1795–1796), by Johann Wolfgang von Goethe (1749–1832), which traces the hero's aesthetic and social education toward becoming a complete human being. Yet the humanist ideal of the Bildungsroman clashed with modern reality; as early as in his first novel, *Buddenbrooks: Verfall einer Familie* (Buddenbrooks: Decline of a Family, 1901), Mann's writing was ironic and critical of this tradition.

The decline of the Buddenbrook family over four generations from 1835 to 1877 is depicted by narratively intertwining economic, ethical, and biological forms of decay to represent each generation as weaker than the previous one. In keeping with Aestheticist ideals, however, decline is not dealt with negatively. It is presented in a matter-of-fact way, most notably in the objectified descriptions of Thomas Buddenbrook's and Hanno's deaths, or it is seen in the context of a heightened sensibility, implying that decadence leads to artistic creativity. The central theme of decline allowed Thomas Mann to achieve a high degree of epic integration (which is defined as the relating of all narrative elements to each other), to the extent that the novel can be seen as "a complex metaphor for the way art is born out of a dying culture" (John Fletcher and Malcolm Bradbury, in Bradbury and McFarlane 406). While the novel moves from the great-grandfather's vigorous self-reliance to the grandfather's holding on to bourgeois values, the third generation, that of Thomas Buddenbrook and his siblings with their abstract sense of duty, provides the focal point and frame of the novel. The decline reaches its final stage for the family with the death of the musically gifted Hanno, the fifteen-year-old son of Thomas Buddenbrook. Nevertheless, the fact that the novel begins and ends with scenes showing Thomas Buddenbrook's sister, Tony, who is characterized by a certain childish immaturity, both as a little girl and as an adult, might indicate that there is continuity in life at different levels.

*Buddenbrooks* marked a watershed between nineteenth-century Realism and Modernism. It introduced experiments in form that went beyond traditional realism, as well as beyond a mere borrowing of themes from Aestheticism. Above all, there was the narrative irony (a measure of the author's awareness of the complexity involved in narrating a complex world expressed in the detachment between author-narrator and the narrated characters and events), which became Thomas Mann's trademark as a storyteller. A second aspect was the integration of ideas into the narrated events by means of essayistic presentation of psychological insight.

What was so modern about Mann's narrative irony was its foundation in the modern human condition of life in isolation and alienation; dehumanized life was reflected by a dehumanized narrative form, which nonetheless retained a spark of humanity — hence the irony. Both Thomas Buddenbrook and his son, Hanno, die a modern death without metaphysical comfort; they are simply specimens of humankind that succumb to a fatal medical condition, which, in turn, is the subject of a medical case history rather than a traditional novel. The description of

Thomas Buddenbrook's seizure reflects this detachment. His collapse in the street, with all its pathetic and humiliating details, is by no means presented from an outside view. The third-person inside view, however, does not show an individual's emotional response but rather the final failure of a mechanical doll whose brain "is being thrown around by some force at an increasing, horribly increasing speed in large and then smaller and smaller concentric circles" [sein Gehirn . . . von einer Kraft mit wachsender, fürchterlich wachsender Geschwindigkeit in großen, kleinen und immer kleineren konzentrischen Kreisen herumgeschwungen].

Hanno's death is described with even greater detachment. No longer given an inside view, the reader has to connect the medical discussion of typhoid to Hanno. After a long chapter that presents a typical day in Hanno's life, the next chapter begins quite abruptly with the announcement: "Now, a typhoid infection proceeds in the following way" [Mit dem Typhus ist es folgendermaßen bestimmt]. The remainder of the chapter discusses, in medical terms and without reference to any character in the novel, the course of the disease to its fatal end. A few paragraphs into the next and final chapter, the information that Hanno had been buried for about six months is almost casually related.

The second aspect that made *Buddenbrooks* modern was its essayistic character, which went hand in hand with a psychological emphasis. Hanno's emotions are presented through his music, and Thomas Buddenbrook's attitude toward life is presented through his response to reading Schopenhauer. Here the Modernist search for the center, for a new myth, becomes operative; like the protagonists in stories by James Joyce (1882–1941), Thomas Buddenbrook experiences an epiphany. In the middle of the night he cries out: "I will live!" [Ich werde leben!]. Ironically, like Hans Castorp in Mann's *Der Zauberberg* (The Magic Mountain, 1924), Thomas Buddenbrook forgets his insight and allows the traditional order to take over again, symbolized by his returning the book to its proper place on the bookshelf.

This context emphasizes that the world of ideas meets the real world in *Buddenbrooks*. While similar meetings in realist novels lead to the affirmation of the real world, the situation here has changed. Thomas Mann's novel depends on an affirmation of events and ideas as they interconnect, to the extent that the ideas add to the story rather than take away from it. The epic integration of all narrative elements supplies the novel with its own syntax of ideas. The main idea of decline not only lends a consistent logic to the novel but also contains the basic Modernist experience. The ultimate irony may lie in the fact that the novel presents modern complexity in the guise of surface realism.

Heinrich Mann took the opposite route to in-
*Heinrich Mann:* cluding modern life in the realist tradition; he
Professor Unrat used social criticism and satire to distort reality,
while his narrative techniques — which he con-
sidered secondary to plot and social relevance — generally remained
within the tradition. In contrast to his brother, Heinrich Mann understood himself as a political writer; indeed, he was the only openly
democratic writer of major stature in Germany at the time. More than
his brother, he was influenced by French realist writers in particular,
but like his brother, he structured his works in terms of dichotomies,
including the one of artist and society. The main dichotomy in his
works, however, was clearly political: mind versus power. Often played
on the concretely human level with love as a motivating factor, the
treatment of this dichotomy expressed Heinrich Mann's optimistic belief in humanity's progress toward democratic ideals.

His optimistic belief in changing the world, his opposition to
power, and his willingness to use novels as a fictional means of documenting the utopian — in short, his assumption that literature and
politics go hand in hand — have an affinity to the later Avant-Garde
movement. His 1909 novel, *Die kleine Stadt* (The Small Town), which
has been called his masterpiece, celebrates the potential of humankind.
A summary of its main plot reads like the gospel of the later Avant-
Garde, because art and life are merged and because the *neue Mensch*
(New Human Being) is evoked. Political tensions in a small, idyllic
Italian town are brought to the fore by the rehearsals and performance
of an opera, which the audience understands as a representation of its
world. After the tensions are calmed by the major antagonists' public
reconciliation, the artists are rewarded, and the social function of art is
recognized.

Heinrich Mann's social criticism still remains valid; this is especially
true of *Der Untertan* (The Loyal Subject, 1916). Written during the
first decade of the twentieth century, his novel *Professor Unrat oder das
Ende eines Tyrannen* (Small Town Tyrant, 1905) is particularly noteworthy. The 1905 novel also had tremendous popular success in its
1930 movie adaptation, *Der blaue Engel* (The Blue Angel), with Emil
Jannings as the secondary-school professor and Marlene Dietrich in the
role of the seductive music-hall actress Rosa Fröhlich. Heinrich Mann
welcomed the cinema as a new means of expression for democracy,
emphasizing his belief that art is a form of public life.

*Professor Unrat* shows two sides of Raat, whose nickname, *Unrat,*
means "garbage." One side enjoys public approval; as the teacher, he
represents power in a nationalistic and imperialistic system. The other
side suffers public condemnation as an anarchistic attempt to under-
mine the morals in the small town. What the novel reveals, however, is

that these are not simply two sides of the same person but also two sides of the same tyrannical power that destroys human life in the name of what it considers right. *Professor Unrat* is a case study of the decline of an authoritarian personality who, after initial attempts to protect society, turns against it. At the same time, the novel calls attention to the destructive potential of the society that makes such a personality possible.

Instead of eliminating what he considers the corrupting influence exerted by the artist Rosa Fröhlich over some of his students, the fifty-seven-year-old Professor Unrat himself falls under Rosa's spell and loses his bourgeois respectability and his teaching position. He marries Rosa; after spending all of his money, they start entertaining at their home, giving rise to rumors about orgies and attracting even more people. In this way Unrat takes revenge on the society that shunned him, and he regards the moral decline of the town as his personal triumph. Despite his love for Rosa, Unrat's true emotions are defined by his exercise of power and fluctuate between fear and triumph.

The novel's plot is set in motion by Unrat's decision concerning one student, Lohmann: "to eliminate *this* student, to protect human society from *this* contagious material" [*diesen* Schüler zu beseitigen, vor *diesem* Ansteckungsstoffe die menschliche Gesellschaft zu behüten]. To destroy people's bourgeois existence is Unrat's main motivation throughout the novel. This endeavor is not a reaction to his being shunned by society, because it precedes his association with Rosa and has been his usual attitude toward students. In the end, it is Lohmann who brings Unrat down. After an absence of two years, Lohmann comes back to town at a time when the relationship between Unrat and Rosa is strained psychologically and financially. Unrat confronts Rosa and Lohmann, grabs Lohmann's wallet, and runs. Ironically, Lohmann, the one whom Unrat wanted to bar from bourgeois society, responds to being robbed "in a quite bourgeois way: with 'police'" [ganz bürgerlich mit "Polizei"].

The novel ends with Unrat disappearing into the darkness of the police car, where he is reunited with Rosa, who has also been arrested. This indeterminate ending invites speculation as to whether the novel is a social-psychological case study of an authoritarian personality, whether Unrat engaged in an anarchist revolt against society, and whether Unrat and Rosa will return and keep threatening the moral fiber of society.

*Emphasizing the nonrealistic mode* — Other novelists took an approach that even more strongly emphasized a sense of, or a search for, that which is beyond reality. While the nonrealistic mode could be incorporated into novels in many ways, two developments were particularly important for the history of the novel: the emergence of the lyrical novel, which constituted a major Modernist innovation, and the continuing tradition of fantastic literature.

*Toward the lyrical novel*

The Modernist combination of realistic and nonrealistic modes favored a concept of objectivity that emphasized the lyrical process over the narrative description. This process is described by the famous dictum of the Swiss painter Paul Klee (1879–1940) that art does not reproduce that which is already visible; rather, art makes visible. Applied to literature, it meant that the modulation of images that express human experiences had become more important than the human being himself or herself. Novels of this kind during the first decade of the twentieth century laid the foundation for the explosion of Modernist creativity that began around 1910 and that gave rise to novelistic excursions into the lyrical and essayistic. This development is central for the Modernist novel and includes the works of Franz Kafka (1883–1924) and Thomas Mann, in spite of the latter's great indebtedness to realism. During the twentieth century's first decade, Robert Musil's *Die Verwirrungen des Zöglings Törless* (The Confusions of the Pupil Törless, 1906) and Robert Walser's novels were the masterpieces of this development.

Musil's *Törless*, although a third-person narrative, evokes the atmosphere of an Austrian military boarding school rather than realistically describing it, because the central consciousness, young Törless, is in a state of confusion. The surface plot was based on the author's own experiences and was in keeping with other works about conflicts of adolescents with authority and among themselves. The main conflict concerns a group of students who take it upon themselves to punish another student. Reiting deduces that only Basini could have been stealing money from Beineberg and the others, so he and Beineberg punish Basini sadistically in secret nighttime meetings in which Törless joins as an observer rather than an active participant. He is both attracted to and repulsed by the sadistic events and the homosexual acts in which Basini engages in separate meetings with each of his punishers. In the course of a few weeks Törless matures, and as the other two plan to expose Basini publicly, Basini, on Törless's suggestion, turns himself in to the headmaster. Törless testifies in the ensuing investigation, and it is decided that he should leave the school.

The surface plot, with its sadistic and sexually charged elements, contributed to the novel's success, the only great success Musil enjoyed during his lifetime. Beneath this plot lies the more profound problem of power in general: how society's class structure is reproduced in the totalitarian institution of the school; how the group dynamic among the students again reproduces this order; and how it escalates into violence. Later, the novel invited political interpretations as prefiguring the political sadism of Nazism in the behavior of Beineberg and Reiting.

At the core of the novel, however, is a profound crisis resulting from the alienation that originates in the conflict between reality and nonreality. This was a driving force in the development of Aestheticism; like Lord Chandos in Hofmannsthal's fictitious letter, the adolescent Törless experiences the existence of another reality behind normal reality, of the irrational, which remains for him unfathomable. Testifying during the investigation, he tries to explain it when he says that he sees things in two forms while he knows that things are things and will always remain things. Even though he cannot express the duality in words, he clearly feels that it will remain a part of his life. At this point, Törless has taken a crucial step in the process of his individuation, because he accepts the combination of rationality and irrationality, of the bourgeois order and the adventurous disorder, that Musil himself attempted to achieve. The fact that his confusions have been cleared up finds expression in the metaphor of his regaining his ability to distinguish between day and night and in the adult sexual gaze with which he is now able to see his mother, who comes to take her son home. The novel convinces because it depicts with psychological subtlety the achievement of autonomy by an individual mind that is confused but not weak.

*Jakob von Gunten* (1909), subtitled *Ein Tagebuch* (A Diary), is considered the most important of the three Berlin novels by Robert Walser (1878–1956). The narrator, Jakob von Gunten, attends the Berlin institute for the training of servants headed by Mr. Benjamenta. Although the institute is presented as real, it remains mysterious throughout the novel. From the first sentence, which states "one learns very little here" [man lernt hier sehr wenig], to the last, which bids farewell to the institute, the narrative has a dreamlike quality; even Jakob's self-assertiveness at the end of the novel seems strangely carefree. Realizing that he amounts to nothing, Jakob is sure that God will be with him, even though he does not have to think about it: "God is with those who do not think" [Gott geht mit den Gedankenlosen].

In his passion for all that is small, Walser wrote a novel about servants, people who are small in terms of social significance. As though in ironic reversal of Goethe's *Wilhelm Meisters Lehrjahre*, Walser sent this young student with the aristocratic name on a journey to a diploma that would entitle him to serve. In the narrator's psychological journey, the realm of the unreal is extended and then suddenly confronted with reality and imploded. The institute's inner rooms are usually forbidden to students and are the subject of fantastic speculations; when Jakob finally is allowed to go there, the mystery disappears, and everyday banality takes over: there is the fish tank that has to be cleaned.

A development toward initiation only occurs in Jakob's psyche. After Mr. Benjamenta's sister, Lisa, has died and the institute, which had been losing students and faculty, has been closed, Jakob follows Lisa's wish and stays with Mr. Benjamenta, although the latter made a mysterious attempt on Jakob's life. Now they will go into the desert together. This destination allows for multiple interpretations, from biblical implications to foreshadowing failure in the search for selfhood. Jakob, because he is so undefined, is a lyrical hero, around whom the novel's imagery is modulated. The lyrical novel was continued especially with Rilke's *Die Aufzeichnungen des Malte Laurids Brigge* and novels by authors who admired Walser, for example, Franz Kafka and Hermann Hesse.

Thematically, Hermann Hesse's *Unterm Rad* (Beneath the Wheel, 1906) belongs in the context of novels about adolescents attempting to grow into the adult world. In contrast to the novels by Musil and Walser, *Unterm Rad* was a more directly satirical attack on the contemporary educational system. Its aggressive realism made it more like the straightforward German school novel, or *Schulliteratur*, such as *Freund Hein* (Friend Death, 1902), by Emil Strauß (1866–1960). Hesse's autobiographically informed novel shows how a sensitive boy is pushed by his philistine elders beneath the wheel of formal boarding-school education, which metaphorically crushes him to death. The boy is sent back to his small rural hometown, where he eventually commits suicide. Yet the novel is not entirely pessimistic, because it concentrates only on one possible story. The boy's soul mate leaves the school and novel mid-narrative; his name (Heilner, possibly related to the verb *heilen*, to heal) and his poetic inclination suggest that he will go the way of the heroes in Hesse's later novels: from the external to the internal world. Hesse's early novels are important points in his artistic development toward the lyrical novel because they simultaneously show him as a realist and romantic. They prefigure much of his later fiction by exploring the tension between the real and the nonreal and by setting up a dualistic relationship between characters for such an exploration.

*Fantastic literature*  Fantastic literature would seem ideal for unfolding the premise of Aestheticism about creating objects and events that can exist only in language. Nevertheless, this genre has never been at the center of German literature, although it has been a crucial element in many works. The range of fantastic literature extends from pure imagination to an irreality that intrudes into reality. Especially in the latter case, only

a fine line separates "fantastic" literature from "mainstream" texts, such
as *Törless*.

Paul Scheerbart (1863–1915), an intriguing and important outsider
to mainstream German literature, wrote predominantly in the fantastic
vein. Even where his work dealt with technology, it was not typical science fiction, because it was naive to the point of believing one could
create a perpetual motion machine (which Scheerbart not only tried to
do, but he also documented his attempt). His writing was visionary in a
mystical sense. Other writers with similar mystical interests in cosmic
events include Alfred Mombert (1872–1942), Theodor Däubler
(1876–1934), and the circle of the *Kosmiker* in Schwabing (Munich)
around Karl Wolfskehl (1869–1948).

Revolution in Scheerbart's sense meant imagining cosmic events in
organic terms and changing the world into a work of art. Nevertheless,
in his short narration *Rakkóx der Billionär* (Rakkóx the Billionaire,
1900), an architect's proposal "just as an experiment to transform an
entire mountain into an architectural work of art from top to bottom"
[versuchsweise mal einen ganzen Felsen von oben bis unten in ein
Kunstwerk zu verwandeln] in order, ultimately, to change the entire
planet within the next thousand years is placed in the scenario of global
warfare. An antimilitarist and antimaterialist attitude defined the other
side of Scheerbart, the social critic as humorist who fled into fantastic
literature out of rage. At their most fantastic, such as in *Die wilde Jagd*
(The Wild Chase, 1900), Scheerbart's mystic visions of the cosmos created images that can exist only in language and that celebrate an aesthetic model not of reality but of potential existence and fulfillment.

While Scheerbart pushed for the far reaches of liberating fantasy,
Alfred Kubin (1877–1959) focused on the intrusive quality of the fantastic. Doubly talented as a writer and a graphic artist, he wrote a great
fantastic novel *Die andere Seite* (The Other Side, 1909). In the tradition of Edgar Allan Poe (1809–1849) and E. T. A. Hoffmann (1776–
1822), the novel presents the narrator's attempt to make sense of the
distortions of normality by fantastic occurrences that begin with an invitation to come to a "Traumreich" [dreamland]. Created by Claus
Patera, the narrator's former classmate, the dreamland is described as
located in remote China and appears so real that the narrator, a graphic
artist like Kubin, includes a map of its capital in his report, which constitutes the novel.

Chronicling the slow but inevitable self-destruction of the dreamland, *Die andere Seite* proceeds in a matter-of-fact description from one
terrifying detail to the next, from the death of the narrator's wife to his
final vision of Patera, the ruler of the dreamland, as an androgynous
being. The dreamland is no happy utopia; rather, it is literally "the
other side" — the dark side — of the human psyche, which encom-

passes contrary forces that are identified in the novel as the principles of life and death. The contradiction is so terrible because "this contradictory double play is continued within us" [sich dies widersprechende Doppelspiel in uns fortsetzt] and because it makes reality increasingly elusive. The ruler of the dreamland remains inaccessible, even to his former classmate, the narrator. The way to him leads through a labyrinth of rooms and hallways — scenes that prefigure aspects of Kafka's castle. Moreover, nothing is what it appears to be. The population consists of dreamers who have been invited to join the dreamland; but is the novel itself a dream? And do the dreamers dream Patera into existence or he them? Patera metamorphoses into several beings and people, even into his adversary from America; at least, that is what the narrator sees. Everything and everybody seems to be "the other side," not just of its respective counterpart but of itself, himself, or herself.

Scheerbart's influence can be seen during his own time, especially in the poetry of Morgenstern and Joachim Ringelnatz (pseudonym of Hans Bötticher, 1883–1934); in general, his work was well received by the early Expressionists of the *Sturm* circle. Kubin's novel showed a great affinity to Kafka's work, but its influence continued independently of Kafka's. In retrospect, *Die andere Seite* was often understood as an anticipation of the atrocities of Nazism. In the immediate years after the Second World War, West German literature's version of magic realism in works by authors like Hermann Kasack (1896–1966) and Wolfdietrich Schnurre (1920–1989) was indebted to Kubin.

### Toward Expressionist Drama

*Frank Wedekind*

Frank Wedekind (1864–1918) rose to fame during the first decade of the twentieth century, partly through plays that he had written and published earlier but that had not been performed before because of censorship. These plays were revolutionary on two counts: they anticipated Expressionist drama, and they advocated a new role for sexuality. Thematically, Wedekind radicalized aspects of the contemporary discourse, such as youth and sexuality, by means of exaggeration and the grotesque. The anti-illusionist tendency of both devices ran counter to Naturalism and Aestheticism but led toward Expressionism. His opposition to Naturalism was also ideological, because he believed that literary movements, such as Naturalism, and social movements, such as workers' and women's liberation, sold out to bourgeois society by trying to improve elements of a fundamentally bad society rather than trying to create a better one.

Rather than dominating nature, actualizing it by means of a new role for sexuality was Wedekind's way to a better society. His emphasis on sexuality touched on social taboos, and his attitude was that of an artist who, in order to pronounce the truth, had to shock his audience, especially because he felt that values could only be presented in their negation. Cases in point are Wedekind's cynical songs about shocking subjects, such as slaughtered aunts, performed by himself at political cabarets. His most significant achievements were the plays *Frühlings Erwachen* (Spring's Awakening) and *Lulu*.

*Frühlings Erwachen* (published in 1891, premiered in 1906) was one of the first works in German literature to participate in the contemporary discourses on youth issues. *Reformpädagogik*, the reformist movement in education, proposed radical changes in the traditional school system, whose authoritarian character was also exposed in literary works of the time. The adolescents, who in Wedekind's play represent natural beings, can only under great suffering grow into an adult world that has become devoid of anything natural — if they grow up at all. Wendla, a girl who is pregnant by the protagonist, Melchior, dies as a result of an abortion her mother forces her to undergo. Moritz, Melchior's friend, is weak and commits suicide after he fails at school. Melchior, a free spirit, is suspended from school, and his parents decide to send him to a correctional institution.

The drama's anti-illusionist style is obvious in the way the play is broken up into short scenes that often jump from one place to another, violating the traditional unity of place. The clash between realistic scenes and farcical nonrealistic scenes suggests that the world in Wedekind's play is out of balance on the surface. It is unified, however, in its underlying perspective that no longer privileges the sphere of the dialogue, which provided the basis of classical plays. Not only do people no longer really talk with each other in *Frühlings Erwachen*; a scene can also be an expression of one consciousness rather than the meeting of two. The farcical scene (III, 1) of the faculty meeting is more than a searing attack on an authoritarian school system; it can also be understood as a representation of how the students see their teachers. The final scene in the cemetery, where "the Masked Gentleman" [der vermummte Herr] rescues Melchior from following the invitation of Moritz's ghost to join him in death, is more than a nonrealistic dream scene: it is a scenic representation of Melchior's quite realistic inner conflict.

Wedekind's most notorious work and greatest achievement was *Lulu*, the 1913 recombination of a play that was originally planned as a unit but had to be published in two phases: *Der Erdgeist* (The Earth Spirit, published in 1895, performed in 1898) and *Die Büchse der Pandora* (Pandora's Box, published in 1902, performed in 1904). Lulu is the natural being par excellence; therefore, her decline is inevitable in an unnatural world. The drama's central conflict — the inevitability of Lulu's downfall and her struggle against it — is determined by two mutually exclusive moral concepts. Lulu's amoral and innocent sexuality becomes a death trap for men who behave according to bourgeois morality; she, however, eventually becomes the victim of a world dominated by men. *Der Erdgeist* and *Büchse der Pandora* are about Lulu's rise and fall, respectively. Lulu's uninhibited sexual behavior is not evil, yet it attracts and creates evil in a society that is so different from her.

At the end of *Der Erdgeist* Lulu kills her husband, Dr. Schön. This is the end of a complex relationship of love, dependency, and exploitation. Dr. Schön had picked up the young Lulu from the streets, but instead of officially tying himself to her, he had maintained a clandestine sexual relationship with her, while seeing to it that she was involved in other, official, relationships. Dr. Schön realizes that he is dependent on her, finally gives up his plans to marry someone else, and marries Lulu. Yet in the long run, just like her previous two husbands, he is killed by her uninhibited promiscuity. While Dr. Goll died of the shock over the realization of Lulu's nature and Schwarz killed himself for the same reason, Dr. Schön tries to get Lulu to kill herself but thereby causes his own death.

*Die Büchse der Pandora* picks up where *Der Erdgeist* left off, with Lulu in prison for the murder of Dr. Schön. In a self-conscious reference to the first play, Alwa, Dr. Schön's son, is the author of a play called *Erdgeist*, and he wonders whether a person sentenced to prison can be the hero of a modern drama. In the meantime, Lulu has actually been freed from prison through a grotesque plan of the lesbian Countess von Geschwitz. When she returns, Lulu and Alwa kiss, and he pulls her down onto the sofa on which his father had bled to death. The next act shows Lulu and Alwa in Paris, where they continue their social decline and finally have to flee from the police. The final act finds them in London, where their lack of funds forces Lulu into prostitution. But the woman whose nature is defined by sexuality is clumsy at being a prostitute. Natural sexuality and practice of sexuality as defined by bourgeois society are presented as two entirely different behaviors. The catastrophe, then, is imminent: one of Lulu's visitors kills Alwa; another, who turns out to be Jack the Ripper, kills the countess and Lulu.

The world of the play is one in which people do not know each other, and for a brief moment of satisfaction "they turn the world into a torture chamber" [machen sie die Welt zur Folterkammer]. Wedekind puts this analysis in the mouth of the Countess von Geschwitz, whose question — whether there have ever been people who were able to achieve happiness through love — is a central question that Wedekind asks his audience. He believed that living his own radical individuality was a legitimate response. While this attitude made his criticism of bourgeois society most radical, it did not offer a general solution. Wedekind's achievement lay in portraying the violent clash of the bourgeois world as torture chamber with the possibility of a different world.

The play also contains anti-illusionist elements that point toward Expressionism. In addition to the elements that it shares with *Frühlings Erwachen* (social criticism, use of exaggeration and the grotesque, decaying dialogue when the characters talk past one another), *Lulu* places greater emphasis on the characters as representatives of types: Lulu as natural sexuality, or "the true animal, the wild, beautiful animal" [das wahre Tier, das wilde, schöne Tier]. The play's structure also points to a typical form of Expressionist drama, since each act presents a distinct station in Lulu's development. Beyond Expressionism, Wedekind influenced Bertolt Brecht and, later, the theater of the absurd and grotesque, especially Friedrich Dürrenmatt (1921–1990).

# 2: The 1910s:
# The First Phase of Avant-Garde
# Literature — Expressionism and Dada

### The Social Foundations:
### A World at War with Itself

A S THE CLIMAX OF ONGOING POLITICAL CHANGES, the First World War was the defining experience of the decade. It was the first great civil war of the European bourgeoisie because a shared value system was one of the many factors — including misjudgments, miscommunication, and fatalism — that contributed to the complex situation before the war. Ironically, in the nations fighting each other in the First World War, one and the same culture, that is, bourgeois culture, was fighting itself. This culture valorized the virtue of duty, which, however, had different meanings for each nation: for "the British 'the white man's burden,' the French 'mission civilisatrice,' and the German 'deutsche Kultur'" (Kern 151).

Territorial conflicts heated up the political atmosphere and ultimately triggered the outbreak of the war. Since Germany had become politically isolated from the other major European powers except for Austria, it oscillated "between grandiose visions of *Weltpolitik* and paranoid fears of *Einkreisung*" (Kern 250). As the Turkish empire retreated, the Balkans became increasingly volatile; the Serbs called for a greater Serbian state, and the Russian empire, during a conflict between Italy and Turkey, annexed European Turkish territory. While Austria prepared for war against Serbia, the Austrian heir to the throne, Prince Franz Ferdinand, believed in a diplomatic solution. But he and his wife were assassinated in Sarajevo on June 28, 1914, and on August 1 the precarious European order erupted into the First World War.

After initial enthusiasm on all sides, the attrition phase of the war brought disillusionment and alienation. Nine to ten million lives were lost during the war. Food rationing and the fact that women worked in weapons factories meant that the civilian population was also affected. The Russian Revolution under Lenin in the spring of 1917 brought a separate peace treaty on the Eastern front, with harsh territorial losses for Russia. On the Western front the United States joined forces with France and England late in the war.

As early as September 1917, General Erich Ludendorff, the second in command in the German army's high command under General Paul von Hindenburg, had asked the government to seek a cease-fire. On October 3, 1918, the German high command repeated its assessment that the war could no longer be won. The same night a telegram was sent to the American president, Woodrow Wilson, asking for a cease-fire. At this point Ludendorff reverted to a hard-line position, demanding that the war be continued. He was discharged in late October 1918, before the cease-fire went into effect on November 11, giving him and other nationalists the opportunity to fabricate the *Dolchstoß-legende,* according to which the German military would have won the war if it had not been stabbed in the back by pacifists and democratic politicians.

The final peace treaty of 1919 imposed harsh conditions on Germany: loss of about a tenth of its population and a seventh of its territory, restrictions on the military, reparations, and the declaration of Germany as the only guilty party. While the declaration of guilt may have been intended as a justification for the harsh conditions that Germany had to meet, the effect was moral condemnation. Many Germans felt resentment because a complex prewar situation had been reduced to a simplistic explanation. Nationalist propaganda of the *Dolchstoß-legende* type caused such general resentment to be transferred onto the leading postwar politicians and the young democracy itself.

Thus, the seed of conflict between democratic and antidemocratic forces was planted from the first moment of the republic's existence. Yet there was another conflict during which the opportunity for a stronger democracy was lost. Germany was declared a republic twice — or, rather, two different republics were declared — within the period of two hours on November 9, 1918. The Social Democrat Philipp Scheidemann declared one republic, the official one (later known as the *Weimar Republic,* after the town of Weimar), after the last imperial chancellor had handed over the government to the Social Democrat Friedrich Ebert. The other republic, a socialist one, was declared by the Spartacist Karl Liebknecht.

This conflict went back to the October 1918 mutiny in Kiel, when sailors refused their admiral's order to attack England after Germany asked for a cease-fire. Across Germany, soldiers and workers formed local councils modeled after the Russian soviet, without the checks and balances of executive, legislative, and judicial branches but with direct representation of the people, who can impeach their representatives at any time. Facing the beginning of a general strike in Berlin on November 9, the Social Democrats, who had led the soviet movement, formed an interim government with Ebert at the helm to counteract the rising influence of the more radical leftist parties. General elections were held on January 19, 1919, from which the SPD emerged as the strongest party. The national assembly elected Ebert president, and he appointed Scheidemann to form an SPD-led government. The Social Democrats had opted for reform rather than revolution and worked together with moderate parties in the young parliamentary democracy.

Paradoxically, the democracy turned to its enemies for defense against the socialist republic. The notorious right-wing volunteer corps, or *Freikorps*, were deployed by the SPD-led government in addition to regular military to quell wide-scale strikes and to defeat the local soviet-style councils during the spring of 1919. However, the *Freikorps* had their own terrorist agenda of political murder; on January 15, 1919, their victims included Karl Liebknecht and Rosa Luxemburg.

At a safe distance from the volatile political situation, the national assembly met in the small town of Weimar to work on the new German constitution. The center of German Classicism, the town had been also selected to reach out to a German tradition distinguished by humanism. In addition, the colors of the liberal movement of 1848 — black, red, and gold — became the national colors of the new Germany. Bearing the mark of the earlier unsuccessful attempt at democracy, the 1919 constitution guaranteed rights of freedom and equality. To strengthen checks and balances, the president was given an amount of power that would actually tip the scale in the president's favor vis-à-vis the parliament; and this later contributed to Germany's political problems.

Germany's first successful attempt at democracy in the Weimar Republic carried the seeds of its own destruction because of the role the antidemocratic elements were allowed to play and of missed opportunities for a deeper democratization that left more radical, yet still democratic, individuals alienated. When the next decade brought economic crises, the young German democracy was too unstable to survive.

## The Literary Spectrum

The First World War altered the actual political landscape of Europe that had been relatively stable for the previous half century. Czarist Russia became the Soviet Union; the Austro-Hungarian empire was dissolved, and Germany, its borders redrawn, became a republic. Just as the political map was redrawn, so was the artistic one. The First World War defined the decade; nevertheless, the experience of an absurd world and its artistic reflection, often in fierce images of war, not only predated the actual war, but the war itself could also be called Modernist. In Modernist art, the background, once "negative" in relation to the foreground, became "a positive element, of equal importance with all others" (Kern 153). In camouflage, war developed its own version of blending background and foreground. The First World War fused art and life into surrealist landscapes — landscapes of an absurd world whose reality, precisely because it was so complex and overwhelming, seemed insubstantial and, hence, beyond the individual's comprehension.

*A Theory of the Avant-Garde*

The Modernist answer to such a complex world was to create a self-conscious art that was itself complex and that set out to find the lost center (or a new one). Aestheticism represented the climax of this development within art: literature had not only become self-aware of language as its own medium but also had withdrawn into the realm of the work of art. Aestheticism considered a work to exist within the institution of literature, a view that assumes a social fabric in which certain ideas about art exist and determine in which manner a specific work is received by the audience. Therefore, literature was not considered to have a direct impact on the real world.

In contrast, the Avant-Garde pushed forward from its counterworld into reality. The Avant-Garde took the linguistic self-awareness of Aestheticism and the political fervor of Naturalism in its radical departure from previous artistic practice. It represented a tremendous politicization that fused art and life in terms of reassigning utmost importance to the social aspect. The center that was the goal of the Modernist quest was considered "found" in terms of a political goal, and literature was believed to provide the map to that goal. Therefore, the Avant-Garde replaced Aestheticism's orientation toward art for art's sake and pure poetry with its own emphasis on *l'art social* and *littérature engagée*.

The Avant-Garde was new because it was not simply literature about politics; rather, it was politics, or even revolution, in the form of literature. This political fusion of art and life had a lasting effect: ever since, it has not been clear what, unequivocally, constitutes a work of art. The Avant-Garde was successful at revolutionizing art because it turned against art as an institution. To the self-awareness of Aestheticist art the Avant-Garde added self-criticism, attacking the status of art in bourgeois society. The Avant-Garde's two fundamental achievements consisted in rendering art visible as an institution and then attacking the institution and in creating a "nonorganic" work (or manifestation) of art.

By fusing art and life, Avant-Garde literature challenged the assumption that literature had no direct consequences for the other spheres of society. Exposing the rules that determined art as an institution, this challenge was political by default, since the political potential of individual works is usually neutralized when the works participate in art as an institution. Dadaism was the most radical movement not only among the three Avant-Garde movements in German literature — the others are Expressionism and epic theater — but within the European Avant-Garde in general, because it directly attacked art as an institution.

The attack on preconceived ideas about art necessarily changed the character of the work of art. The traditional work of art before the Avant-Garde appeared as "organic," that is, as growing from concrete life situations — even using material that was considered to be living — and, thus, as producing a living picture of social totality. In contrast, an Avant-Garde work of art seemed to be "nonorganic" in the sense that it did not endow its material with life but considered it to be just what it was: material. Therefore, linguistic signs were no longer meaningful and representative of totality; rather, they were empty signs that, taken out of their context by the Avant-Gardist, were mere fragments. These fragments were now joined, with the intent of creating meaning — although positive meaning could no longer be guaranteed.

The concept and practice of montage exemplifies the essence of a nonorganic work, since "montage presupposes the fragmentation of reality and describes the phase of the constitution of the work" (Bürger 1984, 73). The montage, which may combine pieces of newspapers or other objects of reality, is a radically different type of work: the signs (or at least some of them) out of which the montage is made no longer point to reality; rather, they are reality. The Avant-Garde fusion of art and life, perhaps, should no longer be referred to as a work of art but as a type of manifestation. While the Avant-Garde was ultimately perceived as art, its challenge to the very concept of the artwork still continues.

The Avant-Garde represented a reintegration of the supposedly autonomous social spheres under the dominance of the political. Such a reintegration is problematic. It would be an antimodern vision of a unified world if it did not correspond to the status of the autonomous spheres. The Avant-Garde, however, operated in response to actual developments of the modern world, such as the emergence of economic capitalism as defining all other spheres via its political manifestations. Furthermore, such reintegration might produce a literature that successfully fuses art and nonart but in the process loses its "literariness" in favor of its rhetorical function, as literature becomes one political strategy for change among others, such as propaganda or advertising. The questions to consider are whether literature is capable of producing social change — and, if not, whether its failure to effect change is owing to the fact that the intended reintegration has no basis in reality or to the fact that literature is not significant in a social reintegration. Either reason for failure would, paradoxically, attribute a special, if not autonomous, status to literature; after all, insignificance also allows for freedom to experiment.

Regardless of these theoretical limitations of political literature, Avant-Garde literature understood itself as a literature of revolution. Continuing the Modernist expression of alienation, resistance to hierarchies, and criticism of the bourgeois lifestyle, the Avant-Garde introduced a democratizing spirit into literature. In the 1910s, most Avant-Garde authors in Germany understood revolution in leftist terms.

*European contexts* The year 1910 marked a radical change in human character, as Virginia Woolf (1882–1944) pointed out. The early 1910s, indeed, brought a tremendous change in European artistic styles as the result of increased experimentation. The proliferation of *isms* — Italian Futurism, Cubism in France, Imagism and Vorticism in English literature, and Russian Futurism — was an expression of the relativity that defined the Modernist mode at the same time as the search for the center continued in increasingly political terms, especially after the First World War.

Italian Futurism, driven mainly by Filippo Tommaso Marinetti (1876–1944), is central for assessing the political content of the Avant-Garde. First, Futurism influenced German Expressionism through the circle around the magazine *Der Sturm*, edited by Herwarth Walden (1878–1941). Second, similar to the attraction of some Expressionists to National Socialism, Futurism had a distinct fascist streak, leading to the general question of the direction of the Avant-Garde's political options. Marinetti's 1909 *Futurist Manifesto* was a creed of speed and violence, celebrating modern technology and attacking everything old, presenting a glorification of war, and instrumentalizing language for an intensification of communication. Valorizing "machine-gun language" and preferring an automobile (or, later, an airplane) as a work of art over the Venus de Milo are cases in point.

In April and May 1912 the Futurists Umberto Boccioni (1882–1916), Giacomo Balla (1874–1958), and Marinetti himself joined the early Expressionists in Berlin for a successful exhibit in the *Sturm* art gallery. Yet the relationships between Futurists and Expressionists were full of disappointments and irritations. Typical of the naiveté and vagueness in political direction of early Expressionism, Walden never focused on the fascist side of Futurism but saw an artistic affinity in elements, such as destruction of syntax combined with concentration of thought into words or phrases, that clearly influenced his own theory of *Wortkunst* (Art of the Word), which in turn was best exemplified in the poetry of August Stramm (1874–1915). Early Expressionism longed for war as a spiritual experience as long as there was no war; during the First World War the Expressionists overwhelmingly embraced pacifism.

In contrast, Marinetti — after envisioning a more democratic Futurism in 1918 to 1920 — remained a fascist until his death in 1944.

The German literary Avant-Garde began under the strong influence of Aestheticism and became politicized as a result of the war experience; the Avant-Garde's second phase, during the 1920s, was openly political. The first phase of the Avant-Garde encompassed Expressionism (1910–1925) and the even shorter-lived Dada movement (1915–1922). Expressionism revolted primarily against society but did not strongly challenge art as an institution, although it did aim at the destruction of language. Dadaism was most radically Avant-Garde and revolted against everything, including Expressionism and art in general. Among contemporary European Modernist developments, Expressionism was native to German-language literature; Dada was decidedly international.

*Modernist (Non-Avant-Garde) literature*

Expressionist and Dadaist innovations emphasized the expressive function of language, because projections of the author's thoughts as reality took priority over the author's perception of reality. Of course, the literary spectrum was much broader and included literature produced for mass consumption and for a nationalist readership. The latter type of literature is usually interesting for social or political but often not for literary reasons. Major literary achievements, however, were not restricted to Expressionist or Dadaist writers in the narrow sense. During the 1910s Kafka, Rilke, and Hesse, who were less openly political than the Avant-Garde writers, produced major works that showed close affinities to emphasizing the expressive function of language and redefined, if they did not invent, the modern narrative. Other works continued to be written more directly in the vein of the earlier literary movements of Naturalism and Aestheticism.

Gerhart Hauptmann, who had dominated German Naturalist drama, remained a major force during the 1910s and was awarded the 1912 Nobel Prize for literature, an indication of his international stature. Early on, he had oscillated between writing Naturalist texts and those that approached Aestheticism. His successful play *Die Ratten* (The Rats, 1911) is an example of the continuation of the Naturalist tradition. While its title is symbolic of human alienation, Hauptmann presented the conflict of the drama primarily in terms of the social determinism that was typical of Naturalism's political conception of reality. He was a prolific writer until his death in 1946; during the 1920s he assumed the role of a literary elder statesman after declaring his support for the Weimar Republic from its beginning. After a brief flirtation with National Socialism, Hauptmann lived a secluded life.

The major Aestheticist writers — Arthur Schnitzler, Hugo von Hofmannsthal, and Stefan George — kept producing texts that were predominantly within the Aestheticist tradition. Nevertheless, these writers also developed in often idiosyncratic ways more "public" texts, for example, Hofmannsthal's opera libretti, such as *Der Rosenkavalier*, and plays with festival character, such as *Jedermann*. With his attack on anti-Semitism in *Professor Bernhardi*, Schnitzler created another politically charged drama that premiered in Berlin in 1912 but remained banned in his native Austria until after the First World War.

With the novella *Der Tod in Venedig* (Death in Venice, 1912), Thomas Mann produced a short Aestheticist masterpiece that has been compared to Oscar Wilde's *The Picture of Dorian Gray* (1891) and *The Immoralist* (1902), by André Gide (1869–1951), in its depiction of a life's destruction by a sudden intrusion of passion. The protagonist, Gustav Aschenbach, is a successful writer whose work is defined by the artistic will and mastery with which he also attempts to style his life. Aschenbach ignores his emotional side, and the resulting imbalance in his life leads to his death when he is seized by a vague urge to travel (he has a vision of a luscious jungle) and goes to Venice. There he is infected with cholera (whose geographic origins are identified as the luscious jungle of his vision) and falls in love with a beautiful boy (related emotions attack Aschenbach in a dream of a Bacchic orgy, whose depiction mixes images of the luscious jungle and Aschenbach's mountain home). Unable to resolve the conflicts within and without, Aschenbach dies.

Mann was expanding on the dichotomy of the bourgeois versus the artist that was present in his previous successes, *Buddenbrooks* and his early short stories. This and corresponding dichotomies, such as North versus South, health versus sickness, sobriety versus intoxication, and rationality versus irrationality, not only structured Mann's entire oeuvre but were also representations of the Nietzschean polarity of the Apollonian versus the Dionysian. "Myth plus psychology" was Mann's phrase for his method of writing. With Aschenbach's experience of his own homoerotic desires and his resulting confusion, Mann introduced into his writings influences of Freud's psychoanalysis. In the young, yet sickly, Polish aristocrat Tadzio, Aschenbach sees the beauty of a Greek god, Apollo. But his repressed homosexual desires for the boy expose Aschenbach to a state of delirious intoxication in which dream images of the "fremde Gott" [strange god] mix with his cholera-induced fever, and Aschenbach, a lifelong disciple of Apollo, succumbs to Dionysus. Ironically, the Dionysian triumph is presented in the masterly, or Apollonian, style of Mann's novella.

## Inventing the Modern Narrative

When Rainer Maria Rilke's lyrical novel *Die Aufzeichnungen des Malte Laurids Brigge* appeared in 1910, it was not recognized as one of the most important literary innovations of the prewar period: the first truly modern novel of European literature. Malte, the protagonist and narrator of Rilke's novel, is a typically modern individual who lives in frightened isolation in the highly industrialized cityscape that requires new ways of perception. Franz Kafka went even further by taking the individual's isolation and modern society's impersonal structures as a point of departure to encode angst, the quintessential Modernist emotion, into the structure of his narratives. Kafka's unique way of combining this emotion with an open form has placed him among the most important prose writers of world literature.

*Experiencing new realities: Rilke's lyrical novel* Reflecting Rilke's experiences in Paris at the time he was developing his thing poems, *Malte* was the first work to achieve a synthesis of poetic language and modern reality by using language to confront the world. The crisis in language, as experienced by Hofmannsthal's fictitious letter writer a decade earlier, was now replaced by a crisis in perception. This led, above all, to acknowledging the centrality of fear both within and without. Malte repeatedly states that he is learning to see the world in all its frightening ugliness. He experiences the new reality as a world fragmented into things that exist independently of each other: "The existence of the horror in every particle of air" [Die Existenz des Entsetzlichen in jedem Bestandteil der Luft].

He breathes in the new horrors with the particles of the air. In addition, "all lost fears come back" to Malte [Alle verlorenen Ängste sind wieder da]; they are heightened by his new experiences. Thus, the world's fragmentation into separate things takes over the individual's mindset, and the individual's inner world is projected onto the outer world. Malte shares Baudelaire's prototypical Modernist experience of the city: solitude and multitude become contingent on the individual's perception. Solitude, in the form of "fear of death" [Todesfurcht], attacks Malte "in the crowded city, right among people" [in der vollen Stadt, mitten unter den Leuten].

Particular fears — "that some number will start growing in my brain until it has no longer room inside me" [daß irgendeine Zahl in meinem Gehirn zu wachsen beginnt, bis sie nicht mehr Raum hat in mir] — took on an intensity that pointed to Expressionist language. Indeed, the clash between subjectivity and reality that showed in Malte's shocked recognition of death, with which the novel opens, was closer to the Expressionist attitude than to Rilke's own usual Aestheticist approach: "So, this is where people come to live; I'd rather think it would be a place for dying. I've been out there. I've seen: hospitals. . . . Now there's dying being done in 559 beds. Factory-style, of course." [So, also hierher kommen die Leute, um zu leben, ich würde eher meinen, es stürbe sich hier. Ich bin ausgewesen. Ich habe gesehen: Hospitäler. . . . Jetzt wird in 559 Betten gestorben. Natürlich fabrikmäßig].

Rilke created a masterpiece by giving the major themes of the Modernist experience (city, fear, death, decay, dehumanization, and alienation) a new form: the lyrical novel. Continuing on the path away from realism, this form explored subjectivity and a different concept of objectivity by no longer emphasizing narrative structures but rather the lyrical process, which Ralph Freedman defines as a process that reaches a specific intensity by modulating images. The lyrical process places experiences and themes, instead of characters and actions, in the foreground.

The lyricism of *Malte* is usually acknowledged in regard to the two main components of its lyrical process. First, the partial disappearance of the narrator, who is more a persona of individual experience than a real character, into the complex time structure is a direct consequence of the underlying lyrical process, which foregrounds the experience of time itself. Second, the associative technique, by tying the themes together, makes the text cohere. Such a description applies to the overall design of the novel as the texture of imagery that foregrounds experiences and themes. The shift of attention to a formal design was a further extension of the Modernist preoccupation with language.

Language is Malte's tool for making sense of the world's fragmentation, as well as of his own mind and identity. Utterly alone, Malte, the last in a long line of Danish nobility but now destitute, has just arrived in Paris. He tries to cope with the overwhelming and frightening experiences of the city by keeping a journal of precise observations and nightmarish responses. These trigger memories of his childhood (in the novel's first part) and reflections about history (in the second part). Both memories and reflections aim at establishing options of human existence and lead to reflections about love, which culminate at the end of the novel in Malte's version of the parable of the prodigal son.

While Malte's fate remains unresolved in the city's dynamics of disorientation and reorientation, there is a clear movement in the novel, and the reader is drawn into it. The movement is away from fragmented existence and toward an attempted totality: from Malte to the prodigal son, from reality to image, from temporality to timelessness. The parable of the prodigal son presents the first-person narrator Malte and a third-person protagonist in a lyrical combination that fashions experience as imagery, repeating the central themes of the novel and, thus, representing Malte's final mode of awareness.

The novel's version of the parable identifies the prodigal son as one who left home because he did not want to be loved. When he returns, he is ready to love and be loved. It is a different kind of love, however, one that is identified with God, who is the only one capable of loving the prodigal son. Yet, in a reversal, the novel's last sentence says about the one person who is capable of loving: "But he did not yet want to" [Der aber wollte noch nicht]. God as a metaphor for recognition and forgiveness is an image for an absolute form of spirituality that can ensure totality. Malte's experiences and his retelling of the story of the prodigal son are images of the Modernist quest of the center, for which Rilke was to give a valid answer a decade later in his *Duineser Elegien* and *Sonette an Orpheus*.

*Modernist angst and open form:*
*the two-world condition of Kafka's stories*

The writings of Franz Kafka, who was born into the Jewish minority within the German-speaking minority in Prague, are seminal contributions to world literature. The 1913 story "Das Urteil" (The Judgment) is generally considered the first major narrative in which Kafka found a combination of theme, tone, and narrative form that was clearly Modernist and yet unique. The theme of the experience of alienation was expressed as Modernist angst; the tone evoked a nightmarish mood; and the narrative form radicalized the Modernist redefinitions of realism.

As lyrical heroes, Kafka's protagonists are personae of a narrative consciousness, because their perception of the world in images is at the same time a projection of their emotions and because their experiences are allegorical for the modern Everyman. The underlying pattern of the narrative is determined by the conflict between reality and irreality. The same conflict led to openly lyrical language in Rilke's *Malte*, but Kafka's language was of realist precision and terseness. While other authors, from Rilke to Musil, attempted to integrate reality and irreality into one world as part of the Modernist quest, Kafka's narratives presented a two-world condition with fundamentally separate worlds that could not be connected in any meaningful way: the visible world (reality, normality, everyday life, and logic) versus the invisible world (irreality, mysterious bureaucratic super-systems, and dream logic).

In Kafka's texts awareness of the two-world condition is divided unevenly between the protagonist and the reader in an ironic narrative situation. The protagonist uncritically assumes the existence of one world and hopes to find the rules that make the irrational elements cohere with the rational ones; in contrast, the reader experiences the a priori incompatibility of the two worlds. Even for the reader, however, the focus on the protagonist's perspective foregrounds the question of knowing one world's rules rather than the choice between different worlds.

Because the division of awareness encodes angst narratively by juxtaposing the protagonist's inevitable failure and the reader's choices, it leads to a heightening of the Modernist sense of ambiguity to a sense of overdetermination. A text is overdetermined if its gaps of meaning may be filled in such a diversity of ways that the text seems to be telling different stories at the same time. This quality accounts for the vastly different interpretations that Kafka's stories have received. His texts, however, are not vague: the text's coherence favors those readers' choices that do not support authoritarian interpretation but valorize the modern individual's struggle against authoritarian systems. This interpretative diversity has contributed to keeping Kafka's texts — from his stories to his three novels (the latter were published posthumously in the 1920s) — "modern" to the present.

In Kafka's "Das Urteil," Georg submits to his father's judgment after rebelling and drowns himself. The plot suggests an autobiographical interpretation, because the failure of this and all other of Kafka's protagonists to assert themselves or to understand their existence can find an explanation in the author's strained familial relationships, especially with his domineering father. Similar to the Expressionist treatment of the father/son conflict, however, the father represents the old, authoritarian system that had to be overcome.

In fact, the achievement of Kafka's stories lies in the way they create general significance. Such significance depends on the reader's choices, which are informed by the reader's own background and interests but guided by the text's coherence. The many interpretative options include understanding the story as a private search for acceptance by the father and the family or as a general quest for meaning in a meaningless world, for humanity in an impersonal and bureaucratic hierarchy, even for God himself.

Reflecting Kafka's own experiences, his protagonists are the victims of private and general conflicts. In Kafka's best-known story, "Die Verwandlung" (The Metamorphosis, 1915), Gregor Samsa wakes up one day and realizes that he has turned into a "monstrous vermin" [ungeheueren Ungeziefer]. The reader is assured that this is no dream, but as a literary metaphor the metamorphosis into a bug can be two things at the same time: Gregor is a bug and he is not. In the latter sense, he is a dysfunctional human being who has lost his humanity.

This choice is complicated by the issue of how the characters in the story react to Gregor's metamorphosis: how do they know that the bug is Gregor? The question's answer supplies a key to understanding Kafka's stories in general, because it goes beyond arguing that Gregor's change is not real but indeed metaphorical. Instead, the focus moves from how the metamorphosis happened to where it happened. In fact, regardless of whether he really changed or not — everything is related to the protagonist's consciousness. In other words, everything is Gregor's projection in a nightmarish situation, which makes his dehumanization not any less real but firmly establishes Gregor as a lyrical hero.

The exploitation that deprives Gregor of his humanity is a metonymic process. The family exploits him, because all family members depend on him for their living, and so does society. Gregor is exploited by his own father, who stands at the beginning of a series of father figures: the office manager, who inquires about Gregor's absence; the boss, who remains anonymous in the story and is merely a function of the big machine of bureaucracy; and (perhaps) God or some other transcendent meaning that may or may not exist. The family members are repulsed by Gregor's dysfunctionality, because they see it as the result of their own inhumanity; after all, they caused him literally to work himself to death to support them. When Gregor dies and is put in the trash, the family members, who in the meantime have taken jobs to support themselves, feel relieved for their own sake. While the failure of Kafka's protagonists is inevitable, the other characters in his narratives are not necessarily better off. "Die Verwandlung" ends with the family taking a day off in a celebratory mood that seems to affirm life. No longer able to live by exploiting Gregor, however, they have entered the workforce, where they, in turn, are subjected to the same mechanism of exploitation that destroyed Gregor.

### The Expressionist Revolution against Society

During the 1910s the antibourgeois attitude moved from the private to the public sphere, from aesthetic enjoyment to an ethical call to action, from a timeless myth to the politics of the day, and from a celebration of decline to a conviction that the decline was caused by industrial capitalism. While the antibourgeois attitude had led to the Aestheticist proclamation of an artificial world of art separate from the bourgeois world, Expressionism created a counterworld in which art and life were one, often focusing on extreme human and social situations to foreground marginalized characters, especially madmen. The Expressionist proclamation of a new world for the new human being, or "der neue Mensch," was supposed to change the real world; therefore, Expressionism was revolutionary in a political sense.

*Literature of revolution*

Such a revolutionary direction was the central aspect of the Avant-Garde, and it raises concerns about the rhetorical use of literature and the reintegration of literature and life. Specifically, the question is whether Expressionism is to be considered a success or a failure. After all, the real world did change, but it could be argued that the new human being had the face of National Socialism. The *Expressionismusdebatte* (debate on Expressionism) centered on the question of whether or not Expressionism played into the hands of conservative politics, even paving the way for National Socialism in Germany, although National Socialism considered Expressionism degenerate and banned it. The debate was a reaction to the shock that literature had not been able to prevent fascism. Of course, other parts of society — above all, politics and the economy — had also failed. In regard to literature, however, the question was fundamental: what is the place of *littérature engagée* in a socially differentiated world?

Literature can create counterworlds by way of thought experiments to interact with and comment on other spheres and, in the process, imagine and practice new modes of behavior in a world that is incommensurate. This goal was behind Modernism's search for the center and is still an issue today. Literature can perceive reality; and, as Expressionism emphasized, it can create its own realities. To determine whether these literary realities have changed the world is to measure political or social success.

Conversely, literature must use the medium of language to present its thought experiments. To determine how language has been used to represent reality or to create new realities is to measure the success of literature as literature. Although the revolutionary ideas expressed in Expressionism failed in the area of politics, Expressionism was a literary success. It developed the medium of language to a new precision, derived from linguistic abstractions and their recombinations in creative visions and driven by individuals who were uncompromising in their art.

*Destruction of reality and of language through literature*

The revolutionary idea of the new human being that defined the Expressionist project was strongly influenced by Friedrich Nietzsche's philosophy, since the latter shaped the responses to nihilism. Nietzsche's transvaluation of all values found its expression in the demolition of reality and language, *Wirklichkeitszertrümmerung* and *Sprachzertrümmerung*, which Expressionist writers attempted in their texts on the levels of content (world) and form (language). Such destruction of the bourgeois world and its values and attributes (including language) was conceived as the prerequisite for the appearance of the new human being in a new world of brotherhood and equality. The source of the destruction was the writer's imagination of truths and experiences, which were projected as reality. The resulting emphasis on what the writer envisioned and expressed, rather than what impressed him or her, warrants the term *Expressionism*.

The writer's imagination created its own reality by destroying the traditional aesthetic forms, because a new language was necessary to express new realities. This destructive mode was indicative of the Expressionist surging energy that made possible such revolutionary visions as a new human being, a new world, and a new language. Stylistic devices were more than mere mannerism; they were aimed at overthrowing the rule of traditional hierarchies of syntax and word classes. Expressionist texts displayed, for example, syntactic innovations (telegram style and other deformations), concentration of words (especially nouns and adjectives), and extreme imagery (to represent abstract ideas). While the variety and combinations of these stylistic devices often appeared to be chaotic, the variety itself was typical of Expressionism — a situation compounded by the fact that Expressionism produced only a few great writers but many writers who produced one or two great Expressionist works. Typical also was a hurried (*gehetzt*) pathos as a unifying element of Expressionism; its effect of combining the political and ethical impulse with experiments in literary form was expressed in the slogan *new rhythm*.

Areas from which images were taken included the city (especially the metropolis), the machine, and, ultimately, war, in apocalyptic as well as utopian visions, which would give rise to the new human being. The father/son conflict became more than a central motif of Expressionism; it was prototypical for the conflict of old versus new. In the process of such destruction of the old and creation of a new world, the pathos could become ecstatic and transcend into a cosmic sense of humanity. As a consequence, Expressionist texts often emphasized collective experiences and typifications over individual human beings.

Expressionism as a relatively short-lived movement was centered in the 1910s. Although it mainly reacted against Aestheticism, Expressionism was also strongly influenced by Aestheticism. Both lyrical poetry and the drama were dominant throughout the Expressionist project, although traditional forms were altered. Expressionist poetry tended to be more rhythmically determined than previous poetry, and Expressionist drama stressed lyrical elements to represent the protagonist's struggle for transformation. Furthermore, prose can be considered typical of the Expressionist project, because its lyrical and/or dramatic changes were even less traditional. Often the programmatic quality of prose was in keeping with the rhetorical purpose of revolutionary literature: to incite change. For the same reason, programmatic statements and manifestos became important with Expressionism. Also central to the development of literature were literary magazines, especially *Die Aktion* (Action, 1911–1932), edited by Franz Pfemfert

(1879–1954), and Herwarth Walden's *Der Sturm* (Storm, 1910–1932).

The three main phases of Expressionism reflect the movement's interconnection with political events. First, the early years (1910–1914) were often experienced by the writers as paralyzing in their boredom and oppression by industrial capitalism, hence the poetry with intense apocalyptic images idealizing war and destruction as the opportunity for change that was, for most writers, just vaguely political. The idealization of war also explains the initially positive response to the First World War, which, however, literally silenced some of the most promising Expressionist writers, who were killed during the war. Second, during the years of the First World War (1914–1918), experiencing first-hand the reality of the war politicized most writers. Drama became the dominant form to proclaim, especially after 1916, pacifist ideals. Third, the immediate postwar period (1918 and 1919) allowed the hope for a radical political change of German society in which several German writers — such as Ernst Toller (1893–1939), Erich Mühsam (1878–1934), and Oskar Maria Graf (1894–1967) — actively participated. Once the more moderate parliamentary democracy of the Weimar Republic had been established, the revolutionary impulses of Expressionism dwindled, too. Toller, for instance, wrote major Expressionist dramas about his ideas on nonviolent revolution after his participation as a leader of the failed first Bavarian soviet republic, but by 1922 he had turned to a more realistic style. By 1925 Expressionism had been replaced by New Objectivity as the predominant literary style. In politics the practitioners of Expressionism had moved on to other positions, spanning the entire spectrum from resignation to Communism and fascism.

*Poetry: emphatic visions and abstractions*

One of the signature poems of early Expressionism, "Weltende" (End of the World, 1910) by Jakob van Hoddis (pseudonym of Hans Davidsohn, 1887–1942), was lauded by fellow poet Johannes R. Becher (1891–1958) as the "Marseillaise of Expressionist rebellion." The eight-line poem illustrates the new Expressionist pathos proclaiming the end of the bourgeois world, which is literally blown away by a storm. The poem's matter-of-fact tone presents the insignificance of human technology in the face of the forces of nature, which the poem equates with the force of revolution. As is typical of Expressionism, the destruction of the old is seen as the prerequisite for something new — an attitude that is underscored by the almost frivolously humorous tone of the poem, for instance, when two roofers are blown from the roof and, in a strangely nonhuman manner, "go to pieces" [gehn entzwei]. The contrast between the serious and the banal, the tone of sarcasm and caricature, similar to that of the paintings and sketches of George Grosz (1893–1959) and the early poems of Gottfried Benn (1886–1956), was a typical mode of Expressionism.

*The apocalypses of Georg Heym and Georg Trakl* An opposite, yet equally typical, mode was the one of serious apocalyptic gloom as exemplified by Georg Heym (1887–1912) and Georg Trakl (1887–1914). The two most important poets of early Expressionism, they both suffered untimely deaths: Heym in an attempt to save a friend from drowning in an ice-skating accident and Trakl, a longtime drug addict, of a cocaine overdose after witnessing the brutality of war while he was serving as a medic.

In their combination of materialistic and morally corrupt reality with demonic visions, Heym's apocalyptic poems achieved an overpowering sense of threat. Lonely, mad, and sick people live in twilight worlds that suggest the imminent doom of the middle-class world. The modern industrial city is a central motif. At night the city succumbs to the man-eating and fire-spewing demon who rules it in "Der Gott der Stadt" (The God of the City, 1910), just as, during the day, the city succumbs to the factories. The city's nighttime ordeal links with images evoking war when the demon extends his butcher's fist into the darkness and sends a sea of fire chasing through a street. The intensity of the metaphors culminates in the ecstasy of inescapable destruction. Heym celebrated war with the same imagery in his 1911 poem "Der Krieg" (War); war became an image of the destruction that Heym felt was necessary to overcome the old bourgeois system.

As was the case with many Expressionists, Trakl's early poetry was influenced by the French Symbolists. The poems he wrote after 1910, however, are considered an ultimate achievement of early Expressionist poetry. Born into one of the wealthiest Salzburg families, he had a troubled childhood, which left him to cope with a drug problem and a strong sense of guilt derived from his incestuous feelings for his sister. Less an Expressionist revolutionary than an eccentric individualist, Trakl extended his personal guilt into the themes of universal suffering and general guilt, which, in turn, provide the focus for his hermetic poetry.

Trakl achieved the hermetic quality of his poems by using ellipsis and illogical word combinations, as though words had lost their communicative function. This technique is especially striking when comparing individual versions of the same poem reveals that he often replaced words with their antonyms (for example, *winter* with *summer*). The difficulty in understanding these poems brings the communicative function of language to the fore. It has been argued that all of Trakl's poems could be read as one poem expressing a general dualism of good versus evil, where the yearning for harmony gives way to a feeling of decay and loss of meaning. The loss of meaning in the world is duplicated by an evasiveness of meaning in Trakl's poems, which are particularly challenging with their color metaphors in combinations like "black dew" [schwarzer Tau], "red evening wind" [roter Abendwind], and "bluish sleep" [bläulicher Schlaf]. Color metaphors and other idiosyncratic combinations were typical of Expressionism in general.

"Grodek," the last poem Trakl wrote, is often considered the ultimate Expressionist war poem. It is about the battle of Grodek, soon after which Trakl died. Here "a wrathful God" [ein zürnender Gott] inhabits "red clouds" [Rotes Gewölk], and "all streets lead to black decay" [Alle Straßen münden in schwarze Verwesung]. The flame of the "Geist," which translates as "mind" or "spirit," is so hot because it is fed by an enormous pain: "The unborn grandchildren" [Die ungeborenen Enkel], suggesting the waste not just of current life but of life's future itself. Ecstasy of vision blends with the chaotic experience of reality; the absence of a benevolent God is appropriately expressed in a chaos of rhythms and images. Trakl's poetic chaos was more than a rebellion against the conventional way of seeing things; it expressed the concept of seeing things in a diversity of ways.

*The new rhythm*    While Heym's and Trakl's poems share a sense of doom, they also exemplify the two major sides of the Expressionist "new rhythm." On the one hand, there is the emphatic pathos, whose expression ranges from the dark ecstasy of destruction, as in Heym's poems, to transcending such destruction and evoking a human community in the optimistic and celebratory exclamation of "O man" [O Mensch]. The latter is connected to visions of salvation — either in a new socialist state, for which Johannes R. Becher wanted to recruit soldiers, or in a religious and often messianic, Christian sense. For instance, Franz Werfel (1890–1945), who, despite his Jewish roots and socialist outlook, experienced late in life a conversion to Catholicism, exclaimed that his sole wish was to "be related to you, o man" [Mein einziger Wunsch ist, Dir, o Mensch, verwandt zu sein].

On the other hand, Trakl's poetry pointed toward the increasing abstraction evoked through far-reaching syntactic reduction. This abstraction extended to the word level in the poems of August Stramm, who also died an untimely death. Stramm went through phases of writing Naturalistic dramas and Aestheticist poetry but eventually developed a lyrical language that often reduced syntax to relationships between individual nouns and arranged them in short lines, sometimes with one word per line. Supported by Walden's *Der Sturm*, and advocated by Walden as foremost examples of *Wortkunst*, Stramm's poems attributed autonomous status to the word. Most of his poems allow a realistic reading, but the composition does not follow traditional grammar, even in more syntactically coherent poems, such as "Patrouille" (Patrol), where the first line uses a noun as a verb. Unusual personifications surprise or shock the reader throughout the poem as it tries to convey the author's war experience: "Stones are enemying / A window grins deceit / Branches choke / Mountains shrubs are leafing rustlingly / Screams / Death" [Die Steine feinden / Fenster grinst Verrat / Äste würgen / Berge Sträucher blättern raschlig / Gellen / Tod]. Stramm's war poems, written between 1914 and 1915, were collected in *Tropfblut* (Dripping Blood, 1919).

The two options of Expressionist poetry reproduced those of the Aestheticist rejection of realism: either creating a representation of an artificial world (the Expressionist emphatic visions of destruction or creation) or inventing a new artificial language (abstractions of the *Wortkunst* type). In spite of this close affinity to Aestheticism, the two options unfolded in an entirely different context in the practice of Expressionist art. First, Expressionism no longer attempted to achieve the rarified atmosphere of Aestheticism; second, as vague as the political position of Expressionism was at times, meaning unfolded within the political project of the Avant-Garde in contrast to the overtly apolitical attitude of Aestheticism. The emphasis on the rhetorical function of Avant-Garde literature no longer invited aesthetic enjoyment of a world separated from life; rather, it primarily incited political change by way of suggesting a counterworld that aimed at bringing art and life together.

In addressing the contemporary political issues, Expressionist poetry reflected a broad range of influences from Aestheticism to technology. For example, Else Lasker-Schüler (1869–1945) combined Judaic, Christian, and Middle-Eastern elements into a personal mythology. Her early poem "Mein Volk" (My People, 1905) exhibits her rootedness in the Jewish faith and her hope for a new beginning when, inside her, her people screams to God. Both Ernst Stadler (1883–1914) and Gerrit Engelke — the latter being the only of the major *Arbeiterdichter* to become an Expressionist — embraced modern technology, which, in contrast to Heym, they did not demonize but integrated into a hymnal and cosmic, quasi-religious experience that encompassed technology and humanity. Stadler concludes his celebration of a train ride in "Fahrt über die Kölner Rheinbrücke bei Nacht" (Ride Across the Rhine at Cologne During the Night, 1914) ecstatically with: "And with fire and passion / Toward the ultimate, giving blessings. To the celebration of procreation. To pleasure. To the prayer. To the sea. To destruction"

[Und Glut und Drang / Zum Letzten, Segnenden. Zum Zeugungs-
fest. Zur Wollust. Zum Gebet. Zum Meer. Zum Untergang].

*Gottfried Benn* Typical of the valorization of the experiment, Stadler equated form with passion. Gottfried Benn emerged as a central figure of Expressionism, especially because his lyrical practice combined both emphatic vision and abstraction. Although his writing underwent major changes in tone and form, moving from emphatic vision to increasing abstraction during his long career, Benn remained an Expressionist in the sense that he always expressed his absolute subjectivity with an emphasis on the formal aspects of that expression. Beginning with the metaphysical assumption of the lost center, Benn considered the word the only reality. Consequently, the word — and, with it, the whole text — became autonomous signifiers. Yet this was not just theory; it had a concrete meaning for Benn and others. The word had to be special; as an almost explosive reservoir of energy, it had to be unusual and shocking.

Unusual and shocking were indeed Benn's early poems in *Morgue und andere Gedichte* (Morgue and Other Poems, 1912), *Söhne* (Sons, 1913), and *Fleisch* (Flesh, 1917), with their themes of death and disease, as well as their surreal and visionary imagery, all explicitly expressed in a crass language that demolished both the world and itself. Benn became the foremost practitioner of *Wirklichkeits- und Sprachzertrümmerung* and a related aesthetics of negativity when he dissected reality using images of medical dissections in *Morgue*, thus reducing any metaphysical assumption to naught, or when he added a cosmic dimension through nightmare and drug-induced visions in *Fleisch*.

Behind such provocative language lurked desperation about nihilism, which assumed a world that no longer had a functioning value system. Such ambiguity between visionary destruction and quiet desperation proves crucial for understanding the general ambivalence of Expressionism, which Richard Sheppard (in Bradbury and McFarlane, eds.) describes in reference to Benn's *Morgue*: "his coldness conceals a compassion that fears to express itself lest it become part of the dissolution" (384). Consequently, Expressionism seemed both involved and detached in relation to both reality and vision, hence the polarity of *Realitätsferne* and *Realitätsnähe*, or detachment from and closeness to reality, that is mediated within one and the same text. Although Expressionist visions are seen as removing literature even further from reality, the same visions are understood as a political challenge to reality.

As ecstatic as the texts were, they were also diagnostic of the times. Human beings were seen as reduced to insignificance in the real world with no ties to each other. Characteristic of Expressionism and, at the same time, combining emphatic vision and abstraction in a unique way, humans were typified as carriers of properties in Benn's poetry. A famous example is the *danse macabre* of the lonely hearts in his "Nacht-café" (Night Café, 1912): "Grease in hair / talks to open mouth with tonsil / Faith Charity Hope around the neck" [Fett im Haar / spricht zu offenem Mund mit Rachenmandel / Glaube Liebe Hoffnung um den Hals].

Benn's rejection of Western civilization was complete. His poems provided rhetorical slogans for this attitude, such as: "Europe, this booger / in a Sunday School student's nose" [Europa, dieser Nasen-popel / in einer Konfirmandennase]. Benn mourned the "Ich-Zerfall" (ego-disintegration), but he also celebrated the creation of new subjectivity as an act of irrationality and resistance in "Fleisch" (Flesh, 1917). In the same poem Benn, a medical doctor, considered the brain to be the wrong path of human development. Therefore, the source of creating a new world could not be the same as the source of Western rationality. It had to be at an irrational level, though still located in the physiology of the isolated human mind, which is often pushed to the brink of madness in its effort to create a new reality. This option was precisely what Benn explored in his prose texts.

*Prose: between lyricism and realism* The poles of emphatic vision and abstraction that defined the options for lyrical expression also defined the prose works of Expressionism, because the overriding principle of Expressionist literature — the claim that the world was contained in the individual's subjectivity — favored the lyrical mode. The short narrative form was clearly dominant in Expressionist prose; no major long novels emerged except by Kafka and other writers who, despite some affinities to Expressionism, did not fully belong to the movement. The long epic form presupposes a sense of totality that Expressionists could not derive from outside reality; instead, they turned to inside the human psyche, which, in a twilight world of dream and hallucination, envisioned a totality in creative bursts that were too short to sustain long narratives. Expressionist prose refused to understand the mind in terms of conventional psychology; on the contrary, it emphasized explosive acausality and the deformed human beings who were reduced to an elementary level where the line between sanity and madness had been crossed.

In their appropriation of emphatic vision and abstraction, Expressionist prose texts tended toward terseness and developed two basic strands of narrative emphasis. One was labeled "autonomous" or "absolute" prose and overlapped with the lyrical novel. Carl Einstein (1885–1940) is the major representative of autonomous prose, although Gottfried Benn's *Rönne* cycle (1915–1916) is better known.

The other strand eventually developed toward the New Objectivity of the 1920s and is exemplified by Alfred Döblin (1878–1957), both with short prose and novels, including *Die drei Sprünge des Wang-lun* (Wang-lun's Three Leaps, 1915).

*Autonomous prose*   Carl Einstein proclaimed that the narrative needed to focus on movement in terms of creative arbitrariness, thus turning "the absurd into reality." Although Einstein rejected conventional lyricism, his concept of autonomous prose valorized the modulation of images, which is typical of the lyrical process. Therefore, Einstein's prose was a version of the lyrical narrative. His major work, the slender novel *Bebuquin oder Die Dilettanten des Wunders* (Bebuquin, or The Dabblers in Miracles, 1912), demonstrated how the Expressionist agenda of the new world could be accomplished. Independent of causality and psychology, the principle of arbitrary playfulness was supposed to take the fragments of reality and of divergent plot lines and arrange them into new patterns. In this way the work created its own symbolic, not mimetic, reality. The work became an autonomous space for thought experiments independent of objective description of reality. The process of textual self-generation is ironically broken by the protagonist's failure to be a creator in his own right after weeks of trying: "But his exhausted will was not able to generate one speck of dust" [Aber sein erschöpfter Wille konnte nicht ein Stäubchen erzeugen].

Bebuquin's hectic search for the miracle, which can be understood as a manifestation of the world's totality, ends in pathology as a last resort of creation *ex negativo*. Again, it can be seen as in keeping with the Expressionist agenda of the new world that presupposes the destruction of the old world. After half a year of carnival celebrations, the townspeople go crazy and start killing each other. Bebuquin believes that all options for dealing with life lead to madness. At the end of his final three nights (also the end of the book), he uses his willpower to destroy his life and, with it, reality, since he cannot create reality. Such a manner of narrating also foregrounds the very process of narration. The movement from one plot element to the next, as Bebuquin explores the options for the miracle of creation, is playful; exploring the miracle of narration, however, Einstein's prose also is self-referential and theoretical.

*Bebuquin* exemplified Einstein's consistently radical thinking and pushed the limits of what could be expressed. It was especially influential for Dada and, most immediately, for Gottfried Benn. While Bebuquin fails, Benn's Werff Rönne succeeds in creating his own world. Einstein's protagonist coolly and systematically destroys his own mind. In Benn's *Rönne* cycle, madness becomes fully irrational: the mind —

or, rather, the brain — is a blank that is filled by life. The stories of this cycle, "Gehirne" (Brains, 1915), "Die Eroberung" (The Conquest, 1915), "Die Reise" (The Journey, 1916), "Die Insel" (The Island, 1916), and "Der Geburtstag" (The Birthday, 1916), were published together in the collection *Gehirne* (1916).

Their protagonist is a young doctor, Werff Rönne, who suffers from an identity crisis. In "Gehirne" Rönne in a sense diagnoses himself, observing that he is losing touch with reality because his brain is ceasing to function. Throughout the story the image develops of Rönne holding a brain in his hands after a dissection. Finally, he expresses his own predicament in this image: "Now I'm always holding my own (brain) in my hands and must continuously search for what I can do with myself" [Nun halte ich immer mein eigenes (Gehirn) in meinen Händen und muß immer danach forschen, was mit mir anzufangen sei].

No longer centered by his brain, Rönne's subjectivity is overwhelmed by the sensory input from reality. Following the principle of irrationality, Rönne looks inward and, in "Der Geburtstag," not only turns thirty but also experiences a rebirth. After ups and downs he reaches a state of liberation from material reality, living his own visions that are typical of Benn: they are visions of the Mediterranean, and their source is the irrational level of the brain. In his mind Rönne addresses people: "my ladies, . . . Allow me to create you" [meine Damen, . . . Gestatten Sie, das ich Sie erschaffe], and he creates them. The story ends in an apotheosis: "There was someone floating, radiant, . . . boundless: he, Rönne" [Da trieb einer, glühend . . . unabsehbar: er, Rönne].

In the destruction of the old world lies the creation of the new one. The pathos of radical subjectivity is meant quite seriously and is embedded not only in religious allusions (Rönne is thirty, the age of Jesus when he began his ministry) but also in an Expressionist language that attempts to be new. Language becomes abstract in a subjective way; for example, instead of "he heard a sound," the sentence reads: "A sound happened" [da geschah ein Ton], perhaps suggesting that Rönne made it happen. Or sentences are reduced to the word level, similar to some Expressionist poetry: "An oar-stroke: Taking breath; a bark: Support of the head" [Ein Ruderschlag: Ein Eratmen; eine Barke: Stütze des Hauptes].

*Apsychological realism* Alfred Döblin took a narrative approach that was quite different from autonomous prose; he valorized the realist tradition of Homer (eighth century B.C.), Dante (1265–1321), Cervantes (1547–1616), and Feodor Dostoevski (1821–1881). In this way he approached anew the old ideal of totality in the sense that each moment of our life is a complete reality, as well as a realist mode of presentation that privileged life over art. The writer's task, for Döblin, was to bring life and art together by narrating life in simple and descriptive language, avoiding both psychologism and a heavy-handed style.

Döblin's early phase was Expressionist, because he avoided psychologism, which would supply causality to his narratives; rather, like other Expressionists, he focused on pathological states of mind, on acausal and irrational behavior. The basis of his narratives, however, remained realist in the sense that reality was perceived in exacting detail, yet the perception was distorted, because reality was typically seen through the eyes of a pathological protagonist. Döblin, the neurologist and psychiatrist, presented a collection of neurotic people in his often grotesque stories.

In Döblin's early story "Die Ermordung einer Butterblume" (The Murder of a Buttercup, 1904), the world surrounding the protagonist corresponds exactly to his unstable emotional state. The thoughtless act of decapitating a buttercup leads to pangs of guilt that take on pathological dimensions, from his smelling the odor of the decaying plant's corpse to his opening a bank account for the dead flower. Atoning for the murder of one buttercup, he keeps another in a pot at home. When the cleaning lady accidentally breaks the pot and throws away the flower, the protagonist feels relieved from all guilt. The reader sees him disappear into the forest, ready to go on a killing spree of countless flowers.

The focus on an antipsychological account of pathological minds unified Expressionist prose by various writers, including Georg Heym, Carl Sternheim (1878–1942), and Georg Trakl. Differences existed in the type of narrative treatment, which either emphasized the autonomy of the thought experiment and its language, as in Einstein's and Benn's texts, or foregrounded the realistic embedding of the pathological episode, as in Döblin's story. Formally, Expressionist prose was at least as experimental and innovative as the other genres, if not more so; however, the political orientation that made Expressionism part of the Avant-Garde was less pronounced in prose than in poetry and especially less pronounced than in drama, the most directly political genre of Expressionism.

*Drama: between abstractions and pacifism*

The crisis of the theater that had begun at the end of the nineteenth century when, determined by economic factors, the inbetween of human communication — the dialogue and, with it, the very possibility of drama — seemed impossible in the mutual antagonism of social hierarchies and fragmentation. With fragmentation the coherence of events was challenged and so was the presentation of coherence on stage. Finally, since the possibility of dialogue and coherence was gone, the ability to create the illusion of the play as something absolute and primary — as something that could create its own world for the duration of the performance — was also gone.

The answer of Expressionist drama to the crisis was radical. Building on earlier experiments by Frank Wedekind and the Swedish writer August Strindberg (1849–1912), Expressionists dramatized the absent inbetween of human communication in the monodrama, or *Ich-Drama* (ego-drama). No longer tied to the classical unities of time, place, and plot, the monodrama could extend into irreality, develop in separate episodes, and be topical while being universal. First, dialogue was no longer primary, because the drama existed as an extended monologue by an alienated individual searching for his fellow human beings; the stage became the projection of that individual's monologic mind. Second, events no longer had to cohere as a continuous stage presence, because the individual mind and its development were the focal point, and these were portrayed jumping from one episode to the next (or one station to the next, hence the German term *Stationendrama*). Finally, the stage reclaimed its absolute and primary status, because it not only embodied the protagonist's vision but, metonymically or collectively, humankind's struggle; thus, the Expressionist stage became an almost sacred place to celebrate both individuality and humanity.

This approach to drama was even more radical because of the interrelationship between the politics of its thematic elements and the abstraction of its structural elements. The political orientation centered on transformation and favored the same themes as poetry did — above all, the creation of a new humanity via individual rebellion against alienation. Rebellion unfolded in such images as the father/son conflict, war and its effects, and city and machine.

*Archetypal conflicts: father/son, man/woman*

Formally, the individual's rebellion was expressed in abstractions, suggesting a universal revolution. Often the characters did not have names but represented types, such as the Father, the Son, the Mother, the Man, or the Woman. Characters, such as "Mr. Audience" [Herr Publikum] and even "The Poster" [Das Plakat] in the parodistic *Der Ungestorbene* (The Man Who Didn't Die), part of *Die Unsterblichen* (The Immortals, 1920), by Yvan Goll (pseudonym of Isaac Lang, 1891–1950), are indicative of an increased use of pantomime. As an emphatic gesture, pantomime emerged to parallel the pathos of the word, which, similar to its role in poetry and prose, still reigned supreme as the expression in the emphatic vision of a new humanity in both terse, intense, telegram-style exclamations and long, eloquent speeches.

Ernst Barlach (1870–1938) and Oskar Kokoschka (1886–1980) wrote some of the first Expressionist plays. Both authors also left their primary marks in the history of art as sculptor and painter, respectively. The conflicts that were felt to erupt in society were often expressed in archetypal images, such as father versus son or man versus woman. In Barlach's *Der tote Tag* (The Dead Day, 1912) both archetypal conflicts are combined in a mystical atmosphere where the mother (the principle of the earth) and the long-lost father (the spiritual principle) try to win the son over to their side. It becomes clear that the father represents the divine principle that should be followed; nevertheless, mother and son commit suicide.

Kokoschka's *Mörder, Hoffnung der Frauen* (Murderer, Hope of Women; published in 1910, premiered in 1917) postulated the battle of the sexes as a universal conflict between abandon and liberation in a mythical antiquity where a man and a woman confront each other, supported by a chorus of men and women, respectively. Kokoschka intended the play as an attack on the thoughtlessness of male society and depicted love between man and woman as a vicious circle of violence that only murder could end. After the woman dies at the touch of the man's fingers and after he kills the other men and women, he is left desperate when he realizes that he cannot save himself from the devil embodied by male society and, ultimately, by the character himself. Central to the play's impact was the symbolism of the stage, with light effects and choreographed action, such as the pantomimed rape of the woman.

While these two plays by Barlach and Kokoschka are largely spiritual and even mythical, Expressionist plays became more and more openly political as a reaction to the First World War. Plays by Georg Kaiser (1878–1945), the most important playwright of Expressionism and the most performed German author between 1918 and 1933, illustrate the dominance of the political. Kaiser's perhaps most famous play *Von morgens bis mitternachts* (From Morn till Midnight, published in 1916, premiered in 1917), a typical Expressionist monodrama, shows a bank cashier on the run, not just because he took 60,000 marks but also because he can no longer bear his meaningless existence. The episodes take him through places where he expects to find real life yet finds only alienation. Money, the centerpiece of capitalism, turns out to be "the most miserable fraud of all frauds" [der armseligste Schwindel unter allem Betrug], because the cashier comes to understand that money clouds the real issues. Finally, he is completely exhausted and alone, and suicide is his only option. As he sinks down with his arms extended, his posture alludes to the crucifixion of Christ; however, the cashier's suicide is not sacrifice as in other Expressionist plays, such as *Die Bürger von Calais* (The Burghers of Calais, published in 1914), but social accusation.

*The new human being in plays before the war* The play that made Kaiser famous, *Die Bürger von Calais*, was first performed in 1917 about three months before *Von morgens bis mitternachts*. Calmer in pace, less episodic, and almost classical in its three-act structure, the drama introduced the ultimate ethical goal of Expressionism: the new human being. In the historical setting of this play, the survival of a medieval French town under siege is at stake. The king of England promises to spare the town if six volunteers surrender to him to die. Kaiser's emphatic use of language underscores the ethical conflict when seven townspeople volunteer, a conflict intensified when one of them does not show up at the crucial moment, early in the morning — until his dead body is carried past the group in a small funeral procession. He sacrificed his own life so that one of the remaining six could live. Ironically, the town is spared anyway, because the king's son was born during the night. Nevertheless, in Eustache's sacrifice, a selfless act that restores meaning to dying, the town has also "seen the new man — in this night he was born" [den neuen Menschen gesehen — in dieser Nacht ist er geboren].

Walter Hasenclever (1890–1940) tied the elements of new man, father/son conflict, and Expressionist rhetoric together into what came to be considered the prototypical Expressionist play, *Der Sohn* (The Son, 1914). The play was generally understood as an expression of the human pursuit of freedom and happiness that is shown in the son's defying the father's obsolete authority. Hasenclever himself stressed the political impulse with the claim that the play's goal was to change the world. As a monodrama, the play presents the episodes of the archetypal quest in terms of projections of the son. In a highly emotional confrontation during the second act, the son offers the father a solution: "Tear down the fetters between father and son — be my friend" [Zerreiße die Fesseln zwischen Vater und Sohn — werde mein Freund]. When the father refuses, the son realizes that they will be enemies until one of them is victorious. At the end of the play only the father's stroke prevents patricide.

Not all sons get off, however, with clean hands. The conflict took on several variations, including *Vatermord* (Patricide, published in 1920, premiered in 1922), by Arnolt Bronnen (1895–1959), a play that has been called "unappetizing" and whose psychopathological plot and climax have been linked to fascist tendencies (Bronnen, indeed, later turned to National Socialism). The father/son conflict was so central to the Expressionist project of evoking the new human being because the father represented everything that had to do with the old human being and his social system. Franz Werfel's novella "Nicht der Mörder, der Ermordete ist schuldig" (It's Not the Murderer, It's the

Murdered Who Is Guilty, 1920) epitomizes the justification for patricide, arguing that any guilt of the son presupposes the father's guilt, because fathers are "monsters of *authority*" [Ausgeburten der *Autorität*] and because everything, from religion to the state and factories, falls under the "domination of the father" [Herrschaft des Vaters].

*The war experience*

In the course of the First World War, some of the Expressionist visions of destruction found their cruel counterparts in reality, and the development of Expressionism in the direction of politics was radicalized. Drama, especially, became outright revolutionary, in the sense that the transformation presented in the plays could no longer be understood as merely spiritual. The plays were now clearly antiwar and anticapitalist. In *Seeschlacht* (Sea Battle, 1917), Reinhard Goering (1887–1936) presented the suggestive power of war far from the glorification of war typical of nationalist literature. Ernst Toller portrayed his own conversion from nationalist volunteer to pacifist in *Wandlung*. Finally, Georg Kaiser focused on the inherent link between war and industrial capitalism in his *Gas* trilogy.

Goering's one-act play *Seeschlacht* zeroed in on how seven sailors in a battleship's gun turret cope with the imminent Battle of Jutland. Individual identities are not important; the sailors remain unnamed and are just referred to by number. Each represents a different approach to the war, including the fifth sailor's skepticism, which almost leads him to mutiny during an argument with the other sailors. The battle explodes right into the middle of this argument and emerges as a power that is beyond human control. It draws all seven sailors into the rush of killing, even the fifth, who had considered mutiny but now cries out: "my pulse sings the battle, battle above us" [meine Pulse singen Schlacht, Schlacht über uns]. In the end, all the sailors die. While the resignation and the depiction of meaningless death made *Seeschlacht* an antiwar play, war itself was not portrayed as functioning in primarily political terms but rather as a mythological fate that seemed inescapable. The suggestive supernatural, fatelike force of the rush of blood that war exerts on man is akin to topoi of National Socialism (an ideology to which Goering later was attracted), but in *Seeschlacht* this force is embedded in antiwar images, such as referring to the sailors as "calves who are being slaughtered" [Kälber, die abgestochen werden].

The new human being who was created as a result of the destruction around him is presented in Ernst Toller's *Die Wandlung* (The Transformation, 1919). The play shows the hero's transformation — as he begins to understand the political and social structures that underlie reality — from volunteer to pacifist and, finally, to activist in six phases. As a result of his transformation, his family (except for his sister) withdraws from him, but he finds a new family of brothers and sisters: a large crowd of people to whom he preaches the gospel of love and revolution. After he reminds the crowd that they are but "distorted images of the real human being" [verzerrte Bilder des wirklichen Menschen], they cry out in recognition of their own humanity. Then the hero incites them to revolution by nonviolent means. For example, he charges the poor people to open their hearts to the rich, whose false castles need to be destroyed: "Yet be gentle with them, for they, too, are poor people who have lost their way" [Doch seid gütig zu ihnen, denn auch sie sind Arme, Verirrte].

*Die Wandlung* ends with the crowd's cries for revolution, stopping at the ecstatic moment when revolution — happiness and freedom for all — seems possible. In the real world of politics, the "revolution of love" seems to have been the beliefs that led to Toller's participation in the first Munich soviet republic, where he raised his voice for moderation and nonviolence. He wrote his pacifist and revolutionary plays in prison after actual revolutionary attempts in Germany had failed.

*The tragedy of the new human being*

The tragedy of the new human being is the topic of Kaiser's *Gas* trilogy, which describes the seemingly inevitable destruction of humankind. Along with amplifying the sense of social alienation from play to play, the trilogy increasingly typifies the characters, shifting from Billionaire and Engineer to "Blue Figures" [Blaufiguren] and "Yellow Figures" [Gelbfiguren]. While *Die Koralle* (The Coral, 1917) introduces the setting, central characters, and themes of the trilogy, Kaiser developed *Gas I* and *II* as two effective revolutionary plays that expose the dehumanizing effects of industrialization. In *Gas I* (1918) the son of the Billionaire in *Koralle* has made all the workers shareholders in his father's company, which he is now running. After an explosion that could not be avoided, the son proposes that they close the factory and all start a new life as farmers. But the Engineer incites the workers' passions by painting a great picture of their industrial domination of nature. When the son attempts to resist, the government steps in to guarantee production of the gas, which is needed for military purposes. The son is killed by the workers, who willingly return to the work that will only exploit them.

*Gas II* (1920) is set two generations later and is even more stylized than the previous play. The state now controls the production of the gas, which is needed in a war. The factory and its workers are under siege by the Yellow Figures. As the ultimate solution, the Great Engineer offers a new invention to the workers: poison gas. The Billionaire-Worker, the grandson of the Billionaire's son, rejects this offer because he believes in nonviolence. When the workers themselves demand to use the poison gas, he sees no way out but to throw the gas bomb, sacrificing himself and killing everyone else — workers and Yellow Figures — but also destroying the poison-gas weapon.

*Satires and absurd plays*  While *Von morgens bis mitternachts, Die Wandlung,* and the *Gas* trilogy include grotesque and distorted elements, they were all serious plays. But there were also humorous Expressionist plays. Above all, there were the early social satires of Carl Sternheim (although some critics prefer not to group him with Expressionism but stress similarities between him and that literary movement). Other humorous plays include late ones by Expressionists revisiting their own beliefs with hindsight, such as Yvan Goll's *Die Unsterblichen.*

The works for which Carl Sternheim is best known consist of the cycle of plays *Aus dem bürgerlichen Heldenleben* (From the Heroic Life of the Bourgeoisie), dealing primarily with prewar society: *Die Kassette* (The Money Box, performed 1911, published 1912), *Bürger Schippel* (Burgher Schippel, 1913), and the *Maske* tetralogy, consisting of *Die Hose* (The Bloomers, 1911), *Der Snob* (The Snob, 1913), *1913* (published 1915, performed 1919), and *Das Fossil* (The Fossil, performed 1923, published 1925). In the tetralogy, Sternheim traces the rise of the Maske family from their modest middle-class origins to the aristocracy. The name is telling: the civil servant Theodor Maske and his family use the inconspicuousness of their bourgeois respectability to mask their ambition. Although events expose bourgeois values as often ridiculous and dangerous, there also seems to be an ambivalent admiration for the energy of the bourgeoisie. In this sense, Sternheim's plays are less radical in their attack on bourgeois society than the typical serious Expressionist plays. Sternheim did not believe in the possibility of changing society; therefore, he felt that he had to attack it with satire. In addition, the terse language of his plays is Expressionist.

In *Die Hose* Theodor Maske emerges as the most vital among the competitors for the affection of his wife. *Der Snob* presents Theodor's son Christian, who distances himself radically from his past, including his family, in order to marry into the aristocracy. *1913* shows the confrontation between an aging and dying Christian and his children, especially his daughter Sophie, who represents him in business affairs during his illness and closes a weapons deal to which Christian morally objects. She no longer sees human beings but only masses that she can exploit; therefore, with Christian's death, whatever humanity that had been left in the family's approach to the world has disappeared. *Bürger Schippel* presents the embourgeoisement of a worker. Thus, the vicious process of society, as Sternheim saw it, is complete: the working class emulates the middle class; the middle class emulates the aristocracy;

and, in the process, all humanity is lost. The only hope lies in the revolutionary ideals of Expressionism; Sternheim dedicated *1913* to fellow Expressionist Ernst Stadler, and one character in the play who represents revolutionary ideals is called (Friedrich) Stadler.

As, by the mid-1920s, the Weimar Republic stabilized to a degree, the failure of a radical political alternative in Germany and the restoration of conservative and reactionary aspects directly affected the revolutionary momentum of Expressionism. After the emphatic literary proclamations of change and the new humanity, reality was sobering, and many writers turned their backs on their fervor, which now seemed outdated. Exploring other modes of expression, Hasenclever and Toller turned to comedy. Yvan Goll considered the Expressionist fight to have turned grotesque. This is what Goll caricatures in *Der Ungestorbene.*

The new man has deteriorated into the intellectual Dr. Gulfstream, whose topic on the lecture circuit that night is the new man. The reporter, who is also an insurance salesman, persuades Dr. Gulfstream to die in order to emphasize his message that the superman has appeared. To ensure his wife's financial well-being, Dr. Gulfstream buys life insurance from the reporter. After the lecture, Dr. Gulfstream's wife Veronica ignores her husband to be with the reporter, and Dr. Gulfstream exits "into death" [In den Tod!]. At six o'clock the next morning, however, he is still alive, while the morning papers announce his death. He finds himself in an absurd situation in which almost everybody ignores his existence. The reporter reminds Dr. Gulfstream that things cannot be changed. At that moment, however, things do change, as though the previous events had been a dream: Veronica enters, rebuffs the reporter, and is with her husband as if nothing had happened. Dr. Gulfstream, without mentioning the ordeal of the previous night, announces the topic of the new evening lecture — which is on bugs — and the reporter asks him for an interview.

Goll, bilingual in German and French, had lived in Paris since 1919. He belonged to the pioneers of the absurd theater and had joined the Surrealist movement in France. In his grotesque play *Der Unsterbliche,* Goll used and parodied Expressionist themes and devices, but he also attempted to present a new drama, the *Überdrama* (sur-drama), that included a world beyond empirical reality, the *Überreale* (surreal).

*The legacy of Expressionist drama and film*  Expressionist drama has often been considered too radical to find immediate successors beyond the Expressionist decade. Some of the emphatic visions may seem overacted today, and the consistency with which the spirit was placed over matter may appear naive after politics shaped reality in quite a different way. Nevertheless, the burst of creative energy alone made Expressionism at the very least an important transitional phase. Contrary to the often-heard criticism of Expressionism and literature in general, literature is under no obligation to present political solutions. But literature is successful on its own terms when it expresses the need for a counterworld in ways that are at the cutting edge of artistic innovation, as Expressionism most vigorously did.

Expressionist drama, in particular, was to prove influential, not only through the texts but primarily through actual stage productions. Kaiser's theoretical position paved the way for epic theater; in a multiple pun on the German word for theatrical play (*Schauspiel*; literally, "see" plus "play"), he called for the *Denk-Spiel*, a play that emphasizes the pleasure of thinking over the pleasure of watching. In practical terms, Max Reinhardt — who directed the premieres of early plays by Reinhard Sorge (1892–1916), Goering, Hasenclever, Kokoschka, and Kaiser — and later Erwin Piscator were instrumental in creating the stage for the epic theater. Piscator is connected with Bertolt Brecht, who wrote his first plays, including *Baal* (published 1922, performed 1923), as a direct response to Expressionist drama. The influence of Expressionist drama extended to Carl Zuckmayer (1896–1977) and, with its emphasis on the grotesque and absurd elements, to Max Frisch (1911–1991) and Friedrich Dürrenmatt.

The ultimate Expressionist medium, however, was film, whose main Expressionist phase developed during the 1920s. With adaptations appropriate to film, the conventions of Expressionist stage presentation were expanded and have remained influential to this day. The cityscape of the modern cult movie *Bladerunner* (1982), which, in turn, left clear marks on movies for mass consumption, such as *Batman* (1989), would not have been possible without the influence of the seminal silent film *Metropolis* (1926), directed by Fritz Lang (1890–1976). *Metropolis* presents a science-fiction story, reminiscent of Georg Kaiser's Expressionist *Gas* trilogy in its theme of dehumanization as a result of industrial capitalism, where the few exploit the many by subjugating them, as workers, to the machine in the big city. From their subterranean quarters the workers attempt a rebellion but are held back by the girl Maria. A scientist builds a robot to look like Maria in order to incite the workers' rebellion. Using the father/son conflict, the movie resolves the impending catastrophe by uniting Maria and Freder, who has been in love with her for some time, with Freder's father, the master of Metropolis.

The earlier *Das Cabinet des Dr. Caligari* (1919), directed by Robert Wiene (1881–1952), was the first Expressionist film. In the tradition of the monodrama, the movie presents a story of madness from the perspective of madness. The set applies the principles of Expressionist painting, where lines and forms express inner visions, that is, how a madman would perceive the world in a distorted, nightmarish way: streets appear labyrinthine and houses are crooked. This movie can serve as an illustration of Expressionism's strengths (the energy and innovative potential in the search for a new world) and weaknesses (the vagueness of the ideas about what the new world should look like).

Because movies address a much larger mass audience than the theater, Expressionist films were typically not as radical as Expressionist plays. *Metropolis* can be placed in a conservative context, because the film's happy ending seems to restore the social order. There is a strong affirmative undercurrent in *Caligari*. It departed from the original script that tried to unmask the madness of all authority by equating the mad criminal with the director of the mental institution. In contrast, the movie presents the authority figure of the director as benevolent and his identification with the criminal as a hallucination of the hero.

### The Dadaist Revolution against Everything

If the underlying goal of the Expressionist project can be described by the key phrase "spiritual-political transformation of humanity," Dada is defined by one key word: randomness. While Expressionism was the rhetoric of destruction, Dada was the practice of destruction. Dadaists were disappointed by the hopes that Expressionism had raised in art, especially in its proto-Dada aspects, and then had not fulfilled. From the Dadaist perspective, Expressionist practice was but a version of Aestheticism. Now it was up to the Dadaists to develop a truly and consistently radical practice to fuse art with life "in the entirety of its brutal reality" [in seiner gesamten brutalen Realität] as "a simultaneous confusion of noises, colors, and spiritual rhythms" [ein simultanes Gewirr von Geräuschen, Farben, und geistigen Rhythmen]. Thus the Dadaists wrote in their first manifesto in Berlin on April 12, 1918. Transcending traditional political options, they concluded: "If you are against this manifesto, you are a Dadaist" [Gegen dieses Manifest zu sein, heißt Dadaist zu sein].

*Art as anti-art* — While in Expressionism the underlying political goals seemed to determine art, Dada was complete anarchy: Dada denied any meaning, subverted all politics, and aimed to destroy the concept of art itself (after all, art should be indistinguishable from life) — Dada was art as anti-art. But Dada was more than mere negation. There was a method to this madness; it was called *Zufall* (randomness). Randomness ranged from free association to taking any object — including a text — apart and rearranging the parts. In the process, the Dadaists not only hinted at such ultimate questions as whether man is the product of chance, but they also had fun and used humor (from ironic provocation to self-irony).

Dadaism was action; the Dadaists were performance artists; and the "happening" was their main medium and provocation their main intent. When most people were prowar, Zurich Dada was against the war; likewise, when most people leaned toward pacifism, Berlin Dada was against it. It was symptomatic that Berlin Dada, a movement that became known for its political aggressiveness, was inaugurated on 22 January 1918 with a speech by Richard Huelsenbeck (1892–1974), who earlier had gone to neutral Switzerland to avoid the war. But now he nonchalantly claimed to be prowar and stated that things were still not cruel enough. Nevertheless, politically Dadaists leaned toward the left and anarchy; they considered the Weimar Republic a restoration of the old reactionary powers in a new guise. The Berlin Dadaists caused their greatest public provocation when they demanded of the National Assembly that the executive powers be transferred to a "Central Bureau of Dada" [Dadaistisches Zentralamt]. His business card identified Raoul Hausmann (1886–1971), among other things, as the "President of the Sun, the Moon and the Lesser Earth (Inner Surface)" [Präsident der Sonne, des Mondes und der kleinen Erde (Innenfläche)]; Johannes Baader (1875–1955), the Berlin "Chief-Dada" [Oberdada], declared himself president of the universe.

But the Dadaist project was not childish. As a new kind of creation, it was an adult and sensitive reaction to reality, though playful and radical. Above all, the emphasis on randomness can be seen as Dada's insight into the enormous meaninglessness of the social and political system that nevertheless insisted on having meaning. In response, Dada was the creative attempt to experience nonsense as meaningful or, perhaps, as the hope that what looked like randomness was not true randomness but rather an extreme complexity that provided meaning after all. It was this attitude that tied the Dadaists to the Modernist search for the center. They valorized randomness and negation and embraced nothingness, but they generally did so to find the absolute.

The polarity of randomness and meaning was already expressed in the name for the movement: *Dada* — which means "nothing at all, i.e., everything" [Gar nichts, d.h. alles]. Of course, the Dadaists added a question mark after this definition. *Dada* is a word in many languages (French for "hobby horse," Romanian and Russian for "yes-yes," and the repetition of the German word for "there" used in baby talk) and a word of no known language. And several Zurich Dadaists claimed to be the true originator of the name for the movement.

The main phases of Dadaism were related to their geographical centers. The birthplace of Dada was Zurich, as early as 1915 but at the latest in spring of 1916. Zurich Dada began falling apart in 1917 with the departure of Hugo Ball (1886–1927), and in 1918 Dada moved to Berlin. It reached its climax there in 1920, after which it, too, started to decline. Overlapping with the second phase, Dada spread to other places in Germany, especially Hanover and Cologne, and elsewhere, especially Paris. In addition, Marcel Duchamp (1887–1968) was the main representative of a similar but independent movement that began in New York in 1915. Although individual authors, such as Hans Arp (1887–1966) and Kurt Schwitters (1887–1949), continued practicing their versions of Dada, the Dadaist movement was exhausted as early as 1920 and superseded by other movements, especially Surrealism, by the mid-1920s.

*Zurich Dada*      In Zurich an international group, though mainly German-speaking, formed around Hugo Ball. Members included Emmy Ball-Hennings (1885–1948), Hans Arp, Marcel Janco (1895–?), Tristan Tzara (pseudonym of Sami Rosenstock, 1896–1963), Hans Richter (1888–1976), and Richard Huelsenbeck. Perhaps because of their dependence on the host country to provide a safe haven from the war, the Zurich Dadaists were more abstract and less outspokenly political than the later Berlin Dadaists; still, the artistic clean sweep that they intended was clearly a reaction to the war that was devouring Europe.

In February 1916 Zurich Dada first went public in an exhausting six-month, six-days-a-week run of their *Cabaret Voltaire*, mixing entertainment to bring in money (as demanded by the owner of the bar where the cabaret performances took place) and radical provocation. Performed were cabaret songs by Frank Wedekind and provocative Expressionist poetry; there were guest performances by other artists, such as Arthur Rubinstein and dancers from the Laban School. But there were also Zurich Dada creations. Although Ball claimed to have invented a new genre of poetry, these "poems without words" or sound poems — for example, his "Karavane" (Caravan), which he first performed in June 1916, begins with these two lines: "jolifanti bambla o falli bambla / großgiga m'pfa habla horem" — had been predated by Morgenstern's and Scheerbart's lyrical experiments. The Zurich Dadaists had *Dada*, their own publication; however, Dadaism achieved its visibility by performing its poems as provocation. Ball performed his sound poems dressed in Cubist-style costumes; other poems were performed in conjunction with gymnastic movements, as though the poems were abstract dances. Indeed, there was a whole series of new poetic forms, such as bruitist, simultaneist, and static poems.

The bruitist poem, such as Huelsenbeck's "Ebene" (Plane), appears on the page as little more than a nonsense poem that combines existing and invented words in distorted syntax as in the line "or or birribound birribound the ox whizzes round in a circle" [oder oder birribum birribum saust der Ochs im Kreis herum]. As a bruitist poem, a form introduced by Italian Futurism, it was meant to be performed with interspersed real noises in order to bring poetry closer to life. The simultaneist poems, another form adapted from Italian Futurism, incorporated rhythmical elements, such as rattles, whistles, and drumbeats, with several speakers reading out loud (ranging from loud to very loud) their divergent sound segments of the poem, similar to singers singing their individual themes simultaneously. The sounds were supposed to represent the human soul caught in a destructive world. The static poem (not to be confused with Benn's use of the same term) was supposed to express the absurdity of life by pointing to the arbitrariness of the word and its parts. During the performance of a static poem, the syllables and letters of words, written on large cards, were displayed in changing sequence.

The linguistic experiments aimed at relating language directly to reality; thus, Dada moved away from traditional use of words toward live performance because the latter could both introduce elements of actual reality (noises of all sorts) into the text and free language from the abuse it had suffered at the hands of bourgeois society. The resulting abstraction and fusion of arts were among Ball's central concerns for reaching a synthesis.

In the same way that this synthesis challenged traditional language use, the role played by chance in creating abstract texts challenged the traditional role of the artist. As part of the fusion of art and life, everyone was considered an artist: the "artist" and each member of the audience. Randomness was at the heart of the process of bringing reality into art, because live performances not only included a chance element by definition but also further altered the role of the artist by applying randomness to creating art. In their version of working with objets trouvés — ordinary objects treated as objects of art — Dadaists randomly combined elements that they found ready for their use from their own writing or from already published materials, such as newspapers.

*Berlin Dada*    Zurich Dada was weakened in part because of conflicts between Tzara and Ball; the latter left the group in May 1917. In January 1918, Richard Huelsenbeck brought Dada to Berlin, where an artistically less abstract and politically more aggressive version of Dada emerged in the collaboration between Huelsenbeck, Raoul Hausmann, Johannes Baader, George Grosz, Wieland Herzfelde (1896–1988), and others. The April 1918 Dadaist Manifesto was signed by major Dadaists from Zurich and Berlin. The last Dada evening in Zurich took place in April 1919.

In Berlin, Dada became much more political, because its main protagonists were no longer emigrants in a host country but citizens. Late in 1918 Grosz and others joined the Communist Party. In contrast, the self-proclaimed "German Group" (including Hausmann and Huelsenbeck) of the "Dadaist Revolutionary Central Committee" called for radical Communism, which they, however, parodied at the same time by demands, such as introducing the simultaneist poem as the Communist state prayer.

In their artistic work the Berlin Dadaists also turned away from abstraction, emphasizing the aspect of performance even more than the Zurich Dadaists had. It was but a short step from the linguistic play with randomness of Zurich Dada to radicalizing the collage technique. Texts, such as Hausmann's optophonetic poetry (for which he used ready-made letters of various types and sizes), emerged. Above all, the photomontage was invented; it seems to have been invented at the same time by Hausmann and John Heartfield (pseudonym of Helmut Herzfeld, 1891–1968) independently of each other. Baader took a step further with his *Plastic-Dada-Dio-Drama*, a three-dimensional version of the photomontage that assembled objets trouvés into a sculpture.

Huelsenbeck's *Dada Almanach* and the International Dada Fair were the two main achievements of Berlin Dada in 1920. That was also the year the movement began to fall apart; Huelsenbeck himself was missing from the Dada Fair, and so was Kurt Schwitters, who had not been admitted to the Club Dada because of Huelsenbeck's aversion toward him.

*MERZ by Schwitters*

Schwitters developed his own version of Dada, which he called MERZ. Reportedly derived from truncating the name of the German bank Commerzbank, it uses not just ready-mades but also objects that had been thrown away — a montage technique with which Schwitters breathed new life into objects. MERZ differed in one crucial aspect from Dada: it was art, not anti-art. Best known are Schwitters's nonsense poems that make sense — just not the usual sense, in the same way that Schwitters did not restrict himself to the usual five physical senses. His 1919 love poem "An Anna Blume" (which Schwitters himself translated as "Anna Blume," but which literally means "To Anna Flower") identifies Anna Blume as "the beloved of my twenty-seven senses" [Geliebte meiner siebenundzwanzig Sinne]. The poem takes the reader through an accordingly distorted reality with statements, such as "Blue is the color of your yellow hair" [Blau ist die Farbe deines gelben Haares], and an equally playful disregard of linguistic rules, while following a grammar of the heart, such as in the poem's last sentence: "Anna Blume, you trickle beast, I love your!" [Anna Blume, du tropfes Tier, ich liebe dir!].

Schwitters's *Ursonate* (Primal Sonata) was similar to Ball's sound poems, such as "Karavane," but longer. Similar to the simultaneist poems, *Ursonate* came with a complete score but had only one performer. In contrast to Dadaist provocation that could lead to disruptive confrontations, Schwitters did not perform his *Ursonate* (premiere in 1924 or 1925) to alienate the audience by shocking it. Rather, he shocked his listeners into pleasure, into enjoying themselves and their reaction to hearing language in a way they had not heard it before: as the play of modulated sounds.

To the degree that MERZ was pro-art, however, it was more radical in the fusion of art and life because Schwitters lived his art. Everything became MERZ; there was MERZ art, the MERZ journal, the MERZ stage, and even MERZ building. The latter grew out of the *Schwitters-Säule* (Schwitters's Column). Reminiscent of Baader's *Plastic-Dada-Dio-Drama*, the *Schwitters-Säule* started out as a kind of abstract plaster sculpture in a room of Schwitters's house in Hanover, but Schwitters kept adding to it. Hans Richter recalls seeing it for the first time in 1925, when the *Schwitters-Säule* filled about half the room and reached almost to the ceiling. It was a structure of concave and convex shapes, with hollow spaces in between that contained objects relating to a person that had meaning to Schwitters's life; for instance, a thick pencil that belonged to the architect Ludwig Mies van der Rohe (1886–1969) was in the "Mies van der Rohe hole." Over the years the column grew to fill the entire room and, through a hole in the ceiling, into the upstairs rooms. In the *Schwitters-Säule* art and life were one; Schwitters continued the endeavor all his life, always remaining a Dadaist. When he had to flee from the Nazis, he started building it over again, first in Norway and then in England, where he died in 1948.

Internationally, Dada was primarily a precursor of Surrealism. André Breton (1896–1966), Louis Aragon (1897–1982), Marcel Duchamp, and Man Ray (1890–1976) — all major players in the Surrealist movement — had Dadaist roots. In Paris Dada, Tzara's emphasis on negativism, which early on in Zurich was in conflict with Ball's interest in synthesis, now stood in sharp contrast to Breton's position, which had close affinities to that of Ball and other Dadaists. In 1921 Breton defined Dada in the same way he later defined Surrealism: "What keeps Dada going is its wonderful faculty of reaching two different realities without leaving the realm of one's existence and, by bringing them together, of obtaining a spark." Dadaist inventions — such as automatic writing, objet trouvé, and photomontages — were among the hallmarks of Surrealism, facetiously dubbed "Dada for successful artists."

In the end Dadaism fell apart as a movement, because it could not merge art with life in the way that was necessary in order for it to be an anti-art movement. Ironically for Dada, the artistic movement that did not want to be art but life was still appreciated by the audience as art. The legacy of Dadaism is ubiquitous in modern art, including textual experimentation with collage techniques, concrete poetry, object art, and performance art.

## The Sum of the Era

By the end of the 1910s, literature and art in general had seen their most radical innovations, which challenged not only bourgeois society; Expressionism attacked the medium of literature, and Dada challenged even the practice and status of art in bourgeois society. Modernist literature had developed its major resources or models between 1890 and 1920 with the various modes of Aestheticism, the Avant-Garde, and the ongoing Modernist redefinition of realism. Around 1920 these modes began to converge into the innovative synthesis that constituted the high Modernist mode.

While Modernist works on either side of the turning point of the year 1920 can be considered equally important artistic achievements, the change raises theoretical issues of how to evaluate Modernism. On the one hand, the years before 1920 could be discarded as a period of artistic failure because the Avant-Garde movements did not reach their self-proclaimed political goals. This view ignores the fact that, setting out to revolutionize art and life, Expressionism and Dadaism successfully revolutionized art during the 1910s through formal innovations and challenges to the concept of the work of art. On the other hand, the years after 1920 could be judged as a period of mere artistic reprise on the premise that the Modernist modes before 1920 had exhausted all innovative options and that any gesture of protest had become inauthentic after the failure of the Avant-Garde's political goals. The charge of inauthenticity, however, misses the point of a literature that attempts to be a part of life, because life seems to require that some fights be fought over and over again, which does not make the repetition inauthentic.

As the 1910s came to an end, the title of the most important collection of Expressionist poetry summed up the Expressionist vision of creating a new humanity by destroying the old: *Menschheitsdämmerung* (1919), edited by Kurt Pinthus (1881–1975), means ambiguously *Dawn of Humanity* or *Twilight of Humanity*. The years 1918 and 1919 also brought other attempts to sum up an era that at the same time reflected the Expressionist decade and prefigured later literary explorations of the conditions that had led to the First World War: Hermann Hesse's *Demian* (1919), Karl Kraus's *Die letzten Tage der Menschheit* (The Last Days of Humanity, 1918–1919), and Heinrich Mann's *Der Untertan* (The Loyal Subject, 1918).

In *Demian* the dawn of a new humanity is presented. In a departure from his earlier works, Hesse created with *Demian* a fully developed lyrical novel within the confines of a Bildungsroman. In contrast to realistic description, the novel presents a gradual internalization of the outer world in the process of the hero's attaining his goal, which can be understood as "soul," or a state of inner awareness. Each step that the hero, Emil Sinclair, takes toward achieving his goal makes it clear that it is not an achievement of the final goal but only a preparation for the next step. At the end he finds himself wounded in war and lying in the hospital bed next to the bed of his mentor Demian, who dies after their symbolic embrace that sets Sinclair free to live his own life (unless he, too, dies of his injuries, which is left open in the novel). Sinclair's inner journey paralleled the development of Hesse's generation, whose spokesperson Hesse became with the great success of the novel.

*Demian* resulted from Hesse's reaction to the First World War, as well as the psychotherapy that Hesse underwent to deal with his problems. He needed to make sense of the nonsensical; like the early Expressionists, he saw the war as a necessary step toward a better world. A new humanity is forming somewhere deep down: "A giant bird was fighting its way out of the egg, and the egg was the world, and the world had to be destroyed" [Es kämpfte sich ein Riesenvogel aus dem Ei, und das Ei war die Welt, und die Welt mußte in Trümmer gehen]. The ancient Roman image of bird and egg becomes the central image of the book, because it encompasses the individual rebirth, the rebirth of humanity in terms of Jung's collective unconscious, and the emergence of a new humanity, perhaps along Nietzschean lines.

The bird is identified in the novel as "Abraxas," a deity that combines all opposites — good and evil, male and female, human and animal — within itself. Sinclair seems to find Abraxas in Demian. However, identities are fluid in lyrical novels and are often only projections of the symbolic hero, so it is possible that Demian does not really exist or that he is Sinclair's daimon. In addition, the name *Sinclair* itself can also be understood as an Abraxas-like combination of opposites: the English word *sin*, representing the dark, and the French word *clair* (clear), representing the light side of life.

In this union of polarities, a fundamental dichotomy in the basic understanding of *Demian* emerges, which is also symptomatic of the understanding of much of early Expressionism. Some critics see the novel as displaying the liberating process of searching for an authentic self (which is in keeping with Hesse's own humanist comments about his novel); other critics detect conservative, if not fascist, tendencies in the spiritualization of war. The search for the grand harmony of *Geist* (spirit) and *Macht* (power) was the center of the hopes for national renewal that paved the way for the First World War. But society's broadly supported prowar attitude, initially also held by Hesse, was typical of all belligerent nations and was an extension of their bourgeois value system. Like some early Expressionist texts, *Demian* has an unsettling textual property: it not only suggests and supports political readings that the author intended but also allows for fundamentally divergent ones.

Postwar Expressionism, on the other hand, was intent on indicting war. Although Karl Kraus's dramatic style had clear affinities to the movement, he did not consider himself an Expressionist. His montage technique, combining news reports, military orders, and official announcements, as well as his epic gesture of presentation, was influential beyond Expressionism. A clear antiwar attitude is one hallmark of the satiric play *Die letzten Tage der Menschheit*, which Kraus published in special issues of his famous journal *Die Fackel* (The Torch) in 1918 and 1919. Totaling about 700 pages, and comprising over 200 scenes and several hundred characters, this amazing play presents the twilight of humanity, as its title promises.

Concentrating on life at home, Kraus depicts an everyday existence of ignorance and superficiality that make mediocrity and political crime possible. War seems to be only an extreme extension of this dehumanized life. Kraus was convinced that Austria started the war and that the media had helped prepare the public for the war by desensitizing people's minds. Nevertheless, the play gradually moves to include Germany, whose hollow patriotism Kraus exposed. He referred to his play as Mars Theater; the cosmic dimensions seemed more accommodating to the proportions of the play than the human theater. In the epilogue Mars destroys the earth with meteors; after a pause, God's voice is heard, ironically repeating Kaiser Wilhelm's comment about the war: "I did not want this" [Ich habe es nicht gewollt].

A similar analysis of the Wilhelmine spirit is presented in Heinrich Mann's *Der Untertan*, the major satirical novel of twentieth-century German literature. In his 1910 essay "Geist und Tat" (Spirit and Action), Mann demonstrated his commitment to democracy and attempted to reconcile the tension between spirit and action, which are usually considered the main ingredients of militant nationalism, by calling for a synthesis of artists and people, of art and life. He thus had provided the key words *spirit* and *action* for the German Expressionist movement, as well as the central belief that literature is a form of public life. His own approach to this fusion was less revolutionary but more analytical. In *Der Untertan* Mann analyzed why the revolution did not happen in Germany: because of the political identity of tyrant and subject.

Following the formal pattern of the Bildungsroman, Mann's novel satirizes the education of the bourgeois Diederich Heßling (whose name sounds like *häßlich*, German for "ugly"). For Diederich education means climbing the social ladder in the name of materialism and self-interest, all of which is connected with Heßling's reactionary ideal of manhood, hunger for power, and anti-Semitism. While Heßling is a gentle child and could have developed into a sensitive and socially responsible adult, he is caught in the clutches of the hierarchy of Wilhelmine Germany and emerges in the double role of tyrant over his own small realm and loyal subject of the German emperor.

That Diederich Heßling identifies with Kaiser Wilhelm II unmasks society's authoritarian fabric; this identification is carefully developed in the novel. The first high point occurs at the end of the first chapter, when, in a brief and silent public encounter between the two, Diederich is awed, slips, and falls into the mud; the emperor sees this and laughs, recognizing "a loyal subject" [ein treuer Untertan]. Diederich styles himself after the Kaiser, and his greatest achievement is erecting a monument in honor of Kaiser Wilhelm. The storm that starts during Diederich's dedication speech corresponds to the belligerent content of the speech, which is directed against France. Therefore, the end of the novel presents the final climax of Diederich's identification with Kaiser Wilhelm in the revelation of their symbolic true character: they embody the same authoritarian ideals. Old Buck, a participant in the failed 1848 democratic revolution in Germany and the only positive character in the novel, suddenly recognizes who (or what) Diederich really is: "He has seen the devil!" [Er hat den Teufel gesehen!].

Heinrich Mann's position stood in stark contrast to that of his brother, Thomas. In his essay *Betrachtungen eines Unpolitischen* (Observations of an Unpolitical Man, 1918), the latter shared his brother's analysis of the synthesis of artist and people in European democracies, such as France, but he considered politicizing the spirit to be the true crime of democracy against humanity. Thomas Mann argued an essentially Aestheticist position, which was a conservative one, even though Aestheticism included a subversive potential. While Thomas Mann argued polemically against the totalizing tendencies that politicization effects on the artistic spirit, Heinrich Mann's novel presented a satirical analysis of the totalizing tendencies of politics on all of life.

At the heart of the conflict between the brothers lay the question of the role of politics in literature and, conversely, the role of literature in politics and the rest of life. These questions raise the issue of literature as an institution. Both Heinrich and Thomas Mann remained within the confines of literature as an institution in a bourgeois society. This stance, in turn, raises the question of whether all political content is potentially neutralized if expressed within institutional limitations, or whether literature needs to go beyond those limitations and become anti-art if it is to be politically effective. In sum, the 1910s presented various models of how art and life could be combined; the Avant-Garde approach was the most radical one and gave this decade its imprint.

❧    ❧    ❧    ❧    ❧    ❧    ❧

# 3: The 1920s: High Modernism and the Second Phase of the Avant-Garde — Surrealistic Elements and New Objectivity

## The Social Foundations: Promise of a Democratic Society

THE PROMISE OF A DEMOCRATIC SOCIETY in Germany had only limited options between the opposition of the extreme right, whose dreams of military grandeur had ended with the First World War, and of the extreme left, whose hopes for a Communist or more radically democratic society had been thwarted by the reality of the Weimar Republic. Although Germany had become a parliamentary democracy, weak general support of the democracy was a problem for the republic from the outset. It was particularly harmful that leading representatives of German cultural life, such as Thomas Mann, were slow in coming out in public support of the Weimar Republic. Much of the support seems to have been a matter of reason and not of the heart (hence the term *Vernunftsrepublikaner*).

The 1920s encompass the three phases of the development of the Weimar Republic. Economic chaos and inner turmoil that at times reached the magnitude of civil war characterized the initial phase (1920–1923). The middle phase (1924–1928) brought general stabilization and economic recovery that made these five years appear to be the *goldene Zwanziger* (Golden Twenties). The final phase (1929–1933) began with renewed economic trouble and ended in the replacement of the Weimar Republic by the Nazi dictatorship.

The first parliamentary elections in 1920 were marred by violence, and as early as March 1920, the first major coup was attempted by the extreme right. It was carried out under the command of Wolfgang Kapp (hence its name, *Kapp putsch*) and General Walther von Lüttwitz by the infamous *Freikorps*, which, along with the regular military, had just been used by the SPD government to quell the leftist uprisings of 1918 and 1919. The government had to flee Berlin when the military high command refused to follow orders. The coup's collapse after a few days became one of the most hopeful signs of popular support in the history of the young German democracy, because it was primarily a general strike by the workers, with support from other groups, that ended the coup attempt.

But the lagging democratization of workers' participation in their companies and a general strictness against violence from the left, combined with a lax attitude toward violence from the right, provoked the formation of a Red Army and led to leftist uprisings in the area of the Ruhr River, in Saxony, and in Thuringia. This time the military interceded, with support from the reactionary *Freikorps*. An analysis of politically motivated murders between 1919 and 1922 reveals that the unequal treatment of political violence favored the political right, contributing to the Weimar Republic's problems. Of twenty-two political assassinations committed by leftist radicals, only four murderers went unpunished, and ten received the death sentence; in contrast, of 354 murders by the extreme right, 326 murderers went unpunished, and not a single one received the death penalty.

The Treaty of Versailles brought additional challenges in the form of reparations that Germany was required to pay but that exceeded German economic capabilities. By 1931 Germany had paid a total of 53 million Reichsmark. Economic realities during the early 1920s, however, were defined by an unprecedented inflation: the value of one mark in gold before the war, in 1914, had fallen to ten Reichsmark in December of 1919 and to 1,000,000,000,000 Reichsmark in November 1923. The impoverishment of large sections of the population contrasted starkly with gigantic financial windfalls stemming from speculations that only a few could afford. In a bold move in 1923, the new coalition government stopped the inflation when it introduced a new and solid currency, the Rentenmark, by signing securities that guaranteed the temporary currency with gold.

The year 1923, however, brought further crises. In January, French and Belgian troops occupied the Ruhr region, overcoming armed resistance. In October, Communist participation in state governments in Saxony and in Thuringia was brutally ended by the military; an earlier coup attempt from the right, in Munich, collapsed after a day when local police dispersed the crowd. The coup leaders, among them Adolf Hitler, were given light sentences. As 1923 ended, so did the first phase in the history of the Weimar Republic. While the tensions remained unresolved under the surface, Germany recovered economically.

The recovery was also tied to foreign-policy successes. German policy was oriented toward the West, and in 1925 Germany reentered the international scene as a member of the League of Nations. Also in 1925, the French and Belgian occupation of the Ruhr region ended. But the period of stability was short-lived. Conservatives held key administrative, economic, and military positions. After the death of the Social Democrat Friedrich Ebert, the first president of the Weimar Republic, efforts to get another true democrat elected as president failed. Field Marshal Paul von Hindenburg became president in 1925.

Though loyal to the Weimar constitution, the conservative monarchist Hindenburg was actually an ersatz Kaiser. The economy started to slow in 1928, and with Black Friday in New York (October 24, 1929) the industrialized nations spiraled into a worldwide economic crisis — and Germany spiraled with them. Thus began the final phase of the Weimar Republic, with widespread unemployment that led to profound social and psychological displacements in the population.

### The Literary Spectrum

The 1920s (and the early 1930s) saw climactic developments for German literature written in the Modernist mode, a literature whose content mirrored the democratic versus reactionary political confrontations that tore through the Weimar Republic. Some writers were caught in the middle. Hugo von Hofmannsthal and Stefan George had emerged as Aestheticist authors and, despite their tendencies to open up their works to an idiosyncratically defined social level of broader reach, their generally conservative politics invited misunderstandings and controversial interpretations.

Hofmannsthal's speech "Das Schrifttum als geistiger Raum der Nation" (Literature as a Nation's Spiritual Space, 1927) and George's collection of poems *Das neue Reich* (The New Empire, 1928) displayed, even in their titles, elements that were used as key words in National Socialist phraseology — for example, German *Schrifttum* as opposed to allegedly un-German *Literatur*, and the central idea of a new empire, or *Reich*. Hofmannsthal most likely meant his phrase "conservative revolution" in a spiritual sense; George left Germany just before his death and right after the Nazis had come to power.

These examples suggest a broad range of conservative attitudes, but they do not suggest a necessary development toward National Socialism. Nevertheless, it has been argued that the terms, and with them the concepts, were vague and that, in the historical situation of the 1920s, a German audience needed clarity, not vagueness. Rather than implying that the writers and their texts alone could have prevented National Socialism from taking power, this argument expresses shock that none of the attempts at resistance by intellectuals was successful, and it also expresses disappointment in many of the foremost intellectuals in the German-speaking culture who either seemed blind to the dangers of National Socialism or even contributed, however unwittingly, to a general intellectual atmosphere in which National Socialism could gain acceptance.

*Modernism versus Anti-Modernism*  Beginning with *Heimatkunst* at the turn of the century, authors emerged whose political views were clearly nationalist, reactionary, and antidemocratic. They rejected modernity (not just Modernism). For most of these writers, the political problems of Germany started when the Enlightenment forced its rational approach onto what they considered the profoundly irrational German soul. The Modernist fusion of rationality and irrationality, therefore, appeared to be equally un-German. The major antimodern works were written before 1933: *Volk ohne Raum* (Nation without Space, 1926), by Hans Grimm (1875–1959), and the *Paracelsus* trilogy (1917–1926), by Erwin Guido Kolbenheyer (1878–1962). By creating a nationalist and irrational myth, they propagated an ideology sufficiently close to that of National Socialism to be considered crucial in opening the door for a fascist mindset in their readers. In fact, these works constituted a central element in the National Socialist literary canon, and most of the reactionary authors were active supporters of the Nazi regime.

Democratic and reactionary attitudes met head on, especially in the subgenre of the war novel, toward the end of the 1920s. While most of the war novels share a proximity to popular literature, their forms and contents show significant differences. So-called democratic war novels generally took an antiwar stance, as did, for example, *Der Streit um den Sergeanten Grischa* (The Argument Concerning Sergeant Grisha, 1927), by Arnold Zweig (1887–1968); *Krieg* (War, 1928), by Ludwig Renn (pseudonym of Arnold Friedrich Vieth von Golßenau, 1889–1979); *Heeresbericht* (Army Report, 1930), by Edlef Köppen (1893–1939); and *Im Westen nichts Neues* (All Quiet on the Western Front, 1929), by Erich Maria Remarque (pseudonym of Erich Paul Remark, 1898–1970). The last novel was by far the most popular antiwar novel, with 3.5 million copies sold within the first year and a half of its publication.

In the formal context of New Objectivity, antiwar novels attempted to create a sense of authenticity by documenting events of war, usually from the perspective of the average soldier, in a realistic language whose tone is matter-of-fact and casual. The linguistic objectivity of these novels precluded metaphoric speech that would glorify or romanticize war; on the contrary, the objectivity concerning language extended to seeking sense in war, which is being unmasked as senseless. The heroes of the democratic antiwar novel suffered a fate that is equally meaningless; for example, the protagonist-narrator of *Im Westen nichts Neues*, Paul Bäumer, dies even though (as the novel's two final, third-person paragraphs relate) the official report states that all was quiet on the Western front.

Reactionary war novels — such as *Die Gruppe Bosemüller* (The Bosemüller Group, 1930), by Werner Beumelburg (1899–1963), and *Glaube an Deutschland* (Belief in Germany, 1931), by Hans Zöberlein (1895–1964) — were more than simply prowar in their glorification of violence. What made them politically significant was the idealization of community, which fed into a core belief of National Socialism. The early and overrated war diary by Ernst Jünger (1895–1998), *In Stahlgewittern* (In Storms of Steel, 1920), belongs in this context. The reactionary prowar novels suggested that war was the ultimate and meaningful experience of a new nation's birth in the spirit of the community among brothers in arms. The metaphoric and sentimental language of these novels corresponded to the political idealization that they presented.

*High Modernism*

Based on the diverse Modernist models that had emerged before 1920, the high Modernist mode presented a synthesis that itself developed a variety of styles, from surrealistic elements to a New Objectivist mode. On the international scene, high Modernism emerged with T. S. Eliot's *The Waste Land* (1922); James Joyce's *Ulysses* (1922); and the last volumes of *Remembrance of Things Past* (1920–1927), by Marcel Proust (1871–1922) and lasted into the 1950s.

Especially influential for German literature was the translation of *Ulysses* (1927 and 1930), "both as a literary case-book and as a spiritual inspiration" (Mitchell 90). Although Schnitzler's story "Leutnant Gustl" presented the first sustained interior monologue in German literature as early as 1900, the breakthrough of the technique came with Joyce's demonstration of how to use interior monologue together with other techniques, as well as how to adapt interior monologue itself. The latter application moved from still mainly logical and grammatical organization, as in Gustl's monologue, to allowing free association to dominate narrative structure and linguistic form itself. Similarly, Dada had invented the montage technique. Joyce's use of the montage technique, however, both as variation within shorter text passages and across the chapters, inspired literary imagination.

While German Modernism thus developed in a parallel fashion to international Modernism, its public stay in Germany and Austria was cut short by the Nazis' taking political power in 1933. During the early 1920s, Rilke's poem cycles *Duineser Elegien* and *Sonette an Orpheus*, Thomas Mann's novel *Der Zauberberg*, and Kafka's three posthumously published novels explored the tension between rationality and irrationality. They formed, together with the works of Eliot, Joyce, and Proust, as well as later ones by Robert Musil and Hermann Broch (1886–1951), the body of literary high Modernism.

These works belong to the Aestheticist tradition because of their emphasis on the lyrical aspect of an inner vision, yet the high Modernist mode continued to aim at a more authentic rendering of reality. Particularly in German and Austrian literature, such an infusion of reality was connected to the First World War and the new social realities in which it had resulted. While the works mentioned encountered reality in terms of the polarity of rationality and irrationality, Modernist literature of the 1920s also included styles that dealt with reality in a more direct and somewhat coolly detached manner. The political impetus of the Avant-Garde lost its former anti-art and destructive orientation but around the mid-1920s found its way into the publicly political literature of the New Objectivity, or *Neue Sachlichkeit*. While the tone of New Objectivity ranged from pessimism to optimism (or, more specifically, from melancholy disillusionment to revolutionary calls to action), its primary characteristic was its political perspective on reality.

In terms of the modern and democratic attitudes, an affinity can be detected between the New Objectivist approach and the International Style, as it was exemplified in Walter Gropius (1883–1969) and Ludwig Mies van der Rohe's Bauhaus (1918–1933) in Germany. *Bauhaus* means "Building Institute" and has been defined as a technical school of design emphasizing the industrial arts, including architecture, and the study of new materials and methods. Neither Bauhaus nor New Objectivity mindlessly accepted the world as they found it; rather, both tried to assess more pragmatically the real conditions and possibilities of change. The much-abused Bauhaus creed of "form follows function" was the result of objectivity, detached coolness, and skepticism. At the Bauhaus, Lothar Schreyer (1886–1966, a cofounder of the Expressionist *Sturm* stage), Oskar Schlemmer (1888–1943, who focused on a mathematics of the relationship between man and space on the stage), and Laszlo Moholny-Nagy (1895–1946, who studied the new aesthetic media of film and photography in relation to the theater) continued Avant-Garde experiments with theater, especially stage design, to create a theater of totality.

It was also in the context of Modernism in general, and parallel to political developments during the 1920s in particular, that women began to gain more influence. Indeed, the emergence of the female voice was a major innovation of Modernism, although that voice remained primarily embedded within a patriarchal consciousness. The New Woman in the literature of the 1920s was usually stereotyped as sexually aggressive, dominant, or active, yet still judged by male standards. It has been argued that these stereotypes define the presentation of women in works by female authors, such as *Stud. chem. Helene Willführ* (Helene Willführ, Student of Chemistry, 1929), by Vicki Baum (1888–1960) — a novel, despite being criticized for reconventionalizing the image of the modern woman, usually credited with bringing the image of the New Woman to popular literature.

Contemporary literature focused on the struggle to achieve rights and independence for women. Marieluise Fleißer (1901–1974), for example, expressed in her works the right of women to determine their own lives against the narrow-mindedness of male antagonists. Her play *Pioniere in Ingolstadt* (The Corps of Engineers in Ingolstadt, performed 1928) exposes the sexual exploitation of women; disappointed by the casualness of sex, Berta complains: "We've left out love" [Die Liebe haben wir ausgelassen]. In contrast, the woman in Fleißer's novel *Mehlreisende Frieda Geier* (Frieda Geier, Traveling Saleswoman, 1931) is the 1920s New Woman with leather jacket and short haircut, who leaves her husband rather than sacrifice her independence. In addition, novels by Irmgard Keun (1905–1982), such as *Gilgi — eine von uns* (Gilgi — One of Us, 1931), can be interpreted in terms of women's struggle against traditional roles as sexual objects, mothers, daughters, and wives.

Challenged by political confrontations of the Weimar Republic and attempting to find new modes of expressing human consciousness, high Modernist literature functioned within the parameters of literature as an institution. Furthermore, realism played a stronger role during the 1920s, whether it was in those works that explored the tension between realistic and surrealistic elements or in the detached coolness and skepticism of New Objectivity.

## Surrealistic Elements: Rationality and Irrationality

The polarity of rationality and irrationality had provided the playing field of previous works, from fantastic literature (Paul Scheerbart) to Ironic Realism (early Robert Musil and Thomas Mann). This tradition was continued by exploring various manifestations of irrationality and its interactions with reality. The term *surrealism* needs to be used with care, however, and not be confused with the French Avant-Garde movement of Surrealism, which continued Dada practices of randomness, such as automatic writing, to achieve a new political understanding. These were neither the main motivation nor the technique of the German writers discussed in this section. Furthermore, while the German writers sought visible evidence of a spiritual world and explored ways to connect the visible and invisible, the French Surrealists primarily sought to create the marvelous. The latter aspect is more akin to later versions of magic realism in German literature than to the works of the writers discussed in this section. Nevertheless, with Yvan Goll's sur-dramas and works by Hesse and Kafka, German literature clearly included elements that were surrealistic in the sense that the simplistic concepts of reality and rationality gave way to a creative presentation of visions and dream experiences that allowed concepts of a different reality.

The works considered here were influenced by the Aestheticist tradition to the extent that their focus on the unique and separate world of the individual intensified the feelings of fragmentation and alienation that they expressed and tried to overcome. More symbolist that surrealist, Rilke's poetry succeeded in finding meaning in the poet's task of linking the material and the spiritual worlds in his praise of the material world. Other works, such as Hesse's *Steppenwolf* (1927) and Mann's *Zauberberg*, at least allowed glimpses of possible salvation. Still other works, such as those by Kafka and Jahnn, stressed insurmountable human limitations. They all, however, opened up ways in which the Modernist fusion of rationality and irrationality might point to meaning: Kafka explored angst caused by the experience of the clash between the visible and invisible; Hesse considered the mediating power of laughter; Mann emphasized the centrality of love as an almost transcendental force; and Hans Henny Jahnn (1894–1959) revealed the fundamental existence of the human body as central. These explorations in terms of content went hand in hand with experiments in literary form.

***Rilke's lyrical poetry*** The greatest achievements in lyrical poetry during the early 1920s and the defining German lyrical works of the first half of the twentieth century were Rilke's conclusion of his *Duineser Elegien*, begun earlier at Castle Duino but interrupted in part by the First World War, and the creation of its companion piece, *Die Sonette an Orpheus*. Formally, Rilke equaled the Expressionists in radicalness of language, although his choices were different. In terms of content, he evoked a new liberating transcendence that provided meaning to human life by bridging life and death, rationality and irrationality, exemplifying the typical Modernist mythmaking. Rilke believed that he had found the answer to his quest for eternal truths in his *Elegien*. There he transcended the human condition by recognizing lyrical poetry itself as a means of ensuring meaning through the communication between the human world and a higher realm, which is expressed in the unconventional symbol of the angel as "terrible" (schrecklich). The process of communication itself consists of praising the simple things to the angel. In keeping with Aestheticist tradition, the poet, as the singer of this praise, is also a prophet; the prophet-poet, in turn, became the main theme of the *Sonette*.

**Duineser Elegien** The ten *Elegien* continued the German elegiac tradition of Friedrich Gottlieb Klopstock (1724–1803) and Friederich Hölderlin (1770–1843) but opened up its form to rhythmic variations and moved from lament to triumphant celebration. This movement is also a central formal aspect, since the *Elegien* embody the principle of change, one of Rilke's core beliefs, in the cycle's structure. Change also affects the angel as the element that provides unity to the cycle. At first a terrifying and distant symbol of the absolute, the angel remains distant but develops into a bridge between mortal human existence and eternity.

The first five elegies lament the general human condition of loneliness (particularly unrequited love in the first elegy) and alienation. Especially in contrast to the terrifying magnitude of the angel — a representative of the invisible world for which humans yearn — the human capabilities are dwarfed (first and second elegies). Yet humans are also threatened from the inside by man's "wild inner nature" [seines Inneren Wildnis], which is the source of the will and the unconscious (third elegy). The will fractures human existence, and even the puppet is closer to the angel because while the puppet has no will, it has unity (fourth elegy). The climactic fifth elegy presents a family of street acrobats, an allusion to Pablo Picasso's (1881–1973) painting *La Famille des Saltimbanques*, as a symbol of human life where perfect movements are performed without emotional participation and, hence, without meaning.

These five elegies belong in the corpus of great pessimistic literature; however, not only do the *Elegien* as a whole cycle break out in jubilant optimism, even the pessimistic first five elegies can be seen as carrying the seed of human affirmation. The realms of liminal existence "within the gap between the world and the toy" [im Zwischenraum zwischen Welt und Spielzeug] are open for humans to experience that which is beyond the human. Throughout, the cycle refers to people in these realms, which include children, lovers, and dying or dead youths, because death is a transition and not an ending. Also, the hero is close to such liminal experiences; beginning with the sixth elegy's praise of the hero, the tone of the cycle prepares the reader for the shift from lamenting human limitation to celebrating human potential: "His rising is existence" [Sein Aufgang ist Dasein].

The seventh elegy presents the acceptance of the here and now, including the possibility of fulfilled love. This elegy moves from the experience of alienation in the first elegy to the jubilant affirmation: "Life here's glorious" [Hiersein ist herrlich]. This requires another transformation toward the interior: "Nowhere, beloved, can world exist but within" [Nirgends, Geliebte, wird Welt sein als innen]. The realm of such interiorization is the imagination, for which Rilke had created the term *Weltinnenraum* (the world's inner space) in his 1914 poem "Es winkt zu Fühlung fast aus allen Dingen" (It Beckons to Feeling from almost Everything).

The eighth elegy returns to the original lament of human will, or the consciousness that man is outside the chain of being. Again, however, the liminal realms of childhood, love, and dying open bridges that humanity can take, according to the ninth elegy, by embracing liminality, as the seventh elegy had claimed. The ninth elegy elaborates that the transformation of the visible into the invisible connects humanity with eternity because through it man expresses what is alien to the angel: the here and now of everyday existence.

The evocation of things achieves eternity. The poet's imagination, however, does not try to describe the invisible, as Rilke's thing poems did. The inner vision of the *Elegien* is not focused on the essence of an object but on the very process of communication between the realms of mortality and eternity. The earth's invisible emergence within the human imagination is the poet's task, which is accepted at the end of the ninth elegy. The tenth and final elegy establishes a balance between lament and celebration by once again referring to the liminal situations, including dying and death, in order to identify the lament as ultimately leading to suffering as "the source of joy" [die Quelle der Freude].

**Die Sonette an Orpheus**
*and beyond*

The *Sonette* are an extension of the *Elegien*. They not only center on praise as the poet's task but also demonstrate the process of interiorization that the *Elegien* evoke — hence the symbol of Orpheus as the ideal poet whose "word transcends life here" [Wort das Hiersein übertrifft] when he sings about ordinary things, such as the apple, the flower, and the tree. Oscillating within the "dual realm" [Doppelbereich] between visible and invisible, the *Sonette* challenge the reader to explore the possibility of meaning for himself or herself, and they establish the dichotomy of communication: Orpheus, the prophet-poet, depends on being heard. At the center lies existence, which is identified with poetry and change; the latter is even formulated as an imperative: "You must wish for change" [Wolle die Wandlung, II, 12].

Not only is the rigid form of the sonnet handled by Rilke with great and relaxed subtlety and suppleness, but its very form in the Italian tradition, with the turn from problem to solution occurring between the octave and the sestet, perfectly encodes the dual realm in which, according to Rilke, unifying meaning should emerge. The new myth of Orpheus's communicating with the angel was a paradox itself, since it presented a myth for a postmythical time. This paradox, typical of an antimodern element within Modernism, can be seen as the focus of Rilke's last poetic phase during the remaining four years after the *Elegien* and *Sonette*. These final texts are terse, rigidly built yet relaxed, and usually short poems. They express a newly found clarity and naiveté of vision that continues the transformation of the visible into the invisible to an extent that suggests the term *présence absente*, or language of absence. Such a language approaches silence, a characteristic that was important for other poets, too, especially Paul Celan after the Second World War. The aphoristic three-line poem that Rilke chose for his epitaph may serve as an example of his last poems: "Rose, oh pure contradiction, delight / in being nobody's sleep under so many / eyelids" [Rose, oh reiner Widerspruch, Lust / Niemandes Schlaf zu sein unter soviel / Lidern].

A complication emerges in the differing evaluations of the message of Rilke's work that readers have derived, especially in political terms. As in many cases, the issue is complex, because Rilke was a man of many contradictions. He welcomed the democratic changes after the First World War, and Walther Rathenau, a liberal and democratic politician assassinated by nationalists, was among his friends. But as his Bohemian, antibourgeois attitude and extreme individualism increased, Rilke — for a short period toward the end of his life in 1926 — came to admire Italian fascism under Mussolini by transferring to the political realm his aesthetic experience of obeying the dictate of poetic imagination. Rilke's use of myth is not representative of the fascist wish to return to simple premodern times, because his myth is a Modernist expression of the complex human need for meaning in the modern world. Nevertheless, it is legitimate to raise the question of whether fascist values are encoded in any poet's works. The treatment of Rilke's works by the National Socialists was itself marked by contradictions. While certain elements made it easy for National Socialism to appropriate specific works, some Nazi publications accused Rilke of "liberal, racial, and artistic" degeneration (Schwarz 1975, 295).

*The lyrical novel and a theory of the novel* In contrast to the classical epic, which is considered a representation of a self-evident totality, Georg Wilhelm Hegel (1770–1831) and Georg Lukács (1885–1971) called the novel the epic of the modern bourgeois world, because its form developed parallel to the socially differentiated world of modernity. Evolving into the most typical and successful bourgeois literary genre, the novel has been just as flexible in its many transformations as the bourgeoisie. While the novel originally foregrounded characters and action in the private realm of bourgeois life, it expanded that realm into a general description of a segment of life and then turned to an inner vision by gradually foregrounding experience and theme, elements traditionally considered lyrical. The development of the lyrical novel reached an important turning point at the beginning of the twentieth century with a stronger emphasis on psychology in the tension between rationality and irrationality with writers like Rilke, André Gide, and Virginia Woolf.

But the genre of the novel also became problematic, because it encompassed a multitude of divergent forms, styles, and themes that seemed to dissolve the genre. Not only had the scope of the novel expanded from focusing on the individual to focusing on society or the collective unconscious, but the novel also relied on language, which was perceived to be in a state of crisis, as expressed in Hofmannsthal's Chandos letter. As a result, everything done with language appeared tentative. Yet the novel also proved to be resilient; it was able to accommodate the multitude of forms and to incorporate the tentativeness into its structure: it became essayistic in two ways. On the one hand, the novel itself was an essay in the sense that it attempted a tentative approach to reality. On the other hand, the novel adapted the discursive tradition of the literary essay to reflect its relationship with reality.

The basic mode of the novel has always been the search; therefore, it was a logical consequence that the novel developed into the predominant literary form of the twentieth century. The motivation of the search that underlies the novel is the anthropological factor of hope corresponding to the Modernist hope of finding the center, either as a totality or, at least, as an individual identity. The search, however, changed over time to include the feeling of resignation. The hope was no longer individual but rather abstract: people no longer loved and hoped — instead, they lived according to a principle of love and a principle of hope. That was the state of the human condition expressed by Modernism.

These developments in the novel had begun before 1920 and led to the defining elements of the Modernist novel (and Modernism in general): modernity, complexity, and intensity. Modernity derived from a dehumanized presentation of the human being, who is seen as being directly dependent on psychological and/or social factors. Complexity incorporated the overwhelming abundance of experience in a way that resulted in formal changes, such as interior monologue and montage technique. Intensity mirrored fragmentation by zeroing in on specific aspects, thereby amplifying modernity and complexity. The high Modernist novels that adapted Aestheticism and Ironic Realism built on these three elements by reinforcing the inner vision of the novel's protagonist.

*Kafka's novels*    In addition to his short stories, Kafka wrote three novels, all of which remained unfinished and were published posthumously. Before his death Kafka had given the manuscripts to his friend Max Brod (1884–1968) with the understanding that they would be destroyed. Kafka worked on *Amerika* (1927) from 1912 to 1913, on *Der Prozeß* (The Trial, 1925) from 1914 to 1915, and on *Das Schloß* (The Castle, 1926) from 1921 to 1922. *Amerika* is superficially the lightest in tone of the three, yet it, too, portrays the protagonist's small failures that prevent him from achieving his goal of being successful in America. This is a variation of the basic plot that all three novels share: each protagonist attempts to get in touch with an invisible force that seems to have some kind of power over him, but fails.

*Der Prozeß* begins with a speculation that is typical of Kafka's stories, because it attempts to make sense of a situation that does not and cannot make sense: "Someone must have denounced Joseph K., for one morning, without having done anything bad, he was arrested" [Jemand mußte Josef K. verleumdet haben, denn ohne daß er etwas Böses getan hätte, wurde er eines Morgens verhaftet]. Josef K. has to face charges against which he is unable to defend himself, because he never fully understands what they are. At the end of the novel, he is led away into a small quarry and killed without having ever faced the court. At the moment before his execution, "K. now knew exactly that it would have been his duty to take the knife . . . and thrust it himself into his body" [K. wußte jetzt genau, daß es seine Pficht gewesen wäre, das Messer . . . selbst zu fassen und sich einzubohren]. His refusal to do so appears to him as a refusal to redeem himself fully in the eyes of the authorities. One of the men stabs K. in the heart, turning the knife twice. The novel ends with K. being aware of the men bending over him as if to observe his decision to accept death: "'Like a dog!' he said; it was as though the shame was meant to survive him." ["Wie ein Hund!" sagte er, es war, als sollte die Scham ihn überleben].

The crucial structural element of Kafka's narrative world is obvious in the novel's ending: the two-world condition in which the protagonist, though doomed to failure, frantically attempts to interpret what is happening. He cannot connect his visible world to the invisible world that has power over the visible one — a predicament that the protagonist does not want to perceive. The inaccessibility of the invisible world and the mutual exclusion of the two worlds are, however, clear to the reader. The surreal, nightmarish events are in stark contrast to the matter-of-fact tone of the narrative and express the Modernist theme of angst.

Yet the ending also points to another central aspect that complicates the interpretation (of any of Kafka's stories, for that matter): the text's dream quality strongly suggests an understanding of the events as a projection of the protagonist's inner world. The ultimate paradox lies in the construction that, although the invisible world is perceived a priori as inaccessible from the visible world, there seems to exist some kind of shared but elusive knowledge, after all.

The ending expresses the idea that, somehow, Josef K. knew what his duty would have been at the time of his execution. What is more, his death seems to be his decision; the two executioners bend down to see what the decision will be: his death occurs because he accepts it. The shame that seems to want to survive him appears to be a response of the visible realm to the invisible one. Kafka's protagonists are good middle-class citizens, because they try to remain respectable (an aspect of visibility in the bourgeois value system) through it all. From the beginning of the novel, Josef K. seems to have some knowledge of what is happening; for example, he admits that he is surprised by his arrest but adds, "I am not very surprised at all" [aber ich bin keineswegs sehr überrascht].

Josef K. attempts to integrate everything into his respectable world. He keeps working at the bank, which symbolizes a visible and rational social organization, while he attempts to get in touch with the court, which is prosecuting him and represents another kind of organization: invisible, irrational, elusive, but perhaps not a social organization after all. It has received various interpretations from literally standing for the law to representing God, an abstract concept of guilt, or even disease. The invisible realm remains inaccessible; nevertheless, there are links that cannot be attributed to the protagonist's interpretation of events.

Admittedly, Josef K. could believe that he knows what he was supposed to do during his execution without having any basis for this "knowledge." Yet there are elements in *Der Prozeß* that do not make sense unless there is some elusive connection. When Josef K. is in the labyrinth of rooms and hallways on his search for the committee that will take his deposition, he happens upon a woman and feels that he cannot ask her, so he invents a name and pretends to be looking for that person. The woman, however, sends him to the committee. The next chapter suggests an explanation when K. again meets the woman, who identifies herself as the wife of a messenger of the court. Yet her relationship to the messenger does not explain how she recognized K. when he first met her.

Narrative gaps of this kind are typical of Kafka's narratives and need to be filled in by the reader. Assuming Josef K. to be a lyrical hero locates the origin of the gaps inside his mind; it does not, however, explain the significance of these gaps. It also does not make the invisible world accessible; it simply construes a point of origin or connection that makes the inaccessibility all the more frustrating. At first it seemed as though the reader's task is to interpret not only the meaning of the court but K.'s interpretation of the court. Now it turns out to be even more complicated: the reader needs to interpret the court as K.'s interpretation of something that is already K.'s interpretation in the first place, that is, a symbolic representation offered by K.'s unconscious. Such a multi-refracted process of interpretation reflects the problematic readability of the world of the twentieth century.

As an expression of the ultimate unintelligibility and futility of life, Kafka's narratives struck a strong chord with readers. The plot of *Das Schloß* is encapsulated in the first paragraph of the novel, which says that K., who later identifies himself as a land surveyor, arrives late in the evening; the village is covered in snow, and he cannot see the castle or the castle's hill because of the fog and darkness: "For a long time, K. stood on the wooden bridge, which led from the country road to the village, and looked into the apparent emptiness" [Lange stand K. auf der Holzbrücke, die von der Landstraße zum Dorf führte, und blickte in die scheinbare Leere]. This is perfectly descriptive of the protagonist's situation in general: as much as he tries, he never reaches his goal, the castle. Throughout the novel he remains staring into the emptiness where he knows the castle is, just like humanity is trying to fathom the modern world.

Hermann Hesse explored inner visions that
*Hesse's* **Steppenwolf**    were autobiographically determined by his cultural conservatism and mysticism, which themselves were influenced by his interest in Nietzsche and in Eastern philosophies. Hesse addressed the potential failure of an inward journey in his novel *Das Glasperlenspiel* (The Glass Bead Game, 1943) when the master of the game, which symbolizes spiritual unity and discipline, begins to question the practice of withdrawal from life and decides to leave his religious order. In contrast, in the short novel *Siddhartha* (1922) individual asceticism is presented as the goal of the journey toward true meaning. Siddhartha's smile, which is that of the Buddha, reveals that he has finally found inner peace in accepting life and abandoning his desires. The novels *Demian* and *Der Steppenwolf* transpose the mythical quest into a contemporary context, which serves to underscore how difficult the quest has become. Set in the Jazz Age of the 1920s and influenced by Hesse's own psychoanalysis, *Steppenwolf* is the most Modernist, and most controversial, of his novels. The warning "for madmen only" [Nur für Verrückte], repeated throughout the novel as a leitmotif, refers to the maddening affirmation of human nature and modern life. But the journey is the same: the protagonist, Harry Haller, sets out to master the game of life; to do so, he needs to learn to laugh about life. Siddhartha's smile returns in Harry's quest for laughter.

The complex structure of the novel as a cabinet of mirrors suggests the subject matter of insight into human existence, where things are infinitely refracted and not always what one would like to see. The triad is an important structural device whose individual elements mirror each other, but at the same time there exists an underlying duality. On the global level, the novel consists of three major parts, but, as in a cabinet of mirrors, the boundaries are not quite clear. On the one hand, there are three central passages: a fictitious editor's introduction, the "Tractat vom Steppenwolf — Nur für Verrückte" (Treatise of the Steppenwolf — For Madmen only), and the visit to the "Magic Theater" [magisches Theater]. On the other hand, three related but different parts form the novel's entirety: the fictitious editor's introduction; the novel proper, which consists of "Harry Hallers Aufzeichnungen — nur für

Verrückte" (Harry Haller's Notes — For Madmen only); and, embedded in Harry's notes as a third and independent part, the "Tractat vom Steppenwolf," which usually appears in a different font but has even been printed on different paper stock so that it literally seems to be what Harry says it is — a leaflet he picked up. The plot of the novel proper, however, develops in two steps: first, Harry's quest for meaning culminates in a first answer, the "Tractat vom Steppenwolf"; second, Harry's exploration of that answer culminates in his visit to the Magic Theater.

The fictitious editor's introduction to the novel proper is important to the flow of the work. He introduces the fifty-year-old Harry, who refers to himself as the *Steppenwolf*, or lone wolf, and evaluates Harry's notes from a bourgeois point of view — an aspect of Harry's own thinking that he futilely tries to eradicate. Expressing his fascination with Harry's liminal experience, the editor places Harry outside of what is considered normal by the editor. Misunderstanding the notes, he assumes that Harry has fallen through the cracks of time. On the contrary, Harry is more at home in his time than the bourgeois editor.

Harry's notes begin by identifying him as an outsider searching for meaning for his fragmented life. The search takes him to the entertainment the city offers: variety shows, movies, evening dance, and jazz. None of the usual options for entertainment appeal to him. At one point, he passes a sign advertising the Magic Theater, but in his endeavor to find out more about this entertainment, he only runs into a man who gives him the "Tractat vom Steppenwolf." Harry observes that it has the typical appearance of a self-help leaflet.

When he reads it, however, Harry realizes that the "Tractat vom Steppenwolf" is uniquely about him. There can be no doubt, because the treatise begins with: "Once upon a time there was a man named Harry who was called Steppenwolf" [Es war einmal einer namens Harry, genannt der Steppenwolf]. It proceeds to identify the dual nature of the Steppenwolf: part human, part wolf. This duality is explored further in terms of the duality of the bourgeois and the artist. The Steppenwolf's independence is the other side of his isolation, which brings him close to suicide. Regardless of his endeavors, the bourgeois element remains a central aspect of his thinking. Similar to the dualities and triads being just the beginning of the novel's self-reflexive mirroring, the treatise explodes the Steppenwolf's identities: "Harry does not consist of two beings, but of one hundred, of thousands" [Harry besteht nicht aus zwei Wesen, sondern aus hundert, aus tausenden]. Beyond the dualities lies the third option: humor. This option gives direction to the path that the treatise calls Harry to follow: reject suicide and start developing a human existence.

The "Tractat vom Steppenwolf" also introduces the fundamental Modernist duality of reality versus illusion that underlies the novel and is fused in Harry's mind. Hesse presents both reality and Harry's illusion about reality without accentuating the boundaries. Therefore, it has been argued that the "Tractat vom Steppenwolf" is in reality not about Harry at all; rather, it is one self-help leaflet of many. It is Harry's suicidal state of mind that makes him see everything in connection to himself, and because he needs consolation, he reads it into the leaflet; only by way of his reading does it become the "Tractat vom Steppenwolf." Consequently, Harry is a symbolic hero, and the novel, as projection of its hero's inner vision, is a lyrical novel.

His mind set on developing a human existence, Harry probes into areas — the demimonde of sleazy bars and prostitution — that are beyond those of bourgeois life. As the repressed other of the bourgeois world, however, the demimonde is not really capable of overcoming bourgeois values. The "Tractat vom Steppenwolf" has already identified the category of the bourgeois as an ever-present condition of humanity in terms of the ideal of harmony between the extremes of human behavior. Harry's world remains a bourgeois world after all, while he attempts to transcend it by means of humor. His explorations culminate in a visit to the Magic Theater, which is, most likely, a drug-induced hallucination.

On the level of relationships among characters, the oscillation of duality and triad is repeated. On the one hand, Harry encounters three people who are central to his search for meaning: the prostitutes. Hermine and Maria and the musician Pablo. Hermine is Harry's Other — his mirror, as she herself says. Their names relate them to each other. Harry is the Americanized Jazz Age version of Hermann (the author's name); Hermine is the feminine version of the same name. For the ball, Hermine dresses in male clothes and goes by the name of Hermann. Furthermore, she appears (in reality or in Harry's illusion) to be interested in Harry's progression to human existence and becomes a kind of teacher for Harry; his educational goal is laughter, as an expression of not taking things too seriously and of accepting life as it is. On the other hand, the close relationship of the characters allows the reader to understand them in terms of human characteristics rather than individual personalities: Hermine's name and behavior suggest a hermaphroditic or androgynous quality; Maria is the natural and sensuous woman; Pablo represents the masculine side. They can even be understood, in terms of the archetypal concepts of anima and animus, to constitute the human psyche as a whole. In addition, the three characters' homosexual relationships further function to blur the boundaries between individual identities.

In a step-by-step development reminiscent of the educational program of the traditional Bildungsroman, Harry encounters sexual love with Maria, who has been sent by Hermine, whom he then meets at the masked ball. Pablo is also present and invites Harry to enter the Magic Theater to learn how to laugh. Pablo's role as magician is tied to his dispensing the drug that induces Harry's hallucinations of visiting a cabinet of mirrors that leads to several doors. Each door is labeled, and each label promises the attraction behind that door, for instance, "All Girls are Yours!" [Alle Mädchen sind dein!] and "On with the Hunt! Big-Game Hunting for Automobiles" [Auf zum fröhlichen Jagen! Hochjagd auf Automobile]. At the surface level these labels sound frivolous; the latter label even leads to Harry's witnessing cars that chase and kill pedestrians; in turn, Harry joyfully participates in shooting the cars. At a deeper level, however, the doors that Harry chooses to enter lead him to confront his own inner demons, including the long-denied admission that sexuality and aggression are human emotions.

Now that he feels ready for Hermine, the door with the label "How to Kill with Love" [Wie man durch Liebe tötet] triggers unpleasant memories and, when Harry finally opens it, leads him to Hermine and Pablo, who lie asleep in each other's arms. The narrative does not distinguish between, but rather fuses, reality and illusion; therefore, this scene can be interpreted as Harry slowly coming out of his hallucinations yet still unable to see things clearly. Out of jealousy Harry stabs Hermine to death when he sees her in an embrace with Pablo. But the realistic evocation of the murder gives way to irreality: Pablo admonishes Harry for having spoiled the humorous theater and having "soiled our pretty world of images with spots of reality" [unsere hübsche Bilderwelt mit Wirklichkeitsflecken besudelt]. What had seemed real now appears to be a part of a game in which Hermine is but a play figure: Pablo "took Hermine, who in his fingers soon shrank into a little play figurine, and put her into the same pocket of his vest from which he had just before taken a cigarette" [nahm Hermine, die in seinen Fingern alsbald zum Spielfigürchen verzwergte, und steckte sie in ebenjene Westentasche, aus der er vorher die Zigarette genommen hatte]. Thus, Hermine's murder did not happen the way it was first presented: Harry did not kill a human being but rather the emotion that she stood for and that Harry could not handle. Harry's jealousy proves that he has not yet developed the sense of humor he needs to accept the world the way it is — or seems to be.

At the novel's end, yet another triad blends together. There are Harry, the demimonde, and the ideal that Harry wants to achieve — the ideal of lightness of existence that he attributes to immortals, such as Goethe and Mozart. In a dream Goethe tells Harry not to take life, including dead old people, too seriously. At the illusionary level, Harry seems to imagine the members of the urban demimonde as intermediaries between him and the immortals; therefore, in the end he sees Pablo and Mozart as identical. As a result, despite its generally acknowledged cultural pessimism, the novel ends on a positive note. Harry feels that he eventually will learn to play the game of the figurines or, in other words, to handle his responses to reality with humor.

*Thomas Mann's Zauberberg* — Mann's major novel *Der Zauberberg* is about time and about the times (a seven-year period ending in 1914), because its Modernist narrative structure ties the content together by reproducing the flow of time. To achieve such a sense of time, Thomas Mann created a narrator who is limited omniscient in a specific way: not only does he not know everything; his knowledge is also restricted to the setting in the mountains. Once characters leave the setting, such as the main character at the end of the novel, the narrator loses them from his sight. The narrator's position epitomizes Mann's narrative irony. While the narrator identifies himself within the tradition of the old-time "murmuring conjuror of simple past tense" [raunenden Beschwörer des Imperfekts], his narrative is structurally innovative.

In the exclusive and rarified atmosphere of a sanatorium in the mountains of Davos, Switzerland, the young protagonist Hans Castorp is exposed to major prewar philosophical approaches to the world, and he finds his own understanding of the world's meaning in the central chapter. This insight is so significant that in the 700-page novel it is the only sentence set in italics: *"For the sake of kindness, man shall not allow death to take dominion over his thoughts"* [*Der Mensch soll um der Güte willen dem Tode keine Herrschaft einräumen über seine Gedanken*]. Hans Castorp's fundamental insight itself is subject to time: as time elapses and becomes more and more immaterial, the memory of the insight's significance fades.

Hans Castorp, an embodiment of the average man, comes to visit his cousin in the sanatorium but succumbs to the magic of the place, which is defined by a sense of freedom deriving from the proximity of illness and death. Hans starts feeling ill, becomes a patient himself, and stays for seven years. During this time he encounters four major ways of dealing with the world, each of which enters the novel's plot in the form of a character. First, the Italian Settembrini represents the Enlightenment's optimism and belief in progress. Second, Naphta, who is a Jesuit of Jewish descent, preaches an extreme medieval version of a Communist dictatorship founded on ascetic discipline. Third, with his vitalistic emphasis on pleasure, Mynheer Peeperkorn embodies life itself. Fourth, the beautiful Russian Clawdia Chauchat represents an Oriental passivity and sensuality. Hans is receptive to all these influences, yet he also keeps his independence from them, since each influence not only displays in its proponent its attractive side but also its shortcomings.

The tension between these ideas, rather than the ideas themselves, determines Hans's intellectual development in the heightened and feverish atmosphere of the sanatorium, which follows its own routines — routines that appear distant from hectic everyday life. This spatial detachment has its correlation in the development of time toward timelessness as the novel progresses. In the absence of normal orientation points (specifically, time and space), Hans can form his own opinion on the clean slate of the sanatorium's "alchemist, hermetic pedagogy" [alchimistisch-hermetische Pädagogik].

The novel develops toward timelessness in a well-executed progression from chapter to chapter. The first two chapters are brief and furnish an introduction to the setting and the character: the protagonist's arrival at the sanatorium, where he is told that time "doesn't pass at all" [vergeht überhaupt nicht], and his first night there that brings confusing dreams (first chapter), followed by background information on Hans (for instance, that he is an engineer) in the second chapter.

The next three chapters move in successively larger periods of time so that it eventually feels as though time is standing still. The third chapter, in which Hans meets Settembrini and Madame Chauchat, presents his first full day in an hour-by-hour rhythm; thus, the unchanging daily routine at the sanatorium is established. The fourth chapter progresses primarily in a day-by-day rhythm and covers three weeks, the original amount of time planned for Hans's visit. Shortly after the chapter's beginning, reflections on the sense of time prepare the reader for the effect of emptiness and monotony. The fifth chapter narrates the first seven months primarily in a week-by-week rhythm. Hans notices that the concept of time in the mountains is different than in the flatland — a realization that he experiences as a liberation.

The sixth chapter addresses the question "What is time?" [Was ist die Zeit] but leaves it — identifying time as a mystery — unanswered, just like the question about life in the previous chapter. Nevertheless, the chapter continues to telescope time so that it can be experienced through the narrative progression, which is now primarily month-by-month. Naphta arrives, and he and Settembrini start their arguments. Hans is told that, except for his raised temperature, he is physically healthy. But Hans is not ready to leave because he suffers from a metaphysical illness. Not even a brief visit by an uncle can persuade him to return to everyday life. Embedded in the sixth chapter is the section "Schnee" (Snow), which constitutes the novel's climax.

The snowy mountain region of the Alps is the ultimate extension of Hans's timeless and spaceless existence in the sanatorium. One afternoon when Hans is alone on a hike, he gets caught in a surprise snowstorm. In the storm's "nothingness, white, whirling nothingness" [das Nichts, das weiße, wirbelnde Nichts], which is marked by an absence of time and space, he has contradictory visions that, nonetheless, together constitute the totality of human life: Apollonian visions of a Mediterranean *locus amoenus*, complete with green trees, the sound of harps, small harbors, and horses, on the one hand, and, on the other hand, a Dionysian vision of bloodthirsty sacrifices. In response, Hans partially awakes from his daydreams and feels that he knows everything concerning humankind. He realizes that both Settembrini and Naphta are "wind-bags" [Schwätzer] and that "man is the master of contradiction" [Der Mensch ist Herr der Gegensätze]. He resolves the contradiction of life and death, which has been troubling him for a long time, with the insight that it is up to humanity to allow death dominion over life, but because of kindness and love, humanity should choose not to do so. This fundamental insight is reached near the end of the snowstorm; by dinnertime, however, the insight's significance is already fading.

Hans's spiritual education is not yet complete, because he does not know how to use his insight. The concluding seventh chapter relates the final four and a half years that Hans spends in the sanatorium. During this time Mynheer Peeperkorn arrives. Time has become insubstantial; referring to the reading room where Hans used to have conversations, the narrator parenthetically interjects: "this former time is vague; narrator, hero and reader are no longer certain about the degree of its past" [dies Einst ist vage; Erzähler, Held und Leser sind nicht mehr ganz im klaren über seinen Vergangenheitsgrad]. Hans's mentors abandon him: Madame Chauchat, with whom he once had been in love, leaves the sanatorium; Mynheer Peeperkorn and Naphta commit suicide; and Settembrini's health is declining rapidly. The sanatorium's seclusion can no longer provide stimuli for Hans; appropriately, the reason for Hans to move on comes from outside.

With the outbreak of the First World War, time and reality intrude and claim Hans. The narrator's position remains fixed in the mountains, so narrator and reader lose sight of Hans in the chaos of battle: "And thus, in the tumult, in the rain, in the twilight, he walks out of our sight" [Und so, im Getümmel, in dem Regen, der Dämmerung, kommt er uns aus den Augen]. In the novel's last sentence the narrator wonders whether there will be a time when love will rise again from "this worldwide festival of death" [diesem Weltfest des Todes]. This question refers back to the insight of not granting death dominion over life because of love. It may be argued that the novel reduces all ideologies to relative truths and establishes itself as the only absolute value that is capable of mediating between contradictions. Moreover, the novel's last sentence introduces a political dimension: war is the domination of death over life.

The creation of the timeless Magic Mountain resulted from myth-making, incorporating elements of Greek mythology, mysticism (for example, the number seven), and alchemy. Since myths are stories that explain the world, Hans's spiritual education intensifies his awareness and culminates in his insight about the meaning of life. Paradoxically, such an insight gained through the experience of timelessness is only as valid as its implementation in life, which is necessarily tied to time. While Hans fails to do so, the narrator formulates the challenge for humankind to grant love power over life, which it must do by following the democratic process of allowing opposing views to meet in discussion. This is the democratic stance of *Der Zauberberg* and, in general, of Thomas Mann's use of myth, which remained important for his later work. The democratic reworking of the tradition of the Bildungsroman is intriguing because Mann's turn to democracy had been so recent; he had not come out in public support of the Weimar Republic until 1922. From then on, however, he evolved into an active spokesperson for democracy in general and against National Socialism in particular, both in his literary and nonliterary work.

**Jahnn's Perrudja**     If Hans Henny Jahnn's novel *Perrudja* (1929) seems radically different from the previously discussed novels, it is because this author's works were radically different, which, in turn, might explain why he has become the forgotten one of the major early twentieth-century German prose authors. This difference has less to do with the Modernist techniques that were informed by Joyce's *Ulysses* than with the sexually and morally charged content that found its formal expression in a passive type of antihero and in unusual imagery.

Jahnn's narrative was radical, and his attempt to make it even more so by adding interior monologue and structural devices, such as word-plays and catalogues, becomes apparent in the comparison of the published version with the revisions of the unpublished first draft. The past tense is the principal tense of the third-person narrator's report of the draft, but the published novel moves back and forth between past-tense descriptions and present-tense evocations: "He unlocked a heavy iron box. . . . The well-being of his life lay inside it. Perrudja is young. Perrudja is very young" [Er schloß eine schwere eiserne Kiste auf . . . Das Heil seines Lebens lag darin. Perrudja ist jung. Perrudja ist blutjung]. The third-person perspective of Perrudja's vision of himself as young shifts to a first-person point of view in the next paragraph: "I roam through the woods on the back of a black horse. Immense" [Ich streife auf schwarzem Pferd durch Wälder. Unermeßlich]. These quotations demonstrate the relative simplicity of Jahnn's syntax, which tends both to paratactic constructions and to fragmented hypotactic constructions. On the one hand, the short sentences and phrases or clauses resonate with the many lists of things (including different types of soups and fruit jams) that expand into play with language. On the other hand, the brevity of linguistic units corresponds to a powerful prose style that suggests an urge to uncover what is basic in life. And that is exactly what Jahnn's novel is about: the immediacy of experiencing the body.

It is fitting that Perrudja's round and dark nipples become one of the leitmotifs that weave through the novel. Corporeality is an antidote to dehumanization yet is also a part of it. Jahnn's radical affirmation of the body places the human being back within the context of nature, where man is animal's equal. Consequently, the first time love is mentioned in the novel, it is Perrudja's love for a horse. Later, when Perrudja courts Signe, it strikes her that what he said expresses his wish "to be half animal, half human" [halb Tier, halb Mensch zu sein]. As part of their courtship Perrudja and Signe encounter each other in animal form. Each of them, while in animal form, explores the other's human shape. Perrudja is first a leopard and black panther, licking Signe's body while she enjoys it: "Signe believed she had to be dying of pleasure" [Signe glaubte vergehen zu müssen]. But when she turns into a tigress to explore Perrudja's body, he feels ashamed of his meek body.

Such unusual imagery is typical of Jahnn, and Perrudja's almost conventional sense of shame is a sign of how alienated humans have become from their own bodies. The encounters between Perrudja and Signe are metaphoric: they mean what they describe (animal love), and they mean something else (human love as instinctual as animal love). They can be understood as imaginary (wishful thinking) and as imaginative (playacting in the sexual encounter). But relationships are fragile; therefore, it is significant that Signe's brother Hein briefly observes the encounter as a "young buck" [junger Rehbock]. In Perrudja's uncertainties concerning his own identity and origins, man and woman seem like "blood that is alien to itself" [Blut, das sich fremd]. At this point, homosexual love emerges as an option for a human relationship that makes understanding possible.

The extent of love for animals, as well as that love's symbolic potential for other taboo sexual behaviors, might have been shocking for readers, although the naturalness with which Jahnn portrayed these behaviors aimed at liberation, including a liberation from conventional morality, which is in the tradition of Modernist writing in general. But the novel goes further: to get rid of Hoyer, his rival for Signe's love, Perrudja teams up with Hein. As officers of the mountain police, they hunt down Hoyer, who is poaching: "The police officers became public prosecutors and judges" [Aus den Beamten der Polizei waren Staatsanwalt und Richter geworden] — and executioners, for Hoyer is ambushed and, although both Perrudja and Hein each fire a shot, killed by only one bullet. When Signe confronts Perrudja, he denies killing Hoyer, and she believes him. She would have understood and remained silent; when Perrudja finally admits to the crime on their wedding night, she immediately withdraws and ultimately leaves him because she cannot forgive him for lying to her. After Signe refuses to consummate the marriage, Perrudja again turns to Hein for love and companionship. As in his other homosexual encounters, Perrudja is confronted by sadomasochistic experiences. Like the quality of the language, the homosexual subject matter that Jahnn wrote about was down-to-earth and immediate, not sublimated as in Thomas Mann's treatment of homosexuality in *Der Tod in Venedig*.

Perrudja is explicitly identified as a nonhero in the summary of content that is prefaced to the novel. As a nonhero, he is reactive and passive, and his imagination plays a great role in digesting books and in developing visions for his future. While this treatment is in the tradition of the symbolic hero, because it focuses on the inner vision rather than on probability, it is also grounded in the intellectual milieu of the 1920s with its visions for the future of humankind. Perrudja's personal life has failed to achieve a lasting love relationship, be it with animals, male friends, women in general, or Signe in particular. She has not consummated her marriage with Perrudja but, living in another town, finds sexual pleasure with her male servant.

After Signe leaves Perrudja and he turns to Hein, the plot shifts to a political level. In a surprise revelation, Perrudja learns that Mr. Grigg, who has been bankrolling him, is just the secretary of a vast industrial complex to which he, Perrudja, is heir. Perrudja finds himself the world's richest man. While enjoying his wealth with Hein, Perrudja becomes aware of responsibilities that equal the vastness of his power. Developed together with Mr. Grigg, Hein, and others, Perrudja's plans include the creation of an island empire populated by a new human race. In stark contrast to contemporary nationalist thought, the racial ideal for Perrudja is the "bastard," the racially impure human being. Technology — the machine, neither virtuous nor evil — has to be put to appropriate use. The goal of world peace requires a global war fought with technological and military grandeur: electrically powered boats, airplanes, and weapons of mass destruction are mentioned in science-fictionlike scenes, and dreadful visions of destruction emerge. Such visions, especially given the actual German politics at the time, could not be brought to a literary conclusion. While Jahnn's bleak scenario for humanity's future — "Everything is wasted: things, animals, people" [Es ist alles vergeudet: die Dinge, die Tiere, die Menschen] — revealed human existence as dark and unfathomable, the narrative got caught up in history, which is referred to as "the great book of forgeries" [das große Buch der Fälschungen]. Jahnn's attempt to write a second part of *Perrudja* remained fragmentary; the existing passages do not bring resolution to any of the conflicts.

Despite the project's fragmentary character, the first novel is complete as an artistic achievement, including its complexity and indeterminacy. It incorporates various digressive elements, from catalogues to self-contained short narratives. The stories reflect major themes of the main plot and often function as foreshadowing devices. Mostly, they are integrated into the main plot as texts that Perrudja reads or tells himself. This is, of course, a correlative to his status as a nonhero, who is passive in life and withdraws into the realm of fiction, where he finds his own life mirrored.

Hans Henny Jahnn, who had been known for his controversial dramas before *Perrudja*, mirrored his own life in this novel. As a convinced pacifist, he had lived in Norway during the First World War with a male friend with whom he also tried but failed to establish a pagan community Ugrino, in spirit not unlike Perrudja's island empire. Jahnn's works were banned by the Nazis. He was an activist for animal rights and, after the Second World War, against the atomic bomb. His matter-of-fact language in *Perrudja* certainly achieves a high degree of realism, although the nonhero's individuality is dissipated in Perrudja's own narrative project of reading and telling stories and in the exploration of the complex underlying and dark bodily side of human existence. The complexity suggests mythological patterns, such as the epic of Gilgamesh with its two male heroes and the goddess Ishtar, or the Great Mother, as the model for Signe.

The side of high Modernism that evolved in conjunction with Ironic Realism was defined by the polarity of rationality and irrationality. While it dealt with reality, it could also encompass inner visions and mythological aspects, as did the works by Kafka, Hesse, Thomas Mann, and Jahnn. Quite in contrast, the other side of the high Modernist mode that emerged during the 1920s emphasized rationality over irrationality and led to a new sense of objectivity.

## New Objectivity

After the exuberance of Expressionism and Dada, as well as after the sobering and disappointing social conditions of the years immediately following the First World War, the focus on mainly leftist politics and twentieth-century phenomena, such as technology and urban life, was combined with a sober and skeptical look at reality. The fact that the resulting literature was often maligned by the political right as *Asphalt-literatur* — literally, "asphalt literature," where *asphalt* is meant to have the negative implication of "gutter" — points to more than political enmity. It also emphasizes a shift in aesthetics: New Objectivity valorized coldness, mobility, and diffusion. Therefore, it could experience urban anonymity as liberation and see beauty in serial production of industrial goods. The latter was a legacy of the objet trouvé so that New Objectivity can be understood as the second phase of the Avant-Garde. Some Expressionists, such as Toller, Hasenclever, Werfel, and Döblin, turned to the new movement. As the Bauhaus had done for art and architecture, New Objectivity took Avant-Garde literature into the mainstream.

The aesthetic shift led to the final acceptance of the complex world of social modernism, which was scandalous to those who preferred to ignore the way the world had become, but it was the source of the aesthetic appeal of New Objectivist writing. Prose texts explored objective forms that approached documentary literature; poetry dealt with emotions rationally; and drama emphasized disillusion and thus went against the entire history of the theater, which had been based on illusion.

A crucial point of origin of New Objectivist politics was the Enlightenment, which was a problematic but an undeniable element of New Objectivity — for the truly radical innovation of Brecht's epic theater, it was even the necessary element. Like the Enlightenment, New Objectivity used reason as a tool and believed in progress. Paradoxically, the coolly rational assessment of reality often led to the emotional realization that the world fell short of the ideal. In turn, this meeting of the Avant-Garde and the Enlightenment led to a tone of sentimental melancholy that characterized a large part of New Objectivity.

*Objective narratives* The discussion of New Objectivity is complicated by the fact that the range of prose grouped into this literary movement is considerable. It includes experimental texts of high literary quality in the Avant-Garde tradition, such as Alfred Döblin's *Berlin Alexanderplatz* (1929), as well as works of lower quality whose objectivity often consisted of crude surface realism. The common basis for all these works was a documentary emphasis meant to achieve authenticity.

*Documentary and proletarian texts* The reorientation toward objectivity in literature during the 1920s was influenced by the increasing availability of information through the new media of radio and film. While some authors integrated essayistic elements into their literary works — the primary example is Robert Musil's *Der Mann ohne Eigenschaften* (The Man without Qualities, 1930–1943) — essays and even journalistic reports were developed into a literary art form. Important representatives of the latter subgenre were Joseph Roth (1894–1939), whose literary production of these years also was New Objectivist, and the journalist Egon Erwin Kisch (1885–1948). Kisch's popular newspaper reports were collected in books; the title of one collection capitalized on his professional reputation, which earned him his nickname: *Der rasende Reporter* (The Racing Reporter, 1925). While Kisch's approach was defined by a cool objectivity, he was not a mere observer but a writer of *littérature engagée* that aimed at changing society.

The boundaries between fact and fiction became flexible, and documentary literature emerged. Works that claimed to be completely documentary posed a challenge to aesthetics. In the wake of the Avant-Garde, and especially Dada, the question of what was art had become unanswerable unless in reference to some kind of strict but controversial criteria. Nevertheless, even leftist writers and critics, such as Kurt Tucholsky (1890–1935) and Georg Lukács, supported a clear distinction between art and documentation.

Such a distinction flew in the face of the endeavor to create a revolutionary and predominantly documentary literature by workers for workers. This concept of literature was advocated by the BPRS (*Bund proletarisch-revolutionärer Schriftsteller*, or Union of Proletarian and Revolutionary Writers). Founded in 1928, the BPRS saw itself in sharp contrast to treatments of working-class issues in what it considered bourgeois literature that was produced either by *Arbeiterdichter* or writers who belonged to the bourgeoisie, from Richard Dehmel to Josef Winckler. While most of the *Arbeiterdichter* had been workers, the variety of their ties to politics, including the Social Democrats and Christian churches, was dismissed as bourgeois by the BPRS. For the BPRS, *Arbeiterdichtung* failed because it did not focus on rallying workers for class struggle but, instead, adopted bourgeois values for literature. The members of the BPRS, such as Johannes R. Becher, Willi Bredel (1901–1964), and Ludwig Turek (1898–1975), were typically also members of the Communist Party and aimed at creating a revolutionary literature that did not compromise with bourgeois values.

The split between the BPRS and *Arbeiterdichtung* was indicative of the split that went through both the working class and the intellectual left. The BPRS institutionalized the endeavors that had begun earlier, and it participated in the Communist International; after the Second World War, its members became models for the literature of the German Democratic Republic. Among these novels — which included *Ein Prolet erzählt* (A Proletarian Tells His Story, 1930), by Ludwig Turek, and *Des Kaisers Kulis* (The Emperor's Coolies, 1929), by Theodor Plivier (1892–1955), who spelled his name Plievier after 1933 — *Brennende Ruhr* (Burning Ruhr, 1929), by Karl Grünberg (1891–1972) is an exemplary work for the BPRS's Rote Eine-Mark-Roman (Red One-Mark-Novel series). It describes the armed struggle of the workers in the industrial area of the Ruhr River against the reactionary Kapp putsch in 1920.

The novel's portrait is historically correct: while the reactionary coup is thwarted, the Communist cause of the Red Ruhr Army is not successful, because "conservative" leaders of the Social Democrats and of the labor unions withdraw from the proletarian people's front. Personal experiences and historical events are combined with Communist role models in a style that itself combines elements of documentation and sentimentality. Descriptive prose sections alternate with vivid but stereotyped dialogue that presents political and often heated arguments. For example, at the novel's beginning, the reactionary legend of the *Dolchstoß* (the "stab in the back" that allegedly caused the German defeat in the First World War) is set straight: "I know that the stab in the back came from behind — that is, from the military leaders behind the lines" [Ich weiß, daß der Dolchstoß von hinten kam — nämlich aus der Etappe]. The novel's protagonist, the student Ernst Sukrow, comes to the Ruhr area to look for work. In Swertrup he at first finds a place to stay with the family of Peter Ruckers, whom he met on the train and for whose daughter Mâry he experiences an unrequited love. Sukrow is exposed to a variety of political opinions and the experience of "the proletarian's life between the dark coal mine, ugly holes of houses, smoky bars and stale prayer halls!" [Proletarierleben zwischen dunklem Kohlenschacht, häßlichen Wohnlöchern, dunstigen Kneipen und muffigen Betstuben!]. In the face of mounting nationalism, he decides to join the Social Democratic Party.

But he quickly becomes disenchanted with the SPD; when the Kapp putsch begins, Sukrow feels that the SPD-led government deserves to be overthrown if the boring and superficial local party meeting is typical of the party as a whole. Moving between sections with subplots or background information and sections focusing on Sukrow, the novel gives a detailed description of how the general strike is carried out. After he receives information about the plans of the right-wing side, which has been trying to recruit him, Sukrow joins the workers' resistance. When they are attacked, he takes charge and emerges as the commander of the Red Battalion Swertrup. After the coup is overthrown, the military disbands the Red Ruhr Army in a brutal campaign. Sukrow's political development has left him unsure of the German political parties, but he remains committed to the revolutionary ideals he has acquired, admiring the Soviet revolution. In addition to a matter-of-fact, yet partisan, presentation of historical events in an entertaining way that made the reading easy, the novel was meant and understood as a rallying cry for Communist ideals, because the defeat in 1920 was seen as a first step in the long but necessary revolutionary fight.

*Literary quality and social criticism* Crude surface realism that voices its social criticism in conventional forms and predictable plots is considered to be of less literary quality than works with innovative form and challenging plot. The choice of surface realism, however, was deliberate because the message of the text's social criticism was aimed at a larger audience; indeed, these works often met with wide public success. Yet these works no longer belong to Modernism proper for two reasons: first, they are not complex in form; second, their political function, which would align them especially with the Avant-Garde, is diluted. Their crowd-pleasing form rendered any critical content into affirmation — in the sense that the reader might feel emotionally touched by the narrated experiences but not encouraged to actual participation in politics. In addition, the conventional and sentimental form may suggest that these experiences should remain within the realm of literature. The Avant-Garde movements of the 1910s were aware of this affirmative function and tried to counteract it by way of form.

Nevertheless, because surface realism addressed issues of twentieth-century modernity, the realistic documentation of social criticism is shared as a point of departure with truly Modernist New Objectivist works. While the feeling conveyed by surface realism is immediate and authentic, the emphasis on reading pleasure generates a proximity to forms of the *Trivialroman*, including adventure plots and sentimentality. Although a terminological differentiation between social criticism in conventional form and Modernist New Objectivity might be helpful, the boundaries are not clear-cut, as works by B. Traven (?–1969), Hans Fallada (1893–1947), and Erich Kästner (1899–1974) illustrate.

B. Traven — an elusive author and cult figure whose real name is believed to be Ret Marut and whose adventurous life led him to Mexico — is best known for the novels *Das Totenschiff* (Ship of the Dead, 1926) and *Der Schatz der Sierra Madre* (The Treasure of the Sierra Madre, 1927), which was made famous by John Huston's 1948 movie version. Traven combined the form of the adventure story with the message of social criticism, exposing inhumanity, exploitation, and violence. In *Das Totenschiff* he took aim at modern forms of slavery and exploitation for financial gain: the ship with its entire crew on board, including the narrator, is sunk to collect insurance money. From the beginning, however, the realistic foundation of the narrative is clear, because the traditional romanticism of sailor's stories is dismissed and the usual cliché of the adventure story is undermined. Traven's treatment of Mexican Indians in later novels went beyond idealization and colonial gaze, attempting to portray their social reality in a critical manner.

Hans Fallada's novels — perhaps best known is *Kleiner Mann, was nun?* (Little Man, What Now?, 1932) — delivered an almost documentary objectivity by means of a detailed and authentic description that exposed and criticized social wrongs, such as poverty, joblessness, and conditions in prisons. In addition to a conventional presentation, a narrative characteristic was a tone of warm and sentimental humanity that originated in the possibilities of idyllic conditions in the private realm. This style not only reduced the force of the social criticism and conflicted with New Objectivist skepticism and coolness but also explains Fallada's success: over two million paperback copies of his novels had been sold by the mid-1960s.

*Erich Kästner's* Fabian    Erich Kästner's novel *Fabian* (1931), which is often cited as an important example of narrative New Objectivity and considered a brilliant satire, is also criticized for its apparent sentimentalism and a hidden affirmation of political conditions. The latter criticism has also been leveled even more strongly against his children's books, such as *Emil und die Detektive* (Emil and the Detectives, 1929), *Das fliegende Klassenzimmer* (The Flying Classroom, 1933), and *Das doppelte Lottchen* (The Double Lottie, 1949). While such criticism has some justification, it falls into the tradition of the Avant-Garde argument that only literature that directly calls for political revolution is capable of being political literature. The underlying question, of course, is whether or not literature can have any effect on politics.

New Objectivity emphasized the pose of a cold, uprooted intellect but typically in conjunction with social criticism, which could be voiced in various ways but mostly stemmed from moral thinking in the tradition of humanism. Disillusionment with social and political reality (with or without a faint sense of hope) was characteristic for writers, including Kästner, and has been referred to as "leftist melancholy." This enlightened-bourgeois attitude was particularly clear in Kästner's poetry but also in *Fabian*, which is subtitled *Die Geschichte eines Moralisten* (A Moralist's Story) and whose original title, rejected by the publisher, was "Der Gang vor die Hunde," a nominalization of the phrase "gone to the dogs."

The novel's goal, Kästner wrote in the preface twenty-five years after the first publication, was to warn its readers "of the abyss that Germany and hence Europe were approaching" [vor dem Abgrund warnen, dem sich Deutschland und damit Europa näherten]. Kästner continued, stating that such warnings, no matter by what literary means, were often hopeless. In spite of his growing personal resignation, Kästner held on to the position of a moralist: "His motto has always been and still is: However!" [Sein Wahlspruch hieß immer und heißt auch jetzt: Dennoch!].

The novel's protagonist Jakob Fabian, whose perspective as a participating observer dominates the third-person narrative, experiences the abyss in the metropolis of Berlin. There the thirty-two-year-old doctor of literature lives in a sublet room and works in the advertising department of a cigarette company. His path toward the abyss is complete with observations of sexual promiscuity and political extremism. As far as its inhabitants are concerned, the city has long resembled a madhouse. Yet small-town, provincial Germany does not hold any answer either. Fabian soon realizes that he has simply exchanged the city's feverish atmosphere for the chilling narrow-mindedness of the small town when he returns home after everything that held his life together has gone: he loses his job; his girlfriend leaves him for a rich movie producer to further her career; and his only friend Stephan Labude commits suicide because of an intrigue by a petty and jealous research assistant. The surprise ending — Fabian, who cannot swim, drowns in an attempt to save a boy from drowning — has been interpreted as a parable of the moralist who cannot survive in an immoral and inhuman world.

Kästner's matter-of-fact style, which combines cool detachment with irony and colloquialism, enters into a dialectical relationship with his didactic humanism. The disinterested description of lost values is but the reverse side of an interest in retaining values, such as reason, understanding, and commitment. The dialectical relationship is made more complex by the way Kästner addresses the challenges of modernity. While the sequence of catastrophes in Fabian's life seems to suggest fatalism, Kästner's humanism upholds enlightened values. For example, Cornelia complains about the modern character of love as a commodity: "Then, one gave oneself away as a present and was kept like a present. Today you get paid and one day, like any commodity that's been paid for and used, are given away" [Früher verschenkte man sich und wurde wie ein Geschenk bewahrt. Heute wird man bezahlt und eines Tages, wie jede bezahlte und benutzte Ware, weggetan]. Fabian agrees; however, when he and Cornelia fall in love, he confesses that he believes he had only been waiting for the opportunity to be faithful. Ironically, he is later left behind like a commodity by Cornelia.

In his walk toward the abyss Fabian exemplifies the 1920s. Together with Labude's political dreams of a bourgeois revolution in the name of reason, Fabian's passive position as an unhappy observer who would like to become involved, if only he could get exited about something, illustrates bourgeois attitudes in a volatile political situation. Fabian describes this situation as "a great waiting room, and it was called Europe" [einem großen Wartesaal, und der hieß Europa]; summing up disillusionment and disorientation of a generation of bourgeois intellectuals who saw their humanistic ideals destroyed once during the First World War and challenged again in an imminent new crisis.

In his suicide note to Fabian, Labude writes that he should have become a schoolteacher, since "only children are ready for ideals" [nur die Kinder sind für Ideale reif]. Kästner himself took this conviction to his writing of children's books, where his utopian vision of humans living in harmony tended toward idyllic solutions. In a speech in 1953 he emphasized that, given the desolate state of the world, only those people who believe in humankind will be able to help the youth. The point of departure for his children's books was a realistic and authentic perception of childhood as including moments of pain. That point, although often developed into a modern fairy tale, was quite different from traditional children's stories. What is more, in contrast to Kästner's escapist novels, such as *Drei Männer im Schnee* (Three Men in the Snow, 1934), *Fabian* never leaves the authenticity of a down-and-out reality. The pending political crisis affects the private realm, and brief moments of private happiness seem only to pave the way for more unhappiness. Fabian, like Franz Biberkopf in Döblin's novel, is caught in a vicious circle of events that he cannot control. Because the challenge for the protagonists in both novels is to keep trying, the challenge is passed on to the audience with Fabian's death and by way of the balladesque detachment in *Berlin Alexanderplatz*.

**Döblin's Berlin Alexanderplatz**   Although the book's subtitle *Die Geschichte vom Franz Biberkopf* announces the story of Franz Biberkopf, any plot summary — a lower-class man, full of good intentions, fails to turn his life around after prison but gets another chance — does not address the formal aspects that make the work one of the greatest novels of the 1920s. It is not by accident that the main title designates a major public square in Berlin, because the work is the novel about a metropolis: Berlin.

The formal innovations, inspired by Joyce's *Ulysses*, attempt to evoke the experience of life in the big city. Interior monologue renders immediate responses to the city environment, and Döblin's montage technique incorporates bits of the city's reality directly into the novel. This includes actual icons, such as the bear from Berlin's city seal. Names of streets, shops, and newspapers are given, as well as headlines and excerpts of actual articles, including advertisements and political and general-interest topics. The manuscript shows that Döblin literally cut out sections from newspapers and pasted them into his text. Franz Biberkopf's story intersects with the story of the city, because his life is subjected to the dynamics of disorientation and reorientation that is typical of life as portrayed in city novels and that also reflects Döblin's ambiguous opinion about Berlin, with its dynamism and technological feats in conflict with dire social conditions.

An additional dimension of mythology connects directly with the theme of the city in references to the ultimate biblical symbol of the big city as the whore of Babylon and indirectly with sections that suggest a parallelism between the story of Franz Biberkopf and the biblical stories of Isaac and Job. Linguistically, Döblin adapts passages from the Bible in Martin Luther's German translation, whose solemn and prophetic tone contrasts with other passages that are dominated by colloquialism, especially Berlin dialect. Franz's story, too, is one of a human who becomes a victim of fate — fate understood biblically as God's will or in modern terms as the city's superindividual dynamics, which turns Franz into a member of a collective, the city's masses.

The mythical dimension leads to two other aspects: the function of the narrator and the structure of the novel. Like God, who talks with Job, the author (or, technically speaking, the narrator) interacts with his story's personnel in *Berlin Alexanderplatz*. The narrator, who also addresses the reader from time to time, talks to Franz beginning with the first page, where Franz's reaction to his release from prison is questioned: "terrible, Franz, why terrible?" [schrecklich, Franze, warum schrecklich?]. The narrator, while using colloquial language, appears godlike in his omniscient role that is an expression of the Modernist focus on mastery. This focus is, ironically, broken by the fact that the modern city is a world without gods.

Döblin's portrayal of the modern city in all its complexity and fluidity — using a complex, yet casual and down-to-earth, style — contributed to the novel's modernity and its commercial success. About 50,000 copies were sold within the first five years, and later adaptations include a made-for-television fourteen-episode miniseries directed by Rainer Werner Fassbinder (1980). While practicing Avant-Garde techniques, *Berlin Alexanderplatz* reached the mainstream through its playfulness. The narrator's comments, addressing Franz or the reader with moral suggestions, are tongue-in-cheek and contribute to the novel's quality of an extended street ballad. Franz learns a paradoxical lesson. Instead of staying away from criminal elements, Franz is drawn to them, and his reliance on people compounds his problems; nevertheless, he still has to rely on people: "You don't start your life with nice words and good intentions; with insights and understanding is how you start it, and with the right neighbor" [Man fängt nicht sein Leben mit guten Worten und Vorsätzen an, mit Erkennen und Verstehen fängt man es an und mit dem richtigen Nebenmann]. The tone of the street ballad is suggested by the rhyming words (*an* and *mann*). In the end it is by no means clear that Franz has learned to tell the right people from the wrong; therefore, he again appears as a small player in a larger field.

The mythical element is also encoded in the structure of *Berlin Alexanderplatz*. Despite the apparently random montage technique and the association-driven interior monologue, the novel is symmetrically arranged around the fifth, or middle, chapter: the first and ninth, second and eighth, third and seventh, and fourth and sixth chapters reflect each other. Franz is released from prison and ready to begin a new life (first chapter). He tries to stay honest (second chapter) but is betrayed, thus suffering a first blow (third chapter). Franz is depressed but gets back on his feet (fourth chapter) only to suffer the next blow when he loses an arm as the result of yet another betrayal (fifth chapter). He seems fully to embrace a criminal lifestyle (sixth chapter) and is dealt the third blow when Reinhold, who is Franz's antagonist but pretends to be his friend, kills Franz's girlfriend Mieze (seventh chapter). Franz finally quits his life as a criminal (eighth chapter); and, after his release from the psychiatric clinic, he starts over again (ninth chapter).

It is also possible to superimpose the structure of a classical Greek tragedy onto the symmetrical structure of the novel by considering the first chapter the exposition and combining the other chapters into groups of two. As in a classical tragedy, the plot can be seen to unfold by revealing the hero's flaw or fault (his *hamartia*), bringing about the turning point (*peripetia*) after the last of the three blows dealt to Franz, and leading to a psychological change (*catharsis*) in Franz — and probably in the reader because of the open ending. The novel's concluding two paragraphs are set in italics, like the summaries at the beginning of each chapter. Therefore, as is appropriate for Franz's attempt at starting over, the ending is not an end but a beginning.

Yet it is an ambiguous ending, and one much debated. In the context of a similar passage a few pages earlier, the final passage, where Franz seemingly falls into line to the sound of a drum, can be read as the temptation by nationalism to which Franz succumbs — it is the kind of collective that would not just correct his narcissistic egotism (like the collective existence in the city) but completely efface his individuality. Therefore, the apparently idealistic and optimistic ending in the sense of Döblin's ethical socialism, which seems just added on to the novel, reveals a possibly quite realistic and pessimistic reading and remains ambiguous. The temptation to revert from enlightened behavior to barbaric myth challenges both Franz (in the novel) and the German people (in real-life politics).

The combined effect of the novel's formal elements, which include the use of leitmotifs, scientific observations, and parody of scientific observations, makes the readers aware of the fact that they are reading fiction, just as Brecht's epic theater wanted the members of the audience to be aware that they are watching a play. This anti-illusionist effect, in addition to the novel's general orientation toward the New Objectivist approach of humanistic coolness and skepticism, makes *Berlin Alexanderplatz* significantly different from the novels that belong to Ironic Realism.

The formal radicalness of *Berlin Alexanderplatz* contributed to challenging the concept of the novel. Döblin himself was reluctant to categorize his work as a novel; therefore, he chose, when pressed by the publisher, to use the term *Geschichte* (story) in the subtitle. The genre of the novel evolved as an expression of the will of the bourgeois value system to achieve harmony; nevertheless, it expresses the disharmony of reality. The novel is the most "modern" literary genre because its prose form attempts to harmonize all disharmony into a specific order while keeping that order itself flexible. One prime example of how the novel combines order and flexibility is Döblin's *Berlin Alexanderplatz*.

*Political poetry* New Objectivist poetry centered on everyday situations and depicted, with detachment and disillusionment, people's emotional responses to those situations. The style was prose-oriented, either abandoning rhyme or favoring lyrical forms, such as the ballad, that allowed casual and colloquial speech. As in prose, there was a distinct difference concerning the role of social criticism in poetry; bourgeois writers aimed at raising political awareness while the revolutionary writers aimed at an even more ambitious goal: changing the world.

Bertolt Brecht, although of upper-middle-class background, belonged to the revolutionary writers. His first book of poetry was ironically titled *Hauspostille* (Book of Family Prayers, 1927). It presents harsh, but not yet revolutionary, social criticism because it contains poetry mainly written prior to 1926, the year of Brecht's turn to Marxism. The poems parody conventions of advice giving and emphasize their own use value; in this manner, the ballad of the unwed young girl who kills her baby does not evoke a sense of moral indignation toward her but an indictment of society. Brecht grouped the poems together into larger sections ironically referred to as "Lektionen" (Lessons). The final lesson, the poem "Gegen Verführung" (Against Seduction), warns against political seduction by religion and capitalism. In his lyrical production, Brecht developed a materialistic approach, both in his political message to change the world and in his language. In spite of its colloquial character and prosy tone, Brecht's poetry began to evolve toward an eloquence and elegance that made him one of the most important poets of his time and has established him as a classical author.

"Über die Bauart langdauernder Werke" (On the Construction of Long-lasting Works, 1931) is a key poem because it is an early illustration of Brecht's classical tone and his theoretical reflections about the interaction of author, text, and reader. The poem's first five lines ask the question of a work's duration and answer with regard to the challenge that it poses: "How long / do works last? As long / As they aren't finished. / As long as they require effort / They do not decay" [Wie lange / Dauern die Werke? So lange / Als bis sie fertig sind. / So lange sie nämlich Mühe machen / Verfallen sie nicht.]. The "construction workers" [Bauleute] — the readers of a text — who make a work last are identified as those yet unborn. Working for a future world was an important aspect of Brecht's poetics; as a materialistic and political thinker, however, he was aware that literature also had to confront immediate problems. The poem warns: "He who addresses the unborn / Often doesn't contribute to birth" [Wer sich an die Ungeborenen wendet / Tut oft nichts für die Geburt]. The dialectical relationship between the aesthetic quality of works and their political function also defined Brecht's attempt to establish a classical, yet revolutionary, tone of his own that was unique and, therefore, in stark contrast to the tone of leftist melancholy.

*Leftist melancholy* Erich Kästner, Kurt Tucholsky, and others, such as Walter Mehring (1896–1982) and Lion Feuchtwanger (1884–1958), wrote a type of *littérature engagée* that they considered *Gebrauchslyrik* (poetry for use) to be used in the process of understanding one's own social and political situation. These poets wanted to entertain and teach, and they preferred satires in line with a long tradition of Enlightenment thinking, from Gotthold Ephraim Lessing (1729–1781) to Georg Büchner (1813–1837), in conjunction with a tone that was particularly indebted to Heinrich Heine (1797–1856). New Objectivist poetry also incorporated modern popular poetic forms, such as French chansons, American songs, and political cabaret. The latter, in turn, provided a forum for performing *Gebrauchslyrik*, which was usually published in the journal *Die Weltbühne*. The commitment to bourgeois values that were continuously challenged in the political reality sometimes led to resignation or sentimentality, to which Walter Benjamin (1890–1940) referred as *linke Melancholie* (leftist melancholy).

Moral integrity is the basis of the unfaltering criticism of militarism and exploitation of people that Kästner voices in his poems. He exposes militarism as an abuse of people as "cannon fodder" [Kanonenfutter] and shows urban existence as dominated by capitalism and soothed by a false sense of religion: "So pray: 'Mister Boss, do torture us!' / God wills it so. And his system is great" [Drum betet: "Herr Direktor, quäl uns recht!" / Gott will es so. Und sein System hat Größe] in his first collection of poems, *Herz auf Taille* (Heart on Waist, 1928). Kästner's main goal is to show disillusionment and to create an awareness of life that is threatened in all respects. As the political intrudes into the private realm, the destruction of the world finds its counterpart in the destruction of private relationships. "Sachliche Romanze" (Objective Romance) in the collection *Lärm im Spiegel* (Noise in the Mirror, 1929), for instance, shows a couple whose love has simply disappeared after eight years. Connecting their private problem with a public space, they sit in a café the whole day, unable to say a word. While this type of poem never was idyllic, the author's sympathy — a sympathy that corresponds with melancholy — still shines through. Indeed, Kästner seemed to grow more resigned over the years.

Kurt Tucholsky exhibited a similar but much stronger tendency. As early as 1924 he left Germany and lived in Paris and then in Sweden. Stripped of his German citizenship by the Nazis, he suffered increasingly from depression that was compounded by financial and medical problems so that he finally committed suicide. Nevertheless, Tucholsky — a prolific writer of poetry and various forms of essays, such as literary critiques and satirical sketches — kept writing until and publishing almost until his death. His social criticism was at first directed toward militarism and the reactionary revival that took place during the Weimar Republic; he is credited with being one of the most outspoken critics of National Socialism.

The intention and tone of his poems were similar to Kästner's, but Tucholsky was even more slangy and casual in his language, as well as more polemical in his formulations. In "Ideal und Wirklichkeit" (Ideal and Reality, 1929), he contrasts the ideal woman (tall and slender), according to wishes of the fictitious reader (addressed as "you"), with reality (a short and fat woman), only to move from a perhaps frivolous but private thought to a political observation about how unprepared the German public was for the Weimar Republic, whose reality fell short of the ideal many people had: "Whoever thought under imperial restraint / of a republic . . . and now it's this one" [Wer dachte unter kaiserlichem Zwange / an eine Republik . . . und nun ists die!]. The casualness of transition between private and public realms is underscored by the transition of spelling the French phrase for "such is life" in French at the conclusion of the first stanza, "C'est la vie," and in German mock-phonetic transcription at the end of other two stanzas, "Ssälawih." Tucholsky's 1932 poem "Beschlagnahmefreies Gedicht," whose title proclaims that the poem cannot be confiscated, evokes the gradual process by which democratic forces are flushed out. The reactionary sentiment is satirized, for example, with reference to Adolf Hitler and the nationalist colors of Germany: "Hip, hip. / If only my Adolf I have / until my black-white-and-red grave. / Hurray" [Hipp, hipp. / Wenn ich nur meinen Adolf hab / bis an mein schwarz-weiß-rotes Grab. / Hurra].

## Revolutionary Theater

The creation of a new type of theater is perhaps the farthest-reaching innovation in terms of world literature that originated in the German-speaking countries during the twentieth century. The history of Western European drama had gone through three major phases — ancient Greek theater, the medieval church tradition, and the beginning of the classical style with the theater of the Renaissance — but the basis of all performances remained the creation of illusion. The nonrealistic mode means the creation of a theatrical illusion that openly deviates from empirical reality, and the realistic mode creates only a different theatrical illusion: that of reality. Regardless of how realistic the drama was, it still depended on the audience's suspension of disbelief. And aesthetic pleasure was to be derived from the experience of the difference between theatrical illusion and empirical reality. Since classical theater was also founded on social assumptions, such as intact human communication as expressed in dialogue, the tradition reached a crisis at the end of the nineteenth century when these assumptions became problematic.

Attempts to solve the crisis of traditional drama included Arthur Schnitzler's one-act plays, Hugo von Hofmannsthal's "well-made" plays, and Expressionist monodramas. During the 1920s German-language theater moved farther away from the problematic theater of illusion toward a fourth major phase in the history of drama: the theater of anti-illusion. Major components of anti-illusion in theater — documentary and epic elements — are indebted to New Objectivity. Karl Kraus, with *Die Letzten Tage der Menschheit*, led the way toward a dramatization of the documentary. Ferdinand Bruckner (pseudonym of Theodor Tagger, 1891–1958) and Erwin Piscator were instrumental in this development; the major force, however, was Bertolt Brecht as the theoretician and practitioner (both as writer and stage director) of his "epic theater."

*Political theater*   The history of drama as a literary genre that is meant to be performed and the history of the actual performances necessarily intersect. The production side determines a play's success, and the theatrical culture is often dominated by individual directors and actors. During the first half of the twentieth century, influential directors were Max Reinhardt, Leopold Jessner (1878–1945), and Piscator. While Reinhardt stayed within the parameters of the illusionist theater by developing a decorative style of mass theater, the other two directors worked toward establishing a political theater. Jessner's goal was to liberate the stage of the external decorations that had helped create illusion. Jessner understood the resulting political theater as a general expression of the times, not of any particular political faction. In contrast, Piscator was decidedly partisan in his theater work. From the early 1920s, Piscator worked against the theater of illusion, which he sought to replace with a revolutionary theater.

The German tradition of revolutionary theater in the sense of class warfare reaches back to the early twentieth century with performance groups presenting political propaganda and agitation (agitprop). Since these performances were typically limited in their audience to workers and members of the Social Democratic or Communist Parties, it was ironic that agitprop theater was at odds not only with the tradition of larger organizations, such as the SPD-oriented *Volksbühnen* (the people's stages), whose programming was geared toward making bourgeois culture accessible to workers, but also with the Communist Party, which did not officially endorse this type of theater until the 1920s. It was only with Piscator, who aimed at reaching both workers and the lower middle class, that political theater became more visible to the mainstream.

Later Brecht, having worked both with Reinhardt and Piscator, continued the tradition of the political theater, but usually with plays he had written or adapted himself. Piscator focused on directing and used plays by classical authors, such as Friedrich Schiller (1759–1802), and contemporary ones, such as Ernst Toller, who was one of the most important playwrights of the 1920s with his plays, *Masse Mensch* (*Masses and Men*, performed 1920, published 1921), *Der deutsche Hinkemann* (The German Hinkemann, 1923), and *Hoppla, wir leben!* (Hoppla, We're Alive!, 1927).

*Hoppla, wir leben!* premiered under the direction of Piscator, whose innovations for the stage emphasized the documentary aspects in the play, which deals with the problems of working for the revolution from the left in a time that is becoming more and more right-wing. Influenced by Russian theater, Piscator had developed a political multimedia variety show — in some cases literally, such as in his first big production, the *Revue Roter Rummel* (Red Hustle and Bustle Review) for the Communist Party in 1924. This technique was adapted for theater plays, and it included lighting effects, radio announcements, film spots, and simultaneous scenes (*Simultanbühne*). These elements were meant to enter into a stimulating and challenging interaction with the plot as it was acted out on stage. The results consisted in the dissolution of the self-contained world of classical drama and the emergence of epic theater. After the Second World War Piscator headed the Freie Volksbühne Berlin from 1961 to 1966, where documentary plays by Rolf Hochhuth (b. 1931), Heinar Kipphardt (1922–1982), and Peter Weiss (1916–1982) premiered under his direction.

Plays by Ferdinand Bruckner can be seen in the context of Piscator's *Simultanbühne*. The set allows the audience to see different events as they are taking place at the same time. For example, in *Die Verbrecher* (The Criminals, performed 1928, published 1929) the set is a tenement house, three stories tall and housing seven different groups of people. The montage of simultaneous spaces, events, and persons makes it possible to suggest the complex social conditions of modern society, whose judicial system fails to deliver real justice. The montage is simplified in *Elisabeth von England* (1930), which puts the centers of the two world powers of the sixteenth century side by side. The contrast between the English queen, whose country represents reason, and the Spanish king, whose country represents irrational imperialism, is brought to the fore by the set, which juxtaposes Philip in the Church of San Lorenzo on the left and Elisabeth in St. Paul's on the right; both are praying to Christ and expressing their differences concerning the war. The structural device of simultaneous scenes negates the possibility of dialogue, which is a development consistent with the crisis of the theater, whose central element, the dialogue, had become problematic.

*Epic theater*  Bertolt Brecht's major contribution to world literature was epic theater, which he began developing during his second creative phase, usually referred to as his middle phase from 1926 to 1933. The works of his second phase were influenced by his adoption of Marxism and brought the breakthrough of the new theatrical style. Though not one of his more important works, *Die Dreigroschenoper* (The Threepenny Opera, performed 1928, published 1929), is his most popular one, especially because the music by Kurt Weill (1900–1950) made songs, such as "Mackie Messer" (Mack the Knife), world-famous. During his third phase, after 1933, Brecht wrote his major works in exile. The final decade of his life, from 1945 until his death in 1956, he focused on directing and on the theory of theater.

The story of Brecht's success is a history of affinities to approaches by others, such as Karl Valentin (pseudonym of Valentin Ludwig Fey, 1882–1948) and Erwin Piscator, and of collaboration with colleagues, such as fellow writers Lion Feuchtwanger and Elisabeth Hauptmann (1897–1973), as well as the composer Kurt Weill and the set-designer Caspar Neher (1897–1962). Brecht's theorizing about epic theater has been pointed out as a major difference between him and other artists with interests in a similar theatrical practice. Although Brecht presented his systematic approach in *Kleines Organon für das Theater* (Little Organon for the Theater) as late as 1949, the theory and characteristics of epic theater were almost fully developed during his middle period.

The major premise of epic theater concerned the function of literature. As a Marxist, Brecht believed that humankind could change and that literature should be didactic to help humankind bring about that change. As a writer, he believed that literature should be pleasurable. Brecht brought both aspects together by comparing the theater to the sports arena; the theater audience should view a play the way sports spectators view a sporting event: actively but objectively engaged, with expert knowledge and keeping their distance. Learning and knowledge seemed the most important pleasures of the time, and Brecht wanted to create a theater for a scientific age. A leading force in this scientific age,

Marxist theory analyzed the history of the human attempt to dominate nature as a history of class conflict. For the drama, this analysis explained why the social communication that the dialogue presupposed had become problematic; therefore, Brecht replaced the old theater with a new one. Since Marxist analysis offered a focus and a strong belief in progress and in the meaningfulness of world history, Brecht tapped into this intellectual energy and combined it with didactic elements to make theater useful and learning pleasurable.

The three major formal characteristics of epic theater — the stage narrating the event, turning the audience into observers, and portraying a changing world — present significant deviations from traditional theater. The emphasis on learning and knowledge made Brecht's theater not dramatic but epic: the stage did not embody the event but narrated it. Epic presentation was supposed to allow for the freedom that was necessary to reflect on the social basis of events. In contrast to the dramatic form of theater, epic theater intended to turn its audience into observers by awakening activity, not using it up; by forcing decisions, not making emotions felt; by offering knowledge, not experiences; and by confronting the audience with the staged action, not drawing it into the action. Consequently, the dramatic form of theater was based on illusion, while the epic form of theater was based on anti-illusion. The illusion produced a self-contained world as it existed for the moment of the illusion; the anti-illusion attempted to reveal change as the true character of the world. As a consequence, the epic play's form was open, as opposed to the closed form of classical drama. It thus encouraged its audience to understand its own role and options in a changing world.

To narrate the event, the didactic style is applied to the action on stage. While it no longer attempts to create an illusion, the play remains a play — or, more specifically, a role-play — whose plot, more than the characters, serves as a model for behavior. The audience's attitude is defined by objectivity, which makes it possible to derive positive behavioral choices from the plot, even if the characters are examples of behavior to avoid.

To achieve objectivity, each member of the audience has to become an observer. As a thought experiment, Brecht gave the example of a street scene after an accident: the eyewitness — repeating in part what the parties involved in the accident did but not assuming their identities — demonstrates to those who did not see the accident how everything happened; these people can then come to their own conclusions. Similarly, the theater will no longer hide that it is theater, and the actor will not become fully one with his or her role. Theater will do without illusion and will have practical implications for society.

The detachment needed for such objectivity was to be created by elements that interrupt the dramatic flow of a play. These elements can be hand-held signs that tell the audience to stop gawking, brief plot summaries for the next scene to reduce the suspense so that the audience will be less emotionally involved, or songs that comment on the events in a way that goes beyond the knowledge of the character who performs the song. Such elements remind the audience that actors are playing their roles and create a distance between the action and the audience. This effect is called *Verfremdungseffekt* (defamiliarization effect) or *V-Effekt*, usually referred to as "alienation effect" in English.

The redefined roles of the stage and the audience add to the political message of change. The plot unfolds in a loose combination of episodes, suggesting that history exists outside the theater performance. Consequently, the action of the play can be continued — and should be continued — by the audience's political actions in the real world. These formal characteristics underscore the dialectical quality of Brecht's plays, because critical detachment (through the *V-Effekt*) and understanding the historical character of events and ideologies presented (by way of the episodic organization) are supposed to amplify each other in the sense of dialectical materialism and make options available (hence the didactic style) that would allow for overcoming the conflicts that the plays portray.

During the late 1920s and into the 1930s Brecht wrote his *Lehrstücke* (didactic plays). They were most radically Avant-Garde and most consistent in the development of model situations for teaching behavior in a thought experiment, since the plays assume the learning collective that includes the actors as players in the new theatrical style of the role-play, where actors and audience become identical. The *Lehrstücke* worked as highly party-line theatrical applications of Communist dogma that put the party before the individual. The rhetoric of the plays suggested a revolutionary toughness that included a willingness to sacrifice human life (the lives of others, as well as one's own) for the greater good of the collective.

Today, with retrospective knowledge of the Stalinist excesses in the Soviet Union, these plays appear dogmatic and inhuman. *Das Badener Lehrstück vom Einverständnis* (The Baden Didactic Play of Agreement, performed 1929, published 1930) and *Die Maßnahme* (The Measure, performed 1930, published 1931), especially, have been blasted for their inhumanity. In *Die Maßnahme* the young comrade jeopardizes revolutionary activities by clinging to humanist ideas that are false and inappropriate for the situation. Finally, his four comrades see no other way than to kill him; they confront him; and he dies willingly at their hands. Far from glorifying death, the play explicitly says: "Terrible it is to kill" [Furchtbar ist es, zu töten], but the play makes it equally clear that it is sometimes necessary to kill.

Because of their form, it has been argued that the *Lehrstücke* constitute Brecht's most advanced experimentation and that his later plays, which are usually considered his major works, are a step backward. Brecht's formal experimentation toward a role-playing collective of a potentially self-contained role-play is, indeed, most advanced in his *Lehrstücke*. Still, the effectiveness of such role-playing was linked to the social movements of the working class; as a consequence, Brecht was hesitant to have the *Lehrstücke* performed in regular theaters. When the workers' movement dissolved in the 1930s, the social basis for reception of the *Lehrstücke* was gone, and Brecht took his Avant-Garde theater to the mainstream with the redefined interaction of stage, actors, and audience. Therefore, the plays of his exile years constitute his major accomplishments: they not only were an appropriate artistic response to a changing world (something Brecht asked of his audience, after all), but they also established Brecht as a playwright of a nonclassical classicism.

# II
# *Imposing a Total Map: Fascism*

## 4. The Literary Continuum: From Anti-Modern to Modernist Voices

### Political and Ideological Foundations: A Social Pathology?

AN UNFORTUNATE MYSTIQUE has evolved around National Social-ism — something Susan Sontag has referred to as "fascinating fascism" (71). The crimes committed in the name of National Socialism constitute the single most catastrophic episode in German and world history of the twentieth century. Because the enormity of crimes is expressed in statistics that measure victims by the millions, an eerie abstractness makes it difficult to look at concrete individuals and their choices. Instead, the fascination with the rise and fall of National Socialism has at times been sensationalized by viewing the Nazi movement as a force of fate. This perception buys into Nazi propaganda and reproduces Nazism's self-image of its role in world history.

*The crisis of 1930*    The history of National Socialism is full of contradictions, and its rise had a concrete social, economic, and political background. The crisis began in 1929 with rising unemployment, was compounded by the worldwide effect of the New York stock market crash, and continued into the 1930s. It reached a first political climax in the elections of September 1930 that brought 6.5 million votes for the NSDAP (*Nationalsozialistische Deutsche Arbeiterpartei*, or National Socialist German Worker's Party). The Social Democrats and the Catholic *Zentrum* party held their own, while the other parties suffered severe losses. In a political climate that was not characterized by civilized debate but increasingly by physical confrontation between left- and right-wing paramilitary organizations, it was virtually impossible to find any solid majority to form a government. Consequently, the series of the *Präsidialkabinette* began, which were appointed by the president, who also signed their decisions into law as emergency decrees in accordance with Article 48 of the Weimar constitution. Thus, to a great extent, the political fate of the republic came to rest on the shoulders of President Paul von Hindenburg, whose loyalty to the constitution was not in doubt; in 1932 the Social Democrats even supported his successful bid for reelection to prevent Hitler from being elected president.

The Nazis' coming to power was a process that took time and was a combination of a ruthless drive by the Nazis to seize power and of profound frustration and disorientation on the part of the middle class. The economic crisis, which helped the Nazis gain popularity, had caused about seven million people to lose their jobs; that was about one-fifth of a labor force of thirty-two million. Several industrial cities reported unemployment rates of up to eighty percent. To deal with the crisis, the government became involved in the economy to a larger extent than before; in this way, structures to control the economic sector were introduced that the Nazis were able to expand and abuse. Indeed, the conditions would have been just as amenable to measures taken by a democratic government. In fact, the famed autobahn, as well as other measures to create jobs, had already been planned by previous governments.

The main impact of the economic crisis, however, was psychological. Encompassing such diverse groups as farmers, craftsmen, civil servants, lawyers, and bankers, the traditional middle class had not felt at home in the Weimar Republic. The economic depression added to the feelings of frustration a feeling of disorientation, because the bourgeois ethic of hard work, honesty, and respectability did not seem to amount to anything any more. While National Socialism found support across all segments of German society and was able to recruit an especially large number of young people, it was mainly the middle class, in particular, the lower middle class, who turned to the Nazis for simple solutions. The solutions the Nazis had to offer reflected the core beliefs of their ideology: the creation of a community (rather than a society) based on authoritarianism and racism. The strong leader, or *Führer*, would always be right, and the German race would be superior to and deserve to dominate other races; any social problem in Germany could only be the result of the degenerate influence of inferior races, especially the Jewish race.

The theory that the fear of destitution running through large segments of the German population contributed to the Nazis' appeal can be corroborated by the results of parliamentary elections. On July 31, 1932, the Nazis received 13.5 million votes (37.4 percent). New elections were called soon, and the Nazis won only thirty-three percent; they lost two million votes for two likely reasons: a slightly better economy and voter distrust of the Nazis' brutal tactics. Nevertheless, the impasse of the political parties made it impossible to form a government without the Nazis. Trusting his advisers, who assured him that they and other conservatives would be able to keep Hitler and the other Nazis in the cabinet under control, Hindenburg finally appointed Hitler chancellor on January 30, 1933.

But Hitler was intent on ruling by the constitutional powers of the emergency decree rather than with the parliamentary majority of his coalition. Within the next few days he called new elections, and for this campaign the Nazis used a strategy of expanding their power through the government agencies they controlled, such as the police, and deploying their paramilitary troops. As the chief of police in the state of Prussia, Hermann Göring deputized 50,000 men, 40,000 of whom were members of the paramilitary Nazi organizations, the SA (*Sturmabteilung*, or Storm Troopers, which lost its political power after 1934), and the SS (*Schutzstaffel*, or Protection Squadron), the source of the image of the Nazi storm trooper. When the Reichstag, the seat of parliament, was set on fire on February 27, 1933, the Nazis declared a national crisis in order to pass the *Reichstagsbrandverordnung* (Parliament Fire Decree).

This decree marked the onset of the state-imposed terror that became characteristic of the Third Reich. While it was rumored that the fire might have been set by the Nazis themselves, the Nazis were quick to blame the Communists and used the decree for a political witch hunt. Human rights were suspended. Communist publications were outlawed; the Social Democratic press had to interrupt publication for two weeks; and of the total 7,784 people arrested, ninety-five percent were Communists, including that party's leaders. The arrests and the suppression of the leftist press occurred during the campaign for the elections that took place on March 5, 1933. As a result, the ability of the Social Democrats and Communists to participate in the elections was severely curtailed.

Even under these conditions, the National Socialists were not able to win a majority of votes. Only by combining their votes with those of their conservative coalition partner could they reach a majority of 51.9 percent; the NSDAP by itself won 43.9 percent of the vote. Given the circumstances, the outcome for the left — the Social Democrats received 18.3 percent of the vote and the Communists 12.3 percent — was impressive and proved that, while it was the strongest political force, National Socialism was by no means the only one. But it soon would be.

Hitler, who remained chancellor, sought to expand his dictatorial powers through the *Ermächtigungsgesetz* (Enabling Act), as a further application of Article 48. Presenting the bill in parliament was yet another example of the travesty into which the Nazis had turned the first democracy in Germany. The members of the Communist Party were either in prison or in hiding, so only the Social Democrats, led by Otto Wels with a courageous speech defending the principles of democracy, were left to vote against the bill, which was passed on March 24, 1933. On that day the Weimar Republic effectively ceased to exist.

The republic died of structural flaws, such as splinter parties in the parliament and a shift of balance from the parliament to the president, as well as of a lack of support derived from lukewarm enthusiasm for democracy or ruthless ambition for political power by groups whose antidemocratic orientation had not been properly addressed at the beginning of the Weimar Republic. But most political systems have flaws and varying levels of support; therefore, descriptive summaries hold little explanatory power and might even create the impression that the demise of the Weimar Republic and the installation of the brutal dictatorship of the Third Reich were inevitable. At each step of the development, however, there had been alternative choices — yet none of them were taken. For example, there was no general strike by the left, as there had been in 1920 against the Kapp putsch; there was no concerted effort by the Church to remind its congregations that the Bible's commandment to love one's neighbor included the Jews and other targets of Nazi terror. There was resistance, but it was too little, too late.

*The Nazi regime*     *Gleichschaltung*, which refers to the act of producing conformity in all governmental and social realms, is used to describe the often brutal process of bringing all political and major nonpolitical organizations under Nazi control. Soon there was only one party, one labor union, one youth organization. *Gleichschaltung* extended to the everyday lives of the people, beginning with new or redefined national holidays that commemorated National Socialist achievements and going as far as the substitution of "Heil Hitler" for the usual salutation "Guten Tag."

After President Hindenburg died on August 2, 1934, Hitler also assumed the function of the presidency, using the official title of *Führer und Reichskanzler.* Now that the German military swore its pledge of allegiance not to country or constitution but to Hitler personally, the Nazi rise to power in Germany was complete. But it was not intended to stop there. As early as 1936, at the Nuremberg party rally, Hitler defined German self-sufficiency and independence from foreign products as the goal of his four-year plan. In a secret memorandum he clarified his hidden agenda: he demanded that within the following four years the German army should be ready for deployment in war and that the German economy should be ready to support war.

Less than four years later, Hitler's orders began the Second World War. In the years leading to the war the German economy was turned into a war economy. The military sector of the national budget grew from four percent in 1933 to about fifty percent in 1938, the year before the war. These numbers leave no doubt that the Nazi regime was preparing Germany for war. Numbers also suggest that the war could not be backed by Germany's economic power: in the same period during which military spending grew 1,250 percent, state debt grew about 380 percent, from thirteen billion to fifty billion marks.

The beginning of the war was a giant miscalculation on Hitler's part in other respects, as well. When he ordered German troops to attack Poland on September 1, 1939, Hitler's irrational fixation with England as Germany's true soul mate among the European nations had led him to believe that England would stay neutral. It did not and declared, together with France, war on Germany.

Before starting the war, the Third Reich had annexed neighboring territories without causing the other major European powers to intercede. The first and most important was Austria in March 1938. Because of the political developments in that country, Nazi propaganda was able to present the German annexation of Austria as an *Anschluß*, a term that carries the positive meaning of "joining." In collaboration with the Austrian National Socialists, the military annexation was orchestrated as a public welcome for the German troops in Austria, culminating in the triumphant arrival of Hitler in Vienna. The growing aggressiveness of German foreign policy led to increasing international isolation, and eventually the only allies left were Italy and Japan.

The increasing isolation correlated with the insignificant role that world opinion played within the Third Reich, and as a result, the Nazi terror inside Germany grew — especially against the Jews. From the moment Hitler became German chancellor, one after the other of the civil rights of Jewish citizens had been restricted. This policy was aimed at humiliating the Jews while, at the same time, reminding the German citizens that they belonged to a superior race. This strategy was built on a long-extant and pervasive anti-Semitism and was formalized in the Nuremberg Laws of 1935. These laws forbade sexual relationships, including marriages, between Jews and Germans and stripped Jewish citizens of German citizenship. The most visible climax of persecution during the next few years was *Kristallnacht* (Crystal Night), the pogrom during the night of November 8 to November 9, 1938, in which tens of thousands of Jews were arrested and hundreds of synagogues and Jewish businesses were destroyed.

In September 1941 all Jews were forced to wear the yellow Star of David; in October, Jews were barred from leaving the country, and the systematic deportations to the extermination camps, which were mostly in Eastern Europe, began. When the Second World War ended in Europe on May 9, 1945, most of the estimated fifty-seven million people who had lost their lives in the war had died in Europe, and a large number of them were civilians. Among them were approximately eleven million victims of Nazi persecution, of whom about six million were Jews.

Not only are the numbers mind-boggling, so is the bureaucratic infrastructure that administered the systematic extermination of six million Jewish lives, euphemistically called the "Endlösung der Judenfrage" (final solution of the Jewish question). The enormous organizational effort required not just the physical structures that had to be built, such as extermination camps, and the logistics of transporting millions of people as if they were cattle; it also involved a huge number of personnel, from railroad dispatchers to guards, who knew what was going on. Whether in favor of or opposed to the atrocities, the personnel could try to calm their consciences by disregarding the individual victims and focusing on carrying out the administrative process according to prescribed procedures.

It is the eerily abstract disregard for human life and dignity that is so hard to comprehend. This disregard, however, lies at the core of Nazism. Therefore, understanding it provides a key for approaching not only history but also German literature from the 1930s to the mid-1940s.

*Nazi ideology and fascist aesthetics*

National Socialism was part of European fascism, which has often been compared to Communism as another form of totalitarian rule. All too often, however, such embedding into a larger scenario seems at best to blur the specific characteristics of National Socialism and at worst to tend toward apology. While National Socialist ideology can be described as a conglomeration of various ideas, such as anti-Communism and anticapitalism, it had a basis in a quasi-religious irrationalism that was characterized by two central tenets: the *Führer-Prinzip* and *Blut und Boden*.

The *Führer* embodied National Socialist ideology to such an extent that his word was law. In a kind of apotheosis Hitler appeared as the great warrior whose task was to save Germany from ruin in an all-engulfing battle between the forces of good (Hitler's Germany) and evil (especially the Jews, but really the rest of the world) — a battle that could only bring complete victory or complete defeat. National Socialism's view of history was not only fatalistic but also "heroic" and "tragic." Human beings (even the *Führer*) were perceived as mere instruments of the abstract force of history; however, since Nazism also saw itself as a force whose historical task to rule the world was self-evident, yet not unchallenged, there was the possibility of tragic failure, as well as of heroic victory.

Such a victory was anticipated in the hero worship surrounding Hitler, which was part of a simultaneous militarization and aesthetization of the political realm into a realm for religious experience. Uniforms, masses in formation, the "blood flag," and an elaborate scheme of ritualistic and cultic practices combined to create the shared experience of the National Socialist community that was to replace the democratic concept of society. Up to 1943, when Germany was losing the war, Hitler was able to stay above the everyday realm in which Nazi measures might have been criticized, often with the restriction "if the Führer only knew" — of course, he usually knew.

Hitler himself was behind the so-called Röhm putsch in 1934, a three-day killing spree to get rid of political rivals primarily within his own party and especially the SA leader and his group, who were pushing for a second National Socialist revolution. And Hitler was behind the atrocities committed against Jews, other minorities, and political enemies — he was outspoken against these groups. As early as 1925 and 1926, he had laid his inhuman ideology out in the open for everybody who wanted to know with the publication of his manifesto-style book *Mein Kampf* (My Struggle). Even the confusion that grew out of conflicts between the parallel power structures of the state and of the party ultimately stabilized Hitler's grip on power, because the Third Reich was not a centralized state in a traditional sense but rather a *polycracy* with a number of local and changing centers of power, all of which depended on the *Führer* as the single unifying force.

The key phrase *Blut und Boden* encapsulated the racist ideal of blood [Blut] that was supposed to unite all Germans as a race considered superior to other peoples, in the spirit of a true community (hence the term *socialism* in National Socialism). The Germans allegedly had an innate right to the soil [Boden] that they had owned for generations, since they had paid for it with their own blood. This understanding of soil extended to the belief that the German people deserved more Lebensraum (living space), which was to be taken away from the allegedly inferior races in Eastern Europe. This belief was the basis of the plans to invade Eastern Europe, including the Soviet Union, and to restructure the vast area into Germany's granary. The National Socialist ideology derived energy from the enormous potential of hatred and underlying fear that it was able to set free against specific groups who were perceived as the enemy, especially the Jews. While Nazism built on the extant anti-Semitism, the new sense of the German community was defined in terms of race and, by the necessity of its own logic, excluded the other races. Therefore, the overriding goal of National Socialism was racial warfare on a global scale.

The rootedness in irrationalism led to two fundamental contradictions in the Third Reich. The first was the conflict between a preindustrial ideology and the need for the technology of the industrial age, which revealed that National Socialism did not have the appropriate answers for the twentieth century. The second was the conflict between ideological demands and the practical issues of warfare.

The first fundamental contradiction of National Socialism is of special interest because it defined the manner in which Nazism rewrote the map by which it tried to find orientation in the world. The center, whose loss was experienced by Modernism, had been defined in terms of the *Führer* and *Blut und Boden*. This map was not just anti-Modernist; it was antimodern. It presented a network of idyllically agrarian ideals that were even capable of incorporating technology in its preindustrial version of craftsmanship and engineering. It was not only a total map in that it applied to everybody living in Germany; it was also a total lie because its roads did not lead to the idyllic scenes of preindustrial times. Instead, they led to the unspeakable horrors of death camps and pathological visions of magical-technological domination. This map's function was not to guide but to mislead.

The image of the ideologically constructed map can also be used to refer to the shift from politics to aesthetics. Life in general and politics in particular were aestheticized during the Third Reich in the name of ideals: "the ideal of life as art, the cult of beauty, the fetishism of courage, the dissolution of alienation in ecstatic feeling of community; the repudiation of the intellect; the family of man (under the parenthood of leaders)" (Sontag 96). Neither new at the time nor outdated today on an individual basis, these ideals were blended into a map that identified a certain concept of beauty — the German race — and connected it with goodness. What might merely seem a racist aesthetics, as presented in theoretical and literary works by Erwin Guido Kolbenheyer, was actually the political ideology that led to the Second World War.

*The appeal of Nazi aesthetics*   The public appeal of National Socialism can perhaps be elucidated by emphasizing its aesthetic component, which made it possible for Nazi propaganda to reach the masses. The two main factors were the recent experience of the First World War and the nationalism (with its corollaries, such as militarism, imperialism, anti-Semitism, and anti-Communism) that had been growing in Germany for a long time. The recent war experience provided the model of a new national community by glorifying the wartime camaraderie among soldiers. What made the Nazi blend so explosive was its quasi-religious character: the prospect of psychological redemption, the creation of a mythology, a fascination with technology at a rudimentary level, and a vague and hidden sexualization.

In regard to psychological redemption, National Socialism promised to deliver salvation from what was experienced by many as an existential or spiritual crisis through revelatory and communal experiences of the First World War. The experiences were psychologically real; for example, Hitler himself reported undergoing an epiphany after being wounded in the war. Those were the individual experiences and epiphanies that Nazi ceremonies were designed to re-create on a national level. All genres of National Socialist literature aimed at that same goal.

Redemption psychology was connected to the notion of the "sacred," and National Socialism was intent on creating its own mythology. How far National Socialism reached back into occult or magic sources and how serious it was about them has been an issue of debate. On a strategic level, National Socialism had to counter the hold of the Christian churches on the people's minds by offering an ersatz religion without appearing too sectarian. This goal was part of the orchestration of Nazi ceremonies — above all, the Nuremberg party rallies, as can be seen in the film *Triumph des Willens* (Triumph of the Will, 1935), directed by Leni Riefenstahl (b. 1902). Literature also was replete with absurd religious allusions to Hitler, for example, taking over the role of Christ: "Silent night, holy night / All is calm, lonely watches / Adolf Hitler over Germany's fate" [Stille Nacht, heilige Nacht, / Alles schläft, einsam wacht / Adolf Hitler für Deutschlands Geschick].

The obvious contradiction inherent in Nazism consisted in the fact that the radically reactionary utopia of National Socialism was only possible by means of the most advanced technology. The more profound contradiction, however, was that the Nazis needed science but were reluctant to use it. Because they had replaced rationality with irrationality, their concept of technology was one of preindustrial craftsmanship; at best it was applied science, such as engineering. Science itself was rejected as a child of the Enlightenment and, therefore, as Jewish and degenerate. The famed *Wunderwaffen*, the miracle weapons that were supposed to bring Germany's victory, were all engineering feats, but they came too late: the V-1 and V-2 rockets and the fighter jet. Only the real miracle weapon of the Second World War, the atomic bomb, would have made a difference, but its development was slowed down in Germany, in part because the new physics that it relied on was suspected of being a Jewish science.

"Aryan" science was embedded within a premodern agricultural myth of the good and simple life because what mattered was the extent to which technology was an expression of what the Nazis regarded as the German soul. This was not a new concept but had been presented as early as the second phase of *Heimatkunst*. The protagonist of Gustav Frenssen's *Jörn Uhl* embraces a German engineering whose practice is firmly tied to nature and faith and thus appears as a variation of an idyllic rural work ethic. Technology became integrated into the ideology of *Blut und Boden.*

Paradoxically, while Nazi rhetoric and the Nazi embrace of technology created the appearance of addressing the problems of modern times, the Nazi ideology saw these problems in a black-and-white fashion that did not correspond to the complexity of modernism. The result of ignoring modern science in favor of selected areas of technology put Germany at a qualitative and quantitative disadvantage at the beginning of the war. And it stayed that way; from 1941 to 1944 the Soviet Union alone produced almost twice as many tanks as Germany, and in 1943 the Allies produced five times as many airplanes.

National Socialism's appeal to the masses was not merely a result of the Nazi terror forcing people into subservience. Fascist aesthetics, with its components of redemption, mythology, and a fascination with technology, was an important factor. That this aesthetics could take hold has been interpreted as a rechanneling of repressed sexual energy. Yet the extent of actual sexual repression in Nazi Germany is questionable. Sexuality, though not uncontroversial, remained a strong undercurrent in aesthetic terms: redemption fantasies emphasized the beautiful form of the soldier, and technology's masculine nature was part of the Nazis' irrational approach to technology as a victory of form and beauty. Consequently, the famed technological feat of the autobahn appeared as sensuously flowing structures of concrete hugging the German landscape, an expression of the union with the German soul. Furthermore, while eroticism was often stereotyped or sterile, its use in art, literature, film, and advertising was relatively open. The sinister side, however, is most obvious in the politics of sexuality that included the human breeding programs of the *Lebensborn* (fountain of life) to perfect the Aryan race.

*Elements of social disorder*     Thus emerges a picture of a side of Nazi Germany that is in sharp contrast to the usual image of order and obedience. Promiscuity lurked behind the Nazis' relaxed attitude toward sexuality; for example, from the national party rally in 1936, about nine hundred girls of the BdM (*Bund deutscher Mädel,* the Nazi party's organization for girls) between the ages of fifteen and eighteen returned home pregnant.

In this context, the second fundamental contradiction of the Third Reich is relevant: the goal of the race war was not only irrational but also counterproductive to winning the real war. Because Germany was ready neither economically nor technologically for the war, the war effort itself only made sense as an attempt to achieve spiritual salvation, not a military victory. The Nazis showed their priorities when they continued the deportation of Jews to the death camps, although the trains and the personnel who operated them would have been more useful in the effort to win the war against the Soviet Union. The goal of the Nazi race war meant the willing annihilation of the interests (and possibly the lives) of those groups who were instrumental in winning the real war. The goal of the National Socialist race war "flew in the face of the logic of capitalist profit, Prussian military tradition, traditional German foreign policy, and the engineers' technical reason" (Herf 215).

These considerations again raise the question of how National Socialism could take hold in the masses. A range of motivations has been suggested, from being swept away by the energetic force of Nazi ideology to miscalculations about the extent of personal compromises and giving in to the intimidation of Nazi terror. The question, however, presupposes that the Nazis indeed had the masses under control. While it cannot be disputed that the Nazis' hold was strong and far-reaching, exactly how far it reached is debatable. Hans Dieter Schäfer uses the term "split consciousness" to describe what he sees as a profound contradiction of Nazi ideology and practice: the coexistence of the pervasive Nazi influence with a social realm that was "state-free."

Contradicting the usual image of Nazi Germany as characterized by order and obedience by terror, there were clear areas of disorder and disobedience. Americanism, which had been an important cultural factor during the Weimar Republic, continued throughout the Nazi years. Mickey Mouse, straddling a bomb and wielding an axe, was the mascot of a German air force squadron. And the history of swing music in Nazi Germany is a history of continued disobedience, especially in the last years of the war. Although often vehemently attacked by National Socialism, swing music was allowed to be performed up to the end of the war. While dancing to the music had been forbidden in 1938, concerts were (with some exceptions) allowed.

Such phenomena of social disobedience are usually explained by a combination of factors, including the typical Nazi chaos — both Goebbels and Göring enjoyed swing music — and the impossibility of the party machine being able to control interests that were not restricted to a small and politically marginalized group but involved a large and politically significant group of people, such as the youth and the military. It is also possible that such phenomena constituted a release mechanism, providing an escape from reality in Nazi Germany and, therefore, ultimately functioning to stabilize the Nazi hold on power.

Yet the history of swing music during the Third Reich suggests the limitations of Nazi power. In larger German cities swing music clubs formed, whose members were predominantly working-class youths.

Their clubs had the trimmings of street gangs, complete with a specific style of clothes (plaid shirts or jackets and white scarves), weapons (knives and guns), and slang (including the greeting "Heil Swing"). After a swing gang beat up a patrol of the Hitler Youth in January 1942, sixty members of the gang were arrested. According to a secret police report, however, new demonstrations by club members in April and August 1942 showed that deterrence by terror was no longer effective.

The emerging picture of the Third Reich is complex. There was wide acceptance of the Nazis' radical program, and the threat of Nazi terror was real and pervasive, especially because of an atmosphere of distrust and denunciation. At the same time, there were areas of disobedience and even disorder. And there was political resistance, which, although facing a unified enemy, was itself not unified. When the most significant coup attempt failed on July 20, 1944, the response of the majority of the population was silence or solidarity with the Nazi regime.

A final evaluation of the Nazi period remains to be written. It has been complicated by much reluctance to deal with the issue that important facts still keep surfacing; in addition, an intrinsic complication lies in the contradictions of National Socialism itself. Even anti-Semitism, central to Nazism, was contradictory because Germans and German Jews were each other's Other. When the Germans accused the Jews "of being at the same time pacifists and war mongers, revolutionary socialist and reactionary capitalist" (Schäfer 186), the accusation was reflective of the contradictions in the German self-image. Nazism was, above all, a racial utopia that was so out of touch with reality, yet given so much power over reality, that the war started in the interests of National Socialism revealed National Socialism's most central characteristic: self-destructiveness.

## Political Redistricting of the German Literary Spectrum

In the history of literary movements, National Socialism is insignificant; from 1933 to 1945, though fascist literature in other countries, such as France, was significant in literary terms. German literature continued to develop across the usual literary spectrum that was defined by a continuum from antimodern to Modernist trends. The literature that belonged to the Nazi literary canon was primarily reactionary literature, and most of it had been written before National Socialism emerged — and some continued to be written after Nazism was defeated. The literature that was genuinely National Socialist was fundamentally antimodern and limited; most of it radicalized existing reactionary attitudes and was of inferior literary quality.

On the other hand, National Socialism had a crucial impact on German literature, because it radically altered the conditions of how literature was written, published, and read. When the National Socialists took power in 1933, politics intruded into the realm of literature in an unprecedented manner. By bringing all writers' organizations, publishing houses, and theaters under their influence, the Nazis tried to ensure that literature served only one goal: propaganda for National Socialist ideology. Jewish writers were persecuted; writers whose works were considered degenerate for other reasons were banned from writing and publishing, and some of them were also persecuted. Each author who was allowed to write had to decide whether or not Germany was still the place for him or her to continue writing and, if so, under what conditions. Those who stayed but defied the state's literary doctrine did so at their own risk, tried to hide their defiance between the lines, or did not publish. None of the terms used to describe German literature during the time of the Third Reich is uncontroversial. *Exile literature* and *inner emigration* have become politicized terms in the argument concerning which represents the morally better Germany. *Inner emigration* has become a suspicious term because some former Nazi writers tried to hide their participation in National Socialism as an act of political resistance.

The next two chapters discuss the antimodern and reactionary literature and Modernism as the antipodes in the literary spectrum. The following overview will center on resistance literature, which is typically not concerned with Modernist innovation, and traditionalist literature, which is modern but not Modernist and, for the most part, is literally caught in the middle. The German literary scene was reshaped by the intrusion of Nazi politics. Literature was either supported, tolerated, or persecuted by the Nazis.

National Socialism imposed its total map on Germany with the needle of the compass pointing in one direction, that of the irrational myth of the *Führer* and *Blut und Boden*. All (or the overwhelming majority of) texts published in Germany from the 1930s to the mid-1940s, whether they were supported, tolerated, or persecuted by the Nazis, converged on the themes of the Great Man and of myth in a style that tended toward classicist form and specific literary genres, such as the historical novel. While this observation is true as a generalization, it obscures the fact that the common themes and styles were really incorporated into three different maps, in each case providing a significantly different meaning.

*Nazi-supported literature*     Art and literature played a fundamentally different official role in Nazi Germany than before the Nazis came to power, because public and private lives were politicized and politics was aestheticized. The Avant-Gardist fusion of life and art was perverted in an anti-Avant-Gardist way. Strictly speaking, it was not that art was politicized but, rather, that politics was aestheticized in terms of the preindustrial ideals of the simple life that even subsumed technology in a kind of magic thinking. There was the ideology-based restructuring of daily life with fascist ceremonies and holidays. It seemed almost as though life in Nazi Germany was supposed to become a *Gesamtkunstwerk*, or total work of art. The sole purpose of such an aestheticization of life was to prepare for a racial war.

Literature functioned as a closed circuit in the Third Reich: Nazi-supported literature supported National Socialism by becoming one of the many facets of the Nazi propaganda machine; thus, art became part of politics. As part of politics, literature was not allowed to transcend the limits of what appeared to be reality, according to Nazism. Censorship and persecution were used against any literature that did not function as a mouthpiece for National Socialism. As a result, National Socialist literature was necessarily inauthentic as the appearance of actual appearance; it presented an aesthetic image of an aesthetically construed perception of reality according to Nazi ideology.

The irrationality of the interconnected Nazi core beliefs of the *Führer* principle and *Blut und Boden* gave rise to a literature that was equally irrational and had two main purposes: to exalt the *Führer* by presenting history as a history of Great Men and to create the belief in the German master race, which was destined, through its biological and spiritual superiority, to dominate inferior races and save the world from impending doom. Like the ideology that it expressed, National Socialist literature was defined by intrinsic contradictions. The *Führer* principle and *Blut und Boden* corresponded to the opposite attitudes of egomania and servitude, respectively. The contradictions, however, were unified by the people's acceptance of historical developments as willed by fate and were masked by the energy with which fascist art was staged. Nazi art gave expression to a ruthless pursuit of domination that presupposed a blatant and complete disregard for other beliefs and the brutal annihilation of enemies. National Socialism had a profound "heroic" and "tragic" understanding of its own role in the theater of world history to the extent that the way Nazism presented itself had a strongly theatrical quality. On the political stage, the dressing up of the thugs of the Nazi government in heroic roles revealed the true character of fascism as a travesty — the ironic contrast between high form and low content that is also characteristic of much of National Socialist literature.

*Nazi-tolerated literature*    Literature that was not openly National Socialist inside the Third Reich is difficult to evaluate. At the center of the difficulty is not so much literary quality as the political integrity of the texts, because after the war some writers claimed that their texts were meant as resistance. There is, however, a clear distinction. Literature that voiced its resistance in unambiguous terms was ruthlessly hunted down; these texts were banned, and if the authors were arrested, they usually received death sentences. The trademark of Nazi-tolerated literature is ambiguity; if a particular text was perceived as containing vague criticism, the Nazi authorities tended to censure the author while allowing the book to be published. The generally conservative attitude expressed in the texts tolerated by the Nazis had strong affinities to the reactionary core of National Socialism; above all, the major reason for toleration seems to have been that the Nazis did not consider these texts dangerous.

While styles of Nazi-tolerated literature varied, the traditionalist and conservative modes were dominant. In their function these texts ranged from escapism to criticism, both of which can be construed as having either affirmative or emancipatory qualities in the process of reading. As affirmative texts they provided an escapist release valve for readers who, after reading them, returned to their duties without questioning; or the texts allowed for criticism to be voiced in subtle ways, often to be read only between the lines, thus creating a dual illusion. The affirmative illusion was that criticism was restricted to the world of literature — thus providing an even more subtle release valve — and that criticism was possible after all; therefore, reality could not be too badly repressed. Under an emancipatory reading, even escapist texts can be understood as providing areas where the imagination was free and, consequently, could gain strength to resist National Socialism. The ambiguity that resulted from the contradictory functions is the reason why the evaluation of these texts is so difficult. Each text and each writer deserve to be evaluated anew. But evaluation is a political process, and, as such, it needs to address the specific reasons each text gave to its readers not to join the Nazis. As well-intentioned as many texts were, they did not give such specific reasons.

A prime example of the difficulties in evaluation is Werner Bergengruen (1892–1964). His personal integrity is beyond doubt. It has been reported that after he came in contact with the "Weiße Rose" (White Rose), a resistance group at the University of Munich whose young leaders, Sophie and Hans Scholl, were later executed in 1943, Bergengruen and his wife participated in the group's activities. It is therefore tempting to read Bergengruen's personal convictions and actions into the message of his texts, especially his novel *Der Großtyrann und das Gericht* (The Great Tyrant and the Law, 1935), which sold 155,000 copies by 1943. But the question of the political stance of the novel is an ambiguous one: the veiled protest against the Nazis seen by some readers of *Der Großtyrann* was cancelled out by the confirmation of the *Führer* principle seen by other readers of the novel. For example, the official Nazi newspaper, the *Völkischer Beobachter*, which interpreted the novel as the *Führer* novel of the Renaissance (the historical period in which the novel was set), cannot be conclusively accused of having misread the novel, because such a reading is not ruled out by the text. Nazi literature exalted the *Führer* as its version of the Great Man, who moves history and is himself moved by history.

If it was scrutinized for hidden criticism with the same effort, even Nazi literature can be read against its own intentions. *Der Untergang Karthagos* (The Fall of Carthage, 1938), by Eberhard Wolfgang Möller (1906–1972), did not suggest the eventual fall of Hitler and the Third Reich by drawing parallels to Hasdrubal's and Carthage's demise; the parallelism was the warlike attitude toward life, not the result of the attitude. Though different from straightforward Nazi literature, conservative and even Christian texts, such as Bergengruen's, did not challenge the foundation of the concept of the Great Man. Rather, these traditional texts added a human dimension to the Great Man that was ambiguous at best but at worst served to justify the evils of Nazi terror by putting a human face on the *Führer*.

Bergengruen's tyrant of an Italian Renaissance city-state demands the resolution of a murder within three days. After the activities lead to a chaos of denunciations and self-incriminations, the tyrant reveals that he himself committed the murder to test the people, who would now be judged by him. The priest accuses the tyrant of sinning by assuming himself equal to God; humbled, the tyrant confesses that he indeed sinned in testing his people in this way. An antifascist statement is thus watered down by a focus on forgiveness and the universality of human weakness.

Stefan Andres (1906–1970), a Christian author and not a Nazi sympathizer, ended his historical novella "El Greco malt den Großinquisitor" (El Greco Paints the Grand Inquisitor, 1936) in a similar way that might result in numbing necessary resistance to evil and in exonerating political torturers and mass murderers. The painter El Greco (1541?–1614?) is given the task of painting a portrait of the Spanish grand inquisitor, Cardinal Don Fernando Niño de Guevara, who is a symbol for Nazi terror. Since El Greco understands his task as an act of artistic resistance, he decides to make sure that the picture will reveal the face of someone who despises Christ. But during the sittings for the painting the men develop a respect for each other, to the extent that El Greco includes the portrait of Niño de Guevara among his portraits of saints. The person responsible for the torture of the inquisition now appears to El Greco to be "a sad, sad saint, a sainted executioner" [ein trauriger Heiliger, ein heiliger Henker].

To be allowed to continue publishing in Nazi Germany, authors who did not emigrate had to make compromises, which are usually understood as having been necessary for an author to express his or her hidden antifascist message in the so-called slave language, the language in which those who were oppressed could communicate without their oppressors understanding. Poems by Reinhold Schneider (1903–1958), for example, were circulated in private copies and, therefore, were less subject to censorship. Yet the published works by conservative authors, such as Andres, Bergengruen, Hans Carossa (1878–1956), Rudolf Alexander Schröder (1878–1962), Frank Thiess (1890–1977), and Ernst Wiechert (1887–1950), were by necessity more ambiguous and, thus, problematic.

In spite of the good intentions and personal integrity of many authors, as well as the hidden criticism in many texts, the ambiguity of traditional texts allowed the Nazis to abuse them — and their authors — for the purposes of National Socialist propaganda. How little distance there was between traditionalist writers and National Socialist thought during the Nazi regime, and even after, is revealed, for instance, in Carossa's writing about Hitler in 1951: "Without his raging, there perhaps would not yet be a state of Israel" [Ohne sein Wüten gäbe es vielleicht noch keinen Staat Israel]. Such a statement is historically correct only in the most callous sense; it is, however, in line with the kind of thinking that made Nazism possible.

The Nazi authorities tolerated literature that was non-National Socialist — as long as it was not unambiguously antifascist — for two main reasons. First, the high literary quality of traditionalist writings was appreciated by the educated middle class whose members could be misled into believing that Nazi Germany actually cared about and respected the humanist tradition and culture. While most readers could thus be deceived about the Nazis' political intentions, the close affinity of conservative and fascist core beliefs made it possible to influence those readers who were susceptible to such influence. Second, the escapist and entertainment effects of mildly critical texts were usually affirmative and welcome in a country that was gearing up for or engaged in war.

Not only conservative authors remained in Germany. Erich Kästner stayed for primarily personal reasons but also with the vague hope of later being able to write "the" novel of the Third Reich, which he never did. He survived Nazi Germany by writing only nonpolitical texts, including the screenplay for the escapist movie *Münchhausen* (1943), which he could write only with special permission and under a pseudonym (Berthold Bürger), because he was no longer allowed to publish. And not all writers who published non-National Socialist literature during the Third Reich did so with a hidden antifascist agenda. Nature poetry by writers directly or indirectly connected to the magazine *Die Kolonne* (Convoy, 1929–1932) was an important continuation of Modernist traditions. They were political only in the sense that they postulated a realm that was removed from politics at a time when everything was politicized.

*Nazi-persecuted literature*     Any aesthetic reference to actual reality and its problems, as opposed to the aesthetically construed perception of reality according to Nazi ideology, produced texts that gave their readers reasons why they should not join National Socialism. These texts were not tolerated by Nazism, and their authors could be arrested and murdered. Such a violent reaction toward literature reveals an amount of hatred that does not make sense unless it is seen as an expression of a deep-rooted, existential fear.

On May 10, 1933, books that the Nazis considered degenerate and un-German were publicly burned in German university cities by the Nazi student organization; in Berlin alone about 20,000 books were burned. The authors whose books were burned depicted what the Nazis feared the most: the complexity and confusion of the modern world. The list reads like a who's who of Modernist German literature, from Ernst Barlach to Bertolt Brecht, Erich Kästner, Thomas Mann, Ernst Toller, and Franz Werfel. Oskar Maria Graf was ashamed of not being on the list and, from exile, demanded that the Nazis burn his books, too. Carl von Ossietzky (1889–1938) and Erich Mühsam had been arrested as early as February 28, 1933. Ossietzky died after his release from the mistreatment he had suffered while under arrest; Mühsam was murdered in a concentration camp the year after his arrest. Some authors were also arrested and imprisoned. Some even committed suicide, such as Walter Benjamin, Kurt Tucholsky, and Stefan Zweig (1881–1942). Work as a writer in Germany was only possible if one was a member of the newly installed *Reichsschrifttumskammer* (the National Socialist central literature office). Membership in this body was contingent on proof of "racially pure" ancestry and a declaration of loyalty to Hitler's Third Reich.

As authors who wanted to keep writing were forced into illegality, their choices were to stay in Germany but go underground, or to leave. Resistance literature was directly aimed at fighting National Socialism, and that was the reason for a small number of authors to go underground in Germany. German literature written in exile reflected the wide spectrum of the 2,000 to 2,500 authors who, for many reasons, went into exile after 1933. As conditions for active resistance in Germany worsened, most of the writers who had gone underground went into exile. Their works were usually published and distributed in exile; they were in some cases smuggled into Germany, but in general the plan to smuggle literature into the country did not succeed: the police were too efficient.

*Literature of resistance*     The writers of underground resistance literature put their lives on the line; they did not hide their messages between the lines. Resistance literature was as unequivocally political as its enemy, National Socialism; therefore, its message was clear beyond any interpretative doubt. Moral opposition to the Nazi regime was the basis, but what put a work into the ranks of resistance literature was a political and practical issue: whether or not the text was a weapon against National Socialism. It had to be anti-Nazi, not merely non-Nazi, literature. This literature supplied its readers with reasons not to be Nazis; as a result, the literature and its writers were ruthlessly persecuted by the Nazis.

*Literary resistance activities inside Germany*     In his essay "Fünf Schwierigkeiten beim Schreiben der Wahrheit" (Five Difficulties in Writing the Truth, 1940), Bertolt Brecht summarized the challenges of literary resistance: first, the courage to write the truth; second, the wisdom to recognize it; third, the art of using it as a weapon; fourth, the ability to judge which is the right audience; and fifth, the cunning to disseminate the truth to the audience. The last difficulty points both to camouflaging a political message in a text that seems apolitical and to camouflaging resistance literature as a practical question of smuggling and delivery. After the Gestapo shut down the few illegally operated print shops, antifascist reading material was produced abroad, and some was smuggled into Germany. The materials ranged from predominantly programmatic and canonical Communist texts to literary works. Excerpts from Ludwig Renn's antiwar novel *Krieg* were camouflaged as Werner Beumelburg's prowar *Der Frontsoldat* (Soldier at the Front), and Brecht's essay was smuggled into Germany camouflaged as "Praktischer Ratgeber für erste Hilfe" (Practical Advice for First Aid). The relationship between real content and camouflage demonstrates the way in which irony was turned into a weapon against the Nazis.

A major function of resistance literature was to encourage Germans to oppose the Nazi regime. But another function was to inform the world of what was really going on in Germany (for instance, that even the early concentration camps were already places of almost unspeakable terror that only became worse) and thus demonstrate to the world that there existed another, better Germany that resisted these horrors.

Inside Germany, the anti-Nazi propaganda function of literature was most immediate in *Klebeverse*, short verses printed on pieces of paper that were glued to walls, and in other usually brief literary forms printed on flyers that could be distributed with minimum exposure of the persons performing this dangerous task. An often quoted example is the *Klebevers* ("from farms" is added for purpose of rhyme): "Margarine's up again / Even more so butter from farms: / People to arms" [Die Margarine wird teurer / Die Butter noch mehr: / Volk ans Gewehr]. The three short lines do more than just blurt out a political message without considering the aesthetic form. The poignant contrast between the rising costs of living for the people and the war preparation by the Nazis reveal the latter as the cause of the former; either way, the Nazis made the people pay. In addition, the lines gain momentum through the rhyme pattern that, in conjunction with the forward-pushing force of the colon, speeds the poem up by tying the last two lines together.

While the short form in itself does not present a limitation to poetic quality, especially with respect to the haiku-like *Klebevers* above, most of the *Klebeverse* did not display high artistry. Produced quickly and under most difficult conditions of illegality in a police state where even the possession of antifascist material could result in a death sentence, resistance literature had to make a political point. Poetic subtlety was not an impediment but not a priority, either. This kind of literature had to be poignant, persuasive, and easy to understand.

During the first few years of the Nazi regime the writers who participated in such activities as camouflage literature and *Klebeverse* belonged primarily to the Social Democratic and Communist Parties, especially the BPRS. But the antifascist groups had not been prepared for the Nazis' ruthless abuse of power. By about 1935 the initial phase of resistance was over, its members in exile, arrested, or murdered. During a short period, the writer of resistance literature had become an activist, "hard and disciplined" [hart und diszipliniert], had learned to use literature as a weapon, and, because of the real dangers, saw himself proudly as "a corpse on vacation" [ein Toter auf Urlaub] — a phrase that Nazis would use trying to defame antifascist writers. The achievement of the early resistance literature was to have developed models for active opposition to the Nazis by literary means.

*Literary documents of resistance and persecution* Longer forms of resistance literature paid close attention to documenting life in Nazi Germany with a dual goal: first, to reveal to the world the crimes against humanity that were being committed, especially in the concentration camps; and second, to offer everyone in Germany the courage to hope for a better future. Important examples of this literature are *Unsere Straße* (Our Street, 1936), by Jan Petersen (pseudonym of Hans

Schwalm, 1906–1969); *Die Moorsoldaten* (The Moor Soldiers, 1935), by Wolfgang Langhoff (1901–1966); and the *Moabiter Sonette* (Moabit Sonnets, 1946), by Albrecht Haushofer (1903–1945).

Petersen had been a member of the BPRS and the resistance group of antifascist writers, both of which he led from 1933 to 1935. In this capacity he edited the only newspaper for antifascist writers that appeared illegally during the Third Reich. As the "man in the black mask" (or "black glasses"), he made a spectacular appearance at the First International Writers' Congress for the Defense of Culture in Paris in 1935. He emigrated first to Switzerland in 1936, where he published *Unsere Straße*, and later the same year to England after the Gestapo requested his extradition. The manuscript of *Unsere Straße* had been written in Germany, smuggled out of the country by Petersen, and translated into twelve languages. The book documents in plain language the changes that National Socialism brings, as well as the dangerous and fruitless work of Communist resistance — which also suffered from mistakes made by the party leadership in the early years. As a documentation of the failure of grass-roots resistance in a state ruled by terror, *Unsere Straße* is important for the political discussion of the pervasiveness of National Socialism. The lack of large-scale resistance in Nazi Germany made the actual resistance work all the more difficult and dangerous.

The Nazi violation of basic human rights, especially in the concentration camps, was documented in a number of books, including *Im Mörderlager Dachau* (Four Weeks in the Hands of Hitler's Hell-Hounds, 1933), by Hans Beimler (1895–1936), *Oranienburg* (1934), by Gerhart H. Seger (1896–1967); and Willi Bredel's *Die Prüfung* (The Test, 1935). Published during the Third Reich, these works were important for the morale of the resistance fighters in Germany, where the books were smuggled either as complete copies or in excerpts. Many reports, such as *Gefängnistagebuch* (Prison Diary, 1946), by Luise Rinser (b. 1911), were published after the war. Regardless of their date of publication, however, all works are important and often popular documents both of Nazi crimes and of a better Germany.

The most popular of the autobiographically informed novels about imprisonment in concentration camps is probably *Die Moorsoldaten*, by Wolfgang Langhoff, who was primarily a theater director and actor. Langhoff was held in "protective custody" from February 28, 1933, to March 31, 1934. His novel presents a realistic account of the terror of one of the early concentration camps, which was aimed at breaking each inmate's will into accepting Nazism or committing suicide. The experiences in such an early camp, as brutal as they were, only foreshadowed the seemingly impossible: the even worse terrors of the later death camps.

*Moorsoldaten* describes how the inmates develop as a result of their solidarity in order to survive. As an act of resistance, the solidarity is expressed in the "Börgermoorlied," the song of the inmates at the concentration camp Börgermoor. The song contributed to the book's popularity — and documented the function of literature as a form of opposition inside concentration camps. It describes the inmates' physical isolation, monotonous life, and hard labor. Each stanza concludes with the refrain, which determines the inmates' collective identity: "We are the moor soldiers / And with our spades we march / Into the moor . . ." [Wir sind die Moorsoldaten / Und ziehen mit dem Spaten / Ins Moor . . .]. The inmates do not lose their new identity, which is the result of their solidarity, when the end of the song anticipates their return to freedom and changes the refrain to: "Then the moor soldiers / *No longer* will march with their spades / Into the moor!" [Dann ziehn die Moorsoldaten / *Nicht* mehr mit dem Spaten/ Ins Moor!]. As a resistance song, its literary quality is almost irrelevant. As long as the song was effective in achieving its pragmatic and political purpose, it was a good song — and the "Börgermoorlied" was effective. It has an immediate appeal that clearly communicates the situation of suffering under severe oppression. At the same time, the song expresses an undying hope that is strong, uplifting, and democratic, because its subject is facing political oppression with solidarity. The reason the song has such a moving effect also lies in its artistic composition, which, without aesthetic innovations but in its combination of words and melody, evokes the sense of experiencing oppression and hope.

In the novel, the first performance of the song by the inmates draws an immediate and positive response from the guards. Although the song is soon forbidden by the camp commander, individual guards keep requesting it and even ask the inmates to write down the lyrics for them. The inmates are careful not to say who wrote the song, which is called a collaborative effort — as it was, with lyrics by Johann Esser, music by Rudi Goguel, and refrain by Langhoff. Copies of the lyrics are made available only to those guards who treat the inmates less brutally, and the interest of these guards is used for political discussion. This is not just the stereotypical search for the "good Nazi"; it is significant — and sobering — that in such a discussion the average guard is portrayed as having internalized the *Führer* principle to such an extent that he can disagree with the practices of the concentration camp, which he has to carry out by orders of the local commander, while Hitler emerges as the "good Nazi" representing a highly ethical (and in reality nonexistent) ideal of National Socialism. When confronted with the concept of the *Führer* principle, which has to presuppose that the *Führer* knows what is going on in the concentration camps, the guard takes a long time to think but fails to understand the political reality, because he at-

tributes the illness to the symptoms but not the cause: too many functionaries in cushy jobs have come between the *Führer* and "us," referring to the guards as the average-Joe foundation of the Nazi
movement.

The authors of the books mentioned were predominantly Communists; some were Social Democrats. Conservatives, however, were also
imprisoned in concentration camps. Ernst Wiechert rejected National
Socialism on religious grounds but wrote works that reflected conservative values, such as the simple and idyllic life in a rural setting —
hence the title of his best-known novel, *Das einfache Leben* (The Simple
Life, 1939), which demonstrates, like most of Wiechert's other writings, a close affinity to Nazi ideals, especially of blood and soil. Even
more surprising is that Wiechert wrote *Das einfache Leben* after he had
been imprisoned in the concentration camp in Buchenwald in 1938 because one of his stories was considered critical of the Nazi regime and
because he had spoken out in support of the imprisoned theologians
Martin Niemöller and Eduard Spranger. After his release Wiechert
wrote a fictionalized account of his imprisonment, in which an omniscient narrator tells in a reflective style the story of Johannes, who tries
to survive the concentration camp with composure, thinking about literature and reading the Bible, although "he starts wondering from time
to time whether God hasn't died" [beginnt er manchmal zu fragen, ob
Gott nicht gestorben sei]. Because Wiechert feared for his life under
continued Gestapo surveillance, he reportedly buried the manuscript in
his backyard and waited until after the war to publish it under the title
*Der Totenwald* (The Forest of the Dead, 1946).

While the language is traditionalist in Wiechert's account, the Austrian monarchist Max Riccabona (1915–1997) used Modernist techniques, documenting the six stages of his attempt to write his
autobiographical concentration-camp novel *Auf dem Nebengeleise* (On
the Sidetrack, 1995). In Riccabona's case the problem of finding a language that is adequate for the ordeal and the problem of remembrance
that goes back and forth among several time frames combine into a
complex aesthetic text that remains fragmentary. His Modernist technique is unusual for an autobiographically informed account of imprisonment in a concentration camp.

The differences between concentration-camp novels from the left
and from the conservative perspectives reflect the major rift through the
German anti-Nazi resistance that left the Communist resistance efforts
mostly disconnected from the Social Democratic, bourgeois, and conservative efforts. The texts also differ in their political purposes, which
has an effect on the aesthetics. Although fictionalized at least enough
to protect the actual people involved, the leftist accounts aim — with
the immediacy of their everyday language and matter-of-fact ac-

counts — at an immediate political response, solidarity in resisting the Nazis. The conservative texts are more self-reflective both as far as the language is concerned and in the role of the protagonist. The aesthetic level is higher, especially in Riccabona's text, which was written mostly during the 1960s and, as a poetic strategy, placed daily life into the foreground and the terror of the concentration camp into the background. Above all, the context of reception and the target audience of these texts were different. The difference between the politically conservative novels and resistance literature in a strict sense is that, while the former document humanism and resistance, they do not aim at keeping resistance alive and inciting new resistance efforts.

*Albrecht Haushofer's*
**Moabiter Sonette**

Among the texts of literary resistance are also poems and prose texts that deal with Nazi Germany at a more abstract and reflective level. The story "Esther" (1959), by Bruno Apitz (1900–1979), explores the options of the private sphere that emerges as the realm of dignity, love, and hope in the face of the crushing reality of life in a concentration camp. The novel *PLN* (*Postleitnummer*, or Postal Code, 1946) was written by Werner Krauss (1900–1976), a professor of Romance languages. Its grotesque and baroque style and structure allegorically present a critique of Nazi Germany, down to its economic and social roots. Albrecht Haushofer's *Die Moabiter Sonette* attempt to bring private motivation (Christianity) and political realm (resistance) together in poetic contemplation in the classical tradition. What makes these texts different from others is that they were written while their authors were imprisoned. Each text's primary function of resistance can be seen as that of keeping the author himself sane. Krauss reported that he wrote parts of his novel while handcuffed. Haushofer did not survive; he was murdered by an SS raiding party on April 23, 1945, immediately after his release from Moabit Prison and just a few days before the fall of Berlin. His brother found the manuscript of the sonnets on Haushofer's body, reportedly still clenched in his right hand.

An important aspect of Haushofer's poems is the traditional form, because sonnets of resistance literature consciously reached back to the tradition of humanism and rationality. A carefully constructed movement of thought counterbalances the inherent imbalance that lies in the form of the Petrarchan sonnet, whose parts embody the structure of problem and solution: the problem is accorded eight lines (the octave), while there are only six lines (the sestet) for the solution to take form. Thus, a well-balanced sonnet in the traditional sense is a demonstration of the power of rationality. As a consequence, the mere practice of the sonnet tradition suggested an act of defiance of National Socialism.

Haushofer wrote in a conservative tradition of humanism and Christianity. While such a tradition ran ideologically against Nazism, Haushofer had first to overcome his own ties to Nazism. The son of the founder of geopolitics, an important instrument of National Socialist policy, he too became a professor of geopolitics. Although they were friends of Hitler's deputy, Rudolf Hess, and were protected by Hess, both father and son were critical of Nazi foreign policy. Albrecht Haushofer became Hess's foreign policy adviser but also established contacts to resistance movements. He was arrested for the first time after Hess's mission (or escape) to England. After the failed coup attempt of July 20, 1944, Haushofer was arrested and sentenced.

The sonnets welcome the solidarity of others who are like-minded in their uncompromising and active opposition to Nazism. At times reflective, at times emotional, the language of the poems is strong and appropriate to the classical form of the sonnet, and so is the content. Haushofer addresses the complex situation of the world by contrasting it to the simple minds of his guards, who fail to understand the modern world; they, too, are prisoners, but it remains questionable whether they will ever understand. Pondering the sentences of his coconspirators, he concludes: "True, there are times when madness is used to direct. / Then those with the best minds are hanged by the neck" [Es gibt wohl Zeiten, die der Irrsinn lenkt. / Dann sind's die besten Köpfe, die man henkt].

Haushofer also accepts personal responsibility, both for his family and for himself. He sees his father as an inadvertent participant in the demonic rule of the Nazis by providing the theoretical tools of geopolitics. In contrast to those who tried and sentenced him, he admits his real "Schuld" (Guilt) in the sonnet of that title: "For long I deceived my conscience, / I lied to myself and to others" [Ich habe mein Gewissen lang betrogen, / ich hab mich selbst und andere belogen]. And Haushofer does not mince words about the political situation either. Although he might draw a historical parallel — for instance, to Genghis Khan, who, when building pyramids of skulls, showed mercy to thinkers and artists — Haushofer makes the contemporary application of the parallel explicit in the ironic praise of barbarity that is long past: "All skulls are equal now in our time. / Mass that we are, we are so rich in skulls" [In unserer Zeit sind all die Schädel gleich / An Masse sind wir ja so schädelreich]. Though writing in classical poetic form, Haushofer addresses modern issues directly, without leaving room for political ambiguities. Since his *Maobiter Sonette* speak of a strong commitment to actively opposing National Socialism, they are an important document of literary resistance.

*Exile literature* The distinction between exile literature and resistance literature primarily has to do with the condition and place of production. Both exile and resistance literature were persecuted in Nazi Germany, and they overlapped for two obvious reasons. First, active resistance inside Germany became increasingly difficult, and individual resisters were finally forced to leave the country. Second, many writers who had chosen to emigrate immediately, because they had seen that their lives were in danger, supported resistance from the outside. In their works the conditions in Nazi Germany and in exile are presented in an unambiguously political way. The oldest son of Thomas Mann, Klaus Mann (1906–1949), for example, evolved into an important figure of antifascism both as a magazine editor (*Die Sammlung*, 1933–1935; *Decision*, 1941–1942) and a novelist. Based on Klaus Mann's opinion of Gustav Gründgens, the novel *Mephisto* (1936) portrays an opportunistic actor's career in Nazi Germany. In contrast, in the novel *Der Vulkan* (Volcano, 1939), Klaus Mann treats life in exile as a challenge to all the characters. Anna Seghers (pseudonym for Netty Radványi, nee Reiling; 1900–1983) also deals with the conditions of exile, especially waiting to be allowed passage to safe exile, in her novel *Transit* (1948; first published in Spanish as *Visado de Tránsito*, 1944). Reflecting Seghers's own experience of waiting in Marseilles for her visa to Mexico, the novel describes the grotesque and absurd bureaucratic treatment of the petitioners for political asylum. In her earlier novel *Das siebte Kreuz* (The Seventh Cross, 1942), Seghers addresses the situation in Nazi Germany.

*Das siebte Kreuz* made Seghers famous. In 1939 parts of it were published in the Moscow journal *Internationale Literatur;* in 1944 the Hollywood movie version came out, with Spencer Tracy in the lead role. In montage technique and a matter-of-fact style, which owed much to New Objectivity, the novel presents the question of the possibility of resistance in a police state that, in contrast to expectations on the left, had stabilized and tightened its grip on every aspect of life. Seghers's answer is hopeful because, in the decision of individuals to help the escapee and thus put their own lives in danger, the individual conscience emerges as a realm that Nazi terror does not and cannot control, no matter how tight its grip on the population.

The protagonist, Georg Heisler, is one of seven prisoners who escape from the concentration camp Westhofen, north of Worms. To deter further escapes the camp commander orders seven trees to be set up as crosses; on each cross he plans to display the dead body of a recaptured escapee. But one cross remains empty and becomes the symbol of active resistance and the limitations of Nazi terror. Heisler's seven-day odyssey reaches its conclusion when he boards a boat that will take him to safety; the camp commander is replaced by a new one, who has the symbol of defiance, the trees, quietly removed; and the prisoners, whose report is given in the "we" form, feel a sense of solidarity that is founded in individual conscience — a strong emphasis on humanism and hope.

The latter sentiment, with which the novel closes, is remarkable for the simple reason that Seghers, who was a member of the Communist Party and the BPRS, not only presented the possibility of resistance but reclaimed the tradition of German *Innerlichkeit*, or inwardness, which is usually regarded as a contributing factor to the German mind's vulnerability to fascist thinking and is a typical characteristic of texts of conservative authors, such as Wiechert. Such inwardness held the belief that, as the prisoners express it, they not only feel the power of outside forces that reaches deep down into their innermost being, "but we also felt that there was something in our innermost being that was untouchable and invulnerable" [aber wir fühlten auch, daß es im Innersten etwas gab, was unangreifbar war und unverletzbar]. While the novel thus reaches out to a wide spectrum of readers, it has been criticized from the Communist side for not clearly stating the reasons for resistance that lie in social conditions beyond individual motivation.

Whether such criticism is justified or not, it highlights how difficult it was for the many exile authors to speak with one voice. While there were serious attempts to establish a popular front against the common enemy, they failed because of ideological distrust among the groups of exile writers. The move into exile scattered the authors across the world, although some focal points emerged. Furthermore, the places of exile changed as Nazi Germany expanded its influence. Consequently, the history of exile literature is, to some extent, a history of the material conditions under which the writers produced literature, found ways of publishing it, and reached an audience.

During the first phase (1933–1938), Nazi Germany increased its bellicose rhetoric but refrained from direct military action against neighboring countries. Therefore, these countries seemed attractive to exile authors — especially Austria (despite its authoritarian rule under Chancellor Dollfuß) and Czechoslovakia because of their German-language cultures. German-writing authors depended on a German-speaking audience and on publishing houses that were willing to print their writings. Some publishers had emigrated with their writers; Gottfried Bermann-Fischer, for example, took part of Fischer Publishers to Vienna. The German annexation of Austria in 1938 and of Czechoslovakia in 1939 brought an end to easy access to a German-speaking audience, because Switzerland not only stayed officially neutral but also practiced a restrictive immigration policy.

The second phase of the exile period began with Germany's expansion in 1938, which led to the Second World War in 1939. Other countries in Europe suddenly became less safe. France had developed into a major destination of German authors — especially, Southern France, which attracted Feuchtwanger, Werfel, and Heinrich Mann. As German troops invaded France and Spain turned fascist under Franco, France became a trap; the only option was to leave by way of Marseilles, if one could obtain a transit visa. The Scandinavian countries had not been attractive to literary emigrants — with exceptions, such as Hans Henny Jahnn, Nelly Sachs (1891–1970), and Peter Weiss — but the German invasion of those countries put the emigrants' lives in danger. Less crucial as a place of exile for writers, the Netherlands was most important for the publication of German-language literature with major support especially from the publishing houses of Querido and Allert de Lange, which were brutally persecuted after the German invasion.

With the continued military success of the German army, the only safe Western European country was Great Britain. By 1941, in the last phase of exile, German writers increasingly turned to countries outside of Europe. While a few writers, such as Else Lasker-Schüler and Max Brod, emigrated to Palestine, the three centers of German exile were the Soviet Union, the United States, and Latin America (especially Mexico). While Communist emigrants such as Becher and Bredel were able to work and publish with state support, the Soviet Union never received the number of emigrants the United States did. An obvious reason was Stalinism, which proved fatal for some German exiles, such as Herwarth Walden.

The United States, especially Los Angeles and New York, became the most important country for German emigration. Whether because of a different political orientation, feelings of cultural disorientation, or simply because of the language barrier, most major German writers, including Thomas Mann, Remarque, Brecht, and Döblin, did not find a long-term home in the United States and returned to Europe after the war, though for very different reasons. Mexico was the exile home of Seghers, Kisch, Renn, and Gustav Regler (1898–1963). It was particularly important because of the German-language publishing house El libro libre, which first published Seghers's *Das siebte Kreuz*.

# 5: The National Socialist Literary Canon: The Uneasy Voice of Reactionary Traditions

## The Literary Tension of Ideological Paradoxes

THE PARADOX OF NATIONAL SOCIALIST LITERATURE originated in pretending to speak with one voice, while there was a conglomeration of reactionary traditions that were accumulated into a National Socialist literary canon under the *Führer* principle and correlated tenets of National Socialist ideology. Most of the major works of that canon had already been written before 1933; they are discussed in this chapter to emphasize the ideological connections between them and the literary production of the Third Reich. The criterion is not whether a particular work has all the characteristics of some definition of Nazi literature. Fascist literature was primarily an expression of an attitude toward the world's history and direction; therefore, the important criterion is political: whether or not the work in question had an unambiguous functionality that allowed the Nazis to integrate it into their literary canon. A few young writers — such as Baldur von Schirach (1907–1974), Herbert Böhme (1907–1971), Hans Baumann (1914–1988), Heinrich Anacker (1901–1971), and Herybert Menzel (1906–1945) — followed a hard-core party line with the goal of creating truly National Socialist literature; despite the expectations that were placed on the party-line authors, they did not produce works that were capable of replacing the centrality of the pre-1933 works for the Nazi literary canon.

Nazi literature (a term used here as shorthand for the National Socialist literary canon) also existed within the tension of contradictions that marred National Socialism in general. As an ideology, it led to disorientation, because the irrational construct of a racial myth failed to relate to the real world. In this sense, the state of literature mirrored the state of National Socialism, with its monolithic rhetoric covering up its *Kompetenzwirrwarr*, or lack of clearly defined areas of responsibility between the various elements charged with the same task.

Such a lack of clearly defined responsibilities resulted in a duplication of efforts that was paradoxically productive in the sense that in a totalitarian state without democratic checks and balances, one institution functioned in such a way as to keep a check on the activities of the competing institution(s) and at least assure a balance of power in their particular area. Literature was caught in the middle of such overlapping responsibilities, especially between propaganda minister Joseph Goebbels and Alfred Rosenberg. On the Nazi state's side, Goebbels was the ex officio chair of the *Reichskulturkammer*, and on the Nazi party's side, Rosenberg was the *Führer*'s commissioner in charge of the ideological training and education of the NSDAP.

The state-controlled literary canon deteriorated to an instrument of party-line propaganda; the literary genres were defined by their rhetorical functions: poetry as battle cry, theater as ritual, and fiction as colonialism. The canon was based on an aesthetics of hatred that extolled the virtues of domination and presupposed the annihilation of enemies. Therefore, although the battle cry, ritualistic aspects, and colonial attitudes seem to be particularly strong in one literary genre, they are variations of the same aestheticized ideology and pervade the other genres, too.

As a result, the rhetorical function in the service of a simplistic ideology contributed also to a simplification of aesthetic means. Yet propagandistic use of literature did not turn all literature into simple propaganda, and just because some Nazi literature pretended to portray the profound soul of the German people, this did not become aesthetic fact. The soul that was expressed was often merely the superficial spirituality of the German petty bourgeoisie, which was the original power base for Nazism and the source of Nazi ideology.

This argument can also be reversed: Nazi literature had to cater to the ideals of the petty bourgeoisie, because the latter represented the lowest common denominator in terms of presentation and message. Literature that reached the lower middle class took care of the Nazis' core constituency and, at the same time, gained access to other social groups through the petty bourgeoisie, which was part of the middle class, after all, and shared values with the rest of that class. Moreover, particularly because of social proximity, petty-bourgeois values appealed to the working class as a perception of a better life. The vision of the classless community — as it was envisioned, for example, in the camaraderie of the trenches — seemed to address the needs and insecurities of the petty bourgeoisie.

*Radical antimodernity* The real world's complexity and the corresponding petty-bourgeois insecurity were interconnected and constituted a powerful drive in the rejection of everything that was considered to be different, complex, or threatening. Since modern problems challenged the traditional value systems in the real world, traditional literary concepts were also challenged: experiencing the world as fragmented and simultaneous challenged the linearity and causality of the story; experiencing dehumanization and objectification challenged the role of the hero; experiencing general confusion and miscommunication challenged the possibility of dialogue. These experiences — all part of the realization that the world was no longer understandable through immediate experience — were real. Modernism reflected the limitation of experience in form and content by experimenting with different aspects of perception, truth, and language itself.

In sharp contrast, the rhetoric of the National Socialist literary canon suggested that it was still possible, in an immediate way, to experience the world — which had, of course, become the simplistic world of Adolf Hitler. Combined with social, political, and economic factors that made it possible for the Nazis to reach a large segment of the population by appealing to petty-bourgeois needs and insecurities, it made for an explosive mixture leading to concrete political action that, as in the case of the book burnings in 1933, was accompanied by literature to justify the event. In his "Weihespruch" (Consecration Poem) titled "Feier der Jugend" (Celebration of Youth), Ernst Bertram (1884–1957) encouraged the youthful book burners of May 1933: "Reject what confuses you, / Condemn what seduces you!" [Verwerft, was euch verwirrt, / Verfemt, was euch verführt]. The poem was aimed directly at an "irritating" characteristic of Modernist literature: a conscious and aesthetic irritation that stemmed from the attempt of a complex art to deal with the real and complex world. By rejecting irritating literature that might seduce the reader into thinking about the real world, the book-burning students also rejected that world. The violence that Nazism (as an ideology and as a political movement) displayed against Modernism made obvious that fear of freedom was the cause of the Nazis' flight from freedom.

The writers loyal to Nazism played a public role that is accorded to writers only on rare occasions. New visions were expected from them, emanating "from the mothers, from the blood and soil" [Von den Müttern her, von Blut und Boden her], as Börries Freiherr von Münchhausen wrote in 1934, celebrating the instrumentalization of literature in which poetry and politics became one. Many writers embraced the task of doing their part in the *Führer*'s metaphorical army of all Nazis. Superficially, this meant becoming the mouthpieces for Nazi ideology. Creatively, however, it presented quite a challenge, because it was not just a matter of adulation of the *Führer* and writing about the German mother and the German farmer and soldier.

If the writers were serious, they had to conceal the discrepancies between the orientation National Socialism offered and the modern world. Hans Friedrich Blunck (1888–1961) might have only sensed the extent of the challenge, but he was right on target with his demand to counter "smart and smart-allecky rationality" [klugen und klügelnden

Ratio] with emotion by tapping into "ancient, magic currents" [alter, magischer Ströme] and by juxtaposing chemistry and physics with mystical experience. This was at the core of the contradiction of National Socialist ideology, and the writers were called on to do the impossible: to reconcile preindustrial ideology with industrial society. The central aspect of the Nazis' incorporation of technology (as opposed to theoretical science) into the magic realm of the German soul is central to Blunck's understanding of the Nazi writer's task.

With the arrogance of a totalitarian ideology, National Socialism assumed that it had found all the answers in a regression to the premodern past of a "simple life." As a political movement, it sought means to influence the masses. Within the totalitarian state, literature was used to preach the "simple life" to the masses. To do that, it no longer needed experimentation or a critical, rational approach. Therefore, literature of the Third Reich became Nazi propaganda and could not offer an authentic representation of the world.

### Reactionary Literature before 1933

Reactionary traditions as direct precursors to Nazi literature reached back to the turn of the century and included the works of *Heimatkunst*, Neoclassicism, popular literature, and even *Arbeiterliteratur*. A second phase, often referred to as a *conservative revolution* in analogy to political developments, was defined by the experience of the First World War and is exemplified by the antidemocratic war literature of the late 1920s. The book burnings of May 10, 1933, merely documented a turning point in terms of what kind of literature the Nazi regime was willing to allow in its area of influence; they represented neither the end of democratic literature nor the beginning of fascist literature. The former was forced into an existence outside the official German public. The latter, now in a third phase, during which it was elevated to the status of the official state literature, continued the reactionary trends of antidemocratic, anti-Semitic, racist, and antimodern literature.

*Continued reactionary trends* Written and published before the National Socialists established their reign of terror in 1933, the major works of the reactionary traditions were predisposed to being incorporated into the Nazi canon, which brought into prominence with the literary public and to power in the literary organizations of the Third Reich reactionary writers who had previously been in the background, because of their second-rate, though often quite popular, literary production. Werner Beumelburg, Hans Friedrich Blunck, Paul Ernst, Friedrich Griese (1890–1975), Hans Grimm, Hanns Johst (1890–1978), Erwin Guido Kolbenheyer, Agnes Miegel, Börries von Münchhausen, Wilhelm Schäfer (1868–1952), Emil Strauß, and Will Vesper (1882–1962) were appointed to the *Preußische Dichterakademie* (Prussian Poets' Academy), replacing writers who had been forced out. A few writers refused the appointment, such as Hans Carossa and Ernst Jünger. Ricarda Huch (1864–1947), the only one to leave the academy voluntarily, called the new way of the academy un-German and disastrous in her courageous letter of resignation.

Because many authors loyal to Nazi Germany had established themselves as writers of reactionary, folkish-nationalist literature long before 1933, they had often been independent of National Socialism. Even during the Third Reich some of these authors raised eyebrows. Kolbenheyer expressed his own reactionary views; nevertheless, he actively campaigned for the Nazis, giving lectures in England and France supporting Hitler's policies in 1936. Still, ideologically reactionary texts contributed to the antirational cultural climate and promoted public acceptance of antidemocratic attitudes that culminated in National Socialism. Beginning around 1927 with more or less National Socialist sponsorship, but especially after 1933, the tendency of "convergence" took full effect on these authors, and their texts (as well as their actions) became instrumental to official National Socialist policies.

*National Socialist appropriation of literary traditions*

The works of deceased authors were incorporated into the Nazi literary canon according to the importance of these authors. In the case of authors with a clear reactionary, nationalist orientation, such as Hermann Löns, the incorporation merely reflected the development of nationalist literature from pre- or proto-fascist ideas. Perhaps because of the second-rate literary quality of most of these works, Nazi cultural politics attempted to appropriate works by writers who were considered important.

Of particular interest were "modern" authors, such as Rilke and George, whose personal conservative politics led to formulations in their works that were open for reinterpretation. Within the Nazi *Literaturbetrachtung* (contemplation of literature), which replaced literary criticism after the latter was officially abolished in 1936, such reinterpretations were one-sided and narrowed down the complex network of possible interpretations that marked Aestheticist texts in general. A similar tension underlay the efforts to appropriate authors of early nineteenth-century German Classicism. These writers' humanist ideals had to be reconciled with the radical convictions of National Socialism and the young generation of Nazi writers. Johann Wolfgang von Goethe was suspect because of his association with freemasonry; on the other hand, he was considered the greatest German poet, and his *Faust* was abused as a manifestation of the *Führer* principle. Friedrich Schiller was flatly declared a precursor of National Socialism, a fact that — so went the argumentative twist — was evident only now that National Socïalism had come into existence.

Bringing authors who were considered of value into the Nazi fold found its counterpart in banning authors who were considered degenerate. In the declaration "Wider den undeutschen Geist" (Against the Un-German Spirit), the German Student Association demanded on the occasion of the 1933 book burnings that works written by Jews should appear in Hebrew; if published in German, texts by Jewish authors should be marked as "translations." Of course, the ultimate goal of the Nazi regime was the extermination of any Jewish presence in German culture. Works by Jewish authors that had ineradicably found their way into German culture were an embarrassment to Nazism. In these cases, authorship and text were dissociated; for example, Heinrich Heine's poem "Lorelei" was listed as a "folksong" written by an anonymous author.

Authors who were merely claimed by National Socialism and those who indeed contributed to the reactionary subculture that led to and constituted the core beliefs of National Socialism need to be kept separate. Nazi literature glorified not just some vague idea of violence but a political view whose practice would lead to the most unspeakable and worst imaginable abuses of human rights. National Socialist atrocities happened in reality, not just in the literary imagination.

### The Unwanted Token Modernist
### and the Unwilling Token Reactionary

*Gottfried Benn*

The short-lived affiliation of Gottfried Benn with National Socialism was in part motivated by the dream that his version of Modernism could be the official literature of the Nazi state. Affinities in Modernist thought to fascism were not reciprocated. Even in the case of Italian Futurism, where fascist core beliefs provided the basis for a Modernist movement, Mussolini's fascist Italian state, like Nazi Germany, endorsed imitative classicism as the official art, despite Mussolini's personal friendship and political cooperation with Marinetti, the chief proponent of Futurism.

Another motivation was the role of irrationalism and biologism in his own thinking, which made Benn vulnerable to National Socialist ideology so that he welcomed Nazism as the answer to the threat of nihilism. He embraced specific National Socialist concepts, such as racial purity, heroism, and the *Führer* principle, as an extension of his own irrationalism. Thus, Benn could — in a complete reversal of reality — explain that the *Führer* principle was not a terroristic but a spiritual principle.

Benn's flirtation with Nazism and subsequent recantation — including his retreat into the army, which he had the indecency to glorify as an aristocratic form of resistance — seem ironic. In an attempt to establish his version of Modernism as National Socialist art, Benn celebrated the genesis of art out of power, but as early as 1934 he had to experience that his kind of art was not tolerated by those in power. His early Expressionist poems were still a scandal for the Nazis, who were not appeased by those of Benn's works that could easily be read as in keeping with Nazi ideology, such as "Dennoch die Schwerter halten" (Still the Swords Withstand, 1933); consequently, Benn and his works were attacked in Nazi publications. In 1938 Benn was removed from the *Reichsschrifttumskammer*, which meant that he was no longer allowed to write or publish.

Nevertheless, in 1933 and 1934 there was Benn humming the Nazi mantra of "breeding" [Züchtung] and at the same time having to supply proof of his own pedigree because his name looked Jewish. Soon after Benn took pains to trace his name to a racially pure Celtic source, he recanted the political use of the idea of breeding in his essay "Züchtung II" (Breeding II), where he accuses the Nazis of having perverted the philosophy of his hero Nietzsche. When he equates the political practice of racial breeding with "kidnappers' love for children" [Kinderliebe von Kidnappern], he uses a sharp and brilliant formulation, which is typical of his style and sharp wit, to mask the fact that his own senses had been kidnapped for a short while. Benn is the prototypical example of the failure of the intellectuals, who, because of their incisiveness and brilliance, were expected to have known better; Benn's case was much more disappointing because he rebuked Klaus Mann's attempt to remind him of what Benn had once stood for as a Modernist.

*Ernst Jünger's*
**In Stahlgewittern**
With his war diary *In Stahlgewittern* and other texts, Ernst Jünger belonged to those who helped prepare the intellectual climate for National Socialism. While it had an important political impact, Jünger's war diary has been overrated aesthetically. It is a simple glorification of war, full of linguistic platitudes and juvenile egocentricities; for example, Jünger boasts that eleven of the many shots fired during the war had been directed at him personally. Paradoxically, he uses an utterly unaesthetic style to talk about an aesthetics of horror. The book was so influential, not because it was written by a great author (which Jünger was on other occasions) but because Jünger was saying what many people were ready to hear. While he was radically reactionary and antidemocratic, he probably was not a Nazi; the way the book was written and read, however, encouraged people to turn to radically reactionary ideologies, such as National Socialism.

There are elements even in *In Stahlgewittern* that were not in keeping with Nazism. Most important at a personal level is Jünger's attitude of an elitist, pseudo-aristocratic fairness. Although assuming their mutual intention to kill each other, Jünger explicitly states that he "always endeavored to look at the opponent without hatred" [immer bestrebt, den Gegner ohne Haß zu betrachten]. The use of the term *opponent* conveys the notion of participating in a civilized game rather than a war. Such a display of respect is in complete contrast to the depiction of the enemy as subhuman, expressing a hatred typical of most antidemocratic war novels and of Nazi ideology. It was one of Jünger's typical romantic attitudes that allowed him selectively to turn his back on reality.

Even more important than Jünger's elitist self-image is the fact that he looked at the larger issues. Beyond a fascination with the war's "orgy of destruction" [Orgie der Vernichtung] and its "type of horror that is strange like an uncharted territory" [Art des Grauens, die fremdartig ist wie ein unerforschtes Land], Jünger had an understanding of the economic side of warfare that the Nazis ignored because they thought of war in racial terms. He regretted war's systematic destruction as an expression of disastrous economic thinking: "it also brings more damage than benefits to the destroyer and no honor to the soldier" [sie . . . bringt auch dem Zerstörer mehr Schaden als Nutzen und dem Soldaten keine Ehre]. Even though it was added in a later revision, this passage is consistent with Jünger's thinking.

Such reflective passages of the diary, however, are few in comparison to the descriptions both of the boredom of daily routine, which nonetheless leave room for the idealization of quiet moments as "cozy security" [behaglicher Geborgenheit], as well as storms of steel and walls of fire as "clumps of earth, pieces of brick, and splinters of iron came raining down on us and sent bright sparks flying from our steel helmets" [ein Schauer von Erdklumpen, Ziegelstücken und Eisensplittern hagelte auf uns herab und schlug helle Funken aus den Stahlhelmen]. Passages like this one were seized on, above all, by Jünger himself, in later publications, such as *Der Kampf als inneres Erlebnis* (Battle as an Inner Experience, 1922), which continues where the predominantly realistic diary left off. Now Jünger fully aestheticized war in the fascist vein as a beautiful phenomenon that happens upon mankind like an act of nature or fate, where man finds his true destiny as the ultimate predator who controls destruction: "For all technology is a machine, is random, the projectile blind and without will of its own. Man, however, is driven by his will to kill with storms of explosives, iron and steel" [Denn alle Technik ist Maschine, ist Zufall, das Geschoß blind und willenlos. Den Menschen aber treibt der Wille zu töten durch die Gewitter aus Sprengstoff, Eisen und Stahl].

Works such as this expose the strong affinity between Jünger's beliefs and National Socialism; therefore, it was possible for the Nazis to see Jünger as one of them and even to offer him a seat in parliament, which he rejected in 1927. Similarly, he rejected the appointment to the new and "cleansed" Writers' Academy. It was, Jünger wrote in a letter of November 16, 1933, his "soldier's character" [soldatischer Charakter] that did not allow him to get involved in academic relationships. His refusal, he wrote, was to be understood as a sacrifice that was forced on him by his participation in the German mobilization in the service of which he had been active since 1914. His reactionary politics, therefore, showed more shared values with the Nazis than not. This evaluation can be supported by the fact that Jünger's thoughts found their way directly into Nazi literature. For example, in a dialogue in Arnolt Bronnen's *Roßbach* (1930) the title character Roßbach attributes the phrase "mobilization of the German" [Mobilmachung des Deutschen] to Jünger. Three years before the Nazis came to power, Bronnen's Roßbach is quite explicit about means, such as "extermination of many millions" [Ausrottung vieler Millionen], and the goal "to turn this nation into the territory of a single master-race" [aus diesem Reich das Gebiet einer einzigen Herrscher-Rasse zu machen].

Jünger's militarist, nationalist, and authoritarian beliefs were readily available to be used by National Socialism, and his early writings helped pave the way for National Socialist thought. But in a strange way, he stayed neutral. Jünger reportedly had contact with members of the anti-Hitler resistance, but he had no part in it, just as he never seemed to have developed a sense of personal responsibility. His notion of fate — another core belief he shared with National Socialism — perhaps did not allow such a sense of responsibility. His writings during the Third Reich displayed his personal distaste for National Socialism, yet Jünger's judgment seemed to be one of aesthetics, not ethics.

Jünger's *Auf den Marmorklippen* (On the Marble Cliffs, 1939) is a test case. Usually understood as a critique of National Socialism, it remains ambiguous. The brutal dictator type, the Head Forester, can easily be understood as representing Hitler or Göring — but also Stalin. Unambiguous is only, as discussed in the next chapter, the Modernist quality of that book's reactionary aesthetics.

## Poetry as Battle Cry

The tradition of the reactionary ballad had been established by writers like Börries von Münchhausen and Agnes Miegel, both active long before 1933 and loyal to the Third Reich. Now lyrical production was dominated by the rhetorical function of preparing and supporting the Nazi war effort. Lyrical forms usually were imitative, exploiting literary devices that ranged from classicist to Expressionist. Themes represented by such words as *blood, oath,* and *flag* dominated and were directed at effacing any individual personality, because blood, oath, and flag symbolized an ahistorical loyalty to the community of the German people as embodied by the Nazi state and its *Führer.* All poems became battle cries that were imbued with a quasi-religious, cultlike meaning as they were used in official celebrations. In the context of its use as a text to be performed or sung, the lyrical genre merged with the theater and other forms of performance, such as marching songs.

*War poems*    War poems were calls to arms that did not simply glorify war but encoded the *Führer* principle with its demand of each German citizen's complete abandon to the National Socialist idea. "Entscheidung" (Decision, 1938), by Hermann Burte (1879–1960), reveals the murderous social Darwinian struggle for survival as the true essence of life: "Murder keeps you alive! / Look at nature, / Eat or be eaten, / People, you decide" [Mord hält am Leben! / Schaue Natur an, / Fraß oder Fresser, / Volk, mußt du sein]. War not only appeared as a direct expression of that struggle but also generated the sense of a people's right to a homeland, as in the first two lines of the 1943 poem by Ernst Bertram: "Yet it's the graves / That create a home" [Aber erst Gräber / Schaffen Heimat].

National Socialism also created war poetry from its own history: poems — especially marching songs — that encouraged and glorified the battle in which the Nazis were engaged against the democracy of the Weimar Republic. The most famous song is known simply by the name of its writer, Horst Wessel (1907–1930), whom the Nazis considered a martyr of their movement. This song became the Nazis' anthem and was usually sung after the German national anthem. The first stanza rallies the Nazi battalions: "Hoist the flag! Keep ranks close and tight!" [Die Fahne hoch! Die Reihen dicht geschlossen!]. The following lines reveal that it is an early poem (about 1928) because of its references to the SA, which had not yet been neutralized, and to enemies from the right, such as monarchists. The song proceeds to demand "free reign over the streets for the brown battalions" [Die Straße frei den braunen Bataillonen], referring to attempts by the government in the late 1920s to outlaw paramilitary units, and ends by asserting that the end of the slavery (of democracy) is near.

The flag with the swastika, which is hoisted in the "Horst-Wessel-Lied," is also flying in Baldur von Schirach's poem of 1933, which was the third song printed after the German national anthem and the "Horst-Wessel-Lied" in official party and Hitler Youth songbooks of 1934. It begins with the line "Forward! Forward! sound bright fanfares" [Vorwärts! Vorwärts! schmettern die hellen Fanfaren], and its refrain varies the image of the flag that leads the way into a new era —

like many other Nazi poems that, with more or less originality, varied the same set of imagery including honor, faithfulness, flag, drum, blood, and people.

Another work is often considered the quintessential poem of National Socialism: Hans Baumann's poem "Es zittern die morschen Knochen" (Brittle Bones Are Trembling), famous for its refrain: "And today we own Germany / and tomorrow the whole world" [Und heute gehört uns Deutschland / und morgen die ganze Welt]. It was first published in 1933 with two stanzas, basically completed by 1935 with two additional stanzas, and modified in minor ways from time to time to accommodate changing political trends. The song not only glorifies war and the Nazis' battle against the Communists in Germany; it seems to anticipate the war against the Soviet Union (first stanza) even at the cost of reducing the world to rubble (second stanza).

**Führer** *poems*   The *Führer* principle equated the will of one person, the leader, with the law. It was not based on the idea of majority rule but on that of personality, as Hitler himself explained. The writer became the "poet" in official language, implying his or her function as a seer. Hence the poet was a kind of leader him- or herself. In an immediate and practical sense this was true to the extent that, like other groups of the social and cultural elite that cooperated with Nazism, Nazi writers mediated between National Socialist ideology and the German population. It is precisely in this context that the behavior of nonfascist writers who collaborated with the Nazis appears less innocent and more dangerous.

The ultimate *Führer*, Adolf Hitler, reigned supreme. The entire German people was considered his army, including the poets: "Poets must march / in formation like soldiers" [Dichter muß in Reih' und Glied / wie Soldaten wandern]. These lines by Hans Schwarz (1890–1967) illustrate the role of literature during the Third Reich: like all art, literature had to contribute to achieving the *Führer*'s will to power. Specifically, literature was involved in upholding the metaphysics of power that masked the power of state terrorism in the hands of one man. The claim to power was total; correspondingly, texts written in adulation were often openly religious in tone and imagery. The *Führer-Gedichte* — poems that celebrated the character and achievements of Adolf Hitler — were variations of war poems, because they glorified Hitler's battle to bring greatness to Germany, both as achievement (the Third Reich) and as future (plans for world domination).

In a poem by Heinrich Anacker the speaker addresses Hitler in a conventional way by saying "we all carry in our hearts your image" [Wir alle tragen im Herzen dein Bild]. The poem, however, quickly moves to celebrate the success with which Hitler led his people through "storm and danger" [Sturm und Gefahren]. Rhetorically, storm is characteristic both of the enemy and of the German people's motivation. Hitler emerges as the "leader to freedom and bread" [Führer zu Freiheit und Brot]. Other poems, too, glorify Hitler as liberator, referring to the liberation from "foreign" influences, such as the Jews within Germany, and, internationally, from German subjection to demands by the victors in the First World War.

These poems communicated Nazi propaganda, repeating core concepts of the *Führer* principle. The *Führer*'s word becomes "language, law, and power" [Sprache, Gesetz und Macht], and people and *Führer* are joined in matrimony, thus strengthening the Third Reich in a poem, "Dem Führer" (To the Führer), by Hanns Johst. In another poem of the same title Will Vesper relates the *Führer* principle to premodern times by replacing democratic law with a mythical concept of customs that are placed in Germanic prehistory: "Thus be valid again / our forefathers' custom: / The leader shall rise / from among the people" [So gelte denn wieder / Urväter Sitte: / Es steigt der Führer / aus Volkes Mitte].

The *Führer* poems repeated these motifs in many variations. Some sound tragically ironic after the Second World War — after fifty-seven million people were dead as a result of the war and the Nazi policy of physical extermination of their enemies that also left Germany devastated. For example, Hitler is compared to a great gardener in a poem by Eberhard Wolfgang Möller, while Herbert Böhme's poem "Der Führer" presents Germany as a drum and "he who beats the drum also leads" [der sie schlägt, der führt], a variation on the often used comparison of Hitler with a drummer boy. Other poems illustrate the quasi-religious and tasteless character of Nazi ideology and propaganda, such as the travesty of "Silent Night," written by Friedrich von Rabenau (1884–1945).

*Blood-and-soil poems*   Often nature poems were bellicose, because they expressed a blood-and-soil ideology that not only celebrated the earth and agrarian life in quasi-religious terms but also emphasized the battle in which the farmer defends the tilled soil from any enemy. Two lines from the poem "Deutschland" (Germany, 1937), by Heinz Steguweit (1897–1964), contain the quintessential definition of blood-and-soil ideology: "God has connected our blood / to the furrow that sustains us" [Gott hat unser Blut gebunden / an die Furche, die uns nährt]. Idealized images of the family, mother and father, and the role of woman as wife and childbearer emerged — as well as a Germanicized religiosity.

Kolbenheyer rhetorically admits to ideas that are "antiquated" [rückständig], implying that they represent the right values; after all, he only wants women to be women: "fertile / womb, nursing breasts, instinct / for family" [fruchtbaren / Schoß, nährende Brüste, Instinkt / für Familie]. The praise of the German mother includes an undercurrent of pornographic images, as in "Von Männern und Müttern" (Of Men and Mothers, 1938), by Friedrich Ludwig Barthel (1898–1962): "Mothers are always the same, and always lie the fields / Spread out and suffering the plough" [Mütter sind immer die Gleichen und immer liegen die Äcker / Breithin und dulden den Pflug]. The Nazi image of woman represented a dehumanization that did not reflect, as dehumanization did in Modernist literature, social conditions in the real world; on the contrary, this dehumanized image of the woman represented the Nazi ideal that was to contribute to making the world whole.

Another dimension of *Blut und Boden* was reached when racial ideology was supposed to lead to a new transcendence by retracing the Germanic bloodline back to a prehistoric age of Norse mythology. For instance, Gustav Frenssen wrote *Der Glaube der Nordmark* (The Belief of the Northern March, 1936), in which he celebrated National Socialism as a revival of an "ancient, proto-Germanic belief" [uralte, urgermanische Glaube]. In his opinion, Christianity was not only worthless but dangerous for the Germanic people. Therefore, he saw nothing wrong with turning away from Christianity; after all, Frenssen argued, Jesus himself had been nothing more than "a pious pagan" [ein frommer Heide].

Hans Friedrich Blunck explored Norse mythology, formally attempting to emulate the Homeric verse epic in *Sage vom Reich* (Legend of the Empire, 1941), in order to put Christianity (represented by "Krist" for Christ) and Germanic tradition ("Wode" for Wotan) into perspective in terms of the new empire that had begun with the defeat of 1918. The sonnet "An das Ich" (To the Self), by Hermann Burte, emphasizes a third path taken by the new German man. This path follows a "community" [Gemeinschaft] defined by the ideals of blood and soil — a path that is different from, but in suffering similar to, those of Krist and Wode. What counts in the end is the great individual: "True to oneself, until finally the pain carries him off / Like Krist on the cross and in the ash tree Wode" [Sich selber treu, bis endlich ihn die Pein rafft / Wie Krist am Kreuz und in der Eschen Woden]. The form of the sonnet flows toward the irrational conclusion of the sestet that ties together the great man, *Blut und Boden*, and the new Nazi myth. In the last line quoted, the cross-like structure of the chiasm reflects the "tragic" suffering of the self as the cross he has to bear.

*Literary quality*

Like other National Socialist sonnets, Burte's "An das Ich" stood the argument structure of the traditional sonnet on its head. While the latter worked by applying reason to solve a problem, the Nazi sonnet proceeded by presenting an issue that is resolved by an embrace of intoxicating irrationality. While irrationality in itself is neither bad nor the cause of low literary quality, the radical and complete reliance of National Socialism on irrationality is problematic, especially when a demanding form, such as the sonnet, is filled with propaganda slogans for Nazism. Burte's sonnet feels unbalanced, yet other literary devices, such as chiasm, are handled well. The literary quality of the Nazi canon is generally mediocre, but among the obvious examples of writers of high literary quality within the Nazi fold are Gottfried Benn (prose and poetry), Ernst Jünger (prose), Erwin Guido Kolbenheyer (prose), and Josef Weinheber (poetry).

Weinheber (1892–1945) wrote poems of a virtuosity that set them apart from most other lyrical production by writers loyal to the Nazi regime. His tone is less radical and "bloodthirsty"; however, his combination of subtle use of Nazi themes (hero, fate) and formal mastery was exhausted in imitating classical models, which he meticulously labeled (for example, as Alcaic stanza). The heroic fatalism of Nazism combined with Weinheber's melancholy mood to form an aesthetics whose normative demands have been called imperialist. The sonnet, for example, appeared to Weinheber as the embodiment of a firm order (as opposed to the power of reason). The resulting poems are an expression of political thought that aligned itself with the reactionary view of order and obedience. Consequently, Weinheber's poetry is an example of heroic formalism, the folkish-classicist ideal of Nazi art — a battle cry, after all.

In his last collection of poems, *Hier ist das Wort* (Here is the Word, 1947), written in 1944 before he committed suicide on April 8, 1945, there are indications that Weinheber had begun distancing himself from his involvement with National Socialism. The lines "Time, time betrayed me, / and therefore I bring charges" [Die Zeit, die Zeit verriet mich, / und darum klage ich an] are instructive. First, at a human level, they reveal Weinheber's denial of guilt, which is quite in contrast to Haushofer's acceptance of his guilt. Second, like so many other authors who either tried to compromise with the Nazis or who had second thoughts, Weinheber seems to be like the sorcerer's apprentice. Now he cannot handle the force of time, which he had previously invoked. It is legitimate to judge Weinheber by his own words, because he himself proclaimed that art itself provided the standards: "art is quiet and hard" [Kunst ist schweigsam und hart].

## Theater as Ritual

It is sometimes said that fascism is theater, but not even Nazi theater was just theater. It was real. What is usually referred to as an aesthetization of politics means, above all, that the Nazis staged politics; it was ultimately a theatricalization of politics. The Nazi mastery of theatrical aspects is evident in Leni Riefenstahl's staged film documentaries. The staging of the communal experience of the annual Nuremberg party rally maximized the effect of that community by delineating an inside realm of "us" and an outside realm of "them." Against the dark night sky, 130 searchlights at regular intervals created the "dramatic" effect of the "cathedral of light" [Lichtdom] by casting their beams vertically into the sky. In literary terms, the fundamental distinction between "us" and "them" in the Nazi worldview represented the conflict that underlies each drama as a driving force of the action. The theatrical presentation of party rallies enacted the heroic and tragic National Socialist view of the world. This was yet another reworking of the basic tenets of Nazism. In the combination of the heroic (the *Führer*) and the tragic (the racial war determined by *Blut und Boden*), the whole world was turned into a stage for the new myth that found its expression in the Second World War.

Given the domination of the theatrical in the official displays of the Nazi state, it is not surprising that the most ambitious attempt to create a genuine National Socialist literature was made in the realm of the theater. And given the Nazi self-image of being part of a profound and tragic era, it is also not surprising that Nazi theater would be dominated by the tragic. In addition to imitative classicism (especially in historical dramas) and plays that dealt with the fight of National Socialism to come to power (action drama), the major dramatic form was the *Thingspiel*, an innovation named after the Germanic word *thing* for a form of public trial as it was practiced by early Germanic tribes. Finally, given the Nazi mastery of orchestrating public events as theater, it is not surprising that the stage productions of Nazi plays were similarly effective. Nevertheless, the plays fell short of the expectations the Nazi regime had for them, and older dramas of the classical tradition retained their importance in German theater because they catered to middle-class tastes and because they allowed the Nazis to claim that tradition as well.

*Historical drama* Avoiding confrontation with modern problems meant that the Nazi drama could not deal with the modern world other than through the distortions of ideology. History was supposed to be rewritten to support the Nazi way of solving problems in terms of a racist and nationalist ideology. National Socialist drama expected as much complete identification with the action on stage as possible so that the sense of history would awe the audience into believing the Nazi vision of the German mission. Historical settings in periods that were considered parallel to the Nazi struggle to change Germany dominated. These included Norse mythology (as a representation of German prehistory), the Middle Ages (especially at the time of the imperial idea), and the Prussia of Frederick the Great. Examples include Paul Ernst's *Chriemhild* (1918) along with *Siegfried* (1934), by Ernst Bacmeister (1874–1971); Ernst's *Canossa* (1907) and Erwin Guido Kolbenheyer's *Gregor und Heinrich* (1934); as well as Ernst's *Preußengeist* (Prussian Spirit, 1914), *Vater und Sohn* (Father and Son, 1921), by Joachim von der Goltz (1892–1972), and the series of five dramas about Prussia written by Hans Rehberg (1901–1963) between 1934 and 1937.

Kolbenheyer's *Gregor und Heinrich* was praised by the Nazis as a prototypical historical play. The medieval conflict between the pope and the emperor pitted religious and secular rule against each other concerning the right to appoint bishops and whether the designation of a new pope needed the emperor's approval, but the Nazis understood the conflict as much more far-reaching in two respects. First, it juxtaposed the imperialism of the Roman Catholic Church and the German idea of the *Reich*, or empire, which was a central concept in how the *Führer* state with its blood-and-soil ideology should take political form. Heinrich's early exclamation "it's the hour of the empire" [es ist die Stund des Reichs!] reflects the historical self-image of National Socialism. Second, the confrontation between the Roman Catholic Church and the German empire was seen in racist terms; it was a battle between the Mediterranean and Northern Germanic races. The pope explicitly states not only the racial aspect but also the church's dependence on, and challenge by, Germany as the "fountain of a barbaric youth" [Borne einer barbarischen Jugend], which suggests the Nazi attempt to slowly replace Christianity.

History is experienced as continuous racial warfare, which the Nazis felt had progressed through a long series of conflicts to the final confrontation for which they were now preparing the German people. Heinrich acknowledges defeat as a means of political strategy, and the message is that Emperor Heinrich IV knows that in the course of history he will win, although he has to bow to the pope's political power in the specific historical situation. By the same token, Pope Gregor VII knows that by accepting Heinrich's show of penitence, he will lose in the long run. Indeed, in the end Heinrich states: "Powerful and strong has become the empire within me" [Mächtig ist in mir geworden und stark das Reich]. The play dramatizes one step in German history in the way it should be understood according to National Socialist doctrine;

therefore, the drama is dedicated "to the rising German spirit" [Dem auferstehenden deutschen Geist].

*Action drama*    The National Socialist action drama is often seen in the context of Expressionism, whose forms of presenting ecstatic emotions were now used to convey a message of the extreme political right. The connection to the Expressionist tradition and the thematic focus on the National Socialist revolution explain why the action drama is a phenomenon of the early phase after 1933. While the Nazis understood their rise to power as a revolution, they also declared the revolution completed, did not tolerate any true revolutionary tendencies, and even disposed of the inner-party opposition during the so-called Röhm putsch. In contrast to much of the Nazi self-image, the hero of the National Socialist action play displayed a revolutionary behavior that, after 1934, was not quite appropriate.

The most notorious and successful action drama was Hanns Johst's *Schlageter* (1933), which formulated the Nazis' intolerant inhumanity in dashingly brutal slogans, such as: "When I hear the word culture, I release the safety of my Browning" [Wenn ich Kultur höre, entsichere ich meinen Browning]. The poignant formulation and linguistic play are the play's strong point when they concentrate the Nazi message into quotable form; they are also its weak point when language has to make up for what is missing in an overly romanticized presentation of action and characters.

The presentation, while romanticized, is convincing within the drama's purpose of glorifying the rise of Nazism. Schlageter emerges as the first soldier of the Third Reich rather than being the last soldier of a lost war. This stereotyping puts Schlageter on a pedestal, exactly where the drama wants him. The speeches are enormously one-sided and at times stiff, but they usually flow well. Almost chilling is the scene in the second act where an unidentified high-ranking military commander (most likely a reference to the chief of the German army, General Hans von Seeckt) implicitly instructs Schlageter to join the resistance to the French occupation by explicitly warning him not to. The dramatic irony of Schlageter's failing to understand underscores the scene's effectiveness in putting his individual actions within the much larger context of the antidemocratic undercurrent of the Weimar Republic.

Schlageter's final words before his execution again illustrate the play's strong and weak points: "Germany!!! / Awaken! Catch fire!! / Blaze! Burn in immense glory!!" [Deutschland!!! / Erwache! Entflamme! / Entbrenne! Brenn ungeheuer!!]. The tradition of the Expressionist cry is obvious, but the passage also reveals how dramatic linguistic effects and a bloodthirsty rhetoric have to make up for content that is anemic because of its propagandistic one-sidedness. But contemporary audiences embraced the nationalist content, perhaps because it was based on true events.

A veteran of the First World War and a member of the extremist paramilitary *Freikorps*, Albert Leo Schlageter became involved in the resistance against French occupation of the Rhineland in 1923. He was arrested, tried, and executed amid international attempts to spare his life. He became an instant national hero. The drama's premiere on April 20, Hitler's birthday, was attended by Hitler and was considered a "national event," with an awed audience breaking out into singing the German national anthem and the Nazi anthem, the "Horst-Wessel-Lied."

*The* **Thingspiel**  With its open-air performances in front of mass audiences, the *Thingspiel* aimed at establishing a communal experience in the spirit of National Socialism. Therefore, this dramatic form has been considered the prime example of the aesthetization of politics that was typical of National Socialism. The Nazis referred to the *Thingspiel* as political worship and a trial of the *Volksgemeinschaft*, or community of the people, establishing a link to the historical form of the Germanic tribunal, the *thing*.

The *Thingspiel* also borrowed eclectically from traditions as ancient as Greek drama and as recent as the mass performances during the Weimar Republic. The main character was the German people itself; therefore, the dialogue was monologic and, similar to related forms of cultlike lyrical performances, such as the choric play, determined by a higher and unified will to power. This will was expressed by the chorus. Eventually, audience and actors were merged in the emotional dynamism of the *Thingspiel*; both the audience and the actors lost any individuality and were reduced to props of the will to power. Thus, forms of stage production of the Weimar Republic were deprived of their originally emancipatory function and were instrumentalized for Nazi propaganda. In the mass performance (a performance in Berlin in 1933 used 17,000 SA members as its cast and had an audience of 60,000), the choric tradition of the Weimar Republic was combined with parade and other mass elements of political rallies.

The dramatization of these aspects in the *Thingspiel* served to celebrate — and continue — the National Socialist revolution. The dramatic form of the people's tribunal promised to do justice to the people's troubles. While the concept of justice on stage unfolded as propaganda, the initial popularity of these plays reflected the actual need of the people to address the issues that were brought before the *Thing* on stage — for example, the effects of the First World War, such as loss of national pride and the perceived injustice of the Weimar Republic caving in to the conditions of the peace treaty. Therefore, history itself appeared to be a trial, whose sentence was the National Socialist revolution.

After a grass-roots beginning in 1933 and a short phase of official sponsorship starting in 1934, the *Thingspiel* lost its appeal to the audience and its official support around 1937. Like the action drama, the popularity of the *Thingspiel* had been connected to the promise of the National Socialist revolution. The SA, especially, had a stake in the continuation of that revolution, the "Second Revolution," which was supposed to divide up the power among the revolutionaries who had been passed over. But as early as 1934, Hitler declared the end of the revolution, and the influence of the SA, as an unwanted revolutionary remnant, was eliminated.

Also, the *Thingspiel* was too similar to the equally careful and theatrical mass orchestration of Nazi rallies. Albert Speer's monumental Nuremberg building for party conventions and the actual rallies held there were the ultimate *Thingstatt* (the open-air theater) and *Thingspiel*. The rally was less an involuntary parody of the *Thingspiel* (or vice versa) than an unproductive duplication of form and function. The rallies were the real thing: not just political theater but aestheticized politics mentally preparing the population to wage total war.

*Das Frankenburger Würfelspiel* (The Frankenburg Dice Game, 1936), commissioned from Eberhard Wolfgang Möller, one of the Third Reich's leading playwrights, for the cultural program of the 1936 Olympic Games in Berlin, is considered the high point of the *Thingspiel* movement. However, *Deutsche Passion* (German Passion, 1933), by Richard Euringer (1891–1953), established itself as a model for the *Thingspiel*. As an early example, it showed the development of the genre from the ritual of the *Totenfeier* (memorial service).

In the first scene of *Deutsche Passion*, the evil spirit, representing the democratic era according to Nazism, proclaims his victory, but the fallen soldier is willing to rise again to help the millions of unemployed: "I want to suffer it, the passion" [Ich will sie leiden, die Passion]. The soldier rises from a mass grave, wearing a crown of thorns made of barbed wire in a clear analogy to Christ. In the second scene the nameless soldier does not recognize Germany anymore and is told by a crippled veteran that "criminals and democrats" [Verbrecher und Demokraten] betrayed Germany during the war. In the third scene the evil spirit describes Europe as a whorehouse and, when the people complain, accuses the nameless soldier of being the guilty party.

In the fourth scene the people confront the soldier, but soon the evil spirit is identified with hatred, while the nameless soldier is identified with love. This identification reverses the political realities, in which Nazism (the soldier) is the creed of hatred. In the fifth scene the German people — represented by the crippled veteran, students, the unemployed, the businessman, the worker, the farmer, the priest, and the artist — cooperate to establish the German nation. In the sixth and final scene, the community of German people creates work for everyone. The nameless soldier reveals himself as the good spirit and ascends to heaven. The evil spirit has the last word, only to acknowledge his defeat by nationalism: "That's too much! Why don't you just expire! / This exists after all: A third empire!!?!!" [Das auch noch! Da zerplatz doch gleich! / Das also gibt's: ein drittes Reich!!?!!].

The literary model can be seen in Goethe's *Faust*, where Mephisto and the angels struggle over Faust's soul as the evil spirit and the good spirit struggle over the soul of the German people. The religious element was part of the Nazi staging, yet at the same time Nazi writers had to be careful that they did not evoke a sense of religion that smacked of Catholicism (of which both *Deutsche Passion* and the *Frankenburger Würfelspiel* were accused). The main goal of *Deutsche Passion*, however, was to create a communal experience, as the instructions at the beginning of the play make clear: "The listening people must be able to sing along" [Das hörende Volk muß mitsingen können].

### Fiction as Colonialism

The production of fiction during the Third Reich continued the tradition of the reactionary and antidemocratic popular novel. This continuation on the level of predominantly trivial stories was a result of the National Socialist avoidance of the problems of the modern world, which stands in opposition to the novel's principal orientation toward the social realm. The form and content of the novel of the Third Reich, however, led away from such an orientation, which would have been problematic for National Socialism.

The guiding principle of composition was, again, the *Führer* principle that underlay the National Socialist war novels, historical novels, and utopian novels that celebrated German grandeur in the colonization of the world or the idyllic life of the German farmer. Because the *Führer* figure aimed at making *Blut und Boden* ideology a reality, all novels are utopian and colonialist in spirit — even the historical novel, with which National Socialism attempted to colonize history by rewriting it in the image of Nazi stereotypes.

*Antidemocratic war novel* Ernst Jünger's phrase of "battle as an inner experience" [Kampf als inneres Erlebnis] describes the glorification of acts of war as heroic action and an intoxicating liberation, while ignoring the brutality and senselessness of the First World War with its new weapons of mass destruction, such as poison gas, tanks, and flame throwers. The glorification not only presented war as a biological necessity but also stressed war's utopian element as a magical national sacrifice that created the model of a true community in the sense of the classless camaraderie of the trenches. Although the utopian element regressed into dreams of a heroic past that never existed, it was crucial in the political mission of the antidemocratic war novels: behind the glorification of war there emerged the "new German man."

In the antidemocratic war novels of the late 1920s, the small unit of soldiers in the trenches becomes a total community; it absorbs the individual traits of its members into a reactionary and classless group identity, complete with all the life-sustaining functions of the family. The idealization of simple solutions was problematic because it was contained within a small and easily comprehensible group that could only be integrated with difficulty into larger units of the army or the country. Unconsciously, these novels described the psychology of soldiers who were not able to adjust to peace in the real world and often joined the notoriously brutal and reactionary *Freikorps* after the war.

The wide popularity of these novels can also be explained in part by their psychological appeal in terms of wish fulfillment and latent sadomasochism. The will to power as a fatalistic category appears to be the true subject of these novels; consequently, the individual identity is irrelevant in the face of the new German man's emergence from the camaraderie of the small group. This wish fulfillment, however, was possible only by way of sacrifice, both the sacrifice of individual identity in a subjugation to the group identity and sacrifice of life in the battle where death is beautiful and meaningful. The masochistic combination of pleasure and pain had a sadistic counterpart in the clear-cut concept of the enemy as so subhuman and savage that his ardent destruction is glorified as self-defense. The enemy was not only the soldier of the enemy army but also everybody in German society who did not truly belong to the German community, such as democrats, Communists, socialists, pacifists — and Jews.

Werner Beumelburg's *Die Gruppe Bosemüller* is a paradigmatic antidemocratic war novel. Most important is the focus on the bonding between the men. The novel portrays how, step by step, the military group replaces family bonds until leave at home is no longer relaxing because the male camaraderie of the trenches has become the true home of the men. This attraction to the group is irrational and instinctive, but without understanding it, the men feel that it is right. One of the group, Siewers, breaks down sobbing because he does not want to go home to his mother but would rather return to fighting. The group's irrational appeal is reflected in the awkward description of the comfort he receives: "Quietly, he allows himself to be held in Wammsch's arms, allows himself to be stroked by Wammsch's rough hands" [Er läßt sich ruhig von Wammsch in die Arme nehmen, er läßt sich streicheln von Wammschs harten Händen].

The bonding, however, had psychological reality for those who participated in the war because it was one of the few options for making sense of an utterly senseless environment. When the illusion of immediate and meaningful human interaction emerged in the extreme situation of war, it had a high degree of suggestiveness, especially for National Socialism, which conceived of itself as a warlike group poised for inevitable racial war. The platitude of the language in which Beumelburg offers the communal experience reveals the artificiality and shallowness of the new ideal.

Consequently, during the Weimar Republic the antidemocratic utopian element in reactionary novels was itself a declaration of war against democracy; during the Third Reich it served both to justify the Nazi revolution and to prepare for and sustain a total war. The only major change in literary production after 1933 consisted in the semi-official introduction of National Socialist criteria for war novels. Most important, Nazi war novels emphasized the *Führer* principle, celebrating the war hero as a born leader who is capable of galvanizing his men for the national cause. Similarly, the novels stressed the communal experience of war as an image of a true National Socialist community. Consequently, a Nazi war novel was a narrative narrowed down to a mere propagandist elaboration of political slogans exalting "One Nation, one People, one Führer" [Ein Reich, ein Volk, ein Führer].

The understanding of the war novels as part of the war effort was made explicit in the novels and in Nazi contemplation of literature. Several factors, which all found their ideological justification in *Blut und Boden*, were laid out to make the necessity of war self-evident: the German people needed more living space and had the right to take that space in Eastern Europe; ethnic Germans living in neighboring countries suffered under those countries' governments and should be brought back under German rule by extending German rule over those countries; it was a racial conflict that pitted the white (Aryan) race against the "Asiatic flood" of Bolshevism, and it was Germany's European mission to save the white race by uniting Europe under German control and by defeating Bolshevism.

After Germany started the Second World War in 1939, the war novel increased its propaganda function, to which mass-produced *Kleine Kriegshefte* (Little War Books) also contributed. They first celebrated the victories and later covered up the defeats of the German troops during the Second World War. In the same vein, reports were published by authors who were known for fiction, such as Edwin Erich Dwinger (1898–1981) and Josef Martin Bauer (1901–1970). Bauer contrasted the honest German soldier to the "soulless animality of those narrow-eyed Asians" [seelenlosen Tierhaftigkeit dieser schmaläugigen Asiaten].

*Historical novel*   National Socialist rewriting of history found a major outlet in the historical novel. As with the historical drama, special interest lay in the so-called threshold periods in German history that were perceived as similarly momentous in changing the direction of the German people as the National Socialist "revolution," including Germanic tribal society, the Middle Ages, fourteenth-century mysticism, and the Reformation and Thirty Years' War. The threshold periods also served to illustrate the *Führer* principle as a characteristic element of German history with great men, such as Arminius, Frederick the Great, and Bismarck, who at the same time could be used to justify Nazi expansionist goals in the biographical novel of *Führer* figures; examples include Blunck's *König Geiserich* (King Geiserich, 1936) and *Der Traum vom Reich* (The Dream of the Empire, 1940), by Mirko Jelusich (1886–1969). Among these periods, fourteenth-century mysticism and the Reformation were seen by the Nazis as expressions of a significant conflict between the dogma of the Roman Catholic Church and the German soul. A prime example is Erwin Guido Kolbenheyer's trilogy *Paracelsus* (1917–1926).

The historical figure of the physician and philosopher Paracelsus, whose teachings concerning natural remedies and a healthy lifestyle were shunned by the school medicine of the sixteenth century, was used by Kolbenheyer to create the biography of a Faustian character. Like Faust, the Paracelsus of Kolbenheyer's trilogy is on a search for true knowledge and faith that leads him to study magic and alchemy. Paracelsus leads a predominantly itinerant life, always fleeing gossip and official repression. Although he is isolated and misjudged by most people, he can rely on a small group of friends to the very end. He has mystical visions, but his search for the "new creature" [neuen Kreatur], or new man, remains unsuccessful. Still, toward the end of his life he is able to gain modest recognition. Above all, the visit to his father's grave fills Paracelsus with a "nameless peace" [namenloser Friede]. The sense of inner calm does not leave him even during the long illness that leads to his death in Salzburg. Before he dies, Paracelsus shares his vision of the totality of being: "There shalt all things be divided into goode and evyl, and yet be one with God in Heaven and Hell" [Do werdind all Ding gescheiden sein in Gut und Boes und dennocht eins sein mit Gott im Himmel und Hoellen].

The language, especially in direct speech, is deliberately archaic in an attempt to re-create the flavor of the language of the Lutheran Reformation, which was a movement contemporary with Paracelsus's life and one with which Paracelsus had contact. The description does not go beyond surface realism, even in the mystical setting of the short introductory chapter of each novel. In these introductory chapters, in a vague analogy to the "Prologue in Heaven" in Goethe's *Faust*, each of the three Paracelsus novels begins with an encounter between Wotan and Christ, providing the context in which the Paracelsus plot has to be understood — the context of the Nazi's failed attempt to reduce the influence of Christianity by reviving Germanic mythological concepts. The prologues are all set at night and progress from Advent to Easter and finally Midsummer Night. Never named, the characters are identified by their attributes: Wotan has only one eye, and Christ has the stigmata.

In the prologue to the first novel, Wotan and Christ are talking with each other as equals, although Christ has just returned to earth in the form of a beggar and is comforted by Wotan. He wants to lead the humans back to the right path from which Church dogma led them astray. Wotan warns Christ that they will only crucify him again. The setting is clearly identified as Germany, so Wotan is referring to the Germans when he says: "There is no people like this one that has no gods and forever demands to see the God" [Es ist kein Volk wie dieses, das keine Goetter hat und ewig verlangt, den Gott zu schauen]. Finally, they embrace — although their embrace looks as though they are struggling with each other.

The prologues to the other two novels, however, reveal that Wotan and Christ were not struggling with each other but against the German people. Kolbenheyer rewrites Christianity and Germanic mythology to make the point that each represents a form of religiosity that is no longer appropriate for the German people. After he becomes triumphant for a last time in the Reformation in the prologue to the second novel, Christ is dead in the prologue to the third novel. Wotan understands that Christ will not have the strength for another resurrection and gives him a final burial in the Alps. In contrast, Wotan cannot die, but he simply exists "always" [immer] and has no influence on the German people. Rather, it is his role to observe the German people, "the people of the center of blood" [das Volk der Blutesmitte], as it "must rise and fall like the high and low tides" [muß steigen und fallen wie Ebbe und Flut]. The National Socialist claim to racial self-determination of the German people and its religious implications provide the key to understanding Paracelsus as an expression of the German soul on the way to its racial (and racist) self.

*Utopian novel*  The National Socialist utopian novel centered on colonization. On the one hand, the concept of "inner colonization" derived from *Heimatkunst* and emphasized the ideology of blood and soil. On the other hand, the

Nazi dreams of world domination were expressed in visions of colonization, such as in the *Grenzlandromane* (borderland novels) or even popular utopian and science-fiction novels. These visions of colonization abstracted from real social problems to create an illusion of timeless validity. At the same time, they ultimately aimed at radically changing political reality: they prepared the German population for war.

The *Heimat-* and *Bauernroman* withdrew to the stereotypical symbol of antimodernity: the farm, where life followed the cycle of nature, not the demands of industrial production. Emil Strauß's *Das Riesenspielzeug* (The Giant Toy, 1934) and Hermann Stehr's trilogy *Das Geschlecht der Maechler* (The Maechler Clan, 1929, 1933, 1944) are examples of novels by reactionary authors who had been well established before 1933, but whose mystic and racist understanding of the German soul made them loyal to the Nazi regime and, in turn, favorite authors of the Nazis.

Other novels varied the same agrarian motifs, the fight for the German fatherland, and eventually the fight for fascism in a setting that supported expansionist tendencies by dealing with the lives of ethnic Germans abroad, often in the countries bordering on Germany. These *Grenzlandromane* were a literary mirror in which the political desire for eastward expansion met the description of the unjust treatment of hardworking Germans abroad who deserved to be rescued by Germany, thus justifying eastward expansion. The territories at issue ranged from countries that literally bordered Germany to the Soviet Union, where a relatively large group of ethnic Germans (usually referred to as Volga-Germans) lived. The settings of the novels span accordingly from Bohemia in *Die Brüder Tommahans* (The Tommahans Brothers, 1937), by Wilhelm Pleyer (1901–1974), to the Volga-German territory in *Volk auf dem Weg* (People on the Move, 1930–1942), by Josef Ponten (1883–1940). These novels are a typically German variation of the traditional colonial novel, to which German authors also contributed, writing especially about Africa.

Hans Grimm's *Volk ohne Raum* (People without Space, 1926) combined the agrarian ideals of the *Heimatroman* and the expansionist chauvinism of the *Grenzlandroman* with two other elements. First, it has a strong utopian element, less in the action of the novel than in the protagonist's teachings concerning Germany's future. Second, it shared the goal of colonizing Africa with colonial novels, from Gustav Frenssen's *Peter Moors Fahrt nach Südwest* (Peter Moor's Journey to the Southwest, 1906) to *Kinder der Steppe* (Children of the Savanna, 1935), by Hans Reepen (1887–?). While the idea of world domination was not in contrast to Nazism, the Nazis' initial goal was the German colonization of Eastern Europe, for which the title of Grimm's immensely popular book, indeed, supplied the phrase, because it describes the plight of the German people as a nation without space.

The four parts of Grimm's novel reflect the development of Cornelius Friebott, the protagonist, into a socialist and finally into a nationalist in four major steps, each step signified by the title of the respective part. From the experience of home and the spatial narrowness of Germany, Friebott moves to enlisting in the navy and seeing Africa for the first time (first part), to fighting in the Boer War in the foreign space of Africa (second part), to living in the German colonial space in Africa (third part), to visiting Germany and finally returning there after the First World War to preach his ideas about the nation without space (fourth part). The ideological conclusion that Friebott draws from his experiences and his readings is that the social question is a spatial question. The German people is simply a farming people, so it is wrong to industrialize Germany to feed a rising population. Since the conflicts in Germany are not caused by capitalist ownership of property but by simple lack of space, according to Friebott (and Grimm), socialism cannot solve the conflicts, while nationalism in the form of colonialist expansion can.

Grimm begins his book by setting the nationalist tone, literally, with the tolling of bells in the first paragraph. In the second paragraph he identifies the territory where the bells toll within the boundaries of Germany, as delineated in the fifth and sixth lines of the German national anthem's first stanza; this underlines the colonialist and nationalist connection when Grimm adds southern Africa to the list. The next few pages explain that everybody participates in the cycle of life as defined by agriculture, while only a few rely exclusively on farming for their livelihood. Friebott joins the navy for four years and then finds work in a mine until he leaves for Africa, where he works at odd jobs and tries his luck as a farmer; in between, he enlists in colonial military campaigns because of a vague sense of masculine duty.

In Africa, Friebott finds his belief confirmed that "the races, the white one and the colored one, must not mix if the white race is to prevail in its spiritual domination and its small yet irreplaceable human good of cheerfulness, objectivity, and mysticism" [die Rassen, die weiße und die farbige, sich nicht vermischen dürfen, wenn die weiße Rasse dauern sol (*sic*) in der geistigen Herrschaft und ihrem kleinen, aber unersetzlichen menschlichen Gute an Heiterkeit, Sachlichkeit und Mystik]. This concept mixes things that do not mix well: racism and humanism, objectivity and mysticism. After his return to Germany, Friebott's central speech culminates in his rhetorical questions uncovering the unjust suffering of a Germany that is kept small by its enemies and his assertion that change must come from the people who suffer.

The depth of argumentation and the superficial realism of the style hardly ever go beyond the quality of the passage excerpted above. Direct speech is stiff, and even where the action flows quickly, as in the description of the mining accident, the language remains conventional and plodding. A narrative twist, designed to lend authenticity, consists in the fact that a character named "Hans Grimm" appears in the third-person novel. He meets Friebott in Africa and later again in Germany. Roughly fifteen pages before the 1,279-page novel's end, the reader is informed that "in the month of Christmas, Grimm began writing the story 'A People without Space'" [Im Weihnachtsmonat fing Grimm die Erzählung "Volk ohne Raum" zu schreiben an], with Cornelius Friebott as protagonist. This twist does not constitute self-referentiality in the sense of Modernist complexity but is a variation of the framed story, or story within the story, that belongs to the nineteenth-century Realist tradition.

The development of reactionary and fascist utopian literature can be divided into three phases. First, during the years immediately after the First World War, utopian novels celebrated a return to monarchy in one way or another, for example, *1934: Deutschlands Auferstehung* (1934: Germany's Resurrection, 1921), by Ferdinand Eugen Solf (1876–1928), and *Bismarck II: Der Roman der deutschen Zukunft* (Bismarck II: Novel of the German Future, 1923), by Adolf Reinecke (1861–?). Second, during the stabilization of the Weimar Republic the reactionary utopian novel turned increasingly to myth, such as in *Deutschland ohne Deutsche* (Germany without Germans, 1929), by Hans Heyck (1891–1972).

The third phase began with the Nazis' coming to power and was marked by an optimism that was correlated to the idea of domination inherent in National Socialism that seemed to be coming true in the real world. For example, Titus Taeschner's novel *Eurofrika: Die Macht der Zukunft* (Eurofrica: The Power of the Future, 1938) revisited Hans Grimm's expansionist dreams and extended them into a racial science-fiction novel, where the final onslaught by subhuman Jews and their allies is averted only by the ingenuity of German engineering.

What is surprising, however, is how close Hans Dominik (1872–1945) was to the racist and mythical stereotypes of Nazism, because he is usually considered a mainstream science-fiction writer. He is the most successful German writer of science fiction. His fifteen novels sold a total of more than 2.5 million copies by the 1960s, about the time that his commanding influence on the new generation of German science-fiction writers started to wane. His novels typically centered on the struggle for world domination, and his heroes were German engineers. The achievements of technology, however, were not explained but, rather, mystified as early as his first science-fiction novel *Die Macht der*

*Drei* (The Power of the Three, 1922). The power consists in heat rays, harnessed from atomic energy, that are capable of melting airplanes and ships. It is also a power that is to be shared, and the plot is one of abuse of power, which is finally righted; however, it is set within a mystic realm of an ancient prophecy and the three rings of an old Tibetan abbot.

After 1933 Dominik's earlier works, which had emphasized global conflicts and the white race in general, fit seamlessly into the National Socialist literary canon; between 1940 and 1945 the sales of his books peaked, although he apparently did not receive specific sponsorship from the Nazis. Dominik's science-fiction novels written during the Third Reich centered on conflicts that were more specifically related to making the German fatherland stronger — for example, with a new island in the Atlantic in *Befehl aus dem Dunkel* (Order from the Dark, 1933).

The science-fiction novel, with its technical emphasis, at first seems to be the most difficult genre to integrate into the National Socialist literary canon. Science fiction, however, fit perfectly into the Nazi project of returning to a preindustrial world where science is really a craftsmanlike technology that has its source in the ancient currents of magic and racial myth but not in rationality. In real life this was the final goal toward which the *Führer* led the German people in a total war. In literature the irrational that is capable of subsuming technology in a rudimentary sense had been prepared as early as *Heimatkunst*. It would be more precise to refer to Nazi science-fiction novels as magical-technological novels. These novels — because the real-life dismissal of science was at the core of National Socialist ideology and its self-destructiveness — constitute the one literary genre in which Nazi ideology showed its true face most clearly.

# 6. Modernist Literature: The Many Voices of Defiance

THE MID-1930S WERE A TURNING POINT for Modernism because both Germany and the Soviet Union rejected Modernism in the official literature of the state. The National Socialist canon of literature became the favored form in Germany in 1933, and the 1934 decision by the ruling Communist Party of the Soviet Union prescribed the dogma of Socialist Realism for the literatures in its area of influence. These regulations affecting literary production went hand in hand with changes in the availability of literature to the reading public. In Nazi Germany, while authors were persecuted and books were banned, the greatly reduced, yet continued, presence of Modernism was important when Modernism was revisited by German literature after 1945. There were not only German literary developments within German Modernism that managed to coexist with National Socialism, but even international Modernist works, such as novels by William Faulkner (1897–1962), were still available, though they were increasingly difficult to find after the beginning of the Second World War.

Up to the 1930s, Modernist works had evolved in an interaction between reality, traditional modes, and the individual Modernist modes. Aestheticism had emphasized the power of the word, the Avant-Garde the power of action, and Ironic Realism the power of the story; as a result, Modernism had given rise to innovations, such as the prose poem, the epic theater, and the lyrical and psychological novel. These innovations were brought to their culmination during high Modernism in the 1920s. After 1930 great works were still published in this tradition, including Robert Musil's and Hermann Broch's ambitious novelistic projects, and written, such as Brecht's major plays in exile and magic realism inside Germany. Nonetheless, there were no new major Modernist innovations during these years. The emphasis on "Make it new!" — the driving force behind the Modernist quest for literary style and spiritual meaning — seemed exhausted. While this observation does not take away from the literary quality of the Modernist works that were written, it points to a paradigmatic shift concerning the role of innovation. In fact, the formal achievement of German Modernism of the 1930s and 1940s lay in adapting traditional forms to its specific needs.

## The Final Years of the Democratic Era

Earlier literary movements were still present. Hugo von Hofmannsthal's novel fragment *Andreas* (1932), written between 1907 and 1913, was published posthumously. Gerhart Hauptmann returned to his Naturalist roots with his play *Vor Sonnenuntergang* (Before Sunset, 1932). Because of his early opposition to the Wilhelmine empire, Hauptmann had developed into an elder statesman during the 1920s. Now seventy years old, Hauptmann published this tragedy whose plot (a variation of the *King Lear* plot that shows the demise of the bourgeois value system) is usually understood as a political warning against National Socialism. Nevertheless, during the Third Reich, Hauptmann allowed himself to be celebrated by the Nazis. Still, he withdrew into a secluded life, and his works of that period, especially his *Atrides* tetralogy (1941–1948), revealed his humanism.

The 1920s movement of New Objectivity and the tradition of Ironic Realism continued into the 1930s. As New Objectivity started to wane, some of its most typical and popular works were published, such as novels by Kästner and Fallada. Zuckmayer's and Horváth's adaptations of the *Volksstück* (folk play) also belonged in the New Objectivist context. Ironic Realism culminated in major novels by Austrian writers.

**Volksstück** Works by Carl Zuckmayer and Ödön von Horváth (1901–1938) exemplify the scope of the New Objectivist folk play, which was usually written in dialect but presented a more urban equivalent to the dialect comedies set in rural villages. Zuckmayer voiced his social criticism through an optimism that seemed to derive from his belief in indestructible humanism. In contrast, Horváth's social criticism combined with humanism to unmask the mentality and unconscious protofascist elements of the petty bourgeoisie.

While Zuckmayer's *Der fröhliche Weinberg* (The Merry Vineyard, 1925) was considered a triumph of New Objectivist drama, his best-developed and most successful play was *Der Hauptmann von Köpenick* (The Captain of Köpenick, published 1930, premiered 1931), subtitled *Ein deutsches Märchen in drei Akten* (A German Fairy Tale in Three Acts). Based on true events that happened in 1906, the play is an ironic fairy tale of a simple man's elevation to power, a short-lived success made possible by the politically dangerous mix of militarism, bureaucracy, and submissiveness. In the play Zuckmayer places great emphasis on establishing Wilhelm Voigt's motivation. Voigt is not a con artist but an ex-convict who has once done wrong and is caught now in a bureaucratic double bind: without proof of residency he is unable to get work, and without proof of work he is unable to get proof of residency. For his attempt to steal a passport, Voigt is sent to prison for ten years.

There he learns everything he can about the military, and after his release he uses his knowledge to outsmart the system. Dressed in an old army captain's uniform — the symbol of the power of militarism and the people's blind obedience — he takes control of a group of soldiers and then of the Köpenick city hall. But he fails to reach his goal; because the city hall does not issue passports, he cannot get one.

The irony of the play rests on the incongruity between the ex-convict in an old uniform and the effect the uniform has on people — an effect that reveals the people's mentality. The tailors in the play put this role of the uniform and of militarism into words. First, the statement "It's the better skin, so-to-speak" [Das is die bessere Haut, sozusagen] makes the uniform more important than the human who wears it. Second, the military hierarchy accentuates the inequality of Wilhelmine Germany, because the degree of humanness depends on the military rank: "the human being just begins at the rank of lieutenant" [der Mensch fängt erst beim Leutnant an]. Third, militarism is so pervasive that "the officer of the reserves is the open door" [der Reserveoffizier ist die offene Tür] to all important sectors of society. Finally, the concluding exclamation "Impossible!" [Unmöglich!], by Voigt, when he sees himself in the uniform for the first time in a mirror, acknowledges not only the play's major incongruity but also the social incongruity between humanism and blind obedience.

The satire is carried by the play's atmosphere of real life, just as Zuckmayer's interest lay with real people rather than with abstract ideas. Thus, Zuckmayer revealed with humor and humanity the Weimar Republic's dangerous fixation with militarism. Its ability to please an audience in the tradition of the illusionist theater accounted for the play's popularity. If seen as an early 1930s attempt to exorcise the evil spirits of militarism, however, Zuckmayer's play was not nearly as successful politically, for about a year and a half later Hitler became chancellor, and Zuckmayer went into exile.

Ödön von Horváth, too, was forced into exile; he was killed in 1938 by a branch falling from a tree under which he had sought shelter during a storm in Paris. From 1926 to 1936 he wrote seventeen plays, all of which he considered tragic, but he called them *Volksstücke* to stress his role as a chronicler of ordinary people's lives. His works went through a renaissance in the 1960s after they had been all but forgotten. *Geschichten aus dem Wienerwald* (Tales from the Vienna Woods, 1931, also the title of a waltz by Johann Strauss, which is played in the drama) is considered Horváth's most complex play. It is a melodrama with an apparently happy ending to Marianne's bitter disappointments with her involvement with the demimonde, which mirrors the (real or impending) social dislocation of the middle class to which she belongs.

Marianne is to marry the simple and outwardly good-hearted butcher Oskar, whom she has known since childhood. From the beginning, however, the connection with Oskar smacks of an arranged marriage because her father's toyshop is faltering and Oskar's business is secure. In an argument, Marianne calls Oskar an idiot, and the moment she sees Alfred, a good-for-nothing who is having an affair with the owner of the nearby tobacco store, she is attracted to him. On an outing to the Vienna Woods the following Sunday on the occasion of Marianne and Oskar's engagement, Valerie, who owns the tobacco store, seduces Erich, Marianne's cousin from Prussia, and Marianne falls for Alfred and throws the engagement ring in Oskar's face. He says that he will continue to love her.

The four scenes of the *Volksstück*'s first part foreshadow the catastrophe that is played out in the rest of the drama. Marianne has a child with Alfred; they put the child in the care of Alfred's mother; Alfred leaves Marianne, who is forced to take a job as a dancer, poses nude in a cabaret, and finally attempts a petty theft. When she is released from prison, Erich has left, and Oskar has mediated Alfred's getting back together with Valerie. Marianne reconciles with her father, and when the entire company arrives to pick up Marianne's son in the country, where Alfred's mother lives, they learn that the child has died of a cold (presumably of neglect that left the cold untreated).

Marianne's desperation does not bring her to an understanding of the causes of her misery, but she voices her pain clearly by accusing God of misleading her. The other characters show neither insight into their own social and moral displacement nor any true understanding of Marianne. Oskar's commitment to her sounds more like a threat: "I told you before, Marianne, you won't evade my love" [Ich hab dir mal gesagt, Marianne, du wirst meiner Liebe nicht entgehen]. Her giving in is, indeed, a giving up of any chance of having her own identity. As is typical of Horváth's plays, the characters' inability to gain insight into their own situation is used to expose the disillusionment and oppressive tendencies of the petty bourgeoisie.

*Austrian novels of the democratic era* The disintegration of the vast Austro-Hungarian Empire was strongly perceived as a decline of Western civilization. While Germany, for better or worse, had placed its dreams in future grandeur, in Austria the literary imagination was still focused largely on coming to terms with the deep sense of loss caused by the radical change in the cultural life and political role of the now small country. The old Austrian double monarchy, encompassing the *Kaiserreich* (empire) of Austria and the *Königreich* (kingdom) of Hungary, was often referred to by the initials *k. u. k. (kaiserlich und königlich*, or imperial and royal), which Musil used to dub the country "Kakanien" in his *Mann ohne Eigenschaften*. In a long list, Musil evokes Kakanien with affectionate irony as an often misunderstood country that was like any other, only without the excesses of other countries.

The important Austrian works after the First World War shared this focus, which made the decline of the old world a dominant theme. Joseph Roth is an author who experienced the political and social changes at a personal level as an irretrievable loss of his political home. His protagonists share a yearning for that past; they feel like expatriates, since they no longer live in the old Austria. *Radetzkymarsch* (Radetzky March, 1932) is Roth's major work. It describes the development of four (with emphasis on the last two) generations of the Trotta family as it intertwines with the Austro-Hungarian Empire from the moment when the fictitious Lieutenant Joseph Trotta saves the life of the young Austrian emperor Franz Joseph during the battle of Solferino in 1859 from a sniper's bullet and takes the bullet himself. Trotta is promoted and elevated to the nobility. This rise takes Joseph away from his rural roots, which are embodied by his father. Joseph's son dies the day the emperor is buried in 1916. Joseph's grandson, the last in the line of Trottas, had died even earlier, at the beginning of the First World War. In an ironic contrast to his grandfather's heroic saving the emperor's life, the grandson's death is the result of unnecessarily risking his life to get water for his soldiers.

*Radetzkymarsch* and its 1938 sequel, *Die Kapuzinergruft* (The Capuchin Crypt), which deals with Austrian history up to the Nazi annexation and thus the complete termination of the *k.u.k.* traditions, do not present an explicit political analysis; the reader has to derive such an analysis from the discrepancy between the characters' apolitical views and their demise through political events. Roth was critical of the *k.u.k.* tradition as a hollow way of life; he even mildly satirizes Joseph Trotta's decision to resign his post and become a farmer — a decision that would, on the surface, seem to be in keeping with the sentimental valorization of simple life or even blood-and-soil ideology. But Roth presents this move ironically as a retreat into pettiness: Trotta "became a small Slovenian farmer" [wurde ein kleiner slowenischer Bauer], who does not derive much satisfaction from his existence. On the other hand, especially in the 1938 sequel Roth idealized the outlived mode of the *k.u.k.* way of life, although the idealization can be seen primarily in contrast to emerging National Socialism.

The other two major Austrian novels of the democratic era also focused on the decline of the old world. Their experimental combining of plot and theoretical analysis made the novels of Robert Musil and Hermann Broch significant contributions to the Modernist tradition.

*Robert Musil's* **Der Mann ohne Eigenschaften**

Robert Musil's major work *Der Mann ohne Eigenschaften* is one of the most important Modernist novels. It was published in two parts in 1930 and 1933 during the author's lifetime, and a third part was published posthumously in 1943. The central topic — experiencing life in a decaying world and trying to find meaning — corresponded to the Modernist quest. The novel prefigured the demise of the bourgeois world through Nazism, but its setting is the Austrian monarchy before the First World War. While its similarities to all large cities are immediately pointed out, Vienna is named as the specific setting on the first page.

By the same token, action is not as important as the novel's essayistic structure and the texture of its individual components. The plot can be quickly summarized. The protagonist Ulrich is the man without qualities (or characteristics), who, ironically, does have certain qualities, such as his profession; however, these qualities appear insubstantial, so he decides to explore his potential. Generating the novel's underlying irony, Ulrich's participation in the planning of festivities in honor of the Austrian emperor's seventy-year reign to be celebrated in 1918 will be for naught, because — as author and readers know — Emperor Franz Joseph will have died in 1916, and the defeat in the First World War will put an end to the empire.

The irony is heightened because the celebration is planned in competition with a similar anniversary of the German emperor, which the First World War also makes obsolete, and because the planning committee attempts to define the Austrian mission, which turns out to be as elusive as Ulrich's attempts to define his own life. The world has fallen apart into too many separate pieces; it can no longer be brought to a point, and an individual can no longer understand his own life. At the beginning of the novel the thirty-two-year-old Ulrich cannot make up his mind when he starts decorating his new home, a mansionlike little palace. He begins dreaming, gives up, and puts himself at the contractors' mercy; whatever they deliver, he uses. In a similar way Ulrich's life remains undefined, because definition implies a sense of reality, or *Wirklichkeitssinn*, which is founded on knowing boundaries and having basic convictions — all values embodied by Ulrich's sixty-nine-year-old father; in contrast, Ulrich has a sense of possibility, or *Möglichkeitssinn*.

A sense of possibility opens up multiple options. If Ulrich thinks about boundaries, it is to dissolve them. This is typical of the essayistic approach, which Ulrich, the mathematician, takes to everything, even his profession. For him, mathematics is a science, but it also has a magical side; it is "a ceremony of the highest power of heart and brain" [eine Zeremonie von höchster Herz- und Hirnkraft]. In such an interaction of rationality and irrationality, possibilities emerge and, with them, a utopian element — the antidote to "man's enormous loneliness in a wasteland of fragments" [das ungeheure Verlassensein des Menschen in einer Wüste von Einzelheiten].

From the utopian thought follows the experiment of observing life itself in a typical Modernist fusion of exactitude and uncertainty, courage and involuntary ignorance of life. Ulrich understands himself not as defined by any given reality but as a man without qualities (or characteristics), that is, as a potential man in terms of his possibilities. The best way to explore one's potential is by means of hypothesis, which Ulrich connects with the concept of the essay. Ulrich feels that he has to approach life "like an essay, in the sequence of its parts, considers an object from many sides without fully comprehending it" [wie ein Essay in der Folge seiner Abschnitte ein Ding von vielen Seiten nimmt, ohne es ganz zu erfassen]. The meaning of essay in this endeavor, then, involves the unique shape that the inner life of a human being takes. Ultimately, Ulrich's utopian essayism leads to his preferring the history of ideas to the history of the world.

Ulrich's essayism is also descriptive of Musil's own writing endeavor. Both assume a principal difficulty in describing the world, a difficulty that results from the crisis of rationality. As a result, the novel — and, with it, Ulrich himself — has become impossible to narrate. If epic is defined as a simple order of clear chronological events, then Musil's *Mann ohne Eigenschaften* no longer has the fundamental epic quality, despite the omniscient and ironic narrator. The epic structure of the novel has been redefined in terms of the protagonist's problems in dealing with the world: essayism instead of action.

Ulrich's thoughts have become so complex that it is difficult for him to make simple decisions. Furthermore, the novel is centered on Ulrich, in the tradition of the lyrical novel; the people with whom he interacts are as much characters of the real world as they are personifications of Ulrich's own potential. Characters on the planning committee also represent options for escaping the increasing complexity of thought: war (General Stumm), strong leadership (Arnheim, a literary giant, patterned after Walther Rathenau), and irrationality (Meingast, a false prophet, patterned after Ludwig Klages). All the characters in the novel are incomplete in some respect. In their search for completeness, they all seem to gravitate toward Ulrich, who is not just the protagonist without properties, but the novel's center of attention and attraction.

The connection of the novel's characters to Ulrich receives a theoretical foundation in the presentation of the relationship between Ulrich and his sister Agathe. Their incestuous attraction reflects their "shadowlike duplication" [schattenhafte Verdoppelung] in terms of Ulrich's utopian project as an attempt to bridge the difference between the visible and invisible world. This attempt had been at the center of

Musil's attention as early as 1906 in his first novel, *Die Verwirrungen des Zöglings Törless*. Ulrich's speculations about the possibility of a "seraphic love" [seraphische Liebe] give way to his attempt to live the myth of the androgynous being from Plato's *Symposium* (about 380 B.C.). After the gods divided the whole human being into man and woman, who now strive to restore that wholeness, the real problem is, according to Ulrich, that "nobody knows which one of the many halves that are running around is the missing one" [Kein Mensch weiß doch, welche von den vielen herumlaufenden Hälften die ihm fehlende ist].

Ulrich's close bond with his sister, whom he only now really gets to know since they grew up separated from each other, evokes other mythical patterns, such as Isis and Osiris. Ulrich and Agathe refer to this bond as one between twins, even Siamese twins, although they are not biological twins. Their love is a possibility that, as Ulrich defines it, is tied to specific circumstances. Once detached from these circumstances by a withdrawal of brother and sister from their environment, the possibility has a utopian potential, which encompasses an irrational element in addition to Ulrich's previous essayistic attempts that were rational. This love, which fails, is not an immoral impossibility but an expression of the Modernist search for style and meaning. In other words, the love of brother and sister stands for overcoming all conflicts, like Thomas Mann's myth in the *Joseph* tetralogy (1933–1943). *Der Mann ohne Eigenschaften* is a culmination of this quest, where the mode of searching is more important than the goal. Therefore, Ulrich's and Musil's essayism is not the goal but the style of the search. Nevertheless, essayism contains the possibility of meaning; at least, it provides artistic unity to the wildly branching novel with its many digressions and subplots (including one involving a pathological murderer).

The unity is fragmentary because the novel itself remained fragmentary. It is assumed that the novel was intended to encompass four parts. The first book publication included the first two parts, which present the issues to which the following two parts suggest solutions. The second book publication presented the third part; the final fourth part, however, was never completed. Because of the way the novel grew — Musil kept revising, as though the style of essayism prevented closure — it remains open as to how everything would have played out.

**Hermann Broch's**
**Die Schlafwandler**
The novels of Hermann Broch's trilogy *Die Schlafwandler* (The Sleepwalkers, 1931–1932) trace specific stages in the "Zerfall der Werte" (decay of values), a phrase Broch used as the title of the epilogue to the last novel in the trilogy. Without values, he saw the existence of the world as endangered. The First World War, as the climax of illogic, proved to Broch that this danger was real. The

historic stages in the development in Germany that the Austrian Broch described were the ones that he saw leading to the war: romanticism, anarchy, and objectivity. The dates that he attributed to his novels span the years 1888 to 1918, which correspond to the reign of German emperor Wilhelm. Each stage is exemplified by the respective protagonist's behavior in one of the three novels: *1888: Pasenow oder die Romantik* (1888: Pasenow, or Romanticism, 1931), *1903: Esch oder die Anarchie* (1903: Esch, or Anarchy, 1931), and *1918: Huguenau oder die Sachlichkeit* (1918: Huguenau, or Realism, 1932). This development found its formal expression in moving from a conventional narration in the first two novels to the open form of the third one.

The protagonist of the first novel, the young officer Joachim von Pasenow, already experiences the decay of values, which leads to self-deception, including the protagonist's repressed sexuality, and his search for a simple world, a process Broch identifies with romanticism. The protagonist of the second novel, the bookkeeper Esch, is driven by desires that will lead to failure, hence the stage of anarchy. In the third novel the protagonist, the businessman Huguenau, suffers like Musil's Ulrich from man's enormous loneliness in the wasteland of fragmented reality. Huguenau surpasses the protagonists of the two previous novels, who reappear in the third novel: Pasenow goes mad, an end becoming to a romantic; Esch is murdered by Huguenau, an end becoming to an anarchist; and Huguenau adapts to the new value system as a realist. But as a murderer and an opportunist, he is part of the fragmentation of reality and thus participates in the decay of values.

Broch's *Schlafwandler* attempted more than a portrait of the decay of values; as a Modernist novel, it aimed at creating a new center. Its process of mythmaking was typically Modernist. It took the relative truths that it found in the complex and fragmented world and elevated these relative truths to the level of the absolute. While this was the task of Modernist art, art itself is not absolute. According to Broch, however, art presented the "closest approximation to the idea" [größtmögliche Annäherung an die Idee] of totality. This in itself was the great achievement of Modernist literature in the era of the decay of values.

In the epilogue to *Huguenau*, the novel's participation in the Modernist quest is stated by referring to the ideal center of values that defined the Catholic Middle Ages. But that center had been lost, and the totality had been replaced by a variety of partial systems. The final unit of the decay of values was the human individual, who in his isolation and freedom from values also became the victim of irrationality, and eventually, as in the First World War, the "hangman of a world" [Henker einer Welt]. In his desperation, man is likely to wish for a strong leader, who would, however, not be able to make a difference.

Broch's argumentation, like Musil's essayism, is interconnected with the novel's plot; at the same time, it is at an abstract level of theorizing about historical events. *Die Schlafwandler* is not unlike the theoretical discussion by Max Horkheimer and Theodor Adorno, who argue that Enlightenment thought will necessarily revert to myth. Broch understood this in terms of his concept of the "polyhistoric novel," which encompasses all levels from the unconscious to the conscious, including theorizing. But the novel's specific position on the power of love and the principle of hope — which it shares, for instance, with Thomas Mann's *Zauberberg* and *Joseph* tetralogy — suggests not a criticism of Enlightenment but rather an attempt to save the Enlightenment project of rationality by means of a typically Modernist fusion of rationality and irrationality, of logos and myth; as a result, the novel's epilogue ends by evoking the myth of the logos. In utter isolation and darkness a timid voice that connects the past with the future is heard "in the silence of the logos yet is carried by it" [im Schweigen des Logos, dennoch von ihm getragen]: "it is the voice of man and of the peoples, the voice of comfort and of hope and of immediate kindness: 'Do not do any harm to yourself! for we're all still here!'" [es ist die Stimme des Menschen und der Völker, die Stimme des Trostes und der Hoffnung und der unmittelbaren Güte: "Tu dir kein Leid! denn wir sind alle noch hier!"].

This passage illustrates two fundamental differences between Modernist and antimodern texts of the 1930s. The content of Broch's novel is determined by a humanistic attitude; the aesthetics is one of love and hope, not of hatred. And the linguistic structure — its rhythm and its abstract level — defined literary quality, as opposed to the flat surface realism and pseudo-profound thought that is characteristic of the National Socialist literary canon.

### Authors in Exile

Long before 1933, Modernist writers, such as Toller, Tucholsky, Kaiser, and Kästner, had taken aim at growing nationalist and reactionary sentiments in Germany. It came as no surprise that Modernism, when it was forced into exile after 1933, continued its criticism of National Socialism. At the same time, Modernist writers focused on their situation in exile, often aesthetically refracted as a historical narrative or drama, much in the same way that the current political circumstances in Germany were approached in literary works. In contrast to Modernism inside Nazi Germany, however, lyric poetry did not play as great a role in exile as did prose and drama.

*Lyric poetry*    Thematically, exile poetry often centered on the poet's personal experience of suffering and the Nazi terror in Germany. Louis Fürnberg (1909–1957) and Erich

Weinert (1890–1953) continued writing political poems, while poems by other authors, such as Max Herrmann-Neiße (1883–1941) and Franz Werfel, often displayed a tone of lament. Yet Werfel's main contribution to exile literature was not in poetry. Still, there were a good number of poets of all generations who searched for opportunities to publish, such as in collections by the Austrian Centre in London, whose *Mut: Gedichte junger Österreicher* (Courage: Poems of Young Austrians, 1943) included poems by Erich Fried (1921–1988), as well as by Jura Soyfer (1912–1939), who was arrested when he attempted to go into exile; he died in a concentration camp. Other important lyric poets in exile included Else Lasker-Schüler, Karl Wolfskehl, Yvan Goll (who after 1933 wrote mostly in French), Paul Zech (1881–1946), Hans Sahl (1902–1993), Walter Mehring, Stephan Hermlin (1915–1997), Johannes R. Becher, and Nelly Sachs.

Nevertheless, Bertolt Brecht's assessment is right: exile from Nazi Germany was not conducive to writing poetry; these were "bad times for poetry" [schlechte Zeit für Lyrik]. Ironically, it was the poetry that Brecht wrote during exile that represented a culmination of narrative and politically didactic poems, especially in his collection *Svendborger Gedichte* (Svendborg Poems, 1939). In the last poem of this collection, addressed to those born after him ["An die Nachgeborenen"], Brecht acknowledges that life goes on in the apparently privileged situation of exile, but that fact does not affect the need to fight: "What kind of times are these that / A conversation about trees is almost a crime / Because it includes being silent about so many atrocities" [Was sind das für Zeiten, wo / Ein Gespräch über Bäume fast ein Verbrechen ist, / Weil es Schweigen über so viele Untaten einschließt]. The poems in the collection range from satirical attacks on the Nazis to analyses of capitalist exploitation as the root of all evil (which, according to Communist theory, eventually led to the Nazis being able to seize power).

In "Schwierigkeit des Regierens" (The Difficulties of Governing), Brecht satirizes the pompous self-aggrandizement of the Nazi regime, which portrayed itself as necessary for everything to function properly: "Indeed, it is quite questionable / Whether the sun would rise in the morning / Without the Führer's permission, and if it did, / It would be in the wrong place" [Ja, ob die Sonne früh aufginge / Ohne die Genehmigung des Führers / Ist durchaus fraglich, und wenn, dann / an der falschen Stelle]. Brecht's satiric intent is to expose the Nazi lies about how the people are exploited. He makes this intent clear by ending the poem with the question of whether the real difficulties of this kind of government do not originate in the fact that such exploiting and lying have to be learned. This is, of course, a rhetorical question, because it provides the answer in question form.

In his best poems Brecht engages the reader in a more active role. Two of his most famous poems, "Fragen eines lesenden Arbeiters" (Questions of a Worker While Reading) and "Der Schneider von Ulm" (The Tailor of Ulm), are included in *Svenborger Gedichte*. "Fragen eines lesenden Arbeiters" formulates a series of questions that are more suggestive than rhetorical; the answer is not clearly provided, placing the reader in the worker's shoes. The worker reads a history book, and the list of glorious victories or tragic defeats of great men seems to leave out most of real life, which is the life the worker knows. Like the worker, the reader has to figure out what has been left out and why. The second half of the poem poses questions, such as: "Young Alexander conquered India. / He alone? / Caesar defeated the Gauls. / Did he not even have a cook by his side?" [Der junge Alexander eroberte Indien. / Er allein? / Cäsar schlug die Gallier. / Hatte er nicht wenigstens einen Koch bei sich?]. These questions provide their own answers: these great men were not alone. But the real question — "Who picked up the tab?" [Wer bezahlte die Spesen?] — and its political consequences remain for the reader to contemplate.

Brecht's answer is suggested by juxtaposing the evoked reports of the great men's deeds and the explicitly stated questions. In the Marxist theory of history, humankind progresses from one social system that is defined by exploitation (the slaveholding society under Alexander and Caesar) to the next, until all antagonisms are resolved in an ideal Communist society. In the poem the worker is on the brink of gaining insight into these patterns of history and of understanding the historical differences in the exploitations described in terms of specific class antagonisms. The worker then can transfer his insight to his present situation and understand it in terms of the exploitation of the working class by the capitalists, who own the means of production.

Brecht's poetry, like his other works, was inherently tied to his political convictions, which his poems communicate effectively. The simplicity of the language and the easygoing rhythm emulate colloquial speech, which hides the poems' artfulness and makes them immediately accessible. They are most effective where the reader is challenged the most. For example, "Der Schneider von Ulm" proceeds even more subtly than the poems that pose rhetorical and suggestive questions. Brecht uses the historical event of a tailor who was killed in an attempt to fly by donning wings and jumping from the church roof in the city of Ulm in 1592. The bishop's opinion, repeated in the refrainlike second and fourth stanzas, not only summarizes the tailor's failure but by way of the generalization, "No man will ever fly" [Es wird nie ein Mensch fliegen], invites the reader's contradiction. The poem's ironic historical incompleteness — suggested by leaving out the modern technology that makes flight possible — is also an aesthetic and political incompleteness that the reader has to fill in by supplying the "missing" final stanza himself or herself.

Modernist texts often provide textual gaps that they allow the individual readers to fill, within the limits of the possible interpretations supported by the text in question. Because reader (or audience) participation is at the core of Brecht's work, it is for the reader to agree or disagree with the opinions, and interpretations of Brecht's works vary. While it might be possible, however, to derive meanings that are not Marxist (but, for example, existentialist), nonpolitical interpretations are most likely not supported by the text and say more about the interpreter. Brecht's exile poetry represents the best of his own lyrical production, as well as that of German exile literature, although these years, as Brecht points out, were bad times for poetry, but it was Hitler's speeches that horrified Brecht into writing poems — against Hitler.

*Historical novel* Prose literature written during the exile years can be thematically divided into two groups. In the first group are works that focused on the situation of exile itself, such as Anna Seghers's *Transit* and Klaus Mann's *Der Vulkan,* or that dealt with the situation in Nazi Germany that made going into exile necessary, such as Seghers's *Das siebte Kreuz.* The second group encompasses works that approached the same issues by way of historical analogy.

The category of "history" is problematic for literature. A novel that deals with contemporary conflicts is involved with history as soon as these conflicts do not evolve in a fictitious "now" but are conflicts of the *Zeitgeschichte* (contemporary past). In this case, such as with Heinrich Mann's *Der Untertan* or Thomas Mann's *Der Zauberberg,* the present is treated in a historical perspective as a matter of storytelling. This suggests an almost uncritical self-evidence of the description and explanation of the present in terms of the contemporary past. Whenever the barrier from contemporary past to actual historical past is crossed, such self-evidence is lost, and the treatment of history has become problematic within the fictional realm.

The much-debated theoretical problem of historical fiction concerns the connection of present and past; it is exemplified by the vastly different uses of the historical novel by National Socialism and by Modernism. The question was not simply whether the historical novel was used to justify and even glorify the present (as in works of the Nazi literary canon) or whether it was used to explore options of the present and attempt to change it. The question was whether a historical novel, regardless of its goal, could not help but justify the present. The reasoning behind this question was that suggesting a model from the past for the present would blur any difference and make the connection of past and present appear to be eternal recurrence — a paralyzing experience that caused Nietzsche's Zarathustra to undergo a nervous breakdown. The vicious circle of the eternal return led to the breakdown of the historical novel as an instrument for using a historical scenario to understand and change the present; the logical conclusion seemed to be that the historical novel was necessarily escapist.

Assuming such a breakdown of historical fiction's emancipatory potential is itself ahistorical. A historical novel can be — and Modernist historical novels often were — ahistorical in a positive sense; they did not assume a historical model to understand the present; rather, they used a historical guise for present issues. The novel, then, really never was about the past but always about the present, and its emancipatory potential did not depend on the power of its historical analogy but solely on its critical power to analyze the present (in whatever guise). Furthermore, where the historical novel took the past to be a model for the present, the novel could overcome the problem of the eternal recurrence in two basic ways. First, as Heinrich Mann did in his two-part history of the French King Henri IV, the historical counterimage of the human king versus the implied present inhuman dictator emphasizes difference over recurrence (even if this were understood as an eternally recurring conflict between good and evil, it would not necessarily be fatalistic). Second, as Thomas Mann demonstrates in his *Joseph* tetralogy, historical fiction could confront the issue of repetition head-on and find a solution in the paradoxical nature of repetition itself, for repetition includes the very element that it seems to deny — change.

The 1930s and the first half of the 1940s saw such a flood of historical fiction that it seems as though almost all exile writers wrote works of this kind. Lion Feuchtwanger wrote several historical novels, including the *Josephus* trilogy (1932–1942), about the Jewish historiographer Flavius Josephus. So did Alfred Döblin, with his *Amazonas* trilogy (1938–1948), and Hermann Kesten (1900–1996), with *Ferdinand und Isabella* (1936) and *König Philipp der Zweite* (King Philip the Second, 1938). The main achievements in the realm of historical fiction, however, were the aforementioned works by Heinrich and Thomas Mann, although Franz Werfel's *Das Lied von Bernadette* (The Song of Bernadette, 1941), translated into English in 1942, was a great popular success and well known through its cinematic version (1943).

In addition to dealing with average men, Modernist texts also dealt with great men in order to debunk the myth of the Great Man by embedding him in the context of social responsibility and of the collective. In his novels *Die Jugend des Königs Henri Quatre* (Young Henry of Navarre, 1935) and *Die Vollendung des Königs Henri Quatre* (Henri Quatre, King of France, 1938), Heinrich Mann presents the French king as central in bringing peace to a France torn by religious strife.

Despite his greatness the king is presented on a human level and has limitations. His decisions arise out of skepticism and humanism, qualities lacking in the reactionary image of the Great Man. Moreover, Henri IV is not led by his humanism to a sterile and self-defeating sense of tolerance but encouraged by it to take a firm stand that, nevertheless, allows for compromises and failures.

While myth became completely irrational in National Socialism, Modernism was a fusion of rationality and irrationality, in which myth could represent either the fusion or the irrational side. Thomas Mann went one step further by reclaiming myth not only from National Socialism but also reclaiming it for rationality. In a speech about his massive reworking of the biblical story of Joseph, Mann explained in 1941 that Joseph's early exuberant subjectivity is brought back into the collective, where the contrast of individual and collective is resolved in a mythical realm, just as Mann wished to see the modern contrasts of individual and collective, of artist and bourgeois, resolved in the realm of democracy.

In the novels Mann presents his concept of myth as something that happens in the lives of all individuals as a process of imitation "that views the task of individual existence as filling in given forms with the present and as letting them be flesh again, a mythical pattern founded by the fathers" [die die Aufgabe des individuellen Daseins darin erblickt, gegebene Formen, ein mythisches Schema, das von den Vätern gegründet wurde, mit Gegenwart auszufüllen und wieder Fleisch werden lassen]. Central to this myth, however, is rationality. Joseph evolves from a narcissistic boy who imitates God to a rational and intellectual adult who repeats the mythical pattern of divine revelation when he reveals his identity to his brothers. The difference lies in the fact that the latter mythical pattern is applied consciously; therefore, it is not a matter of emotion and irrationality but of rationality. Furthermore, it implies that the pattern has already been changed; simply being conscious of the pattern adds an element to the myth's repetition that did not exist before. Finally, changing the myth in that way makes change itself become possible, and new elements are capable of emerging. This is how Joseph achieves a new sense of social responsibility.

This paradoxically timeless, yet changing, concept of rational myth fits well into Mann's complete oeuvre. It is not only similar to the use of myth in *Der Zauberberg*, but Joseph's conscious repetitions of myth are related to the "as if" attitude, with which the artist-heroes of other works by Mann do not fully participate in bourgeois life but merely repeat aspects of it. Embedded in a complex narrative that integrates discussions of myth and of the limits of storytelling, the rational myth gives an artistic coherence to the tetralogy, from the first novel, *Die Geschichten Jaakobs* (The Stories of Jacob, 1933), which provides the

208 • Before 1945: Fascism

prehistory to Joseph's story and introduces the concept of imitating a myth, to the last one, *Joseph der Ernährer* (Joseph the Provider, 1943), which presents Joseph's final triumph as the savior of Egypt and of his brothers and father from famine.

The positive vision that is upheld in the fourth novel by Joseph's sense of social responsibility was most likely so strong as a result of Mann's experiences with democracy in the United States under Franklin Roosevelt's New Deal. This understanding of the novel puts into perspective the claim that National Socialism dominated all German literature. During the 1930s to the mid-1940s, Modernist German literature obviously responded to Nazism, but its environment was its own Modernist literary tradition, as well as the democratic tradition of the Western world.

*Theater and drama* During the exile years the connection between theater performances and the writing of drama increasingly deteriorated. With German-language theaters closed to exile authors — with the exception of theaters in Switzerland, especially the Zurich Playhouse, and a few small and often short-lived theaters abroad — there was virtually no opportunity for performing the approximately seven hundred German plays written in exile.

The division of exile literature into two groups also applies to drama. First, there were the plays that tried to expose the brutality of Nazism, such as *Professor Mamlock* (1934), by Friedrich Wolf (1888–1953), and Ferdinand Bruckner's *Die Rassen* (The Races, 1933), or that dealt with the exile situation, such as Wolf's *Die letzte Probe* (The Last Test, 1946). Second, the historical drama was represented by Bruckner's *Napoleon der Erste* (Napoleon I, 1936) and Wolf's *Beaumarchais* (1941). Many of the playwrights, even Ödön von Horváth, Franz Werfel, Georg Kaiser, and Walter Hasenclever, made formal compromises and wrote entertaining plays for commercial theaters, trying to reach a wider audience. This did not mean that quality was completely compromised, nor did it mean that these plays were uncritical. Rather than exposing the Nazi crimes in a serious setting, Nazi self-aggrandizement and contradictions were exposed to laughter.

An important example of the anti-Nazi comedy is Franz Werfel's *Jacobowsky und der Oberst* (Jacobovsky and the Colonel) because of its success on Broadway. It was written between 1941 and 1942, and in 1944 it premiered first in English in New York and then in German in Basel, Switzerland; in 1958 it was turned into a movie, *Me and the Colonel*, starring Danny Kaye and Curd Jürgens. The play juxtaposes the Polish Jew Jacobowsky and the colonel of the defeated Polish army

MODERNIST VOICES • 209

as unlikely allies against the common enemy: the German occupation forces in France. As the result of several complications, mostly caused by the colonel's stubborn sense of honor and overcome by Jacobowsky's wit and ingenuity, the colonel grows to appreciate Jacobowsky and revises his anti-Semitism. In the end Jacobowsky is allowed to board the English submarine that will take him and the colonel to safety.

The play was criticized for emphasizing comedy while forcing the tragedy of Europe in general, and the fate of the Jews in particular, into the background. Such criticism, however, is political, not aesthetic. It misses the point because Werfel used the interaction of politics and aesthetics creatively, as indicated by the ironic subtitle: *Komödie einer Tragödie* (Comedy of a Tragedy). This duality points to the existence of the horrible just beneath the surface of the play, and the horrible is barely averted from happening to the little group of four people. Exile itself, however, was at least a partial triumph over the Nazi terror and was sustained by the hope of driving the Nazis from power. This hope needed to be kept alive as much as the Nazi terror needed to be exposed.

The play's achievement as a tragicomedy is based on its presenting the fragility of resistance. Jacobowsky is called an optimist, but this designation is qualified by his typical behavior of wishing for the best, yet also preparing for the worst. As he goes into the final scene, he has two bottles — one with pills for seasickness if he makes it on board the vessel, the other with poison if he does not. The conflicts caused by anti-Semitism are not resolved either. The colonel slaps him on the shoulder, reminding him that their duel has only been delayed; Jacobowsky responds: "Our duel is eternal" [Unser Duell is ewig]. Such constant reminders of the underlying tragedy make the comedy of Werfel's play stronger and more realistic.

*Bertolt Brecht*     Any drama like Werfel's play that was written in the tradition of the illusionist theater encountered difficulties because its basic concepts had become problematic. Brecht's anti-illusionist theater proved to be a particularly appropriate response to these problems. Between 1938 and 1945 Brecht wrote the main plays of his epic theater, which also represent the high points of exile drama, including *Leben des Galilei* (Life of Galileo, 1943) and *Mutter Courage und ihre Kinder* (Mother Courage and Her Children, 1941), which he began writing in 1938 and 1939, respectively.

To debunk the image of the Great Man, Brecht went further in his portrayal of Galileo in *Leben des Galilei* than Heinrich Mann did in his depiction of the French king in *Henri Quatre*. Brecht continued to revise the play to communicate his interpretation of history more clearly.

Brecht takes pains to explain to the audience the significance of Galileo's physics for the common people at the time. The new theory of physics is based on a world in motion, which suggests, by extension, a changing society. Therefore, the implications for the people are vast, and they can be summarized in one word: freedom. Galileo's historical failure was, according to Brecht, to have yielded under the threat of torture at a point in time when, if he had defended his ideas, the people would have supported him. Therefore, Galileo became guilty of causing centuries of exploitation of people, deprived of freedom by church dogma. Galileo does not exemplify a Great Man; rather, like all humans, he has a chance for greatness. Greatness, however, is meaningless if it only affects the individual; it finds meaning only in combination with responsibility and social commitment.

While Galileo's situation can be understood as analogous to a scientist's existence under the Nazi regime, it also reflected the conditions of exile. Although, like *Mutter Courage und ihre Kinder*, it was not called a didactic play but a parable play, both plays lead the audience through a learning process. While Galileo is aware of his failure, Mother Courage does not achieve any such insight; it is the audience who has to understand what Mother Courage fails to learn. When Courage's daughter Kattrin sacrifices her life in a successful attempt to save the lives of others, especially children, by warning a city of an imminent attack, her action constitutes an important model, because it shows the possibility of changed behavior — behavior demonstrating that people can learn to rise beyond the fatalism exhibited by Mother Courage. The epic theater's montage of structural elements contributes to the learning process by creating the audience's detachment from the action.

The episodic progression of *Mother Courage* tells the story of Mother Courage, a camp follower who peddles provisions to the soldiers during the Thirty Years' War. She is trying to make a living from war to feed her children, while keeping them away from the war. Nevertheless, her children, one after the other, die as a result of the war. The story unfolds over a period of twelve years, and the individual episodes show Mother Courage as a representative and, at the same time, a victim of the capitalist way of life, in which war is simply a special way of doing business. After losing all her children, she still tries to carry on with her business. The time gaps between the episodes are filled by titles and brief summaries of the following episode that are projected on the stage so that the audience understands the context and is able to observe the action in a detached manner. The songs that interrupt the flow of the plot also function as anti-illusionist elements, because they express a knowledge that goes beyond what the character who performs the song can know; therefore, the songs have been interpreted as an articulation of the "epic subject" of the play.

## Continuity of Nonreactionary Modernism inside Nazi Germany

*"Modern classicism"* The trend of the 1930s was toward classicist forms, and the term *modern classicism* is sometimes used for the Modernist application of traditional forms and themes for its own purposes inside Germany. To understand the condition of German literature in Nazi Germany, it is important to realize that the Modernist tradition had never been fully interrupted there. The continuity can be explained in terms of the Nazi attempts to generate the public image of a country that was open to the world and to give its upper-middle-class citizens the impression that the state was interested in culture as a zone free from politics.

After Nazi Germany began the Second World War, the conditions for Modernist literature deteriorated, but before the war international literature was available on the German book market, including Modernist texts. The only works that were effectively banned were texts by German exile authors (with the possible exception of some works by Thomas Mann). The removal of books largely took place through "voluntary" measures on the part of individual booksellers, since the blacklists were intended primarily for public libraries. Young German authors who wrote in the Modernist tradition were also able to read Modernist works by authors from Franz Kafka to Marcel Proust and William Faulkner. For example, Faulkner's *Light in August* was published in German translation as *Licht im August* in 1935, and *Absalom, Absalom* in 1938. Although Faulkner was misunderstood by some as a racist writer, even Ernest Hemingway (1899–1961), an American author with clear antifascist credentials, saw the English-language publication of his *The Sun Also Rises* in 1937 by a German publisher. Before the war it was also possible to special-order books from Switzerland.

The first few years of the Nazi regime even brought a limited debate on whether or not to establish a form of Modernism, such as Benn's style of Expressionism, as the official art of the state. These efforts were an indication of the artists' misunderstanding of what Nazism was really about, and the effort came to an end in 1937 when Hitler himself declared that the cultural scene had to be cleaned up just like the political scene before it. Over the following two years, Nazi control over this area, including the publishing houses, was expanded. Many young authors were to a large degree apolitical, or at least did not seem to understand their writings as a politically motivated inner emigration as the writers of the older generation did. The attitude of the young generation can perhaps be best described in the often quoted words of Marie Luise Kaschnitz (1901–1974): "Preferably surviving, preferably still being there, continuing to work when the charade was over" [Lieber überleben, lieber noch da sein, weiter arbeiten, wenn erst der Spuk vorüber war].

Yet the young authors did not remain silent. Within Germany, and later the German-speaking areas that had been brought under German control, Modernist literature was written and, to some degree, also published, especially before 1939, in literary magazines and the arts section of newspapers. While some of these publications, from the *Frankfurter Zeitung* to *Das Reich* and *Das Innere Reich*, had a nonfascist profile, they were not overtly or even covertly antifascist.

The fate of Jewish writers who could not or did not leave the Nazi sphere of influence was horrific. The victims of systematic, yet at times deceptive, persecution, Jewish writers were given their own cultural organization, the *Jüdischer Kulturbund* (Jewish Cultural Union), on May 11, 1933, the day after the book burnings. This was, however, part of the National Socialist attempt to isolate the Jews. Until 1937 there were twenty-seven Jewish-owned publishing houses and sixty-one Jewish-owned book distributors in Germany. When the Nazis started the Second World War, they radicalized their treatment of Jews, and in September 1941 the *Jüdischer Kulturbund* was outlawed. But the problem for Jewish writers was not simply a question of having access to an organization; it was a question of physical survival.

Paul Celan (pseudonym of Paul Antschel; 1920–1970) emerged as one of the most significant new Modernist voices of the 1950s and 1960s. He was born into the Jewish minority within the German-speaking minority in the multicultural environment of Romania, the southeastern part of the recently defunct Austro-Hungarian empire. He was strongly influenced by the Modernist traditions of Trakl, Rilke, and the French Symbolist poets. Stronger still were the traumatic experiences he suffered during the German occupation of Romania in 1941. His parents were deported and murdered, and he was placed in a forced-labor camp. Among the poems Celan wrote during this period but which were not published until after the war was "Todesfuge" (Death Fugue), which made him world-famous.

Gertrud Kolmar (pseudonym of Gertrud Chodziesner, 1894–1943?) stayed in Germany after 1933 because of her father. She, too, was exploited for forced labor in 1941 and was deported in 1943, which was the last time she was seen — she most likely became a victim of the systematic mass killings by the Nazis at Auschwitz. Her increasingly mythological poems reflect her conflicts with traditional gender roles, her own growing isolation, and the history of the Jewish people. In "Die Jüdin" (The Jewish Woman) she confronts her alienated existence in the sentence, "I am a stranger" [Ich bin fremd], which stands separate from the four-line stanzas in which she explores her "own ancient land" [mein eigenes uraltes Land] of the Jewish people's long history. In 1933 some of Kolmar's poems were published in an anthology edited by Elisabeth Langgässer (pseudonym of Elisabeth Hoffmann, 1899–1950). The next year Kolmar published a collection of poems, *Preußische Wappen* (Prussian Coats of Arms, 1934). She was able to publish another book, *Die Frau und die Tiere* (The Woman and the Animals), in Germany as late as 1938. But after her relocation into a ghetto the same year, her last book was pulped.

Celan and Kolmar were persecuted simply because they were Jewish. Works of other writers had been removed from the German public because they were considered degenerate for reasons of form and content: they were Modernist works. But writers kept producing Modernist texts. The war diary of Felix Hartlaub (1913–1945) is an example of a text that would have been too political for publication during the Third Reich. Published posthumously under the title *Von unten gesehen* (Seen from Below, 1950), it used the popular New Objectivist form of the diary to explore the eerie nonreality of war, where orders seem to be disconnected from reality. As a historian, Hartlaub worked on the official war diary for the *Führer*'s headquarters. His personal diary, especially from 1943 on, was often written in the form of individual prose texts. The most famous one is the last one, titled "Im Sonderzug des Führers" (In the Führer's Special Train) by his sister Geno (b. 1915), who edited his diary. The text ends with the description of an endless tunnel, in which the *Führer*'s train, disjointed from the surrounding reality and representing the country's fate, disappears into an abyss.

Still, young non-Nazi writers who were just starting out could publish Modernist literature in a variety of genres if these texts, in spite of their authors' personal antipathy toward National Socialism, did not question the Nazi exercise of power. These writers often continued their disengagement from political issues that stemmed from earlier disappointments with the Weimar Republic. Günter Eich (1907–1972) and Peter Huchel (1903–1981) wrote radio plays. From 1933 to 1939, about seventy radio plays that Eich coauthored with Martin Raschke were broadcast. Among prose works, the novel *Schwarze Weide* (Black Willow, 1937), by Horst Lange (1904–1971), is considered especially important. Many of the works by young authors explored the Modernist fusion of rationality and irrationality with a tendency to the hermetic, if not magical, which led to these authors' being loosely grouped under the label of *magic realism*.

*Magic Realism*   Though most often used in reference to Latin American literature, the term *magic realism* has also been applied to works of German literature. It is usually defined as a modern form of realism describing a concrete reality that contains elements symbolic of a secret meaning and a sense of

214 • Before 1945: Fascism

totality. In the context of New Objectivity, German magic realism is seen as a response to Expressionism. Like New Objectivity, magic realism rediscovered reality as its subject; the attitude, however, is quite different. New Objectivity displayed skeptical and disillusioned coolness and social criticism. In contrast, magic realism ambiguously meant a warmth of feeling that derived from a sense of secret meaning or an irritation that stemmed from the secret demonic character of the world. Furthermore, magic realist texts turned away from direct social commentary.

*Magic realism* is typically used in a narrow sense for German literature, while it lacks clarity when it is used in a broad sense. In the latter meaning, reactionary authors, such as Ernst Jünger, are also included in magic realism. Furthermore, magic realism remained important for postwar literature — for instance, in works by Wolfdietrich Schnurre and Günter Grass (b. 1927). Other attempts to define the term *magic realism* are even broader; they focus on the irrational in general because they include a wide spectrum of writers from Hans Henny Jahnn to Reinhold Schneider. Clarity can be achieved by regarding magic realism as a Modernist mode, which implies that the mere existence of irrationality in a work does not suffice; for a work to be considered magic realism, it has to be part of the typically Modernist fusion of rationality and irrationality. In addition, to belong to magic realism, a work should be significantly different from other Modernist modes — specifically Symbolism and Ironic Realism. It can be argued that the approach toward reality and the specific quality of the symbol constitute a significant difference between magic realism and Symbolism and that the difference from Ironic Realism lies in the fact that many works of magic realism do not display a sense of ironic detachment but rather one of magic involvement. Conversely, the term *magic realism* could, in general, refer to all surrealist, magical, and ironic Modernist redefinitions of realism in German literature (and could replace the term *Ironic Realism* that has been used in this book).

**Naturmagie**     In a narrow sense, German magic realism coincides with the term *Naturmagie* (nature magic), a magic that is seen to unfold within the realm of an ambivalent nature. It is connected to writers who published in the journal *Die Kolonne* (Convoy, 1929–1932) or were associated with them. While some *Naturmagie* texts were published earlier, 1930 is usually given as the approximate beginning of this literary movement. Among its main authors were Peter Huchel, Günter Eich, Horst Lange, Elisabeth Langgässer, Wilhelm Lehmann (1882–1968), and Oskar Loerke (1884–1941).

Loerke, who began his literary career as a prose writer, is considered the precursor to this new kind of nature poetry that contrasted with the contemporary poetry of the big city. Loerke's poetry, however, illustrates the wide scope of *Naturmagie*, because it is capable of including the city, too. In his early collection of poems *Wanderschaft* (Journey, 1911), he sets the tone both by searching for revelation in symbols that nature provides and by incorporating aspects of the city into his poems. "Der dunkle und der lichte Gott" (The Dark God and the Bright God) not only suggests the contrast of city and civilization versus country and nature, but it also attempts to reconcile both into a poetic unity; sights and sounds of the city merge with visions and rhythms of nature.

Nature is not mere subject matter; it is a medium for poetic expression. Nevertheless, nature and humanity cannot completely come together, since the meaning of existence that is contained in nature is not understood by the poet-speaker. The ultimate meaning is suggested in nature's symbols by way of magical elements. The poem "Garten" in Loerke's collection *Der Silberdistelwald* (The Carline Thistle Forest, 1934) has been interpreted as a prototype of the modern German nature poem in regard to both form and content. Stanzas, consisting of four short lines and an *abab* rhyme, vary the linguistic material in a playful, musical way while the diction is matter-of-fact and colloquial. The content, at the same time, withdraws into the magic of nature and asserts a social element without direct political statement.

The magic of nature typically unfolds, as it does in this poem, as the interaction between mythical or magical characters and nature imagery (landscapes, plants, and/or phenomena). In "Garten" the setting is a group of mountains in the south Tyrolian Dolomites that is known in German as the *Rosengarten* (rose garden, a word that is not used in the poem itself); the plants are roses, as well as others, such as lavender; and the natural phenomena are the "soothing winds" [besänftigender Winde]. The mischievous king of dwarfs, Laurin, is called the "master of the roses" [Herrn der Rosen]. He was familiar to German readers from the medieval legends of Dietrich von Bern, which identified Laurin as the master of the *Rosengarten* mountains.

The evocation of magical-mythical nature is connected to a sense of reality that often seems alien to nature, as if the reality were a residue of that which man attempted to forget in nature. In "Garten" the winds sweep away bad things that came from the world: "so much hardship, / So much torture, so much guilt" [soviel des Harten, / Soviel der Qual, soviel der Schuld]. This was the extent of direct social statement in Loerke's poetry; nevertheless, since he was clearly not a Nazi, Loerke had to deal with Nazi repression in his job as an editor for the Jewish publisher Samuel Fischer and felt increasingly depressed as a result of the political situation. He sought relief in writing poems as an attempt to overcome social alienation. Some poems suggest an antifascist read-ing of their imagery, such as his "Leitspruch" (Motto, dated November 1940): "Each empire built on blood / Caves in like a mole hill. / Each word born of light / Radiates through the darkness on and on" [Jed-wedes blutgefügte Reich / Sinkt ein, dem Maulwurfshügel gleich. / Jedwedes lichtgeborne Wort / Wirkt durch das Dunkel fort und fort].

Loerke's approach to writing nature poems was influential for the group of writers associated with the magazine *Kolonne*. Most of these writers belonged to the next generation, with the exception of Wilhelm Lehmann, who was two years older than Loerke but had come late to writing poetry. Other genres were also important; for example, Elisa-beth Langgässer favored prose. In Loerke's tradition, however, nature poems were especially popular with Peter Huchel, Günter Eich, and Georg Britting (1891–1964).

Nature was no longer innocent; it had nothing to do with the tra-ditional sentimentalized images. The nature of *Naturmagie* could be a threatening realm that included aggression, battle, and even all-out war; therefore, its tradition could also extend into the postwar years. Peter Huchel's "Späte Zeit" (Late Time, 1941) evokes the scene of a forest in terms of a battlefield; the natural cycle of seasons becomes a symbol of an underlying struggle when "autumn fired its shots" [Herbst schoß seine Schüsse ab] with "acorns like ammo" [Eicheln wie Patronen]. Lehmann's "Atemholen" (Taking a Breath, 1948) creates a sense of warfare, as if war went on all the time somewhere at a distance: "The war of the world is faded history here" [Der Krieg der Welt ist hier verklungene Geschichte].

The sense of a complex world, which makes these poems Modern-ist, is even more complex beyond its surface appearance because the lost center of the visible world can be sensed in the invisible world. Therefore, the magic still resonates. Huchel's "Späte Zeit" ends with the evocation of a demonic realm: "Fog drifts and so do demons" [Ne-bel ziehen und Dämonen]; similarly, Lehmann's "Atemholen" ends with a confirmation of the timeless quality of existence: "Time stands still. . . . / . . . Cordelia's quiet laughter echoes / Through the centu-ries. It has not changed" [Die Zeit steht still. . . . / . . . Kordelias leises Lachen hallt / Durch die Jahrhunderte. Es hat sich nicht geändert].

This magical realm of timeless and changeless existence, however, is a literary construct. Poems of *Naturmagie* can be understood as voic-ing the concept of a world counter to the existing world of disorienta-tion (both during the Nazi regime and immediately after the war) without being too openly political. The poems express a sense of yearning for a meaning that was felt to have existed in long-ago magical times or realms. The visible world of complexity that is subject to time and mutability is no longer connected to the magical realm — a sense of loss that is intensified by the continued withdrawal of the magic. Lehmann's "Oberon" (1935) says that the king of the fairies, who used to take a particular path through nature, "has long since faded into the time of legends" [ist längst die Sagenzeit hinabgeglitten].

The only remnant of the connection between the visible and the magical worlds is the symbol that the poems evoke but of which they do not express any understanding. The demonic presence that evokes images of warfare is acknowledged as a potentially threatening message but not explained; neither are potentially positive messages. A jay's feather, which gives the title to Eich's poem "Die Häherfeder" (1948), brings the speaker of the poem closer to a secret, because he realizes that the feather is a symbol, but he does not know what it symbolizes beyond the connection to a secret. Georg Britting's "Krähenschrift" (Crow's Writing, 1944) describes the human lack of understanding; looking at the flight of birds whose movements in the sky appear as some kind of writing, we are "like a child who cannot yet read / And holds the page upside-down in his hand" [Wie ein Kind, das noch nicht lesen kann, / Und das Blatt verkehrt hält in der Hand]. Poetic speech became incantation, conjuration, and interpretation, but it had to stop short of fully understanding the symbol.

As a result, *Naturpoesie,* the attempt to realize poetically the ideal of the safe haven in nature, seemed to be a legitimate literary response to a lack of orientation. All the poet and the reader have is the symbol, which they cannot understand. This can be seen as an evasion of responsibility in a world that needed clear statements, not an apolitical evocation of vague symbols that might be construed as implying a counterworld. Although it was Modernist and nonfascist, its realist approach to nature, lack of clear statements, and vague references to myth made *Naturmagie* seem close enough to Nazi concepts to be tolerated — though grudgingly, as evidenced by the fact that *Kolonne* no longer appeared in Nazi Germany. Making clear statements after the war no longer came at the risk of one's life; consequently, some writers — most importantly, Günter Eich — began to change their styles after 1945, while remaining indebted to *Naturmagie.* Furthermore, younger poets, such as Ingeborg Bachmann (1926–1973), whose works were influenced by magic realism, demonstrated how nature imagery can communicate a political message.

Magic realism used language in the Modernist tradition of Symbolism, which attempted to connect this world with the other world by means of the symbol, something from this world that unlocked the secret other world hidden beneath it. Compared to George's poems as an example of German Symbolism, the poems of *Naturmagie* during the 1930s and 1940s were both more matter-of-fact and precise in their approach to reality and more focused on an emotional and often foreboding sense of a miracle that acknowledged not understanding the symbol. Conversely, Symbolism exhibited a more subjectively intellectual fusion of rationality and irrationality in which the meaning of the symbol was suggested; at least, the poet-speaker implied that he had knowledge of the symbol's meaning, which, nevertheless, remained vague.

The texts of magic realism operate, first, by assuming a one-world condition by way of an underlying unified totality (as opposed to the two-world condition in Kafka's texts) and, second, by a realistic presentation of the visible world into which the invisible intrudes by means of symbols. The effect is a text that is at the same time stable (formally grounded in realist presentation) and paradoxical (containing an ultimately inexplicable symbol).

### Reactionary Modernism

Since its beginning, Modernist literature had often been created by writers whose personal politics were conservative. Still, because of their strong antibourgeois bias and their complex structure that incorporated a subversive element, Modernist texts rarely came across as straightforwardly conservative. Modernist writing, regardless of whether it was done from a conservative or a progressive perspective, by definition reflected the world's complexity in an intricate artistic structure that fused rationality and irrationality.

The more reactionary a writer's perspective became, the less the world's complexity was approved of. Disapproval and rejection of the complex world were legitimate Modernist responses as in Hofmannsthal's Chandos letter. However, when the perspective became politically too reactionary, it became also aesthetically too narrow-minded to the point that the world's complexity was no longer disapproved of but, rather, ignored. Since such ignorance led to simplistic responses that had to be shored up against criticism, rationality as the means of criticism was ignored as well, and irrationality was wholeheartedly embraced. This response was no longer a Modernist one; even Brecht's hard-core Communist party-line didactic plays, by virtue of activating the audience's capacity to reason, were founded on rationality; therefore, they were complex and (perhaps unintentionally) open to criticism and divergent opinions. Complete irrationality no longer presented the fusion of rationality and irrationality typical of Modernism; instead, it was the antimodern response and embrace of premodern concepts in much reactionary writing. It did not in itself have to be National Socialist in the sense of being in complete agreement with the tenets of Nazi ideology in order to move toward and help prepare the acceptance of Nazism.

It can be argued that while Modernism and Avant-Garde may have a reactionary side, there was no National Socialist Modernism or Avant-Garde. The Avant-Garde was not focused exclusively on an embrace of politics and technology but, while including that focus, was firmly embedded within Modernism; therefore, Italian Futurism occupies a position between Avant-Garde and fascism. It is usually considered an example of a fascist Avant-Garde; Futurism, however, was not embraced by the Italian fascist state. Similarly, German National Socialism favored a mixture of classicist, realist, and folklorist appearance in the works of art that received official approval. It is significant that German Modernists, such as Benn or the painter Emil Nolde (1867–1956), although they tried hard to establish their conservative versions of Expressionism as the official art of an envisioned futurist and National Socialist state, had no chance of succeeding. Their art remained, necessarily, "degenerate" by the standards of National Socialist ideology and aesthetics. Even Ernst Jünger, once he moved away from his protofascist texts to a Modernist style, raised the suspicions of the Nazis.

**Ernst Jünger's**
**Auf den Marmorklippen**

Reactionary Modernism is exemplified by the writings of Ernst Jünger, though not in his influential, yet overrated, *In Stahlgewittern*, but in his later works. Jünger became a Modernist at the moment when, while remaining an elitist reactionary, he moved toward inner opposition to the Nazis. At that moment his world turned complex in a way that he could not ignore. *Auf den Marmorklippen*, which is the primary literary example of this change, might be an ideologically objectionable work because of its reactionary quality, but extending this opinion into an aesthetic judgment capitulates before the challenge of dealing with a variety of Modernism that expresses reactionary thought. Form and content, of course, cannot be separated from each other in any simplistic manner. First of all, there is no agreement concerning the novel's political evaluation. It has been read both as a novel of resistance and as a mere allegory that makes no statement about the real world other than Jünger's own elitist attitude. There is no doubt that Jünger despised the Nazis, but whether his novel was read as a resistance work might say more about what the individual reader brought to the text than what the text had to offer.

Within this political tension, the novel can develop its aesthetic momentum. As opposed to Jünger's earlier works emphasizing the collective will over the individual, *Auf den Marmorklippen* moved toward a revaluation of the role of the individual that is central in Jünger's later work. In *Marmorklippen* the individual's possibilities are limited — which is, on the one hand, an ironic paradox for the individualist Jünger but, on the other hand, a logical consequence of his fatalistic view of history. The plot develops in a mythical realm with characters who are more like archetypes than true human beings. In the tension between the novel's reading as a myth and its reading as a roman à clef (because of obvious similarities to people and events in Nazi Germany), the reader moves from poetic evocations of specific scenes to general contemplations about the fate of mortals or the role of remembrance. Evocations and contemplations can be disapproved of as overdone and too general, respectively; they also, however, successfully function as invitations to individual readers to re-create the evoked atmosphere in their minds, fill in the gaps left by the generalities, and feel themselves in agreement with the contemplations.

The novel begins: "You all know the wild melancholy that takes hold of us when we remember times of happiness" [Ihr alle kennt die wilde Schwermut, die uns bei der Erinnerung an Zeiten des Glücks ergreift]. The elegiac tone, which is sustained throughout the novel, and the direct address of the reader invite identification at a personal level. The process of identification is supported by the aforementioned elements of the mythical realm and the archetypal characters. The mythical realm in which the plot takes place is a representation of a landscape that is defined by a shared central and southern European culture and geography with references to the landscape around Lake Constance, where Jünger began writing the novel.

Mythical meaning is also implied in the plot of *Marmorklippen*. The narrator-protagonist flees to the country of Marina from war and the slowly expanding reign of terror of the Head Forester [Oberförster], complete with places of torture and death that are hidden deep inside the high forest, the original power base of the Head Forester. The protagonist used to be a friend of the Head Forester, but he is reminded that "a misjudgment becomes a mistake only if one insists on it" [ein Irrtum erst dann zum Fehler würde, wenn man in ihm beharrt]. He tries to live a peaceful and withdrawn life with only a few friends, dedicated to the study of nature. Finally, despite the narrator's participation in Marina's defense, that country, too, is overrun by the Head Forester's forces, and the narrator has to move on to Alta Plana for refuge.

This plot is part of the archetypal pattern of the story of the dragon slayer — not in a vague sense that assumes that all stories are variations of archetypes, but in a concrete sense that is supported by the elegiac and mythical tone of the text. The protagonist-hero is the dragon slayer, and the antagonist, the Head Forester, is the dragon. Brother Otho is, in part, the double of the hero and, in part, the wise, old mentor. Father Lampros is the hero's mentor, and Biederhorn is Lampros's evil counterpart. Belovar is the true friend of the hero, while

Lampusa is the false friend. This list of the archetypal patterns can be continued all the way to good and evil animals (the dogs of Belovar and those of the Head Forester, respectively). And the novel's plot itself can be retold in terms of archetypal patterns, specifically, the three tests of the hero, the last of which leads to the hero's defeat when the Head Forester takes control of Marina. The hero, however, overcomes the defeat through the archetype of rebirth when he is saved by his son and their pet snakes. He finally reclaims his right of freedom, but it is his own personal freedom stemming from his elitist position as hero, not general freedom.

As much as Jünger had personally contributed to the rise of Nazism through his earlier writings, the underlying aesthetics of *Marmorklippen* is not one of hatred or of a cold-blooded and inhuman technology. Jünger formulated a clear renunciation of violence in the protagonist's decision "to resist by the pure power of the spirit alone" [allein durch reine Geistesmacht zu widerstehen]. This renunciation put Jünger in the context of humanism; as conservative as it still might have been, it was not in keeping with Nazi ideology. Furthermore, the world had become complex for Jünger's protagonist; for example, he notices that language is no longer satisfying; he is reliving the experience of Lord Chandos in Hofmannsthal's letter. He senses, "almost painfully, that the word has separated itself from the appearances" [fast schmerzhaft, daß das Wort von den Erscheinungen sich löste].

Jünger's reputation as a singular figure in German literature rested on his importance for the intellectual preparation of Nazism through his early works that soon developed at a stylistically high level. The close proximity to National Socialist core beliefs made Jünger's quiet dissent all the more poignant, which perhaps led to an overrating of this aspect of his career. Above all, Jünger was able to stylize himself into playing the role of a singular literary phenomenon that he appeared to be by sheer biographical coincidence. When he died in 1998, he was 102 years old, and, as had been remarked ironically on the occasion of Jünger's hundredth birthday, he had been keeping a diary (his main form of publication) for eighty years. In the wider context of literary history, however, Jünger belonged to a large group of reactionary writers.

# Part Two

# AFTER 1945:

## MODERNISM REVISITED
## AND POSTMODERNISM

# III

# *Defining Local Maps:*
# *The Second Phase of Modernism*

## Late Modernism as Establishment Culture

AT THE BEGINNING OF THE COLD WAR after the Second World War, literature changed again. Modernism, although not completely repressed during the period of Nazi rule over Germany, was revisited by German-language literature that was, once again, produced and published where its audience was located. The high Modernist mode was at the center of attention because it had been in full swing when its reception in Germany had been curtailed by the Nazi terror. After the war, the Modernist traditions evolved into establishment art in part as a result of the paradox of internal depoliticization and external politicization.

*Internal depoliticization* The first aspect of the paradox occurred within Western societies, where Modernist literature became depoliticized — ironically, because it was valorized on account of its perceived political orientation: it was perceived as fundamentally democratic. The Modernist writers who were persecuted by Nazism and who had spoken out against it certainly supported this perception, while the attraction of fascism to which some Modernist writers had succumbed was often overlooked. The diverse Modernist traditions, while including an anti-bourgeois element — even in their most bourgeois representatives, such as Thomas Mann — were accepted to such an extent that they eventually became establishment art in Western Europe and the United States.

By the 1950s and 1960s, as a result of an increasing depoliticization, late Modernism had come to be seen as being identical with culture. While Modernist works retained their political dimension — some were even decidedly partisan, such as the early postwar works of Wolfgang Koeppen (1906–1996) and Arno Schmidt (1914–1979) — many works could be read as trying to have it both ways: as affirming social conditions and, at the same time, subverting the same social conditions. This pattern had been observed early on in Modernism when even conservative writers produced works that, in part, subverted existing social conditions by articulating an antibourgeois, keen awareness of the fragility of identity at all levels, which could range from personal to linguistic and social. This affirmative-subversive pattern was at the core of Modernist ambiguity, because no reading could be the final reading. Nevertheless, this pattern also came more and more to underlie popular literature, such as some of the novels of Johannes Mario Simmel (b. 1924). This in turn made it even more controversial to determine the role of popular literature within any canon of German-language literature.

In the West Germany of the 1950s and 1960s, the writers of the Group 47 came to personify not only new contemporary German literature but also Modernist traditions and innovations that were decidedly political, although the political aspect was voiced mostly as a matter of private concern (either of author or fictional character) up to the end of the 1950s. Only then did German literature find a voice that was its own and that was strong enough to withstand the controversies that it sparked. Yet there is a twofold measure of the Group 47's unintended establishment status. On the one hand, the sometimes ferocious attacks from the political right (including the conservative government — the real political establishment) revealed disappointment that a type of literature that did all of these controversial things had established itself as the generally accepted art form. On the other hand, it became apparent that Modernism was perceived as aligned with the real political and social establishment when the Group 47 (in strong contradiction to its self-image) was attacked by the left-wing counterculture of the late 1960s.

*External politicization*  The second aspect of the paradox of depoliticization and politicization emerged in the scenario of the Cold War, during which the West, under American leadership, was pitted against the East, under Soviet leadership. During the Cold War, the East came to regard Modernism as more than merely a formalist aesthetics opposed to anti-Modernist Socialist Realism, which the Soviet Union had proclaimed as its ideal in art as early as 1934. More than simply being decadent, Modernism was seen as a weapon of the West — an evaluation that reflected the postwar identification of Modernism with culture in the Western countries.

Late Modernism after 1945 continued the search for a center. From the immediate postwar years to the end of the 1960s, the mood of the public in the West was torn between giving in to apocalyptic visions of impending global nuclear destruction, on the one hand, and, on the other, reaching for the stars with space exploration. This torment evolved within a period of economic growth and prosperity during which everything seemed feasible in a manner that, in hindsight, can be considered naive (all of which found its mirror image in the East). The "giant leap for mankind" from Earth to the first landing on the moon in 1969 was the ultimate achievement of Modernist thinking, for which that last frontier of space promised the chance to reestablish a sense of direction and accomplishment.

But the scope of Modernist thinking had changed. It still attempted to master the world in its quest for meaning; however, the mental maps that it could provide for this goal became more limited the more ambitious they were. In a sense, they became localized. Modernism was limited to the West. Eastern writers who explored Modernist elements in violation of the Socialist Realist dogma — and most of the important ones did — were accused of Westernization. Furthermore, the tension between apocalyptic nightmares and technological dreams seemed to impose limits on the extent to which orientation could be provided. Total maps, like the ones drawn in accordance with National Socialist ideology, had to be totalitarian constructs that ignored the way the world really was. Consequently, even a little amount of orientation was valuable. In contrast to the great works of high Modernism, most late Modernist models of this world or of a possible counterworld appear to be less ambitious and, in the metaphor of the map, more localized.

Late Modernist thinking operated on the premise that the experience of fragmentation could be overcome by regaining a sense of totality. This means that it remained based on the mainstream Modernist response to the modern condition of society. The other Modernist response was pushed into the background — as it usually had been, with the exception of some of the Avant-Garde movements, especially Dada in Germany. This other Modernist attitude understood the fragmentation as a condition of contemporary existence that had to be embraced rather than overcome. While scientific and technological triumphs of the 1960s, such as the moon landing, epitomized the belief that nature could be mastered, scientific and social changes at the same time challenged the limits of that belief. The beginning of nonlinear systems theory in science and the emergence of the counterculture movement both contributed to a sense that fragmentation cannot be dealt with by the search for the lost totality. This changing approach to fragmentation ultimately laid the foundations of postmodernism, which emerged (with a few earlier precursors) in German-language literature in the 1970s.

# 7:1945–1949: The Immediate Postwar Years — Defining Different Traditions in East and West

## Social Foundation: Competing Political Systems

ON MAY 8, 1945, THE SECOND WORLD WAR ended in Europe; on that day the German military capitulated. The major Nazi leaders, including Hitler and Goebbels, had committed suicide in the *Führer's* bunker in Berlin on April 30. The entire country, much of which lay in rubble after the Allied air raids, had become occupied territory under the control of the Allied forces. At the July 1945 conference in Potsdam, the victors decided on the geographical division that foreshadowed the Cold War. The Western Allies agreed to Germany losing its territories in the East, which came under direct Soviet or Polish rule, and to the four occupation zones each being subject to the respective occupying country's military government in accordance with general principles, such as the "4-D" program (demilitarization, denazification, decentralization, deindustrialization).

Less than two years after the end of the war, the Truman Doctrine to contain the influence of Communism was announced, and Germany's strategic importance, particularly as a result of its geographical location between the two geopolitical power blocs, led to the American Marshall Plan for Western Europe (especially the three Western occupation zones of Germany). While the Soviet Union kept bleeding its occupation zone of industrial structures, the West German industrial potential was rebuilt, and a federalist governmental structure with some centralized aspects was established. This policy resulted for all practical purposes in a suspension of the denazification effort, because the expertise of former Nazis was needed in rebuilding the country, and it brought about a hotly debated remilitarization in the 1950s.

Immediately after the war the challenge consisted of rebuilding the life of an entire country that had suffered the loss of half its housing and experienced a large influx of refugees. The political infrastructure, too, had to be renewed. In Nuremberg the Allies held the war crimes tribunal for high-ranking Nazi functionaries. The Social Democratic Party revived its democratic traditions, and even the two newly founded parties — the Christian Democratic Union (CDU) and its Bavarian sister party, the Christian Social Union (CSU) — included in their

1947 party platform a strong call for social reform. Only later did the CDU, which initially had a program of Christian Socialism, take on a distinctly conservative program.

The political parties in East and West soon went their different ways. In the Western zones each party developed its own profile. In contrast, in the Soviet-occupied zone the leading Communist party, which had returned from exile with the Soviet forces, did not enforce the political system of soviets. Rather, in the tradition of the popular-front call for an antifascist and democratic renewal of Germany, the East German Communist Party forced a merger with the East German Social Democratic Party into the new Communist-controlled SED (*Sozialistische Einheitspartei*, or Socialist Unity Party). The other East German parties, while they existed throughout the forty-year history of the independent East German state, formed a bloc that usually voted with the SED.

In spite of occasional calls for German unity, the political momentum was toward a stabilization of the two major ideological blocs with the Iron Curtain running right through the middle of Germany. The situation was even more complicated because in the heart of East Germany — the Soviet-occupied zone, which, in 1949, became the German Democratic Republic, or GDR — lay the former capital Berlin. The city, divided into Eastern and Western sectors like the country itself, epitomized the East-West conflict and became that conflict's symbol as early as 1948, when a new currency was introduced in the West.

The German division into a political entity in the West, bound to the Western Allies, and a political entity in the East, bound to the Soviet Union, became a de facto reality when, by decree of the American, British and French military governments of Germany, the *Bank deutscher Länder* (Bank of the German States) introduced the Deutsche Mark, effective as of June 20, 1948. The new currency gave rise to the myth of a political and economic success story: because each adult German living in the Western zones received forty Deutsche Mark, the myth was that of a democratic new start with equal chances for everybody. However, in reality the new, hard currency not only created an incentive for people to work hard, but also for producers to make available their products, which they had kept stashed away while there was no profit to be made other than on the black market.

This development in the Western zones excluded the population of the Soviet occupation zone, and it provided the Soviet Union the provocation for beginning the Berlin Blockade. From July 1948 to May 1949, the Western Allies, above all the Americans and the British, airlifted all necessary supplies into Berlin, as the world's attention was focused on Berlin as a symbol both of freedom and of an armed conflict that threatened to erupt between the two ideological systems. As a result of the increasing tensions, the military governments gave the prime ministers of the states in the Western zones the directive to form a federal state. On May 8, 1949, the *Grundgesetz* (Constitution) was passed by the Parliamentary Council; it went into effect on May 24, 1949. It was based on the old Weimar constitution and a draft of the 1848 constitution, but modified so as to take into account the bad experiences of recent history. In addition to guaranteeing human rights, it strengthened the position of the federal chancellor by reducing the president to representative functions, while strengthening the judiciary by establishing the *Bundesverfassungsgericht* (Federal Constitutional Court, equivalent to the U.S. Supreme Court). The first federal elections brought about a conservative majority coalition government and the defeat of the KPD and SPD, and Konrad Adenauer became the first chancellor of the Federal Republic of Germany in August 1949.

While the early political goal of the Soviet Union had most likely been a unified Germany at a time when history had appeared to be open to more than the choice between the two systems, the Soviets did not want to see unification under West German law. And the Western allies did not want to return to exercising joint control over Germany. The de facto division of Germany became a legal reality with the creation of the German Democratic Republic on October 7, 1949 — despite its name, not a democracy but a centralist and Communist "people's republic." Thus, the status quo of two different, if not competing, political and ideological systems was established with an underlying sense of instability, because no formal peace treaty had been signed.

Another part of the European status quo was the role of Austria. Like Germany, Austria had been divided into four occupation zones and Vienna into four sectors. Since it had been annexed by Germany, Austria could claim to have been the first country to fall victim to Nazism. Austria finally regained its independence in 1955, after protracted negotiations that led to its political neutrality. Switzerland had remained neutral during the Second World War and continued this tradition after the war. Austria's own underlying fascist tendencies and Switzerland's questionable business transactions with Nazi Germany were not openly addressed until much later.

### The Literary Spectrum: The Search for Literary Traditions

The year 1945 was one of tremendous political significance, but even though it brought closure (above all, with the end of the Second World War), it can, like any other year, be described both in terms of change and continuity. The same terms apply to literature. During the immediate postwar years of 1945 to 1949, everything was in flux. When the first German writers' congress after the war met in October 1947, authors from East and West attended and proclaimed the unity of Germany against the background of the two Germanies drifting apart. Only authors from the three Western zones attended the next writers' congress in 1948. But there was a continuity of another sort: everybody — from the Nazi writer to the literary resistance fighter — was still there. Some remained silent or inconspicuous for a while, but by the 1950s restoration was in full swing in the West in literature, as well as in economics and politics. The immediate postwar years were part of such a literary continuity; what makes these years interesting, however, is the way in which the continuity appeared open to debate. Much of it was rhetoric, but there was a chance to define the role and function of literature as part of a conscious effort either to connect with older traditions or to make a fresh start.

*Poetry after Auschwitz*  The most famous example in this context was the 1949 dictum by the philosopher Theodor W. Adorno that "to write a poem after Auschwitz is barbaric" [Nach Auschwitz ein Gedicht zu schreiben, ist barbarisch]. Auschwitz, a major Nazi death camp, came to stand as a symbol of the Holocaust, and Adorno was pointing to the difficulty of writing in the face of knowing about such enormous crimes against humanity. He was particularly aiming at *Naturpoesie*, whose tradition was being continued — for instance, by Wilhelm Lehmann — as a kind of absent-minded lyrical evocation of beauty that could be understood as callous, because it upheld an inhuman attitude of ignorance (and of a desire to remain ignorant) about the Nazi crimes. Such an idyllic celebration of beauty seemed barbaric.

Adorno's dictum went right to the heart of the matter if it is understood as expressing the moral claim that after the Holocaust poems should not be written the way they used to be written. Nevertheless, it was still absolutely necessary to write poetry. Adorno himself later clarified that suffering had its own right to expression. Indeed, literature had helped writers to resist the Nazi regime; and after the war almost all major German-language writers, such as Paul Celan, Ingeborg Bachmann, Jurek Becker (1937–1997), Botho Strauß (b. 1944), and Günter Grass, addressed the Holocaust and the fascist way of thinking that had made the Holocaust possible. In his poetics lectures, *Schreiben nach Auschwitz* (Writing after Auschwitz, 1990), Grass emphasizes that it was important and even necessary to keep writing after Auschwitz "because Auschwitz belongs to us . . . and . . . made possible an insight that could be put in these words: Now, finally, we know ourselves" [weil Auschwitz zu uns gehört . . . und . . . eine Einsicht möglich gemacht hat, die heißen könnte: Jetzt endlich kennen wir uns].

The trauma of the Holocaust, which brought into focus what Nazism represented, emerged as the defining point in creating a new literary tradition and in altering the old ones. While most major writers can be seen in this light and while Nazism has remained an important literary topic, the literary renewal during the first postwar years, which had turned toward restoring naive and apparently innocent literature, offended Adorno. The danger was that in a perhaps understandable and even well-intentioned attempt at stressing the positive aspects of the German cultural tradition after the evils of the Third Reich, it had been forgotten that the evils had to be confronted.

*Exile versus inner emigration*

The search for literary traditions that could bridge the years of the Nazi regime in Germany and reestablish democratic values led to a head-on confrontation between the two most visible forms of nonfascist literature. It was a sometimes ugly and personal debate concerning who had the right to represent the truly other and better Germany: writers who had left Germany and lived in exile or those who had stayed and gone into inner emigration. Missing the chance to deal with the emotional issues of loyalty, democracy, and abuse of power and to exorcise Nazism effectively, the literary debate looked like a sideshow to the political developments leading to the Cold War and left the issues of fascism strangely unaddressed.

The primarily West German literary debate began with an exchange of open letters. In 1945 Walter von Molo (1880–1958) extended an invitation to Thomas Mann to return to Germany as soon as possible, "like a good physician" [wie ein guter Arzt], to examine the causes of Germany's political illness. Such an examination is what Thomas Mann presented in his *Doktor Faustus* (1947), but it was not embraced as such. Rather, in both more and less subtle ways, writers of the inner emigration expressed resentment toward exile writers. Molo implied that living in exile was a privilege by using inconspicuous formulations, such as his reference to the many millions of people who could not have left, because "for them there would not have been any other place on earth but home" [für die kein anderer Platz auf der Erde gewesen wäre als daheim]. The enormity of this apologetic attitude toward compromises with Nazism becomes evident if Molo's statement is seen in the context of speculation in which it is made. Such a context invites other speculation; for instance, if the many millions had stood up for their rights with a general strike, or if they had left Germany, it would have meant an effective drain of power from Nazi Germany and possibly a quick demise of the dictatorship. This reveals, as Thomas Mann pointed out in his response, the guilt that Molo hides behind his statements: the many millions of people did not leave because they did not want to.

In his open letter of August 18, 1945, Frank Thiess added a more openly aggressive tone by also addressing Mann and inviting all emigrants to return, while at the same time insulting them with the qualification "those who today still feel that they are Germans" [die sich heute noch als Deutsche fühlen]. The clause "With this I do not want to reprimand anyone who went away" [Ich will damit niemanden tadeln, der hinausging] highlights that the opposite was Thiess's intent. He was right in saying that the chance to gain wisdom existed for those who had stayed behind in Nazi Germany, but he was wrong and offensive in suggesting that they all, morally superior to the exile authors anyway, had been successful in gaining that wisdom. After all, his attack on exile authors did not display wisdom of any kind, and the writers of the inner emigration included some who retained their personal integrity, some who had made questionable compromises — and now, after the war, also some who had been well-known contributors to the National Socialist literary canon. Most significantly, Hans Friedrich Blunck, the first president of the Nazi *Reichsschrifttumskammer* from 1933 to 1935, claimed that even then he had been an "antifascist at the helm of the *Schrifttumskammer*" [Antifaschisten auf dem Sessel der Schrifttumskammer].

Thomas Mann's response was, for the most part, more measured and conciliatory. But one central passage of his letter documents the difficulty of reconciliation: Mann calls all books published in Nazi Germany "less than worthless" [weniger als wertlos] and concludes that "they all should be pulped" [Sie sollten alle eingestampft werden]. The controversy between the two factions continued, often as an undercurrent, with charges from those who had stayed that those who had fled Nazism had betrayed the German people.

Much of the polemics of the immediate postwar years needs to be put into perspective. For instance, the observation that German literature had three options for effecting a renewal — drawing on the established exile authors or on the established authors who had been in inner emigration, or turning to new young talents — is just part of the picture. On the one hand, the ideas that were entailed in the terms *exile* and *inner emigration* were politicized. On the other hand, some of the new talents were not that young anymore and, although Modernist and nonfascist, had published during the Third Reich. The need to make a fresh start, even to the point of starting one's career over again, is understandable; the rhetoric of change, however, obscured the strength of the continued Modernist tradition.

## Redefined Continuity, Part I:
## Exile Authors Returning to the East

The official cultural policy embraced the exile authors as a reflection of the East German political leadership, because the *Gruppe Ulbricht*, the small Communist leadership group, had itself returned from exile in Moscow to rule East Germany. While the Communist Party could not be sure how many of its sixteen million subjects had been Nazis, the party's antifascist rhetoric glossed over this difficulty, and the GDR portrayed itself as a participant in the victory over Hitler's Germany. Still, distrust ran deep through East German society; later, the widespread spying by the East German secret police, known as *Stasi* (*Ministerium für Staatssicherheit*, or Ministry for State Security), on its own population ate away at the fabric of the East German state.

*Antifascist prose*      The renewal of East German literature took place within the well-established antifascist tradition of exile and resistance. The returning exile authors represented a wide spectrum, from writers who were closely identified with Communism to those with a bourgeois, though liberal, worldview. In the first category were Anna Seghers, Bertolt Brecht, Willi Bredel, and Johannes R. Becher. Becher, one of the dominant lyrical poets, returned from exile immediately after the war as an influential politician and, in 1954, rose to the position of first minister of culture. Bourgeois authors who returned to the eastern part of Germany would have included Heinrich Mann, who had made plans to go to East Berlin before he died in American exile in March 1950.

The beginning of prose literature in the East reflected a wide spectrum of writers. Several eyewitness reports on the concentration camps revisited the Nazi years from the victims' and enemies' perspectives, including Ernst Wiechert's *Der Totenwald* in 1947, which had been published in Munich in 1945. Such inclusiveness was the policy of the *Kulturbund zur demokratischen Erneuerung Deutschlands* (Cultural Federation for the Democratic Renewal of Germany), which, led by Becher, not only encompassed conservative and Communist writers but also tried to become heir to the classical-humanist tradition. Problems with such an inheritance involved the vagueness of how those ideals related to Communist goals and became obvious when Goethe's Faust was now claimed to be a worker's hero whose belief in progress mediated between humanist and socialist ideals.

It was under this interpretation that the works of Heinrich Mann, Lion Feuchtwanger, Leonhard Frank (1882–1961), and Thomas Mann were published in the Soviet occupation zone (and later in the GDR), although these authors neither lived in East Germany nor were Communists. While they were praised by GDR critics as "bourgeois humanists" and "critical realists," such praise increasingly went hand in hand with a condemnation of "formalist" writers from German-speaking countries (such as Kafka, Broch, Musil, and Jahnn) and abroad (such as James Joyce, Marcel Proust, William Faulkner), where *formalism* was a derogatory term for Modernism. As Socialist Realism and antiformalism took hold as artistic dogma, especially in the 1950s, East Germany's great achievement of making the exile works available was tinged by provincialism, and the few Modernists — such as Brecht, Huchel, and Hermlin — were lone voices.

The novel *Die Toten bleiben jung* (The Dead Stay Young, 1947), by Anna Seghers, was an important step toward Socialist Realism. The title refers to the sentimental hope that the antifascists will win because their tradition is carried on. At the beginning of the novel the Spartacist Erwin is murdered by a small band of fascists in 1918, but his son Hans, under the guidance of their close friend Martin, continues the antifascist fight. At the end of the novel Hans is shot on the order of one of the murderers of his father, but his girlfriend is pregnant. While Seghers's novel fell short of some expectations of Socialist Realism — the presentation of the fascist side was criticized as being too colorful, and Martin was not stylized into a heroic mentor — it exemplified the goal of creating clarity about the national and individual past, which was important for Socialist Realism.

Johannes R. Becher's novel *Abschied* (Farewell, 1940 in Moscow, republished in East Berlin in 1945) describes the conversion of the hero from his bourgeois roots to a new proletarian identity. While this work became a model for later GDR novels with similar conversion plots, it also retraced the history of German fascism and antifascism. Like Seghers and Becher, other writers chronicled more than just the Nazi years; they went back to the First World War or Bismarck's Germany — for example, Arnold Zweig in his novel cycle, *Der große Krieg der weißen Männer* (The Great War of White Men, 1927–1958) and Willi Bredel with his trilogy — *Die Väter* (The Fathers, 1948, first published under a different title in 1943), *Die Söhne* (The Sons, 1949), and *Die Enkel* (The Grandchildren, 1953). Other writers focused on Nazi Germany; with his novel *Stalingrad* (1945), Theodor Plievier provided the keyword for the painful liberation from Nazism. Shortly thereafter he turned his back on Communism and moved to the West.

*Poetry between classicism and Modernism*

Johannes R. Becher embodied the attempt to reclaim the German literary tradition under socialist ideals. His lyrical production was in keeping with an antifascist and democratic renewal of an inclusive ideal of the popular front. His works

236 • AFTER 1945: MODERNISM REVISITED

did not welcome the more aggressive proletarian and revolutionary literary traditions of many Communist authors, such as Erich Weinert in poetry and Friedrich Wolf in drama, although the latter tradition found a continuation in the poems of Kuba (pseudonym of Kurt Barthel, 1914–1967). Becher's poetry integrated classical forms, such as the sonnet and even religious motifs; for example, the poet-speaker says in the poem "In diesem Sinne . . ." (In this Sense . . ., 1948) that he carries "the pain / Of the people as a cross through his poem" [das Leid / Des Volks als Kreuz durch sein Gedicht].

This poem is typical of Becher's tendency to reach past the Nazi years to sing the "old songs" [alten Lieder] again, as he wrote in another poem. Like the old songs, however, his new poems were in the style of a conventional classicism. Worse, often vague and sentimental references to pain and sorrow did not afford any help in understanding what had happened to his native country that Becher loved so much and that he glorified in his poems. This characteristic made his poetry prototypical of a tension that ran through lyrical production in East Germany into the 1970s. On the one hand, the poem was supposed to fulfill a political role (and Becher also wrote poems about how the nationalization of power plants improves the world); on the other hand, the poem aspired to a form that was beautiful in some way or even classicist.

This tension can be found in poetry by Peter Huchel and Stephan Hermlin, two of the few practitioners of Modernist poetry, which was in conflict with East German doctrine. Huchel, who had been close to the poetic circle around the magazine *Kolonne* before the war, added a sense of history to his nature poems in the collection *Gedichte* (Poems, 1948). Thus, nature was less a symbol of a secret meaning beyond humanity than an expression of human experiences and political issues, such as war and freedom. This contrast to *Naturmagie*, which was becoming increasingly popular in West Germany, was characteristic of the different treatment of landscape and nature in poems by younger GDR poets. In addition, Huchel exerted a great influence as editor of the magazine *Sinn und Form* (Sense and Form) from the magazine's inception in 1949 until his forced resignation in 1962, after he had printed many texts that were considered formalist and were not welcomed by the official cultural policy of the GDR.

Stephan Hermlin had relocated to East Germany in 1947, and while the country was slowly moving toward Socialist Realism and anti-Modernism, he attempted to express antifascism in Modernist form and to give a political function to hermetic poetry. He had been especially influenced by Expressionism and Surrealism; for example, in his collection *Zwölf Balladen von den großen Städten* (Twelve Ballads of the Great Cities, 1945), the vision of the new city "like forests of marble" [wie Wälder aus Marmor] emerges from social commitment but, echoing Baudelaire's phrase "forests of symbols," is also expressed in a rarified and stylized language that obscured the poems' political intent. In the 1950s Hermlin stopped publishing poetry, and his approach to Modernism did not find direct successors.

*Theater and the new focus on* **Aufbau** The theater in the eastern part of Germany was revived in a strong effort; however, *Die Illegalen* (People in the Underground, 1946) by Günther Weisenborn (1902–1969) was the only postwar play that had a significant success there. To let the world know that many Germans had been willing to fight and, if necessary, die for humanity, Weisenborn documented the "illegal," but moral, behavior of the resistance, in which he had participated and which he had paid for by being imprisoned by the Nazis for three years. Without the use of superficial glorification, the play's effectiveness lay in the emotional impact of its scenes. It had performances in fifteen theaters in the East; in contrast, it was performed in only four in the West. Conversely, the two most successful new plays in the West, *Des Teufels General* and *Draußen vor der Tür*, were not performed in the East because they were considered to be apologetic for the Nazi past.

The theaters in the East performed classical and modern plays, as well as exile plays, such as Georg Kaiser's *Der Soldat Tanaka* (Private Tanaka, 1940) and Friedrich Wolf's *Professor Mamlock* (1933). Wolf, who had returned to East Berlin in late 1945, moved away from his earlier agitprop plays and wrote dramas in the Aristotelian tradition in order to turn the theater into the workers' battle stage. The foremost German playwright of the time and major opponent of such an Aristotelian aesthetics, Bertolt Brecht, did not come to East Berlin until the fall of 1948, and it was July of the following year before he was able to open his own theater, the Berliner Ensemble. Brecht adapted his theatrical style by retaining the epic element, but entertainment took on a new importance, because he assumed that he had to reach an audience in a different way after the German people had suffered twelve years of Nazi indoctrination. While Brecht did not write major plays after his return to East Berlin, he established a theatrical tradition that was influential and controversial in both East and West Germany — controversial in the West because Brecht's Marxism was suspect and in the East because his plays were often understood as antirealist and decadent.

By 1949 demands increased in the East for literature to refocus on the new achievements in the process of building socialism and rebuilding the destroyed country. These demands ushered in the new era of *Aufbau* literature, where *Aufbau* means "building up" in a political sense. The model for *Aufbau* literature had been provided by Soviet

Socialist Realism of the 1930s and 1940s and came to bear on East German literary production primarily in the 1950s. This contributed to the rift between East German literature and Modernism. At the same time, it created a curious parallelism: in both the Western and Eastern German zones (and later states), a real and profound analysis of National Socialism did not happen. Both Germanies were too busy rebuilding their own lives.

## Redefined Continuity, Part II: Celebration of Inner Emigration in the West

The literature of the Western zones was determined by the writers of the inner emigration who continued the classicist tradition, while, in their treatment of modern issues, their literary products could merge with Modernism. The later work of Stefan Andres, who was, with Rudolf Hagelstange (1912–1984), one of the youngest in this group, was Modernist. Older authors include Gertrud von Le Fort (1876–1971), Werner Bergengruen, Hans Carossa, Ernst Penzoldt (1892–1955), and Rudolf Alexander Schröder.

*Conservatism in poetry*

Bergengruen had a considerable impact after the war. His collection of poems *Dies irae* (Day of Wrath, 1945) documented the author's moral integrity, conservative Christianity, and traditional poetics. His five-stanza poem "Die letzte Epiphanie" (The Last Epiphany) was reportedly written in 1944 and secretly passed from reader to reader. It is an uncompromisingly critical poem that updates the message of the Bible: God comes to earth, is killed by mankind, and returns to judge. It is an immediately gripping poem in which three individuals symbolize major groups who fell victim to Nazi terror and exploitation: the "pale Hebrew" [bleicher Hebräer], the "mentally retarded old woman" [geistesgeschwächte Greisin], and the "orphaned boy" [verwaister Knabe]. These are not only the meek, who should have deserved the care and love of their German neighbors but instead were killed by them; they also personify the divine, for which all humans are equal, regardless of whether they consider themselves the master race. The poem ends with the foreboding question: "Now I come as judge. Do you recognize me now?" [Nun komm ich als Richter. Erkennt ihr mich jetzt?].

While Bergengruen's moral attitude was beyond reproach, the religious embedding took Nazism out of the individual's realm of responsibility. Two related, yet fundamentally different, issues were confused. On the one hand, there was the political issue of undeniable guilt and responsibility for Nazi atrocities; on other hand, there was the humanitarian issue of the German civilian population's suffering, especially from the air raids and from the vast postwar dislocations. Both issues were real and legitimate, but public opinion often forgot the issue of the Nazi atrocities in favor of the German suffering. The confusion was not on Bergengruen's part, but his poems, such as "Die Stimme" (The Voice), seem to invite such a confusion. The voice addresses presumably the German people, asking: "Where is thy brother Abel?" [Wo ist dein Bruder Abel?]. While this implies that the people are the guilty ones who have slain their brother, in their ensuing suffering they discover "the ancient secret: 'Abel — that's you'" [das Urgeheimnis: "Abel — das bist du"]. Embedded in Christianity, universal suffering also allows for universal forgiveness and salvation. Such an awareness could have given strength in addressing the political issues of responsibility, as it probably did to Bergengruen, who wanted his people to change its way of thinking, hence the last poem in *Dies irae* ends with the imperative: "Metanoeite" (change your way of thinking). Overall, however, religious and spiritual awareness was more typically used to avoid dealing with the past other than understanding oneself as a victim of the times.

Another example of restoration, Gottfried Benn's comeback as the dominant Modernist force in poetry (and essay writing) in West German literature up to about the mid-1950s is symptomatic of the public interest in Modernist art forms combined with a reluctance to deal with political issues that went beyond generalities, such as an evocation of cultural decline. Since Benn was banned from publishing in Germany not just by the Nazis but also after the war by the Allies, his *Statische Gedichte* (Static Poems) appeared in Switzerland in 1948 after it was first published privately by Benn in 1946. These poems are distinctly Modernist and reflect Benn's withdrawal from political issues after his short-lived flirtation with Nazism. His creative nihilism now was centered on the separation of the world's history and artistic consciousness. Art and science provided the forms with which individuality could express itself in a meaningless world. In this manner, history became accessible after all, but only in an abstract sense.

This sense of history became geological with Benn. "Decay, discharge, downfall — / in toxic spheres, cold / some stygian souls after all, / lone ones, tall and old" [Verfall, Verflammen, Verfehlen — / in toxischen Sphären, kalt, / noch einige stygische Seelen / einsame, hoch und alt]. The poem from which these lines are taken, "Quartär" (Quaternary), evokes the passing of time on vast geological scales encompassing "quarternary cycles" [Quartäre Cyclen] with the Sphinx, Babylon, huge brains, and divine dreams. All of this is done with formal mastery and in the relaxed rhythm in which great poetry expresses an existential experience — of Benn's monstrous subjectivity, as it has been called by some critics.

The continuation of *Naturlyrik* belongs in this context, at least in part. After Oskar Loerke's death, Wilhelm Lehmann emerged as the leading proponent of this type of poetry. More than just evoking nature, Lehmann attempted to create a form that was itself natural. The cycles of nature supplied a remedy for the wounds inflicted on humankind, and Lehmann let grass grow over the war and its aftermath. Yet there remained a sense of foreboding; the speaker seems alone with nature (and art). In "Entzückter Staub" (Enchanted Dust), which gave Lehmann's 1946 collection of poems its title, the scenery is devoid of people, even when a farmyard is mentioned. For Lehmann's poems, as for much of *Naturlyrik* in general, the ambiguity of apolitical escapism and political potential was characteristic. The combination of looking at reality and not having to confront political issues (while also understanding that this type of poetry had just barely been able to survive as nonfascist poetry during the Third Reich) contributed to the popularity of *Naturlyrik* immediately after the war and in the 1950s. The political potential of *Naturlyrik* was expanded by younger authors in East and West, such as Erich Fried, Stephan Hermlin, Peter Huchel, Karl Krolow (1915–1999), Walter Höllerer (b. 1922), and Ernst Meister (1911–1979).

**Exile authors in West Germany**

Exile writers were not as well represented in the West as were inner emigration and the young writers. The exile authors' return to the West was often not a full return, reflecting the West German reluctance to welcome them. Thomas Mann, Erich Maria Remarque, and Carl Zuckmayer, for example, all returned to Europe from the United States but settled in Switzerland. Mann's *Doktor Faustus* is one of world literature's intellectually and formally most well-rounded novels; it could have been a great contribution toward coming to terms with the Nazi past if it had not become enmeshed in the politicized debate of exile versus inner emigration.

*Doktor Faustus* is the fictitious biography of the composer Adrian Leverkühn, narrated by Serenus Zeitblom, who, as Leverkühn's friend since their childhood, is also a character in the novel. In the interaction of two time frames — Leverkühn's life in the first third of the twentieth century and the political situation from 1943 to 1945, when Zeitblom writes his friend's biography — the story of Leverkühn's tormented soul merges with the commentary on Germany's problematic history. The narrative parallelism suggests that the regression into accepting archaic and demonic principles is both an individual and a general process — a parallelism made explicit in the novel's last sentence, which asks God to have mercy on "my friend, my Fatherland" [mein Freund, mein Vaterland], and reinforced by the novel's combining of various aspects from German intellectual and cultural history, such as Arnold Schoenberg's twelve-tone music and episodes from Friedrich Nietzsche's life. The allusion to Nietzsche emphasizes the symbolic character of Leverkühn for Germany's path into National Socialism because Nietzsche's philosophy (while also claimed by other traditions) had supplied important impulses to nationalist and reactionary thought.

Leverkühn is passionately attracted to music's duality of mathematical strictness and magical ambiguity. He experiences the confrontation with the Modernist challenge of rationality and irrationality as a threat of artistic sterility, which he battles with increasing irrationality. Events that are associated with the demonic weave through his life and, as leitmotifs, structure the narrative. Leverkühn unconsciously enters into a pact with the devil by knowingly infecting himself with syphilis in 1906 — a variation of the motif of a terminal disease whose progression produces artistic greatness. His self-admitted lack of human warmth foreshadows the final intrusion of the demonic into his life in 1911 or 1912, when his conversation with the devil, who radiates the coldness that is necessary to live in hell, takes place. Similarly, Leverkühn forsakes love to acquire the coldness that is necessary to endure the heat of brilliant artistic creation. The account of sealing his pact with the devil is told by Leverkühn himself; Zeitblom, an embodiment of reason, merely copies his friend's report, which he interprets as a document of Leverkühn's mental torment rather than of real events. Leverkühn spends the following years in growing isolation and composes brilliant music. In the absence of love, life's burning intensity is dominated by death — a reversal of Hans Castorp's insight in *Der Zauberberg*. After the completion of his major work and its presentation to his friends in 1930, Leverkühn collapses; he never recovers from this attack of dementia and dies ten years later.

Carl Zuckmayer, who had returned to Germany as a civilian working for the American military government, went back to the United States but finally settled in Switzerland. His play *Des Teufels General* (The Devil's General, 1946) was among the most successful dramas of the immediate postwar years. It presented an authentic picture of inner emigration and resistance, although it was written by an exile author while he was living in exile. Moreover, the play was controversial because the motivation of the hero was nonpolitical; he rejected the Nazis as a matter of the heart, while still working for the Nazi war machine. General Harras (based on the real-life air force general Ernst Udet) is such an avid flyer that he cannot stand not being involved in building up the air force; therefore, he becomes the devil's (Hitler's) general, even though he detests the Nazis. Under false suspicion of sabotaging airplanes, Harras comes across a resistance movement and covers for it with his life by flying a plane he knows has been sabotaged. The presentation of his heroic death was seen by some critics as an exoneration of the German military before its role in the Third Reich had been fully assessed.

Nevertheless, the first version of the play was dedicated to the memory of three resistance fighters who had been murdered by "Germany's hangmen" [Deutschlands Henkern]. The flat character of Oderbruch, the resistance fighter, corresponds to the relative insignificance of the resistance movement in Germany. General Harras identifies the root of all evil that needs to be purged — Hitler. And he admits that, as the devil's general in this life, "he must also arrange accommodations for him in hell" [der muß ihm auch Quartier in der Hölle machen]. This attitude amounts to taking responsibility without making wrongs right, and Zuckmayer's criticism of the traditional hero is dulled by Harras's verbally swashbuckling gusto. But the ambiguity of Zuckmayer's play highlights the urgency that was felt by some writers to move beyond the traditions of inner emigration and exile and to start over again.

## The Radical "Rediscovery" of Modernism in the West: Point Zero

There was no *Nullpunkt* (Point Zero) for German literature: no such privileged start from scratch existed in the *Nullstunde* or *Stunde Null* (Zero Hour) of the *Kahlschlag* (clearing a place by leveling everything) — not even for the young authors, many of whom had published before 1945. Nevertheless, while Modernism had not been completely suppressed, certain Modernist traditions, such as the American short story, took full effect on German writers only after the end of the war. Also, the war had left Germany in rubble, and it is conceivable that literature experienced a similar rupture — at least in the way younger writers viewed their literary options. Consequently, the Zero Hour was a psychological perspective — less a physical reality than a feeling that a new start was necessary.

Just as reality had been radically altered by the war, literature about the new reality was expected to be radically different. Wolfgang Weyrauch (1907–1980) used the term *Kahlschlag*; Heinrich Böll (1917–1985) spoke of *Trümmerliteratur* (literature from the rubble); and other young writers used similar terms to express their poetic creed that literature had to take stock and examine reality with X-ray vision to get to the bottom of the matter. These programmatic declarations found their exemplary application in the way Wolfgang Borchert (1921–1947) revealed the fundamental disruption in human relationships as a result of the war in short stories such as "Das Brot" (The Bread, 1949). While this was the rhetoric of a strict realism, in practice the new literature often used the tradition of magic realism.

*Taking stock and "strict" realism in poetry*

Günter Eich created a landscape of experiences devoid of direct human presence yet unthinkable without it. In the poem "Latrine," most basic human functions render cultural achievements questionable, and Eich rhymes "Hölderlin" with "Urin" (but he still rhymes). He published poems that dealt with his experiences in American POW camps in the magazine *Der Ruf* and in his 1948 collection of poems *Abgelegene Gehöfte* (Remote Farms).

Life in a POW camp was also the background of "Inventur" (Inventory), Eich's best-known poem and the signature poem of the Zero Hour. It exemplified the new laconic approach to reality in the sense of a strict realism; at the same time, it pointed to the tradition of magic realism and the related attempt to use metaphors in more or less hermetic ways to grasp the enormity of the Nazi legacy. In seven unrhymed four-line stanzas the speaker takes stock of his worldly possessions in a simple naming process: "This is my cap, / this is my coat, / here is my razor / in the bag of linen" [Dies ist meine Mütze, / dies ist mein Mantel, / hier mein Rasierzeug / im Beutel aus Leinen]. These seemingly artless lines evoke a sense of bare survival and achieve the virtually impossible: they create art (a poem) out of nothing — or, more precisely, out of a reality that has been reduced to very little and is experienced as nothing. After classicist mystifications of reality and magic mediation via a secret symbol, Eich's poetry was perceived as quite fresh in tone and content.

Still, "Inventur" also contains hints that go beyond immediate reality (other than the mere fact that the poem as an art form, by necessity, transcends reality); after all, Eich came from the tradition of *Naturlyrik*, which is more obvious in other poems. The POW's most prized possession is the "lead of a pencil" [Bleistiftmine], because it does something that has no immediate practical function: "During the day it writes verses / which I thought up at night" [Tags schreibt sie mir Verse, / die nachts ich erdacht]. In subtle self-referentiality, the poem suggests that reality needs to be assessed, but since reality has been reduced to nothingness and meaninglessness, meaning must be found somewhere else. Thus, celebrating the pencil metonymically celebrates the power of poetry. The radical newness of tone and implied approach to reality becomes evident by comparison, for instance, with "Tabula rasa" (Clean Slate, 1949), by Hans Egon Holthusen (1913–1997), who voices the same sentiment of making a fresh start. His tone and poetic means, however, are traditional. While "Tabula rasa" declares that "we say stuff without rhyme or reason" [Wir reden ungereimtes Zeug], the poem itself rhymes; it also alludes to a vague personification of meaning "murmuring in secret" [raunend in Verborgenheit].

*The older generation of prose writers and magic realism*

Some authors of the older generation, mostly of the inner emigration with works influenced by magic realism, saw their postwar works in a more directly political way than, for example, Wilhelm Lehmann saw his poetry. Representative authors and works include Hermann Kasack with *Die Stadt hinter dem Strom* (The City Beyond the River, 1947), Elisabeth Langgässer with *Das unauslöschliche Siegel* (The Indelible Seal, 1946), and Ernst Kreuder (1903–1972) with *Die Gesellschaft vom Dachboden* (The Society of the Attic, 1946).

All successes with the reading public, these works typically treated reality as a nightmare, so it was difficult to take stock other than to turn inward to parable and religious experience — be it specifically Christianity (Catholicism in Langgässer's novel) or general spirituality (Kasack, Kreuder). The parabolic view of reality could suggest eternal values and fatalism, which often seemed close to — and hence apologetic of — the fascist concept of history. Kreuder's short novel, however, was well received internationally and welcomed with rave reviews in unlikely quarters in Germany, such as from Alfred Andersch (1914–1980) in *Der Ruf*, the major magazine promoting a new political and literary beginning in Germany.

*Die Gesellschaft vom Dachboden* was a new adaptation of magic realism that struck a chord with younger writers because it presented imagination as an option for voicing protest instead of obscuring reality in evoking a metaphysical realm. The narrator and the five others he joins in a secret association know that it takes more to survive than simply observing their city's reality; survival requires a creative impulse, and nothing is more opposed to creativity than stupidity, which, in turn, is nothing but a lack of imagination. Therefore, in a romantic and Dadaist fashion, the group proclaims that "each one become his own visionary" [jeder sein eigener Phantast werden]. Their ideas, conversations, and adventures are bizarre and imaginative; they involve the idea of the secret society itself, conversations about literature, a treasure hunt, and the rescue of a young girl who is to be married off against her will.

Most important, however, is that in these activities the relationship to reality is always present, because reality is the prerequisite for survival. But for humankind's survival, reality needs to be addressed with imagination, and this is what the group does. For example, the group keeps revising its seven principles. In their first discussion, the members decide to replace the principle of peacefulness with independence, because they are, after all, fighting ignorance. Much later they decide to get rid of the unrealistic principle of invincibility in favor of flexibility because they understand that, as a result of the war, not even large empires are invincible.

In addition to the older and established writers,
*The short story* there was the young (or, at least, predominantly
younger) generation of the *Kahlschläger*, or writers
of Zero Hour literature. Influenced by the contemporary American
short story, a new form of brief narrative emerged and remained a
dominant genre of German prose literature throughout the 1950s in
the work of most young authors, including Ilse Aichinger (b. 1921),
Wolfgang Borchert, Heinrich Böll, and Wolfdietrich Schnurre. The
short story was usually contrasted to the novella, which evolved during
the Renaissance with Giovanni Boccaccio (1313–1375) and is defined
as a narration of a singular event in a tightly organized structure that
follows the pattern of a classical drama (exposition, rising action, turning point, falling action, resolution); the significance of a novella can
often be objectified in one symbol. The modern short story, in contrast, narrates everyday life. Consequently, its structure is less tightly
organized; its ending is usually open, and, since an everyday event is
narrated, the beginning often appears open or arbitrary. As the action
continues, everyday life receives a symbolic meaning through an interruption, while the mode of presentation is realistic. The characteristics
of the short story played well in the context of Zero Hour literature because the short story's emphasis on everyday life invited the presentation of basic human experiences, the related realistic mode
accommodated a matter-of-fact and laconic language, and its principal
openness and brevity allowed expression of disillusionment and unresolved issues appropriate to the contemporary mood.

During the early years the search for a simple language dominated,
as did the theme of war, where "war" represents a wide thematic field
from war events themselves to the effects of war's aftermath on civilian
life. In the wake of Germany's total defeat and collapse, disorientation
was often expressed as the individual's subjection to blind fate. This was
a disillusioned fatalism that did not have much in common with the
fascist sense of fatalism, where man was subject to history yet still destined to ride the crest of history. Extended into the postwar German
situation, this image meant that the human being had fallen off the
crest and had little hope of recovering from the injuries sustained in the
fall, because it was like a fall from grace. The short story's fatalism, as
much as it reflected the actual contemporary mood, prevented a more
thorough social analysis (which was the reason for the rejection of the
short story by the GDR). Borchert's "Das Brot" and Schnurre's "Das
Begräbnis" (The Funeral) can stand as exemplary for the immediate
postwar years in the West. However, both writers produced many other
short stories of equal quality, and so did other authors.

Borchert has remained the prototypical writer of Zero Hour literature not just because of the significance of his short stories and the pre-

dominance of his only play, *Draußen vor der Tür*, but also because his work was restricted to this literary phase as a result of his early death at the age of twenty-six, the day before his play's premiere in 1947. Borchert's prose ranges from short stories that focus on plot to manifesto-style texts, such as "Das ist unser Manifest" (This is Our Manifesto) and "Dann gibt es nur eins" (Then There Is Only One Thing). The latter is a passionate plea to "say NO!" [sag NEIN!] to any attempt at making war. The stories portray, as part of the general war theme, life in a country reduced to rubble. They take the reader directly to the ruins, as in the story "Nachts schlafen die Ratten doch" (But the Rats Sleep at Night).

Although not explicitly mentioned, the brutal, yet everyday, postwar reality is also the background for "Das Brot," a story of starvation and broken trust. In the middle of the night an older woman is awakened by a noise and surprises her husband in the kitchen; he has been secretly eating bread, because the daily ration of three slices leaves him hungry. But he hides the fact, and she has to deduce it from evidence, such as his chewing and the crumbs on the table. The next evening the woman gives the man four slices, which reduces her ration, but she tells him that her stomach does not tolerate bread well in the evenings anyway. After a long while, he sits down at the table with her. This plot summary is not much shorter than the story, which is about two pages long. Except for brief and matter-of-fact descriptions, the story consists of laconic dialogue that reveals in its repetitions the everyday banality of life.

But it is no longer truthful dialogue; both the wife and the husband use it to lie to each other. It is in their actions that the dilemma of betrayal and loyalty becomes visible. The bread is the symbol of the breakdown of the marriage, as well as the chance for redemption. The husband lies to hide his selfish act, and the wife commits a selfless act of sacrifice that underscores both that she understands what happened (although he tried to conceal it) and that she loves her husband. The way the husband hesitates at the end of the story suggests that he knows that she understands. The husband's final hesitation could imply the moment that he needs to accept his wife's sacrifice in triumph or the moment he needs to realize in humility how much she loves him. Either reading leaves the story open-ended, because husband and wife still do not talk about the real issues, and there is no indication that they will. The issue remains unresolved, as did many issues in postwar Germany.

Yet the bread refers to more than the material world. It is a symbol of the state of a particular marriage, but it is also the symbol of the importance of communication, love, loyalty, and other intangible human values. Consequently, even in its most condensed and laconic form, literature of the Zero Hour assessed more than just factual reality. "Das Brot," however, does not include phenomena that do not occur in reality. Wolfdietrich Schnurre's short story "Das Begräbnis" takes that additional step from strict realism toward magic realism. In addition, Schnurre's story was significant in the history of postwar German literature because the author read it to fellow authors in 1947 at what turned out to be the first meeting of the legendary *Gruppe 47* (Group 47).

"Das Begräbnis" displays a laconic language similar to Borchert's story, but Schnurre's style reduces the linguistic material even further. Terse, rhythmical, and colloquial, the tone of "Das Begräbnis" creates a sense of hectic casualness. The fragmentation of language includes reduction of words to single sounds, for example, *n* and *m* for the articles *ein* and *dem*, respectively. It also includes one-word sentences and telegram-style sentences — for example, "(I) pick it up" [Nehm ihn] — and absorption of the subject into the verb by syntactic inversion, such as "Klopft's" for "es klopft" (somebody is knocking). These devices create an offhand tone that contrasts with the possible metaphysical implications of the story. At the beginning of the story there is the knock on the door, but nobody seems to be there; then the call "Hallo!" being heard, but again nobody seems to be there; however, a letter lies on the table.

There is no discernable agent; thus, the letter has appeared out of nowhere. It turns out to be an announcement for a memorial service for God, who, "loved by nobody, hated by nobody, died today after long suffering endured with heavenly patience" [Von keinem geliebt, von keinem gehasst, starb heute nach langen, mit himmlischer Geduld ertragenem Leiden]. The realistic tone and setting of the story make it conceivable that someone just dropped off the announcement and that, although the funeral is grotesque (the coffin slips, and the dead body falls out), the dead man's last name is Gott, since it says "H. Gott" on the coffin. The name could be a pun on the German "Herrgott" (God the Father). The mysterious beginning points beyond strict realism. While its potential is only touched on in Schnurre's story, magic realism became more important later for some writers of the *Gruppe 47*, which began with a strictly realistic program of Zero Hour literature.

In addition to the established groups of exile and inner emigration and the emerging group of Zero Hour literature, there were authors who asserted their independence from any group. One of the great German literary outsiders of the second half of the twentieth century, Arno Schmidt, began publishing with the three stories in the collection *Leviathan* (1949). Schmidt turned to cosmic and mythological treatment of experiences of total war that shattered his own and his generation's idealism.

*The drama about
an absurd world*

Drama literally returned to a world in rubble, because the theaters, just like the rest of German cities, lay in rubble. While this situation could have meant the end of live performances, there was a need for theater. People came to watch plays in makeshift theaters, at times paying not with money but with barter currency, such as coal to heat the building. The first theater programs were dominated by German Classicist plays — such as Goethe's *Iphigenie* (1779), Schiller's *Don Carlos* (1787), and Lessing's *Nathan der Weise* (Nathan the Wise, 1779) — and the translations of contemporary American plays, including *Of Mice and Men* (1937), by John Steinbeck (1902–1968), and *Our Town* (1938), by Thornton Wilder (1897–1975). These plays received the military government's support as part of the re-education efforts, which did not put a premium on theatrical innovation. Plays by Brecht, Toller, and other authors who had gone into exile and by French authors, such as Albert Camus (1913–1960) and Jean Paul Sartre (1905–1980), were greeted with less support; however, French existentialist plays would strongly influence the German theater of the next decade.

In addition, much drama was written for radio, which was a major focus of literary life in the postwar years. Political cabaret was revived, with Erich Kästner leading the way by establishing *Die Schaubude* (The Show Booth) in 1945 and *Die kleine Freiheit* (The Little Liberty) in 1949, both in Munich. Other cabarets of the early postwar years — for example, the Berlin *Stachelschweine* (Porcupines), founded in 1949, and the Düsseldorf *Kom(m)ödchen* (Little Comedy/Commode), founded in 1947 — contributed to the genre's growing popularity, which went beyond the successes political cabaret had enjoyed during the Weimar Republic. The programs of the postwar cabarets were later broadcast on radio, then on television; they were especially popular until the 1960s, when political changes resulted in other outlets for voicing criticism of a materialistic and increasingly wealthy Adenauer Germany.

In the context of Zero Hour literature, Wolfgang Borchert's *Draußen vor der Tür* (The Man Outside, 1947) was the most significant play (it was originally a radio play), and in the context of the entire theatrical production in Germany before 1949 it was one of the three dominant plays; the others were Zuckmayer's *Des Teufels General* and Weisenborn's *Die Illegalen*. Borchert transposed the immediate postwar experience into an effective play about a disillusioned soldier named Beckmann, who returns to a meaningless world that, while reduced to rubble, has proceeded on without him. The play was a huge success because it remained within the tradition of illusionist theater by offering a tremendous source of personal identification to its audience. At the same time, it presented a political statement and could be understood as an accusation of the nascent political restoration. Following the tradition of Expressionist drama, however, the play failed to establish its own theatrical tradition, and it stopped short of a direct analysis; instead of revealing the reasons for the political situation, it proclaimed a general pacifism.

Like Expressionist monodramas, Borchert's play moves from one station of the protagonist's development to the next, but this time no change is effected other than an awareness of utter isolation. As a symbol of his different view of the world, Beckmann continues to wear the goggles of his gas mask. In his initial desperation he tries to drown himself in the Elbe; however, the river, personified as a woman, refuses to take his life. The Other [der Andere], Beckmann's alter ego — or, rather, the personification of Beckmann's optimism and will to live — is in constant dialogue with Beckmann as he tries to start a new life. But he has to come to terms with a series of failures to connect to people, including the following: Beckmann finds his wife in love with another man. He meets a girl, but the girl's husband, a missing soldier like Beckmann, returns. His wartime colonel now refuses to accept responsibility for the death of his soldiers, a responsibility that Beckmann has on his conscience and wants to give back to the colonel.

At the end Beckmann falls asleep during a dialogue with the Other and has a dream: he meets God and Death, allegorical characters who were introduced in the prelude to the play. God is a disoriented and powerless old man, wailing about humankind's fate: "My poor, poor children!" [Meine armen, armen Kinder!], and Beckmann is disgusted by him. Death is just raking in his dues; when Beckmann meets him, he looks like a road sweeper. Finally, Beckmann briefly encounters everyone he has met throughout the play again. He wakes up and, suddenly, is aware that he has to go on living but also that he is all alone; even the Other has disappeared. Beckmann's return to Germany has so far been a dialogue with himself. For survival in the real world, however, he needs real dialogue with real human beings, but they are not there, and the play ends with his desperate outcry: "Doesn't anyone answer???" [Gibt denn keiner Antwort???].

Borchert's message of pacifism and self-criticism was soon out of fashion as social and political restoration progressed. But the play's view of the modern world as a world of anxiety, alienation, and the absurd in combination with its grotesque elements, connected it loosely with plays by the Swiss authors Max Frisch and Friedrich Dürrenmatt during the immediate postwar years. Frisch showed how war guilt is dealt with by presenting nonrealist visions in which the dead walk among the living but cannot be heard in *Nun singen sie wieder* (Now They Sing Again, premiered 1945, published 1946). In *Die chinesische Mauer* (The Chinese Wall, premiered 1946, published 1947) history follows its own dynamic in a farcical plot that takes place both today and in ancient China, with historical personalities from Brutus to Napoleon showing up. Dürrenmatt's *Romulus der Große* (Romulus the Great, premiered 1949, published 1958) exploits the grotesque contrast of the last Roman emperor's stoic retirement to country life with the upheaval that ends in defeat for his empire. Frisch and Dürrenmatt established themselves as preeminent playwrights in the 1950s.

### *Der Ruf* and the *Gruppe 47*

The political magazine *Der Ruf* articulated the Zero Hour belief of a generation of young authors and, after its short life, led to the establishment of the informal *Gruppe 47*, named after the year of its first meeting. The list of participants in the group meetings reads like a who's who of contemporary German-language writers from Ingeborg Bachmann and Peter Handke (b. 1942) to the Nobel Prize winners Heinrich Böll and Günter Grass. The link between the magazine and the group was the magazine's coeditor and the founder of the *Gruppe 47*, Hans Werner Richter (1908–1993). Ideologically close to the Communist Party, Richter had attempted active resistance against the Nazis and had been arrested in 1940 under suspicion of being the leader of the pacifist youth movement, but he was released and drafted into the military. As a POW in American camps, he worked for newspapers and magazines for his fellow prisoners, including *Der Ruf*, which was edited by Gustav René Hocke (1908–1985) and Alfred Andersch. When Andersch went to Munich to edit *Der Ruf* as a magazine "of the young generation" [der jungen Generation] after the war, Richter followed as coeditor. The first issue of the new *Der Ruf* appeared on August 15, 1946.

The rhetoric in *Der Ruf* was characterized by a pervasive dichotomy of *old* versus *young*, rather than of *old* versus *new*; a problematic generalization of "young generation"; and the difficulty of starting a genuine dialogue with other discourses. *Der Ruf*, literally meaning "the cry" or "the call," indeed called out to its readers, the young generation. While the contrast of *old* versus *new* is functionally unstable because the new does not exclude the old as long as the latter has been renewed, the contrast *old* versus *young* is more radical: youth is opposed to that which never will be young again. Therefore, the rhetoric of *Der Ruf* created the impression of an irreversible division.

The definition of the magazine's target group, the young generation, was problematic, because this category could not be well defined. Still, the editorial in the first issue of *Der Ruf*, "Das junge Europa formt sein Gesicht" (Young Europe Develops Its Face), attempted a definition: the young German generation comprised men and women between eighteen and thirty-five. The two categories that follow are descriptive of the young generation as a whole rather than restrictive in order to narrow down the group. Its "non-responsibility for Hitler" [Nicht-Verantwortlichkeit für Hitler] and its "experience of the war at the front and of imprisonment" [Front- und Gefangenenerlebnis] were seen to separate the young generation as a whole from the older and younger generations. This definition is perfectly descriptive of the magazine's self-image, which fell short of reality; for example, Richter himself did not meet the age criterion for the young generation — he was about three years too old. The editorial presented an ideological construct of the magazine's projected audience rather than a theoretical definition.

With the privilege of hindsight, the programmatic, speculative, and ideological character of the editorials becomes obvious, because the postwar renewal of Germany turned out to be a restoration and not a "spiritual rebirth in an absolute and radical beginning from scratch" [geistigen Wiedergeburt in dem absoluten und radikalen Beginn von vorn] that the young generation of *Der Ruf* hoped and worked for. Since restorative tendencies in German politics could already be felt in 1946, the polemic in *Der Ruf* against such restoration is easy to understand. It can be speculated that the discourse in the editorials of *Der Ruf* did not aim at a dialogue with other discourses but rather, because of the onset of a restoration, purposefully aimed at a polemical confrontation. To effect changes, however, dialogue between social groups and their specific forms of discourse was necessary.

The need to develop a new discourse for *Der Ruf* was clearly perceived by Hans Werner Richter, and he employed the rhetoric of the Zero Hour when he condemned the Nazis' "linguistic trash" [Sprachwust]. Consequently, the achievement of *Der Ruf* has to be measured against the goal of overcoming the Nazis' linguistic legacy. The influence of fascist rhetoric was still pervasive, because there is evidence that *Der Ruf* was not able to overcome the linguistic legacy of the Nazi past in its own discourse, such as in *Der Ruf*'s claim: "Fanaticism for the right of mankind to freedom is . . . the great teaching that Europe's youth derives from the experience of dictatorship" [Fanatismus für das Recht des Menschen auf seine Freiheit ist . . . die große Lehre, welche die Jugend Europas aus der Erfahrung der Diktatur zieht].

The problem does not lie with the commitment to human rights but with the way this commitment was expressed. The use of the word *fanaticism* is in the fascist tradition. Victor Klemperer (1881–1960) devoted a short chapter to "Fanatisch" in his personal account of the linguistic history of the Third Reich, *LTI: Notizbuch eines Philologen*. (*LTI: A Literary Scholar's Notebook*, 1947 in East Berlin; *LTI* stands for *Lingua Tertii Imperii*, or language of the Third Reich). Although Klemperer traces the transvaluation of the word *fanaticism* from a vice into a virtue back to French Enlightenment, he insists that never before the Third Reich were the German words *Fanatismus* and *fanatisch* used in a completely positive way — the same way *fanaticism* was used in the *Der Ruf* editorial after the war.

Considering the need for a new start and the resistance to the political and linguistic Nazi legacy, the editors' choices become understandable as a polemic aimed at objecting to some political developments, while affirming others. But a critical self-examination of the basic political assumptions of *Der Ruf* and their rhetorical presentation could have made a dialogue with others more likely. Such a dialogue did not even evolve between Richter and Andersch, on the one hand, and the military government, which decided on licenses for publication, on the other. For example, Richter believed in a third option, a specifically German path between capitalism and Communism, based on the premise that not just the Allies, but the German young generation, too, had won the war. This belief implied the potential of conflict between the editors of *Der Ruf* and the American military government. In regard to the official Allied position on the collective guilt of all Germans, *Der Ruf*'s dichotomy of young versus old suggested the contrast of individual guilt of the politically responsible versus collective guilt, or in brief: guilty versus not guilty. In a commentary on the Nuremberg trials a straightforward distinction was made between those who are guilty (individuals, such as General Keitel) and those who are not guilty (collectively, the young generation). In this way, the polemical rhetoric of *Der Ruf* was part of the editors' difficulties with the military government in terms of the underlying dichotomy of young versus old and its implications that were not in the interest of Allied politics.

After the American military government took *Der Ruf* away from Andersch and Richter in 1947, Richter planned to start a new literary and satirical magazine *Der Skorpion*. The galleys (still with blank spaces for advertisements) of that magazine's first issue exist, but it was never printed, because Richter could not obtain a license. What had been intended as a preparatory meeting of authors in September 1947 to plan the new magazine evolved into regular meetings of an informal group whose membership was determined by Richter's invitations to attend. Over the years a ritual developed for the readings during *Gruppe 47* meetings: Richter would call the group to order by ringing a bell; an author, seated on the "electric chair," would read from one of his or her texts; then the text would be critiqued without the author having the right to justify or explain it.

The *Gruppe 47* dominated the literary scene throughout its twenty years of existence. One of its main functions was to provide a meeting place for authors, critics — and publishers. In this respect, the group can serve as the perfect example of the transformation of Modernism into an establishment art after the Second World War. The *Gruppe 47* changed how authors and publishers interacted with each other within the broader institution of literature. The group represented a wide range of attempts to renew a democratic literature, and, ironically, its criticism of the political situation in Germany became representative of German literature. The group meetings themselves became media events. A generally Modernist conception of literature had become absorbed into the official understanding of what literature was. To say that contemporary West German literature was the literature of the *Gruppe 47* would be an exaggeration, but this statement encapsulates both the real and the perceived influence of the group, which had become part of a kind of cultural imperialism in spite of its own progressive self-image and intentions.

During the late 1960s, criticism of the group as a literary club for establishment writers increased. The *Gruppe 47* is a textbook example of David Harvey's general observation about the relationship between Modernism and the beginning of the counterculture: "for the first time in the history of modernism, artistic and cultural, as well as 'progressive' political revolt had to be directed at a powerful version of modernism itself" (37). During the meeting in 1967, the group was confronted by a student organization that demanded the authors' commitment against the conservative newspaper mogul Axel Springer.

The 1967 meeting was the last, although the Group was never officially disbanded. The meeting in Prague, planned for 1968, could not take place because of the Soviet-led invasion of Czechoslovakia by Warsaw Pact troops. Richter decided that the group would not meet again until it was possible to do so in Prague. When authors were finally able to meet as a group in Prague after the collapse of Communism in Europe, it was not a revival of the *Gruppe 47* but a one-time celebration of the group's achievements. Thus ended, in 1967, contemporary West German literature's most enduring literary force — a force that had begun twenty years earlier, only two years after the end of the Second World War.

# 8: The 1950s: Modernism or Formalism — Nonconformist Literature in the West vs. Socialist Realism in the East

## Social Foundation: Cold War and Restoration

THE COLD WAR between the Western countries (led by the United States) and the Eastern countries (led by the Soviet Union) was perceived as threatening to escalate into a Third World War, especially when local conflicts, such as the two that broke out in 1950, pitted the interests of the superpowers against each other. First, in January 1950 the war in Vietnam started. Second, in June, the Korean conflict began.

The war in Korea helped the West German economy: the "Korea-Boom" aided in a quick recovery that was referred to as the *Wirtschaftswunder* (economic miracle). The policy of combining a free-market economy with social responsibility — the *soziale Marktwirtschaft* proclaimed by Ludwig Erhard — had been politically controversial, but it received the stamp of approval through its success. Industrial production in West Germany in 1948 was only sixty percent what it had been in 1936; in 1952, however, it was 144 percent of the 1936 level. Nevertheless, more that one million households still lived below the poverty line in 1955; seventeen percent of the West German population owned seventy-five percent of the private property. Furthermore, the Nazi legacy proved difficult to overcome; in particular, members of the civil service of the Third Reich were usually rehired because their expert knowledge was needed regardless of their activities during the Nazi regime.

Internationally, both German states were incorporated into a wide network of international treaties. But an underlying and (until 1990) unresolved problem was that neither German state possessed full sovereignty under international law, because no peace treaty had been signed for all of Germany. While each bloc recognized its respective Germany as a sovereign state (in 1954 for the East and in 1955 for the West), the status of Berlin served as a constant reminder of unfinished business. In contrast, Austria regained full sovereignty in 1955 as a neutral nation. The immediate postwar map of central Europe was established when, after a referendum in 1955, autonomous Saarland was officially transferred from French to West German control in 1957.

The East-West confrontation between the superpowers seemed immediately mirrored in the relationship between the two German states. On the one hand, Cold War scenarios projected the two Germanies as the major battlefield of an impending Third World War. This outlook, combined with the knowledge of the Nazi legacy, affected artistic and political awareness in Germany. On the other hand, as time passed and the prospects of reunification dwindled, each German state saw itself in competition with the other to be regarded as the "better" Germany. Typically, a political action in one German state was followed by a reaction in the other. For instance, the newly established West German military accepted its first volunteers on January 2, 1956; and the East German parliament established the GDR's army on January 26 of that year.

While integration with the West (including membership in NATO and in the European Community) was generally accepted as a political goal in the Federal Republic, there was disagreement about specifics. When, bypassing parliament and even his own cabinet, West German chancellor Konrad Adenauer suggested remilitarization as early as August 1950, the event marked the beginning of a long confrontation between proponents of remilitarization and rearmament versus proponents of pacifism. During the 1950s the central issues of the confrontation were remilitarization, NATO, and the atomic bomb. The "fight against death by nuclear war" [Kampf dem Atomtod] became a broad-based movement in 1957 and 1958 that was strongly supported by Social Democrats and labor unions. By 1960 this movement had been superseded by a more independent anti-nuclear-weapon movement that is known as the *Ostermarschbewegung*, because its protest marches were held at Easter. It is generally regarded as a precursor to the protest movement of the late 1960s.

During the same period East Germany took great strides toward building a socialist society with an ambitious first five-year plan that aimed at increasing industrial production by ninety percent. The plan went into effect after the national bloc, including the SED, won 99.7 percent of the vote in the first general — but not free — elections in 1950. The early 1950s brought fundamental changes: the agricultural production cooperatives replaced individual farmers and landowners; the five member states of East Germany were dissolved into fourteen districts; and the East German secret police was established.

After Stalin's death on March 3, 1953, liberalization in the Soviet Union resulted in uncertainties that caused popular uprisings in the Communist countries. June 17, 1953, brought a workers' uprising in East Germany, which was particularly embarrassing for the government because the GDR had portrayed itself as the "state of workers and farmers," the *Arbeiter- und Bauernstaat*. A spontaneous strike against an increase in prescribed productivity spread from East Berlin on June 15 and 16 to over 350 East German cities and towns after the call to join the protest was broadcast to the entire GDR by RIAS, a West Berlin radio station. The revolt was suppressed by Soviet tanks, and twenty-one demonstrators were sentenced to death by Soviet courts-martial or East German courts; twenty East German police and forty Soviet soldiers were also executed for refusing to shoot at demonstrators. The East German revolt of June 17 and the uprisings in Poland and Hungary later in the same year caused only minor disruptions in the GDR, and by the mid-1950s the East German state stabilized after fundamental changes affecting the structure of retail business and education were implemented. Nevertheless, while the number of people who left East Germany for West Germany via the open border peaked at 300,000 in 1953, decreased slightly to 280,000 in 1956, and dropped to 145,000 in 1959, the GDR was still losing its most valuable resource: its citizens.

## The Literary Spectrum

*The doctrine of Socialist Realism and censorship*

Literary developments in the two German states, especially concerning the atmosphere in which literature was produced, exhibited many parallels. The most obvious difference was the doctrine of Socialist Realism, with which the GDR attempted to promote the development of a German socialist literature on the model of the Soviet Union. This literature, which was considered a necessary expression of the new socialist conditions in East Germany, was charged with two additional tasks: overcoming all holdovers of decadent and formalist literature, as Modernism was called, and laying claim to the German literary heritage from classicism to the poetic Realism of the nineteenth century.

Socialist Realist literature was defined by five key criteria. First, it had to relate to the people's interests and needs. Second, the presentation had to be partisan, both in the choice of social reality as subject matter and in describing the world as it was supposed to be according to Marxism. Third, reality had to be mirrored by literature in a concrete way based on understanding social reality as being determined by objective historical forces that would ultimately lead to a Communist society. This criterion provided the keyword *Widerspiegelung* (mirroring). Fourth, typifications were to be generalized from individual cases, in keeping with the belief that class consciousness, not individual subjectivity and irrationality — the obsolete concepts of tragedy and fate — mattered. Fifth, the hero was to be positive but to have minor defects that he or she overcomes in the course of the plot. The hero's final and complete embrace of socialist ideals was supposed to invite reader identification. Since the characters were nontragic (in the sense of the fourth criterion) and represented class consciousness, they all served to glorify socialism.

Socialist Realism was declared the official state literature of the GDR in March 1951 by the Central Committee of the SED. Measures to ensure compliance developed over the years into various levels of censorship. Socialist Realism was embraced by many writers, including Anna Seghers; however, almost all major writers at one point or another broke loose and explored Modernist modes. Such explorations led the state to question the authors' loyalty as citizens and as Communists because Modernism was officially considered not only decadent and bourgeois but something much more dangerous: an ideological weapon of capitalism.

*Reactionary and popular literature in the West*  During the Cold War suspicions of a Communist threat ran high in the West. In spite of its antidemocratic tendencies, reactionary literature was able to thrive in the climate of restoration because of its anti-Communist stance. Not only were new editions of older works published, such as Edwin Erich Dwinger's novel *Die letzten Reiter* (The Last Riders, 1935, new printing, 1953), but Nazi writers remained actively committed to their old ideology. For example, Hans Grimm continued the prewar tradition of his Lippoldsberg Meetings of reactionary poets and became a central figure in German neofascism as an apologist for National Socialism.

Josef Martin Bauer's popular novel *Soweit die Füße tragen* (As Far as the Feet Can Go, 1955) continued the tradition of the adventure novel based on reactionary stereotypes of the good German (the novel's hero escapes from a POW camp in Siberia) and the evil Russian. The success of the novel (within the first six years it sold about half a million copies) coincided with the German chancellor's trip to the Soviet Union in 1955 to negotiate the return of the remaining German POWs. As real as the German people's suffering was, the novel failed to examine the causes that had led to that suffering. Instead, the epilogue advocated the "mercy of forgetting" [Gnade des Vergessens]. The reduction of history to adventure and anecdotal stories struck a chord with many readers and corresponded to the political restoration.

The 1950s also brought the first big successes of three major writers of popular literature, which is referred to as *Trivialliteratur* in German: Heinz G. Konsalik (1921–1999) with *Der Arzt von Stalingrad* (The Physician of Stalingrad, 1956), Johannes Mario Simmel with *Ich gestehe alles* (I Admit Everything, 1954) and especially *Es muß nicht immer Kaviar sein* (It Must Not Always Be Caviar, 1960), and Hans Hellmut Kirst (1914–1989) with the *Null-Acht-Fünfzehn* trilogy (1954–1956;

258 • AFTER 1945: MODERNISM REVISITED

the title, *08/15*, is the military expression for "standard issue"). Regardless of quality, popular literature usually outsells "serious" literature. Internationally, Kirst's trilogy alone sold 2.5 million copies by the mid-1970s; by the mid-1990s the total number of copies sold of all their novels was more than fifteen million for Kirst, about seventy-three million for Simmel, and more than eighty million for Konsalik. Few writers of serious literature are able to match such success; by the time Günter Grass received the Nobel Prize for literature, the total number of copies sold of all his works was about fifteen million.

Yet these numbers are dwarfed by statistics for the lowest-quality fiction: dime novels, mass-produced cheaply on rotation presses, such as the popular German Jerry Cotton thriller series, which was published with a weekly run of 1.8 million copies in the mid-1960s; by the mid-1990s the total sales topped 300 million copies, making Jerry Cotton the world's most successful thriller. The number of copies of dime novels sold just in 1965 is estimated at 130 million. One of the most significant icons of popular culture, the comic book, sold a total of 600 million copies from 1950 to 1960. In contrast, of the books published during the 1950s, Thomas Mann's *Bekenntnisse des Hochstaplers Felix Krull* (Confessions of the Confidence Man Felix Krull, 1954), which could be read with the adventure plot overpowering the novel's complex and parodistic elements, was the only work by an established author of major literary status that had sold more than half a million copies (approximately 700,000) by the early 1960s. Günter Grass, who began publishing in the mid-1950s, was another exception; his *Die Blechtrommel* (The Tin Drum, 1959) sold four million copies by 1999.

While popular literature, by definition, caters to popular taste, usually by varying certain sets of stereotypes, there are different levels of literary quality and of political consciousness with which writers achieve popular success. Clearly, Bauer's *Soweit die Füße tragen*, which belonged in the context of 1950s popular literature, preserved a reactionary core whose stereotypes have often been used in *Trivialliteratur*. Konsalik was accused of concealing a reactionary message under the good-versus-evil dichotomy. *Der Arzt von Stalingrad* begins with the pervasive and familiar smell of cabbage soup and a laconic description of a POW camp, which is reminiscent of Eich's camp and Zero Hour poetry. Yet it immediately gives way to sentimental descriptions of nature and home, evoked by a primrose. The presentation of life in the Soviet POW camp is mixed with plot elements of the *Arztroman*, a genre of the dime novel that has a physician as its hero. In Konsalik's novel, the German prisoners appear as members of the master race who are now morally winning the war that was lost against the subhuman Russians: "something of the ancient wisdom of the Asian shimmered behind the mask of civilization" [etwas von der uralten Weisheit des

Asiaten schimmerte hinter der Maske der Zivilisation]. Any respect the
Russians command is based on their power as the military victors, but it
serves to distance them as alien from the Western world, to which suddenly the Germans belong, as if the Nazis had not tried to eradicate
Western civilization. Nazi crimes are mentioned to explain the hatred
with which the Soviets treat the Germans. Emphasizing the mistreatment of German POWs in Soviet camps, the novel's anti-Communism
appealed to a wide readership in Cold-War West Germany; behind such
politically opportune statements, racist notions were hidden.

Yet popular literature was not necessarily reactionary. Kirst's *Null-
Acht-Fünfzehn* trilogy was billed as an attack on the brutality and
meaninglessness of military drill and war. When the protagonist, Private
Asch, is told that he will never make a good German, he counters that
there first needs to be "a good Germany" [ein gutes Deutschland]. The
novel names the Nazis as guilty of starting the war; its criticism, however, remains at a surface level; the German soldier is presented as a
good soldier, so he fights the Nazi war anyway. In the same vein, the
sentiment that all soldiers, friend or foe, are "poor bastards" [arme
Schweine] is an important step away from the Nazis' universal hatred,
but it neither stops the fighting nor makes the crucial distinction between those who attack another country and those who defend their
own country. The critical potential of Kirst's novel indicates an antiwar
attitude, but it seems hidden behind the presentation's crude realism.
The section "In Place of an Epilogue" [An Stelle eines Nachwortes]
ends the trilogy; it contains a speech given by a retired army captain at
a veterans' reunion in 1954. The captain claims that the German soldier is still the world's best soldier; that, although he had been betrayed, his behavior has always been honorable; and that with the
remilitarization of West Germany that is just beginning, the proud tradition of the German soldier can be continued. The reaffirmation of
militarism in this speech corresponds exactly to the attitude of which
Kirst's novel has been accused. However, the novel does not end with
this speech but with the chilling response to it that defines the novel's
position against militarism: "After these words by Captain Schulz loud
applause began. Only a few stayed silent. Not one of those present
protested" [Nach diesen Worten des Hauptmanns a.D. Schulz erhob
sich ein lebhafter Beifall. Nur wenige schwiegen. Keiner der Anwesen-
den protestierte]. The novel is vulnerable to being read against its intentions because its antimilitarism is as timid as those who remain silent
after the captain's speech.

Simmel's work shows another dimension of popular literature. His
specialty is treating controversial topics of the time in an entertaining
format, such as the spy thriller and detective story, which has earned
him praise for his mastery of *Unterhaltungsliteratur*, which literally

means "entertainment literature" and is descriptive of the gray area between *Trivialliteratur* and serious literature — an area in which literary critics usually place few German works but many popular works of American literature. At the same time, Simmel was attacked for creating a sense of social criticism while covering up the real problems. Although such an analysis might be accurate as applied to individual works, it does not do justice to his works as a whole because it dogmatically assumes popular literature to be reactionary and ignores Simmel's political perspective as a self-proclaimed Social Democrat. This perspective has informed the social criticism in Simmel's works, which have been praised as democratic commercial literature.

*The Modernist tradition* After the Second World War, the West embraced Modernism, which it equated with democratic and anti-Nazi art. While Gottfried Benn and Ernst Jünger were controversial, they were mostly regarded as belonging to inner emigration; as a result, even they were able to jump on the anti-Nazi bandwagon as part of a general restoration. The truly democratic, artistically daring, and generally nonconformist Modernism — exemplified by the *Gruppe 47* and notable outsiders, such as Arno Schmidt — interacted in an ambiguous way with Adenauer Germany, which had a reactionary undercurrent. On the one hand, whether or not all readers wholeheartedly accepted nonconformist literature, they considered it to represent contemporary German literature. On the other hand, the reluctance to accept nonconformist literature, especially if it was considered representative, led to court challenges that alleged pornographic and other violations perpetrated by literary works. While this was not state censorship, which had been declared unconstitutional, it raised the specter of censorship in the West. In light of the youthfulness of democratic freedoms in West Germany, any infringement on freedom of speech had to be a sensitive issue.

The 1950s also saw the completion of the works of major prose writers, primarily in the tradition of Ironic Realism: Thomas Mann's *Felix Krull* (1954), Hermann Broch's *Die Schuldlosen* (Those without Guilt, 1950), Hans Henny Jahnn's *Die Niederschrift des Gustav Anias Horn* (The Manuscript of Gustav Anias Horn, 1949–1950), Alfred Döblin's *Hamlet* (1956), and the posthumous publication of Heinrich Mann's later works. As a result of the deaths of these authors, as well as of Bertolt Brecht and Gottfried Benn during the 1950s, the voices of the major representatives of prewar Modernism, who had contributed to the international status of German literature, fell silent.

While the 1940s had not seen major new writers emerge, German-language literature closed the gap with world literature during the

1950s. In poetry Paul Celan (from exile in Paris), Nelly Sachs (from exile in Sweden), the Austrian Ingeborg Bachmann, and the West German Hans Magnus Enzensberger (b. 1929) were the most significant new voices. Theater continued to be dominated by Brecht's tradition, especially in the East with playwrights like Heiner Müller (1929–1995). New dramatic experiments by the Swiss writers Max Frisch and Friedrich Dürrenmatt created the theater of the absurd and grotesque. The radio play was taken to new heights by a large number of writers, foremost among whom was Günter Eich. Prose literature had many important representatives, but the two overwhelming achievements that put the new Modernist German novel onto the map of world literature were both published in 1959, as if to usher in the new era of 1960s literature: *Die Blechtrommel*, by Günter Grass, and *Mutmassungen über Jakob* (Speculations about Jakob), by Uwe Johnson (1934–1984).

### Poetry between Restoration and Political Statement

*The classical status of two Modernists* During his withdrawal into the army, Gottfried Benn found his way to classicist perfection in a type of poetry he called "static poems" — hence *Statische Gedichte*, the title of his 1946 collection. These poems are considered the climax of Benn's career and contributed to his status as the preeminent poet in West Germany in the 1950s, a decade when poetry was popular. His poems in *Fragmente* (1951), *Destillationen* (1953), and *Aprèslude* (1955) returned to a more open form and, at times, to his earlier aggressiveness, while unhurried to the point of melancholy and resignation.

Benn's poems exemplify his conviction that form precedes content and that "a poem hardly ever comes into being — a poem is made" [Ein Gedicht entsteht überhaupt sehr selten — ein Gedicht wird gemacht]. Benn's point was that everybody shared in the common ideas that define the content; therefore, nothing really new could be said in terms of content, and only form could make a new statement. Benn explored aspects of content by evoking the remainders of myth that he thought were still present in the twentieth century (such as the self, the word, suffering, and visions of the Mediterranean). He voiced cultural criticism and self-criticism in an ironic tone that oscillated between laconic off-handedness and resignation. His poems ranged from attacks on contemporary civilization to attempts at dealing with human isolation, such as in his last poems, "Worte" (Words, 1955) and "Kommt — " (Come — , 1955). In "Worte" Benn voices the poet's loneliness in his dependence on words; he builds on this insight in "Kommt — ," where language appears as life-sustaining: "Come, let us talk together / he who talks is not dead" [Kommt, reden wir zusammen / wer redet ist nicht tot]. Even here, form (the process of talking) precedes content (what is being talked about).

.The audience not only appreciated the artistic quality of the poems but also Benn's classical status. That Benn also began influencing younger writers can be explained by his combination of formal mastery and thematic focus on processes of alienation. His poems did not address politically or socially sensitive areas; his criticism was a cultural and existential one, so for the general reader it was safe to embrace Benn's poetry in the awareness that such an embrace was a participation in the Modernist tradition that predated National Socialist control of Germany. The Modernist quality of Benn's poems originated in their formal openness, their tightly woven structure, and the artistic control that underlay form and structure. The same formal characteristics, however, define the poetry of Benn's counterpart.

The great ideological and poetic antithesis to Benn, the cynic and nihilist, was Bertolt Brecht, the moralist and socialist, whose poetry was openly political and, through a masterly colloquialism, had achieved its own classicism. The posthumous *Buckower Elegien* (Buckow Elegies, 1964) express Brecht's fundamental humanism and feelings of resignation concerning the political situation in the GDR, especially in his response to the suppression of the workers' uprising of June 17, 1953, which he addressed in "Die Lösung" (The Solution), whose final four lines have become famous: "Wouldn't it be / Easier after all if the government / Dissolved the people and / Elected another one?" [Wäre es da / Nicht doch einfacher, die Regierung / Löste das Volk auf und / Wählte ein anderes?]. Still, Brecht remained loyal to the GDR because he perceived it as an opportunity to build a "better" Germany.

The poetic language of Brecht's final years is simple and straightforward, its imagery that of everyday events and nature, yet it displays a more strongly aesthetic tone than his early poetry, one that combines the beauty of life and nature with cheerful lightness or mild resignation. At the same time, the poems' dialectical complexity derives from the intertwining of politics and human beings. In contrast to Benn's geological time scale and to *Naturpoesie*'s poems without people, Brecht's poems are situated in the here and now and are centered on human life, on humanity itself. In the five-line poem "Der Rauch" (Smoke), Brecht evokes the image of a house on a lake and observes that the scene would look "desolate" [trostlos] if there were no smoke. Smoke from the house implies the people who made the fire and the life that they lead, sustained by the fire that gives comfort and cooks food.

The lightness of Brecht's poetry is the result of great artistry: form and content complement each other so that the poems sound authentic. The late poems reconfirmed his status as one of the most important German poets. The dialectical structure of his poetry engaged his readers — and younger poets. In terms of influence on younger poets — including Wolf Biermann (b. 1936), Günter Kunert (b. 1929), Hans Magnus Enzensberger, and Erich Fried — Brecht was more important for the second half of the twentieth century than any other German poet.

*The private realm of politics*
Traditionalist poetry slowly lost its predominant position largely for the same reason that it had become successful after the war: its traditionalism, which at first gave people something to fall back on but which later was perceived as not being able to say much new. The new aspects of poetry, however, still did not include directly political statements; rather, the political dimension was implied or held in the background as if it were not more than a private opinion. Modernism was tempered in this way, and during the 1950s a wider audience was exposed to and appreciated Modernist literature. While German writers had remained in (increasingly weakened) contact with Modernism between 1933 and 1945, after the Second World War Modernism was still to be discovered by the German public. In addition to Gottfried Benn (Expressionist-existentialist poetry) and Bertolt Brecht (political and dialectical poetry), Wilhelm Lehmann (nature poetry) and Hans Arp (Dadaist poetry) served as models for younger German poets.

Karl Krolow and Günter Eich were major West German postwar poets and emerged from *Naturpoesie* with their own poetic vision. Influenced by Modernist French and Spanish poetry, Krolow's poems became more playful and surrealistic in the mid-1950s as in *Tage und Nächte* (Days and Nights, 1956) and *Fremde Körper* (Foreign Bodies, 1959). The latter collection has been considered a high point in Krolow's career. His poems presented imaginary events in the form of lyrical anecdotes; for example, in the playful ending of the poem "Der Wind im Zimmer" (Wind in the Room), the sleeper wakes up "With a strange wind rose in his hair" [Mit einer fremden Windrose im Haar].

Eich's *Botschaften des Regens* (Messages of the Rain, 1955) demonstrates a close affinity to Lehmann's apolitical program of *Naturlyrik* in the sense of an existential loneliness in which all that is left to the poet is nature — and art that is used to turn nature into poems. For Eich it was a logical consequence of this position to evoke the flight of birds as "the scaffolding of the trigonometric point" [das Gerüst des trigonometrischen Punktes] in a poem and to consider poems trigonometric points that provide him with orientation. In sharp contrast to Lehmann's nature poetry, however, Eich's poetic visions of word and object becoming one were highly political. They were poems of protest and defiance; they voiced mistrust of everything that could be ideologically problematic, including nature itself. The "messages of the rain" were messages of desperation, poverty, and reproach. The texts were increasingly terse and, while poetic, without the pathos of poetic exclamations. Again, there is the symbol of bird flight, but its message is not worth being deciphered because it is preempted by death. To his radio play *Träume* (Dreams, 1950) Eich added a poem of the same title; the poem ends with a direct appeal to be politically aware and to exercise one's own judgment: "Be inconvenient; be grit, not oil in the machinery of the world!" [Seid unbequem, seid Sand, nicht Öl im Getriebe der Welt!].

Poetry in the GDR showed characteristic differences from and similarities to developments in the West. On the one hand, there was poetry written largely to affirm socialist achievement by older poets, such as Johannes R. Becher, Erich Weinert, and Louis Fürnberg, as well as younger poets, such as Heinz Kahlau (b. 1931). The early 1950s also saw poems in praise of Stalin or Ulbricht, even by Hermlin and Huchel. On the other hand, there were outstanding poems by authors who went beyond uncritical celebration of the GDR and beyond traditional depictions of surface reality. As though to emphasize such transgression, these poetic oeuvres often had a private "feel." Of the older generation among these poets were Brecht and Peter Huchel, the latter also having had a great influence on younger GDR poets. Reiner Kunze (b. 1933) and especially Günter Kunert were the most important younger poets. Huchel's achievement consisted in taking up the tradition of *Naturlyrik* and putting nature back into an interaction with humanity. While Brecht treated nature imagery in a similar way, Huchel's poems were often more subtle because they also allowed a nonpolitical evocation of nature that had to be correlated by the reader to a political statement. In the mid-1950s, for example, the words *Herbst* (autumn) and *Winter* not only evoked the seasonal cycle but could also imply the rigidity of GDR society.

Günter Kunert's great theme, the process of change, was biographically founded in a "childhood that was messed up by the state" [staatlich verpfuschte Kindheit] because of his Jewish roots. Kunert's typical approach to the grotesque aspects of reality is humor, especially the paradox. While his early poetry contributed to the antifascist canon of GDR literature, Kunert moved from the positive view he had held during the 1950s to a negative assessment of reality in the 1960s. Yet already in his early poems, laconic irony pointed beyond Socialist Realism by revealing the potential for fascist tendencies in the GDR. For instance, in "Über einige Davongekommene" (About a Few Who Got Away), the human being [der Mensch] who was rescued from the rubble of his house after an air raid says about war: "Never again. / At least not right away" [Nie wieder. / Jedenfalls nicht gleich].

Hans (Jean) Arp, who wrote in German and in French and lived in Switzerland and France, stood for yet another tradition. One of the cofounders of Dada in Zurich in 1916, he kept this tradition alive by writing grotesque and humorous literature; for example, one of his "Dada-Sprüche" (Dada Sayings, 1955), reads: "Dada is a rose that has a rose in its buttonhole" [Dada ist eine Rose, die eine Rose im Knopfloch trägt]. Arp explained that Dada had accosted the fine arts to destroy art's arrogance but not to create mere nonsense; Dada was without meaning in the same way that nature does not have meaning. The Dada tradition intersected here with the beginnings of concrete poetry, which was met with reservations in the 1950s but achieved a breakthrough during the 1960s.

In the 1950s some poets in the West were for the most part independent of the models of Benn, Brecht, Lehmann, and Arp; Marie Luise Kaschnitz and Christine Lavant (pseudonym of Christine Habernig, 1915–1973), however, did acknowledge Rilke's influence. Kaschnitz combined classicist and modern characteristics in her poems and moved consistently toward a disillusioned treatment of reality, often with death as her thematic focus. Mostly personal, her poems also included political issues. In "Hiroshima" in the collection *Neue Gedichte* (New Poems, 1957), Kaschnitz imagines that "he who threw death upon Hiroshima" [Der den Tod auf Hiroshima warf] became a monk, committed suicide, or went mad because he felt haunted by the ghosts of the hundreds of thousands killed by the atomic bomb. But these thoughts are illusions, which she cuts short with the statement: "Nothing of all of this is true" [Nichts von alledem ist wahr]; in reality, the man lives in a suburban home with a yard. Still, "the eye of the world" [das Auge der Welt], the photographer who recorded the scene in the yard, symbolizes the unresolved conflict between forgetting in the private realm and the need to deal with issues in public.

Poetry appears to have provided Lavant the means for survival through various crises caused by illness, poverty, and her resistance to traditional gender roles in the rural and strongly religious region of her native Austria, which the motifs of her poems never left. Exploring emotional extremes, the poems of her major collections in the late 1950s and early 1960s, including *Die Bettlerschale* (The Beggar Bowl, 1956), oscillate between protest and resignation but always express emotional pain and the unfulfilled wish to overcome the suffering, of which titles (and first lines), such as "It smells like the end of the world" [Es riecht nach Weltuntergang], are characteristic. Unusual compound nouns and complex metaphors are held in check by regular syntax and the traditional poetic devices of meter and rhyme.

*Major new lyrical voices*  The major new voices who found their audience during the 1950s were Paul Celan, Nelly Sachs, Ingeborg Bachmann, and Hans Magnus Enzensberger. Johannes Bobrowski (1917–1965), who started publishing poems in magazines in the mid-1950s, reached a wider public with collections of poems during the 1960s. All of these poets built on lyrical traditions in their own ways. Along with other poets of the 1950s, they treated the private realm in a way that implied a political meaning by each poem's venturing out into the public sphere. Even where the political statement moved into the foreground, in the 1950s political opinions seemed to have been regarded as opinions of individual, private citizens.

Paul Celan focused his poems on one existential and traumatic wound: his experiences as a Jew persecuted in his native Romania after Nazi occupation during the Second World War. Living in France after the war but writing in German, Celan struggled to find a language that was appropriate to the subject matter. His solution to the poetic dilemma placed him among the major poets of world literature. He increasingly condensed and intensified his metaphoric language in an attempt to objectify the linguistic function of reference to reality. He did so to an extent that his poems became simultaneously enigmatic and evocative. Readers and critics were stunned by his provocative and paradoxical combinations that encoded subjective meaning in an objective way into the poems' artificial language. These combinations were considered hermetic, but they never obscured the reality of the Holocaust. On the contrary, because of the metaphoric quality and precision of Celan's language, every detail of reality is there: the death camp, the torture, and the agony.

The best-known example of Celan's poetic language is the oxymoron "black milk" [schwarze Milch] in his most famous poem, "Todesfuge" (Death Fugue), first called "Todestango," which was written in 1945 and published in the collection *Mohn und Gedächtnis* (Poppy and Memory, 1952). Genitive metaphors combine concrete elements, such as *milk*, with elements evoking abstraction, such as *daybreak*, into "milk of daybreak" [Milch der Frühe], whose evocative imagery is made even more ambiguous by the addition of the color adjective *black*. This process is the reverse of the normal linguistic process, in which the meaning of the modified noun becomes more specific with the addition of each attribute. Such a reversal exemplifies the difficulty of finding the appropriate means to describe unprecedented horrors and alienation; the resulting poetic language also tried to resist the corruption that language had suffered by Nazism. As provocative, evocative, hermetic, or dark as Celan's poetic language might seem at first sight, in a typically Modernist fusion the irrationality of the poetic trance implied by the "poppy" of the title was always based on concrete experiences that had to be recalled in the rational process of "memory" work.

The poem "Todesfuge" evokes the horrors of the extermination camps with their gas chambers and cremations through the metaphor "grave in the air" [Grab in den Lüften]; it delineates the historic situation as that of the Nazi death camp by the metaphorical statement: "Death is a master from Germany" [der Tod ist ein Meister aus Deutschland]. The rhythm of the poem's long lines with their many repetitive elements invites a reading of the poem that accelerates in speed and becomes almost breathless. The reader's gasping for air is a mimetic correlation to the "grave in the air," the constant reminder of the situation in the Nazi death camps where each breath could have been the last. The black smoke from the crematorium defines the experience of daily life just as milk used to provide sustenance for life: "Black milk of daybreak we drink it at dusk / we drink it at noon and in the morning we drink it at night" [Schwarze Milch der Frühe wir trinken sie abends / wir trinken sie mittags und morgens wir trinken sie nachts].

Ultimately, Celan attempted to explore the meaning of human existence; therefore, his poems emphasized the problem of language, of communicating in language, and specifically, communicating in the language of the murderers, German. Often the poems were dialogic, addressing a "you" who could be understood as the speaker himself. "Todesfuge" presupposes the communal experience of suffering in the plural form of the poem's voice: "we" [wir]. Here also resided Celan's major theoretical and practical problem: suffering is a shared experience but cannot truly be put into words. Therefore, his lyrical method attempted to approach the unspeakable, and it faded more and more into an intensification of language that appeared formally minimalist as the place that takes the author's and reader's words and breath away — hence the title of a later collection: *Atemwende* (Breath Turn, 1967). Celan's own life approached silence, and he committed suicide in Paris in 1970.

Nelly (Leonie) Sachs survived Nazi persecution because of the support of the Swedish author Selma Lagerlöf. Sachs emigrated to Sweden, where she lived for the rest of her life. In exile, she developed her own poetic voice. The reception of her works in Germany was slow, especially since her early exile poems did not mince words about the guilt of the Germans for the Nazi crimes. The title of the poem "Ihr Zuschauenden" (You Onlookers) not only addresses the German readers but is modified with an indictment in the first line: "Under whose gaze killing was done" [Unter deren Blicken getötet wurde]. She explored the pain of the Holocaust by blending influences from Judaic and Christian mystical sources that are evident in her metaphors and symbols. Her free-rhythmical diction showed the influence of the Old Testament, especially the Psalms. During the 1950s Sachs found more and more readers in Germany; in 1966, she was awarded the Nobel Prize for literature.

Like Celan and other authors, Sachs wrote to make remembrance possible. The success of Celan and Sachs, however, may have allowed some readers to consider the Nazi legacy resolved while they avoided confronting it themselves. In the mid-1950s Sachs broadened her poetic agenda by attempting a universal approach to contemporary issues, culminating in her 1961 collection that also included earlier poems, *Fahrt ins Staublose* (Journey into the Dustless Realm). The title implies that the journey itself is more important than the destination. This antithesis to "dust," which evokes death and decay, promises a cosmic perspective. Sachs, too, approached the realm that could no longer be easily expressed with language yet needed to be addressed: "Behind the lips / the Unspeakable waits / tearing at the umbilical cords / of the words" [Hinter den Lippen / Unsagbares wartet / reißt an den Nabelsträngen / der Worte].

Although Ingeborg Bachmann did not suffer persecution, she experienced the Nazi annexation of her native Austria during her childhood as traumatic. Her main themes — love, loss, and death — were variations of the dark side of human nature. Bachmann equated male-dominated society with fascism in her later radically feminist prose works. While this political aspect was not yet in the foreground of her poems, they were equally radical in evoking imminent change and probing unknown regions of subjectivity in an increasingly meaningless world. The evocation of the dark side of human nature pointed to a political reading of her poetry, which was based on nature-magical traditions but changed, as Eich and Huchel had, with poems in which damaged nature implied damaged human life.

Her lyrical debut, *Die gestundete Zeit* (On Borrowed Time, 1953), and her second collection of poems, *Anrufung des Großen Bären* (Conjuration of the Great Bear, 1956), established Bachmann as a major poet with a new and powerful voice. Her poetic production, however, was almost entirely limited to the 1950s. She did not write much poetry after 1956 because she began to doubt the "beautiful word" and because the reception of her work ignored the profoundly dark and political meanings in favor of the aesthetic pleasure that the poems allowed. Media attention to a brilliant and intellectual woman (she had written her dissertation on Heidegger) who was one of the most outstanding female writers in a literary scene that was dominated by male writers contributed to her work's achieving almost cult status. Bachmann's poems come alive in the tension between their formal brilliance and the tremendous suffering they express. While some poems evoke the consequences of the Holocaust, others present fascist tendencies and the threat of war — or, war itself — as having unnoticeably become part of everyday life. "War is no longer being declared / but continued. The incredible / has become commonplace" [Der Krieg wird nicht mehr erklärt, / sondern fortgesetzt. Das Unerhörte / ist alltäglich geworden], Bachmann writes in "Alle Tage" (Every Day). In light of the changed circumstances, courageous and honorable behavior consists in astounding reversals; therefore, medals are no longer awarded for "courage" in the face of the enemy but "in the face of the friend" [Tapferkeit vor dem Freund].

Hans Magnus Enzensberger's prolific literary production established him as one of the greatest contemporary German poets. In addition, he had an equally important influence on West German literary and political culture through his editorship of the magazine *Kursbuch* (Timetable). His poems were from the beginning — with his first collection *verteidigung der wölfe* (in defense of wolves, 1957) — political poems critical of the shallow materialism resulting from the postwar German economic miracle. Their satirical tone and critical subjectivity showed Brecht's influence, just as their aggressiveness showed an affinity to the American poet Allen Ginsberg (1926–1997). Enzensberger's poems ushered in a new era of openly political poetry. Criticized by some and praised by others, he was indeed the first angry young man of postwar West German literature.

In Enzensberger's poetry, life in the 1950s became satirized as so dull that even love had to be "allowed by the police" [polizeilich gestattet]. Nature metaphors were replaced by concrete reference to social wrongs; for example, in "Geburtsanzeige" (Birth Announcement), each of the six five-line stanzas reveals different ways in which the newborn will be "betrayed and sold" [verraten und verkauft] before it has had a chance. Rhetoric and metaphors were thoroughly political in expressing — similar to Eich and Bachmann — a sense of danger in a country where democratic traditions were young and the threat of repression and fascism not adequately dispelled. Even in Enzensberger's metaphors, as in the title poem, "Verteidigung der Wölfe gegen die Lämmer" (In Defense of the Wolves against the Lambs), his biting irony is clearly directed against restorative tendencies in the Federal Republic, where Hans Globke, who had done work for the Nazis on anti-Semitic laws, could become a top adviser to the chancellor. The antidemocratic forces, the "wolves," ironically appear as models of democratic virtues, but they still run in "packs," revealing the true quality of their brotherhood as a fraternity of dangerous brothers-in-arms. But the fault does not lie entirely with the wolves; they can achieve their goal of domination, because the lambs are willing victims who do not resist: "To be torn apart / is your wish. You / won't change the world" [Zerrissen / wollt ihr werden. Ihr / ändert die Welt nicht].

## Radio Plays

The origins of the radio play reach back into the 1920s when Brecht, Kästner, and Döblin were among the first to experiment with the new genre. In keeping with his general approach of engaging his audience, Brecht formulated his ideas of turning the radio, until then only an apparatus of distribution (of information, etc.), into an apparatus of true communication that required active participation on the part of the listeners. In the 1930s and early 1940s the National Socialists used the radio primarily for propaganda purposes. After the Second World War, West German law decentralized radio broadcasting — creating several powerful public radio stations, each to serve a designated region — and mandated each station to include participation by all socially relevant groups, including churches, unions, and political parties.

While such participation often evolved into partisan politics because of the state parliaments' control over their respective regional radio stations, early successes in audience participation have been noted. In 1950, for example, 80,000 listeners sent in responses to broadcasts by Ernst Schnabel (1913–1986) on Northwest German Radio. At the time, literary radio plays and journalistic radio features were still housed in one department, which allowed a creative interchange between the two genres. Moreover, since 1951 the prestigious *Preis der Kriegsblinden* (Prize of the War Blind) has been awarded for radio plays, indicating public acknowledgment of the new genre.

During the 1950s the radio play became more lyrical (although individual authors still preferred the realistic tradition), which meant that it evoked dreamscapes that were less openly political than the journalistic radio features. Nevertheless, the genre continued to experience a booming popularity. The radio version of Borchert's *Draußen vor der Tür* was a success in 1947 before the play's stage premiere the same year. Moreover, contributing to the new genre were the major authors of the 1950s, such as Ilse Aichinger, Heinrich Böll, Friedrich Dürrenmatt, Max Frisch, Dieter Wellershoff (b. 1925), Wolfgang Weyrauch, and Günter Eich, whose radio play *Träume* (Dreams, broadcast 1951) is generally praised as the culmination of the lyrical radio play of the 1950s and of this author's popularity.

Eich's play is also a case in point that a lyrical evocation of dreamscapes is not necessarily aimed at creating an apolitical realm. On the contrary, Eich's intention was the creation of nightmare visions to make people aware of the existential threat under which he perceived the world of the twentieth century to be found. Therefore, the author emphasizes that everything in the radio addresses the listeners' issues in the same way dreams address the dreamers' issues. After the end of the first dream, when the sounds of the speeding train have faded, the listener is reminded of the political context: "Remember: / Nowhere on the map lie Korea and Bikini, / but in your heart" [Denke daran: / Nirgendwo auf der Landkarte liegt Korea und Bikini, / aber in deinem Herzen]. Still, the play's dream setting was criticized for not clearly stating the issues because the dream would only allow feeling, not analysis; responding in 1953 to this criticism, Eich added the lines encouraging the listener to take responsibility and "be inconvenient." The dream scenes take the listener around the world, and all share the materialization of some threat in a hostile environment that is brought to the point of catastrophe as the result of some anonymous power exerting its influence.

The first dream in *Träume*, which particularly irritated listeners, makes the evocation of the condition of human existence all the more dire because it suggests the Holocaust. The radio play takes one step in the process of murdering the Jews — their transportation to extermination camps, mostly in cattle cars, under inhuman conditions that foreshadowed the ultimate horrors to come — as a point of departure and generalizes it into a statement about humanity. Many years after being abducted by men in strange uniforms, the members of a family have been locked up inside a moving railroad car that is sealed so that they cannot look out. It has been for so long that only the grandparents are able to recall how the world outside looked. Remembering the once-ubiquitous dandelion is the current permutation of the Blue Flower of German Romanticism, and the parents instruct their child that the grandparents are wrong: "There are no yellow flowers, my child" [Es gibt keine gelben Blumen, mein Kind]. For them, life in the moving railroad car has become normal; when a tiny crack opens to the outside, they seal it in order to avoid seeing what does not conform to their perception of normality. This dream scene is, ironically, a reminder that reality should not be treated as though it were a bad dream.

### Different Theatrical Visions

*Slow return of the Avant-Garde* Writers of poetry and prose — particularly Paul Celan, Günter Grass, and Uwe Johnson — were able to close the gap with world literature. In contrast, drama lagged behind because the theater's more public character had resulted in tighter control by the Nazis so that the audience had been weaned from Modernism by a steady diet of classical and National Socialist drama during the twelve years of the Third Reich. Nevertheless, after the war Modernism was more widely available because a great number of German Modernist authors had lived in exile — but there were reservations about welcoming exile writers back to West Germany, while in East Germany dramatic production was subject to socialist doctrine. Under these circumstances, the emergence of two Swiss writers, Max Frisch and Friedrich Dürrenmatt, as the most important and innovative German-language playwrights of the 1950s is not surprising.

International drama, and specifically theater in the Avant-Garde tradition of Dadaism and Surrealism, played a great role in postwar West Germany. The political situation there favored French existentialism and its theater (Jean-Paul Sartre), as well as the theater of the absurd (Samuel Beckett, 1906–1989; Eugène Ionesco, 1912–1994), because their approaches to the universal predicament of the human condition could instill in a German audience the sense of making the correct political choice without challenging the audience to address the real issues of the Nazi legacy. Being an existentialist soon became a fad; moreover, the emphasis on action based on absolute free will as the only possibility of meaning in an absurd world helped pave the way for the political movements of the 1960s. The theater of the absurd, in contrast, suggested that everything had become meaningless.

The developments of grotesque and political approaches in German-language theater in the 1950s followed the dichotomy of giving up on meaning and yet searching for it. The basis was the acknowledgment that the world was becoming more and more complex. The grotesque approach had been part of absurdist theater; however, as a shocking and revealing juxtaposition of elements that are considered mutually exclusive, the grotesque does not negate meaning but creates new meanings. Examples of the grotesque tradition include "unnatural" combinations of plants and animals in murals in Roman grottoes (hence the term *grotesque*) or literary combinations of the tragic and the comic (such as tragicomedy and black humor). Dürrenmatt assumed that the age of classical drama had come to a close; he argued that together with today's abstract and anonymous social structures, which have essentially become invisible, the prerequisite for classical tragedy had disappeared. In a reversal of Adorno's dictum about the impossibility of poetry after the Holocaust, Dürrenmatt saw the threat of nuclear extinction posing a different threat to the arts: in the nuclear mushroom cloud "mass murder and beauty become one" [Massenmord und Schönheit eins werden]. He concluded that the contemporary theater had only one option: grotesque comedy.

Conversely, the political approach of epic theater understood the world as constantly changing, which demanded a theatrical presentation that reflected the changeability. The difference between the absurd-grotesque and political approaches originated in different beliefs concerning the effect that human action could have in a world that was becoming more and more absurd. This was not the position of Socialist Realism in East Germany, which considered the absurdist approach, like any other Modernist approach, decadent and dangerous. When writers of this political approach transcended the dogmatic constraints of their ideology, the political and absurdist traditions could be combined — for example, in the later works of Heiner Müller.

Absurdist and epic theater share an anti-Aristotelian foundation; they are open forms of drama, as opposed to the closed forms of classical drama. While some critics — including Wolfgang Hildesheimer (1916–1991), who was also one of the few German practitioners of absurd theater — stressed the independence of the absurdist tradition, absurdist theater can also be considered a radicalization of epic theater. Although Brecht was instrumental in the definition of, and experimentation with, the building blocks of epic theater, his was only one way to put those building blocks into practice. The mode of presentation turned the staged event into a narrated object or object of demonstration for the audience's observation. Both epic and absurdist drama demonstrate their events. Consequently, the difference between Brecht's political application and the absurdist tradition appears to be one of ideological statement and radicalization. The epic device of *Verfremdung* (defamiliarization) became transposed into a symbol of *Entfremdung* (alienation) in the theater of the absurd.

*Absurd and grotesque plays in the West* — Absurdist theater operated with a minimalist stage presence that took its most radical form in Samuel Beckett's plays, including *Waiting for Godot* (1953). It meant a consistent reduction of human personality; such dehumanization approached mechanization and was the central theme of absurdist drama: to unmask the condition of complete alienation and fragmentation in today's world. As a result, plot was dispensed with, and so were characters and dialogue (people talked at or past each other if they talked at all). Consequently, characters no longer had a firm identity or psychological reality and appeared puppetlike so that choreography often replaced language. Such a theatrical presentation created the experience of an ahistorical and absurd reality.

Wolfgang Hildesheimer and Günter Grass understood themselves as being in the tradition of absurdist theater; nevertheless, the grotesque element seems to dominate their works. Hildesheimer's personal experience of the meaninglessness of the world drove him to question the possibility of communication to the extent that in the 1970s he turned to writing biography and finally declared that writing itself had lost its meaning for him. In the 1950s he began exploring the absurd experience in radio and theater plays, such as the radio play *Prinzessin Turandot* (1954) and its stage adaptations *Der Drachenthron* (The Dragon Throne, 1955) and *Die Eroberung der Prinzessin Turandot*

(The Conquest of Princess Turandot, published 1961, premiered 1967). In the confrontation between con artist and man-eating princess, the possibility of escaping the despotism of power seems to be within reach because the two characters, who usually do the wrong thing, are right for each other. The utopian element of the happy ending in the second adaptation points to Hildesheimer's political position of searching for meaning in postwar Germany. With other plays — published together under the title *Spiele, in denen es dunkel wird* (Plays, In Which It Is Getting Dark, 1958) — he took a step toward the antidramatic form of absurdist theater.

Günter Grass, whose success as a novelist overshadowed his dramatic and poetic works, had originally studied fine arts. Throughout his career, he used his drawings and lithographs and his poems to gauge elements that he considered treating more extensively. Referring to his first creative phase from 1955 to 1959, Grass described his poems as expanding and, with added stage directions, growing into his absurdist theater plays, such as *Onkel, Onkel* (Uncle, Uncle, premiered 1956, published 1965) and *Die bösen Köche* (The Wicked Cooks, premiered 1961, published 1970). In a strict sense, these plays are more grotesque, because they suggest meaning by way of parable. In the same sense, Grass's one-act plays, especially *Noch 10 Minuten bis Buffalo* (Still 10 Minutes to Buffalo, premiered 1959, published 1970), are more absurdist than grotesque. It was Grass's most successful play because of its playful, yet nonsensical, plot.

The experiments with adaptations of the absurdist theater were short-lived and confined to the late 1950s and early 1960s. The grotesque, however, evolved into the defining characteristic of a new from of drama that was exemplified in the 1950s and 1960s by the works of Max Frisch and Friedrich Dürrenmatt. The parabolic character of the plays, with characters as personifications and with means of presentations ranging from satire to farce, was still designed to unmask the alienated and absurd character of the world. However, to create a more specifically historical, yet still universal, setting, it did not use the radically minimalist approach of the theater of the absurd.

Frisch's play *Biedermann und die Brandstifter* (The Firebugs, 1958), as well as its 1953 version for the radio, presents the parable of how evil is allowed to spread through cowardly behavior in the figure of Biedermann (the name of a businessman that also implies the simplemindedness of the petty-bourgeois worldview that avoids conflict at all costs), because he lets arsonists live in the attic of his house. From there they start an all-consuming fire for which Biedermann has given them the matches in an irrational hope that he might be spared. This parable can be understood as a polemical attack on Swiss provincialism or as an allusion to the way German intellectuals underestimated Hitler.

Like Frisch's other theatrical parable *Andorra* (1961), which deals with racism, *Biedermann* addressed political issues in a universal way while avoiding specific questions; in this sense it was epic theater without Brecht's ideology.

Dürrenmatt's *Die Ehe des Herrn Mississippi* (The Marriage of Mr. Mississippi, 1952) has been called a grotesque dance of death, and his great successes, *Der Besuch der alten Dame* (The Visit, 1956) and *Die Physiker* (The Physicists, 1962), vary the mode of the grotesque and the theme of death in the conflict between moral and material values. These plays are grotesque, because they not only allow but presuppose meaning. In his essay "Theaterprobleme" (Problems of the Theater, 1955), Dürrenmatt emphasized that despair is just one possible response to the world's hopelessness; the individual has the choice to be courageous and to prevail "like Gulliver among the giants" [wie Gulliver unter den Riesen].

In *Der Besuch der alten Dame* the grotesque display of the corruptibility of an entire town, whose inhabitants sacrifice one of their own, Alfred Ill, to the revenge of his former lover Claire Zachanassian, is contrasted with the development of Alfred's individual moral awareness as he comes to accept his guilt. Abandoned by her lover, Claire left town forty-five years ago; at first she was reduced to prostitution, but she eventually became the richest woman in the world. Now she returns, demanding complete revenge. She offers immense wealth to the townspeople if they kill Alfred; they initially resist, but ultimately they do kill him. They all crowd around him, and when they stand up, Alfred's dead body remains lying on the ground. A doctor diagnoses heart failure, and the reporters, who have just arrived, echo the mayor's statement, "Death by joy" [Tod aus Freude], referring to Alfred's alleged joy over the town's impending wealth. Fitting for a Europe that was recovering from the Second World War and that concentrated on material values, the play ends with a prayer to ensure the newly found prosperity without questioning the political, spiritual, and moral costs at which it was acquired.

*The political Brechtian tradition in the East*

After the exile years, Brecht concentrated on writing his theoretical essays and working with his own theater, the Berliner Ensemble in East Berlin, where he directed adaptations of plays by authors, such as Sophocles (496?–406 B.C.), William Shakespeare (1564–1616), and Molière (1622–1673), as well as exemplary stage productions of his own works. Despite his major status as a writer and his Marxist beliefs, Brecht's work was criticized in the GDR as being too Modernist and not Communist enough in the sense of Socialist Realism. Nevertheless, Brecht's influence remained commanding, and many GDR playwrights — Helmut Bairl (b. 1926), Peter Hacks (b. 1928), Erwin Strittmatter (1912–1994), and, above all, Heiner Müller — wrote in the Brechtian tradition.

Helmut Bairl had his first theatrical success with *Die Feststellung* (The Determination, 1958), a Brechtian didactic play. In other plays, Bairl varied themes and motifs from plays by Brecht; for instance, the comedy *Frau Flinz* (1961) portrayed a Mother Courage-like woman learning the lesson that Mother Courage did not learn and becoming active for socialism. Peter Hacks also began with plays strongly influenced by Brecht, such as *Die Schlacht bei Lobositz* (Battle at Lobositz, premiered 1956, published 1957). But beginning in the 1960s, Hacks moved toward what he called a "postrevolutionary" theater.

Erwin Strittmatter was primarily a prose writer who came to writing through the *Volkskorrespondenten* (people's correspondents) movement. His play, *Katzgraben* (the name of a village; literally, Cat Ditch, published 1954), first commissioned and then rejected by the state-run youth organization FDJ (*Freie Deutsche Jugend*, or Free German Youth), finally premiered in 1953 under Bertolt Brecht's direction in collaboration with Strittmatter. The play gave Strittmatter his first success, and it gave Brecht the play about contemporary issues that his theater was expected to present. Brecht praised *Katzgraben* as the first play to bring to the stage the modern class struggle in a village setting. The issue of progress is exemplified by the construction of a street. The conflict pits the progressive forces against the forces of the past, because feudalism and capitalism still influence the way many people think; even after the land reform, the rich farmers still treat the poor farmer women like servants. In the end, progress is victorious; the street is built.

The issue of all-round modernization (social and technological) is at the core of *Katzgraben*. Ironically, the need for the street is caused by the old trail being literally undermined by a coal mine. The new street, however, would also mean a change in the people's way of life, inasmuch as the village would become accessible by bus and the means to challenge the dominance of the rich farmers could be brought to the village. After a failed vote the previous year, street construction is approved by a majority of the citizens, but the project runs into problems because of the drought. Finally, all progressive forces rally behind the cause; and, with the help of tractors from the city, all obstacles are overcome. Even the threat of the baron's return is no longer effective, as social progress toward Communism makes the old structures of exploitation obsolete.

The conflict is defined in terms of haves and have-nots and is set in the postwar years prior to the establishment of the GDR. One rich farmer's wife explicitly states the conflict in class terms by justifying exploitation: "What is good for the little people, Erna, / often isn't good for our kind" [Was für die kleinen Leute gut ist, Erna, / ist oft nicht gut für unsereinen]. Class conflict does not disappear with the triumph of the progressive forces in the village of Katzgraben, but that triumph is presented as a step in the right direction. At Brecht's suggestion, however, the language of the play is anything but progressive: contemporary language was put into metrical form, modeled after the blank verse (unrhymed iambic pentameter) of Shakespeare and Schiller. Strittmatter's play, then, fit well into the East German literary agenda of combining Socialist Realism with anti-Modernism and the classicist heritage.

Heiner Müller emerged as one of the leading German-language playwrights of the twentieth century, but his career was a difficult one. His early works, such as *Der Lohndrücker* (The Scab, 1958), one of the didactic plays he wrote in collaboration with his wife, Inge Müller (1925–1966), were influenced by the Brechtian tradition. Even during this early phase of *Produktionsstücke* (Production Plays), Müller asserted a strongly independent artistic position, which led to his dismissal from the East German Writers' Guild in 1966. He reestablished himself with adaptations from the classical tradition. His work continued its focus on exploring subjectivity and history; along this path, however, Müller left the Brechtian premise of teaching and engaged in a search for a new theatrical language. This search proceeded in two major steps. First, in the 1970s, the montage of monologic passages still allowed for a sense of dialogue in a world that is depicted as a slaughterhouse; second, mainly in the 1980s, Müller used the montage technique to move away from the spoken word and to assign more importance to the other elements of the stage performance.

*Der Lohndrücker* owed much to the thematic program of Socialist Realism. Müller supported socialism, not because of the way in which it was practiced in the GDR but because of what he believed to be its potential for creating a better society. Therefore, the theory of the Production Play considered literature a productive force; furthermore, the play's subject matter was industrial production in accordance with the official demands on literature to deal with contemporary efforts to build a socialist society. *Der Lohndrücker* was based on a true story. A bricklayer, called Balke in Müller's play, suggests a method of repairing huge industrial ovens one chamber at a time, thus avoiding a shutdown of the entire oven and the resulting loss in production. His suggestion is met with skepticism on the assumption that capitalism would have come up with this method, if it were feasible. Balke, then, proves the superiority of socialism because "the working class creates new realities" [Die Arbeiterklasse schafft neue Tatsachen].

Müller, however, did not provide a glorification but an astute analysis that was not blind to social contradictions. The new repair method in the play also reveals another, uglier side of the new realities created by the working class, as a character retorts: "But exploitation is not a new reality" [Aber Ausbeutung ist keine neue Tatsache]. The problem consists not only in the conditions of performing the repair work, which means that the bricklayers have to work at a temperature of 212 degrees Fahrenheit. It also implies that Balke's innovation depresses the wages, because the oven is not shut down and the other workers have to work more for the same money; the "norm," the expected output of production, is raised (or "erhöht," hence the term *Normerhöhung*). The result is politically volatile: some of the workers are openly hostile toward Balke — just as workers were toward the GDR when *Normerhöhung* was announced, leading to the uprising of June 17, 1953.

Müller's treatment of the issue was in direct conflict with a state in which Marxist orthodoxy, by definition, understood class antagonism as an issue of the past. The play ends with an uneasy compromise of cooperation that is likely to lead to the successful completion of the repair; it does not, however, celebrate the success itself as a completed fact. For the doctrine of Socialist Realism this compromise was especially problematic where it entailed, as in *Der Lohndrücker*, the new and innovative forces of socialism (in which Müller did believe) having to cooperate with the old conservative forces, even former Nazis. Balke, who is only in a limited sense the hero that Socialist Realism demanded, has to deal with Nazism in his own past. These complexities showed Müller's reluctance to present the victory of the new when he still saw the continuing struggle between the old and the new. The play's resulting openness is characteristic of epic theater. In retrospect, and in contrast to the uncritically affirmative plays of Socialist Realism by authors ranging from Strittmatter to Helmut Bairl, *Der Lohndrücker* is the outstanding contribution to the Production Plays.

### Prose on the Way toward World Literature

**Aufbau *literature* in the East**
The building of a socialist society from the foundations upward was the task to which the GDR also committed its authors. While Peter Demetz surmises that the hidden agenda of the SED was to "create an anti-intellectual counterforce of factory-writers and people's correspondents" (114) in order to keep its own potentially unruly intellectuals in check, the movement of the *Bitterfelder Weg* (Bitterfeld Way) of April 1959 was also a logical consequence of the state-imposed Socialist Realism. East Germany encouraged workers to write, and it sent writers to work in industry and agriculture. Officially hosted by the Mitteldeutscher Verlag, a publishing house in Halle, the conference on

the role of Socialist literature met in the town of Bitterfeld, one of the new East German industrial centers, and brought approximately 150 writers and 300 workers together. In the same year, about 9,500 workers were people's correspondents writing for local newspapers, and hundreds of writers' groups were formed by workers.

The official goal of the Bitterfeld model was to eliminate the division between the artist and the people in the socialist sense that everybody was working for the construction of socialism, some with their hands and others with their minds. While the readers' tendency to passivity was overcome by inducing many to write themselves, the importance of the Bitterfeld model remained largely localized with forms such as the *Brigadetagebuch* (diary of the work brigade). As a result, the ambition to create a point of departure for a new German national literature remained unfulfilled. Dogmatic application of the Socialist Realist doctrine turned literature stale or propagandist, and the authenticity of many texts could not make up for their lack of literary quality. While the doctrine remained important for official criticism of literature, it lost its importance for more and more writers.

The formulation of the Bitterfeld model can also be seen in part as an answer to the waning of the Production Novel, or *Produktionsroman*, novels that centered on topics from the world of industrial production and the new socialist methods of production, just as the Production Plays did for drama. As a matter of fact, Eduard Claudius (pseudonym of Eduard Schmidt, 1911–1976) wrote about the same incident involving the innovative repair of the oven that was featured in Müller's *Lohndrücker*. Claudius's novel *Menschen an unserer Seite* (People on Our Side, 1951) is usually seen as ushering in the type of work that became known as the Production Novel. Erwin Strittmatter's trilogy *Der Wundertäter* (The Miracle Worker, 1957–1980) applied the pattern of the picaresque novel to narrating the life of Stanislaus Büdner from the early twentieth century. In the first novel Strittmatter presented a mainly apolitical hero who learns to think in political categories after the end of the Second World War, the period covered in the following two novels.

In addition, the 1950s saw a continuation of antifascist literature in the GDR. The stories by Franz Fühmann (1922–1984) and the concentration-camp novel *Nackt unter Wölfen* (Naked among Wolves, 1958), by Bruno Apitz, were conspicuous popular successes. Both authors relied on their own experiences: Fühmann as a member of the Nazi army who eventually turned antifascist and Apitz as a member of the Communist Party who spent most of his life under National Socialism in Nazi prisons and camps. While in Fühmann's story *Kameraden* (Comrades, 1955) the desertion of one soldier shows that he is turning away from the Nazi ideals, the story's ending leaves the question of where the soldier will finally turn unresolved.

Apitz's novel was the most successful of the concentration-camp novels; it sold more than 400,000 copies in the GDR in the first two years and about two million copies internationally in the first fifteen years. The novel's title, *Nackt unter Wölfen*, alludes to the existence of a three-year-old child who is smuggled into the camp. The novel has been criticized for the use of clichés from *Trivialliteratur* in resolving the conflict between the human emotion of wanting to help the child and strategic decisions of political and physical survival. The SS guards in the camp are searching for the child, whose very existence jeopardizes the resistance movement; its members, however, take care of the child, who becomes the symbol of the final triumph in the novel. The criticism in terms of *Trivialliteratur* stresses the adventure-story characteristics and the privatizing of the problems, which result in neglecting the historical reasons for National Socialism. But these aspects worked together to idealize a picture of Communist resistance to the Nazis as free from internal contradictions and to offer emotional identification to the readers.

*Prose between affirmation and criticism in the West* Literary developments in the German-speaking countries outside the Eastern political bloc were quite different. While the West German market, for which Swiss and Austrian writers wrote as well, emerged as central, Austrian literature in particular seemed ideologically divided during the 1950s. Young writers, such as Ilse Aichinger and Ingeborg Bachmann, defined new trends in German-language literature through their involvement in the *Gruppe 47*. Another trend in Austrian literature of the 1950s was enlightened and conservative. It was exemplified by authors of the older generation, such as Fritz von Hermanovsky-Orlando (1877–1954), whose works, except for two early books that appeared in the 1920s, were published posthumously beginning in 1957; Albert Paris Gütersloh (pseudonym of Albert Conrad Kiehtreiber, 1887–1973); and Heimito von Doderer (1896–1966).

Doderer's early publications, dating back to the 1920s, did not bring the success that he had expected. His membership in the NSDAP, which he suspended in 1938, canceled in 1941, and considered a "barbaric error" [barbarische Irrtum] throughout his later life, added a further critical dimension to his complex postwar texts, which encompass an undercurrent of sexuality and the precariousness of happiness. The Vienna trilogy established Doderer as the preeminent Austrian writer of the 1950s: *Die erleuchteten Fenster oder Die Menschwerdung des Amtsrates Julius Zihal* (The Lighted Windows, or

Julius Zihal's Becoming a Human Being, 1950), *Die Strudlhofstiege oder Melzer und die Tiefe der Jahre* (The Strudlhof Stairs, or Melzer and the Depth of the Years, 1951), and *Die Dämonen* (The Demons, 1956). The first short novel is an overture to the following massive novels, which complement each other in the sense that a well-defined topic (social decline into a authoritarian state) is given a diffuse presentation in *Dämonen*, while *Strudlhofstiege* treats a diffuse topic (chaotic life in the 1920s) in a structure with closure.

The Strudlhofstiege, open-air stairs that connect two streets, and Melzer are, respectively, one place and one person out of many. Doderer emphasized the priority of the associative form of the novel over its content for several reasons. It was, first, a result of his attempt to handle chaotic reality with the language of an anachronistically omniscient narrator. Second, the novel's positive ending and the positive role of language contrasted with the younger generation of writers, whose skepticism toward the world and language Doderer criticized as a fashionable surrender to desperation, or *Desperatismus*.

In *Strudlhofstiege* the action centering on Melzer holds the events in the novel together through Melzer's acquaintance with many of the other characters. The big picture is composed of an interconnection of tragedy and comedy that makes up the drama of society from 1910 to 1925, but the conflicts are mostly personal while the social realm seems unimportant. The upper middle class experiences one tragedy after another, which can be interpreted as a comment on the decline of this class. In contrast, Doderer considered the lower middle class as "Genie in Latenz" (latent genius), appropriate for the republic. Pettybourgeois life is the material of comedy. The novel ends on a positive note, since Melzer joins the lower middle class by means of a typical device of comedy: engagement to be married. Nevertheless, Melzer's happiness is contrasted with many other people's failures, and the institution of marriage itself is not depicted as unproblematic. While the novel suggests that an order exists, it does not suggest that this order can be taken for granted.

The writers of the young and middle generations had to survive in an environment in the 1950s that became increasingly conservative as a result of the political restoration in the West, and they had to compete with conservative trends in literature. As far as public opinion was concerned, politics was a private issue. The young writers, in this sense, were a silent generation, who dealt with politics in an indirect way: as a private issue of the fictional characters whose political involvements were often rendered in a nonrealist mode as the experience of an absurd world. That such a privatization of politics in literature indeed occurred is easily illustrated by the scandals caused by the novels of Wolfgang Koeppen, who was more political than Arno Schmidt and

Hans Erich Nossack (1901–1977); but all three were great literary out-siders of the 1950s. In the novels by Max Frisch the private realm con-stituted the novelistic core. The most significant young German novelists, all associated with the *Gruppe 47*, were Martin Walser (b. 1927), Siegfried Lenz (b. 1926), Heinrich Böll, Günter Grass, and Uwe Johnson. The debut novels by Grass and Johnson in 1959 were the most important novelistic achievements of the 1950s.

Wolfgang Koeppen's prewar novels did not find a strong echo, but he found himself at the center of attention with his 1950s trilogy about West German society's fascist undercurrent — but not with the re-sponse that he had expected; he finally withdrew from publishing. *Tau-ben im Gras* (Pigeons in the Grass, 1951), *Das Treibhaus* (The Greenhouse, 1953), and *Der Tod in Rom* (Death in Rome, 1954) combined the high Modernist traditions of James Joyce and Alfred Döblin with political commentary. Of Koeppen's novels, *Tauben im Gras* made the most use of the Modernist devices of montage tech-nique and interior monologue, which stood in contrast to traditionalist classicism or the less provocative Aestheticist line of Modernist tradition that dominated the literary market in the early 1950s. The characters appear as disoriented and uncertain about their lives as do pigeons in the grass; the individual has become homeless in a reality that is dan-gerously fragmented into East and West. The images of airplanes with which the novel begins and ends are menacing symbols whose reference to contemporary reality is made clear by the mention of the air-raid si-rens that, for the time being, remain silent. The public and the literary critics, with few exceptions, were not ready for such an attack on West Germany and accused Koeppen of glorifying ruins and for not having the right sensitivity for contemporary issues. This reaction showed that Koeppen was on target with his unmasking of political restoration in Germany.

Formally the most innovative and radical of this group of outsiders, Arno Schmidt also drew criticism as far as his subject matter was con-cerned. He was even investigated on charges of sacrilegious and porno-graphic writing for "Seelandschaft mit Pocahontas" (Seascape with Pocahontas, 1955). His main works of the 1950s were *Brand's Haide* (Brand's Heath, 1951), *Schwarze Spiegel* (Black Mirrors, 1951), *Aus dem Leben eines Fauns* (From the Life of a Faun, 1953) — published as a trilogy in 1963 under the title *Nobodaddys' Kinder* (Nobodaddy's Children) — and *Das steinerne Herz* (The Heart of Stone, 1956). Schmidt's subject matter was the attempt of individual human beings to redefine their lives in response to National Socialism (*Aus dem Leben eines Fauns*), to the end of the war (*Brand's Haide*), to an apocalyptic utopia (*Schwarze Spiegel*), and to the monomaniacal desire to collect historical books in divided Germany (*Das steinerne Herz*).

In these stories Schmidt dissolved the continuum of the narrative flow so that the new form expressed an analogy to the lost sense of life as a continuum. To accomplish this effect, he developed a *Raster* (grid) technique that moved from one fragment to the next, mixing interior monologue, first-person narration, and precise observations. Typographically, each fragment is identified by the first phrase that suggests its topic; the phrase is printed in italics, and the rest of the fragment follows in hanging indentation. The language mixes various stylistic levels, literary allusions, and foreign words. The punctuation follows expressive needs and gives some passages a staccato pulse: "Flame: I: woe: night!!" [Flamme: Ich: weh: Nacht!!]. The spelling, which Schmidt continued to radicalize, is idiosyncratic.

The notion of an extended realism that added the realm of the invisible to visible reality was central to Hans Erich Nossack's *Nekyia* (1947) and *Spirale* (1956), a novel consisting of five stories, where the author emphasized the cyclic way of thinking by means of analogies and associations in the image of the spiral. The middle story, "Unmögliche Beweisaufnahme" (Impossible Taking of Evidence), demonstrates Nossack's extreme doubts concerning language. Accused in the disappearance of his wife, a man describes the breakdown of communication between them, which is also a failure of communication between the man and the court, in the image of snow that falls between people while they keep talking: "The snow wants to bestow the gift of loneliness, but they do not accept the gift. Until they suffocate" [Der Schnee will ihnen Einsamkeit schenken, doch sie nehmen das Geschenk nicht an. Bis sie ersticken]. The wife has emigrated into nothingness. Nossack also used the concept of people "remigrating" back into reality from nothingness, although such a remigration often appeared on the surface as failure. The monologic quality of his works, emphasizing the role of the author or narrator in the fragile attempt at finding himself in an uncertain reality, links Nossack's works to those of Max Frisch.

Frisch's novels appear as a continual self-exploration of his identity and of his existence between subjective and objective reality; the diary form provides the basic structure for his works as an attempt to overcome the lack of language that is appropriate for reality. The man in his novel *Stiller* (1954) who claims to be someone else — hence the novel's first sentence "I'm not Stiller" [Ich bin nicht Stiller] — experiences life from a solipsist perspective, from which everything is a dream and he seems locked up not in prison but in his own body. The result is an achronological reconstruction of his life, written while he is in prison. After his earlier attempt to take on a new identity in America as Mr. White failed, he returns to Switzerland and is forced to resume his old identity and his old life with Julika. Stiller, however, seems to find a sense of identity only after his wife dies. At this point, he no longer needs language: "his letters were meager. Stiller stayed in Glion and lived alone" [seine Briefe waren karg. Stiller blieb in Glion und lebte allein], the novel's short second part, which consists of the state attorney's report, concludes.

While solipsism dominates in *Stiller*, Frisch's following novels, *Homo faber* (1957) and *Mein Name sei Gantenbein* (Gantenbein, 1964), more clearly add social embedding to the process of individuation. For example, in *Homo faber* the protagonist fails, because he tries to master life with technology and leaves out the human factor; as in a Greek tragedy, hubris leads to his downfall when he commits incest with a young woman whom he does not recognize as his daughter. All of Frisch's protagonists are afraid of a life of repetition; however, their escapes do not provide a solution. While Stiller returns from his escape to accept his shortcomings, Walter Faber's attempt to escape as a matter of principle leads to his downfall. *Gantenbein* suggests that, while individual identity cannot be clearly defined but remains fluid, it is based on an awareness of social reality. The novel does not present a social analysis but rather focuses on the fluidity of identity as a liminal experience in a world that is increasingly meaningless.

Making sense of the world, and specifically of contemporary Germany, meant coming to terms with the war experience and the postwar social and political structures. While many German writers shared this goal, they differed in political perspective and narrative approach. Martin Walser, Siegfried Lenz, and Heinrich Böll were similar in their realistic approaches; in contrast, Günter Grass and Uwe Johnson remained grounded in reality but went beyond realism. The works of these authors can be read as a commentary on the history and contemporary situation of Germany because of the their openly political dimension. In his novels, such as *Ehen in Philippsburg* (Marriages in Philippsburg, 1957), Walser centers on middle-class people and examines the tensions that result from the characters' attempts to establish careers and find happiness. Walser refrained from direct political commentary. So did Lenz, although the author's didactic intentions seem to be more open — perhaps because Lenz understood himself as a moralist. His most successful novel, *Deutschstunde* (German Lesson, 1968), deals with the moral problems of the Nazi legacy that were still prevalent during the 1960s.

Heinrich Böll's works evolved in a close interaction with the development of social reality in Germany, a process that often put Böll, a liberal and an unorthodox Catholic, at odds with public opinion, especially when he spoke out against what he considered inhuman — whether those inhuman conditions were abroad, in the GDR, or in his own West Germany. Over the years he gained a moral authority unprecedented for an author in Germany, and since his works treated political issues, discussions of them usually emphasized the subject without doing justice to Böll's formal gifts as a writer. In the first phase of his career, Böll understood his writing in terms of the literature of the Zero Hour, examining the hard times of the average person. After the publication of *Wo warst du, Adam?* (Where Were You, Adam?, 1951), he moved to his next phase. There he remained true to his focus on the average person but examined the lives of those who remained excluded from the economic miracle. Böll's considerable satirical talent exposed hypocrisy and sentimentality in the hilarious and simultaneously sad stories of *Nicht nur zur Weihnachtszeit* (Not Just during the Christmas Season, 1952) and *Doktor Murkes gesammeltes Schweigen und andere Satiren* (Doctor Murke's Collected Silence and Other Satires, 1958).

The culmination of this phase was the novel *Billiard um halb zehn* (Billiards at Half-Past Nine, 1959). It narrates the involvement of three generations of the Flähmels, a family of architects, in German history from the Wilhelmine empire to the years after the Second World War, including the fascist undercurrent in post-1945 political thought and life, which defines the conflict between the die-hard Nazis and their victims. The focal point is the Abbey of St. Anton, which was built by the first generation of the Flähmels, was destroyed by the second during the war, and is to be rebuilt by the third. The action of the novel is condensed into one day and presented in flashbacks and interior monologue. The novel's complex structure has been compared to novels by William Faulkner and to the French nouveau roman. After this novel Böll developed a more direct way of integrating his political commitment in his writing, which he understood in terms of an "Ästhetik des Humanen" (aesthetics of humaneness).

**Günter Grass's
Die Blechtrommel**

*Die Blechtrommel* was a milestone in bringing the German novel back to the level of world literature in 1959 and earned Günter Grass the Nobel Prize for literature in 1999. The novel is a complex work with a distinct political and progressive impetus. The novel's focal point is its narrator-protagonist Oskar Matzerath, through whose eyes the reader witnesses the rise of Nazism in the free city of Danzig (now Gdansk, Poland), the Second World War, and after Oskar's flight to the West, the postwar years and the economic recovery in West Germany. Together with *Die Blechtrommel*, the novella *Katz und Maus* (Cat and Mouse, 1961) and the novel *Hundejahre* (Dog Years, 1963) constitute the *Danzig* trilogy.

The narration begins with the conception of Oskar's mother, Agnes, in a potato field. Oskar's own birth, told in the third chapter, is summarized in the sentence: "I first saw the light of this world in the form of two sixty-watt light bulbs" [Ich erblickte das Licht der Welt in

Gestalt zweier Sechzig-Watt-Glühbirnen]. As a result, the beginning chapters establish the novel's blend of satiric nonrealistic exaggeration and tone of precise realism that allows narration of any topic, including sexuality, without taboos. In fact, sexual relationships are crucial for *Blechtrommel* because they cause tremendous disorientation for Oskar, who does not know whether Alfred Matzerath or his mother's cousin, Jan Bronski, is his real father. As promised by his mother, Oskar receives a tin drum for his third birthday, but he stops growing when he falls down the cellar steps the same day. This event completes the novel's central image — Oskar as the boy with the tin drum who maintains the appearance of a three-year-old until he starts growing again at age twenty-one but is left slightly crippled.

As the years pass, Oskar causes various bits of mischief with his high-pitched voice and his nerve-wracking beating on his tin drum. In 1936 Oskar's mother dies of food poisoning, which she induces by eating as much fish as she can because she is pregnant again. In the meantime, the Nazis have taken power in Germany, and their steadily growing influence on everyday life provides the background of the novel. The first book ends with an eerie evocation of *Kristallnacht*, the infamous nationwide Nazi rampage against Jews and their property on November 9, 1938. Markus, the Jewish owner of the toyshop that kept Oskar supplied with new tin drums, commits suicide during the turmoil. This chapter is a good example of Grass's style, which uses grotesque distortions and — not in spite but because of this — remains centered on reality. Nazi brutality appears so incomprehensible that a great number of the chapter's paragraphs start with the formulaic beginning of fairy tales: "Once upon a time" [Es war einmal]. Most significantly, this does not take away from reality but rather intensifies the events by metaphoric transposition; for instance, Hitler's genocide of the Jews is indicted as is the German people's blind faith in Hitler: "The entire people of a credulous nation believed in Santa Claus. But Santa Claus was really the gasman" [Ein leichtgläubiges Volk glaubte an den Weihnachtsmann. Aber der Weihnachtsmann war in Wirklichkeit der Gasmann].

The beginning and end of the second book of *Blechtrommel* coincide with the beginning and end of the Second World War. Alfred, who turned Nazi, and Jan, who is Polish, have been pitted against each other for a while. Oskar leads Jan, his uncle and "presumed father" [mutmaßlicher Vater], to Jan's workplace, the Polish Post Office, which is currently under siege by local Nazi troops. The surrender of the postal workers means death for them, including Jan, and it signifies the beginning of the war. As the novel progresses, Oskar seduces Maria, who was hired to help in the household, but Alfred marries Maria, who is pregnant. Oskar joins Bebra and his ensemble of Lilliputians to entertain German troops during the war; since one of their engagements takes him to Normandy, he becomes an eyewitness to the Allied invasion. He returns to Danzig, where he becomes the mascot of a youth gang. When Soviet troops occupy the town, Oskar causes Alfred to choke on the Nazi party pin, and a startled Soviet soldier shoots Alfred to death. Oskar throws his drum into his father's grave but also falls into the grave himself — and starts growing again. Oskar, Maria, and Kurt, who is Maria's son with either Oskar or Alfred, leave for Düsseldorf in the West, where Oskar begins his adult life.

In the third book of *Blechtrommel* Oskar has a career as a musician. Under Bebra's management, he takes his success as a drummer to a cult following, a phenomenon dubbed "Oskarnismus." In the meantime, Dorothea, a nurse Oskar tried to seduce, is found murdered, and he is a suspect. After fleeing to Paris, he turns himself in and identifies himself in three languages, including English: "I am Jesus." The charges against Oskar are soon dropped, and a nurse is accused of the crime. In a mental hospital Oskar writes down his story and turns thirty — the age, he points out, that Jesus started gathering disciples and perhaps the year that Oskar will start a new life. When Oskar has finished telling his story, the song of the "Black Witch" [Schwarze Köchin; literally, Black Cook], of whom he is afraid, concludes the novel. The Black Witch has been understood as a metaphor for reality in general or for women in particular. Various autobiographical elements run through the novel, including Grass's German father and Kashubian-Polish mother, as well as Grass's training in stonemasonry.

The novel is a satire of the petty-bourgeois mindset that made Nazism possible. Consequently, the critical aspect of the satire centers on the issue of guilt. The humorous aspect is determined by Grass's use of the grotesque, which often functions as an anarchic antidote to the taboos of the petty-bourgeoisie. In this way, *Blechtrommel* is an artistically unified work of art of great complexity and moral standards. Two creative challenges for the reader, however, make this novel a literary tour-de-force: the protagonist-narrator's reliability is more than questionable, and the relationships among the characters can be understood as symbolic.

The first challenge becomes immediately obvious when Oskar opens the novel with the somewhat disconcerting admission that he is confined to a mental institution. What tests the reader's suspension of disbelief even more is that Oscar clairvoyantly knows things that he could not have known first-hand, although that is what his narration suggests. Between the lines, however, the suggestion emerges that his narration is a fabrication. For instance, on his third birthday Oskar decides to throw himself down the cellar stairs. As result he stops growing and, while maturing on the inside, maintains the appearance of a three-year-old for eighteen years. During that time Oskar possesses two destructive weapons: his tin drum, with which he is able to "drum the necessary distance between myself and the grownups" [zwischen mir und den Erwachsenen eine notwendige Distanz ertrommeln], and his shrill voice, with which he "screamed and sang glass to pieces" [zerschrie, zersang, zerscherbte (Glas)].

Oskar's narrative presents himself, in his own words, as "a little demigod whose business it was to harmonize chaos and intoxicate reason" [ein kleiner, das Chaos harmonisierender, die Vernunft in Rauschzustände versetzender Halbgott]. The association of Oskar with both Jesus and Satan seems to remove the novel from its realistic foundation. Central to Oskar's fall into the cellar that halted his growth is the question whether it was willed by Oskar (as he claims) or whether it was an accident caused by Alfred's negligence (as the adults think). Understanding Oskar as an abused child (because of various types of neglect, including the parents' emotionally destabilizing love triangle) provides an explanation of the paradox of subjective and objective versions of events in terms of Oskar's need to see himself in a position to exert control over those who have power over him. Child abuse as an interpretative pattern does not restrict the metaphorical force of the novel; rather, it underscores the foundation in reality, and it supports a political reading that goes deeper than understanding historical reality as a background for the adventures of a modern picaro.

The second challenge involves the symbolism of a multitude of the novel's elements. Above all, Oskar's impotent need to control his destiny and his perspective on history from below correspond to the needs and perspectives of the petty bourgeoisie, whose members appear both as victims and as perpetrators. Readings have been suggested for political implications of the initially happy ménage à trois, which suggests the political chaos of the time. It fails because of Agnes's suicide, which results from the rising National Socialist influence, whose stereotypes of motherhood no longer allow alternative lifestyles — or a metaphorical mediation (Agnes) between German (Alfred) and Polish (Jan) interests. Behind Oskar's narrative lies a considerable critical power to analyze historical events that help the readers recognize Oskar's blind spots. His critical power is reasoning taken to an extreme form; like his tin drum and piercing voice, it is not only destructive of the society it analyzes but also potentially self-destructive. In Oskar's hypercritical attitude, a world of total war brought forth total reason.

*Uwe Johnson's*
**Mutmassungen über Jakob**

Uwe Johnson's novel *Mutmassungen über Jakob* gained prominence over other major contemporary novels for two reasons: it was the most experimental one, and it focused on the East-West conflict rather than on the Nazi legacy. Jakob is killed crossing the railroad tracks, although, as a railroad dispatcher in East Germany, he has always done so — hence the novel's famous first sentence: "But Jacob always cut across the tracks" [Aber Jakob ist immer quer über die Gleise gegangen]. The speculations are twofold. On the one hand, the circumstances of Jakob's death are mysterious; it could have been an accident, suicide, or murder. Rohlfs, an officer of the East German secret police, is investigating. On the other hand, almost as a by-product of the investigations, questions emerge about the human being Jakob.

Often compared to Faulkner's use of multiperpectivism, the speculations about Jakob are presented in three distinct, but intertwined, modes: interior monologue, dialogue, and third-person narration. The monologues are those of Rohlfs, Gesine Cresspahl, who loves Jakob, and Jonas Blach, an assistant in the English department at the university in East Berlin, who is in love with Gesine. The monologues are set in italics but not identified as to speaker. The dialogues are set off by dashes to indicate a new speaker. The narrator's text is printed without any special markers. The narrator provides transitions and background information but does not answer the questions that are raised in the monologues and dialogues. The speculations do not allow for an omniscient narrator because Jakob means something different to each character. The technique of flashback dominates the flow of the novel, and the plot line — as it emerges from the fragmented information provided by monologues, dialogues, and narration — unfolds within the five main parts of the novel, each of which spans a period of about a month. It is the reader's challenge to put everything together to form a picture of Jakob.

The picture, however, remains vague. More clearly established are the personal relationships and the political involvements, while they, too, remain diffuse. For instance, interaction with Rohlfs, as an officer of the secret police, is always determined by second-guessing. But he does not behave in a dogmatic way; for example, he allows Gesine to return to West Germany after one of her visits to her father, Heinrich Cresspahl, who lives in the East. The chronology that emerges begins when the thirteen-year-old Gesine and the eighteen-year-old Jakob meet for the first time. Jakob and his mother arrive, as refugees from Pomerania at the end of the Second World War, in the village where Gesine and her father live. For Gesine it is love at first sight, yet for many years they have only a close brother-sister relationship. The novel contains a highly poetic expression of love, which is, significantly, not said to Jakob himself, but to Jonas so that he will understand with whom Gesine is in love: "It is my soul that loveth Jakob" [Es ist meine Seele, die liebet Jakob]. Only after Gesine has left East Germany and begun a new life in the West working for NATO, and Jakob's mother, too, has left for West Germany, do Gesine and Jakob become intimate when he is on a state-authorized visit to his mother but stays with Gesine for several days. Although Gesine asks him to stay with her in the West and Jakob asks her to return with him to the East, they seem to know that neither arrangement can work. It is after this visit that Jakob, on the way to his job in the morning, is hit by a locomotive and dies.

His life's end point becomes the novel's point of departure. Personal identity and reality become liminal, and the novel explores boundary conditions rather than solid phenomena. The village, or small town, of Jerichow, for example, where Gesine and her father live, is as fictitious as William Faulkner's Yoknapatawpha County. Also, while finally out in the open, the love between Jakob and Gesine is not elaborated on until later in the *Jahrestage* tetralogy (Anniversaries, 1970–1983), Johnson's masterpiece and one of German literature's most significant prose accomplishments of the second half of the twentieth century.

What made *Mutmassungen* controversial was that it does not present simple rights or wrongs in regard to the political systems of the capitalist West and the Communist East. Just as Jakob struggles to make the Soviet intervention in Hungary fit into his value system, Gesine is disgusted with the military solution to the Suez crisis by the West. Jakob decides not to delay a Soviet troop and tank transport on its way to Hungary, because he thinks that a delay of ten minutes, or even a day, would not make a difference; in contrast, Gesine quits her job with NATO. Consequently, both systems are criticized. While some readers in the West might have wondered about the positive portrayal of the secret-police officer, the novel was in conflict with the demands of East German Socialist Realism, whose typical elements included an idealistic Communist (Rohlfs), a wavering intellectual (Jonas), a citizen who is seduced by the West (Gesine), and another citizen who resists this seduction (Jakob). But the hero (Jakob) dies, and the "negative" foil (Gesine) is not presented in negative terms. What is more, the speculative approach to the novel's issues, especially the East-West conflict, runs counter to the Socialist Realist demand of partisanship.

Against this background a symbolic and political reading of the novel emerges, suggesting that objective truth cannot exist in a society (West or East) in which truth is a commodity and a construct of competing propaganda machines. Consequently, Jakob's death can be seen as symbolic of the political situation of the Cold War. His cutting across the railroad tracks is like "cutting across the tracks" of social systems. Caught between the two social systems, Jakob cannot develop a true identity (no wonder people can only speculate about him!) and is ultimately destroyed. Shortly before the novel's publication, Johnson left East Germany; although he remained true to East German themes, he evolved into a writer of both Germanies. In addition to the grotesque perspective on politics in Grass's *Die Blechtrommel*, the psychological and political speculations in *Mutmassungen über Jakob* indicated that the German novel was poised to become more political in the 1960s.

ğ   ğ   ğ   ğ   ğ   ğ   ğ

# 9: The 1960s: Change in Literary Awareness — Politicization in the West and Emancipation of Subjectivity in the East

## Social Foundations: Generation Gap

THE FISSURES BETWEEN the superficial materialism of the economic-wonder years and the need, especially of the younger generation, to find means of self-expression widened. It all had begun innocently and nonpolitically enough with the musical revolution of rock 'n' roll, which most German radio stations did not play until the mid-1950s. The confrontation between the older and younger generations escalated to street fighting in the Munich neighborhood of Schwabing in 1962 when authorities responded to complaints about noise by rather heavy-handedly arresting street musicians, who fought back for three nights. The political dimensions of the underlying social conflict slowly came to the fore during the 1960s.

The focal points for German society in the 1960s were manifestations of the Cold War and of the counterculture movement. After 2,690,000 people left East Germany for the West between 1949 and 1961 — 47,000 during the first twelve days of August 1961 alone — on August 13, 1961, the GDR fortified its borders with West Germany and West Berlin, which lay like an island within East German territory. The initial barbed wire was soon replaced by a permanent and heavily guarded concrete wall, not just around West Berlin but along the entire border between the two German states; nevertheless, it was the Berlin Wall that became a worldwide symbol of the German division and the East-West conflict.

Although several temporary improvements made it possible for West Berliners to visit family members in East Berlin, the 1960s did not see major changes in the relationship between the two German states until toward the end of the decade as the politics of détente commenced. Important social changes, however, occurred within the German states during the early and mid-1960s. For example, the West German public's awareness of its own history was strongly heightened by war crimes tribunals. For the first time, crimes that had been committed in the Nazi concentration camp of Auschwitz were tried in German courts between 1963 and 1966, receiving extensive media coverage. At the time when the image of the "ugly German" had to be confronted, the trust in West German economic strength was also shaken — furthermore, both issues combined in the question of how minorities were treated in West Germany. From about 1955 foreigners had been recruited to work in West Germany to keep the economy booming; the total number of "guest workers," as they were euphemistically called, had steadily climbed to approximately 1,244,000 in 1966. The boom hit a snag, however, when the economy experienced not only structural challenges, such as the closing of many coal mines, but also a recession during which unemployment quadrupled within one year to a peak of 400,000 in June 1967.

After a government crisis in 1966, the conservative CDU/CSU formed a grand coalition with the Social Democrats. The new government — while its overwhelming parliamentary majority was perceived as a threat to democracy — was effective, because it overcame the economic crisis. It also paved the way for the shift in political leadership at the end of the 1960s. After the 1969 federal elections Willy Brandt, the vice chancellor of the previous CDU/CSU-SPD government, formed a coalition with the Free Democrats (the party of economic liberalism) and became the first Social Democratic chancellor of the Federal Republic of Germany.

Chancellor Brandt's inaugural address was as much a sign of the times as it was a speech that raised eyebrows when it promised to "dare for more democracy" [mehr Demokratie wagen]. It went beyond merely reflecting a pervasive will for political renewal; it was also a response to a general politicization of West German society that had especially radicalized the younger generation. Left-wing anticapitalist tendencies were galvanized on two issues — anti-Vietnam War protests and resistance to new West German legislation to increase state control in the event of a national emergency — but were directed against one target: the state authorities. In 1966 hundreds of students held an anti-American rally in West Berlin; in 1967 a student at a demonstration against the Shah of Iran's visit was shot to death by police in Berlin; and in April 1968 Rudi Dutschke, a radical and charismatic student leader, was severely injured in an attack, setting off protests throughout West Germany. By mid-1968, however, the energy of the protest movement had waned; protests had failed to prevent the new emergency legislation, which was passed in May 1968. A crucial aspect of the counterculture movement was that its political activism took a stand against the state and its institutions; significantly, it called itself APO (*Außerparlamentarische Opposition*, or Extra-Parliamentary Opposition). After their political failure, there remained for the young activists two major choices short of resignation: either continue on the path of violence that had already begun with several fire bombings or try to reform the political system from within. Brandt's inaugural address in 1969 was an invitation to the younger generation to opt for democratic reform instead of revolutionary terror.

In spite of the competing political blocs, developments in East Germany showed some similarities to those in the West. Building of the Wall was supposed to stop the flight of East German citizens to West Germany. According to party-line reasoning, however, the Wall should appear as an attempt not to keep East German citizens locked up but to keep them safe from the West — as suggested by the phrase *antifaschistischer Schutzwall* (antifascist wall of protection). In practical terms it meant that the GDR government could concentrate on internal affairs and consolidate its power. The New Economic System for Planning and Guidance (NÖSPL, or *Neues Ökonomisches System für Planung und Lenkung*) of 1963 applied cybernetic and other scientific principles, as well as profit orientation, to the state's economic policies. The central claim of the plan was that the GDR had reached the stage of socialism, which, according to Marxist theory, is one step away from achieving a fully communist society. This claim had sweeping implications: culture, including literature, fell under regulation of NÖSPL, since all cultural activities were regarded as productive elements in the economy. While the renewal of the economic sector ran into short-term problems, it ultimately raised the standard of living in the GDR significantly above that of other East bloc countries.

The GDR experienced a large-scale counterculture influence only within the confines of cultural phenomena. For example, rock music by the Rolling Stones and jeans were no longer condemned as Westernization. The initial relaxation of cultural policies can be seen as the result of the Wall, because writers had the option of accepting the political situation as an opportunity to focus on their state's internal aspects and — taking the Communist value of self-criticism seriously — demand such self-examination and self-criticism from their socialist state, for instance, in questioning the role of the individual within a socialist collective. And the GDR had enough self-confidence in the beginning of its new self-seclusion from the West to allow such discussion of socialist values in Wolf Biermann's poetry. But soon the SED declared any such discussion detrimental and cracked down on its intellectuals. While writers could no longer voice their criticism, the rock music and jeans remained — although they, too, were integrated into state-controlled youth movements.

## The Literary Spectrum

On both sides of the Iron Curtain, German literature responded to a sense of weakness within the respective political systems. The Berlin Wall meant for the East German writers ideological isolation from their

West German colleagues, such as Böll, Grass, and Enzensberger, who protested the building of the Wall. And when an initial phase of relaxed state control ended in December 1965, it meant an even stronger demand for *Ankunftsliteratur* (literature of arrival), which was supposed to illustrate, in the style of Socialist Realism, that East German society had arrived at the phase of socialism. In contrast, a new subjectivity evolved in a process of emancipation of GDR writers who posed the question of how to develop a sense of self within a socialist state; such a semiprivate concern about political views was similar to movements in West German literature in the 1950s. *Der geteilte Himmel* (Divided Heaven, 1963), by Christa Wolf (b. 1929), and *Die Aula* (The Lecture Hall, 1965), by Hermann Kant (b. 1926), were important attempts to mediate between *Ankunftsliteratur* and subjectivity. While defining subjectivity within socialism led to a wave of lyric, yet still political, poetry — such as poems by Sarah Kirsch (b. 1935) and Wolf Biermann — three novels are outstanding explorations of the issue in prose form: *Levins Mühle* (Levin's Mill, 1964), by Johannes Bobrowski; *Buridans Esel* (Buridan's Ass, 1968), by Günter de Bruyn (b. 1926); and *Jakob der Lügner* (Jacob the Liar, 1969), by Jurek Becker.

In the second half of the 1960s the emancipation of East German literature became stronger, and the crisis of political awareness culminated in West Germany (and other Western countries, including France and the United States). Literature in the West was asking a question related to the East German question about subjectivity within socialism. Leaving behind a period during which literature (and art in general) had made political statements as though in a private and subjective realm, literature in the West did not ask about subjectivity within capitalism; instead, its questions were more fundamental: What is capitalism? What is reality? Questions of this kind drew attention to political issues that went beyond immediate local concerns and included the Third World and anti-Vietnam War protests. The theoretical inquiry about the status of the world was also an important step toward the postmodern mode.

The inquiries into reality also entailed inquires into language and the relationship — and ultimately the discrepancy — between reality and language. The resulting literary experiments brought attempts at new forms, such as Helmut Heissenbüttel's (1921–1996) "texts," and a revival of Avant-Gardist traditions from Dadaist sound poems, reborn as concrete poetry, to works akin to New Objectivist documentary literature emerging especially in prose and in the theater. Other authors made more directly political statements in their poetry and prose. In addition, *Die Palette* (1968), by Hubert Fichte (1935–1986), exemplifies literary works that seemed highly subjective but contained a political element because of their countercultural character. Finally, in theaters in both West and East Germany the influence of Bertolt Brecht was waning, and the 1960s drama brought further attempts at finding new forms.

## New Lyrical Awareness

*Changing Traditions*

Greater lyrical assertiveness meant that the responsibilities of the writers' consciousness were deliberately placed above social and political expectations, implying a stronger emphasis on subjectivity for East Germany and on political statements for West Germany. Yet these were two sides of the same coin, because asserting one's subjectivity under the expectations of a Communist state was, of necessity, a political statement. Along with the emergence of a new generation of writers and its new subjective politics, poetry by the older generation of poets also changed.

By the mid-1960s, Karl Krolow had achieved the status of "classical modernist." He increased his use of both lyrical impressions and political allusions, and toward the end of the 1960s, as his collection *Alltägliche Gedichte* (Everyday Poems, 1968) demonstrates, Krolow added a more laconic and skeptical tone, as well as images that are more immediately related to the basics of human existence. For instance, the matter-of-factness of "Alltägliches Gedicht" indicts domestic violence in the context of social attitudes: "A man thinks the Prussian way, / punishes his wife, his children. / She takes off the earring, / when he takes measure, / he who has practice in this matter" [Einer denkt preussisch, / straft sein Weib, die Kinder. / Sie nimmt den Ohrring ab, / wenn der ihr Maß nimmt, / der hier Übung hat].

Günter Eich, too, found his way to a new degree of terse and matter-of-fact poetic language that was tinged with resignation and melancholy. While his late short prose texts, which he titled "Maulwürfe" (Moles), were characterized by biting wit and punning irony, the poems of Eich's last years, which were marked by his declining health, displayed less bite and more suffering. Faced with a decision, the speaker of the poem "Timetable" (1966) withdraws: "I prefer / to place lettuce / on a sandwich and / keep being wrong" [Ich ziehe vor, / Salatblätter auf ein / Sandwich zu legen und / Unrecht zu behalten].

While Krolow and Eich were well-established writers in the West before the 1960s, Rose Ausländer (1901–1988) and her work had to wait to find a wider audience. Hidden in a cellar, she had survived the Nazi persecution of the Jews and had emigrated to the United States after the war. In 1965 she returned to Germany. Of great thematic importance were the childhood memories of her birthplace in Romania, but even more important were her Jewish faith and the horrors of the

Holocaust. During the mid-1950s Ausländer found a way to express her themes that was distinctly different from her earlier, more traditional approach: unrhymed and laconic everyday language. Drawing strength from her faith and childhood memories, she believed in the possibility of communication and in the power of the word. *Blinder Sommer* (Blind Summer), her first collection of poems since the 1930s, was published in 1965, yet it took until the 1970s for her poetic stature to be generally acknowledged.

Georg Maurer (1907–1971), Erich Arendt (1903–1984), and Peter Huchel had an important presence in East German poetry during the 1960s. In contrast to Arendt and Huchel, Maurer displayed in his poems a clear affirmation of the GDR's way of building socialism. Teaching at the prestigious Leipzig Institute for Literature from 1955 to 1971, he actively shaped the younger generation of poets. Arendt came to the GDR from exile having written primarily antifascist works, but he turned to skepticism in the late 1950s. With *Ägäis* (1967) he presented the poetic summation of his visits to Greece. The Greek archaic landscape and mythology became, for Arendt, a symbol of human history that had taken a turn for the worse as a destructive product of self-destructive man. With such a subject matter and an increasingly laconic language, Arendt had a great influence on the younger generation of East German writers.

As the independent-minded editor of the influential magazine *Sinn und Form*, Huchel had printed texts that he considered to be of high literary quality, mostly Modernist works by authors of whom the official party-line aesthetics was suspicious. In 1962 he was forced to resign, but not before he published another issue of the magazine that included six of his own poems. Expressing resignation but also resistance, these poems — in particular "Der Garten des Theophrast" (The Garden of Theophrastus), dedicated to his son — were Huchel's literary testament. "Der Garten des Theophrast" can be read as a political allegory, because the speaker calls on his son to remember those who once planted conversations the way trees are planted. The garden can be interpreted as East Germany and the "olive tree" [Ölbaum] as the tree of poetry and freedom and, by extension, Huchel's magazine. But now, the poem concludes, the order has been issued to cut down the tree to its roots, just as the magazine was taken away from Huchel.

*Political subjectivity in the East*    Important in the development of more private, subjective modes of poetry within a state that expected political partisanship from its authors were Johannes Bobrowski and Günter Kunert. Bobrowski began publishing poems in the mid-1950s. The two collections that included these earlier poems, *Sarmatische Zeit* (Sarmatian

Time, 1961) and *Schattenland Ströme* (Shadowland Streams, 1962), made Bobrowski, along with Paul Celan and Ingeborg Bachmann, one of the most significant and influential voices of postwar German-language poetry. Bobrowski's poetry has two main centers: nature, which includes humanity, and Sarmatia, which is an old name for the Eastern European area between the Vistula and the Volga. Since his vision of Sarmatia encompasses a specific landscape and the history of the peoples who lived there, he evoked the historically problematic relationship between Germany and Eastern Europe. In the contemporary situation Bobrowski saw the Sarmatian landscape and nature still bearing signs of earlier violence.

For Bobrowski, whose self-acknowledged model was the German poet Friedrich Gottlieb Klopstock (1724–1803), his poems were a private matter, but they can be understood as a dialogue between past and present. They are characterized by a tone of melancholy and resignation, and often they are invocations. The poem that opens his first collection is called "Anruf" (Invocation) and begins with an apostrophe to Vilna and Novgorod, identifying the Sarmatian landscape typical of Bobrowski's poems; it ends by quoting the forefathers' wisdom: "Bid welcome the strangers. / You'll be a stranger. Soon" [Heiß willkommen die Fremden. / Du wirst ein Fremder sein. Bald]. The poem's tone is close to everyday speech; in sharp contrast to such an easygoing tone, the metaphors are difficult. In the evocation of the landscape of "Die sarmatische Ebene" (The Sarmatian Plain), the narrow paths appear like "crushed glass / made of tears" [zerstoßenes Glas / aus Tränen] and form a "trace of ashes" [Aschenspur]. This image suggests that extreme suffering and violence in the past — ashes being an allusion to cremation or scorched earth — have shaped the present.

Günter Kunert was only a few years older than the "young" generation of poets, but he was already an established writer and was productive in various genres, such as with the novel *Im Namen der Hüte* (In the Name of the Hats, 1967). During the 1960s, Kunert expressed an increasingly negative assessment of the political realities, posing questions about the nuclear threat and social alienation. These questions were not opportune in the GDR. As defined by Communist theory, alienation could not occur in Communist countries but only in the capitalist West; therefore, an author's depiction of alienation in the GDR was — in the eyes of the SED — not just a deviation from the expected partisanship but a sign of a dangerous subjectivity.

In "Der ungebetene Gast" (The Uninvited Guest), the title poem of Kunert's 1965 collection, the silent guest is unwelcome because he is a reminder of the Holocaust. Although his history is never explicitly stated, his attributes identify him as a survivor or ghost of the ghettoes and death camps so that his presence at the table makes the morsels of food taste like ashes. The five rhymed four-line stanzas that describe the guest alternate with six single lines that are instructions to take the guest into the group at the table; after the food tastes ashen and everybody has a guilty conscience, the poem ends with an instruction to get rid of the guest: "Then move the chair away again" [So rückt doch den Stuhl wieder fort]. The poem suggests that, in contrast to official GDR rhetoric, fascism still existed in the minds of people and had not been adequately confronted. At an even more subjective level, the poem implies that Kunert himself was an uninvited guest in the GDR. Indeed, the collection had been completed in 1963 but had to wait for publication, and Kunert left East Germany in 1979.

The shift to subjectivity in East German poetry is connected with the emergence of a young generation of poets who, with a few exceptions, came from the former state of Saxony: Heinz Czechowski (b. 1935), Reiner Kunze, Rainer Kirsch (b. 1934), Karl Mickel (1935–2000), and Volker Braun (b. 1939). Their mentor, Adolf Endler (b. 1930), spoke of a Saxon School of Poets. Others not from that area who belonged to the new generation included Kurt Bartsch (b. 1937), Sarah Kirsch, and Wolf Biermann. The works of these poets are characterized both by an embrace of East Germany as the better country — an important anthology of these authors, edited in 1966 by Endler and Mickel, was titled *In diesem besseren Land* (In this Better Country) — and by an exploration of their own subjectivity. The anthology was at the center of a public discussion about poetry. Behind the criticism of subjectivity was the Communist suspicion that autonomous and Modernist art was hardly functional in the sense of Socialist Realism.

Czechowski had a reputation for writing poems with a quiet quality that focused on concrete experiences. In the development of his poetry, however, there was a movement similar to that of many of his colleagues: a movement toward doubt. This critical attitude brought the authors into conflict with the state to such an extent that many eventually left the GDR. For example, Kunze left in 1977 and Bartsch in 1980. But it did not mean that the writers automatically embraced the West. Although Kunze's collection *Sensible Wege* (Sensitive Paths, 1969), which brought his literary breakthrough, was published only in West Germany and is usually considered as a document of solidarity with the dissidents of the Eastern bloc countries, the poem with the concluding lines "Man / is an elbow / to man" [Der mensch / ist dem menschen / ein ellbogen] is significantly titled "Düsseldorfer Impromptu," referring to a city in West Germany.

Sarah Kirsch attended the East German Institute of Literature in Leipzig from 1963 to 1965; in 1977 she moved to West Germany and developed into the most important female German-language poet. From her first publications, such as *Gedichte* (Poems, 1967), Kirsch has dealt with the themes of love and nature. In "Dann werden wir kein Feuer brauchen" (Then We Will Need No Fire), she evokes a forest steaming with warmth, and the poem ends with the affirmation: "Tomorrow you will be in paradise with me" [Morgen wirst du im Paradies mit mir sein]. What appears to be artistic naivete, however, reveals its darker dimension when the ambiguous images are read as allusions to a nuclear explosion. The clouds are "a mighty tree of clouds" [ein mächtiger Wolkenbaum], whose brightness makes the sun look pale. And the poem's speaker and her loved one have lost their corporeality; now their silvery bodies "radiate warmth from brightness / is within us" [strahln Wärme aus Helligkeit / ist in uns]. With an innovative emphasis on female subjectivity, Kirsch's poems center on the precarious balance between humankind and nature and between trust and disillusionment. Her laconic tone becomes melancholy when she explores loneliness and disorientation, but it can also turn to subtle humor when Kirsch expresses a sense of hope.

Wolf Biermann left West Germany for East Germany in 1953. But his criticism of the GDR's political system was met with occasional restrictions as early as 1963, and in 1965 he was generally forbidden to publish or perform his texts in East Germany. Most of his early works were published by Wagenbach in West Berlin, such as *Die Drahtharfe* (The Wire Harp, 1965) and *Mit Marx- und Engelszungen* (With Marx and Engels' Tongues, 1968, a pun on the German idiom for "smooth talking" and the founders of Communism). The poems were performed as songs by Biermann himself in an interaction of text, voice, and instrument (the guitar) to underscore the aggressiveness of his message. The typographical presentation in "Warte nicht auf bessere Zeiten" (Don't Wait for Better Times, 1965) indicates the intended performance with fading intensity: "And the best method against / Socialism (I do speak up) / is that you're the ones to / BUILD IT UP!!! Build it up! (build it up)" [Und das beste Mittel gegen / Sozialismus (sag ich laut) / ist, daß ihr den Sozialismus / AUFBAUT!!! Aufbaut! (aufbaut)].

These lines reveal the tensions between Biermann and the state that he had chosen. Although he considered himself a Communist, he criticized the bureaucratic practice of socialism in the GDR, and he did not follow the tenets of Socialist Realism. Biermann's poems are always political, even when they express private issues. This statement can also be reversed: because Biermann insisted on his independence and critical distance from the GDR, his poems always express his subjectivity, even when they are political. A high degree of sensitivity and vulnerability has been considered a likely source of his poems' aggressiveness. This aggressiveness and the GDR's response took an unprecedented and polarizing turn in the 1970s.

*Political poetry in the West*

There were clear affinities between the critical poems by critical East German authors, such as Biermann, and poems by West German poets. Franz Josef Degenhardt (b. 1931) even referred in a poem to Biermann as his "brother in song" [Sangesbruder]. Among the political poets in the West, the Austrian Erich Fried certainly provided a model for the younger generation and was himself highly prolific. A large number of authors wrote political poetry, among them Degenhardt, Volker von Törne (1934–1980), and, most importantly, Hans Magnus Enzensberger.

In 1938 Fried emigrated to England, which remained his place of residence until his death (although he died on a visit to West Germany). He continued to write in German and was best known for poems that explored issues from love to politics with a linguistic brilliance that included well-executed wordplays. While he leaned toward socialism, he never became ideologically inflexible; in fact, he wrote poems attacking such inflexibility. In the mid-1960s, he turned to openly political poems with his *Warngedichte* (Poems of Warning, 1964). His collection *und Vietnam und* (and Vietnam and, 1966) is usually considered a high point in the development of outspoken political poetry. In this collection Fried appealed to his readers' sense of civic duty in a much broader context than that of one specific war that was the occasion for the writing of these poems. For example, he lists several "Gründe" (Reasons) in a poem of that title for not getting involved in anything, which are merely lame excuses, such as "They do what they want anyway" [Sie tun ja doch was sie wollen]. The poem ends with a reminder of the self-destructive consequence of such noninvolvement: "These are causes of death / to be written on our graves // which won't be dug anymore / if these are the causes" [Das sind Todesursachen / zu schreiben auf unsere Gräber // die nicht mehr gegraben werden / wenn das die Ursachen sind].

Franz Josef Degenhardt is perhaps best known as a songwriter and performer with albums of songs, such as *Spiel nicht mit den Schmuddelkindern* (Don't Play with the Dirty Kids, 1965, referring to children from the wrong side of town; the same title was used for his 1967 collection of poems). Degenhardt turned to radical political expression in his poems; for instance, in "Für wen ich singe" (For Whom I Sing) he makes it clear that he does not sing for those who treat their "wives like / steaks" [Frauen so wie / Steaks] but for those who resist the Western way of life and will not rest as long as "Napalm is still food for the poor" [Napalm noch die Speise der Armen ist].

Volker von Törne was paradigmatic for the generation that became aware of its involvement in Nazi crime through its parents. Törne's social and Christian convictions led to an unusual unity of life and work;

he headed the Berlin office of *Aktion Sühnezeichen* (Action Sign of Atonement, an organization that worked to improve West Germany's relationship with Israel), and he wrote poetry that, as another form of atonement, embraced personal and collective guilt but also a commitment to preventing fascism. In conjunction with social developments, Törne's poetry, which has a relaxed and colloquial quality, became more and more political. "Amtliche Mitteilung" (Official Announcement), in *Fersengeld* (Taking to Your Heels, 1962), uses proverbial sayings in unexpected juxtapositions that pretend to understand these sayings literally and thus suggest a discrepancy between the powers that be and the needs of the people: "They are playing with fire: / we shall not freeze" [Sie spielen mit Feuer: / wir werden nicht frieren]. *Wolfspelz* (In Wolf's Clothing, 1968) is more aggressively political.

The most important political German poet is Hans Magnus Enzensberger. His major lyrical publications during the 1960s were *landessprache* (language of the country, 1960) and *blindenschrift* (writing for the blind, 1964); the latter brought to a close Enzensberger's first phase of poetry, whose political tone ranged from aggressive to skeptical. His poem "Landessprache" begins with an outcry, "What am I doing here / in this country" [Was habe ich hier verloren / in diesem Land], mixing an aggressiveness similar to that of Allen Ginsberg's poems with a mock-serious allusion to Rilke's *Duineser Elegien*, which suggests that just as none of the orders of angels will hear Rilke, nobody will answer Enzensberger's question. The Rilke allusion is later made more explicit by the ironic quotation "Being here is glorious" [Hiersein ist herrlich], but in the course of "Landessprache," Germany is unmasked as "a pit of murderers" [Mördergrube]. The contrast between tradition and reality underscores the intellectual's ambivalent situation, which Enzensberger articulates explicitly: he declares his independence from the reality of German political division and, at the same time, insists that he belongs: "my two countries and I, our ways have parted / yet I persist in staying here" [Meine zwei Länder und ich, wir sind geschiedene Leute, / und doch bin ich inständig hier].

"Abgelegenes Haus" (Remote House) in *blindenschrift* is a less aggressive, yet equally effective, political poem. The six-stanza poem, dedicated to Günter Eich, evokes nature, technology, and a homey kitchen scene in the first three stanzas. At the end of the third stanza the radio is turned on, and the fourth stanza consists of fragments of the broadcasts: news, commercials, and songs. The news pertains to the "Caribbean crisis" [Karibische Krise]. In contrast to the actual Cuban missile crisis, which was resolved without military conflict, the poem's fifth stanza implies large-scale destruction. The last stanza is an allusion to the expression "to bomb someone back into the stone age," which was one of the feared effects of a nuclear holocaust: "I don't know how to lay traps / and to make an ax of flintstone / when the last blade / has rusted away" [Ich weiß nicht, wie man Fallen stellt / und eine Axt macht aus Flintstein, / wenn die letzte Schneide / verrostet ist].

Because of his fascination with American pop art as an expression of a new sensitivity, the writings of Rolf Dieter Brinkmann (1940–1975) illustrate the transition from the political 1960s to the sensitivity of the 1970s, which did not necessarily preclude the political. Brinkmann was a prototypically rebellious and struggling artist. During the 1960s, he established himself as West Germany's leading representative of pop and underground literature, especially in *Die Piloten* (The Pilots, 1968). In his prose and poetry Brinkmann aimed at new images of banality and brutality. In a quite realistic style, he looked at the small and ephemeral emotions of everyday life and consumerism. The speaker in the poem "Selbstbildnis im Supermarkt" (Self-Portrait in the Supermarket) is so shocked by his reflection in the supermarket window that he becomes disoriented and unable to move, standing in front of an empty wall: "From there someone will / certainly pick me // up" [Dort holt mich später dann / sicher jemand // ab].

*Konkrete Poesie* (concrete poetry) started in the *Concrete poetry* 1950s, but the political climate was not favorable for experiments. In the 1960s, however, the endeavor took off so rapidly that it has been remarked that by the time the public responded to it, the "movement" was almost over. Production of, and public interest in, concrete poetry began to wane in the 1970s. Like its Avant-Garde predecessors, concrete poetry was more than mere play with sounds. In addition to an anarchical pleasure in playing with linguistic material in a way that was not prescribed by social norms or linguistic rules, these poems aimed at political meaning by making the reader aware of the fact that life in a society can be as empty as linguistic rituals. Concrete poetry unfolded according to rules inherent in the linguistic material, with no constraints. The resulting texts exhibit marked visual and/or acoustic qualities.

Eugen Gomringer, a Swiss author who was born in Bolivia in 1925, is the main theoretician of concrete poetry; he is also credited with applying the term "concrete art," in use since the 1930s, to the new poetic endeavor in 1955. His own concrete poetry was first published under the title *konstellationen* (1953). As is generally true of concrete poetry, some texts depend on language-specific puns and permutations and resist easy translation; others translate easily; and yet others even apply the anarchic playfulness to a language other than German. Gomringer wrote poems in several languages; the full title of his 1953 publication repeats the same word in German, English, and Spanish: *konstellationen constellations constelaciones*. One of his better-known concrete poems, "Schweigen" (Silence, 1960), is an example of constructing an interaction between word meaning and visual effect. *Silence* means the absence of communication, but being silent means something, too. Ironically, the typographically empty center is really silent and embodies the idea of silence, while the repetition of the word for "silence" appears to be quite noisy:

Schweigen Schweigen Schweigen
Schweigen Schweigen Schweigen
Schweigen               Schweigen
Schweigen Schweigen Schweigen
Schweigen Schweigen Schweigen

Concrete poetry demands to be seen on the printed page, because it eludes description and analysis; in this quality lies its political dimension. By refusing to be fully encompassed by rational discourse, concrete poetry resists the claim that rationality rules all aspects of modern life; the rest is silence. This is a universal concept, which, together with Gomringer's multilingual production, suggests the possibility of a universal poetic language. Other poems are more directly visual, such as Reinhard Döhl's "Apfel mit Wurm" (Apple with Worm, 1965), which consists of the repeated word for "apple" in about fifteen lines, cut out in the shape of an apple and, in the lower right-hand corner, interrupted by one occurrence of the word for "worm."

Practitioners of concrete poetry came from all German-speaking countries. Gomringer was from Switzerland; Döhl (b. 1943) and Franz Mon (pseudonym of Franz Löffelholz, b. 1926) were from West Germany; and there was a small Stuttgart Group around Max Bense (1910–1990), a professor of mathematical logic and the philosophy of science who developed an aesthetic theory based on cybernetics and information theory. Nevertheless, Austrian authors, whose interest in possibilities and problems of language had historically been quite strong, were in the forefront of writing concrete poetry. The *Wiener Gruppe* (Vienna Group, 1952–1964) encompassed Friedrich Achleitner (b. 1930), Gerhard Rühm (b. 1930), Konrad Bayer (1932–1964), and Oswald Wiener (b. 1935).

H. C. Artmann (1921–2000) was closely connected with the Vienna Group, but his collection of dialect poems *med ana schwoazzn dintn* (with black ink, 1958) marked not only his artistic breakthrough but also the beginning of his independence from the *Wiener Gruppe*. In 1953 Artmann wrote an "Acht-Punkte-Proklamation des poetischen Aktes" (Eight-Point-Proclamation of the Poetic Act), which included the claim that a person can be a poet without writing or publishing a single word. Strongly influenced by Dada and Surrealism, Artmann developed a fantastic-realistic style.

Ernst Jandl (1925–2000), who, though he was Viennese, did not belong to the *Wiener Gruppe,* is the best-known author of concrete poetry. He did not restrict himself to linguistic play but aimed at creating experiences and insights in which his readers could participate. Even his early poems, which were influenced by Brecht, display an awareness of the world's fragmentary character, while maintaining traditional syntax and word choices. Jandl's sound poems, however, mostly abandon traditional linguistic form and present the fragmentary world — in poems that are composed of linguistic fragments. Yet they are usually referential, as is his perhaps most famous poem, "Schtzngrmm" (derived by deletion of all vowels and slurring of the ending from the word *Schützengraben,* referring to a trench used in warfare), which is dated 1957 but was first published in book form in *Laut und Luise* (Loud and Louise, 1966, Luise is a pun on the proper name and on *leise,* the German word for "quiet"). The word *Schtzngrmm* evokes war by providing the sole linguistic material for the poem, which repeats the word in variations and fragments to re-create the sputtering sound of machine-gun fire: "scht / tzngrmm / tzngrmm / t-t-t-t-t-t-t-t-t / scht."

### Literary Genres and Innovation

Iconoclastic challenges that declared the death of literature or of the narrator were survived by the element whose death had been announced. Still, these challenges were consequential because they proclaimed what was missing in literature by claiming the end of an older literary practice. Yet old forms were not abandoned but redefined; consequently, the epic, lyric, and dramatic genres still provide the basic parameters, within which new forms establish themselves. This holds true for concrete poetry, documentary literature, and the two most radically new genres of the 1960s: the "new radio play" and the "text."

At the beginning of the 1960s a new phase emerged in the development of the radio play that is referred to as the "new radio play." While radio had incorporated sound effects before, in the 1960s experimentation with a wider variety of sounds, including recordings of actual sounds, montages, and stereophonic sound, increased. Paul Pörtner (1925–1984) was one of the early pioneers of the form. Similar experimentation was used in other works that explored the options of the medium of language, especially concrete poetry and new forms of theater, such as Peter Handke's experimentation with *Sprechtheater.* Traditional boundaries — not just between the literary genres but also between the literary and the nonliterary — were crossed.

The resulting strong focus of linguistic and paralinguistic material celebrated as an autonomous sound event engaged the listener in a more active role than did the radio play of the 1950s, for instance, in

*Paul oder die Zerstörung eines Hörbeispiels* (Paul, or the Destruction of a Radio Example, 1970), by Wolf Wondratschek (b. 1943). The new radio play's self-reflexivity not only included the danger of becoming self-contained but also made minimal references to political reality. The beginning of the 1960s marked another change that affected the radio play: the radio was increasingly replaced by television as the entertainment medium of choice. As a result, the radio play lost its significance, although many authors, such as Elfriede Jelinek (b. 1946) in the 1990s, continued to contribute to the genre.

*"Texts"* The most radical literary experiments of the 1960s can be subsumed under the term *text*, which embodied a new (or renewed) understanding of language as a material phenomenon: everything was a text. Literary texts were on equal footing with nonliterary ones, ranging from advertising to computer-generated materials. Three main issues determined the role that "texts" played in the literature of the 1960s: the scope of "texts," the general problem of innovation, and the goals that writers pursued by creating "texts."

First, the new concept of "text" was often experienced as a great liberation from the traditional restrictions of literary aesthetics; the genres did not matter any more; and, consequently, neither did the problem of how to define the genres. Max Bense was a theoretician and practitioner of the new "texts" that have random and serial qualities; for example, "walls and walls made of walls of walls made of walls of walls made of walls" [Mauern und Mauern aus Mauern von Mauern aus Mauern von Mauern aus Mauern] (no title, 1961). This "text" shows a close affinity to concrete poetry; others, such as his "Der Monolog der Terry Jo" (Terry Jo's Monologue, 1968, written with Ludwig Harig, b. 1927), are grouped into the category of the "new radio play." The two best-known writers of "texts," Jürgen Becker (b. 1932) and Helmut Heissenbüttel, showed affinities to concrete poetry but also significant differences in regard to the status of innovation and the goals of their "texts."

Second, the concept of innovation had become questionable and, in a strict sense, irrelevant for literature. If literature is a sphere autonomous of other social spheres, then it is restricted to three creative choices: exploring its relationship to reality, exploring its own qualities, or attempting to break out of its autonomous status. These choices had been taken by Realism, Aestheticism, and the Avant-Garde, respectively. Therefore, all options seemed exhausted, and the literature of the 1960s appeared to be an "encore" of neo-movements: neo-Realism (for instance, by Dieter Wellershoff), neo-Aestheticism (concrete poetry), and neo-Avant-Garde (documentary literature). Such sensitivity toward the exhaustion of literature led the way to postmodernism, which is both the product of the crisis of Modernism in the 1960s and an attempt at redefining the role of innovation.

Heissenbüttel was serious about the second-hand quality of literature. His position marked a central awareness that is important in moving toward postmodernism. The contemporary writer, who no longer could create anything that had not been created in the centuries before, had to work instead with the material that she or he found. The "text" producer, therefore, was evolving from a writer into a collector. The primary means of working with this existing material was the quotation that could be reduced, combined, and reproduced. In an extreme understanding, the writer as collector was nothing more than a keeper of an inventory, which was not aesthetically satisfactory in the long term. In contrast to the proclamation of abandoning the priority on innovation in favor of syncretism, the concept of innovation remained crucial for "texts" in two respects: neither the method (for example, montage) nor the material (such as quotations from earlier literature) have to be new to give rise to a result that is experienced as an innovation, because it reduces, combines, and reproduces old elements in a way that had never been done before. And, above all, the goal of these endeavors was to create something entirely new: a liberated language.

Third, that goal itself was not new, but it had never been achieved. In writing "texts," Heissenbüttel attempted to liberate language from the restraints of grammar. Here the affinity to the predominantly experimental language game of concrete poetry is obvious. But "texts" went beyond concrete poetry because of their stronger political potential. While concrete poetry may reveal meaningless social ritual in analogy to a poem's linguistic rituals, "texts" aim at creating new social reality by means of the liberated language. The radical dissolution of the subjectivity of the author and the traditional lyric "speaker" in Heissenbüttel's "texts" was an indication of this goal, and so was the dynamism between proximity and distance from reality in Jürgen Becker's "texts."

During the 1960s, Heissenbüttel published his "texts" in six collections, from *Textbuch 1* (Textbook 1, 1960) to *Textbuch 6* (1967). In *Textbuch 1*, "Lehrgedicht über Geschichte 1954" (Didactic Poem about History 1954, first published 1956) ends with the proclamation of the author's project as a collector of encyclopedic material; at the same time, however, the proclamation is retracted, suggesting the status of the individual subject as a "cluster of speech habits" [Bündel Redegewohnheiten] and as multiple realities created by speech: "To recapitulate // To recapitulate that's my topic / To recapitulate that's my topic / To recapitulate that's my topic // Not to recapitulate" [Rekapitulierbares // Rekapitulierbares dies ist mein Thema / Rekapitulierbares dies ist mein Thema / Rekapitulierbares dies ist mein Thema // nicht Rekapitulierbares]. Punctuation is abandoned or follows a different grammar that is used to reveal political layers usually hidden beneath language. Such revelation occurs when poetic language "hallucinates" a reality that is shockingly close to our perceived reality; therefore, language itself can be a political tool. "Politische Grammatik" (Political Grammar) in *Textbuch 2* (1961) varies the word for "persecute" in three paragraphs to unmask the vicious circle in ideological confrontations and results in the phrase: "persecuting persecuted persecutors" [verfolgende verfolgte Verfolger].

Jürgen Becker's search for reality confronted the "shrinkage of words" [Schwund der Wörter] and approached the margins of reality, as suggested by the title of his collection *Ränder* (Margins, 1969), with which he continued his experimental "texts" in *Felder* (Fields, 1964). *Umgebungen* (Surroundings, 1970) completed this attempt at achieving objectivity by way of subjectivity before Becker turned to lyric poetry in the 1970s. In a transitional phase, his skepticism toward language culminated in a brief shift to photography in *Eine Zeit ohne Wörter* (A Time without Words, 1971). This collection of black-and-white photographs, however, does not do entirely without words: language still provides the titles.

Fragments of reality (specifically, of Cologne and its surroundings) are presented in detailed descriptions that show an affinity to Naturalism and the French nouveau roman, especially in *Felder* and *Umgebungen*. The structure of *Ränder* reflects a slow approach toward those margins of reality that can no longer be communicated. The mirrorlike structure of the eleven sections, of which the sixth provides the axis, functions to take the reader from observations into silence and out of silence back into communication. The first and last sections present subjective, unordered descriptions of everyday events and scenes in prose paragraphs that are matter-of-fact and immediate in their use of deictic elements (such as "there," "this," and "today"): "There hangs the map, all walls are white, this is the country, these are the shores" [Da hängt die Landkarte, alle Wände sind weiß, dies ist das Land, dies sind die Küsten]. Over the next sections the syntax becomes more and more dissolved, and while section three is one long fused prose paragraph, section four, with its fragmented thoughts and observations, is typeset like a poem. Section five presents words arranged freely in groups and individually on two pages, just barely following syntactic rules:

                                                          it ends
        in this way, again
                              until

[ endet es
so, wieder
bis]

Section six consists of two blank pages, suggesting the impossibility of communicating experience and thus the marginality of communication itself. Section seven picks up where section five left off in midsentence and, thus, begins the process of reentering into communication that is completed in the following sections.

## Prose between Subjectivity and the Death of Literature

**Ankunftsliteratur *in the East***

*Ankunftsliteratur* (Literature of Arrival), a term most likely derived from the title of Brigitte Reimann's (1933–1973) *Ankunft im Alltag* (Arrival in Everyday Life, 1961), reflected the party-line position that East German society had "arrived" at the stage of socialism. To show this arrival, the GDR was the central subject matter of *Ankunftsliteratur*, which presented the proper place of each individual after solving the problems of life (including erotic ones) in an industrialized and socialist society. The new literary phase was based on a continuation of the literature of production but also brought about a movement toward subjectivity. The latter aspect placed more and more emphasis on the analytical and critical potential of literature. Novels by Erwin Strittmatter, Christa Wolf, and Hermann Kant exemplify how texts that were written mainly within the parameters of *Ankunftsliteratur* went beyond the constraints of Socialist Realism.

In a plainly realistic narrative mode, the life of Ole Hansen, called Ole Bienkopp, because he used to be a beekeeper, unfolds in his conflicts with the Communist Party in Erwin Strittmatter's novel *Ole Bienkopp* (Ole Beeshead, 1963). The conflicts are not about political goals but about the best way to achieve them. A perennial innovator who succumbs to his anarchic impulses, Ole has to do everything his way and thus meets an untimely end when he dies after three exhausting days of digging for marl by himself. While the machines, which can do the job without risk to anyone's health, are arriving, Ole is struck down by a fever and dies: "There he lies: no angel, no devil — a human being" [Da liegt er: kein Engel, kein Teufel — ein Mensch]. The character of Ole was understood by the reading public as a dreamer who could not be content with a socialism that no longer allowed dreams; therefore, perhaps more than Strittmatter intended, Ole's death was perceived as criticism of socialism, causing a public discussion about the role of literature.

Criticism also began to play an increasingly important role in Christa Wolf's works. *Der geteilte Himmel* — a huge public success —

followed some parameters of a Socialist Realist plot that includes sexual tensions. The protagonist reconfirms her socialist ideals in a traumatic confrontation of choices after her lover defects to the West; in this confrontation, political conviction triumphs over an individual's feelings. The success has been explained, however, as a result of the novel's violation of taboos of content and form. Public mention of the German division was a taboo but is alluded to in the title and made a central issue when the protagonist's lover remains in West Berlin after the Wall is built. Formally, the novel broke with East German narrative tradition by presenting the events in flashbacks as the protagonist tries to sort out her life in the fall of 1961 after an event that was another taboo: her attempted suicide.

Wolf's next novel, *Nachdenken über Christa T.* (The Quest for Christa T., 1968), was formally even more challenging, with its elusive narrator and its use of a montage of memories to reconstruct the life of Christa T., who had died young. These elements were Modernist — from an author who had previously advocated party-line anti-Modernist views. The novel was a watershed in Wolf's development as a writer. By expanding her narrative attitude of subjective authenticity, which remained the trademark of her texts, she departed from her earlier affirmation of the GDR system. Wolf remained loyal to her socialist beliefs, but she became thoroughly critical of the exercise of power in general. Quite independently of any thinking along the lines of the East-West conflict, an increasingly significant aspect of Wolf's writing was the failed arrival of women in a world dominated by men, which first emerged in *Nachdenken über Christa T.*

Closely in line with party demands of literature, Hermann Kant's *Die Aula* is typical of the *Ankunft* novel that moved thematically away from antifascism and toward the GDR's own self-declared positive history. Historically, the ABF (*Arbeiter- und Bauern-Fakultät*, or Workers and Farmers College) played an important role during the construction phase of the GDR by giving qualified workers and farmers the education they needed to attend a university. Now that socialism had been achieved, the ABF was no longer necessary. Its closing was an occasion to celebrate the ABF's significance and the "arrived" status of GDR society, in which the formerly exploited classes (the workers and farmers) had become the ruling class.

In 1962 Kant's autobiographical narrator Robert Iswall, an ABF alumnus, is preparing a speech to be given at the closing of his ABF. He visits other ABF alumni and recalls their experiences during the years between 1949 and 1952. The resulting blending of temporal layers, memories, and reflections on those memories, however, constitutes a departure from Socialist Realism in favor of a complex and modern narrative form; at the same time, the modern form updates the narration of the educational process that the novel's characters undergo. This process includes temptations and failure to resist temptation, but the novel remains affirmative of the GDR. The work is written with great skill and with a pervasive sense of optimism and humor suggesting that all conflicts will be solved — if not in the novel, then later, as the last sentence suggests with reference to the speech, which was canceled because of a program change: "and things will be spoken about after all" [und hier wird schon noch geredet werden]. Kant's novel is prototypical of a socialist realism that itself "arrived" on the literary scene by closing the gap with the formal standards of Modernism.

**Jurek Becker's Jakob der Lügner** Among the novels of the 1960s in East Germany, Jurek Becker's *Jakob der Lügner* (Jacob the Liar, 1968) was an exceptional text; it is still exceptional in the context of German literature — if not world literature — because Becker (1937–1997) deals with the Holocaust in a humorous way. First written as a screenplay, the work was rejected in East Germany as an inappropriate treatment of a serious subject. Rewritten and published as a novel, it became the basis for a new screenplay in 1974. Becker defended his use of humor as an attempt at setting free the audience's imagination, which might otherwise be inhibited by tragic reality.

The issue of humor in Becker's novel touches on a general taboo. In a brief review of Philip Roth's (b. 1933) *Portnoy's Complaint* (1969), Anthony Burgess praises Roth for breaking the post-Holocaust taboo against depicting Jews as people who make the same mistakes other people make. This taboo remains largely unbroken for German literature, probably because — as a result of the Holocaust — there is no strong Jewish presence in contemporary German literature. And of the writers with Jewish roots, many do not consider their Jewishness material for literary exploration; Jurek Becker, Maxim Biller (b. 1960), and Rafael Seligmann (b. 1947) are among the chief exceptions to this rule.

The taboo against some forms of depicting Jews in literature is compounded when the presentation of the Holocaust employs humorous elements. A slowly changing attitude can be detected in the evolution of the discussion in regard to the films *Europa, Europa* (1991), *Life is Beautiful* (1997), and the Hollywood remake of *Jacob the Liar* (1999), with Robin Williams. One of the reasons Becker was successful lay in the readers' (and critics') knowledge that Becker himself had survived the Nazi persecution, during which his mother died. He had grown up speaking Polish and only learned German when he, as a nine-year-old, was reunited with his father after the war. To write the book, Becker traveled to the ghetto archives in Łodz, Poland, because his memories were too scant and his father would not talk about his experiences.

The plot of *Jakob der Lügner* is simple in premise but develops gradually into comic complexity. Ordered briefly inside the ghetto's German control post for questioning, Jakob overhears a radio message about the advancing Russian army. Jakob's dilemma is that, on the one hand, he cannot tell anyone that he got out of the German control post, because that would make him suspect as a collaborator; on the other hand, since no Jew in the ghetto is allowed to own a radio, he does not have one. Despite his fundamental honesty, Jakob decides that hope is the only thing that can keep many of his fellow sufferers in the ghetto alive; therefore, he feels that he has to lie to make them believe the truth. From the moment the Jews in the ghetto think that Jakob owns a radio, they expect more information about the advancing army, and he is compelled to keep fabricating lies that liberate. Thus, the comical element is juxtaposed with the daily tragedy of the ghetto.

It is significant that the comical element in *Jakob der Lügner* relies on a narrative technique from the oral tradition. The technique consists in slowing down the events by narrating details and reflections, while the events are never out of sight but drive the action forward; the flow of perception seems out-of-sync with the speed of the unfolding events. This narrative technique unfolds best over longer passages; for example, it develops the ironic incongruity between what the searchlight makes visible (the pavement) and what is implied (Jakob's walk to the control post, which has a potentially deadly outcome): "The searchlight accompanies him, makes him aware of the pavement's unevenness, makes his shadow grow longer and longer" [Der Scheinwerfer begleitet ihn, macht ihn auf die Unebenheiten im Pflaster aufmerksam, läßt seinen Schatten immer länger werden] until Jakob's shadow is ominously cast on the door to the control post.

The fundamental uncertainty about life in the ghetto is reflected by the incongruity of the narrative slowing-down and by the novel's two endings — the device of multiple endings became increasingly popular with postmodernism. In one ending, referred to as the invented one, Jakob dies while attempting to escape — ironically, just before the camp is liberated. In the other ending, referred to as the real and trivial one, all of the Jews are put on the train like cattle. While their trip is presumably to an extermination camp, it includes moments of faint hope; for example, the narrator sees trees, which had been absent from the ghetto. The uncertainties of the dual endings and the subdued affirmation of life provided by the trees reveal a function of subtle humor: showing hope for a better future.

*The critical novel in the West*

To be more realistic, prose literature in East Germany had to turn toward the exploration of the subjective element in a socialist society; in contrast, for prose literature in the West to be more realistic required that it become political. In the West the theoretical debate focused on the slogan "death of literature," which Hans Magnus Enzensberger had used in his essay "Gemeinplätze, die Neueste Literatur betreffend" (Commonplaces Concerning the Most Recent Literature) in the November 1968 issue of *Kursbuch 15*. Enzensberger and others who argued in a similar way were often misunderstood as advocating the end of all literature. While noting that many people "celebrate the end of literature" [feiern das Ende der Literatur], Enzensberger emphasized that "'death of literature' itself is a literary metaphor" ["Tod der Literatur" ist selber eine literarische Metapher] that expressed the fact that modern literature's continual crisis had been the motor that had kept literature going. This view suggested that there had not been much new for bourgeois literature, yet Enzensberger saw something that had changed: the author's awareness of his or her text's functionality in an "imperialistic" society, where market forces control literary production.

While other people were obsessed with the end of literature, Enzensberger argued for the beginning of a new kind of literature, one that fell between the extremes of a technocratic literature and a literature of mere political agitation. What Enzensberger described in terms of small steps was a tall order, as he admitted: "The political literacy of Germany is a gigantic project" [Die politische Alphabetisierung Deutschlands ist ein gigantisches Projekt]. Yet it was not entirely new. Enzensberger referred to the literary tradition of the pre-1848 years, which was exemplified by authors such as Ludwig Börne (pseudonym of Löb Baruch, 1786–1837). Contemporary works that he believed had pointed in the right direction (for example, the reports of Günter Wallraff, b. 1942) favored a new realism in terms of documentary literature, which rather suggests the death of the author (or narrator) than of literature.

New documentary realism was not the only mode of critical prose literature written and published during the 1960s. The way the Nazi legacy shaped contemporary society and the exploration of what was under the surface of the economic miracle continued to be central themes. These themes were treated in a variety of modes, ranging from the traditionally realistic in works by Heinrich Böll and Siegfried Lenz to the grotesque in those by Günter Grass and verging on the subcultural in the works of Hubert Fichte. Although Fichte began publishing in the 1960s, his works took on greater significance in the 1970s.

*New realisms*

Dieter Wellershoff developed a concept of realism, called the "Cologne School of New Realism" (after the city, where he lived), that he pursued in his own novels, such as *Ein schöner Tag* (A Beautiful Day, 1966) and *Die Schattengrenze* (The Shadow Line, 1969), as well as in his support for other authors in his capacity as editor of a literary publishing house. Because the Cologne School emphasized that the facts of social reality should speak for themselves, it occupied the middle ground between social criticism and the grotesque mode. Because it was mainly defined in terms of what it rejected rather than what it represented, most authors soon abandoned its tenets, including Rolf Dieter Brinkmann and Renate Rasp (b. 1935).

Another kind of realism emerged with a revival of the traditions of workers' literature of the early twentieth century — traditions that had been mostly ignored in West Germany. Named in analogy, but also in opposition, to the *Gruppe 47*, the *Gruppe 61* was founded in Dortmund in 1961 with the program of placing in the center of its endeavors a "literary and artistic critical analysis of the industrial work world and its social problems" [literarisch-künstlerische Auseinandersetzung mit der industriellen Arbeitswelt und ihren sozialen Problemen]. The program attracted such authors as Angelika Mechtel (b. 1943), F. C. Delius (b. 1943), and Peter-Paul Zahl (b. 1944). In a combination of realistic and documentary elements, the novels of the group's best-known author, Max von der Grün (b. 1926), such as *Irrlicht und Feuer* (1963, The Will-o'-the-Wisp and the Fire), incorporated his own experiences as a worker. The theoretical position of the *Gruppe 61* was open to any kind of workers' literature, and not restricted to texts by workers for workers — a principle of the Bitterfeld model of East German Socialist Realism that the *Gruppe 61* found too restrictive.

The openness of the group, which was criticized as a "bourgeois" orientation, was one of the reasons for the its official demise in 1972. At the end of the 1960s, however, a new group came together with a more radical program and some of the same authors. The *Werkkreis Literatur der Arbeitswelt* (Workshop Literature of the Industrial World) took a less bourgeois and more partisan approach that followed the East German model. The activities of the *Werkkreis*, which included organizing workshops for workers interested in writing, took place mostly in the 1970s. The aesthetic problem of not getting beyond a moralizing human-touch approach led to more radical experiments with elements of the documentary tradition. For example, Erika Runge (b. 1939), who was a member of both the *Gruppe 61* and the *Werkkreis*, used reporting techniques, although her *Bottroper Protokolle* (Bottrop Protocols, 1968, Bottrop is an industrial city) are not unedited transcriptions of conversations but rather the product of artistic selection and arrangement.

The reports of Günter Wallraff are the best-known examples of literature from the working world in West Germany. The result of aggressive and usually undercover investigative journalism, they were highly controversial. With self-irony and a sense for West German reality, Wallraff titled one of his collections *13 unerwünschte Reportagen* (13 Unwanted Reports, 1969). Wallraff was repeatedly sued by companies for publishing reports that exposed unethical or illegal practices. His technique of undercover investigation yielded his greatest success when he published an account of his experiences disguised as a Turkish worker in West Germany. These reports appeared in 1985 under the title *Ganz unten* (Far Down) and sold over a million copies in a few months. Though companies considered his reports unfair and some critics lamented that Wallraff perpetuated the image of the guest worker as victim, the book struck a chord. Its terse, unsentimental, and journalistic style did not hold up an aesthetic smokescreen between the reader and an unpleasant part of German life: exploitation of and discrimination against foreign workers.

*Social constraints and individual resistance* Other authors explored the constraints of society in a less documentary, yet nonetheless realistic, manner; among them were well-established writers, such as Martin Walser and Uwe Johnson, as well as newcomers, such as Peter Bichsel (b. 1934). Walser continued to focus on the everyday middle-class conflict between career and happiness in the novels *Halbzeit* (Half Time, 1960), *Das Einhorn* (The Unicorn, 1966), and *Der Sturz* (The Fall, 1970), which form a trilogy about the rise and fall of Anselm Kristlein. Johnson also pursued the subject matter that he had chosen for his earlier works: the German division. In *Das dritte Buch über Achim* (The Third Book about Achim, 1961) the West German journalist Karsch's planned book about an East German athlete becomes impossible because of the growing distance between the two Germanies. Johnson remained focused on the characters from his groundbreaking *Mutmassungen über Jakob* in the stories collected in *Karsch, und andere Prosa* (Karsch and Other Prose, 1964), thus preparing the rich background for his magnum opus, the tetralogy *Jahrestage*.

Bichsel's slender collection of stories *Eigentlich möchte Frau Blum den Milchmann kennenlernen* (Actually Mrs. Blum Would Like to Meet the Milkman, 1964) was an immediate success. It and the following two volumes, *Die Jahreszeiten* (The Seasons, 1967) and *Kindergeschichten* (Children's Stories, 1969), established Bichsel as an important influence on Swiss storytelling, although he withdrew from writing for about a decade. The stories in his 1960s collections have a static quality that corresponds to the quality of the lives the characters lead. Hardly anything significant happens, as much as the characters may wish for it to; they do not have what it takes to turn their lives around. Above all, language is not only insufficient to deal with the world, but it also increases the characters' isolation. When characters muster all their courage and make a change, it may just add to their isolation. In Bichsel's best-known story, "Ein Tisch ist ein Tisch" (A Table Is a Table, 1969), a man reinvents language; for example, he no longer uses the word *table* to refer to the object commonly referred to as a table; rather, he now calls it a "carpet." Eventually, he forgets the old language and is no longer able to communicate with other people. While the story asserts the rights of the individual over social constraints, such as linguistic rules, it is a quixotic rebellion.

The same right to resist and rebel against social constraints that limit individuality is at the core of works by Heinrich Böll and Siegfried Lenz. Böll entered into a third phase of literary productivity in the 1960s, which was determined by an increasing confidence in one's own political position, characteristic of the politicization of West German literature. For Böll this meant a reassessment of resignation in the light of hope. He turned more and more to portraying outsiders who assert their individuality through acts of rebellion against social constraints and in whose possible failure and resignation there still resides a spark of hope. A political *Ästhetik des Humanen* (aesthetics of humaneness) was the basis of Böll's realistic literature, but he also lived by it as an activist.

Böll's novel *Ansichten eines Clowns* (The Clown, 1963), the pivotal work in the transition to his third phase, and the short novel *Ende einer Dienstfahrt* (End of a Mission, 1966) exemplify his emphasis on human values that he saw repressed in a materialistic society. In contrast, he considered literature and art in general "the only recognizable manifestation of freedom on this earth" [die einzig erkennbare Erscheinungsform der Freiheit auf dieser Erde]. While an aesthetics of humaneness can be voiced in any literary mode, there is a close fit between Böll's aesthetics and his style of writing, which is more complex than is acknowledged by simply labeling it "realism."

*Ansichten eines Clowns* consists of Hans Schnier's inner monologue over the course of one day — occasionally interrupted by dialogues, which are all phone conversations, with the sole exception of a visit by Hans's rich father, who leaves without giving his son any financial support. The monologue is idiosyncratic yet realistic; the staccato of its compound sentences reveals the narrator's nervous and hectic state of mind. Two of Böll's major themes, love and religion, intersect in this novel. Hans diagnoses himself as suffering from melancholy and mo-

nogamy, but Marie, the only woman whom he is able to love, has just
left him after six years and married another man. Sinking deeper and
deeper into melancholy, Hans sits, at the end of the novel, in his professional clown outfit on the steps of the train station in the middle of
many other costumed people who are celebrating carnival. He has sunk
very low, considering the humiliation that is possible if Marie and her
new husband arrive at the station on their return from their honey-
moon.

As much as this last scene evokes resignation and humiliation, it also
contains the seed of resistance and hope: Hans is not giving up. Train
stations are symbols not only of departures but also of returns. Hans
feels that Marie is his wife, although they were never married. For
Hans, the atheist, Marie had been Catholic in such a natural way that
he had encouraged her to keep her ties to the church. Now he feels
betrayed by the church because it does not respect the biblical concept
of two people in love giving each other the sacrament of marriage; instead, members of a progressive Catholic group encouraged Marie to
leave Hans, and one of the group married her. This is not the attitude
religion should use in dealing with people; it is not forgiving and mer-
ciful. Hans demands a morality that corresponds to Böll's aesthetics of
humaneness, and Hans already lives by it despite all his failures. As a
clown he collects moments in time, although he knows that it can be
dangerous; after all, it is easy to forgive the big things " — but who
forgives you, who understands the details?" [ — aber wer verzeiht einem, wer versteht die Details?]. He admits that he is overburdened by
the great number of details. It is, however, in these details that humanity can be found: "Strangely enough, I like those of whose kind I am:
people" [Merkwürdigerweise mag ich die, von deren Art ich bin: die
Menschen]. Hans is the prototypical lonely and misunderstood artist.
Being a clown is not just a job; it is his life.

The action that gives the title to *Ende einer Dienstfahrt* — the
burning of an army jeep — is seen as an artistic act, a happening. The
story is a courtroom drama that unfolds slowly in realistic tradition but
uses narrative delays and satirical elements to play with that tradition.
The major delay concerns the importance of burning the jeep as an act
of civil disobedience and an artistic statement that undermines the
state's authority, so the state has a vested interest in downplaying the
whole affair. This downplaying includes ensuring that the case is as-
signed to a lenient judge. Consequently, the light sentence is an ambiguous triumph, because it is both an affirmation of opposition and an
affirmation of the interests of the state.

As the story unfolds, a group of people who feel an affinity for each
other is formed. It is a small community of outsiders who come together in the courtroom; it includes the defendants, the judge, and a

rich old lady who makes the happy ending perfect by announcing that she will pay the fine for the defendants and finance their future happenings. What is more, there is no generational conflict, because the defendants are father and son. When the son is sent on the senseless mission of driving an army jeep around so that the increased mileage will warrant an inspection, he burns the jeep with the help of his father. These elements are satirical, because they present utopian criticism of the state's authoritarian structure by means of a counterworld of human compassion that is evoked by humorous devices. This nonrealistic aspect of *Ende einer Dienstfahrt* illustrates why Böll held the works of Ernst Kreuder in high esteem.

The intensity of the father/son conflict in Siegfried Lenz's successful novel, *Deutschstunde* (The German Lesson, 1968), corresponded to the generational confrontation in the political arena of the 1960s and foreshadowed a 1970s literary phenomenon: the "father books," which were, typically, written to allow the authors to confront their own fathers' involvement in Nazism. In *Deutschstunde* the premise is slightly different because the narrator Siggi is old enough to have been involved in his father's activities. Lenz's novel can be read as a case study of an authoritarian personality's devastating influence on a son's life.

Under the Third Reich Siggi's father had the task, as the local police officer, of enforcing the Nazi decree banning the artist Nansen from painting. The painter, who is not an unambiguously positive character, becomes a father figure for Siggi. Police officer and artist, once friends, become enemies, although Siggi's father insists that he is only doing his duty. That this is not so is evident when the father, after the war, remains obsessed with finding and destroying Nansen's works. Siggi gets in trouble with the law when he steals the paintings for their protection. Sent to reform school, Siggi has to write an essay for his German class. The topic, "the joys of duty" [die Freuden der Pflicht], is ironic, because his father's warped sense of duty, representing an entire generation's sense of duty, deteriorated into compulsive obedience to fascist ideology and caused Siggi's problems. In addition, the thinly veiled hidden curriculum is unwittingly exposed in the teacher's explanation: "You may write as you wish, but the essay must be on the joys of duty" [Jeder kann schreiben, was er will; nur muß die Arbeit von den Freuden der Pflicht handeln]. While the overt curriculum is written in the language of democracy, the values that are taught by the hidden curriculum perpetuate the same authoritarian system that equates duty with compulsive obedience.

Like Oskar Matzerath in Grass's *Die Blechtrommel*, the narrator is institutionalized, and the narrative situation is fundamentally ambiguous, because everything is presented from the unreliable narrator's perspective. Such ambiguity seems appropriate for the moral dilemma that originates in inculcating democratic behavior while, beneath the surface, authoritarian values are still operative. The "German lesson" that Siggi learns does not provide a solution to the dilemma but continues the problem at a different level: moral laws have to be violated when they justify crimes against humanity.

Günter Grass, one of the initiators of a more strongly political literature, commented even more directly in his literary works on contemporary developments in politics. Completing his Danzig trilogy with *Katz und Maus* and *Hundejahre* in the early 1960s, he explored how the Nazi past led to the West German reality of the 1950s. Toward the end of the 1960s, Grass's narratives arrived in the politicized present; for example, in *Örtlich betäubt* (1969, Local Anesthetic) a teacher reflects on the role of evolution and revolution in the context of the unrest among students while the dentist's anesthetic is taking effect.

Grass wanted to do more than write literature that was political or even "operative" in the sense of having an effect on political controversies. Therefore, he became active for the Social Democratic Party during electoral campaigns. This was an activism that Grass shared with other writers, artists, and intellectuals, including Heinrich Böll. In the 1960s it became acceptable for writers to discuss their social and political opinions and visions no longer simply as a private matter but as one of public interest. It stayed this way for the remainder of the twentieth century, as is proven by the vivid public discussions of controversial statements by authors, such as Peter Handke on the role of the Serbs in the Balkan conflicts beginning in the mid-1990s or Martin Walser on the importance of remembering the Holocaust in the late 1990s.

## Drama after Brecht

*From Brecht to grotesque theater*

Brecht exerted a commanding influence on German drama. From the 1960s to the 1980s he was the most-performed German playwright in Germany (of all writers performed, he was second only to Shakespeare). The history of the interruptions in the stage presence of his plays before the 1960s illustrates more than the practical difficulties faced by political drama in the politicized era of the Cold War; it also illustrates the slowly growing political assertiveness of literary life. In the West, Brecht was attacked as a playwright of Communist East Germany, and his plays were boycotted for a large part of the 1950s. At the beginning of the 1960s, however, the declaration by sixty-six theater directors rejecting any outside influence on their artistic freedom put an end to the boycott of Brecht's plays.

The Swiss authors Max Frisch and Friedrich Dürrenmatt were the next most influential German-language playwrights of the 1950s and early 1960s. Dürrenmatt's *Die Physiker* was based on his belief that the grotesque (as opposed to the absurd) allowed a precise observation of reality; in sharp contrast to Brecht, he no longer considered the world to be capable of change. *Die Physiker* unmasks any attempt to save the world from nuclear destruction as futile. In this sense, the play can be interpreted as a countermodel to Brecht's *Galilei*. Dürrenmatt's play sets the unavoidable catastrophe in a mental hospital that serves as a symbol of the modern technological world. The three main characters are all sane, although they are mental patients. Moebius is a scientific genius, whose discoveries would revolutionize but also, most likely, destroy the world; therefore, he has decided to withdraw from the world by feigning insanity. The other two are spies for opposing political powers. When they understand the vast implications and dangers of Moebius's discoveries, they agree with Moebius to keep the knowledge secret. But it is too late: the psychiatrist, who is, ironically, the only truly insane person in the play, has stolen Moebius's secrets and has built an industrial empire that is threatening to engulf the world. History has taken the worst possible turn.

Epic theater traditions were continued in terms of presenting issues for the audience's consideration in grotesque plays, such as *Die Physiker*. In another sharp departure from Brecht's conception of political theater, however, the grotesque plays did away with the didactic impulse. They provided analysis but no lesson to be learned. In his observations on *Die Physiker*, Dürrenmatt explained that the audience can be exposed to reality but not forced to deal with it. According to his theory of the theater, the tragic was still possible but only as part of a comedy; the comedy, in turn, became grotesque but not absurd, because the play did not produce nonsense but meaning *ex negativo*. What remained crucial for the further development of German-language theater was an increasingly disillusioned view of the world. The central aspect of Brecht's approach had been a world that could be changed by human beings. The absurdist-grotesque view implied that the world was changing but that the change was out of control, and the human being was no longer in any position to be an agent of history. The place in which individual playwrights fall in terms of this polarity of changeability and out-of-control change determines the extent of their departure from the Brechtian model.

*East German drama from realism to mythology*

The important East German playwrights — Peter Hacks, Volker Braun, and Heiner Müller — fit into the general trends of GDR drama. They moved away from the Brechtian model; they wrote plays about agricultural and industrial production; and they discovered themes from history and classical mythology. In contrast to plays that are more affirmative of GDR reality, plays by Hacks, Braun, and Müller often had difficulty in receiving permission to be performed by East German theater companies. As the public increasingly turned to literature for political information that could no longer be obtained from the news media, state control of literature increased and was particularly noticeable in the theater.

Hacks, who had moved to East Germany in 1955 and begun as a student of Brecht, increasingly turned from Brecht's theater to a more classical concept that he later called "postrevolutionary" drama. In his plays Hacks portrayed humanity as the master of history, which meant that his move away from Brecht implied a shift from the political toward a treatment of humanity in general. Loyal to the political system of the GDR, Hacks aimed at achieving a "socialist classicism," which he thought possible, because he believed that a form of society was within close reach in which all conflicts (in the sense of the Marxist theory of class conflict) had been resolved, and he presupposed such a society in his plays of the 1960s. His plays could be understood as critical of political conditions in East Germany and, at the same time, politically noncommittal in their happy endings; as a result, they were also popular in West Germany.

Hacks's *Moritz Tassow* was written mostly according to the guidelines of Socialist Realism and unmasked the dangers of radical idealism (embodied by Moritz Tassow) as opposed to the realistic approach of building socialism one step at a time (embodied by Erich Mattukat). Although the play was written in 1961, it did not premiere until 1965, and the SED intervened the next year because it was felt that Hacks had portrayed the party too negatively. Hacks abandoned topics from contemporary GDR reality in favor of history and classical mythology, as in *Amphitryon* (premiered 1968, published 1969).

Like Hacks, Volker Braun tried to go beyond Brecht's theater, because he, too, saw class conflicts as having been overcome. For Braun new contradictions, which were no longer "antagonistic" in the Marxist sense, existed between the new socialist — and non-alienating — mode of production and the unchanged demands stemming from capitalist production, which was seen as alienating the worker from the product. In contrast to the plays of Peter Hacks, Braun's dramas have usually been regarded as still in keeping with orthodox Marxism, which is why they were not well received in the West. Yet Braun also had difficulty in finding an adequate response in the GDR.

For example, Braun's play *Die Kipper* (The Dumpers, meaning the mine workers whose job it is to dump the slag), in various versions from 1962 to 1972, showed the dangers of radical idealism that raised the question of individuality within a socialist state, especially within the realms of agricultural and industrial production. Braun's protagonist, Paul Bauch, works to improve the productivity of his crew but for the wrong reasons — basically because he can. Only after causing an accident does he understand that the quality of the work, not the quantity, needs to be improved. He realizes that the collective (his crew) has adopted his principles and, therefore, no longer needs him. While this thought was in keeping with Marxism, the amount of individuality with which the play deals went beyond the expectations of Socialist Realism.

In the GDR of the 1960s, the works of Heiner Müller were also slow to be performed because they were considered too critical of socialist reality in East Germany, despite their author's loyalty to Communism and the GDR. For example, Müller's *Der Bau* (The Construction Site) was written between 1963 and 1964, printed in *Sinn und Form* in 1965, immediately rewritten after criticism, but not premiered in East Germany until 1980. Like other playwrights, such as Hacks and Karl Mickel, Müller turned to themes from history and classical mythology. Among Müller's classical adaptations, *Philoktet* (written between 1958 and 1964, published in West Germany in 1966, and premiered in West Germany in 1968) was the most important for two main reasons. First, as part of the second phase of his artistic development, it was a step toward Müller's own distinctive style. Second, its premiere at the Munich Residenztheater in 1968 is generally considered Müller's break-through on his way to international acclaim.

In Sophocles' play *Philoctetes* (409 B.C.), the character of Neoptolemos, Achilles' son, after initial wavering, remains true to his nature and will not lie to betray Philoctetes; therefore, Heracles is needed as a *deus ex machina* to ensure that the conflict is resolved according to the myth. In contrast, Müller's adaptation presents a manipulated and fragmentary world without gods. Müller's Neoptolemos, who goes through similar tribulations of doubt, ultimately proves easy to manipulate; as a result, the play becomes understandable as a critique of the abuse of language.

In Müller's three-character play the mission is still to find Philoktet, whose festering wound — emitting a foul odor and driving him to screaming fits — is why Odysseus had abandoned him on an island. Now Philoktet is needed in the war against the Trojans to motivate his men and to use his weapon, the bow that had belonged to Heracles. Odysseus and Neoptolemos arrive, and Odysseus, knowing that Philoktet hates him and is unlikely to join them, convinces Neoptolemos to lie to secure Philoktet for their cause. Neoptolemos is to convince Philoktet that they both hate Odysseus and that he, Neoptolemos, is on his way home from the Trojan War. The first part is an easy task for Neoptolemos, because he does hate Odysseus. It is precisely because of their mutual hatred and need for each other that Odysseus chose

Neoptolemos for this assignment; he knows that "you will lie believably with the truth" [glaublich wirst du lügen mit der Wahrheit].

Indeed, although he is mistrustful, Philoktet falls for Neoptolemos's lie, which is the first time in ten years that he has heard another human being speak. But Neoptolemos breaks down and reveals the truth. Finally, Odysseus appears, and he and Neoptolemos fight. When Philoktet picks up the bow and threatens to kill Odysseus, Neoptolemos realizes that the Greeks need Odysseus to win the war and stabs Philoktet in the back. The play's imagery of lies and truth, which is woven through the play, is varied when Odysseus explains his new plan: "If the fish won't swim into our net alive / May the dead one be useful as bait" [Wenn uns der Fisch lebendig nicht ins Netz ging / Mag uns zum Köder brauchbar sein der tote]. He proposes to report that just as they arrived, a band of Trojans tried to abduct Philoktet but killed him instead. Neoptolemos threatens to kill Odysseus and says that he, too, could tell a lie about nonexistent Trojans killing both Philoktet and Odysseus. But Odysseus counters that Neoptolemos needs him as a witness. Language is unmasked as an instrument of power that makes truth and lies indistinguishable from each other. Odysseus is the master of the abuse of language; he even boasts that he will later tell Neoptolemos a lie that would have gotten Neoptolemos out of appearing responsible for killing Odysseus had Neoptolemos carried out his threat. But Neoptolemos has already been corrupted by power and has become, like Odysseus, both hero and murderer.

Partisan interpretations tried to fix the meaning of *Philoktet* as either a condemnation of imperialism or a critique of the GDR. The play is both, since Müller emphasized that he wanted to present not meanings but attitudes, and not history but a model. If Odysseus exemplifies the instrumentalization of language for the sake of political lies and propaganda, this suggests an understanding of the play as a parable of the conflict (embodied by Neoptolemos) between the interests of the state (Odysseus) and the interests of the individual (Philoktet). The attitudes described by Müller are manifest in any system that is based on the hierarchical exercise of power.

The farcical-grotesque and the documentary-epic elements of the play support this interpretation. First, the prologue is spoken by the actor who plays Philoktet, wearing a clown's mask and warning the members of the audience that they will be led by the "play into the past / When man still was man's mortal enemy" [Spiel in die Vergangenheit / Als noch der Mensch des Menschen Todfeind war]. When the actor takes off the clown's mask, a skull is revealed. Second, an annotation at the end of the script suggests that, during the prolonged exit of Odysseus and Neoptolemos from the stage, images of war could be projected, ranging "from the Trojan War to the Japanese War" [vom

Trojanischen bis zum Japanischen Krieg]. In terms of the model that he was presenting, Müller was specifically thinking of German wars (ranging from myth to history, from the Nibelungs to Stalingrad), implying the fascist legacy.

*Innovations and*
*renewals in the West*

During the 1960s German-language plays in the West, like those in the East, did not establish new forms that were generally accepted as replacing the old theater. There were significant experimental plays, as well as renewals of earlier traditions, especially of the *Volksstück* and documentary literature, that often presented a mixture of classically dramatic and epic forms.

Among the more radical experiments to renew the theater (and perhaps even go beyond the traditional theater, for example, with happenings) are the *Sprechstücke* (speech plays) by the Austrian author Peter Handke. They consist entirely of speech and dispense with the traditional plot and characters; instead, segments of the text can be distributed among several speakers in various ways. Sharing the linguistic playfulness of the *Wiener Gruppe*, Handke understands these plays as presenting the world "in the form of words" [in der Form von Worten] that refer back to "the world within the words" [die Welt in den Worten]. The most famous of his Sprechstücke, *Publikumsbeschimpfung* (Offending the Public, 1966), gives the audience a good tongue-lashing; still, as Handke admitted, the play needs the audience as its addressee.

In *Kaspar* (1968) Handke continued his exploration of language but added plot elements inspired by the historical events of the early nineteenth century surrounding the foundling who was called Kaspar Hauser. Like the tongue-lashing given to the audience, *Kaspar* displays language as an instrument of torture. Kaspar is like Frankenstein's monster, this time not created by science but formed and deformed by language. At first, Kaspar's movements are mechanical, and he repeats the same sentence over and over in different modulations without seeming to understand its meaning: "I want to become such a person like another was once before" [Ich möcht ein solcher werden wie einmal ein anderer gewesen ist]. And he does: he becomes a human being by learning language in response to voices coming from offstage. When he finally asserts himself with the same sentence with which God revealed himself in the Old Testament, "I am who I am" [Ich bin, der ich bin], his identity is threatened by other Kaspars appearing on stage. At the end he realizes: "With my first sentence I already fell into the trap" [Schon mit meinem ersten Satz bin ich in die Falle gegangen]. But he does not resist and becomes a prisoner of language, just like Othello in Shakespeare's tragedy became a prisoner of language when he fell for

Iago's lies. It is appropriate for Handke's play to end with Kaspar repeating the phrase "goats and monkeys" [Ziegen und Affen], which are the same words that Othello uttered after they — and their implications of sexual infidelity — had been fed to him by Iago.

Furthermore, the 1960s brought a rediscovery of Marieluise Fleißer and Ödön von Horváth, both of whom had renewed the *Volksstück* in the 1930s. Martin Sperr (b. 1944) and Franz Xaver Kroetz (b. 1946) continued the tradition, consciously referring to Fleißer as a mother figure in terms of their dramatic endeavors. Their plays used Bavarian dialect to express the limitations of being able to express oneself, and they emphasized outsiders, characters who, for various reasons, were marginalized in narrow-minded environments. Rainer Werner Fassbinder (1946–1982) is internationally known as a director of the New German Cinema. He is often mentioned in the context of the *Volksstück*, because his work was influenced by Fleißer. For instance, his *Katzelmacher* (1968) uses the typical rural (dialect) setting and the outsider (this time a Greek foreign worker). Furthermore, until the early 1970s, Fassbinder saw his work as antitheater in the sense that he tried to subvert traditional concepts of beauty and heroism, as well as passive consumption of art. Typical for Fassbinder was a creative interaction between theatrical and cinematic forms.

*Documentary theater*   While the impact of *Sprechstück*, *Volksstück*, and antitheater should not be underestimated, the most significant dramatic change during the 1960s was the rediscovery of documentary theater. Although often seen in the tradition of the epic theater, which is usually equated with Brecht, documentary theater evolved from various sources, particularly Erwin Piscator's political shows during the 1920s. In the 1960s Piscator was still active, and many of the most important new documentary plays premiered under his direction in his theater, the Freie Volksbühne Berlin: *Der Stellvertreter* (The Deputy, 1963), by Rolf Hochhuth; *In der Sache J. Robert Oppenheimer* (In the Matter of J. Robert Oppenheimer, 1964), by Heinar Kipphardt; and *Die Ermittlung* (The Investigation, 1965), by Peter Weiss.

Documentary theater met with controversy. Critics could not agree on a precise definition. Documentary theater is epic because of its didactic impulse and because it documents real life, whose interpretation in dramatic scenes presents an object for observation by the audience. At the same time, documentary theater is also a reaction against the parable quality of some epic and grotesque plays. Furthermore, the use of documented material varies from plays that rely almost completely on such material (the usual example is Weiss's *Ermittlung*) to plays that integrate fictional and documentary material, such as Hochhuth's *Stellvertreter* and Kipphardt's *Oppenheimer*.

Furthermore, some critics took issue with the premise of documentary theater. They assumed that by using real-life material, the playwrights were denying their creativity and presenting nothing but a staged form of journalism. But when playwrights asserted their creativity by selecting and arranging documentary material, and at times integrating it with fictional material, to make a subjective and political statement, they were faulted for negating the documentary character of their plays. Such plays, the critics argued, should not be called "documentary" but rather thesis plays (*Thesenstücke*). The underlying conflict involved issues of politics and literature, as well as the extent to which aesthetic and informative functions could be combined, especially in a theatrical scenario that often did not make the fictional quality of the documentary visible.

An often cited example is Kipphardt's play, which was based on the true story of the nuclear physicist J. Robert Oppenheimer, who had been investigated in 1954 concerning his loyalty to the United States. In the postscript to the play Kipphardt emphasized that he had written "a theater play, not a montage of documentary material" [ein Theaterstück, keine Montage von dokumentarischem Material]; still, the real Oppenheimer protested that he had never regretted having been involved in building the atomic bomb — quite in contrast to Kipphardt's fictitious Oppenheimer, whose closing monologue admits that the physicists "did the work of the military . . . did the work of the devil" [haben die Arbeit der Militärs getan . . . haben die Arbeit des Teufels getan].

Such criticism of documentary theater, however, misunderstands the genre's qualities. The use of "literary truths," as opposed to mere factuality, is nothing new for literature. There is no literary reason why an author, to raise the issue of the danger of nuclear weapons, should not present a well-known nuclear physicist as having insights that are not those of the real man. This controversy, as many others, was about politics under the guise of aesthetics. Yet Kipphardt's play might have been both aesthetically and politically stronger if he had played fact and fiction against each other in the drama itself rather than mentioning this conflict only in the epilogue.

The main appeal of documentary theater rested in the authenticity of its material. Even as a highly artistic montage of documentary and fictional elements, each play engaged the audience in a different way than the traditional theater of illusion. In documentary theater, the audience took the information presented in the play seriously; knowing that the play used parts of documented reality prevented the audience from disregarding the staged events as mere products of the playwright's imagination. The documentary theater operates not by suspension of disbelief but by activation of belief.

A number of authors in addition to Kipphardt, Weiss, and Hochhuth wrote plays that can be grouped under the heading of documentary theater, including Tankred Dorst (b. 1925) with *Toller — Szenen aus der deutschen Revolution* (Toller — Scenes from the German Revolution, 1968), Günter Grass with *Die Plebejer proben den Aufstand* (The Plebeians Rehearse the Uprising, 1966), Hans Magnus Enzensberger with *Das Verhör von Habana* (The Havana Inquiry, 1970). *Marat/Sade* (1964) by Peter Weiss is often considered to be the outstanding example of the genre; however, Rolf Hochhuth's *Der Stellvertreter* is the most controversial of all documentary plays.

*Marat/Sade* is the generally accepted shorthand form of the play's full title: *Die Verfolgung und Ermordung Jean Paul Marats dargestellt durch die Schauspielgruppe des Hospizes zu Charenton unter Anleitung des Herrn de Sade* (The Persecution and Murder of Jean Paul Marat Presented by the Ensemble of Actors of the Hospice at Charenton under Direction of Mr. de Sade). Following Weiss's micronovels in a style similar to the French nouveau roman, the 1964 premiere of *Marat/Sade* marked the beginning of Weiss's international success and his shift from individual subjectivity to political statement. In *Marat/Sade* Marat's radical revolutionary attitude is in conflict with Sade's equally radical individualism. Their confrontation, however, is strangely balanced as a play-within-a-play. Sade is the director of the play, and Marat is a character in that play. If Marat has the last word, it is Sade's decision, a decision understood by some critics as a form of verbal sadism that Sade enjoys. While Sade's prominence in the play might suggest that Weiss leaned toward the individualist position, Weiss took Marat's position and came out in strong support of socialism with his next plays, *Die Ermittlung* about the West German trial of Auschwitz war criminals and another play commonly known by its shorthand title, *Viet Nam-Diskurs* (Discourse on Vietnam, 1968).

The performance of the play-within-the-play of *Marat/Sade* is supposed to take place in 1808, but it portrays the murder of Marat in 1793. The difference in time (Napoleon had assumed power in the meantime) intensifies the problematic aspects of the revolution — its violence and the unchanged situation of the poor people, which the chorus proclaims in couplets: "Marat what happened to the revolution that was ours / Marat we're no longer willing to wait for hours" [Marat was ist aus unserer Revolution geworden / Marat wir wollen nicht mehr warten bis morgen]. The confrontation of the mutually exclusive ideologies of individualism and revolution comes out in the arguments, rendered in free verse, between the character and the director, which is based, in documentary fashion, on writings by Marat and Sade.

The play's setting allows for the creation of "total theater." The inmates of the mental institution, among them Sade (formerly Marquis, but now, after the revolution, simply Monsieur), perform the play for the warden and his family. The inmates display a variety of behaviors; some inmate-actors have to be supported by nurses or, when they become too involved with their role, are removed from the stage by the nurses; for instance, one male patient-actor continues to make sexual passes at the female patient who plays Charlotte Corday, the murderess of Marat. Some of the patients who do not seem to be involved in the performance are seized by fits and interrupt the play-within-the-play — one, for example, with a satanic Lord's Prayer. Sade is whipped by the inmate who plays Corday. Some patients perform pantomimes, including a copulation pantomime in the thirtieth scene, and the play ends in general chaos during which the warden has his personnel beat the patients. Sade laughs triumphantly, and the warden ends the play by having the curtain dropped.

The options of total theater, in which Weiss included elements of Antonin Artaud's (1896–1948) theater of cruelty, can be expanded in various ways from one production to the next. The mental institution becomes a symbol for the world, and the temporal refractions of 1793 (year of the murder), 1808 (year of the fictitious performance), and allusions to the world of the 1960s suggest the general applicability of the conflict. The fact that *Marat/Sade* did not present a clear solution to the conflict has been considered a factor in the play's success, which is, however, usually attributed to Weiss's mastery of the theatrical medium. In conjunction with stronger partisan statements, his plays after *Marat/Sade* more strongly emphasized the documentary element.

*Rolf Hochhuth's* **Der Stellvertreter** The possibilities and limitations of the genre of documentary theater come to the foreground in the plays of Rolf Hochhuth, one of the most successful and most controversial German playwrights. While the playwright's position in *Der Stellvertreter* was still that of a masterful montage artist who creatively combined the accumulated documentary material, Hochhuth had already attempted to mediate between fact and fiction. In the fifth act of *Der Stellvertreter* the stage presentation becomes problematic, as the author was well aware, because the setting is the death camp of Auschwitz. With reference to extreme experiences of the twentieth century, the introductory remarks to the fifth act state the paradoxical situation of literature. While "no imagination is sufficient" [Keine Phantasie reicht aus] to imagine such extreme experiences, "documentary naturalism can no longer be a stylistic principle" [Dokumentarischer Naturalismus ist kein Stilprinzip mehr]. The solution, then, had to lie in a mediation between literary imagination and documentation. While in his later plays Hochhuth moved more and more toward literary imagination, an underlying appeal of his plays remained their documentary elements.

*Der Stellvertreter* incorporates documentary material, such as quotations from diaries and biographies, into a classical five-act structure to demonstrate a political hypothesis: the pope should have publicly denounced the crimes against humanity committed by the Nazis, especially the extermination of the Jews, but did not do so because of political considerations. Modern aspects of the presentation include Hochhuth's instruction to have groups of characters, such as the high-ranking SS officer Adolf Eichmann and a factory owner who was a prisoner of the Gestapo, played by the same actor to illustrate the arbitrariness of being victimizer or victim in today's world. The play is dedicated to the memories of Father Maximilian Kolbe and Prelate Bernhardt Lichtenberg, whose biographies are combined in the fictitious character of Father Riccardo Fontana. Kurt Gerstein, who becomes an SS officer to work against the Nazis from within, is based on a historical figure whose controversial biography is highlighted by additional documentary material in the play's appendix. Gerstein confirms Riccardo's information about the genocide, and Riccardo feels the need to become active. Riccardo and Gerstein try to convince the pope to renounce the concordat with the Third Reich and expose the Nazis' crimes against humanity. They see this as the only possible way to stop the genocide. After their attempt fails, Riccardo willingly goes to Auschwitz by pretending to be one of the Italian Jews who were rounded up right next to the Vatican.

The classicist tradition comes to the foreground in the humanist idealism of the play and the possibility of human beings to be the masters, and not merely the objects, of history. In a world that many other writers regarded as absurd, Hochhuth upheld the option for individuals to act responsibly and make a difference. Riccardo and Gerstein are positive heroes; they do not achieve their goal, but they die trying. The Roman Catholic Church is not presented as evil in an undifferentiated way; several of the clergy are sympathetic with Riccardo's and Gerstein's cause, and the assistance given by Catholics to help hundreds of Jews escape is mentioned. Hochhuth believed, however, that these aspects do not excuse the failure of the pope to exert the kind of leadership that humanity had a right to expect from Christ's deputy on earth.

Two main criticisms of *Der Stellvertreter* concern the level of dramatic presentation. First, the detailed introductory discussions to individual acts and scenes make exciting reading but could prove cumbersome for a stage production. Second, Hochhuth's mix of modern and epic with classicist and humanist elements did not convince some critics. Especially problematic was the fifth act, which brought together several previously separate strands of the plot in the setting of the death camp; the critics did not approve of the sentimentalized and simplistic black-and-white resolution. As a consequence, the revised version of the play replaces the fifth act with a changed version of the third scene of the third act. In this scene, Riccardo is taken into Gestapo custody along with others; in this way, his journey to the death camp is no longer explicitly presented on stage.

Hochhuth's play was also heavily criticized for his partisan view of the Vatican's role during the Third Reich, which was not far from historical truth, as became clear in the late 1990s when the Catholic Church itself began to apologize publicly for some of its past mistakes. Hochhuth had picked, as he continued to do, a controversial topic and started a debate about it. Literature, it could be argued, proved to be more than merely taking a position in the sense of *littérature engagée;* it became "operative" literature, which meant that it took effect.

That the role of literature had changed in West Germany can be illustrated by the reaction from the political arena. During the 1965 federal election campaign Ludwig Erhard, who had succeeded Adenauer as chancellor of the CDU-led West German government, referred to Hochhuth as a *Pinscher* (yapping cur). This (and similar name-calling of other authors and groups of authors) was an indication that politics responded to literature as a public event rather than as a private citizen's free speech. The politicization of literature produced such frustration on the part of some politicians with certain literary works to the extent that public condemnation was the surrogate for illegal censorship. The conflict between the public role of literature and politics in both East and West Germany continued in the 1970s.

# IV

# *Adding Partial Maps:*
# *Elements of Postmodernism*

## A Different World, Again

LIFE IN THE INDUSTRIALIZED NATIONS was radically changed during the 1960s, and compared to the period up to that decade, the world was a different one. The term *postmodernity* has been suggested for the world's current condition — a social reality characterized by factors that include a heightened North-South conflict and postindustrial, information-oriented work environments in the Northern Hemisphere. This reality, furthermore, is characterized by such fluidity that it has been described in terms of confusion. It should not be surprising that art reacted to the changed conditions and that it and other discourses on these changes added a further chapter to the development of modern thought.

*From Modernism to the 1960s counterculture and beyond*

Within the complex interaction between art and the world — involving the work of art, its creator, and its audience, as well as the specific institutions that influence the dissemination of art — twentieth-century art evolved as a response to a massive increase in the world's complexity. Modernism — the art that did not turn away from the complexity but, whether disliking or welcoming that complexity, dealt with it by encoding it into art's form and content — emerged as the predominant artistic tradition of the twentieth century. As antibourgeois as Modernism generally was, it became aligned, especially in Western societies after the Second World War, with the cultural mainstream and was identified with culture itself.

It was a logical development when the counterculture movement attacked Modernism — or, more precisely, that version of Modernism that had developed into establishment art. The counterculture focused, according to David Harvey, on "individualized self-realization" by way of "a distinctive 'new left' politics," "anti-authoritarian gestures," "iconoclastic habits," and "the critique of everyday life" (38). Therefore, it had the potential to touch every individual's choice of lifestyles. Politically, the landscape in the United States changed in the wake of the counterculture movement of the 1960s. Its effects ranged from the aesthetic (for example, Woodstock in 1969) to the political (for example, the civil rights and antiwar movements). The 1960s saw worldwide unrest crystallize into an antiwar movement, often with an anti-American sentiment since American involvement in Vietnam was the focal point of the antiwar demonstrations. In Germany, as before with the Expressionist outburst, the conflict was generational; in particular, the younger generation felt the need to deal with the unfinished business of their parents' involvement with Nazism. In the United States, on the other hand, the Vietnam War also split the younger generation.

The counterculture soon lost its direct political impact after the worldwide student protests of 1968 and their attempt to effect immediate social and political change on a grand scale failed. In contrast, the movement's repercussions still run deep. What came out of the counterculture focus on individual self-realization was, ultimately, distrust of any attempt to find totalizing solutions. In other words, the Modernist project of renewing the sense of totality by way of ever more innovations had lost its appeal.

In the overall picture of historical change, the counterculture was an important but not the only contributing factor to a slowly evolving view of the world as thoroughly defined by plurality — including the notion that events are unpredictable. This development challenged the 1950s and 1960s mainstream belief that times were getting better and that everything desirable was achievable through technological progress. The 1960s initiated a change that was to alter the experience of life in as similarly profound a way as the changes that had occurred at the turn of the nineteenth to the twentieth century. Counterculture movements of the 1960s envisioned a shift in one area: culture. While these envisioned effects encompassed a wide range, including everyday choices of culture with a lowercase *c*, the changes occurred on a much wider scale in global power politics, the labor market, and science.

First, long before the end of the Cold War, which focused on the East-West conflict, the North-South conflict between the industrialized and developing nations began to emerge as a major challenge in an era after colonialism. Second, in a global economy industrial production moved to the low-wage labor market of the developing or emerging economies; in the industrialized nations the trend was toward a growing service sector. As computers became ubiquitous, analysts, such as Alvin Toffler, declared a revolution on the scale of the industrial revolution: the information age was being ushered in. Because of an ever-increasing explosion of computer applications, changes occurred in almost all sectors, from education to leisure activities. At the end of the 1990s, the Internet had changed the way in which many people do business. Third, a new scientific approach to "chaotic" phenomena challenged the assumption that each scientific problem has one, and only one, exact solution.

The emergence of chaos theory was linked with the success story of the computer, because chaos theory is predicated on the speedy execution of a vast number of calculations that was not feasible before computers were available. According to James Gleick, the new science was pioneered by Edward Lorenz when he ran weather simulations on his computer in 1961 and discovered that a small change in initial input could trigger massive differences in output. This discovery stood the traditional assumption of the proportionality of cause and effect on its head. The ensuing study of nonlinear systems was popularized as "chaos theory" or (since the word *chaos* could be misunderstood as meaning randomness) "complexity theory." Stephen H. Kellert's summary of the central insight behind the new approach is "that systems governed by mathematically simple equations can exhibit elaborately complex, indeed unpredictable, behavior" (ix). The ultimate example is the weather, which exhibits a typical interconnection of order and chaos. It is not likely, for example, that a hot Texas summer day would be followed by a ten-year ice age starting the next day. Such "locally unpredictable but globally stable" behavior is characteristic of complex systems. Furthermore, complexity is not just without; it is also within: "The brain is the nonlinear product of a nonlinear evolution on a nonlinear planet." The last observation, by John Briggs and F. David Peat (166), suggests that, on the one hand, complexity theory intersects with postmodern thought, because it assumes universal validity without being totalizing, and that, on the other hand, complexity theory intersects with other discourses, including literature — which, as the product of the human brain, fit into the nonlinear context that complexity theory explores.

*Modern thought from the Renaissance to postmodernism*

Modern thought began with the Renaissance and was shaped during the Enlightenment. While it emphasized unity in various forms all the way up to and including Realism during the second half of the nineteenth century, modern thought created such unity rather than assuming a preexisting totality, as did medieval thought. A major change of modern thought occurred with the emergence of modernism when an unprecedented social fragmentation challenged the possibility of unity. The literary response, Modernism, not only fused elements of the previous modern movements; it was also a search for something new: a new style or a new myth. Hence, newness became ever more important. Modernism attempted to combine unity and plurality — it took unity as the goal of its quest and included plurality by virtue of responding to

334 • AFTER 1945: ELEMENTS OF POSTMODERNISM

the world's complexity. Postmodernism took the next logical step by no longer attempting to re-create a totality that had been lost; rather, it fully embraced plurality. This historical model invites an intriguing speculation: if indeed there was a movement from unity to plurality, then Modernism — the movement that dominated all of twentieth-century art — was merely a transitional phase.

This speculation runs counter to those theories that hold the "classical" Modernist project from 1890 to 1930 to be the end of innovation in art. Based on the nature of the linguistic sign, these theories suggest that in an environment of separate and independent social institutions (where literature is its own institution) literature has three basic options: it can use language to explore reality (Realism and, for Modernism, Ironic Realism); it can concentrate on language itself and become self-reflexive (Aestheticism); or it can violate the assumed independence of the social realms and postulate the identity of art with life (Avant-Garde). All options have been explored; therefore, literature at the end of the twentieth century is seen as unable to produce anything new (or even different). While this theory of literature's exhausted options is challenged by the speculation that Modernism is merely a transitional phase, that speculation — as part of a definition of postmodernism — needs to address how such a paradigmatic shift from unity to plurality would make innovation possible.

Hindsight will make it possible to determine whether postmodernism was still so greatly influenced by Modernist traditions that it actually was merely a variation of Modernism or whether it was, as it seems to be, sufficiently different from Modernism to be a separate mode. During the twentieth century German-language literature did not fully embrace postmodernism as much as did the works of authors from South America, such as Jorge Luis Borges (1899–1988), Julio Cortázar (1914–1984), and Gabriel García Márquez (b. 1928); or from the United States, such as John Barth (b. 1930), Donald Barthelme (1931–1989), Robert Coover (1932), Thomas Pynchon (b. 1937), and Don DeLillo (b. 1936). For German-language literature, postmodernism was not a literary mode or movement in the usual sense; it was a literary attitude. Postmodernist works were written by authors — such as Peter Handke, Thomas Bernhard (1931–1989), Botho Strauß, Heiner Müller, Christoph Ransmayr (b. 1954), and Barbara Frischmuth (b. 1941) — at the same time that Modernist traditions continued to be practiced and revised.

## Definitions of Postmodernism

Roger Ebert, an American movie critic, justified his top movie selections for 1998 by quoting the German movie director Werner Herzog (b. 1942): "we need new images or we will die." Beyond proving an intertwining of national cultures, this quotation makes a statement about the function of art. Before art can fulfill any function, it must connect human beings with the world in which they live. This connection is becoming increasingly fragile. While art can no longer claim to be comprehensive or universal, it is, at least, a partial connection that exists for some period of time. How much orientation is provided by such a partial, fragile connection can be argued, but images and stories at least provide connections to this world and to possible worlds — and without these images and stories, humanity will lose that by which it has been defined, and, as Herzog said, "we will die."

*Feeling the difference: a basic definition of postmodernism*

Herzog's statement points to another crucial aspect by emphasizing the newness of the images. In a world that is changing so rapidly that it and the adjective "ever-changing" are bound to each other as a truism, images and stories need to be new; they need to keep pace with the ever-changing world in order to provide a connection between that world and the human mind. The changes have affected the very concept of newness and the understanding of the world itself. Ironically, at a time when many critics claim that the possibilities of art have been exhausted and the best that contemporary art can offer is a clever reprise of previous art, a new image of the world has evolved: in an unprecedented way, the world is being perceived as plural.

The category of newness as a measure of artistic quality has been redefined. The insistence on new images emphasizes the fact that art needs to keep pace with the world; at the same time, "new" can be experienced as a matter of degree, resulting from a difference or otherness that is perceived in an artistic utterance, even if it is just a trace of such an otherness. Such an experience defines the postmodernist impulse that is intuitively experienced, for instance, in architecture, where traces of other styles are integrated as quotations into a whole. When people see such architecture, they feel as though they are seeing something new (in the sense that they feel an aesthetic difference between the old element's previous function and its new function in its new context). For literature, the audience's response seems less intuitive.

A definition of postmodernist literature that comes the closest to capturing a reader's intuition is proposed by Brian McHale in his study *Postmodernist Fiction*. His formal distinction between the epistemological dominant (Modernism) and the ontological dominant (postmodernism) approaches the level of intuition when it is rephrased in terms of the primary question that the reader asks. The text is Modernist if it suggests primarily questions of the type: "How can I make sense of this world of which I am a part?" The text is postmodernist, however, if it suggests primarily questions of the type: "Which world is this?" The absence of a stable and universal context has itself become the context for postmodernity.

The distinction between epistemological and ontological dominants explains why Kafka's texts are Modernist. They have received various interpretations, because they suggest a great variety of issues. Nevertheless, the textual strategies evoke the basic mode of operation of the protagonist in each story: he wants to find out what the rules of his world are; he is constantly engaged in trying to make sense of a world that no longer makes sense. That Kafka's protagonist feels himself to be a part of that world contributes to the story's underlying irony, because the reader is aware that two mutually exclusive worlds exist and that the world to which the protagonist does not belong has taken over. Kafka's stories also illustrate that the primary question for postmodernism is also relevant for Modernist texts, although the issue of the world's identity remains in the background.

By the same token, the distinction between epistemological and ontological dominants explains why Botho Strauß's *Der junge Mann* (The Young Man, 1984) is a postmodern text. Instead of a plausible or even chronological plot development, Strauß executes, as he calls it in the novel itself, a program of "scenarios and temporal honeycombs" [Schauplätze und Zeitwaben]. The resulting multiplicity of interwoven stories establishes thematic connections but no others; for example, the main protagonist, the young man, does not appear in all chapters, and when he does appear, his identity is questionable from chapter to chapter. The characters in each chapter and within the stories interspersed in the chapters have no awareness beyond the realm of "their" story. The closest any of them gets to the reader's experience is when a young businesswoman happens on a surreal scenario: a procession, coiling like a snake, is devouring itself. When she tries to intervene, the businesswoman crosses the "barrier of Equal Time" [Schranke zur Gleichen Zeit] and suddenly finds herself "in an entirely different place" [an einem gänzlich anderwärtigen Ort]. Her disorientation corresponds to the text's calculated irritation of the reader. *Der junge Mann* is a postmodern text, because the novel places a priority on the identity of the narrative worlds and the question "Which world is this?"

*Radical plurality: an extended definition of postmodernism*

The way for the postmodern emphasis on a radical sense of plurality was paved by the Modernist attitude that embraced the world's complexity; even this attitude, however, contained an undercurrent that attempted to unify plurality again. Since the Avant-Garde operated on the premise of a fusion of art and life, it presented the most totalizing discourse of all Modernist modes. In contrast to the Modernist fusion of Being and Becoming, postmodernism is completely defined by Becoming; it valorizes plurality by embracing all of its variations, such as fragmentation and chaos. The difference between Modernism and postmodernism lies, first, in the way postmodernism — out of an underlying antiauthoritarian impulse — distrusts all totalizing discourses and, second, in the way postmodernism shifts from seeing fragmentation solely as causing alienation to celebrating plurality as an opportunity for self-realization.

The characteristics of antiauthoritarianism and self-realization reveal the affinity of postmodernism to the counterculture movements of the 1960s. The postmodernist vision of plurality is often hard to capture in conventional political terms, such as "left" and "right." One of the political and social catch phrases of the late twentieth century was *multiculturalism* in the sense of accepting the right of all groups united by a common cause or background to speak for themselves in the ensemble of society's voices. This acceptance coincides with the postmodern interests in otherness and in power and knowledge. A text can no longer provide a master narrative, as was typical of Modernist texts. For postmodern literature, the embrace of plurality means that the search for the center is no longer crucial; this, however, does not necessarily mean randomness and utter confusion, because plurality implies the existence of various focal points, of "local" centers. Nevertheless, neither the counterculture movements of the 1960s nor the multicultural groups (including ethnic minorities, feminists, ecologists, and gays and lesbians) that have since emerged are necessarily postmodernist. They are forces in a political and social environment that has been labeled postmodernity, yet this in no way means that they participate in postmodernism as an aesthetic practice.

Even where otherness and multiculturalism of political movements find an aesthetic practice, it is not necessarily postmodern. Feminist literature, for example, is often predicated on a master narrative, while postmodern literature has given up master narratives as an aspect of a totalizing discourse. The master narrative of feminism is the suppression of women. The issue here is not an ethical one but one of narrative structure. For example, Christa Wolf's *Kassandra* (1983) clearly indicts the suppression of women, but this does not become the master narrative, because the novel remains open to other narratives, such as the pastiche of romantic love between Kassandra and Aineias that evokes the fragile and ultimately doomed promise of equality between the genders. The presentation of the novel as an interior monologue engages the reader in a de- and reconstruction of the past through which myth is rewritten. *Kassandra*, therefore, is primarily a postmodern text;

in contrast, Wolf's *Medea* (1996) focuses on the master narrative and, therefore, belongs mostly within the Modernist tradition.

### Changing Modes of Belonging

*The possibility of innovation*

The distinction between postmodernity as a social condition and postmodernism as an aesthetic phenomenon is reminiscent of assuming literature to be one part of the social whole, which functions as an ensemble of autonomous spheres. The changes of postmodernity, however, may affect the autonomy of these spheres and thus, necessarily, of postmodernism. The way in which the autonomy of the spheres may change is likely to provide an answer to the question whether artistic innovation is possible at a time when all possibilities of producing innovations should, theoretically, be exhausted. There are three options for producing new things in postmodernist literature: first, recycling of traditions; second, the changing world; and third, communication among the autonomous spheres of the social whole.

The first answer sounds ironic, but the cessation of innovation itself could generate conditions conducive to innovation. Since all traditions would become simultaneously accessible as a huge quarry of culture, all ensuing cultural production would be repetition of previous material. As Modernism already demonstrated, however, in Heissenbüttel's "texts" and Thomas Mann's *Joseph*, the conscious repetition of patterns is always based on choice and results in changing the patterns that it could supposedly only repeat; therefore, repetition has the potential of producing something new. Obviously, the category "new" would no longer be identical with the Modernist concept of radical innovation; rather, it would be defined, as Matei Calinescu suggests, in terms of renovation — or, more accurately, in terms of de- and reconstruction. This is the most profound innovation — the paradigmatic shift from radical newness (innovation) to combinatory newness (de- and reconstruction).

The second answer is based on what would appear to be a paradox if literature were indeed not capable of producing new artistic responses in the face of new realities. If it were accepted that the basic linguistic "operations" are restricted by their object of reference (reality) and their medium (language), the logical consequence would not be an exhaustion of literary innovation but an expectation of further innovation — as long as the world keeps changing (and change it did drastically in the 1990s). To the extent that the world changes, the language that refers to it also changes, and both changes provide the basis for literary innovation.

The third answer involves the autonomous spheres of the social whole. Understanding society in such terms is a model that accounts for the effects of social fragmentation — a model that, by its focus on autonomy, emphasizes the independence of the individual spheres rather than their interaction. Yet there are crossovers between the social spheres, which seem continuously to renegotiate their autonomy with each other. As a result, the image of a forever-changing world may be even more complex as social differentiation remains fluid. What is really new is not a matter of what is happening in each of the spheres but what is going on between them. Postmodern literature finds new material in the condition of postmodernity, that is, in the fine fissures and subtle changes of the contours of differentiated society.

Literature's exploration of crossover phenomena between the social spheres is innovative, because it requires a new kind of rationality — Wolfgang Welsch calls it "transversal" rationality — that mediates such crossovers. Since crossing over from one social role to the next constitutes many people's daily routine, transversal rationality is not just a theoretical construct; it is an opportunity to develop new forms of belonging in a society whose growing fragmentation and uniformity render an individual's experience incommensurate. Everybody takes on different social roles, fulfilling each role according to rules appropriate to it — everybody's life is proof that autonomous spheres exist (they define the individual roles) and that the functional differentiation of the social whole is a real experience. And yet each individual yearns for a sense of identity that is preserved throughout all the role switching. The experience of incommensurability and the yearning for identity are not new; what is new is that this experience has become routine.

The aesthetic phenomenon of postmodernism, however, is neither identical with the social condition of postmodernity nor with the critical theories about postmodernity; therefore, postmodernist literature can go past the shock of alienated life and, in addition to the strains and dangers of role switching, can explore its pleasures and new ways of belonging in this and other worlds. Intertextuality plays an increasingly important role, because each text is considered to be built on an older text, just as a new world is built on an older world; indeed, words (texts) and worlds become interchangeable in the sense that social contexts are seen as composed of words. A text establishes its own identity, not despite but because of its intertextuality, and literature can probe venues of transversal rationality that mediate between the social spheres in much the same way as a literary text mediates between its intertexts.

The task of transversal rationality is to propose new options for structuring the lives of incommensurate individuals and for preserving pockets of meaning in a world that oscillates between globalization and localization. Modernist literature did not address these issues because it pursued the goal of unity as defined by Enlightenment rationality.

Consequently, the Modernist answers to the problems of the twentieth century were genuinely new and, at the same time, still determined by older traditions of modernity. In contract, postmodernist literature suggests a profound change, which can be exemplified by the new understanding of history. Postmodernism rediscovered the past for its own sake and as an extension of the present, but not as a model for, or guise of, the present, as is so often the case in Modernist texts. Postmodern attention to the past often operates by excavating the older text that is hidden beneath a newer one. Where the past has taken the form of myths, the archaeological approach often consists in demythification or the creation of a countermyth, such as in Christa Wolf's Cassandra and Medea projects. Such an integration of history is dynamic and adds a further dimension of plurality to postmodernism. In the postmodernist acceptance of radical plurality, the development of modern thought truly had arrived in the twentieth century.

*A different myth: Odysseus revisited*

The Modernist study of the history of rationality by Max Horkheimer and Theodor W. Adorno in *Dialektik der Aufklärung* (Dialectic of Enlightenment, 1944) defines instrumental reason as rationality run amok, not helping humanity to overcome the restraints of nature but, instead, adding its own restraints to those of nature and thereby oppressing humanity even more. In this interpretation Ulysses comes to stand for domination, as well as exploitation; his tricks reveal him as priest and victim at the same time, Horkheimer and Adorno argue. As victim Ulysses has emerged as a major Modernist myth, becoming an archetype for homelessness and alienation in the world. Yet the reference to the myth seems to give a timeless pattern to everyday life, as in James Joyce's *Ulysses*. For Modernism the image of life as one endless odyssey contains the promise of taking the right road and finding the center. Modernist myth suggests a direction to life that postmodernism no longer can uphold.

In postmodern texts, choosing the right road — in contrast to the poem "The Road Less Traveled" by Robert Frost (1874–1963) — does not matter; all roads could be traveled at the same time. This is not an option in reality, but it is one in literature — one that does not explore the necessity of choice but the nature of choice, one that does not ask about establishing one path through one world but about different possible worlds. While the way of approaching reality in terms of possible or alternate worlds has almost become commonplace in popular culture — for instance, in movies from *Total Recall* (1990) to *Sliding Doors* (1998) and in individual episodes of television science-fiction series or entire series, such as *Quantum Leap* and *Sliders* — it is often done in a manner that preserves or restores a sense of unity. Still, some postmodernist texts have clear affinities to the science-fiction genre.

The image of the odyssey could remain as an image of life in a postmodern world; its meaning, however, would be completely altered in comparison to the Modernist myth. At the end of the twentieth century, the myth of the alienated Ulysses seemed in the process of being replaced by the myth of the "passive Odysseus."

Just as, for Modernism, an alienated Ulysses stood for instrumental reason, for postmodernism the image of a passive Odysseus may represent a new form of rationality. The position of the observer has taken on more and more importance in postmodernist literature; for example, Peter Handke writes in his *Mein Jahr in der Niemandsbucht* (My Year in No Man's Bay, 1994), "In life, the place most fitting for me is that of an observer" [Im Leben ist der mir gemäße Platz der eines Zuschauers], and he wonders, "Couldn't watching also be a type of action? Which could intervene in an event and even change it?" [Konnte das Zuschauen nicht auch ein Handeln sein? Das eingriff in ein Geschehen, und dieses sogar verwandelte?]. This perspective is a redefinition of life in terms of "participatory observation," a concept from contemporary social science. It can be framed as a postmodernist literary myth of a passive Odysseus: a myth that presents an option for finding new ways of existence in a world where sensory overload by the mass media has become a daily routine and a myth that goes beyond the Modernist concept of the *flâneur*, which was mainly confined to an individual's aesthetic experience in opposition to — but not in interaction with — the surrounding world.

If Odysseus (in the function of the postmodernist nonjudgmental narrator) is seen as a metaphor of transversal rationality, then the crossovers from one social sphere to another can be understood as an odyssey that, in turn, represents a map of these crossovers. The resulting map would be a partial map, covering only one of many possible odysseys and its specific terrain. Such partial maps, however, have the potential to be more accurate than any global map could ever be. For example, some postmodern texts, such as those by Botho Strauß and Peter Handke, achieve a great precision in observations of their particular worlds, although they no longer pretend to describe the world as a whole. While Modernism was looking for the one center, postmodernism has found many centers; therefore, postmodernism can provide only partial (but perhaps more reliable) maps for orientation.

One can imagine the new Odysseus, the passive, yet participatory, observer of a world in confusion, sifting through a variety of maps in search of the one that provides a match to the world — and, in the process, discovering that several maps, although incongruent with each other, do so. As Odysseus realizes that he has to keep asking which world this is and that the answers continue to change depending on the various local centers from which limited orientation emanates, he has to chart his journey's course through different layers of maps. He knows that there is no master map, only partial ones. In this knowledge Odysseus may, perhaps, not be naively happy, but we must imagine him taking pleasure in tracing layer after layer of maps. Since these are like texts upon texts that are all simultaneously linked with each other, they create a context in which the journey becomes the goal because the ability to maneuver in a confusing world means survival. Ultimately, since this description of textual interrelationships defines *hypertext*, it is but a small step to see Odysseus as a traveler in cyberspace.

# 10: The 1970s: Increasing Plurality — New Sensitivity in the West and Continuing Emancipation in the East

## Social Foundation: Political Hopes and Failures

THE POLITICAL AND SOCIAL CHANGES of the 1970s were fundamental in the way they affected people's relationships to their state. In West Germany the political climate was increasingly contentious because of two issues: *Ostpolitik* and terrorism. The coalition government of Social Democrats and Free Democrats, in power since 1969, began the new *Ostpolitik*, the West German version of détente, which met with major objections from conservatives, who accused the government of selling out German interests to the East with treaties that officially recognized the way the borders had been drawn after the Second World War. Chancellor Willy Brandt's leadership, however, was internationally recognized with the 1971 Nobel Peace Prize. The confrontations over *Ostpolitik* reached a peak when the conservative opposition failed in its attempt to vote the chancellor out of office in April 1972. In early elections in November of the same year, with a record participation of ninety-one percent of the voters, the SPD-FDP coalition won a sound majority.

The attempt to bring all political groups on the leftist fringes of the 1960s extraparliamentary opposition under the umbrella of democracy failed. In May 1970 the RAF (*Rote Armee Fraktion*, or Red Army Faction), a small radical group, began to launch terrorist attacks in its self-styled urban guerrilla warfare against capitalism. After police captured the first generation of RAF terrorists in May 1972, the activities of the second generation of RAF terrorists culminated in the *Deutscher Herbst* (German Autumn) of 1977 with the kidnapping and murder of Hanns-Martin Schleyer, president of the powerful German Employer's Association. When the immediate goal of the kidnapping — to force the West German authorities to release three imprisoned first-generation terrorists, Andreas Baader, Jan-Carl Raspe, and Gudrun Ensslin — failed, the three prisoners committed suicide (a fourth, Ulrike Meinhof, had already committed suicide in 1976). It was not until after the mid-1990s that the last generation of RAF terrorists conceded defeat; during the approximately twenty-five years of RAF terrorism about forty people were killed.

The pursuit of *Ostpolitik* and the defense against terrorism were combined in the government's policies in a significant way, because the government did not want to appear soft on Communism nor on leftist terrorism. It issued a decree that led to the routine background checks of about half a million applicants for city, state, or federal jobs between 1972 and 1976. In retrospect, Brandt considered this decree the gravest political mistake of his administration because it contributed to an atmosphere of distrust between the state and its young people who were beginning their professional careers. This and other changes that West Germany made in its legislation to defend itself against terrorism were criticized as a threat to democratic freedoms. The heated public debate engulfed Heinrich Böll and other literary figures who tried to be voices of reason. The result was a further deepening of mutual mistrust between the state and some of its citizens.

As global crises (for example, the oil crisis of 1973) and technological advances restructured the job market, West German unemployment started to climb and remained a problem for the rest of the century. While people felt powerless in regard to global issues, there was a tremendous surge of people becoming involved in solving more local problems, from redesigning parking lots to fighting for women's liberation, voicing environmental concerns, and protesting nuclear power plants. Most of the *Bürgerinitiative* (citizens' initiatives) were constructive and nonviolent. More importantly, they represented a development that was new for Germany, because they complemented the principle of democracy by representation with a network of grass-roots movements. These movements empowered the people but also signified disillusionment with political reforms and a sense of mistrust because of the state's often heavy-handed and authoritarian response to challenges.

When Willy Brandt resigned as chancellor in 1974 in response to the discovery that one of his top advisers had been an East German spy, the mood of making a new start, for which Brandt stood, had waned; times were ready for the more pragmatic approach of his successor, Helmut Schmidt. The espionage affair highlighted the precarious relationship between the two German states, which had gotten off to a good start after Walter Ulbricht, the first secretary of the Central Committee of the SED, had resigned in May 1971. The successor to this position, which was the most powerful one in the GDR, was Erich Honecker, who was expected to be more liberal and pragmatic. Indeed, Honecker shifted the focus of economic policies toward satisfying the people's wishes for consumer goods, a goal that made him interested in dealing with the West to import goods that were not available elsewhere.

The general liberalization in East Germany also encompassed the cultural sector, but it did not last long. As it became increasingly difficult for the GDR to import consumer goods because of rising prices, measures were taken that resulted in a two-class society: those who had Western currency stood out from those who did not have Western currency and, therefore, were not able to buy quality products in an expanding chain of stores, the *Intershop*, which did not accept the East German currency. This situation led to protests in which writers and other intellectuals participated, revealing the shabby reality of socialism as it was practiced. As early as 1973 repression of critical literature increased; it reached unprecedented dimensions by the mid-1970s, not just in the clandestine activities of the ever-present East German secret police but also in the obvious consequences for the authors, who were treated with alternating hot and cold baths of privilege and repression. While some meetings between East and West German authors were permitted, some East German writers were not allowed to publish — the official reason often given was a paper shortage — or they were even forced to leave East Germany.

In 1976 it could no longer be concealed that the reality of socialism as it was practiced in the GDR and the ideal of utopian socialism, which most writers embraced, had serious trouble coexisting. Wolf Biermann was not allowed to reenter the country after a concert tour in West Germany because of his allegedly defaming remarks about the GDR. The ensuing reaction led to a strain from which the relationship of writers and their state did not recover as long as the GDR continued to exist. A letter futilely protesting Biermann's expatriation and asking for a reconsideration of the decision was published by a Western news agency after the East German news agency refused to publish it. The letter was originally signed by Erich Arendt, Jurek Becker, Volker Braun, Franz Fühmann, Stephan Hermlin, Stefan Heym (pseudonym of Helmut Flieg, b. 1913), Sarah Kirsch, Günter Kunert, Heiner Müller, Rolf Schneider (b. 1932), Christa Wolf, and Gerhard Wolf (b. 1928). More than seventy other authors and artists added their signatures over the next few days. Only a few significant authors, above all, Anna Seghers, Hermann Kant, and Peter Hacks, came out in support of Biermann's expatriation.

The GDR could not and would not keep many of the critical and disillusioned writers in the country. Although a few writers had already left East Germany, the magnitude of the brain drain after 1976 cannot be underestimated. Despite their criticism of the state, some authors — such as Christa Wolf and Heiner Müller — remained in the GDR, yet they had access to privileges, such as travel to the West. Nevertheless, they were important exceptions compared to all those who left East Germany either permanently or on long-term visas; for instance, Sarah Kirsch, Rainer Kunze, and Hans Joachim Schädlich (b. 1935) left as early as in 1977. It was remarked ironically that, as a result, East German literature was literature written by East German authors, some of whom accidentally did live in East Germany.

## The Literary Spectrum

While plurality was the unifying factor in German literature long before political unification was possible, it was the result of an international development in the arts and literature toward a postmodern mode. Although it can be argued that postmodernism never took firm hold in German-language literature, there were crucial elements that departed significantly from what had become the "traditional" usage of Modernism. Some authors, such as Uwe Johnson in prose and Heiner Müller in drama, used postmodern elements in connection with more traditionally Modernist elements.

Multiculturalism, one of the key concepts in the discussion of postmodernity, became more visible during the 1970s. While often highly politicized, the term *multicultural* — emphasizing the equality of group-specific centers, as well as the interaction and dialogues among these centers and with mainstream culture — is perfectly descriptive of German society. As a correlative of pluralism, literature saw an increasing individualization. In the East, literature that attempted to affirm the type of socialism that was practiced there found itself creatively outdistanced by emancipatory literature that explored individual, as opposed to collective, solutions. In the West, German-language literature reacted to the social trends that encompassed the somewhat contradictory combination of an individualistic New Subjectivity and a political *Alternativbewegung* (grass-roots movement), consisting of a variety of citizens' initiatives each of which was potentially the center of a culture of its own. These trends redefined political meaning, which literature explored as an aspect of the private realm.

The developments were strikingly similar for literature in the East and the West, a similarity that went beyond a vague coincidence in the way texts explored a pluralistic world. Above all, they expressed a deep sense of disillusionment concerning the possibility that literature could play a productive role in politics on either side of the Iron Curtain. In the West the 1960s counterculture revolution had failed, and so had the utopia of socialism with a human face in the East. The 1970s saw impressive developments in feminist literature, and a new generation of writers took a fresh and hard, although subjective, look at Nazism in Germany's past and present, paying close attention to everyday experiences. These developments were indications of an emerging multiculturalism. While it is likely to constitute postmodernity in a social or political sense, multiculturalism is a contributing factor in the development of literary postmodernism but is not a sufficient condition. Some of the texts that were produced in the 1970s turned toward realism —

rather than to Modernism and much less to postmodernism — to take stock of the issues involved in finding one's own identity or that of one's group.

Many texts were *Verständigungstexte*, texts that invited immediate identification by "touching" the readers' own lives — hence the quality of *Betroffenheit* (human touch) that was valued as authenticity. To the extent that such texts relied on shared experiences between author or narrator and reader, writers ran the risk of merely articulating banalities. A text's radical subjectivity, however, often went hand in hand with a political aspect that revealed that subjectivity's social embedding. This became obvious in the formal emphasis on experience (rather than on the other literary basic categories of theme, action, and character). While experience would have traditionally been expressed in lyrical modes, the literature of the 1970s was dominated by prose as the form to express subjectivity. The search for subjectivity — as the last resort to avoid confusion in a world that no longer provided orientation — was an "epic" project that relied on narrative structure to suggest a story and thus the existence of meaning, however subjective. This analysis places the experimental texts that articulated this kind of subjectivity between Modernism, whose search for meaning they continued, and postmodernism, which accepted the loss of orientation as a daily phenomenon.

The focus on stories about individuals paved the way for a rebirth of the historical novel based on a perspective critical of traditional historiography. In the 1970s, however, this focus gave rise to a flood of autobiographical writings that ranged from traditional memoirs to literary reflections. The latter category is exemplified by the works of Elias Canetti (1905–1994), winner of the 1981 Nobel Prize for literature, especially *Die gerettete Zunge* (The Tongue Set Free, 1977). Autobiographies of this type usually unmasked a highly political dimension of subjectivity: "daily fascism." This term refers to behaviors (especially in everyday relationships) that remained basically authoritarian even though, after the end of the Second World War, the fascist regime had been replaced by a democratic form of government in the West and an openly antifascist ideology in the East.

### Subjectivity in Poetry

*Simplicity and dangers of everyday life in the West* The 1970s brought changes in poetry in the wake of an attempt to find new poetic modes after major lines of tradition from Brecht to Benn and Celan seemed at an end. Several poets continued to understand themselves in light of their own previous practice; for more traditional and personal poetry this category included Rose Ausländer, Marie Luise Kaschnitz, and Karl

Krolow, and for political poetry it included Hans Magnus Enzensberger and Erich Fried. In addition, there was a new trend toward authenticity that led to a variety of ways in which experiences of daily life, love, and nature were integrated poetically. The central representative of the latter trend was Rolf Dieter Brinkmann. Other poets of this trend were Wolf Wondratschek, as well as Arnfried Astel (b. 1933), Jürgen Becker, Nicolas Born (1937–1979), Günter Herburger (b. 1932), Karin Kiwus (b. 1942), Ursula Krechel (b. 1947), Jürgen Theobaldy (b. 1947), and Rolf Haufs (b. 1935).

Ausländer made her laconic everyday language more hermetic by shifting from concrete themes of her memories and her Jewish faith to a more abstract belief in the potential of language. This was an autobiographical reflection; while her "fatherland" [Vaterland] had been destroyed by Nazism, language had been the source of her survival: "I live / in my motherland / Word" [Ich lebe / in meinem Mutterland / Wort]. In contrast, Kaschnitz and Krolow moved toward a greater colloquialism. Kaschnitz's last collection of poems, *Kein Zauberspruch* (No Magic Spell, 1972), was praised for its new tone that encompassed revisiting daily events, such as trash collection (in the poem of that title, "Müllabfuhr"); the garbage collectors take away her thrown-out poem, leaving behind only a few words glistening on the driveway. She also seemed at ease with expressing the political dimension of her subjectivity in an almost banal language: "What still comes to mind / When I say Germany" [Was fällt mir noch ein / Wenn ich Deutschland sage].

Karl Krolow consolidated his poetic practice of writing about daily life, which he had started during the late 1960s and which provided the title for his collection *Alltägliche Gedichte* (Everyday Poems, 1968). While this was in keeping with the concept of the "Alltagsgedicht" of the New Sensitivity, Krolow rejected the latter's openly political implications. Nevertheless, he achieved a tone that paralleled that of some of Wondratschek's aggressive poems of male identity. For example, in "Mehrmals" (Multiple, 1972), Krolow laconically identifies "life as a multiple orgasm" [Leben als mehrfacher Orgasmus]. This and other formulations pale in comparison to Krolow's collection of pornographic poems, ironically called *Bürgerliche Gedichte* (Bourgeois Poems, 1970) and published under the pseudonym Karol Kröpke.

Erich Fried and Hans Magnus Enzensberger continued the 1960s tradition of political poetry. Fried became increasingly controversial for criticizing Israeli politics in *Höre, Israel!* (Hearken, Israel!, 1974) and the way the West German state reacted to the threat of leftist terrorism in *So kam ich unter die Deutschen* (Thus I Came to Be Among the Germans, 1977). Toward the end of the 1970s, however, Fried also turned his prolific energy to everyday situations. His *Liebesgedichte* (Love Poems, 1979) was an instant success, selling 140,000 copies within five years, and Fried became popular with the middle-class readership that had been suspicious of his politics just a few years earlier.

After a short leave of absence from poetry, Enzensberger returned in the mid-1970s to his next phase of writing poetry, which had become enhanced by a stronger historical vision, often tinged with pessimism about the awareness of civilization's endgame mood. In *Mausoleum: Balladen aus der Geschichte des Fortschritts* (Mausoleum: Ballads from the History of Progress, 1975), Enzensberger critically assesses historical figures, including Niccolò Machiavelli and Che Guevara, in chronological order. The first ballad, "Giovanni de' Dondi (1318–1389)," about a man who spent his life building a clock, ends with the observation about how little times have changed with the ability to measure time. An even stronger tone of pessimism underlies the cycle of poems *Der Untergang der Titanic: Eine Komödie* (The Sinking of the Titanic: A Comedy, 1978), which encapsulates the decline of civilization in the sinking of the allegedly unsinkable ocean liner in 1912.

The demand for authenticity in poetry led to an integration of New Sensitivity with simplicity, directness, and subjective experience. This integration included the dangers of New Sensitivity, which consisted in mistaking mere authenticity for literary quality and banality for significance. Authenticity in poetry, however, depended primarily on redefining the modes and functions of poetry. The new authenticity was supposed to aim at an area where neither esoteric hermeticism nor laconic brilliance could reach: everyday life. The modes of this poetry — anticipated by Walter Höllerer's 1965 definition of the "long poem" ("long" not in the sense of length but of poetic perspective) — involved an open form that would allow for counteracting the traditionally affirmative function of poetry and support poetry's emancipatory function: to evoke possible worlds, not as wishful thinking but as creative subversions of reality.

In his greatest poetic achievement, *Westwärts 1 & 2* (Go West 1 & 2, 1975), Rolf Dieter Brinkmann explored expressive forms with which he hoped to overcome personal and artistic frustrations. Brinkmann's personal frustrations were tied to his financial situation, which made his self-styled image as an antibourgeois artist precarious; moreover, he felt that pop art did not allow the liberation that he sought. While not abandoning elements of pop art, such as brutality and banality, he adapted them to New Sensitivity's concept of everyday life. Brinkmann's forte had always been astute observations of individual moments. These moments offered themselves to Brinkmann in a multitude of ways that he explored in several collage-type texts that make use of the ultimate banalities of objets trouvés.

The poems in *Westwärts 1 & 2* are less radical. Written between 1970 and 1974 and published shortly before Brinkmann's death in a traffic accident in London, they display a new style and the tremendous sense of temporary liberation Brinkmann seemed to have felt when he spent the spring of 1974 as writer-in-residence at the University of Texas at Austin. Autobiographical details make the identity of the poet and the speaker of the poems evident, especially in the title poem, "Westwärts," which even includes the street address of the Villa Capri motel in Austin. The poem's montage technique arranges the segments of the textual flow all over the page, not unlike some of Jürgen Becker's "texts":

> trailers, snakes                                    Here, in this area, with the
>    grass, black big birds,                              moving houses,
>       creaking vending machines in February.    at night.
>
> [Wohnwagen, Schlangen                        Hier, in der Gegend, mit dem
>    Gras, schwarze große Vögel,                   wandernden Häusern,
>       krächzende Automaten im Februar.       nachts.]

The form is essential to the meaning of the poem; without the flowing text, the flow of the sensory input cannot be evoked in its intensity, simultaneity, and — as far as this example is concerned — in its liberating force of realizing that this scenery is "the West" [der Westen]. The United States is the "West" and, as so often in German literature, becomes a sentimental, though not uncriticized, image of self-fulfillment. Symbols like the "West" reintegrate metaphoric language into Brinkmann's poetic register.

Like Brinkmann, Wolf Wondratschek was influenced by the counterculture movement and pop art. But Wondratschek brought to German poetry a more aggressive sound that was upbeat and melancholy at the same time: he emerged as the rock 'n' roll poet of the 1970s. In *Chuck's Zimmer* (1974, Chuck's Room), *Das leise Lachen am Ohr eines anderen* (Her Quiet Laughter in Another Man's Ear, 1976), *Männer und Frauen* (Men and Women, 1978), and *Letzte Gedichte* (Last Poems, 1980), he dealt with the difficulty of being "a real man" and of having meaningful relationships. Like commercial rock 'n' roll music, Wondratschek's poetry was a critical and popular success. His four volumes of poems — each subtitled *Gedichte/Lieder* (Poems/Songs), since Wondratschek wanted to emphasize his poems' musical quality and some had, indeed, been written to be performed as rock songs — were collected in an 1981 edition that was advertised with the reminder that the four volumes had already sold a combined total of 100,000 copies.

The rock 'n' roll quality is reflected in the language of the poems. Through syntax and word choice the poems achieve a linguistic directness that is colloquial and terse. The melancholy tone is a reflection of

New Sensitivity but is often presented with irony. In "Spätvorstellung in der Stammkneipe" (Late Show at the Favorite Bar, 1978), the speaker notices that he shares a loneliness with the other men, who spend their time drinking beer, indicating a sensitivity for a changed world but also a longing for the good old days. The speaker seems to be able to re-create these old times for himself when he leaves the bar as though he has achieved a victory: "I went outside, / with rolling gait like after / a gunfight" [ich ging raus, / breitbeinig wie nach einem / Schußwechsel]. The context of Wondratschek's poems during the 1970s left open whether such an ending was the macho man's swan song, but in the 1980s the macho male made his comeback in his poetry.

*Disillusionment after utopia's failure in the East* Different political circumstances — in the West the failure of the counter-culture and in the East the failure of utopian socialism — shattered the poetic visions, with similar results. The poets withdrew into texts that represented authentic experiences — experiences that, by virtue of being subjective, possessed a political function. This response was especially strong in East German poetry, where expression of subjective truths was seen as direct opposition to the expected affirmation of the state's official truth of the collective, thus leading to a conflict between utopian socialism and the shabby reality of socialism as practiced in the GDR. The disillusionment was made worse by the disheartening experience of being unwanted by the system that the writers, despite their criticism of specific aspects, generally had supported and often continued to support. As a result, after Biermann's expatriation had removed any remaining doubt, the tone of East German poetry was characterized to a large extent by skepticism and a sense of loss, even of mourning.

Poetry could no longer continue contributing to a critical, yet mainly positive, identification with the state, as it had done during the 1960s; rather, it articulated the crisis in images of ambiguous mythological figures and of the destruction of nature. The range of emotional responses went from bitter resignation to faint hope. The mood of resignation was particularly strong for older poets, such as Erich Arendt and Peter Huchel. Günter Kunert's poetry was also generally pessimistic but contained an occasional spark of a "little however," which also describes Sarah Kirsch's approach, especially when she asserts female subjectivity. Among the group of major poets, Volker Braun remained the most loyal to the GDR. After all, a number of other authors, even some of those who had left the GDR, still considered East Germany "their" state, because socialism with a human face — a third option between capitalism in the West and Communism in the East — had at least had a chance. Such utopian opportunity in the past allowed, in spite of all disillusionment, a faint hope that some day such an opportunity might arise again.

The only grand old man of German poetry to remain in the GDR in the 1970s, Erich Arendt had begun to feel the discrepancy between dream and reality soon after his return from exile. The dark and despairing visions of present and future he wrote of during the 1970s were anticipated by his poems of the 1960s. In the last collection published before his death, *entgrenzen* (delimit, 1981), he formulated the final phase of human history with his typical use of adjectives and adjectival compounds, including those with the delimiting prefix *ent-* (hence the volume's title): "stored zeros we / computerized desouled / imprisoned" [gespeicherte nullen wir / computer-entseelt / gefangen].

In contrast to Arendt, Peter Huchel left the GDR in 1971. An essentially apolitical thinker, Huchel had developed an attitude of resignation in regard to a socialist utopia. The mood of his poetry became increasingly dark and his language increasingly terse. "König Lear" (King Lear), in his last collection *Die neunte Stunde* (The Ninth Hour, 1979), expresses a sense of precariousness in a world that offers no protection. Yet this was not the only mood in his poetry. "Der Fremde geht davon" (The Stranger Walks Away), the last poem in *Die neunte Stunde*, presents quite a contrast to "Garten des Theophrast," Huchel's poetic testament after his removal from the editorship of *Sinn und Form*. Now, almost two decades later, the stranger has become the one who is active; he leaves, but he is not sent away: "Seasons, misfortunes, necrologies — / unconcerned, the stranger walks away" [Jahreszeiten, Mißgeschicke, Nekrologe — / unbekümmert geht der Fremde davon].

After the waning of Arendt's and Huchel's productivity, Günter Kunert emerged as the major poetic voice of East German literature — ironically, at about the time he left in 1979 to live in West Germany. The collections of his poetry, such as *Offener Ausgang* (Open Ending, 1972) and *Unterwegs nach Utopia* (En Route to Utopia, 1977), show the common theme of GDR literature: disillusionment with the socialist utopia, which Kunert had expressed earlier than most other poets of his generation. Whether in reference to mythology (Orpheus), history (Alexander the Great or Hitler), or subjective observations of daily life (the dead wasp lying among dead flies on the window sill), Kunert expresses bitter skepticism and deep concern. Describing the painting of Alexander's victory over Darius, Kunert concludes "Alexanderschlacht" (The Battle of Alexander, 1972) with an indictment of the violent history of humankind: "the Occident has been saved for all / future wars" [das Abendland ist gerettet für alle / künftigen Kriege]. Something has gone terribly, yet also quietly, wrong with a world that seems to be standing on its head, as expressed in the surprising image in "Ausschau I" (Lookout I, 1976): "so you float away with the bridge / while the river beneath you / stands still" [so gleitest du mit der Brükke fort / während der Fluß unter dir / stillsteht].

Dystopia replaces utopia while the latter remains a place of longing in "Unterwegs nach Utopia," the title poem of Kunert's 1977 collection. At the same time, he articulated a poetic project of resistance that went beyond resignation, although it was still defined by a sense of mourning. "Gedicht zum Gedicht" (Poem about the Poem, 1970) declares programmatically: "The poem is a condition / that the poem destroys / by way / of emerging from itself" [Gedicht ist Zustand, / den das Gedicht zerstört, / indem es / aus sich selber hervortritt]. Kunert's poems of the 1970s tried to emerge from themselves by presenting their apocalyptic visions in a language of colloquial immediacy and succinct terseness; therefore, most of them are short, free-rhythmical, and without end rhyme. At the same time, while the poem reached out, Kunert did not believe that he could change political reality with his poetry, but at least he could give voice to "the little however" (hence the title of his 1976 collection, *Das kleine Aber*).

A similar quality, both formally and thematically, characterizes the poetry by Sarah Kirsch, yet the "little however" that she voices seems to be embedded at a more subjective level. This tendency was not new for Kirsch; her poem "Schwarze Bohnen" (Black Beans, 1968) had led to official criticism because it merges a brief moment of thinking about the Vietnam War with a series of subjective and banal events, such as the grinding of coffee beans, which is noisy and eventually drowns out the political irritation. Her major collections *Zaubersprüche* (Magic Spells, 1973) and *Rückenwind* (Tail Winds, 1976) were published before she moved to West Germany in 1977. In her poetic explorations Kirsch had an affinity for landscapes and animals, a focus she continued after she moved to a rural area of northern West Germany in 1983.

Of central importance was her emphasis on female subjectivity, which she elaborated in poems addressed to German women writers, such as Annette von Droste-Hülshoff (1797–1848) in *Zaubersprüche* and Bettina von Arnim (1785–1859) in *Rückenwind*. In "Wiepersdorf," Kirsch talks in the familiar "du"-form directly to Bettina, who had dedicated her 1843 political manifesto for freedom to the Prussian king, thus merging politics and Romanticism. The ninth and final section of Kirsch's poem exploits the ambiguity of political and subjective meaning in the unambiguous existential situation of women: loneliness. It does not matter whether women attempt to express their ideas about love or politics, writing "to the kings . . . / Those of the hearts and those / Of the nations" [den Königen . . . / Denen des Herzens und jenen / Des Staats]. The imagined journey back in time to meet Bettina returns to the present, where a woman's heart can be startled by the sound of a car — which can mean, ambiguously, the lover's car or that of the secret police. Despite the central emphasis on disillusionment and skepticism that Kirsch shared with most GDR poets, her poetry is also characterized by a strong self-assertive quality, perhaps as a result of the growing women's movement.

The title of Volker Braun's collection *Gegen die symmetrische Welt* (Against the Symmetrical World, 1974) seems to prepare the reader for a protest against a brave new world where people use machines to dominate nature, only to be dominated themselves by the machines. Such protest could easily be understood as extending to a general cultural and social critique in which East and West are in symmetry with each other in repressing individuality. The poem "Durchgearbeitete Landschaft" (Worked-Over Landscape), however, condones humanity's unbroken taste for domination of nature. In its tone exposing technological culture as dangerous, the poem's first part equates cultivation with colonization, in the process of which the machines used by man violate nature. In contrast to such a critique, the second half of the poem changes in tone and celebrates the achievements of the domination over nature in a way that was also typical of socialism: nature is remade by man into a paradise on Earth. Now that cultivation is complete, man-made nature, as symbolized by the "little oaks without fear" [kleine Eichen ohne Furcht], can relax, and man can rejoice, for the "tender mountain range" [zartes Gebirge], the "blue water" [blaues Wasser], and "the white new-born beach" [der weiße neugeborne Strand] are ready for his use.

### New Centers of Prose Texts

*Feminist literature:*
*Writing about women*
*by women for women*

The most significant development in literature in the German-speaking countries, as well as worldwide, was the emergence of feminist writing. German feminism was strongly influenced by feminists in France, such as Simone de Beauvoir, and in the United States, such as Susan Sontag and Kate Millet. The feeling of many women — that their situation in a male-dominated world was precarious — led to new and provocative ways to see and think about a world that a majority of people had come to see as intact, a view that feminism challenged as wishful and wrongful thinking. As a consequence of the political redefinition of women's role in society, a new way of writing about women by women and for women evolved. While the mid-1970s saw a surge in feminist literature, there were important earlier works by, for example, Ingeborg Bachmann and Elfriede Jelinek.

Feminist texts are written in a genuinely female voice; "voice" refers to a textual property that allows readers to experience a text as authentic. Authenticity is achieved by focusing on domination and repression of one gender by the other. Consequently, authenticity implies a political approach that brings about an aesthetic response. While this view includes an acknowledgment of the role women themselves have played in patriarchy, it furthermore implies an uncompromising defense of women's newly found identity and autonomy — beyond stereotypical gender roles in all areas of society — as well as an unfaltering resistance to hidden patriarchal attempts at domination, often referred to as "daily fascism."

An authentic representation of men as victimizers had to account for much more complicated circumstances. Individual men may also be victimized by a complex network of social conditions that had evolved to give men all the power but that now seemed to be out of control. An analysis of social structures along these lines suggested that men were at the same time exploiters and exploited and, thus, both enemies and potential allies of women. In addition, women repressed by patriarchy themselves reproduced the repression in relationships with their children; hence, women appeared to be their own enemies. Consequently, feminists faced choices that ranged from rebellion to careful cooperation with some men to build a better society. These challenges for political feminism were also challenges for literary feminism.

*The early 1970s: Ingeborg Bachmann's Malina*

Ingeborg Bachmann's *Malina*, published in 1971, established itself as the definitive German feminist prose text of the 1970s. The novel had been planned as part of a trilogy, whose title is an indictment of what male-oriented society had in store for women: *Todesarten* (Ways of Dying). The other parts of the trilogy remained fragmentary but were published posthumously, including *Der Fall Franza. Requiem für Fanny Goldmann* (The Case of Franza. Requiem for Fanny Goldmann, 1978). For Bachmann, an "eternal war" [ewige(r) Krieg] rages between the sexes; fascism is a logical development of patriarchy; and fascist power structures dominate the daily lives of people.

In *Malina* the father is the embodiment of male power. The female narrator is torn between two men: Ivan and Malina. Ivan is a man who could have made it possible for the narrator to live; however, the narrator's male alter ego, Malina, proves stronger. Yet Malina is less an individual than an extension of the deadly power of patriarchal rule, a trait that is established through connecting him with the narrator's father, who is exposed by the narrator's nightmares as representing the death principle. In these dreams, her father assimilates the identity of others without losing his own; likewise, Malina literally absorbs her identity into his without a trace of the disappeared female consciousness. When Ivan calls to talk to the narrator, Malina answers: "There is no woman here. I tell you, nobody of that name has ever lived here" [Hier ist keine Frau. Ich sage doch, hier war niemand dieses Namens].

*Malina* exposes the subtle, yet brutal, ways in which patriarchy represses women by making women identify, at least to some degree, with patriarchy. The absorption of the narrator's identity is authentic in a sense that goes beyond surface realism; the annihilation of female identity is evoked in highly metaphorical terms that represent the way in which patriarchy erases female desire: "Yet the wall opens up; I'm inside the wall . . . a very strong wall no one can fall out of . . . from which no sound can escape again" [Aber die Wand tut sich auf, ich bin in der Wand . . . eine sehr starke Wand, aus der niemand fallen kann . . . aus der nie mehr etwas laut werden kann]. The triumph of the death principle is established in the novel's last sentence, which laconically evaluates the narrator's fate: "It was murder" [Es war Mord].

The evocation of the narrator's disappearing into a wall is significant in two respects. First, the mechanisms of repression are associated with language — or, rather, since the narrator's voice has been silenced, with the repression of one form of expression by another. Malina even has the power to name the novel. Consequently, language itself is an indicator of "daily fascism." This is a key motif in feminist literature. For Bachmann's text it is also crucial that history's character as a process is underscored. As a process, history cannot be final, regardless of the way in which a text ends. Second, the development within women's literature was by no means as linear as suggested by the usual assumption of a first phase that was primarily realistic and more authentic than literary on account of its human-touch qualities and a second phase that produced authentic texts of high quality as a result of textual refractions that transcended immediate surface realism. The more immediate human-touch approach was, indeed, particularly strong at the beginning; both types of women's writing, however, occurred almost at the same time in the mid-1970s. Bachmann's 1971 novel exemplifies that feminist writings achieved considerable literary quality during the early 1970s. *Malina* remains authentic because, building on the narrative challenges of the 1960s that had questioned the status of the individual subjectivity, it illustrates how female individuality is threatened in gender relationships and because it generalizes these observations into a relevant criticism of the male-oriented world at large.

Other women writers also contributed to an emerging feminine aesthetic during the early 1970s, although no other text reached the significance of Bachmann's *Todesarten* project. Among the established authors, Christa Wolf had continuously moved toward a stronger emphasis on women's issues, but it was only after the mid-1970s that she began publishing works that redefined literary feminism. Furthermore, a wide variety of texts, often only loosely connected with feminism in a strict sense, were produced by female authors, for instance, by Friederike Mayröcker (b. 1924) and Gabriele Wohmann (b. 1932). The Austrian Mayröcker is primarily known as a writer of experimental texts, both lyrical and prose, that unfold the ambivalent experience of emotions and events in complex linguistic arrangements. In the 1980s Mayröcker's texts reached an understanding of the destructive contradictions of social conditions and female identity of which Bachmann's prose stopped short; Mayröcker overcame the potential destruction by means of a linguistic precision that freed other potentials, such as playfulness and openness. Wohmann, who published her first story in 1957, treated the private realm with an ironic tone of desperation and aggressiveness that unveiled patterns of exploitation and non-communication, especially in gender relationships. In her analysis of society, however, Wohmann is one of the more conservative authors. In 1975, when most feminist literature voiced unfaltering criticism of traditional social institutions, Wohmann's novel *Schönes Gehege* (Beautiful Preserve) added a new tone of comfort and possible human understanding to her treatment of the private realm.

Some of the younger authors who had not established themselves during the early 1970s went undetected by the general reading public; for example, Brigitte Kronauer (b. 1940) had been publishing in magazines since the late 1960s but throughout the 1970s was only able to have her work published by a small press. Her breakthrough came in the 1980s. Other authors achieved almost immediate attention, such as the Austrian Elfriede Jelinek, who is known for her provocative texts, beginning with *wir sind lockvögel baby* (we are bait baby, 1970). The integration of elements from popular culture, such as horror stories and pornography, remained a characteristic of Jelinek's texts, which typically show women destroyed by brutal, exploitative relationships. Jelinek declared herself a Marxist feminist, pointing to a dilemma of the political analysis that underlies many feminist texts; a feminist would see the root of all evil in the way intimate relationships pit men against women, while a Marxist would see the root of all evil in class society that exploits people in general. The two positions can be reconciled, but the divergences between them explain why feminism does not offer a single answer but a range of responses. Jelinek typically describes intimate relationships that degrade women, placing the description in the context of class society.

*The mid-1970s:*
*a surge in feminist texts*

Building on these immediate precursors, feminist writing came into its own in the mid-1970s. On the side of human-touch literature, authors included Verena Stefan (b. 1947) with *Häutungen* (Shedding, 1975), Karin Struck (b. 1947) with *Die Mutter* (The Mother, 1975), and Brigitte Schwaiger (b. 1949 in Austria) with *Wie kommt das Salz ins Meer* (Who Put the Salt in the Sea, 1977); on the side of literary refractions, Christa Reinig (b. 1926) with *Entmannung* (Emasculation, 1976), Ingeborg Drewitz (1923–1986) with *Gestern war heute* (Yesterday was Today, 1978), the Austrian writer Barbara Frischmuth with her *Sternwieser* trilogy (1974–1979), and from East Germany Brigitte Reimann with *Franziska Linkerhand* (1974), Irmtraud Morgner (1933–1990) with *Leben und Abenteuer der Trobadora Beatriz* (Life and Adventures of the Troubadora Beatrice, 1974), and Christa Wolf with *Kindheitsmuster* (Patterns of Childhood, 1976) and *Kein Ort. Nirgends* (No Place on Earth, 1979).

*Authentic human touch*

Verena Stefan's *Häutungen* was a major breakthrough in its radically female subjectivity. Texts like Stefan's presented a definite dividing line between male and female worlds; ideally, no thought expressed in such a feminist text could be used to support the male world. *Häutungen* takes female sexuality as a point of departure: while heterosexual relationships are depicted as repressive and humiliating to women, female homosexuality emerges as a liberating force. Traditional roles are challenged; motherhood is questioned but accepted, although there is no place for fatherhood other than in a biological sense.

Brigitte Schwaiger's novel *Wie kommt das Salz ins Meer* derives its title from what seems to be an idyllic family outing but actually reveals that men not only have the power to humiliate women but also to force women to humiliate other women. The girl's father answers her question about the salt in the sea: "The fishermen take their boats out, Father says, and they have these little packages, and they scatter the salt carefully in the waves. Mother laughs and caresses me" [Die Fischer fahren hinaus, sagt Vater, und sie haben Pakete, und sie streuen das Salz vorsichtig in die Wellen. Mutter lacht und streichelt mich]. What might seem like a charming tale is experienced as a humiliation — made worse by the mother's participation in it — when the girl finally understands that it was not the truth.

Both novels have been heavily criticized. Stefan's *Häutungen* was faulted for reducing female identity to a few patterns. Criticism of *Wie kommt das Salz ins Meer* was even harsher: Schwaiger was accused of using worn clichés to build nothing but the pretense of a female consciousness — and of hiding that pretense behind the touchy-feely story of a failing marriage. One problem with Schwaiger's novel was that it read and sold well; thus, it could indeed be read as entertainment, curtailing any emancipatory potential it might have. Behind this specific instance lies the general question of whether the popular success of feminist works means that feminism is "selling out." This question has become more important as women's literature and movies moved from serious but entertaining to include comedy-style forms of presentation.

Karin Struck's *Die Mutter* was criticized along similar lines as being too full of reality. For example, the presentation of how giving birth in a modern clinic had become a dehumanizing industrial process was considered not to amount to more than stories by and about midwives. The novel had, however, been written with the ambition of defining female identity — and it was credited with having established the mother-daughter relationship as a topic in German literature. Struck goes beyond superficial realism by evoking motherhood in terms of mystical eroticism. The vision of the "Great Erotic Mother" [Große Erotische Mutter], to which Struck's protagonist, Nora, aspires, was at the center of the criticism: it was seen as both embarrassing and ridiculous — in short, as the kind of irrational female aesthetics that formulated unattainable expectations of salvation through women. It was a mirror image of the male vision of woman as Madonna, which placed women on such a high pedestal that no real woman could live up to the ideal and, therefore, justified the repression of women in this world while hiding the reality of exploitation from them by focusing them on another world.

Amid all this criticism, it is easy to lose track of the novel's achievement, which lies in the learning process that Struck describes. This process that mediates between daily experience and the utopian vision constitutes the core of the novel. As she experiences motherhood as a role that enslaves her, Nora realizes that her hatred of her children originated in her relationship with her own mother. She seeks to break out of this vicious circle of female education by developing a vision of her own femininity; at the same time, she knows that she has to confront the mother-daughter relationship on a realistic level. On this level, she understands that being born means "to break one's mother" [Die Mutter brechen]. Therefore, it is significant that *Die Mutter* ends on this note and with a kind of motto, which is in contrast to the vision of the Great Erotic Mother: "UNFRIENDLY IS / AND HARD TO WIN / SHE WHO IS WITHDRAWN, / WHOM I HAVE ESCAPED, / THE MOTHER" [UNFREUNDLICH IST / UND SCHWER ZU GEWINNEN / DIE VERSCHLOSSENE, / DER ICH ENTKOMMEN, / DIE MUTTER].

The assumption is that reality has to be refracted in specific ways to yield literary quality in a text. The presentation of reality in *Die Mutter* is refracted in two major ways: first, and most obviously, by the mystical eroticism, however problematic it may be; and second, by the learning process that uncovers the psychological history of repression in familial relationships. This interpretation implies a remarkable similarity between *Die Mutter* and *Gestern war heute*, by Ingeborg Drewitz, who was among the critics of Struck's novel. Drewitz's novel was critically acclaimed; still, it contains strong autobiographical elements that invite identification via human touch rather than by literary refraction. But two major refractions are effective in *Gestern war heute*. First, German political history provides the foil for the history of one family. The family portrait spans five generations but centers on three generations of women whose choices are determined by politics: Susanne experiences Nazi Germany as an adult; Gabriele grows up during that era; and Renate is born in postwar Germany. Second, experiences that Gabriele undergoes lead her to formulate a utopian vision of subjectivity and empathy: "I want to make a difference. Not to hurt, despise, hate anyone" [Ich möchte, daß es auf mich ankommt. Daß ich niemand verletze, niemand verachte, niemand hasse]. Gabriele asserts an ambiguous role of motherhood, one that enslaves the self but, at the same time, offers small amounts of freedom; instead of Struck's mystic eroticism, Drewitz's realistic mode evokes a hidden realm of motherhood that exists within patriarchy.

*Gestern war heute* presents motherhood as having a real and positive potential: liberation depends on mothers. Drewitz's novel is effective because it does not give way to grand visions or radical changes but takes the reader through the small steps of slow change, each of which is questioned, since its ramifications can be either positive or negative. Gabriele understands that women are always in danger of sliding back into the role of submissiveness, regardless of how radical their lifestyles might appear to be. This is the point of Drewitz's novel: the emancipatory potential of motherhood consists in each generation of women affirming and constantly reaffirming their freedom, while being able to build on the experiences of previous generations. Therefore, the present always encompasses the past, as Drewitz indicates in the novel's subtitle: *Hundert Jahre Gegenwart* (One Hundred Years of the Present).

***Authenticity and nonrealism***  Drewitz's *Gestern war heute* exemplifies a general development in women's literature. While in the mid-1970s feminist texts showed a preference for the grand vision of complete self-realization and independence in the private and public realms, from the late 1970s onward they displayed a preference for more modest visions of female potential, especially in the private realm. The grand vision could be voiced in a realistic mode, as in Stefan's *Häutungen*; between realistic and nonrealistic modes, as in Struck's *Die Mutter*; or in a nonrealistic mode that ranged from the grotesque, as in Reinig's *Entmannung*, to the mythical, such as in Morgner's *Trobadora Beatriz* and Frischmuth's *Sternwieser* trilogy. The nonrealistic was often embedded within the realistic, as was particularly displayed by Christa Wolf's gradual shift to using realism in the revision of myth.

Nevertheless, like the other generalization — the change in feminine writing from human-touch realism to literariness — the generalization concerning a shift in terms of the vision correctly describes a trend while it de-emphasizes the simultaneity of different models of feminine writing. For example, three early popular GDR novels examined the claim of female independence as it is scaled back to more modest proportions in confrontation with daily reality: *Franziska Linkerhand* (1974), by Brigitte Reimann; *Karen W.* (1974), by Gerti Tetzner (b. 1936); and *Kindheitsmuster*, by Christa Wolf.

In *Kindheitsmuster* the narrator and protagonist, Nelly Jordan, sets out to answer questions about her own childhood. The result of her exploration of the past in the light of the present is a novel with a complex texture that stands in the essayistic tradition. It mixes three temporal levels: first, the period 1972 to 1975 when the text is written down and Nelly usually addresses herself as "you" [du]; second, the time in 1971 when her family travels to Nelly's birthplace, which is now in Poland; and third, the 1930s and 1940s, when Nelly, now referred to as "she" [sie], was a child during the rise of nationalism and the Nazi regime. Her childhood patterns reveal the continuity of daily fascism.

Nelly experiences the difficulty of coming to terms with her own past as a "linguistic disturbance" [Sprachstörung], shifting between "I," "you," and "she" for self-reference, which makes it hard for her to define her identity — an increasingly important theme in Wolf's texts. An ideal precision that relates the structures of experience to the structures of narration, Nelly discovers, does not exist; thus a fourth level, reflection on writing itself, adds to the novel's complexity. Finding an appropriate language that expresses a female identity is a major challenge, because language itself was damaged by the violence of Nazism. Now language has a tentative quality, as though it were kept pending in order to correlate to a sense of pending change. Nelly observes: "Questions, statements or exclamations could not be used any more or not yet" [Frage-, Aussage- und Ausrufesatz waren nicht mehr oder noch nicht zu gebrauchen]. This also describes a crucial quality of the tone of Christa Wolf's own literary language, which is highly evocative yet restrained.

A change for the worse occurred with the increased restrictions on artistic expression in East Germany, which were signaled by Biermann's expatriation. Christa Wolf was among those who protested this decision, and her next narrative, *Kein Ort. Nirgends*, reflected her disillusionment with utopian ideas — the title translates as "no place," or utopia. Artistic individuals and outsiders have "no place" in a society whose basic modes of belonging are authoritarian. In the fictitious encounter of two real-life outsiders, Heinrich von Kleist (1777–1811) and Karoline von Günderode (1780–1806), the failure to carry through with life plans that are different from the norm is obvious: both Kleist and Günderode committed suicide. In *Kein Ort. Nirgends* Wolf shifted her interest from recent, personally experienced history to a historical narrative that focuses on the intersection of lines of development that could have changed the world, since, for a brief moment, history had the chance to strike a different balance between the genders and thus could have escaped the deterioration of intimate relationships into power struggles and, eventually, daily fascism.

*Kein Ort. Nirgends* is pivotal in the development of Wolf's literary productivity. Wolf's basic analysis of society as daily fascism was in place in her 1970s texts, as was the language with which she explored those moments that could have allowed a different balance between man and woman. Such a balance, however, is only alluded to in its failure in the encounter of Günderode and Kleist. The poetic archaeology of power in Wolf's later works shifted to the foundations of Western mythology to find a woman to fulfill the potential that Kleist sees in Günderode: "In this woman . . . her gender could find faith in itself" [In dieser Frau . . . könnte ihr Geschlecht zum Glauben an sich selber kommen].

Other women writers had already moved farther toward the nonrealistic mode. Christa Reinig continued writing in the grotesque mode in her 1976 novel, *Entmannung*. The diagnosis of reality is quite stark and disillusioned; women either submit to men, or they do not and are violated. Otto Kyra, playboy and surgeon, becomes confused in his sexual identity; claiming that he is trying to turn into a woman, he finally runs out of the house dressed in woman's clothes but without a razor, and soon his androgynous utopia is likely to give way to tragicomedy. The novel ends with a surrealistic chapter in which Gustav Gründgens, one of Germany's grand old theater men with unfortunate ties to the Nazis, stages Mozart's *Magic Flute* with himself in all roles except for the that of the narrator; Goethe has a conversation with Gründgens, who was known for his portrayal of Mephisto in *Faust*. At the end Otto's four women, all of whom he has survived, are also back. The fates of the women illustrate the novel's diagnosis: in a man's world, women are either victims or criminals or both. Yet, like Otto, men are equally unsure of their identities.

THE 1970S: NEW SENSITIVITY AND EMANCIPATION • 363

Myth — either as a reference to traditional mythologies or as a new story of the supernatural — played a crucial role in feminist texts. Mythology was generally important for GDR literature because, like the treatment of historical topics, it allowed social criticism in a form that circumvented censorship. The two main examples among feminist writers are Christa Wolf in the 1980s and 1990s and, in the 1970s and 1980s, Irmtraud Morgner with her planned trilogy, of which the first two novels were completed: *Leben und Abenteuer der Trobadora Beatriz nach Zeugnisssen ihrer Spielfrau Laura* (Life and Adventures of Troubadora Beatriz as Chronicled by Her Minstrel Laura) and *Amanda: Ein Hexenroman* (Amanda: A Witch's Novel, 1983).

*Trobadora Beatriz* demonstrates Morgner's approach to history as the history of everyday life that focuses primarily on women but reaches out to all of humanity. The past literally meets today's world in the novel's montage style, which combines documentary and fantasy elements ranging from interviews to magic and lists of curses. Beatriz de Dia, identified as the only woman troubadour, decides "to leave the medieval world of men" [die mittelalterliche Welt der Männer zu verlassen]. She arranges to sleep for 810 years, and in May 1968 — a little early because of street construction that is impeded by her Cinderella-style castle — Beatriz wakes up in the modern world of men, which is being challenged by the student revolt. But she cannot find true freedom in France, so Beatriz goes to East Germany, where women's liberation is supposed to have made great strides. The prudish atmosphere in the GDR, however, comes as a surprise to her. There she meets Laura, an educated woman, mother, and worker who becomes Beatriz's soul mate.

Beatriz's experiences in the modern world from 1968 to 1973 range from humiliating to tragicomic and point to the obstacles that need to be overcome. After leaving her castle, Beatriz hitches a ride, and the driver rapes her. Her personal disillusionment corresponds to the political disillusionment when Beatriz — hung over after celebrating the French leftist half-victory in 1973 with Laura and Laura's nonchauvinistic husband Benno — falls to her death while cleaning a window. But the novel does not end on this sad tone. Instead, there are two allusions to new forms of belonging in gender relationships. First is the story of Valeska, who transforms herself into a man in an attempt to escape her stifling relationship with Rudolf. But in her process of "becoming human" [Menschwerdung], Valeska and Rudolf realize that they truly love each other. Now Valeska changes back into a woman when she sleeps with Rudolf. Second, the last chapter consists of Beatriz's story that Benno repeats to Laura to console her over the death of Beatriz.

Morgner tried to hold on to the belief that life would become meaningless if hope in the future were lost. Therefore, women's struggle continues in the second novel, *Amanda*, in which Beatriz is brought back to life as a siren. Beatriz writes down — in self-referential criticism of the author of the previous novel — the true story of "Laura," who is separated into her two halves, the human Laura and the witch Amanda. The novel ends on New Year's Eve 1980, with Beatriz promising the speedy conclusion of her final report on the witches' victory over male domination. This report was planned as the core of the trilogy's third novel, but Morgner, too, was affected by the general disillusionment with utopian ideals. Yet she overcame her resignation in a fresh start that centered on the more private power of love. In the chapter "Der Schöne und das Tier" (The Beautiful Man and the Animal), published separately in 1991, Beatriz's love for Leander transforms her from a siren into a human being. As the novel's central new development, in another chapter a woman called Hero takes one of her ribs and makes it a man, Leander — as a "hope for the future" [Hoffnung auf die Zukunft]. The novel's many components, including Laura's battle with blindness and cancer, remained fragmentary and were published as *Das heroische Testament* (The Heroic Testament, 1998).

The creative use of myth to explore new options and other worlds in a playful fashion was not unique to GDR literature; the work of the Austrian Barbara Frischmuth is characterized by a combination of reality and fantasy that allows her to explore different ways of life and modes of belonging. Her novels *Die Mystifikationen der Sophie Silber* (The Mystifications of Sophie Silber, 1976), *Amy oder Die Metamorphose* (Amy or The Metamorphosis, 1978), and *Kai und die Liebe zu den Modellen* (Kai and the Love of Models, 1979) form a trilogy that culminates when one of the new forms of belonging is put to the test in the third novel.

Amaryllis Sternwieser, fairy and guardian spirit of Sophie Silber in the first novel, is transformed into the human being Amy Stern in the second novel, where she decides to become fully human by accepting her pregnancy. The third novel examines the challenges and opportunities of her existence as a single working mother. Like Johnson's *Jahrestage*, Frischmuth's novel focuses on the hope for change in the new generation; thus, the utopian element will unfold beyond the novel's confines in the adult life of Amy's son Kai. The models with which mother and son love to play provide a space for ever-changing experiments in role behavior that give Kai the flexibility he may need in the future. Therefore, it is crucial that Amy and Kai reach out to other like-minded people. With Kai's Turkish playmates, old people, and a young man, they transform their chance meeting in the park into a small utopian community that is united by a sense of love and whose playful seriousness is directed at reality.

*Literature about women by men*

The longstanding tradition of providing a literary counterworld to existing reality can serve functions from pure escape to a didactic approach that attempts to change reality. In the 1970s the emphasis was on the didactic aspect, and many feminist texts can be read as an offer of identification with an educational purpose: solidarity and overcoming inequality. These practical goals invite an examination of their feasibility, because any utopia that claims to have relevance has to establish some connection between its options and reality. The 1970s, however, did not provide a consensus as to whether such a utopia should be a new world of women or a world of new and truly equal gender relationships; and, even more confusingly, either utopian scenario left open the question of how to achieve the new world that was envisioned. Another question was: who are the people who can be expected to bring a utopian ideal to life? Male heroes had historically affirmed forms of male domination; therefore, they are not likely candidates for a feminist utopia. It seemed that women had to take the lead in any event, because men were just too entangled in the male-dominated world.

These considerations center around a serious literary issue involving texts that are evaluated in terms of authenticity: the credibility of the future that a text evokes. Putting women in a position where they are the only saviors of the world is suspect, because it imposes such immeasurably high expectations on them that they are destined to fail. Male authors who wrote about female protagonists were often accused of producing texts that were not credible; all these authors supposedly did in their plots was to wait until they were saved by women. An overburdening of women is, indeed, a fatal flaw in the visionary potential of a text. It is, in fact, the flaw that critics saw in Karin Struck's utopia of the Great Erotic Mother in *Die Mutter*. Moreover, the tables can be turned, since some women writers also placed immeasurably high expectations on male characters. For example, Brigitte Schwaiger's *Lange Abwesenheit* (Long Absence, 1980) not only exposes the father as a petty tyrant but as the standard by which the narrator defines her identity.

If authenticity and credibility are important criteria, those literary utopias that acknowledge a need to develop new forms of belonging between men and women have a fair amount of credibility. This does not rule out utopias that center on women who are in charge of arriving at new forms of belonging. In the same sense, however, it no longer seemed sufficient for utopias simply to create awareness that a counterworld was possible. If power was the real issue, true partnerships needed to be examined or redefined as the place in which power begins to accumulate and, at the same time, where it is possible to hold power in check.

The phenomenon of male authors' participating in such an endeavor that might be judged of specific interest to female authors shows how important thinking beyond the stereotypes of masculinity and femininity had become in the 1970s: it was so important that it influenced major works by the three leading male novelists during that decade. While Günter Grass juxtaposed historical options in *Der Butt* (The Flounder, 1977), Heinrich Böll and Uwe Johnson explored new possibilities. Böll wrote *Gruppenbild mit Dame* (Group Portrait with Lady, 1971), and Johnson began his tetralogy *Jahrestage*, one of the crucial texts of post-1945 German literature.

Grass's novel combines diverse elements, ranging from the grotesque to the theoretical, with a comprehensive vision of history that is presented as a history of love and cooking. This fictitious history spans four millennia from matriarchy to patriarchy. Organized into nine chapters, called "months" [Monate], the novel focuses on the lives of nine female cooks in nine historical eras, from Neolithic times to Gdansk in the 1970s. The novel's point of departure is the Grimms' fairy tale "The Fisherman and His Wife," in which the flounder grants the fisherman several wishes. In Grass's novel the Flounder is a being of truly mythical dimensions but also the embodiment of rationality — as well as the adviser of the men, especially the male narrator, whose awareness remains identical throughout the millennia.

The novel paints a superficially happy picture of the Stone Age, when matriarchal rule treated men like children. Stone-Age men are happy for a simple reason: they are suppressed, because the women keep them away from knowledge, especially knowledge of the connection between sex and procreation. Advised by the Flounder, the men finally gain this knowledge, but their happiness also disappears. Rationality, the means by which the men achieved power, becomes repressive, because the men remain focused on power as an end in its own right; thus, love itself degenerates into an instrument with which to suppress women. In the end, when the novel has reached the present, the failure of patriarchy to improve the world has become evident. But neither patriarchy nor, in Grass's analysis, matriarchy allow an existence based on equality and without repression. The narrator's reference to the novel as a kind of dream invites the reader to look for new patterns of belonging beyond those that are historically available.

Böll's aesthetics of humaneness aimed at exploring new ways of belonging, and his *Gruppenbild mit Dame* has been considered a summation of his work in this respect. In the novel, Böll's fictionalized alter ego — the narrator, abbreviated as "Verf." (for *Verfasser*) in the third-person narrative — reconstructs the biography of middle-aged Leni, criticizes political developments from historical Nazism to new xenophobia, and depicts a small utopian community that has its focal point in Leni. Like many of Böll's characters, she lives at the fringes of society. In contrast to Hans in *Ansichten eines Clowns*, she — representing spontaneity and sensuality — finds fulfillment in love; and like the father and son in *Ende einer Dienstfahrt*, she finds protection in solidarity with like-minded people when her livelihood is threatened as her own relatives try to get her evicted from her apartment. Ironically, the radical rejection of profitability with which Leni sublets at below-market rates appears "inhuman" to her relatives, because it "violates equal opportunity" [Chancengleichheit verletzt]. But it makes possible a solidarity of haves and have-nots: the latter — mostly Leni's tenants and guest workers — block the street with their garbage trucks to delay Leni's eviction long enough for the former to put up for Leni the money that she needs to keep her apartment.

The limits of humanity and solidarity were tested as the Federal Republic of Germany tried to cope with the threat posed by the terrorism of the RAF. Böll became embroiled in the political battle when he pleaded that human concern had to be extended even to a terrorist instead of taking political measures that would threaten to turn the democracy into a police state. The controversy increased after Böll published a satire as his response to attacks on his integrity in the yellow press. *Die verlorene Ehre der Katharina Blum oder: Wie Gewalt entstehen und wohin sie führen kann* (The Lost Honor of Katharina Blum or: How Violence Can Be Created and Where It Can Lead, 1974) is a thought experiment that takes as its premise a witch hunt created by the media and analyzes how, as a result, even fundamentally decent people can snap and become violent. The satire is a portrayal, not a justification, of Katharina's shooting of a reporter — which exposes the failure of West German politics.

*Uwe Johnson's*
**Jahrestage**
Published in quick succession in 1970, 1971, and 1973, the first three volumes of *Jahrestage* established the work as Johnson's magnum opus. After a ten-year interruption, the final volume was published in 1983, a year before Johnson's death. The tetralogy embraces German history within an extended present and branches out politically and psychologically. Politically, *Jahrestage* locates the narration's present action in New York City, thus adding an international dimension to German issues, such as the country's division. Psychologically, the novel centers on the pedagogical dialogue between a single mother and her daughter, who turns eleven in the course of the one-year period that the novel chronicles. The mother is Gesine Cresspahl of *Mutmassungen über Jakob*, whose job has taken her to New York, where she is raising her and Jakob's daughter, Marie. Although Marie has made New York her home, she is interested in her German past. Therefore,

she listens carefully when her mother talks about her memories and their family history, which gives Gesine the chance to try not only to achieve clarity about her own identity but also to ensure that Marie develops her identity by becoming connected with her own personal and her country's political past.

The mother-daughter dialogue constitutes the most important utopian element of the novel. While the dialogue is a pedagogical situation, with one party giving information and the other receiving it, the utopia consists in the fact that two people are talking with each other in an atmosphere that is free of repression and that allows them to treat each other, even in the pedagogical situation, as equals. In addition to the mother-daughter dialogue, the novel encompasses Gesine's monologues and real and imaginary dialogues with other people. Moreover, the novel narrates the mother and daughter's daily life in New York, and it documents life in the United States in the 1960s in a more objective way by including excerpts from and summaries of items from Gesine's daily reading of the *New York Times*. Another apparently objective element is the narrative project of *Jahrestage* itself. It is construed as the documentation of the life of Gesine and her daughter on a day-by-day basis over the period of one year from August 20, 1967, to August 20, 1968 — hence the subtitle, *Aus dem Leben von Gesine Cresspahl* (From the Life of Gesine Cresspahl), and the literal meaning of the German title: Days of a Year. This narrative construction, however, soon begins to oscillate between subjectivity and objectivity.

First, the mother-daughter dialogue is a female project, yet it is told by a male author. On the one hand, the mother engages in memory work with the daughter to establish a feminine identity that will ensure the daughter's future existence as an adult. On the other hand, underneath the female dialogue lies a fixation on male identities. For example, Gesine reconstructs her family history as the story of her father's life, in which the positive characters are mostly men. In a similar way, Marie appears particularly vulnerable to father figures because she is growing up without a father. Still, it may be argued that the female project undertaken by Gesine and Marie necessitates a fatherless condition to prepare Marie for a utopian fatherless society in the sense of relationships among equals.

Second, the relationship of female protagonist and male author becomes a dynamic factor as part of the fiction. In addition to details of Johnson's actual two-year stay in New York that correspond to Gesine's fictional life, there is an actual interaction between the real/idealized author and his fictitious protagonist. The report of her life is presented as the fulfillment of a contractual agreement between Johnson and Gesine; Johnson insisted on this construct in lectures and interviews. This, however, complicates the function of the narrator. In an often-quoted passage, a brief fictional encounter between Johnson and Gesine, the issue of narratorship is addressed (as is typical in imaginary dialogues, in italics): "*Now, who's telling this story, Gesine. / We both are. Surely, you can hear that, Johnson*" [*Wer erzählt hier eigentlich, Gesine. / Wir beide. Das hörst du doch, Johnson*]. At this point an overlapping of Modernist and postmodernist approaches becomes obvious. The complexity of empirical reality is approached in terms of the primary Modernist project: to make sense of the one world. In contrast, the narrative worlds are plural, and the question of who is telling the story leads to the primary question of postmodernism: which world is this? There is one narrative world in which Johnson invented Gesine; another one, in which she imagined Johnson, is conceivable. Yet a third one seems to be privileged by the narration itself: it is a world in which Johnson and Gesine exist independently of each other, regardless of who imagined whom.

Third, the nonrealistic oscillation between protagonist and author emerges as the most visible aspect of the novel's general narrative characteristic: multiple overlaid identities. This characteristic is at the core of Johnson's major theme: the boundary conditions of identity. In the oscillation of conflicting truths in a plurality of possible narrative worlds, *Jahrestage* appears as an ideal biography — most likely Johnson's. In this reading of the novel Gesine would be Johnson's projection and a reflection of his own biography; likewise, Marie could be Gesine's projection as the child she always wanted to be. Considering Jakob's elusiveness, Gesine's relationship with Jakob, if not Jakob himself, could be Gesine's projection — or Gesine's speculations, a radical extension of the original *Mutmassungen über Jakob*. This interpretation, finally, would locate everything in Johnson's narrative consciousness.

The novel's considerable formal achievement rests in the way it combines a realistic mode and a nonrealistic abstraction of narrative categories. While the traditional terms *author*, *narrator*, and *character* apply to the novel's surface, the oscillation of mutual projections and reflections of author, narrator(s), and characters radicalizes the Modernist tradition of the lyrical novel and is best described in terms of more-abstract levels of consciousness. *Thematic subjectivity* denotes the common thematic focus of the characters — the boundary conditions of identity in *Jahrestage*. Although the main characters appear to be real people, the novel's oscillation assigns them multiple overlaid identities. Since the construct of the narrative situation also undermines the narrator's identity, the term *narrative consciousness* refers to what makes storytelling possible. Depending on one's interpretation, the narrative consciousness of *Jahrestage* is either centralized into the traditional narrator (Johnson's persona) or plural (in the fictitious collaboration of Johnson and Gesine).

Any final assessment of the novel has to address Johnson's vision of history. Above all, the utopia of the repressionless dialogue is ambiguous. The dialogue has laid the foundations of historical and psychological connectedness, but its test comes when the mother-daughter symbiosis gives way to independence and when new situations are confronted. Marie still has to be told that D. E., whom she adores and whom Gesine had planned to marry, has been killed in an accident. The news of the Soviet invasion of Czechoslovakia on August 20, 1968 — the last day chronicled in the novel — has not yet reached Gesine, who has stopped over in Copenhagen with Marie en route to Czechoslovakia on a business trip that she now will not be able to conclude. These challenges are not resolved within the novel, yet they are not glossed over, either; therefore, they enter yet another oscillation, one that is ultimately tied to reality itself: disorientation and reorientation. It is in this realistic oscillation that Marie, whether or not she is a realistic representation of a young girl, embodies the future in all its ambivalence. Marie's is a normal city childhood. She has learned how to behave in potentially dangerous situations and sets out to explore subway routes on her own. Like all big cities, however, New York is ambivalent. On the one hand, Marie easily finds orientation in New York; on the other hand, the threat of disorientation is always close at hand.

This ambiguity enters into determining whether the vision of history evoked in *Jahrestage* is positive or negative. In the last scene, at the beach in Denmark, the old teacher quotes to Gesine Jakob's belief that "history is a draft" [Geschichte ist ein Entwurf]. In response Gesine hands a 1875-page manuscript to the old man: the novel *Jahrestage*, which is, indeed, one draft version of history. The self-reference is nonrealistic, because the manuscript, of course, contains the scene at the beach, which evokes the beginnings and endings of the preceding three volumes of the tetralogy, all varying similar imagery of childhood and water. Water, ambiguously life-giving and life-threatening, echoes the oscillation of orientation and reorientation, and the waves at the beach suggest an eternal recurrence. The tone of melancholy that permeates the novel and the importance of political issues, such as the German Nazi legacy, the East-West division, and American conflicts concerning Vietnam and racial tensions, point to history being not just a draft but also a task.

The vision of history as history from below, as family history embedded in world history, is not bleak because Gesine, like Thomas Mann's Joseph, becomes aware of imitating patterns that were established by her ancestors and "the social contract that was forced upon them" [die ihnen aufgenötigte Verabredung der Gesellschaft]. The simple fact of such awareness changes the patterns. In the end *Jahrestage* does not present a utopia as a solution, but it offers in form and content a vision of history as draft, task, and dialogue — something that is not grandiose but quite realistic and positive, after all.

*Family history as political history*    The autobiographical and political examination of the self and its family background hit home in a profound way: a generation of young writers had to face the fact that their family history was a history of their families' participation in Nazism. The guilt of their parents' generation was no longer experienced abstractly but quite literally, because their fathers were those who committed crimes against humanity. Books with this content — the *Vaterbücher* (father books) — were a literary phenomenon of the late 1970s and early 1980s.

*Die Reise* (The Trip, 1977), by Bernward Vesper (1938–1971), generated the greatest public attention of the father books with 40,000 copies sold within the first year and over 100,000 in five years. Vesper chronicles his path from a repressed childhood to his leftist activism and, especially after the failure of the protest movement in 1968, his increasing involvement with drugs; however, he did not follow the path into terrorism taken by Gudrun Ensslin, with whom he had a son. Describing the novel in a letter of September 1969, Vesper explained the montage character that combines three different levels: first, "the report of the real trip" [Der Bericht von der realen Reise] from Dubrovnik in Yugoslavia to Tübingen; second, "the so-called 'trips'" [die sogenannten "Trips"] that digress from the real trip and include details of the "subtle fascism" [subtilen Faschismus] that had dominated Vesper's biography, especially under the influence of his father, the Nazi writer Will Vesper. The remembrance reveals a childhood that, in contrast to its idyllic rural setting, was experienced by the author as a living hell. Third is the level of "current perception" [momentane Wahrnehmung] that reinforces the other two levels.

Identifying the book as a "novelistic essay" [Romanessay] rather than as an autobiography, the subtitle points to the work's literary construction and intended aesthetic unity as a fourth level in the face of a severe personal crisis of orientation. This designation puts Vesper's text in the tradition of the Modernist novel, whose divergent elements and fragmentation aim at authenticity. Part of that authenticity also consists in self-exploration during drug-induced trips and the author's radical approach of a hatred that did not stop at his own self: "Writing: Harakiri, I'm ripping my guts out" [Schreiben: Harakiri, ich ziehe meine Gedärme heraus]. His novel is more complex and longer than other father books, in part because it expresses a radical crisis that led to Vesper's real-life suicide.

These textual and biographical elements set *Die Reise* apart from other father books that seem, at least for some critics, to mistake hypochondriacal self-love, exaggerated self-pity, and whiny sensitiveness for genuine sensitivity. These are not aesthetic categories but rather psychological and emotional judgments of a conflict that fuses private and political realms in an unprecedented manner, exceeding the literary and abstract conflict between father and son as portrayed in Expressionism. The conflict of the 1970s was political and concrete: the former, and now perhaps clandestine, Nazis were more than political enemies; they were the young authors' fathers.

A difference in approaching this issue distinguishes two early father books from each other: *Vaterspuren* (Traces of My Father, 1979), by Sigfrid Gauch (b. 1945), and *Suchbild: Über meinen Vater* (Searching Image: About My Father, 1980), by Christoph Meckel (b. 1935). While Gauch abhors his father's Nazi past and postwar beliefs, he also sees the difference between the good and the bad father. Therefore, Gauch is able to reject his father's politics and, at the same time, to love his father as an individual. This result is quite an exception among the father books, in which typically the father himself has to be rejected in order for the son to be able to resist the repressive politics. Meckel's *Suchbild* is prototypical of the kind of father book that metaphorically kills the father. The father's love is judged by the fact that it makes the protest of the young generation more difficult. Hatred, quite understandable at its real-life source, was the general attitude in the father books.

The father books of the late 1970s and early 1980s broke new ground because confronting one's parents, especially fathers in a male-dominated society, was a violation of social taboos. They radically challenged the male dominance of society and, going beyond the father/son conflict, attempted to proclaim a world that was "fatherless" in the sense of abandoning authoritarian, hierarchical social structures. This message fit perfectly into the intellectual climate of the failed student protests of 1968, which gave way to the wave of New Sensitivity that refocused on the private aspects of politics. Father books, predominantly by male but also by female authors, such as Brigitte Schwaiger's *Lange Abwesenheit*, were felt as liberating despite their typical emotional one-sidedness and occasional literary simplicity.

Still, the father books were not the only way in which family relationships were explored in the New Sensitivity: the role of the mother was also examined by male and female authors. Drewitz's *Gestern war heute* and Struck's *Die Mutter* can be seen as such "mother books" in the sense that they represent the conflict with the internalized image of the mother. Typically, the mothers are not perpetrators; instead, they are victims. Consequently, the center of attention is the mother's submission to "daily fascism" rather than the father's active participation in Nazism. Significant mother books include *Wunschloses Unglück* (Perfect Unhappiness, 1972), by Peter Handke, and the short novel *Ausflug mit der Mutter* (Excursion with the Mother, 1976), by Gabriele Wohmann. The latter focuses on the changes that take place after the father's death by emphasizing the daughter's difficulties with what she perceives as her mother's adjusting too easily to being a widow; the novel follows the daughter's learning process until she is finally able to calmly say about her mother: "Yes you are a widow" [Ja du bist eine Witwe].

Similar to father books, which usually not only addressed the dead father but were also often written as a response to the father's death, the narrative motivation of Handke's *Wunschloses Unglück* is the mother's suicide by an overdose of sleeping pills — thus ending in silence a life during which the mother had been condemned to silence. Death reveals a lifetime of repression that had left her no alternatives: "Still her dead body seemed to me dreadfully forsaken and in need of love" [Noch der tote Körper kam mir entsetzlich verlassen und liebebedürftig vor]. This sentence reveals both a close connection between son and mother and a woman's story that is no story. In Handke's view, people in a fragmented and other-directed world do not have a chance to have lives that constitute a story. The mother's suicide remains a sign of desperation that gives no closure. It puts an end to the chance of communication that is emotionally important to the son. The narrative consequence is that the son cannot tell the complete story; the last sentence documents this inability: "Later I will write about all of this more exactly" [Später werde ich über das alles Genaueres schreiben].

*Exploring individual subjectivity*    In the 1970s literature placed great importance on exploring individual subjectivity by reflecting possible ways for the self either to develop into a truly female consciousness in feminist literature or to free itself, as a male subjectivity, from the rule of the father in the father books. Such self-exploration found additional forms of expression within the movement of New Subjectivity, for example, in Nicolas Born's *Die erdabwandte Seite der Geschichte* (The Dark Side of History, 1976) and Peter Handke's *Der kurze Brief zum langen Abschied* (Short Letter, Long Farewell, 1972). Other explorations went beyond the confines of a literary movement as the continuation of great individual narrative projects by some of German-language literature's outsiders, including Thomas Bernhard's *Das Kalkwerk* (The Lime Works, 1970), Arno Schmidt's *Zettels Traum* (Bottom's Dream, 1970), Peter Weiss's *Ästhetik des Widerstands* (Aesthetics of Resistance, 1975–1981), and Hubert Fichte's *roman fleuve*, a huge narrative project that built on his earlier novels. Schmidt and Weiss also represented the summation of their creative visions.

Born's *Die erdabwandte Seite der Geschichte* not only presented the author's radical departure from the Cologne School of Realism but was also welcomed as the most radical novel of New Sensitivity. While it unfolds against the background of the student movement — a topic shared with *Heißer Sommer* (Hot Summer, 1974), by Uwe Timm (b. 1940); *Lenz* (1975), by Peter Schneider (b. 1940); and Vesper's *Die Reise* — Born's novel is a love story that chronicles, step by step, the failures of several relationships. Its achievement lies in prevailing despite failure; the search for true forms of narcissist self-fulfillment continues, despite the fact that the search is like groping in the dark — hence the novel's title.

Handke's *Der kurze Brief zum langen Abschied* is a combination of the American road novel with the German tradition of the Bildungsroman. The road motif enters into the plot as the story of a separation. It begins in New York when the narrator receives the short letter that his wife, Judith, has left him. The narrator does not find Judith until he reaches the West Coast, a journey as an education that brings him in touch with reality. The narrator and his wife visit the film director John Ford, to whom they tell their story. Handke also transposed the prototypical Bildungsroman, Goethe's *Wilhelm Meisters Lehrjahre*, into the 1970s in his script *Falsche Bewegung* (Wrong Move, 1975) for the 1974 movie by Wim Wenders (b. 1945), in which the classical ideal of a complete human being remained only as a vague goal. *Der kurze Brief* marked Handke's shift from questions of language and knowledge toward those of existence, suggesting that merely subjective perception should lead to understanding.

*Das Kalkwerk* — the title refers to the abandoned lime works in whose isolation the protagonist lives — exhibits Bernhard's major autobiographically based themes of emotional coldness: death, decay, isolation, and desperation. Bernhard's work is described as negative, exaggerated, comical, moral, or ambiguously political in the love-hate relationship between author and his native Austria. The work's artistic quality is generally acknowledged, because the themes find their formal correspondences. Decay and desperation are reflected in an overflowing and elliptical syntax. Isolation is expressed in the reduction of the narrator's function, which consists, in *Das Kalkwerk*, in putting together two complementary and at times contradictory reports about Konrad's murder of his wife, as well as in focusing on Konrad's monomaniacal obsession with his unfinished study on human hearing. Konrad is unable to finish it because of his fear of committing his thoughts to the rigidity of written language; he prefers effectively to end his own life by killing his wife.

Schmidt's *Zettels Traum* ("Zettel" is a pun on the German name for Bottom in Shakespeare's *Midsummer Night's Dream*, on the German word for "note card," and on the novel's term for its pages) caused a stir when it was published in 1970 because of its complexity. The plot, however, unfolds in a straightforward way, revolving around the visit that a married couple, Paul and Wilma Jacobi, and their sixteen-year-old daughter Franziska, pay to their friend, the writer Daniel Pagenstecher (the name is a pun on the bookish nature of the narrator). The couple seeks the writer's advice on their project of translating Edgar Allan Poe's works, and a daylong session of discussions and interactions ensues. Finally, after the aging Pagenstecher resists his attraction to Franziska, the couple and daughter leave. The text's complexity originates in its presentation and its digressive character. Each of the encounter's three aspects — material concerning Poe, the visit itself, and associations and speculations by and about the characters — is arranged in a separate column, usually with all three columns present on every double-letter-sized page of the voluminous novel, which is reproduced in a facsimile of the typescript, including the author's handwritten changes.

The novel applies Schmidt's etym theory, a whimsical type of etymology that assumes that words and phrases exhibit influences emanating from the unconscious; Schmidt locates these influences primarily in sexuality. The individual etyms begin with playful, almost traditional puns, such as the equation of *pen* with *penis*. The text's unusual orthography reveals the underlying influences by spelling the word *fixation* as "fucksation" [Ficksation], and the punctuation includes multilingual etym-equations, such as "Erde=earth=arse." Through an analysis of Poe's style, Pagenstecher develops an understanding of Poe's psyche as suffering from tremendous sexual repression, including impotence and voyeurism. The analysis is less scientific than playful and arbitrary; therefore, it also reflects the self-perception of an aging Pagenstecher and, by implication, of the real-life author and recluse, Arno Schmidt.

*Ästhetik des Widerstands* — whose three volumes were published in 1975, 1978, and 1981, the year before Weiss's death — combines the author's autobiography, biographical details of many of his contemporaries, and an encyclopedic, yet unorthodox, Marxist aesthetic into an individual's ideal biography of the years from 1937 to 1945. In contrast to other ideal biographies, such as Uwe Johnson's *Jahrestage* and Christa Wolf's *Kassandra*, discursive-essayistic and self-reflexive elements add a further dimension to Weiss's draft version of history as pushing the limits of the genre "novel." Yet, like these other works, Weiss's novel emphasizes the condition of political homelessness that requires resistance as a condition for survival and social progress. He defines an aesthetics of resistance, which is focused on the basic theme: "Where, at what times have people overcome apparently insurmountable odds?" [Wo, zu welchen Zeiten haben sich Menschen gegen anscheinend unübersteigbare Widerstände hinweggesetzt?].

This theme underlies the treatment of the final years of the Nazi regime in the face of the increasingly hopeless condition of political op-

376 • AFTER 1945: ELEMENTS OF POSTMODERNISM

position in Nazi Germany. The ending of *Ästhetik des Widerstands* shifts to the subjunctive mood when the narrator speculates about the time after the war: "A utopian vision would be necessary" [Die Utopie würde notwendig sein]; and his melancholy fantasy of how he would meet his childhood friends again lets the last volume end where the first one began: in the Berlin museum, under the lion of the altar of Zeus at Pergamon. By integrating excursions on art, Weiss makes his vision of true and free humanity merge with the history of actual resistance in all its hopes and infighting in a book that has been hailed as one of the most exciting, yet also saddest, works of the 1970s.

*The beginnings of Hubert Fichte's* **roman fleuve** In addition to a strong sense of individuality that Hubert Fichte shared with other authors, he understood himself as an embodiment of marginality in familial, political, and sexual terms: he was fatherless, half-Jewish, and bisexual. These biographical coordinates entered into a massive multicultural literary work that constituted one coherent body, a *roman fleuve*, which combined the subjective and the objective in theme and approach: love and research, myth and reason. Fichte's aim was to write a history of homosexuality in the twentieth century: *Die Geschichte der Empfindsamkeit* (History of Sensitivity), as he titled his ambitious epic project that was intended to encompass nineteen volumes. At the time of his death, Fichte had finished only about half of the novels. They were published, posthumously, together with miscellaneous texts and fragments, in seventeen volumes from 1987 to 1993, with the exception of *Die Zweite Schuld* (The Second Guilt), which Fichte had requested remain unpublished until 2006. His early novels (first published in the second half of the 1960s and republished in the 1970s) already belonged thematically to this project; it was also in these novels that he developed his distinctive style, whose fundamental plurality has clear affinities to postmodernism in terms of unstable identities of human individuality and of possible worlds.

From the opening passage of *Die Palette* (Palette's, 1968, the title is the name of a real-life bar in Hamburg that attracted a diverse clientele from subcultural and alternative groups) onward, all space seems connected by some hidden meaning, while Jäcki, the protagonist and Fichte's alter ego, turns out to be unconnected and thus is searching for the connectedness he believes he can achieve by discovering the origins of his individual life and of humanity in general. The space where he gets closer to those origins is a subcultural one, which has been shunned by official Western culture, although it is always present as a subtext. In *Palette* German homosexual subculture emerges quite bluntly as the novel's main text. Fichte is credited with abolishing the taboo of homosexuality — which he explores in terms of androgyny — in German literature.

Spatial connectedness suggests social and psychological connectedness for Fichte. Yet the novel's linguistic self-reflexivity destabilizes the invoked spatial connectedness. Identities blend into a sense of subjectivity: the real author equals the fictionalized author who equals the narrator who in turn equals the people in Palette's. In this dialectic of absence and presence, language and space become identical: both can liberate or enslave. "Everything's words. / Everything's correct. / Palette's is everything: Sesimbra and Palette's. / They're all my words" [Alles Wörter. / Alles stimmt. / Die Palette ist alles: Sesimbra und die Palette. / Alles sind meine Wörter].

Fichte encoded life into literature, thus transcending the boundaries of fact and fiction. He continued exploring such flexible topology of ethnopoetic studies of syncretism, of which the visits to Palette's and its patrons were just the beginning. Already in *Palette* he challenged the reader with a dynamics of evolving worlds, which places the postmodern question "Which world is this" in the foreground. In addition to facts — such as the connection of violence with sexuality, which is linked to fascism — Fichte presents fictions of better worlds, such as a legend of self-help, although it soon turns out to be wishful thinking. The attempts to cope with the real world are defined by the use of sexuality; however, while androgyny possesses the potential for liberation, it not only threatens mainstream society but also threatens Jäcki in his sexual identity. Jäcki experiences himself as doubled, as though living in two worlds. This condition embodies, at the same time, the threat of confusion and the possibility of liberation.

Narratively, the dynamics of confusion and liberation result in innovative prose that was praised by Helmut Heissenbüttel, whose work displays a stylistic affinity to Fichte's. The three distinct modes in which fact and fiction are combined in Fichte's texts contribute to an unmistakable quality, whose progressive plurality is underscored by the typographical arrangement in predominantly short paragraphs or even lines consisting of a few words — giving some passages of the text the physical appearance of a poem.

First, in the realistic mode, alternatives coexist within the real world so that the need to choose is clear; formally, this is often expressed by transitional elements, such as the conjunction "or" [oder]. For example, when Jäcki and a homosexual friend come to pick up Sänti at his parents' place, Sänti's father has several possible responses, but most likely he will not use all of them. The text supplies a list of alternatives from which Sänti's father could choose either a question "or one of the orders: / — Don't stay away that long! / You aren't going to leave here anymore!" [Oder einer der Befehle: / — Bleib nicht so lange weg! / — Du kommst mir nicht mehr weg!].

Second, in the mode that contrasts realistic and nonrealistic options, the alternatives are not consistent with the real world and are marked by the subjunctive mood as wishful thinking, such as Jäcki's utopian speculations about self-help and the progress of love among human beings.

Third, the mode of a radical plurality suggests that the real world has become insubstantial and is no longer privileged with regard to other possible worlds. Formally, real and alternative worlds are treated alike. Thematic subjectivity — the plural identity of author, narrator, and other characters — is an example of this mode. As traditional individuality was dissipated and language was celebrated as creating realities, Fichte began probing into deeper layers of existence that led him into the realm of myth — an approach that he openly embraced in *Versuch über die Pubertät* (Essay on Puberty, 1974). Fichte was aware of the ambivalence of myth and magic; his main interest, however, was in syncretic Third-World Afro-(Latin)American cultures, whose plurality connected him to the plurality of his own life. Thus, his interest in myth became part of a rational project that defined Fichte's epic and ethnopoetic project: finding the origins of his own individuality and those of humanity.

In terms of literary form, *Versuch über die Pubertät* is a radicalization of Fichte's earlier experiments. Complexity theory can be used to describe the narrative structure of the novel, which displays the pattern of locally unpredictable, but globally stable, phenomena. Passages reflecting the bisexual narrator's experiences — with German subculture and Third-World syncretic cultures as thematic attractors — appear to be randomly intertwined; a principle of order, however, exists at a higher level. The novel's first, third, and fifth parts unpredictably repeat material from each other: it is as though the narrative were looping around itself. The second and fourth parts, like narrative islands of intermittent orderliness in the midst of the novel's chaos, present sample biographies of homosexuals.

## The State of the Individual and the Nation in Drama

*From historicity to the end of history in the West*  West German theater of the 1970s was not characterized by major innovations, and New Sensitivity was less visible in drama than in the other genres. Franz Xaver Kroetz, Martin Sperr, and Rainer Werner Fassbinder continued in the tradition of the new *Volksstück*, which they had helped revive in the second half of the 1960s. Other playwrights, including Tankred Dorst, Dieter Forte (b. 1935), and Gerlind Reinshagen (b. 1926), worked on their individual theatrical concepts. The plays by Botho Strauß, however, showed certain New Sensitive qualities, and so did those by Thomas Bernhard — even though Bernhard's texts contained an aggressive and often monstrous quality of individuality that contrasted with the softness of New Sensitivity. Both Bernhard and Strauß had established themselves as leading playwrights in the West by the end of the 1970s.

In the early 1970s, Kroetz emerged as the most representative of the theatrical new *Volksstück* tradition and as one of the most often performed playwrights in general. Sperr's work was slowed down by an accident in 1972, and Fassbinder had turned to the cinema, providing greater international visibility for the social criticism of the new *Volksstück* by including theatrical elements in his tremendous production of more than thirty motion pictures during the 1970s alone. Kroetz's early plays documented the helpless and repressed individual as a victim of a loveless and prejudiced society in the sense of Horváth's and Fleißer's descriptive realism. His first phase ended with plays such as *Stallerhof* (The Staller Farm, 1971); the beginning of the second phase coincided with Kroetz's membership in the DKP (West German Communist Party). He added an activist element to his plays' realism, including a different use of language, which now went beyond imitation of dialect and became the vehicle with which to voice new perspectives. In retrospect, Kroetz regarded as successful those of his plays that derived such a new perspective not from theory but from social experience. Despite some rhetoric by the characters in the plays, the new perspective did not mean a grand vision but much more mundane decisions, such as accepting a pregnancy in *Oberösterreich* (Upper Austria, 1972) or becoming politically active in *Mensch Meier* (Man Meier, 1978).

After early plays in the absurdist and grotesque tradition, Tankred Dorst found his way to political revue in montage form in his 1968 play *Toller*, in which he combined various elements ranging from scenes of plays by Toller to documentary material. This change embedded individual biography within world history. As a result, during the 1970s Dorst's main focus was on writing a realistic chronicle of a family history extending over several independent texts that spanned from the 1920s to the 1960s. Dorst wrote some of these texts in prose — *Dorothea Merz* (1976), coauthored with Ursula Ehler (b. 1940), shows the dissolution of a marriage at the time of the Nazis taking power — and others for the theater. The comedy *Auf dem Chimborazo* (On Top of the Chimborazo, 1974, revised 1977), coauthored with Ehler, also centers on the character Dorothea Merz. Now widowed, Dorothea plans to light a fire on top of a mountain near the border with the GDR as a sign of belonging, but the plan fails because conflicts within the family erupt.

Bernhard's plays, such as *Ein Fest für Boris* (A Feast for Boris, 1970) and *Der Präsident* (The President, 1975), exhibit the same attitude of hatred as his prose. Fundamentally monologic, they demonstrate the impossibility of communication; they present the opportunity for a self-centered individual to voice his monomaniacal obsessions, which can be both oppressive and comical. Interaction that has the semblance of dialogue often takes place between minor characters, who provide key-words for the monomaniacal individual.

The theater of Botho Strauß, despite similarities with New Sensitivity, went beyond the limiting search for an individual subjectivity; rather, the general linguistic brilliance of his plays unmasks literature as an autonomous system that creates multiple relationships within itself but only indirectly to reality. Understanding history as reduced to repeating old patterns, Strauß was one of those writers who assumed the end of history — a meaningless and chaotic world in which literature can no longer tell a linear plot but evokes an uncertain connection of fragmentary plot elements. Integrating such a lack of plot cohesion and uncertainties about the characters and their relationships with each other, Strauß's plays illustrate the failure of the search for belonging and certainty in a world that has nothing to offer but uncertainty. His first plays, *Die Hypochonder* (The Hypochondriacs, 1972), *Trilogie des Wiedersehens* (Three Acts of Recognition, 1976), and his breakthrough *Groß und Klein* (Big and Little, 1978), established Strauß as a popular playwright.

Strauß's *Trilogie des Wiedersehens* covers several phases of an art exhibit's preopening event for the members of the local Arts Foundation, who know each other more or less well because of the nature of this relatively closed group. The plot is loosely held together by underlying, primarily sexual, tensions and attractions, as well as by a conflict between Moritz, the Art Foundation's director, and the board because of Moritz's choice of artworks. The plot is really defined, however, by a constant coming and going of the characters in which no real communication can take place. This is a further emphasis on the breakdown of the very element that used to be a central force of traditional theater: communication in the form of dramatic dialogue.

In the beginning Susanne is engaged in a monologue that is ironic, because she thinks it is a dialogue. While she is in the middle of telling Moritz how she feels about their relationship, he exits, unnoticed by her. She continues talking, and finally, except for Moritz, all the members of the Arts Foundation have come onto the stage and are, "like a chorus, in the background and listen to Susanne" [wie ein Chor, im Hintergrund und hören Susanne zu]. She never realizes that she has not been talking to Moritz; he has returned just in time to hear her last words expressing her feeling that the two of them are, paradoxically, united while their backs are turned to each other. He cuts her off with a noncommittal response: "Indeed. That's the way it is" [Ja. So ist es]. Such failure to communicate is further highlighted by a playful dynamism between absence and presence. While a sense of true belonging is absent, some or even all members of the Arts Foundation always seem to be present in a way that is both eerily unreal and, as a parody of behavior at public cultural events, realistic.

In *Groß und Klein* Strauß abandons the unities of time and place; only the theme of failed relationships — and the central character, a young woman named Lotte — connect the scenes. The passing of time can only be estimated by the measure of Lotte's slow decline into social marginality, which becomes obvious by the deterioration of the dress that she wears in most of the ten scenes. While Lotte's outgoing nature makes some people more aware of themselves as a result of their chance encounters with her, Lotte herself never finds a place where she belongs. The locations of the scenes are arbitrary, but some contemporary places of urban and technological civilization — the telephone booth, the bus stop, the doctor's waiting room — evolve into symbols of isolation and marginalization. Technology does not offer new options but only amplifies the helpless search for belonging. In the scene "Station" Lotte delivers her farewell monologue to her estranged husband in a telephone booth — again evoking the dynamism of absence and presence, because a telephone call is defined by people calling one another into the other's presence while being absent. Communication technology is reduced to a backdrop, since Lotte has not placed her call; therefore, her farewell monologue cannot be heard by the addressee. Lotte's fate suggests that humanity is running out of options.

*Between reality and mythology in the East*   East German theater had a quite different understanding of its operative character from that of theater in the West; it wanted to have an effect in a world that could be changed. But if the effect was not approved by the Communist bureaucracy, even if a play's content was in accordance with Communist beliefs as understood by its author, the play ran the risk of not being performed at all, or of being performed only after a delay of years. Often it joined the ironic status of other East German texts that were available in the West but not the East. Plays by virtually all major playwrights were affected, including Volker Braun and Heiner Müller.

Plays written in the GDR in the 1970s were much more diverse than those written during the previous decade. By the 1970s, the preeminent writer was Heiner Müller, and a major change in GDR drama was beginning with the youngest generation of playwrights — such as Christoph Hein (b. 1944); Stefan Schütz (b. 1944), who left the GDR in 1980; and Thomas Brasch (b. 1945), who left the GDR in 1976 — because they all were more directly influenced by Müller than by Brecht. For them, theater had to provide its own language, but it was less a means of changing the world than of surviving it. Other East German playwrights of Müller's generation included Peter Hacks and Rudi Strahl (1928–2001); the latter produced widely popular comedies. The generation between Müller and the youngest generation of playwrights was represented by Volker Braun and Ulrich Plenzdorf (b. 1934).

The thematic range of the plays was also quite broad. Some plays dealt with contemporary problems of the GDR, though less and less in the tradition of Socialist Realism. Everyday problems supplied popular topics, particularly difficulties of young people who are full of idealism but have trouble growing into the regimented world of the GDR. Of these plays, Plenzdorf's *Die neuen Leiden des jungen W.* (The New Sorrows of Young W., 1972) was the greatest East German theater success of the early 1970s. The seventeen-year-old apprentice Edgar Wibeau drops out and hides in a small summer house of the typically German allotment gardens. There he experiences his life in analogy to Goethe's *Die Leiden des jungen Werther* (The Sorrows of Young Werther, 1774), the classical formulation of individual subjectivity in German literature, which ends tragically in Werther's suicide over an unhappy love. But the analogy to Werther is ambiguous, because Edgar can be seen as a youthfully radicalized outsider figure like Strittmatter's Ole Bienkopp, who still believes in improving the living conditions of his fellow citizens. Edgar is working on an invention with which he hopes to make industrial production easier; he does not die because of an unhappy love but as a result of an accident with his invention, which electrocutes him — or perhaps it was planned as a suicide, after all. The play's energy derives from these fundamental ambiguities, as well as from its linguistic form, which represents more than simply the language of young people in the GDR, it also expressed an extent of countercultural thinking that had been taboo. An example is Edgar's celebration of jeans, a symbol of potential Americanization. For Edgar, it is important not just to wear the only true kind of jeans but also to be a true wearer of jeans: "I mean, jeans are a state of mind, not a pair of pants" [Ich meine, Jeans sind eine Einstellung und keine Hosen].

Instead of using contemporary issues, the most significant playwrights increasingly turned to topics from history or even mythology. Their plays had in common a critique of civilization that was topical because it examined the roots of contemporary issues. Applying across ideological systems, this critique addressed political controversies as primal conflicts of humanity, often in terms of gender relationships that had become power struggles. While running against the orthodox

Marxist analysis of class antagonisms, the mythological approach was an important point of connection between the literary discourses of East and West. In the West similar critiques were voiced, such as in the Flounder's attack in Grass's novel on male domination under capitalism and communism alike.

*Heiner Müller's theater as a slaughterhouse* Heiner Müller emerged as the preeminent German-language playwright of the second half of the twentieth century. His adaptations of classical traditions were intended as models of corruption by power and started his comeback during the 1960s. But it was not until the mid-1970s that he achieved his final breakthrough, first in West Germany and then internationally. During that decade Müller moved toward a more direct presentation of contemporary issues, while opening up their historical dimension. He also radicalized his means of presentation into a montage technique that allowed him to freely combine fragments of his own texts, other writers' texts, history, contemporary reality, and dream and nightmare images. Each of the fragments expresses a specific attitude, and their combination and recombination encourages a continued examination of their validity.

The complex interaction of textuality and intertextuality overlay a dual subtext of subjectivity and politics. The montage was not only an expression of Müller's own subjectivity and his mode of thinking, but the content of the plays also traced the development of political history to reach the conclusion that the "world . . . is a slaughterhouse" [Welt . . . ist ein Schlachthaus], as the Nazi character in *Germania Tod in Berlin* (Germania Death in Berlin, 1977) puts it. Müller's contention was that something had gone terribly wrong in humankind's history (and in German history, in particular) but that this fact had become obscured. The shock value he sought in his plays, such as *Germania Tod in Berlin* and *Die Hamletmaschine* (Hamlet Machine, 1977), was meant to shed light on forgotten history. While his plays seemed to drive toward an inescapable catastrophe, the radicalness of presentation and its implied dissolution of society can also be seen as a last chance for finding a solution.

The montage technique in *Germania Tod in Berlin* moves toward dramatic monologue, although the option of interaction between the characters via dialogue is partially upheld. In the last scene of the play the old worker Hilse, dying of cancer, drifts off into a feverish vision of a conversation with Rosa Luxemburg. The girlfriend of his friend, the young bricklayer, speaks Rosa's words without understanding them; she is just repeating the words that her boyfriend prompts her to say so that the old man's illusion of talking with Rosa Luxemburg is sustained and he can die happy. Ambivalently, this ending reveals the most basic human isolation, but it also creates an image of a profound human understanding between the old and young worker that does not require any words.

Here Müller's theater approached the realm of silence that had been explored by writers such as Paul Celan and Samuel Beckett. Beckett's plays reduced the representation of the human being to basic characteristics of bodily existence. In contrast to Beckett's ahistorical plays, Müller's plays reduced the functioning of human behavior, especially political behavior, to functions of the body as part of concrete history, regardless of its complex metaphoric evocation. Scenes with the workers in the GDR around 1949 provide a narrative skeleton for *Germania Tod in Berlin*, which blends montage fragments from history into a temporary unity to reveal where humankind had gone wrong. The scenes range from the first — set in a Berlin street in 1918, when the hope for a German revolution died — to the last scene, where Hilse dies in Berlin. In between Müller quotes from Tacitus's description of the meeting between Arminius, a German hero for his victory over Roman occupation forces, and his brother, who was in the Roman army. This fraternal conflict is the root of Germania/Germany's bloodstained history. Two significant scenes, "Hommage a Stalin 1" and "Die Heilige Familie" (The Holy Family), bring German mythology into the twentieth century.

In "Hommage a Stalin 1" the defeat of the German army, encircled at Stalingrad, gives way to obscene, nightmarish visions that unmask the obscenity of history itself. After Napoleon and Caesar have walked across the stage, the four Nibelungs — Gunther, Hagen, Volker, and Gernot — enter. Central figures of the definitive Middle High German epic, they became symbols of *Nibelungentreue*, the German faithfulness to the last man that National Socialism perverted into blind obedience. They step over dead soldiers, pick up body parts, and hurl them at imaginary Huns; eventually, they turn on each other, and everyone is beaten to pieces. The scene concludes with the body parts crawling toward each other and "forming . . . a monster made of scrap and human parts" [formieren sich . . . zu einem Monster aus Schrott und Menschenmaterial].

"Die Heilige Familie" presents an obscene travesty of the holy family by placing Hitler and Goebbels in the roles of the father and expectant mother — a homosexual couple who can give birth, but only to evil. During the scene, Germania enters as the midwife, and the Three Wise Men appear with their gifts: torture instruments, a cannon, and a human being to be eaten by Hitler, who is living on a secret diet of human flesh. Finally, Goebbels gives birth to metaphoric evil, a "Thalidomide-Wolf" [Contergan-Wolf]. Germania is tortured by Hitler and tied to the front of the cannon. When the shot is fired, the curtain falls. With the end of this scene, Germania dies yet another "death in Berlin."

The play's title already embodies Müller's montage technique by forcing words and phrases together without tying them together syntactically. By the same token, the audience is challenged to employ its knowledge of theatrical syntax to provide the connections between the fragments of the play's montage. Müller's *Hamletmaschine*, his best-known piece, begins with Hamlet, Ophelia, and other characters from Shakespeare's *Hamlet* and continues with provocative statements, such as "I am the databank" [Ich bin die Datenbank] and "Heil COCA COLA," which oscillate in tone between hymnal and prosaic. The intertextuality also points to an international literary tradition from *Song of Myself* (1855), by Walt Whitman (1819–1892), to Allen Ginsberg's "America" (1955), and "Treasure Holiday" (1969), by William Harmon (b. 1939). The last poem includes the lines "I am the Gross National Product / absorb & including all things all goods Fab with Borax." From this criticism of empty consumerism, it is a small step in *Hamletmaschine* to seeing human beings as numbers crunched by the big machine of history. "Marx Lenin Mao" appear as three naked women, and Hamlet splits their heads. Thus unfolds a sweeping critique and rejection of the entire male-dominated civilization, of capitalism and Communism alike.

Hamlet is ready to resign: "I was Hamlet" [Ich war Hamlet]. He even admits to being an actor and, therefore, to never really having been Hamlet: "Ich bin nicht Hamlet. Ich spiele keine Rolle mehr" [I am not Hamlet. I no longer play a role]. He wants to leave the play because it is the story of a man who made history. That is over; now history makes man. Human individuals are consumed by the machine of history, and humanity's ironic hope is to become a machine itself. "I want to be a machine" [Ich will eine Maschine sein], the Hamlet actor shouts, only to submit to the machine that exploits him — the Hamlet Machine — in the vicious circle of repeating a story that has lost its meaning, since it is no longer capable of dealing with the world. He puts on costume and mask, and is Hamlet again. Ophelia, too, appears and, identifying herself as Electra, renounces and curses the male-dominated world. Yet women will not be able to save the world, either. Ophelia, who no longer commits suicide as in Shakespeare's *Hamlet*, is silenced in a different way: "The men exit. Ophelia remains on stage, motionless, wrapped in white gauze" [Männer ab. Ophelia bleibt auf der Bühne, reglos in der weißen Verpackung]. It is no longer Hamlet or Ophelia, who may or may not be insane; the world is insane. The end of the play signifies the end of history.

The stage productions of *Die Hamletmaschine* displace the spoken text (which comprises only nine printed pages) with images and non-verbal action. Thus, Müller is approaching a theater without text — more specifically, a theater where text and action are separated from each other. *Hamletmaschine* radicalizes the representation of social alienation as the dialogue disintegrates into monologues by characters who, at best, talk at each other. In this new form of endgame theater, an end-of-history perspective and sense of ultimate frustration — similar to, yet more radical than, approaches in West German dramas, such as those by Botho Strauß — even disintegrated the formal dramatic cohesion of text and action.

# 11:The 1980s: New Confusions — Resurgence of Storytelling and Converging Literatures in East and West

## Social Foundation and Literary Spectrum

THE 1980S LEFT MANY PEOPLE feeling increasingly disoriented, because it seemed as though old certainties had been replaced by an "anything goes" mentality. The jobless rate in West Germany had been above 2.5 million since the mid-1970s, and now even those who were employed experienced mounting insecurity. The critique of technological civilization, which once had seemed academic, loomed as a real threat in a rapidly changing job market: instead of making jobs safer, machines took jobs away from people. In response, many — especially, young people — assumed a "no future" attitude. The phrase *die neue Unübersichtlichkeit* (the new confusion) was used to describe these trends.

Literature of the 1980s, too, was often — though not quite accurately — described in terms of "anything goes." But while the political and social changes of postmodernity often threatened the quality of life, literary plurality had an exciting aesthetic quality because of its vast variety of discourses. Literary discourses included an embrace of many possible centers in the creation of postmodern texts, as well as a continuation of the Modernist search for one center of meaning. Literature had always included visions of despairing disillusionment and of utopian hope. In the coexistence of all these discourses, German literature seemed richer and more diverse than ever. Uwe Johnson, Heinrich Böll, Peter Weiss, and Alfred Andersch, who had put their imprint on German literature for many decades, were able to bring their artistic life's work to a sense of closure before they died. Other established authors, including Friedrich Dürrenmatt and Max Frisch, also continued to publish. New poetic voices and visions emerged, including Uwe Kolbe (b. 1957), Thomas Kling (b. 1957), and Durs Grünbein (b. 1962). It seemed as though old modes were not merely being replaced but, rather, complemented by newer modes. For instance, in lyrical poetry the subjectivity of the 1970s was now complemented by a new emphasis on form, which also explained the renewed interest in Gottfried Benn. In prose the challenges of the 1960s and 1970s to basic literary concepts, such as the narrator or storytelling itself, remained productive; however, storytelling was reinvigorated — the historical novel made a remarkable comeback. Yet it was no naive return to practicing traditional patterns, since narratives increasingly became self-reflexive: they not only told a story but also the story of telling a story.

The rhetoric of many literary works of the 1980s — from Christa Wolf's *Kassandra* to Günter Grass's *Die Rättin* (The Rat, 1986) and Christoph Ransmayr's *Die letzte Welt* (The Last World, 1988) — was as skeptical and even pessimistic as the works' visions were apocalyptic. This literary mood closely corresponded to life in Europe of the early to mid-1980s, which seemed to bring humankind ever closer to an apocalypse. Shock waves rippled through the entire population when AIDS and the nuclear accident in Chernobyl were felt as being close to home. Beginning in 1983 the worldwide spread of HIV and AIDS was publicized. This news distressed people because they were affected in the most private and intimate aspects of their lives by a disease that did not discriminate and that could not be cured. The AIDS epidemic also raised the question of how it could still be possible to write love stories if sexual behavior was radically changed. For example, in Elfriede Jelinek's *Lust* (1989) the picture of marriage as the place of brutal war between the sexes further darkens as the husband unleashes the sexual drives that he fears to satisfy elsewhere out of fear of contracting AIDS.

The nightmare of worldwide extinction in a nuclear catastrophe came closer to reality when one reactor at the Soviet nuclear power plant in Chernobyl, near Kiev, melted down at the end of April 1986. As a radioactive cloud moved west and rained down partially on Germany, the public was terrified. Suddenly, the nuclear threat was no longer a topic for academic debate but a catastrophe that disrupted the lives of millions of people in Central Europe right down to daily decisions of what food items would be on the table. Christa Wolf's *Störfall* (Incident, 1987) and Gabriele Wohmann's *Der Flötenton* (The Flute's Sound, 1987) illustrate the immediacy of the literary response, which could be so swift because endgame scenarios had earlier been a crucial part of literary thought experiments. The response also highlights the function of literature as an option for coping.

During the late 1970s, in response to perceived threats to the environment and world peace, the protest potential of citizens' initiatives had begun to grow into a major, though not unified, movement in West Germany. This protest potential was galvanized by NATO's 1979 decision to deploy Pershing II missiles in Europe, including West Germany, in 1983 unless an agreement with the Soviet Union about arms reduction was reached. Hundreds of thousands of people viewed this as further escalating an already heated arms race and took to the streets in protest in West Germany between 1981 and 1983, joined and supported by a number of German writers — most visibly, because of his public stature, Heinrich Böll. In East Germany, under considerably more difficult conditions because of state repression, a small but vocal peace movement evolved. It was largely based in the GDR's Christian churches, which also provided an important alternative way for critical authors to reach an audience with texts that were not allowed to be published in East Germany.

The most tangible result of the protest movement was a significant shift in the political landscape of West Germany, which had effectively been a three-party system, because usually only the conservatives (CDU outside Bavaria, CSU within Bavaria), the Social Democrats, and the Free Democrats were able to reach the five-percent minimum of votes required to win parliamentary seats. In mid-1982, the Free Democrats entered into a new coalition as the junior partner with the CDU/CSU, electing in October 1982 the new chancellor from the CDU, Helmut Kohl, who would remain in office for sixteen years. Despite this general move toward more conservative politics, a large number of the protest movement's members began to organize. As a result, the *Grüne* (Green Party) was formed at local and state levels in the late 1970s; its ability to win parliamentary seats changed the traditional three-party system into a four-party system locally. In 1980 the Greens formed a nation-wide organization and won seats in the federal parliament in the 1983 elections. Distinctly different in their political style from the other parties, the Greens displayed their roots in the *Alternativbewegung* as a matter of political culture.

The actual picture of the West German political landscape was more complex because not all developments took place within the parameters of a general democratic consensus. In the political reality of the 1980s a murky scene with the potential for violence and terrorism emerged at the right-wing fringes, and the string of leftist terrorist attacks contin-ued in West Germany through the 1980s. Terrorism was a sensitive is-sue, with which several authors dealt in works ranging from F. C. Delius's *Mogadischu Fensterplatz* (Mogadishu Window Seat, 1987) and *Kontrolliert* (Controlled, 1988), by Rainald Goetz (b. 1954), to *Ab-gang* (Exit, 1988), by Peter Jürgen Boock (b. 1951), who was serving a life sentence for his participation in RAF terrorist activities when he wrote the novel.

Somewhere between private scares and global threats, the political landscape had normalized in the two Germanies, which was representa-tive of the way the East and the West related to each other in general: each was suspicious of the other but dealt with the other anyway. In an age of confusion, these political oppositions at least suggested that each side knew who the enemy was. Specifically, "normalization" between the two German states meant a network of relationships — from trade agreements to provisions for citizens of one country to visit the other — built on the 1972 *Grundlagenvertrag* (Basic Treaty). The

GDR appeared to have consolidated its political system to such an extent that it seemed to have been accepted, however grudgingly, by most of its citizens. The consensus was that the German division would remain the status quo for a long time.

Yet the status quo was altered in 1987 when Mikhail Gorbachev, who had assumed power in the Soviet Union in May 1985, proposed sweeping changes to salvage the failing Soviet system. Instead of stabilizing the Soviet Union, however, Gorbachev's politics of *glasnost* (openness) and *perestroika* (restructuring) led to a further destabilization of the entire Eastern bloc. In East Germany the political leadership clung to a hard-line position that saw the consolidation of Communist power endangered by Gorbachev's politics. When Gorbachev made the official statement during his visit to the GDR in June 1989 that each state was free to determine its own political and social system, it triggered a development that had been unimaginable even a few months earlier. Thousands of GDR citizens attempted to flee from East Germany through the neighboring socialist countries. Even more took to the streets in peaceful demonstrations, declaring "We are the people" [Wir sind das Volk].

Finally, the Communist system collapsed. In the GDR the country-wide protests not only drew hundreds of thousands of participants but also became a regular event, the so-called Monday demonstrations, a clear signal of a wide-scale and deeply rooted discontent that was not going to go away. Even after hard-line East German leader Erich Honecker resigned in October 1989, the subsequent restructuring of the political leadership could not stop the momentum of the growing protests. One million people demonstrated on Alexanderplatz in East Berlin on November 4, 1989. In the evening of November 9 a press release stated that the people had been granted the right to travel freely to the West. Like many events of recent history, this one has yet to be fully researched and assessed; it seems, however, that the statement was not authorized by the GDR government. Nevertheless, it spread like wildfire, and within hours people massed around border crossings. The same night, apparently without orders, East German border guards opened the borders to the West — and they remained open. Millions of East Germans visited West Berlin and West Germany the following weekend. The mood of a divided nation became that of one big party.

The 1980s ended in a celebratory mood. The future had returned; the "no future" attitude, which had characterized the greater part of that decade, quickly became a thing of the past since a politically fatalistic "anything goes" mentality had been replaced with an optimistic "everything is possible" outlook. The chant "We are the people" soon changed to "We are one people" [Wir sind ein Volk]. Although a few voices — including Günter Grass — urged caution, the trend was toward a speedy unification of East and West Germany. Nevertheless, other options were discussed; for instance, Christoph Hein, who almost exactly two years earlier had courageously attacked GDR censorship, dreamed about establishing a truly socialist society with a human face. The year 1989, which had brought such a dramatic and fundamental turning point in a peaceful revolution by the people and forced an authoritarian regime to step down, ended with high hopes for the future, including the future of literature. Wolf Biermann, whose fate had been a symbol of the divisive relationship between authors and the East German state, was able to return and give a concert in Leipzig in December 1989, thirteen years after his expatriation from the GDR.

## Drama as Crisis

The preeminent playwrights of the 1980s — the West German Botho Strauß, the Austrian Thomas Bernhard, and the East German Heiner Müller — shared a profound pessimism. Attempts to move away from a pessimistic social analysis were limited by a reality that did not seem to favor optimism. Nevertheless, East German drama preserved at least a faint sense of hope in a socialist utopia still to come in spite of the disillusioning reality of the GDR. The only major Western playwright to proclaim hope for humankind was the Austrian Peter Handke. As in his prose texts, Handke turned to a hymnal tone in his play *Über die Dörfer* (About the Villages, 1982); the character Nora proclaims: "Don't allow them anymore to talk you into believing that we would be unable to cope with life, living at the end of time" [Laßt euch nicht mehr einreden, wir wären die Lebensunfähigen einer End- oder Spätzeit]. Nora's sudden appearance on stage seems like the device of the *deus ex machina*. As a result, in this play and in general, the attempts to overcome endgame scenarios were not convincing. In fact, the notion of drama as crisis is descriptive of many well-established playwrights and newcomers during the 1980s.

Friedrich Dürrenmatt presented a new grotesque play, *Achterloo* (1983), in which figures of world history from Napoleon to Karl Marx (the latter broken into three different characters) and of world literature, such as Georg Büchner's Woyzeck, appear. Achterloo is "anywhere" [Irgendwo] in the present world; for example, the anachronisms on stage can be resolved as a commentary on the contemporary Polish conflict between labor leader Lech Walesa and General Wojciech Jaruzelski or as role-playing by inmates of a mental institution. Anachronism, political commentary, and role-playing are combined to raise the issue of political convictions. Extending the action into the present, the indeterminate ending is a further commentary on the state of the world. *Das Alte Land* (The Old Land, 1984), by Klaus Pohl (b. 1952), refers in its title to a region in northern Germany and to the fact that after the initial upheaval of the immediate postwar years people did not create a new country but re-created the old one. The dance at the end is, consequently, not merely to celebrate a marriage; it is a *danse macabre*: the characters have either sold out or have been humiliated.

West German drama of the 1980s can be described as variations on old themes, with lines of development in the nonrealistic mode, as in Dürrenmatt's play, and in the realistic mode, as in Pohl's play. Predominantly, it was political theater that participated in contemporary developments, such as a rediscovery of myth, apocalyptic visions, and new plays by women writers. During the 1980s Franz Xaver Kroetz, who had written more than twenty plays and was West Germany's most successful playwright, began writing plays such as *Nicht Fisch nicht Fleisch* (Not Fish Not Fowl, 1981), in which he expanded his earlier realism to overcome the theater's crisis. Typically, the action in Kroetz's plays is motivated realistically but soon turns to surrealist and often shocking scenes. For example, in *Bauern sterben* (Farmers Die, premiered 1985, published 1986) the characters speak (an artificial) Bavarian dialect; however, in an attempt to generalize the fate of people fleeing their rural existence to make it in the city, Kroetz locates the setting "anywhere between Landshut and Calcutta" [irgendwo zwischen Landshut und Calcutta]. The horrors of the rural home culminate in the scene in which, according to the stage directions, "like a slaughtered animal, Jesus is carved up and gutted by the priest" [wie ein geschlachtetes Tier wird Jesus vom Pfarrer aufgeschnitten und ausgenommen]. The farmer's son and daughter at long last return to their home after the city has had only death to offer. All they have left is their parents' grave. In the final scene, during a nighttime snowfall the daughter crawls out of the makeshift shack they have built over the grave, undresses, and lies in the snow to die.

Among the most provocative dramas of the 1980s was the apocalyptic vision of the trilogy *Krieg* (War, published 1986, premiered 1987–1988), by Rainald Goetz. Like Kroetz, Goetz realized the theater's lack of effect on people and concluded that it was necessary to turn the artist's loss of responsibility into a strength. During a 1983 reading from a novel, Goetz demonstrated his provocative potential by intentionally inflicting a small bleeding wound on his forehead as part of his performance. *Krieg* also shocked the audience. The first part, *Heiliger Krieg* (Holy War), presents a panoramic view of the history of revolution. The second part, *Schlachten* (Slaughters), narrows the history of the world to family history: "War in the night is slaughter: family, art, hatred. The fight continues" [Krieg in der Nacht ist Schlachten: Familie, Kunst, Haß. Der Kampf hält an]. The final part, *Kolik*, turns even more inward to a psychiatric study of language and body.

During the 1980s women writers also established a stronger presence on the stage. Gerlind Reinshagen continued her project of making the stage a potential for new behaviors. Forming a thematic unit, her plays *Sonntagskinder* (Sunday Children, 1976), *Das Frühlingsfest* (The Spring Party, 1980), and *Tanz, Marie!* (Dance, Marie!, 1989) explore the war years, the 1950s, and the 1980s, respectively. In the last play the characters have become old and disillusioned, but Marie refuses to conform to what society defines as appropriate behavior for old people; she wants to dance. Reinshagen, however, was increasingly criticized for the mystical tone of her plays, which was seen as getting in the way of a critical potential for new behavior. In *Krankheit oder Moderne Frauen* (Illness or Modern Women, 1987), Elfriede Jelinek also combined mythological motifs — specifically, that of the vampire from popular literature — with the intention of social criticism. In Jelinek's play the vampires are no longer products of male sexual fantasies; the play's premise is that women lead an existence as vampires, because they are neither dead nor alive in a man's world.

East German drama also primarily continued earlier developments, with a strong emphasis on a general criticism of civilization, usually by way of historical or mythological themes. In the 1980s, Christoph Hein, Volker Braun, and Heiner Müller were the three most important playwrights in East Germany. Hein's play *Die wahre Geschichte des Ah Q* (The True Story of Ah Q, 1983) exposes the dangers of intellectuals being either victims or instruments of political power. Most interesting, however, is Hein's adaptation of the King Arthur myth in his play *Die Ritter von der Tafelrunde* (The Knights of the Round Table, 1989). The monumental West German drama *Merlin* (1981), by Tankred Dorst and Ursula Ehler, also revisited Arthurian myth under the contemporary aspect of disillusionment in utopian ideals. It was hailed as the first great drama of the 1980s; Hein's variation on the same theme was literally one of the last dramas in East Germany. Hein's evocation of the Grail legend can be read as allegory — in general, of postmodern society that has ceased the Modernist search for meaning because the quest for the Grail has been abandoned; and in particular, of East German society, whose struggle to achieve the Communist phase can be understood as having the elusive and futile quality of the Grail quest. Now the knights are old and tired, and the ideals are dead. Mordred, who is Arthur's son, has the Round Table moved into a museum.

Exploring change, Volker Braun emphasized necessary transitions, such as in his first comedy, *Die Übergangsgesellschaft* (Transitional Society, published 1982, premiered 1987 in West Germany, 1988 in East Germany). Braun transposes the main characters from *Three Sisters* (1901), by Anton Chekhov (1860–1904), to contemporary East Germany. Chekhov's play ended with a vague yearning for the future. In

Braun's play that future has already happened but is still not here. Confined to the drab East German reality, the characters can only escape in dreams to the dream world of capitalism; they return from their temporary escape having their hopes renewed that their society is only a transition toward a utopia that still will turn into reality. Consequently, the rundown mansion in which the siblings live may represent the GDR, but its burning down represents a commitment to socialist ideals. The fire breaks the last ties to capitalism, because the house was once owned by a capitalist.

*The three preeminent contemporary playwrights* Thomas Bernhard's plays are monologic and present actors with the chance to play great roles of isolation and anger that voice Bernhard's own disgust for life and for his native Austria — often written with one of the grand old actors of the German stage, Bernhard Minetti, in mind; one play, *Minetti* (1977), bears the actor's name as title, and *Einfach kompliziert* (Simply Complicated, 1986) is dedicated to Minetti. The latter play shows an old actor's life that has been reduced to repetitions that are only interrupted when a girl, the only other character in the play, comes to bring him milk. Beyond the old actor's hatred, there is his tender care for the girl; he explicitly tells her that he hates milk but still has her bring it because he enjoys her company. But since the girl remains silent, theirs is a monologic relationship. The play gains closure through technology in a way that is reminiscent of Samuel Beckett's play *Krapp's Last Tape* (1958). At the end the actor turns on a tape recorder, which plays back the lines with which the drama began. Life is presented in its repetitions on stage, but at the same time, life is a stage. The actor turns off the recorder, repeating to himself a thought that he had uttered at the play's beginning, then turns to eat.

*Heldenplatz* (Heroes' Square, 1988), which premiered shortly before Bernhard's death in 1989, provoked a scandal because of its criticism of Austria; it was also one of Bernhard's most successful plays. *Heldenplatz* begins after Josef Schuster, a professor of philosophy, has committed suicide. In the course of the play a Jewish fate becomes clear. Returning to Vienna from exile in England in the 1950s, the Schuster family took up residence too close to Heldenplatz, the public square where the Viennese population had given Hitler a hero's welcome in 1938. As anti-Semitism is on the rise again after the war, Josef Schuster's wife, Hedwig, keeps hearing the jubilant shouts of 1938. The professor came to understand that as a Jew he had no place to call home in Vienna or in Oxford, to which the family planned to return in 1988. Therefore, he found his home metaphorically in death, as his brother Robert, a professor of mathematics, finds a home in resigning himself to inactivity.

The play has a monologic quality in the single-mindedness of its critical position toward the modern Austrian state. Anna, one of Josef's daughters, says: "In Austria you have to be either Catholic / or National Socialist / anything else is not tolerated / everything else will be annihilated" [In Österreich mußt du entweder katholisch / oder nationalsozialistisch sein / alles andere wird nicht geduldet / alles andere wird vernichtet]. Her uncle Robert emphasizes that anti-Semitism is a European problem. There is, however, a debate about the different ways to react to anti-Semitism. For Josef Schuster the last resort consisted in suicide; the housekeeper's monologue in the first scene is Josef Schuster's monologue to the extent that it largely consists of her quoting what he had told her on various occasions, revealing his anger and hatred for others and himself. In the second scene the uncle, who has been trying to look on the bright side of life, explains to his nieces that he is fully aware of the ominous developments but has resigned himself to being passive; it should be their generation's responsibility to be active. The last scene ends, after much talk, with the collapse of Hedwig, the only one who hears the deafening shouts of the masses from Heldenplatz, signifying the lethal threat of racism that requires a stronger response than suicide or resignation.

Heiner Müller continued his endgame plays, which achieved worldwide attention, including a Heiner Müller Festival in The Hague in 1983 and a New York production of *Hamlet Machine* in 1985, directed by Robert Wilson. On occasion Müller directed his own plays, often juxtaposing several of them in joint performances; for example, in 1988 the fourth scene of *Wolokolamsker Chaussee I–V* (Volokolamsk Avenue I-V, 1985–1987) was performed together with *Der Lohndrücker*. Müller experimented with his own plays' intertextuality, which is a textual property that creates new texts through the relationship of a work with older texts. Especially when Shakespeare's *Hamlet* was integrated into Müller's *Hamletmaschine,* this approach epitomized the use of intertextuality to generate ever new performances that treated the texts as works in progress and invited the audience to participate in deciding the meaning of the plays.

Müller considered nonverbal stage action and text as potentially separate elements. Indeed, the text of Müller's plays is typically short; some scripts, such as *Verkommenes Ufer Medeamaterial Landschaft mit Argonauten* (Despoiled Shores Medea Material Landscape with Argonauts, premiered 1983) and *Wolokolamsker Chaussee*, lack stage directions but have a few annotations. The short introductory statement for the *Medea* project evokes scenes of urban desolation. The description of what Müller envisioned the stage to look like explains the political impetus of the drama, which places the relationship between Jason and Medea in the context of colonialism: "LANDSCAPE WITH ARGONAUTS presupposes the catastrophes on which humanity is working today. The theater's contribution to their prevention can only be their representation" [setzt LANDSCHAFT MIT ARGONAUTEN die Katastrophen voraus, an denen die heutige Menschheit arbeitet. Der Beitrag des Theaters zu ihrer Verhinderung kann nur ihre Darstellung sein].

The five scenes of *Wolokolamsker Chaussee* span Communist history from the Red Army's fight against German troops to the growing disillusionment with utopian socialism up to 1968. Each of the five scenes is a dramatic monologue, but each monologue can be divided into several speakers when it quotes dialogue with other speakers. Moreover, Müller suggests having a young actor and an older one alternate in delivering the Russian commander's monologue in the first scene. The scenes are predominantly realistic, emphasizing the violence from which Communism rose. The first two scenes, "Russische Eröffnung" (Russian Overture) and "Wald bei Moskau" (Forest near Moscow), show a Russian commander struggling with irresponsible behavior; the third and fifth scenes, "Das Duell" (The Duel) and "Der Findling" (The Foundling), deal with conflicts after the Soviet suppressions of the workers' rebellion in Berlin in 1953 and of the Prague Spring in 1968, respectively — all of which flies in the face of the "child's dream / of a socialism without tanks" [Kindertraum / Von einem Sozialismus ohne Panzer].

In contrast, the fourth scene is surrealist; it is called "Kentauren: Ein Greuelmärchen aus dem Sächsischen des Gregor Samsa" (Centaurs: A Horror Story from the Saxon of Gregor Samsa). The scene transposes the metamorphosis of Gregor Samsa from Kafka's Prague to the East German heartland of Saxony. When Gregor wakes up this time, he has grown together with his desk. The socialist utopia has turned into a nightmare of bureaucracy in which the functionaries lose their humanity and become bureaucratic centaurs: half man, half desk. However, because of their precarious situation, the new centaurs are endangered in an ironic ending: "What creaks / In our wood Hey There's a worm Help" [Was knackt / In unserem Holz He Ist der Wurm drin Hilfe].

Theater of the 1980s continued the destruction of the classical elements of drama, such as dialogue and the unities of time, place, and plot. In Botho Strauß's *Kalldewey, Farce* (1981), the dialogue in the battle of the sexes appears choreographed; first literally, when hands, arms, and legs protruding from doorframes signify the presence of characters; then metaphorically, when the characters — according to the stage directions, "seem" [scheinen] to — shed their roles at the end of the play, thus revealing a sense of a script that they had followed. But they remain characters within a play and do not unmask themselves as actors, as if to suggest that there is no security in relying on an identity that is defined beyond the stage.

Strauß also played with traditional forms — for instance, in *Der Park*, which was performed in about twenty theaters in 1984 alone. Not only does the play have a five-act structure; it is also based on Shakespeare's *A Midsummer Night's Dream* (1595–1596) on the creative speculation that "an industrious society . . . would succumb, instead of to a myth or an ideology, to the genius of a great work of art" [eine tüchtige Gesellschaft . . . erläge statt einem Mythos oder einer Ideologie dem Genius eines großen Kunstwerks]. But a German city park is not magical, so Titania and Oberon seem out of place. The patterns of jealousy among the four main human characters cannot be resolved, and Georg's beautiful wife, Helen, turns out to be a racist. In the fourth act, Oberon's assessment summarizes the entire plot: "love has lost" [die Liebe hat verloren]. A great work of art is no more capable of restoring love to humanity than is myth, which Strauß uses in other plays. For example, in *Kalldewey, Farce*, Kalldewey shows magical properties when he disappears from a room. In *Die Fremdenführerin* (The Tourist Guide, 1986), the affair of the older tourist and the young female tour guide remains superficial, as she is drawn to other men. The setting of the ruins of the Greek classical era, the heat of the summer, and the man reading Ovid (43 B.C.–18 A.D.) invite interpretative speculations concerning the myth of Pan as an underlying pattern for *Die Fremdenführerin*.

*Die Zeit und das Zimmer* (Time and the Room, 1989) is characterized by a further demolition of the classical form of theater. The classical form established an absolute presence of the stage, so the play could be experienced as a world that was complete within itself with a clear beginning and end. In Strauß's play, however, the unit of time is dissolved into paradoxes: Marie tells a story about a man who rescued a sleeping woman from a fire; when the woman woke up, the man "continued to live . . . beside her and realized that he was her dream and nothing else" [lebte . . . neben ihr dahin und begriff, daß er ihr Traum war, und sonst nichts]. Shortly after Marie finishes telling the story, a man comes into the room, carrying a woman he has rescued from a fire. The play's main character seems to come walking in from previous plays and be on her way to future ones. This observation applies to some extent to the earlier play *Groß und klein*, but the principle was radicalized in the 1989 play, especially in the eight short scenes of the second part. In each of these scenes Marie is present, but in some scenes she seems to have a different biography than in others; most notably, she has met the right person at the airport in the first scene of the second part, although she had missed him on that occasion according to the first part. While this suggests parallel realities, other scenes seem to cohere with the play's first part but to precede it in time. If the stage is still a world in *Die Zeit und das Zimmer*, it is appropriate to ask the postmodern question of which world it is.

## Storytelling under the Sign of Postmodernism

*The Modernist tradition*

The 1980s continued the development of converging literary trends in the West and the East, especially by attacking abuse of power by the political systems on both sides. In the 1960s East German literature had begun exploring Modernist traditions in defiance of the doctrine of Socialist Realism, and the major prose developments of the 1980s, especially the historical novel and multiculturalism, brought the German-language literatures closer together. Germany, along with Switzerland and Austria, experienced a resurgence of storytelling, although it was not a naive return to the narratability of the world; rather, stories explored all options, including their own possible failure. Playing a more important role than drama and poetry in the 1980s, prose literature was written by a large number of authors.

Significant authors of literature written in East Germany included Christa Wolf, Volker Braun, and Christoph Hein. Hein's novella *Drachenblut* (Dragon Blood, 1983), first published under the title *Der fremde Freund* (The Strange Friend) in East Germany in 1982, became an instant success because it exposes the fact that life in the alleged paradise of socialism has no goal or meaning. The narrator Claudia has become accustomed to numbing her feelings as a means of protection (the dragon motif) to hide her vulnerability behind her isolation. This is only briefly interrupted by her love for Henry (the strange friend), but after his death, she reverts to her former life in isolation. In the novels *Horns Ende* (Horn's End, 1985) and *Der Tangospieler* (The Tango Player, 1989), Hein approached the theme of isolation and identity from different perspectives. Braun's *Hinze-Kunze-Roman* (Novel of Hinze and Kunze, 1985, "Hinz und Kunz" is the German equivalent of "Tom, Dick, and Harry") reaffirms Communist ideals while, in disagreement with the party line, it shows the continued existence of antagonisms between the haves and have-nots. The commodity, however, is not money but power, as exemplified in the relationship between the party functionary Kunze, who has worked his way up the ladder, and his driver Hinze.

Other East German prose writers of the 1980s included Adolf Endler with *Schlichtenflotz* (1987), a satirical travel report from the early twenty-first century, and Franz Fühmann, who contributed major texts throughout his career, such as *Das Judenauto* (The Car with the Yellow Star, 1962) and *Saiäns-Fiktschen* (1981, the title is a phonetic spelling of *science fiction*). While the older generation of writers, such as Erwin

Strittmatter, Stefan Heym, and Guenter de Bruyn, remained productive, younger writers, such as Hans Joachim Schädlich, Jurek Becker,
Monika Maron (b. 1941), and Wolfgang Hilbig (b. 1941), made major
contributions to prose literature. Yet many of the last group and other
writers, such as Erich Loest (b. 1926), left the GDR to live in the West.

Also from East Germany, Uwe Johnson, who had established himself as a major novelist by exploring the German division and boundary
conditions of human existence in general, was able to complete *Jahrestage* in 1983 with the publication of the last volume, on which literary
critics had already given up. Similarly, with the 1981 publication of the
third volume of *Ästhetik des Widerstands*, Peter Weiss, who had never
returned to Germany from his exile in Sweden, was able to finish his
magnum opus before his death in 1982. Within West German literature, the last work Alfred Andersch completed before his death, *Der
Vater eines Mörders* (The Father of a Murderer, 1980), was not the
author's most important work; however, it played a crucial role in the
context of the father books because it took one step further back into
the development of fascism. In the setting of one school period — a
grammar lesson — the high school principal reveals his authoritarian
and inhuman personality, which is the foundation for a hidden curriculum under a superficial humanism. While no direct judgment is
passed within the framework of the narrative, the postscript reveals the
autobiographical basis of the story and makes clear that the principal is
the father of Heinrich Himmler, who was, as the leader of the SS, in
charge of the Nazi death camps. Heinrich Böll was another major
author who died during the 1980s. The dialogic form of his last novel,
*Frauen vor Flußlandschaft* (Women in a River Landscape, 1985), which
is emphasized in the subtitle, *Roman in Dialogen und Selbstgesprächen*
(Novel in Dialogues and Soliloquies), represented a departure from
Böll's narrative style.

After the deaths of these significant authors, the major standing of
Günter Grass and Martin Walser in West Germany was reconfirmed.
But while their works were characterized, respectively, by the grotesque
and realistic traditions of Modernism, most significant works of the
1980s, including Grass's *Die Rättin*, contained elements that were influenced by postmodernism. The dynamism between Modernist and
postmodern elements was particularly significant during the 1980s in
the resurgence of the historical novel and the emergence of multicultural works. The novelistic spectrum encompassed not only young West
German writers, such as Bodo Morshäuser (b. 1953), with *Die Berliner
Simulation* (The Berlin Simulation, 1983), but also writers of all generations and those from Switzerland and Austria as well. From Switzerland there were Hugo Loetscher (b. 1929); Gerold Späth (b. 1936),
especially with *Commedia* (1980); Urs Widmer (b. 1939); Jürg Laeder-

ach (b. 1945); E. Y. Meyer (pseudonym of Peter Meyer, b. 1946); and
Martin R. Dean (b. 1955). Authors from Austria included Joseph Zo-
derer (b. 1934); Gerhard Roth (b. 1942); Klaus Hoffer (b. 1942), especially with the two-volume *Bei den Bieresch* (At the Biereschs', 1979
and 1983); Peter Henisch (b. 1943); and Gert Jonke (b. 1946). Three
writers — two from Austria and one from West Germany — can be
considered paradigmatic writers of the 1980s: Peter Handke, Thomas
Bernhard, and Botho Strauß.

*Paradigmatic prose*
*writers of the 1980s*

Peter Handke turned from studying the fragments of which the world is composed, such as
in *Das Gewicht der Welt* (The Weight of the
World, 1977), to exploring an increasingly
metaphysical vision that reconstitutes wholeness, such as in *Langsame
Heimkehr* (Slow Homecoming, 1979). These visions of wholeness,
which Handke continued to pursue in his novels of the 1980s, presupposed the awareness of the modern world's fragmentation. In *Kinder-
geschichte* (1980, Child Story) he abstracts from autobiographical
experiences by typifications, such as "the adult" [der Erwachsene] and
"the child" [das Kind]. The narrator in *Der Chinese des Schmerzes* (The
Chinaman of Pain, 1983) lives in a state of alienation and between decisions in his professional and personal life; hence, he appears to be a
"Chinese des Schmerzes." The narrator focuses on the traces of the
things that have been lost; fittingly, his hobby is archaeology. The re-
trieval of what has been lost is intensified in *Die Wiederholung* (The
Repetition, 1986), in which the forty-five-year-old narrator repeats a
journey from Austria to Slovenia that he had undertaken twenty-five
years earlier and attempts in vain to find his older brother.

Particularly in the latter novel Handke relied on language — in this
instance, to reflect on language itself and to represent nature. The renewed emphasis on linguistic form and stylistic awareness was typical of
the 1980s literature that replaced an emphasis on human-touch elements; at the same time, authenticity of the experience remained an
important goal. From the tension between stylistic brilliance and
authentic life Handke derived the possibility of epiphanies, often in a
Rilkean evocation of beauty and myth. Most easily accessible to a wide
audience was this approach in the movie *Der Himmel über Berlin* (The
Sky above Berlin, 1987), a film script by Handke and Wim Wenders.
Wender's 1988 movie — released in English as *Wings of Desire* and remade in 1998 as *City of Angels* — evokes Berlin's postmodern cityscape, consisting of people in isolation who live in spaces that are not
connected to a whole and who are involved in ephemeral incidents that
do not cohere. Angels and humans live on different time scales and
cannot directly communicate with each other. Against the entropy of

postmodernity, the movie suggests a Modernist quest for myth and style — the myth of personal identity and belonging (shown in Marion's plans for her future and in the love between her and the angel Damiel) and the style of storytelling (represented in the monologues toward the end of the movie and in the figure of the old man, who suggests the archetypal storyteller Homer). The mythical and romantic quality of such an approach is probably as problematic as it is unavoidable if one is to create a sense of hope.

Resisting any such sense of hope, Thomas Bernhard's novel *Die Auslöschung* (Erasure, 1986) continued his emphasis on hatred — of himself and of his country, Austria. Bernhard is best known for his plays, but he also wrote fiction. From the mid-1970s to the early 1980s, he focused on autobiography, coming to terms with his own past, a childhood that was overshadowed by problems with family and health. In *Auslöschung*, too, the narrator, Murau, attempts to come to terms with his private history and his country's political history. Summoned by a telegram, Murau returns from Rome, his place of residence, to his birthplace, the aristocratic estate of Wolfsegg, for the funeral of his parents and brother, who were killed in a car accident. More than just a place of pleasant childhood memories, Wolfsegg is also a place in which National Socialism had been embraced by Murau's mother. Before he returns to Rome, Murau transfers the deed to the estate, which he has inherited, to the Israelite Cultural Community in Vienna. After his return to Rome he engages in a paradigmatically postmodern endeavor: writing "erasure." He characterizes his report, which he titles "Die Auslöschung," as follows: "what I write down on the page is that which has been *erased*" [was ich zu Papier bringe, ist das *Ausgelöschte*]. The text is intended to be experienced by the reader in a manner similar to a musical event that slowly fades as the music stops.

*Botho Strauß's* **Der junge Mann**

The short pieces in *Paare, Passanten* (Couples, Passers-by, 1981) established Botho Strauß as a major prose writer because of his ability to convert precise observations of everyday situations to exacting prose texts whose pointillist precision allows the essence of being to shine through the flux of superficial events, almost like epiphanies. The novel *Der junge Mann* (The Young Man, 1984) centered on time and love — two of the most important categories for Strauß — in a combination of both in the theme of social and sexual initiation. Strauß's later novels *Niemand anderes* (Nobody Else, 1987) and novel-in-stories *Kongreß* (Congress, 1989) continued to explore the problematics of love. They do not present a simple discourse on love but a discourse on the discourse of love. While Strauß's other texts received critical acclaim, his controversial novel of the mid-1980s, *Der junge Mann*, was one of the most significant texts of the decade.

In its self-declared poetological position as combining the genres of "Allegories. Stories of Initiation. Romantic-Novel-of-Reflection" [Allegorien. Initiationsgeschichten. RomantischerReflexionsRoman], *Der junge Mann* established its claim as a postmodern novel because of its fusion of premodern and modern elements, which encompass the millennia in an expanded now, ranging from archaic initiation rites that the story evokes to a postmodern abundance of textual information. The novel's introduction, furthermore, calls for "scenarios and temporal honeycombs" [Schauplätze und Zeitwaben] as narrative structures that are appropriate for a contemporary awareness. The fact that *Der junge Mann* has no center, therefore, puts into practice the novel's postmodern program of generating an inherent dynamic of content and form, which is defined primarily by thematic subjectivity but also by relativity of time and by flexible topology.

Thematic subjectivity is an abstraction of traditional main characters in terms of their common thematic focus. In *Der junge Mann* all chapters and "scenarios," or self-contained short narratives within a chapter, are thematically focused on social and sexual initiation. The concept of identity has reached such a high degree of dissipation in the novel that even in chapters one, four, and five, in which the narrator is explicitly called Leon, his identity seems almost accidental; for example, a film project that is alluded to in the last chapter as having been crucial earlier in Leon's life is mentioned here for the first time. Also, in the central third chapter, the narrator (or the narrator's abstraction, the narrative consciousness) is not identified by name, and Leon does not refer to the significant observations and initiation processes of that chapter in the following chapters.

While, in specific passages, the novel allows for quite a large degree of complexity, the overall structure and the relationship of the novel's five chapters impose an order onto the narrative so that the scenarios cohere into a form that can be recognized as a novel. The organization itself suggests the dramatic structure of a novella. In chapter one social initiation is begun. The young man leaves home to work for the theater, asserting himself over his father. The turning point occurs in chapter three, where the scenario "Die Frau meines Bruders" (My Brother's Wife) grotesquely portrays sexual initiation. Finally, social initiation is completed in the last chapter. The young man rejects an offer to collaborate on a film project with his aging professional mentor, thus asserting himself over the last father figure. In addition, although fantasy elements break into the first chapter and although the last chapter includes grotesque scenes and a surreal science-fiction setting of a huge and artificially climate-controlled hotel tower, both chapters are mostly realistic and provide the frame for the three complex inner chapters. The latter are characterized by a pervasive fantastic and surreal mood.

This mood also affects the categories of time and space, which become intangible for the entire novel. The young man is one local center that may provide a context within which to determine a time frame; however, he is himself intangible as thematic subjectivity. Another local center is the tower that seems to be capable of generating its own topography, which changes from chapter to chapter; like Leon's, the tower's identity with itself throughout the novel is suggested but not clearly established. In chapter two, for example, the tower has mythic dimensions as "The Tower of the Germans" [Der Turm der Deutschen] but also more realistic ones as the center of a planned settlement. In the next chapter, which is called "Die Siedlung" (The Settlement), a settlement has already deteriorated into an "inscrutable . . . ruin of an earlier founding era" [unerforschliche . . . Ruine einer früheren Gründerepoche], and the small community that practices alternative lifestyles there is observed by a young man.

The possible points of orientation, the thematic subjectivity and the flexible topology, seem to contradict each other in terms of a possible timeline. For example, it is unlikely that the tower would undergo its changes in the few years that are narrated from the young man's life. As a result, narrated time appears to be relative and, therefore, to differ if defined in relation to the thematic subjectivity or the flexible topology. Time is allegorized in *Der junge Mann* by the way in which its passage is encoded in the metaphor of childhood as humankind's inevitable surrender to time. In liminal experiences, such as initiation processes, time becomes part of human experience, only to remain ultimately elusive. Specifically, the third chapter can be read as an allegory, in which each social institution of the alternative community of the "Synkreas" corresponds to a pattern of childhood. After the vast social dislocations resulting from "a cultural landslide" [kulturelle Erdrutsch], the Synkreas' experiment has a new lifestyle defined by "a kinder, richer spirit" [ein gütigerer, reicherer Geist] and is "playful" [verspielt], "dream-shaped" [traumförmiges], and syncretic, because they combine things rather than invent them. These new and dynamic lifestyles have their own social taboos; therefore, they appear not only as one possible version of postmodern society but also as its parody.

Some writers of the 1980s were accused of withdrawing from the world into a vision of their own solipsistic hermeticism; Strauß and Handke were further criticized for replacing political relevance with brilliant stylistics. Such an analysis ignores the fact that, if there were a paradigmatic shift toward postmodernity that began redefining the traditional understanding of political issues, any literature that reacts to that shift would be likely to push the limits. It follows that a text whose sole distinction is its stylistic brilliance is not just perfectly at home in the realm of literature but may also be hiding its political potential. In his early text "Theorie der Drohung" (A Theory of Threat, 1975), Strauß explicitly stated that the "surplus of a text" [Mehr eines Textes] is to be derived "from a political reading" [von einer politischen Lektüre]. In *Paare, Passanten* he explicitly identified the German people's "unique birthplace, German National Socialism" [einzigartige Geburtsstätte, den deutschen Nationalsozialismus] as the center of memory work that is necessary but becomes increasingly difficult with time. Postmodern literature not only typically opts for an antiauthoritarian stance and a sensitivity to ethical problems but also for a renewed interest in history as part of an expanded now.

*The new historical novel between Modernism and postmodernism*

The paradoxically ahistorical Modernist approach to history usually treated the past as a model for present situations by way of analogy but not causality. In the decades after the Second World War, the form of the historical novel became insignificant, perhaps because these decades allowed and needed a more direct expression of ideas and because the Modernist historical novels of the 1930s and 1940s had set such high standards that the form seemed to have exhausted its potential. But the form, once exhausted, became renewed by incorporating major developments. Because the resulting new form was significantly different from the novels of the 1930s and 1940s, the new historical novel was a major literary achievement of the 1980s.

*A theory of the new historical novel*

For the Western consciousness a new postmodernist understanding of the historical continuum gradually emerged with the exploration of possible worlds that may dissolve any cause and effect relationship. The concept of an "expanded present" extends the sense of the current chaotic world's plurality into that of history's plurality, in which everything — past and present — coexists in a multilayered "now." The Holocaust and the 1960s counterculture contributed to the new attitude toward history.

The post-Auschwitz age is defined by an apocalyptic and postcatastrophic awareness in which other catastrophes, from the Soviet Gulag to Hiroshima and Chernobyl, are merely amplifications of the one existential failure of Western civilization, the Holocaust. It could be argued that the Holocaust was such a fundamental shock because, for the first time, atrocities were so far beyond human comprehension that disbelief ("That's not possible!") evolved into disorientation ("What world is this where this is possible?"). The latter suggests a postmodern paradigm of thinking, in which the primary question is no longer how to behave in one's own world, since the world is no longer being experienced as one's own. Now it is a question of knowing what kind of world one inhabits in which such crimes can be committed.

The 1960s counterculture expressed a generational conflict that added fuel to the questions about what kind of world this is. It identified the official world of Western civilization with war and rejected that world in fundamental terms by postulating what gave the movement its name: a counterculture, defined by the ideals of love and self-realization. While the movement failed because — among other things — it was too narcissistic and too focused on the "now," its attitudes had ramifications beyond the 1960s. Both the Holocaust and the counterculture had an impact on world literature, which can be illustrated in regard to German literature.

The centrality of contemporary history, especially the Nazi legacy, for postwar German literature produced a focus on coming to terms with historical developments, including the conditions that had led to National Socialism. What is more, German literature had to legitimize its own existence in light of the Holocaust, because literature itself had, in part, been absorbed by the Nazi propaganda machine or had stepped aside. Major poets of Jewish backgrounds, such as Paul Celan and Nelly Sachs, proved that it was not only possible but necessary to write poetry about suffering. Other German writers, both in exile and in the underground, established another German literary tradition that had attempted to resist Nazi contamination. Nevertheless, after the Holocaust, any German literary tradition was subject to challenge.

It was the achievement of the younger generation of postwar writers, including Heinrich Böll and Günter Grass, to have proven that it was possible to continue writing literature if the text displayed a consciousness of its own historical and political situation. The prose of Böll and Grass also belongs to the long line of precursors of the new historical novel, which explains why it emerged so quietly. Grass's *Die Blechtrommel* and Böll's *Ansichten eines Clowns* were typically not perceived as historical novels but rather as novels addressing contemporary issues. Of course, they were both. The texts addressed contemporary issues of underlying authoritarian structures that had not been abolished with the defeat of Nazism; however, they did so by addressing a variety of historical issues, from the genesis of Nazism to influences of Nazism on individual characters. While these texts extended into the past, they were so close to the present that this past was not felt to be a "proper" historical past but rather *Zeitgeschichte* (contemporary history).

Contemporary-historical texts radicalized their focus on the conditions of individual lives during the 1960s as part of documentary literature, such as the investigative journalism of Günter Wallraff. His journalistic reports attempted to include the life worlds of ordinary people and, thus, to establish a written historical record of those people whose lives usually fall through the cracks of official historiography. The approach could be considered the laying of the foundations for an "antihistory." The counterculture had provided the theoretical and political background for attempts to declare the literary tradition of "beautiful art" to be dead and, instead, to valorize documentary presentation of real life as a socially relevant practice.

The counterculture, although opposed to mainstream Modernism, was still defined by the Modernist quest for the one center by proposing a grand utopian vision for a better society based on love and self-realization (as opposed to war and other-directedness). The emphasis on self-realization, however, caused the movement to fall apart into a great number of individual approaches to happiness. This dissolution epitomized the shift to more modest and more private visions of the future, which were typical of the mindset at the end of the twentieth century. After the disillusionment caused by the failure of the counterculture, German literature responded with New Sensitivity, which found the political to be contained within the private. The father books of the late 1970s and the early 1980s are the most significant example of discovering the "contemporary history" of the Nazi legacy as an inseparable part of the private history of German families.

*The "antihistory" option*
*of the new historical novel*

As the boundaries between fact and fiction, between the political and private realms, and between perspectives on history from official historiography and those from antihistory were further challenged and blurred in postwar German literature, a new type of historical novel emerged during the 1980s as a broad phenomenon — although individual novels of this type had been written before, such as Stefan Andres's *Die Versuchung des Synesius* (The Temptation of Synesius, 1971) and Grass's *Der Butt*. There are three major ways in which German literature incorporated history as a subject: first, as contemporary past; second, as setting; and third, as antihistory. The latter concept refers to history proper, reaching beyond the immediate time frame of the contemporary past but still containing the past within an extended sense of the present. The option of antihistory became particularly productive during the 1980s. The resulting novels typically used postmodern elements, but they could be either primarily Modernist or postmodern. The antihistory option can be divided into two main groups with regard to the narrative mode: the "counterhistorical" novel and the "metahistorical" novel. Each of the groups can be further subdivided with respect to historical causality.

First, the counterhistorical novel presents its version of events as a direct challenge to official history by a kind of creative archaeology that goes back to the source of a particular historical development. The goal of isolating the conditions of a decision that still influences our understanding of history favors realism as its primary narrative mode, as if to meet official historiography on its own terms by claiming objectivity and authenticity. Some novels propose to revise the official interpretation of historical developments. Examples include Andres's *Die Versuchung des Synesius*, as far as the representation of one man is concerned, and Christa Wolf's *Kassandra*, with regard to understanding the entire history of Western civilization in terms of suppressing female identity. While these novels typically establish a different, though often equally absolute, causality within the timeline, other counterhistorical novels challenge the very notion of causality by inventing a pseudo-history of a new past, such as Wolfgang Hildesheimer's mock-documentary *Marbot* (1981).

Second, the metahistorical novel favors the nonrealistic mode, because it uses anachronistic elements to focus on the process of history itself. It goes against official history not by directly opposing it but by using a consciousness (a character or the narrator) to go beyond an empirical understanding of history. The plot device of time travel is used in several variations from Grass's *Der Butt* to Hans Joachim Schädlich's *Tallhover* (1986) and the *Haiti* trilogy (1984–1992), by Hans Christoph Buch (b. 1944). While this device is clearly nonrealistic, it exploits the officially established timeline to establish hidden connections among historical events. In contrast, novels such as *Die letzte Welt* (The Last World, 1988) collapse all timelines and causality. Openly anachronistic elements underscore the fact that history has become plural; everything is available simultaneously in an expanded present.

*Die letzte Welt*, by the Austrian author Christoph Ransmayr (b. 1954), illustrates the success of a clearly postmodern novel; it sold over one hundred thousand copies within a few months. The fictitious character Cotta travels to what seems the end of the world: the city of Tomi on the Black Sea coast, where the poet Ovid (representing individual freedom) has been exiled by the Roman emperor Augustus (representing state authority). Cotta is interested in saving Ovid's magnum opus, *The Metamorphoses*, which he fears had been destroyed; ironically, it is a work (written between 1 B.C. and 10 A.D.) whose textual integrity is well established in actual literary history. Cotta never finds Ovid but does locate the remote house where Ovid had lived. In the garden of the house, stones with mysterious inscriptions are deciphered by Cotta as Ovid's way of making the world of the Black Sea his world. "By narrating *every* story to its end" [indem er *jede* Geschichte bis an ihr Ende erzählte], Ovid had gotten rid of all humans and had peopled the world with the characters from his text. Thus, Cotta's search for a manuscript ironically ends in a postmodern apocalypse of the end of history and the end of storytelling.

Weaving past, present, and future together in a prose that is characterized by metaphors and a smooth style, the novel itself saves Ovid's text not by repeating but by metamorphosing it. In Ransmayr's version of history, the work has not survived as a literary artifact but as an embodiment of its underlying principle, the one Cotta reads early on as one of the inscriptions: "Nothing holds its form" [Keinem bleibt seine Gestalt]: Ovid's text has been transformed into fragments, and Cotta's story is like a textual layer written over *Metamorphoses*, which, in turn, is a text written over myths handed down through oral tradition. As a result, historical periods blend, with anachronistic elements being part of the harsh, foreboding, and decaying world of the Black Sea at the beginning of the first century A.D.; for example, there are lightbulbs, microphones, bus service, and poison gas. Cotta's search for Ovid's manuscript is the search for meaning in the 1980s.

Other metahistorical novels do not collapse all of history into a metonymical expanded present but follow the established timeline, using the continuity of a character or consciousness in a time-travel scenario. Examples include Stefan Heym's *Ahasver* (1981) and Schädlich's *Tallhover*. Tallhover, the eternal police agent, is always on the side of the powers that be. Born in 1819, he participated in major secret-police activities from the nineteenth century up to the GDR secret police. After the East German workers' rebellion of 1953, Tallhover is transferred from active duty to a position as an archivist, which gives him the opportunity to continue another aspect of persecution; when he realizes that persecution and repression must remain an incomplete endeavor, he decides that it is time to die.

A corollary of time travel from the past to the present consists in traveling to the future, as in Günter Grass's *Die Rättin*. The novel presents a dark apocalyptic vision of a "posthuman" history after the nuclear annihilation of all human beings except for Oskar Matzerath and his grandmother, familiar characters from Grass's *Die Blechtrommel*, who survive the catastrophe only for a little while — and except for the narrator, who survives unscathed, because he is orbiting the earth in a small vessel. There a mythical She-Rat tells the narrator how the rats have taken over the posthuman world. The defining structure of *Die Rättin* as a duel of narrations now unfolds, since the narrator resists the story told by the She-Rat, which he claims is only his nightmare about the admittedly real threat that humanity has to face. He then proceeds to tell the story of the world according to the saving powers of hope, good will, and rationality. While Grass embraced the modern project of Enlightenment reason, the novel's structure is postmodern, because it leaves open which one of the two competing stories, which function as protagonist and antagonist, is the master narrative.

The main example of the counterhistorical novel that invents a new past is *Marbot*, by Wolfgang Hildesheimer. It comes in the guise of a serious biography about a historical personality like *Mozart* (1977), also by Hildesheimer. Other postmodern texts in this category are more easily recognizable as fictional — whether they are based on historical characters, such as the British explorer John Franklin in *Entdeckung der Langsamkeit* (Discovery of Slowness, 1983), by Sten Nadolny (b. 1942), or create a surreally monstrous character that they place in a specific historical context, such as in *Das Parfüm* (The Perfume, 1985), by Patrick Süskind (b. 1949). The latter novel is set in France during the eighteenth century; the odorless protagonist is a mass murderer who kills women to distill from their bodies the absolute scent, which would make him irresistible.

The primary aesthetic challenge for the reader of Hildesheimer's *Marbot* is to determine to which world the character Marbot belongs: the real or a fictional one. On the first page of the novel, Marbot says, during a visit with Goethe, "I mistrust any accounts according to tradition" [Ich mißtraue jeglicher Überlieferung], thus implicitly referring to the novel's own challenge. The decision is not an easy one for the reader, because the cover identifies "biography" and not "novel" as the work's genre. Furthermore, Hildesheimer includes passages allegedly from Marbot's letters and theoretical writings, fake references to research literature, and a number of reproductions of paintings showing Marbot's parents and of pictures showing places, such as "Marbot Hall." The discourse engages the reader to participate in the process of painstakingly reconstructing the life of Sir Andrew Marbot. The self-conscious biographer-persona's speculative style creates the sense of a serious attempt to approach a real subject without the biographer and reader being able to enter Marbot's mind and fully understand him.

The intertextuality of *Marbot* has been used to suggest that the text be understood as double-coded: as a fictitious biography and as Marbot's theory of painting — a sublimation of Marbot's incestuous relationship with his mother. Marbot commits suicide because he recognizes his artistic limitations. The novel ends by calling the reader's attention to the fact that Marbot's question, "The artist plays on our soul, but who plays on the artist's soul?" [Der Künstler spielt auf unserer Seele, aber wer spielt auf der Seele des Künstlers?], is still unanswered today. The soul of the artist was a concept that had not been fashionable for quite a while; indeed, the death of the author had been declared in the 1960s. Postmodernism, however, approached this issue again, carefully and giving the reader a large amount of control.

*Christa Wolf's*
Kassandra

In addition to Strauß's *Der junge Mann* and Ransmayr's *Die letzte Welt*, Christa Wolf's *Kassandra* is
one of the most significant novels of the 1980s. Because of its integration of thematic focus, type of
discourse, and textual coherence, Wolf's text, which includes postmodern elements but, nonetheless, pursues a Modernist project in the spirit
of Enlightenment reason, appealed to a wide audience. The thematic
focus is on how political power relationships determine private relationships. The setting is the Trojan War, which Wolf considers the historical period of the patriarchy's victory over matriarchy. Wolf sees that
victory as the source of what has gone wrong with the world, because
men are turned into heroes and women into objects in such a way that
neither men nor women matter as individual human beings. The plot is
derived from Greek mythology and incorporates alternative legends and
Wolf's own additions.

While Wolf turned to classical myth, she did not simply rewrite it
into another myth but demythified it to arrive at its historical foundation. Although she acknowledged in a later essay the subjective attraction she had felt toward a goddess statue, Wolf resisted irrational and
mythological models of femininity; rather, in her lectures about *Kassandra*, she emphasized the importance of rationality for the project.
Pursuing an archeological project, she adopted the view of an originally
peaceful matriarchal culture of Old Europe (Troy) that was replaced by
an invading warlike patriarchal culture (the Greeks). In the 1980s there
was great interest in matriarchal cultures and the goddess mythology.
This interest, together with the importance of the peace movement,
help explain the novel's success.

The antique myth of the ill-fated seeress is secularized and politicized by Wolf. First, the gods no longer exist other than in dreams;
therefore, Kassandra's rejection of Apollo's advances and his curse that
her prophecies will be unheeded — central to the classical myth — are
no longer part of reality but only of her dreams, which she struggles to
understand. Second, Wolf's Kassandra cannot foresee the future; on the
contrary, her official role as priestess and princess makes it difficult for
her to see what is happening around her. Her ways of expression do
not necessarily coincide with those of rational discourse. Most notably,
Kassandra's notion of "this tiny rivulet" [dies winzige Rinsal] of female
oral tradition passed on from the mother to the daughter stands for an
alternative, yet equally effective, form of communication. Wolf's view
was that the female voice has been cut out of three thousand years of
literary tradition; whatever traces of this voice still exist need to be
found — hence her poetic archaeology of power — and this voice will
have a different quality than the written language of male literature.

Wolf's linguistic devices — parataxis, ellipsis, subjunctive, and no question marks for questions — create a sense of openness and tentativeness that suggests authenticity of emotion and experience. The resulting tone coalesces in Kassandra's interior monologue into a remarkable quality. This quality is based on the intense identification of author, narrator, and character, which is obvious in the sentence that shifts from the author-narrator visiting the ruins of Mycenae to the narrator-character: "With this story I make my way into death" [Mit der Erzählung geh ich in den Tod]. The main plot is narrated by Kassandra in a long flashback as she awaits her death in Mycenae. Her remembrances trace the slow degeneration of society, which was paralleled by her growing isolation.

In Wolf's version, which follows an existing alternative legend, Paris abducts Helen but loses her before they get to Troy; however, the royal family would be too embarrassed if this fact became public, so they pretend that Paris has, indeed, returned with Helen. Although Kassandra belongs to the royal family — Paris is her brother — she is deceived as well. She finally finds out and is aghast when she realizes that the Greeks had known all along that Helen was not in Troy but went along with the pretense as an excuse for starting a war. The political reality is much uglier than fighting over the most beautiful woman in the world: the Greeks want Troy for its resources and strategic location. Kassandra eventually understands that as a still largely matriarchal Troy prepared to fight and then engaged the Greeks, it became more and more like patriarchal Greek society; it finally evolves into a police state administered by Eumelos — one of Wolf's additions to the story. His ironic name, meaning "good song," represents patriarchy's destructiveness and foreshadows all future bureaucrats of terror.

Kassandra experiences her life as a place where three worlds intersect. She is tormented by dreams and breaks down because she needs to decide in which world she is living. When she emerges from her feverish "relapse into creatureliness" [Rückfall in die Kreatur], she has finally found her own truly female voice and identity. And her decision is for none of the three worlds. She does not decide in favor of the matriarchal countersociety at Mount Ida, where she has found refuge. Nor can she decide in favor of the patriarchal world. Her third choice is a reciprocal and symmetrical relationship that Kassandra and Aineias share in their tender and profound love. Like the understanding of love in early German Romanticism, their love expresses a utopian hope. At a historical time where matriarchy was defeated and patriarchy was victorious, there emerged in this utopian love, for only a short moment, an option for a radically different world: a delicate balance with the chance for new, emancipatory ways of belonging.

But Kassandra knows that it is already too late for the third option. Aineias has been turned into a hero and, thus, a part of patriarchy. While her love for him is impossible under patriarchy, it remains the source of her hope for a better future. The historical situation of women, therefore, is identified as a no-woman's-land. Kassandra's monologue of remembrance ends with the fall of Troy, when she and Aineias bid farewell to each other. Returning to her present, Kassandra notices her executioners approaching. And returning to the twentieth century, the author-narrator describes the famous lion's gate of the palace at Mycenae, through which Kassandra must have gone to her death.

The achievement of Wolf's texts in general lie in the attempt to create — in the case of *Kassandra*, to re-create — a genuine female voice, which is supported by the moral stature that Kassandra's monologue establishes for the character. The monologue contains an otherness that suggests a feminine aesthetics, while cooperatively extending to all of humanity. Although it is highly artificial written literature, the monologue expresses a tremendous force, not unlike an oral tradition. *Kassandra*, after all, is an effective dramatic monologue, as stage adaptations have proven. Part of the text's effectiveness resides in the appeal to the audience not to consume the text but to complete it. The narrative coherence requires Kassandra to die so that her ideals will live on: her death is necessary to allow the readers to focus their resistance.

*Kassandra* can be read as an ideal biography of resistance against any oppression. It can also be read more specifically as a critique of patriarchal structures in the GDR and as a portrait of its author. Wolf's involvement with the secret police, from 1959 to 1962, was in line with her conformity, which was also expressed in her writing at the time. It is all the more remarkable that she broke away from such conformity as early as in 1963 with her novel *Der geteilte Himmel*. Wolf's development put some distance between her and the GDR in a slow and painful process, similar to Kassandra's growth from naiveté to analytical understanding. While the fictitious character turned her back on Troy, Wolf never lost that last remainder of loyalty toward her state. But, as a critical author, she herself had become the object of secret police surveillance. Her short text *Was bleibt* (What Remains, 1990) dealt with this experience, yet the timing of the text's publication after the fall of the Berlin Wall raised some eyebrows, because it was suspected that Wolf might try to present herself as a victim despite the privileges that she had enjoyed as one of the GDR's major authors. What the text reflected was the state's schizophrenia and paranoia. But Wolf, pondering only having been victimized, missed an opportunity to come to terms with what the state's schizophrenia and paranoia had meant for its citizens, both in terms of an atmosphere of mistrust and of conflicted loyalties — something that is part of Kassandra's own struggles, for instance, when she admits with striking honesty: "The Eumelos inside me forbade it" [Der Eumelos in mir verbot es].

***Toward multicultural consciousness***

Both the discourse on the Third World and minority discourses represent an engagement with issues of domination by one group (the majority) over another (the minority). Such an understanding defines the relationship between the two groups not only in numerical terms but, above all, in political terms of power relationships, although these two aspects are usually interconnected. The German discourse on the Third World is based on the view of First-World authors toward countries where, in the past, these authors would have been representatives of colonialism and members of the small ruling class, which possessed the "majority" of political power but was vastly outnumbered by the people of the colonized countries. On the other hand, discourses from a minority position are constituted by authors who belong to a minority in the German-speaking countries and who write about issues that concern their communities. Postcolonialism and multiculturalism are two sides of the same coin and, as encounters of coexisting or competing cultures, became the defining moment of these discourses.

At a time when the 1960s program of self-realization was embedded in a multicultural context, literature not only took part in an expansion of awareness (both of oneself and of the Other) but also expressed such an awareness in an increasingly postmodernist manner favoring a plurality of perspectives, lifestyles, and narratives. A principal problem, however, is whether or not texts about the Third World can be authentic and do justice to the Third World when the texts are written by an author from the industrialized West — perhaps even a white male from Germany. In contrast, the various minority discourses are typically characterized by an authenticity based on concrete life experiences.

***Discourses on the Third World***

Encounters with the Other remain central to the human condition, although they have become problematic as a result of the history of such encounters as a history of domination. The assignment of superiority to one's own culture and inferiority to another, reflected in the terms *First* and *Third World* (which are used here in awareness of their problematic qualities), has been challenged. As long as "difference" is thought of in terms of the Modernist dichotomy of absence and presence, the focus remains on domination. But postmodernist thinking allowed for quite another approach in terms of diffusion, which no longer sought after an absolute center, because the absence of such a center was no longer experienced as a loss but as normality. This fundamental change in daily experience had a direct influence on the possibilities of how the Third World could be experienced and how these experiences could be transformed into literature. Consequently, the shift toward postmodernism resulted in a growing interest in the Third World. It also became possible to reflect on the effects of colonialism on literary imagination; in fact, that is what the Third World always has been in literature of the First World: an image.

The image of the Third World thrives on its being prototypically different, unfamiliar, alien. Potentially, the encounter between First and Third Worlds on equal terms invites postmodernist modes, because it brings together two worlds in a state of diffusion that begs the question "which world is this." In the interplay of the West's self-examination and self-affirmation, the Third World can function as a model for the world's future, as an evocation of the First World's past, as a political key to past and present colonial attitudes everywhere, and as autobiography.

The last option, as is evident in Hubert Fichte's work from the early novels to his multi-volume ethnopoetic *Geschichte der Empfindlichkeit*, does not have to imply uncritical travel literature; however, it assumes a more personal-poetic approach, which is one of two principal modes of approaching the Third World. The second principal mode consists in a primarily political approach, such as in Hans Christoph Buch's *Haiti* trilogy. Quite a number of authors participated in the discourse of the Third World, including Günter Grass, Bodo Kirchhoff (b. 1948), and Hugo Loetscher, as well as Hans Magnus Enzensberger with essays and Uwe Timm with his social-political novels *Morenga* (1978) and *Der Schlangenbaum* (The Snake Tree, 1986).

The dialectic of self and Other in the encounter between First and Third Worlds opens up an additional realm of imagination in Fichte's work. Through Fichte's psychological concept of imitation, anything alien is absorbed as though it belonged to the self, but it is not colonized. Fichte's motivation for traveling to and writing about the Third World can be seen as a personal one that is focused on sexuality. His own experiences of marginalization led to an interest in understanding his own origins, as well as those of humanity; autobiography became ethnography and vice versa. Blending experiences from the German gay community with those of syncretic cultures, his travels to Bahia, Haiti, and other Afro-(Latin)American cultures and his writings up to the mid-1970s — both his ethnographic travel reports, such as *Xango* (1976), and his novels, such as *Versuch über die Pubertät* — laid the foundations of his multi-volume *roman fleuve*. In his poetic utopia, the shamanlike male, whom Fichte found in Europe and in Afro-(Latin)American cultures, is an embodiment of androgyny: both androgyny and the shaman transcend the official world by threatening it and are, therefore, bearers of hope for a better society. Fichte's specific way of blending rationality and myth gave his works their unique quality that fused his travel reports and his novels into his own ethnopoetic approach.

In contrast, Hans Christoph Buch's Haiti project centered on political and natural history. It also had a personal motivation in the emigration of Buch's grandfather to Haiti, and both aspects — family history and the story of Haiti's fight for liberty — put each other into perspective in a trilogy of novels: *Die Hochzeit von Port-au-Prince* (The Wedding of Port-au-Prince, 1984), *Haiti Cherie* (1990), and *Rede des toten Columbus am Tag des Jüngsten Gerichts* (Speech Delivered By the Dead Columbus on Judgment Day, 1992). Buch's self-admitted Euro- and logocentristic thinking met a genuine challenge, which was perhaps so strong that it enabled Buch to deal productively with otherness without making it all too familiar. For him, Haiti is located at the intersection of several cultures, thus inviting a multicultural way of thinking. In contrast to Fichte, Buch took the more mainstream political approach of writing a postmodern text by using intertextual elements for pastiche and parody: literary and intellectual history met political history.

The prologue to *Hochzeit von Port-au-Prince* anticipates the novel's three main sections by comparing them to three wings of a decayed castle. Buch peoples the prologue's castle with Napoleon Bonaparte, who is kissing his own sister Pauline; with Rousseau and Voltaire in a play by Jakob Michael Reinhold Lenz (1751–1792); and with Anna Seghers, who brings a cup of tea to an imprisoned Heinrich von Kleist, who is rewriting his novella "Die Verlobung von St. Domingo" (The Engagement of St. Domingo, 1811). In Buch's prologue Kleist will never finish, because he never gets the beginning right and has to keep starting over. Kleist's repetition of the novella's first sentence, which refers to the rebellion in terms of the blacks beginning to murder the whites, perpetuates the colonial gaze of the European. In the first section of *Hochzeit von Port-au-Prince* Buch parodies mythology and revolutionary history alike in the story of Haiti's liberation from France told from the perspective of a crocodile. The second section is a mock-serious reconstruction of a real event involving the imprisonment of a German citizen in Haiti in 1897 and the German Kaiser's usual answer in terms of imperialist "gunboat politics." Since Buch uses authentic newspaper excerpts, the parody results from the interpretation that is implicit in the collage of the elements. The third section begins with an account of Buch's fictionalized family history.

Fichte and Buch each use a different master key (sexuality and politics, respectively) to unlock a pluralistic and multicultural reality. Fichte's approach is syncretic, emphasizing the combination of cultures without necessarily acknowledging their differences (or diffusion). This leads to intensely interwoven narratives by way of self-referentiality and plurality, fusing even contradictory levels of reality and of possible worlds. The result is an image of the Third World that contains psychological immediacy and mythical dimensions. In contrast, Buch's approach is multicultural in the sense of stressing the dialogue between cultures while preserving their identities. Buch's narratives are charged with intertextuality and are entertaining through their pastiche-and-parody technique. As a result, Buch's image of the Third World appears to be more concrete in its historical settings and political implications but is symbolic in its display of magic realism.

*Extended minority discourses*     In the 1980s and 1990s minority issues gained a stronger visibility in German literature in a wide range of discourses from writings by gay and Jewish authors to works by ethnic Germans, particularly from Eastern bloc countries, and by authors of foreign roots who write in German. The qualitative understanding of *minority* includes women's literature in this category, if the text in question assumes women are treated like a minority within power relationships. The last category is also an example of the difficulty involved in classifying texts. In the mid-1970s a strongly feminist approach had defined women's literature. In the late 1970s and 1980s, however, this literature became more diverse, including various styles and genres and the full range from private to political themes; consequently, the suggestion was made that it would be best to refer to "literatures by women."

A radical expression of feminism is found in the novels of Elfriede Jelinek. Her use of hatred and aggressiveness has often been compared to that of her Austrian compatriot Thomas Bernhard. A searing attack on the petty bourgeoisie, Jelinek's *Die Klavierspielerin* (The Woman Piano Player, 1983), portrays the body as the root and battlefield of domination and repression. The novel's mother-daughter relationship is masochistic. The sexual encounter with a man, one of her piano students, is another humiliation for the daughter, whose life has been dominated by her mother. Jelinek's experimental novel *Lust* was consistent in its radicalization of sexuality as suffering, of love as rape. While the piano player in the previous novel was attracted to pornography, Jelinek's goal here was to write an antipornographic novel by exposing marriage — or, more precisely, the wife's body — as the battlefield in the war of the sexes. The colloquial character of the novel's language makes the explicit passages produce repulsion, as though illustrating the connection between sexuality and alienation, which the novel describes as: "Sexuality is indisputably our center, but we don't live there" [Das Geschlecht ist zwar unbestritten unser Zentrum, aber wir wohnen dort nicht]. *Lust* was as controversial as it was successful, selling over 100,000 copies during the first year.

Other women writers attempted to explore options for overcoming differences between women and men. Barbara Frischmuth had written earlier about such visions of a new human being; now, in the novel *Die Frau im Mond* (The Woman in the Moon, 1982), she evokes the possibility of such a renewal, which she sees as necessary for humanity's survival. The theatrical presentation of such a model is the goal of a small family of comedic actors. But the fantasy elements of the novel, such as the invisible panther protecting Columbina on her walks through the city at night, also evoke a sense of precariousness that is underscored by the social marginality in which the family lives. Columbina's husband falls back into stereotypical male behavior; therefore, her night journeys can be understood as her searching the bars for her husband, who is out drinking. The model of alcohol and other addictions is suggested for what is wrong with current gender relationships: men have become addicted to power. Since most individual men are essentially powerless, the only objects of their power are women (or children). These old, addictive behaviors stand in the way of developing the new human being. Even Karin Struck, who once proclaimed the myth of the Great Erotic Mother, turned her attention to the goal of cooperation with men, which requires men to shed their addictive behaviors. In this sense, the protagonist of Struck's novel *Bitteres Wasser* (Bitter Water, 1988) is not only a recovering alcoholic but also a recovering patriarch.

The two extremes of rejecting men and cooperating with them defined the developments of the 1970s. In the 1980s, however, literary discourses by women were expanded by their participating in the continuing renewal of the historical novel and of storytelling that included aiming at entertainment. The latter were met with great public success and some critical skepticism, especially from the feminist side, which centered on the question of whether such popularization of gender issues might mean selling out — especially where the stories raise challenging questions but end happily in a girl-gets-boy scenario, as in the novel *Beim nächsten Mann wird alles anders* (With the Next Man It'll All Be Different, 1987), by Eva Heller (b. 1948). The ironic twist of this novel is that the next man is the same as the previous one, from whom the protagonist had separated.

*Die Geschichten der drei Damen K.* (The Stories of the Three Ladies K., 1987), by Helke Sander (b. 1937), contains fourteen stories about the problems that independent women have with men. These stories are framed by conversations among the three Ladies K., which reflect the seriousness of male domination when the women propose the existence of the "super-HE" [Über-ER] in analogy to Freud's concept of the superego. The irony is that some of the men "are not just any old jerks. They are our lovers" [sind keine dahergelaufenen Heinis. Das sind unsere Liebhaber]. One of the four stories in *Liebe Schmerz und das ganze verdammte Zeug* (Love Pain and the Whole Damn Business, 1987), by Doris Dörrie (b. 1955), is "Männer" (Men), which the author-director had turned into a successful movie in 1985, drawing an audience of over five million viewers. It is a comedy about a business-man, the yuppie Julius, who wins his wife back from her younger boy-friend, the hippie Stefan. To accomplish his goal, Julius, adopting a different identity, sub-lets a room in the boyfriend's apartment, be-comes his pal, and makes sure that Stefan gets a job that will turn him into the kind of businessman Julius himself is. Now Julius can return to his wife as someone who does not take being a businessman as seriously as Stefan does.

Classifying authors according to their "membership" in a minority can be difficult if they belong to several minority groups. For example, Herta Müller (b. 1953) is the only major female writer within the group of ethnic Germans who have lived in Eastern Europe for many generations. Like other ethnic Germans from Romania, including the poets Richard Wagner (b. 1952), Franz Hodjak (b. 1944), and Oskar Pastior (b. 1927), she returned to Germany. Their heritage provided a special perspective on life, since they experienced a majority culture and language from the point of view of a minority culture and language.

Müller's first publication, *Niederungen* (Nadirs), is a collection of fifteen prose texts that first appeared in Romania in 1982 and in Ger-many in 1984. Her stories reflect both her rootedness in the rural world as she was growing up and her bleak vision of this world. Most stories develop in the dynamics of realism and surrealism, which leads to nightmarish impressions in which even the most everyday events or items, such as bread dough, have the potential to become metaphors of danger and dread: "And the dough, which they knead, inflates like a monster and crawls, crazed and intoxicated by the yeast, through the house" [Und der Teig, den sie kneten, bläst sich auf wie ein Ungeheu-er und kriecht, irr und besoffen von der Hefe, durch das Haus]. Mül-ler's precise and unsentimental descriptions, which expose rural life as an ugly, backwater narrow-mindedness, have been praised as studies of psychology and social behavior. Experience of the familiar and unfa-miliar also define her subsequent publications, *Der Mensch ist ein großer Fasan auf der Welt* (Man is a Big Pheasant in the World, 1986) and *Barfüßiger Februar* (Barefooted February, 1987).

Gay literature claimed its place in German literature, especially in works by Hubert Fichte and the Swiss author Christoph Geiser (b. 1949), but also by Christian Enzensberger (b. 1931) and Udo Aschenbeck (b. 1939). Fichte is credited with making the formerly taboo topic of homosexuality an acceptable theme in German literature. Geiser, whose first book publications appeared in the 1970s, reconfirmed the literariness of homosexuality for Swiss-German literature. In his novel *Wüstenfahrt* (Desert Journey, 1986), Geiser narrates the history of a homosexual relationship that ends with the narrator's emancipation from his older partner, who is addressed in dialogue form as "you" throughout the novel.

The subject of homosexuality (and bisexuality) was so central in Fichte's work that he is clearly a representative of gay literature; identifying himself, however, as half-Jewish, he also felt marginalized as a member of that minority. In spite of major writers, such as Paul Celan, Nelly Sachs, and Rose Ausländer, there was no postwar Jewish literature in Germany that had a significance similar to that of Jewish literature written in the United States. This is in part the case because the issue of Jewishness was not central in works by major writers, including Hubert Fichte and Wolfgang Hildesheimer. For other contemporary authors, however, their Jewishness was central to their literary works. Edgar Hilsenrath (b. 1926) survived the deportation to a ghetto in the Ukraine and became known with his second novel, *Der Nazi & der Friseur* (The Nazi & the Barber, 1977), in which the Nazi assumes the identity of his murdered Jewish schoolmate to avoid prosecution after the war. Jurek Becker, who also survived the Holocaust, always understood himself as part of the mainstream, being moved by questions that would move most other people. He is best known as the writer of the popular television series about Liebling, a lawyer in the Berlin neighborhood Kreuzberg: *Liebling Kreuzberg* (1986–1990).

But Becker's most significant novels, *Jakob der Lügner* and *Bronsteins Kinder* (Bronstein's Children, 1986), center on the Jewish experience in Germany. From a retrospective viewpoint of only one year after the events that led to his father's death, the young narrator Hans Bronstein tells how he found out that his father, a concentration-camp survivor, took justice into his own hands by kidnapping a former Nazi guard in East Berlin in 1973. Such a role reversal draws attention to the question of guilt and the victims' psychological deformation; it also emphasizes the victim-victimizer relationship, which *Bronsteins Kinder* treats as a political and personal issue because the son understands himself primarily as a German — hence the novel's working title, "Wie ich ein Deutscher wurde" (How I Became a German); indeed, Hans needs to understand what it means to be a German and a German Jew. Authors from the younger generation of German Jews often approach this issue more aggressively. For example, Rafael Seligmann formulates the victim-victimizer relationship provocatively in his novel *Rubinstein's Versteigerung* (Rubinstein's Auction, 1989): "Will the Germans ever forgive us their guilty conscience?" [Werden uns die Deutschen je ihr schlechtes Gewissen verzeihen?].

Literature by minorities of foreign roots had a longstanding tradition. Cyrus Atabay (1929–1996) — whose first collection of poems, *Einige Schatten* (Several Shadows), was published in 1956 — can be seen as a representative of a first phase of postwar writers who wrote in German, although it was not their native language. Other authors included Milo Dor (b. 1923) and György Sebestyén (1930–1990) within what had remained of the multicultural tradition of the Austro-Hungarian Empire. These writers' lives, which were predominantly defined by the experience of exile, were part of a different social and economic context from the work-related migration that began in the mid-1950s and that led to a different sense of the political function of the literary text.

In the 1980s German-language literature written by authors of non-German roots — often called "guest-worker" literature or migrant literature — was able to gain visibility and stature. While a few authors, such as the poet Adel Karasholi (b. 1936 in Syria) and László Csiba (b. 1949 in Hungary), lived in East Germany, broader developments took place in West Germany. One of the contributing factors to literary change was a move away from the emphasis on reality with a human touch, which had political and utopian implications. Above all, guest-worker literature pursued highly political goals by documenting and criticizing the lack of quality of life for the guest workers. Important authors included Aras Ören (b. 1939 in Turkey), with the novel *Bitte nix Polizei* (No Police Please, 1981); Yüksel Pazarkaya (b. 1940 in Turkey), with collected poems in *Irrwege* (Wrong Ways, 1985) and *Der Babylonbus* (1989); and somewhat younger authors, including Franco Biondi (b. 1947 in Italy), with collected stories in *Passavantis Rückkehr* (Passavanti's Return, 1982). The texts were written in German in order for the foreigners with various native languages to communicate with each other, as well as to reach out to that segment of the German population that was interested in what was going on in the lives of those who had been invited to Germany as "guests" to work. The publication modes available for such literature — primarily small presses and sponsorships from interested academic circles — reflected the minority status of guest-worker literature in the West German institution of literature. A corollary to political and social criticism is found in the utopian aspect of hope for a better life after the return to the home country. Such a reality-based human-touch literature was typical of the first phase of the migrant literature that was written by first-generation migrants to Germany.

The shift to the second phase of this type of multicultural literature in the 1980s also coincided with a generational change. The second generation was still a generation of foreigners according to German law, although many of these authors had grown up in Germany or had even been born there. Because of their socioeconomic status and the way they were treated by the majority of the German population, the members of the second generation lived even more between two cultures than their parents. For the younger people the utopian hope for a return home became increasingly weaker as they grew more and more distant from the native country of their parents, ultimately feeling at home neither in the country of their roots nor in Germany, the country in which they had grown up. This experience of living in a space between cultures, languages, and identities emerged as the central theme of the second phase of German-language literature by writers of non-German roots, often in poetry by writers who began publishing in the 1980s, such as the poets Zehra Çirak (b. 1960 in Turkey), Zafer Şenocak (b. 1961 in Turkey), and José F. A. Oliver (b. 1961 in Germany, of Spanish parents). In turn, this literature became truly multicultural, because cultural differences and specifics were not simply explored; they gave way to a search for a new cultural and linguistic identity, including an increasingly large number of texts by women writers. This literature took a step toward a more intense awareness of linguistic exploration and experimentation without losing a firm grounding in authentic experiences.

Gino Chiellino (b. 1946 in Italy), Rafik Schami (b. 1946 in Syria), and Franco Biondi are examples of authors who more specifically belong to a transitional phase between the two generations. They grew up in their native countries but pursued an academic education in Germany; to finance their studies in Germany, they often worked at the low-paying odd jobs typical of the employment available to guest workers. Chiellino carefully explores what it means to feel at home or to feel like a stranger; for example, the terms, *Heimat* (home, homeland) and *Fremde* (foreign parts, foreign country, abroad) are deterritorialized and are perceived as states of mind that intertwine and, as a result, make new experiences possible. The new experiences provide the means for a new identity and language that is alluded to in the title of Chiellino's collection of poetry, *Sehnsucht nach Sprache* (Yearning for Language, 1983). The encounter with German as one language that contributes to the new linguistic awareness also gives way to surprising insights. For instance, the poem "Kapitän Nemo," by Jiří Gruša (b. 1938 in Czechoslovakia, which he left for West Germany after the suppression of the Prague Spring), in the collection of poems written in 1988, *Babylonwald* (Babylon Forest, 1991), ends with a strong sense of surprise about one of the German words for "clock" or "watch": "you mortally amazed / at the Germanword / *zeitmesser*" [du tödlich erstaunt / über das deutschwort / *zeitmesser*]. The German word is an item-by-item translation of the Latin *chrono-meter* (time-meter); but *Messer* is also an independent word that means "knife." The poem suggests that time is sliced up, or even brutally butchered, with the knife; since this is connected with the German surroundings, the political dimension is always lurking behind language.

### Diffusion of Poetic Modes and Meaning

Poetry of the 1980s was defined by a wide diffusion of modes and meanings, including minority discourses. While the 1960s trend toward expressing everyday events had emphasized everyday language in the *Alltagsgedicht* and while the 1970s had focused on self-explorations, poems in the 1980s showed a much wider variety of stylistic modes that reflected different vulnerabilities and uncertain meanings. The range from easy to difficult poems had always existed, but the 1980s did not seem to have a strong preference. Poetry was still subjective, political, or laconically simple, but some poetry was also increasingly hermetic. At the same time, a general formal virtuosity represented a renewed trust in the power of poetic form, which encompassed traditional devices, such as rhyme, as well as traditional patterns, like the ballad and sonnet. Language was no longer mainly accused of being part of the problematic existence of humanity; rather, it emerged as a possible means with which to fight against this problematic existence.

*The perspective of age: reassessing the world*

During the last decade of Rose Ausländer's life, her poems addressed the dangers stemming from her faith in the word as her "motherland." As old age and illness confined her to her room, everything became imagination in her poetic language. Ausländer attempted to transcend her own life in poems of high linguistic intensity with often only a single word per line. The danger of this abstraction — where simple words, such as *mother* and *Moses*, evoke vast symbolic realms of childhood and Jewish faith, respectively — was in the potential loss of the poet's subjectivity. Yet this may be exactly the subjective experience at the threshold of death that is expressed in the poem "Gib auf" (Give Up): "The dream / lives / my life / to its end" [Der Traum / lebt / mein Leben / zu Ende]. Some of Ausländer's poems suggest a sense of resignation, but most insist on the power of language to keep evoking the dream, as in a poem from *Ich zähl die Sterne meiner Worte* (I Count the Stars of My Words, 1985): "Remain / true / to your word // It will / not leave / you" [Bleib / deinem Wort / treu // Es wird / dich nicht / verlassen]. The title of the last collection published during her lifetime announced her continued resistance to death: *Ich spiele noch* (I'm Still Playing, 1987).

Erich Fried, who was twenty years younger than Ausländer, died the same year she did. Fried always remained a political poet, passionately writing against the status quo; for him, the status quo meant that the world was threatened. That he aimed at writing poems in clear language that expressed clear insights — or at least attempted to — was evident in titles, such as *Um Klarheit* (For Clarity, 1985). Ironically, this collection also contains poems, such as "Verkehrte Welt" (Upside-Down World), whose clear indictment of injustice on both sides of the Iron Curtain is saved from sounding like a truism by taking away some of the clarity at the poem's surface. The vowels of the rhyming words are exchanged; for example, *East* receives the vowel from *West* and becomes *Est*. Appropriately, the poem is dedicated to Ernst Jandl, whose playful style of concrete poetry informed Fried's short poem: "In the Est / just as / in the Weast / it's the bust / who often / are resting" [Im Esten / genau wie / im Wosten / verresten / oft grade / die Bosten]. Above all, Fried was a poet of humanism, as he programmatically states in a poem in the collection published the year of his death, *Unverwundenes* (Unresolved, 1988): "Even that which I wrote / against life / I wrote for life // Even that which I wrote / for death / I wrote against death" [Auch was ich gegen das Leben / geschrieben habe / ist für das Leben geschrieben // Auch was ich für den Tod / geschrieben habe / ist gegen den Tod geschrieben].

Karl Krolow remained focused on reality, although in the 1980s he modified his laconic and at times aggressive observations of everyday events. On the one hand, Krolow radicalized his social criticism in poems that vary in tone from the language of cartoons to that of politics. Several poems explore more traditional forms, often with an ironic twist as in "Beinahe ein Sonett, mit Deutschland" (Almost a Sonnet, with Germany, 1982). It is only "almost" a sonnet, because the mystical dimension of Germany seems to make impossible the logical conclusion of the typical sonnet in fourteen lines; instead, the poem requires an additional tercet that proclaims that in Germany everything is illogical "and ends in vagueness: / that will open your eyes dead on / in these fairy-tale goings-on" [und endet im Ungefähr: / da gehn dir die Augen auf / beim märchenhaften Verlauf]. On the other hand, Krolow pondered his own subjective experiences with the aging process, ranging from aggressiveness in "Täglich" (Daily, 1983), "It's just this feeling of walking daily / along the old path to the execution" [Es ist nur dies Gefühl, täglich zu gehen / den alten Weg zur Hinrichtung], to surprise and possible depression.

In the 1980s Ernst Jandl moved away from the practice of concrete poetry to include his reflections on old age and death. At the beginning of the decade the tone of lament and depression seemed to predominate in the collection *selbstporträt des schachspielers als trinkende uhr* (self-portrait of the chess player as a drinking clock, 1983). The title poem displays a quiet disgust, desperation, and fear — keywords for other writers in the early 1980s as well. At the end of the 1980s Jandl's poems in *idyllen* (idylls, 1989) still had a dark quality but also had attained a more relaxed tone — even the poem in which he ponders the time he has left to write in light of the deaths of Erich Fried and Thomas Bernhard: "This is perhaps / the end of the poems / but doesn't have to be / the end of writing" [das ist vielleicht / das ende der gedichte / muß aber nicht / des schreibens ende sein]. This is a remarkable change in comparison to the poem "begebenheit" (event, written 1979), published in *der gelbe hund* (the yellow dog, 1980), which begins: "five / decades / alive / and nil / to report" [fünf / jahrzehnte / gelebt / und nichts / zu berichten]. In the later 1980s irony at times replaced the earlier bitterness; for example, in "kleines geriatrisches manifest" (little geriatric manifesto, 1989) Jandl writes about physical decline: "the latter is / so obvious that everywhere you / will collect compliments for your / mental alertness" [derselbe ist / so evident, daß sie überall / komplimente für ihre geistige frische / einheimsen werden].

Friederike Mayröcker, a year older than Jandl, focused on the ambivalences of experience and continued her experimental style primarily in prose but also in poetry. Some of her poems are based on subjective experience of reality, such as "Zypressen" in *Gute Nacht, Guten Morgen* (Good Night, Good Morning, 1986): "it's windy / white, the / bird / creaks in the / forest — / *embracing* / tender strangeness when / the bud / withers" [es windet / weisz, der / Vogel / knarrt im / Wald — / *umhalsend* / zarte Fremdheit wenn / die Knospe / welkt]. This poem demonstrates the quality of reality as a complex and multilayered phenomenon, in which subjective experience translates into metaphors and rhythm but does not become immediately accessible. In *Winterglück* (Winter's Luck, 1986) the longer poems seem to withdraw even further into the rhythms of language.

*Midlife crisis: personal and political poems*

The works of a broad middle generation of poets reflected a midlife crisis as a generational and political phenomenon, because these poets had been invested in the political realities of West or East Germany, although typically as critics of their respective states. The general disillusionment stemmed from the failure to see the political changes that these authors had supported and was, therefore, felt in an especially strong way by that generation. Thematically, East and West German poetry grew closer together with a shared emphasis on ecology and mythology. The spectrum ranged from light poems of personal happiness to dark endgame scenarios, with many poems in the middle ground trying to resist disillusionment.

Light poems, which did not seem to fit into the apocalyptic mood of the 1980s, were, nonetheless, highly popular. Ulla Hahn (b. 1946) published her first collection of poems, *Herz über Kopf* (Heart over Heel), in 1981 and became one of the most successful poets of the 1980s with love poems that displayed irony but remained within traditional poetic forms. The poem "Ars poetica" contains Hahn's poetological belief that new forms are not necessary; it sings the praises of rhyme and meter. Hahn's poetic practice was criticized as kitsch, an accusation that was also leveled against Wolf Wondratschek. His *Die Einsamkeit der Männer* (The Loneliness of Men, 1983) and *Carmen oder bin ich das Arschloch der achtziger Jahre* (Carmen, Or Am I the Asshole of the Eighties, 1986) combine a clarity of expression with a celebration of a macho attitude that is close to melodrama but is also carried by a sense of raw energy.

The critically acclaimed poetry of the 1980s, however, was characterized by a darker quality. Guntram Vesper (b. 1941) describes a new political and emotional ice age in "Der letzte Winter" (The Last Winter, 1985), which he experiences as a vicious circle: "and the repetition has to / last for all eternity" [und die Wiederholung muß / reichen für alle Zeit]. In this poem Nietzsche's concept of the eternal recurrence is seen as a fact, as the condition of the postmodern world. The concept of the end of history, typical of the 1980s, did not accept Nietzsche's solution, the will to power, because that solution seemed to have exhausted itself. Since the bad things were seen as returning, the situation did not just stay bad; it worsened — the worst part being that not only was it humanity's fault, but humanity was powerless to do anything about it. Such endgame scenarios were typical of poetry by Günter Kunert, for instance, in *Abtötungsverfahren* (Process of Mortification, 1980) and *Stilleben* (Still Life, 1983). Other poets seemed less certain, yet they still considered not just the end of history but that of humankind a real possibility. For example, Jürgen Becker speculated in *Das Gedicht von der wiedervereinigten Landschaft* (The Poem of the Reunified Landscape, 1988): "Perhaps it's us / whose unnoticeable decay will replace / the grand vision of a catastrophe" [Vielleicht sind wir es, / deren unmerklicher Zerfall die große Vision / der Katastrophe ersetzt].

Wolf Biermann wrote poems that expressed this powerlessness in private terms of self-doubt. He wrote in his 1986 collection *Affenfels und Barrikade* (Monkey Cliffs and Barricade): "Why go on scribbling books, pictures / gossip on the guitar, why go on" [Wozu noch Bücher vollschmieren, Bilder / Geschwätz auf der Gitarre, wozu noch]. But Biermann kept on writing — perhaps because he, like an increasing number of other poets, believed in the power of language in the face of an otherwise seemingly universal powerlessness. Although the works of Gottfried Benn went through a revival, the 1980s poets themselves were not as flamboyant nor as absolute in their belief in the word. Their optimism was qualified by their previous disillusionment; Michael Krüger (b. 1943) wrote about literature in his collection *Aus der Ebene* (From the Plains, 1982): "Completely useless / it was not / completely useless" [Ganz nutzlos / war es nicht / ganz nutzlos].

In continuity with her previous practice of postulating the "little however," Sarah Kirsch expressed her resistance to an emotionally cold environment that does not provide orientation and endangers humane ways of life in the collections *Erdreich* (Earth Realm, 1982) and *Katzenleben* (Catlives, 1984). The poem "Katzenleben" identifies the moment of resistance as the reason why poets love cats, whose characteristics of independence and self-determination become models for political behavior. Traditional images of sensuality and sexuality, cats embody the private realm; in a catlike quiet, yet irresistible, way the private is extended into the political realm as the poem evokes mutual mistrust in an atmosphere of denunciation and surveillance, as well as Kirsch's decision to leave the GDR: "While the zealous neighbors / keep noting license plate numbers / The one spied on inside his four walls / Long ago left the borders behind" [Wenn die besessenen Nachbarn / Immer noch Autonummern notieren / Der Überwachte in seinen vier Wänden / Längst die Grenzen hinter sich ließ]. As cats display the positive qualities that humans should have, animals in general are symbols of hope in Kirsch's *Katzenleben*. Birds present the option of revelation, yet animals are also endangered, and the communication with humans fails: "The haircutter sees a bird / Flying backwards does not believe in God" [Die Haarschnitterin sieht einen Vogel / Rückwärts fliegen glaubt nicht an Gott].

The tradition of the nature poem is integrated in the ambivalence between the sensuality of the private realm and, intruding on it, the violence of the political realm: "The tears of demonstrators no grass / Grows over it concrete settles" [Die Tränen der Demonstranten kein Gras / Wächst darüber legt sich Beton]. The poems in *Katzenleben* follow the cycle of nature, but they begin with winter and end with autumn. The mood of the poems is correspondingly dark and cold, as are the titles of individual poems, such as "Die Verdammung" (The Condemnation) and "Dunkelheit" (Darkness). The language of these poems, typical of Kirsch's poetry, slows down the reading process by virtue of its lack of punctuation, its enjambment, and its seemingly simple yet quite complex syntax, which telescopes and overlaps sentences and phrases into each other.

After writing political-topical poetry in the 1960s and political-historical poetry in the 1970s, Hans Magnus Enzensberger turned to more personal poems with the publication of *Die Furie des Verschwindens* (The Fury of Disappearance, 1980), his last volume of poetry until the 1991 collection *Zukunftsmusik* (Music of the Future). The 1980 volume still contained political motifs, such as that of the man who, by buying cigarettes at the vending machine in "Automat," also buys into all of the exploitative and colonial structures of imperialist capitalism: "He buys the cancer / he buys apartheid / he buys a few distant massacres" [Er zieht den Krebs / er zieht die Apartheid / er zieht ein paar entfernte Massaker]. For a brief, personal moment in his reflection on the machine the man looks like a human being; however, with the completed sale, as in a modern version of a devil's pact, the man's humanity has disappeared. The colloquialism of this observation did not reach the analytical or aggressive power of Enzensberger's earlier poems.

Volker Braun was the major East German poet who remained the most dedicated to glorifying the strides that the GDR had taken during its early years — as late as in 1987 in *Langsamer knirschender Morgen* (Slow Gnashing Morning). Nevertheless, he was not blind to the repressive cultural policies that had caused widespread disillusionment among the intellectuals; therefore, when he treated East German problems of the 1980s, Braun could no longer detect many elements of a socialist utopia. As a result, his 1987 volume was published only in West Germany. The language of these poems is increasingly fragmentary, and their montage character corresponds to the disparities of reality. They no longer celebrate the creation of man-made nature; the formerly blue water now is black, and damage has been done to the utopian vision: "Here I went through / With my Tools Cleared- / Away the belief" [Hier bin ich durchgegangen / Mit meinen Werkzeugen Ab- / Geräumt der Glauben].

*Young voices: born into a state of crisis* The outstanding young poets of the 1980s, who were born in the 1950s and early 1960s, turned to experimental and hermetic poetry. Both in the West and in the East the young poets were born into a situation that was defined by ideals that previous generations had fought for and that now had been compromised. These ideals were second-hand for the generation born in the 1950s. Young poetry displayed skepticism both toward reality and toward language, which had been used to articulate the ideals. The clarity of political poetry and the subjectivity of poetry about emotions gave way to a renewed importance of ambiguity, while the modes of expression ranged from linguistic play to precise observation of reality, including subjective responses.

In West Germany, Thomas Kling — with *Erprobung herzstärkender Mittel* (Trial of Heart-Strengthening Medications, 1986) and *geschmacksverstärker* (flavor enhancer, 1989) — continued the traditions of experimental destruction and reconstruction of language into new units of sound and meaning. In his 1989 volume, he writes: "our language fodder real junk food, real / perishable commodity" [unser sprachfraß echt junkfood, echt / verderbliche ware], emphasizing his medium with its fast-paced and short-lived quality that invites consumption (by the audience); at the same time, the poems are not easily consumed "junk food" because of irritating elements, from unusual enjambment to fractured syntax — elements that would remain the trademark of Kling's poetry in the 1990s. Jan Koneffke (b. 1960) published his first collection of poetry in 1989. Taken from one of the poems, the book's title, *Gelbes Fahrrad wie es hoch durch die Luft schoß* (Yellow Bicycle as It Shot High through the Air), signifies the irony and wit with which fantasy elements distort reality. The tone is colloquial and easily accessible; yet similar to other contemporary poetry by Kling but also by Kirsch, syntactic relationships and other formal elements slow down the reading process, encouraging closer reading.

In East Germany the situation was much more politicized, because in the repressive atmosphere of an authoritarian state any skepticism almost automatically registered as political criticism. Uwe Kolbe, a major poet of the first East German generation to be born in the Communist state, provided with the title of his first collection of poems, *Hineingeboren* (Born Into, 1980 in East Germany, 1982 in West Germany), the phrase that expressed the way his generation felt about its lack of political choice. The title poem reveals Kolbe's radical subjectivity, which identifies the lyrical speaker's social isolation as a personal experience. The political aspect is implied: in a country based on a collective and potentially all-encompassing ideology, the speaker of the poem (the poet) can only speak for himself.

Alluding to and playing in a masterly fashion with traditions of German poetry, Kolbe soon developed his own poetic voice. For example, "Hineingeboren" takes inventory, but unlike Eich's "Inventur," Kolbe's poem refers to elusive items as the speaker's possessions in the first stanza: "The wind is mine / and mine are the birds" [Der Wind ist mein / und mein die Vögel]. As in nature poetry, the speaker's experience unfolds in the trigonometrical points of the landscape; Kolbe's, however, is a thoroughly politicized landscape. Like Friedrich Hölderlin's seminal poem "Hälfte des Lebens" (Half of Life, 1805), the second and last stanza takes the promises of the first stanza away, item by item. While the first stanza of "Hineingeboren" ambiguously evokes the plains through which a fence runs, it primarily contains positive images, such as the "sun tree" [Sonnenbaum]. The second stanza presents the elusive possessions of wind and birds as having become alien: "Small green land, narrow, / Barbed-wire landscape. / Black / Tree beside me. / Hard wind. / Strange birds" [Kleines grünes Land enges, / Stacheldrahtlandschaft. / Schwarzer / Baum neben mir. / Harter Wind. / Fremde Vögel].

The skepticism and irony of Kolbe's poetic vision soon caused difficulties with the authorities. Beginning in 1985 he was allowed to travel to the West, and in 1988 he took up residence in West Germany but maintained his East Berlin address. After his second volume of poetry, *Abschiede* (Farewells, 1981 in East Germany, 1983 in West Germany), Kolbe's third collection, *Bornholm II*, received permission to be published only in a revised version in 1986 (in West Germany in 1987) — hence the roman numeral two after the title, the name of the allotment gardens near the Berlin Wall. In *Bornholm II* Kolbe's poetological program becomes more aggressive toward reality and more positive in regard to the role of poetry: "We should again learn that language which lay before the journals and camera's lies, holding its belly, laughing. / I am only one of its messengers" [Wir sollten jene Sprache wieder lernen, die vor den Gazetten und Kameralügen lag, sich den Bauch hielt und lachte. / Ich bin nur einer ihrer Boten].

Kolbe's emphasis on personal experience marked only one side of poetic possibilities; the other side was play with language, which was the preferred mode of expression in the literary and artistic subculture that had developed in the Prenzlauer Berg neighborhood of Berlin beginning in the late 1970s. Kolbe belonged to this group, which provided a small countermodel to the drab reality of the GDR. Even linguistic play could take on a political dimension if it was understood in terms of turning one's back on the demands of the Communist state. One of the important experimental poets was Bert Papenfuß-Gorek (b. 1956), who, like Oskar Pastior and Kling, invented new words and rules of grammar. Other writers from the "Prenzlauer-Berg-Connection" included Stefan Döring (b. 1954) and Lutz Rathenow (b. 1952). However, two prominent members of the group, Sascha Anderson (b. 1953) and Reiner Schedlinski (b. 1956), had spied on their artist colleagues and friends for the East German secret police. While this does not invalidate the achievement of the group as a countermovement, it does reveal the paranoia of the state toward its own writers. The fact that they were spied on showed how seriously this group of artists was taken as a network with an independently operating center — an organizational form that was in tune with postmodernity but diametrically opposed to the GDR's centralist and authoritarian political structure.

Durs Grünbein burst onto the literary scene with his first collection of poems, *Grauzone morgens* (1988, Morning Gray Zone), published only in West Germany. It displayed Grünbein's mastery of precise observation and poetic from. The precision of his observations contrasts with the murkiness of their subject matter, experience of individuality in the gray urban landscapes that are dominated by "the droning / labyrinths of industry" [den dröhnenden / Labyrinthen der Industrie]. Through the shocking and unpleasant reality that Grünbein evoked in his poems, he connected early twentieth-century Avant-Garde traditions with the late 1980s. His poems can be seen as a final development in the attitude of feeling born into a state of crisis. The characteristic coldness or detachment of the poems is a reaction to the coldness of human existence under an ailing Communist system, which had not only deteriorated but had also become so much a daily routine that the sense of disillusionment no longer seems to include anger or mourning: "MORNING GRAY ZONE, mon frère, on the / way through the city / homeward / or to work (what's the difference) — " [GRAUZONE MORGENS, mon frère, auf dem / Weg durch die Stadt / heimwärts / oder zur Arbeit (was macht das schon) — ].

# 12: The 1990s: A New Order of Things — German Issues and Global Themes in German-Language Literature

## Social Foundation and Literary Spectrum

OVER THE COURSE OF THE TWENTIETH CENTURY Germany came a long way from being an authoritarian and imperialistic nation — untested in democracy after the First World War, surrendering to the National Socialist ideology of hatred, and engulfing the world in another terrible war that has haunted Germany ever since — to a modern, highly industrialized democracy trying to cope with its history while building its future in an information age. At the beginning of the transitional phase after the fall of the Berlin Wall on November 9, 1989, political momentum moved East and West Germany swiftly toward unification. Legally, the process consisted of the states of the German Democratic Republic joining the Federal Republic of Germany according to Article 23 of the West German constitution. Linguistically, the use of the term *unification* emphasized the creation of a new democratic Germany rather than a re-creation of the old authoritarian Germany.

The new Germany, often referred to as the *Berlin Republic* after the 1991 decision to make unified Berlin the new German capital, was only able to come into being with agreement by the victorious countries of the Second World War: the United States, Great Britain, France, and the Soviet Union. On September 12, 1990, after Germany agreed to conditions, such as renouncing any territorial claims east of its current borders, the six foreign ministers of the four Allied Powers and the two Germanies signed the treaty that gave Germany back its full sovereignty, making the German unification effective October 3.

The mood that led up to unification was that of a huge party; several voices had cautioned about the dangers of unification or had asked that the process at least be taken more slowly. The situation in the Soviet Union, which soon dissolved into several independent states, was too volatile to assume that conditions would indefinitely remain favorable to German unification. But the celebratory mood was soon replaced by the equivalent of a political hangover: ten years after unification, basic problems still defined the relation between the western and eastern parts of the unified country. Some critics maintain that soon after the Berlin Wall came down, a new wall went up in people's heads. An "us versus them" mentality solidified with the terms *Wessi* for a person from old West Germany and *Ossi* for one from the former GDR. Nostalgic feelings for the former GDR were popularly dubbed *Ostalgie* (combining the German words for "East" and "nostalgia").

The challenges of dealing with a bankrupt East German economy proved to be immense. The privatization of state-run businesses also provided an opportunity for profiteers, leaving some in the former GDR feeling as though their state had been annexed by an economically victorious West Germany. Paradoxically, a growing economy in the 1990s was unable to reduce the nationwide unemployment rate of ten percent, a figure that was much greater in the country's eastern part. In addition, the citizens in the western part of Germany became resentful because they felt that they were being forced to pick up the tab for the sixteen million people in the east. The positive note with which unification began was replaced by yet another experience of profound social and political upheaval, so typical of the twentieth century, with repercussions in all areas of life.

Germany once again was challenged to deal with its history. This time it was the Cold-War division and the clandestine role of the secret police, which, in its attempt to protect the GDR, subverted the trust of many people in their own state. As the Stasi archives, comprising about 120 miles of files, were opened and systematically reviewed, the extent of the spy network — consisting of approximately 100,000 official employees and 300,000 IMs (*inoffizielle Mitarbeiter*, or unofficial informants) and implicating prominent writers, such as Christa Wolf and Heiner Müller — became obvious. Above all, the extent of official paranoia and repressive potential was revealed; for example, to hunt down dissidents with police dogs if the need arose, the Stasi stored pieces of cloth with the dissidents' scent in glass jars.

At the end of the 1990s continuing economic problems, especially unemployment, led to a general feeling that the conservative government of Helmut Kohl, who had been praised as the chancellor of German unity throughout the early part of the decade, was no longer capable of providing the leadership necessary to move the country into the next millenium. After sixteen years in office, the Christian Democrat Kohl lost the federal election in October 1998 to his Social Democrat challenger, Gerhard Schröder, who formed a coalition government with the Green Party. This move also marked the taking over of political responsibility by the generation which grew up during the 1960s protest movement, but the start of the new government was remarkably slow because of controversies over proposed legislation, from phasing out nuclear energy to allowing dual citizenship.

In addition, the highly emotional discussion about dual citizenship raised the old specter of xenophobia in a Germany that struggled to come to terms with the large minority populations within its borders. Of about eighty million inhabitants in Germany at the end of the 1990s, roughly 7.5 million were foreigners, and slightly over four million of these foreigners had lived in Germany for eight or more years. The rethinking of old positions and of the new role a united Germany should play in the world, especially with respect to military conflicts, remained an important element within political discourse. The 1990s began with a double wake-up call, reminding people that even in Europe the post-Cold War era was far from being unproblematic: the two former German states experienced more difficulties in growing together than had been expected, and 1991 brought an international military conflict, the Persian Gulf war, which led to calls for Germany to take on a role that corresponded to its increased political importance. Later in the decade the new government experienced a moral and political dilemma concerning the Serb campaign of ethnic cleansing in Kosovo. Torn between positions exemplified by the slogans "Nie wieder Krieg" (Never again war) and "Nie wieder Auschwitz" (Never again Auschwitz), the government came out in support of NATO military deployment in the Kosovo conflict.

The 1990s were a time to take stock, not just because a century and a millennium were drawing to a close but, more importantly, because the changes symbolized by the fall of the Berlin Wall in 1989 had profound effects in all areas of life. Immediately after the end of the Cold War, hopes were high for a more democratic future because of sweeping changes in Europe; politicians proclaimed a new world order that would no longer be defined by the conflict between the superpowers, the United States and the USSR, which stood for the competing ideologies of capitalism and Communism. With the old enmities gone, the political picture grew more complex. The nuclear threat became (at least in many people's perception) more local and, thus, more real, with the possibility of nuclear bombs controlled by terrorists. And there was the issue of what the victory of industrial capitalism implied in an era moving toward a postindustrial society, as illustrated by job growth in the service area and the increasing significance of information and its electronic transmission.

At issue was a general revaluation of values — Nietzsche was returning! About one hundred years after his death, the social and political changes may well be so fundamental that the "new" that he had been seeking might just emerge. As far as ideological positions are concerned, old distinctions between the political left and right were blurred. In such an altered social and political landscape, literature can provide a playing field and drawing board for new ideas, alternate scenarios, possible worlds — as literature has always done. And literature is itself part of the revaluation. As a social institution, literature determines and is determined by rules involving the aesthetic and economic relationships among participants (authors, publishers, readers, and critics) and venues (bookstores, libraries, book fairs, and festivals). A complete history of a national literature would have to include the role of international literature, since the two together form a nation's literary canon. This is important for a cosmopolitan literary market, such as Europe, and, in particular, for Germany, where about fifteen percent of all books published in the early 1990s were translations.

Literature also provides a forum for rethinking opinions on social issues, which is especially controversial when writers address these issues in less literary genres, such as speeches, open letters, or essays. Major controversies of the 1990s centered on Martin Walser's assessment of the Holocaust in contemporary discourse, Peter Handke's support for Serbia in the Balkan conflicts, and Botho Strauß's thoughts on the role of literature in society, which he presented in his political essay "Anschwellender Bocksgesang" (Rising Goat-Song, *goat-song* is a literal translation of the Greek *tragedy*), published in the news magazine *Der Spiegel* in 1993. Strauß's combination of essayistic-fictional writing style and metaphysical perspective on the postmodern condition made each of his texts — and his "Anschwellender Bocksgesang" even more so — an irritation that was intensified by his outspoken elitist attitude. The public controversies demonstrate that the borders between traditionally firm political positions became fluid in a changed political landscape after the Cold War.

### Shocking Normality as Drama

*New identity between old taboos*

While sex and violence are always good for a scandal, they were no longer real taboos, and even their shock value was fading in the 1990s. While each generation of theatergoers is scandalized anew, cultural memory places sex and violence in the realm of accepted art, where shock values become crowd pleasers — as is illustrated by the bloodstained canvases of Shakespeare's plays. Heiner Müller observed that only two taboos of West German theater were political: anti-Semitism and terrorism. Still operative, they extended the German past — in particular the 1930s and 1940s (when anti-Semitism at its most violent led to the Nazi atrocities) and the 1970s and 1980s (when terrorism threatened West Germany) — into the new Berlin Republic.

*Der Müll, die Stadt und der Tod* (The Garbage, the City, and Death), by Rainer Werner Fassbinder, was published in 1975 but never performed by a German theater. Fassbinder's play aimed to unmask the continuity of the Nazi legacy and was praised for its honesty in dealing with this issue. Other critics, however, saw anti-Semitism at the core of the play, especially in the contrast between the characters of the rich Jew and the old Nazi. The publication of the play caused a controversy that led Fassbinder to resign in protest from his directorship of the Frankfurt Theater am Turm. The planned performance in Frankfurt in 1975 was abandoned after public protests by the city's Jewish community, and a new plan to stage the play at Berlin's Maxim Gorki Theater in 1998 was dropped when that city's Jewish community threatened protests. Ironically, a performance of Fassbinder's play in a Hebrew translation was scheduled for spring 1999 at a private acting school in Tel Aviv. The school's director believed that Fassbinder made it possible for his audience to gain insights into the German subconscious.

Rolf Hochhuth's play *Wessis in Weimar* (1993) serves as an example for assessing German identity, including the potential for violence. The play's subtitle, *Szenen aus einem besetzten Land* (Scenes from an Occupied Country), implies the provocative thesis that the play elaborates on in twelve scenes, each of which stands by itself: the old Federal Republic's capitalism treats the former GDR as an occupied territory. The first scene fictionalizes the assassination of Detlev Karsten Rohwedder, the president of the *Treuhandgesellschaft* (Trust Company), on April 1, 1991. The Trust Company's task was speedy privatization of the business sector of the former GDR, and Rohwedder is presented as the executor of that task — hence the scene's title: "Der Vollstrecker." The scene gained immediate notoriety because conservative politicians and businessmen accused Hochhuth of condoning acts of terrorism in his thought experiment that explored the motivation for violence.

In his introductory commentary, Hochhuth calls Rohwedder's death an insidious and senseless murder. Therefore, Hochhuth considers his rendition of the historical figure, called only "The President" [Der Präsident] in the scene itself, idealized and in the tradition of presentations of kings who have a human side but also stand for the tyrannical system of absolutism, such as in Friedrich Schiller's *Don Carlos*. The President expresses his honest belief that he is doing his best to revive the "economic Sahel zone" [volkswirtschaftliche Sahelzone; the Sahel is a drought-prone, arid region south of the Sahara] of the former GDR "without resorting to the methods of a police state" [ohne sich den Praktiken des Polizeistaates auszuliefern], which he thinks would be the result if attempts were made to screen the investors. The antithesis to his position is presented by Hildegard, who accuses him of not even being aware of the fact that certain questions should be asked. According to the stage directions, he thinks it absurd that, as Hildegard says, "the economy is there for the people / not the people for the economy" [Daß die Wirtschaft für die Menschen da ist, / nicht der

Mensch für die Wirtschaft]. She accuses him of participating in "a variation of colonialism" [eine Variante des Kolonialismus] when he, as she sees it, does not consider the common good of the former GDR citizens but the good of an abstract economic system. When their dialogue reveals no possibility for mediation between their respective positions, Hildegard shoots and kills him. While this scene seemed provocative, both in terms of Hildegard's argumentation and her crime, it also articulates the real anxieties of people in the eastern part of Germany as they faced the new realities.

The anxieties deepened by unification, new realities, and new identities were central to postunification drama, as they were to German literature in general. While no answers were given, the works offered a chance to explore options or, at least, to assess the state of the nation at a particular moment. The fear of being cheated out of a bright future is expressed in Stefan Heym's collection of stories *Auf Sand gebaut* (Built on Sand, 1990) and Christoph Hein's drama *Randow* (1994). The dangers that run beneath the political surface of the 1990s point back to the Nazi legacy. In the play *Ich bin das Volk* (I Am the People, 1994), by Franz Xaver Kroetz, the problems contemporary Germany experienced with refugees intertwine with events in German history. When the foreigners' petition for asylum is rejected and they are forced to leave their refuge, a concentration-camp memorial church, Christ himself appears and spits on the priest. As the political debates of the 1990s demonstrated, dealing with minorities, especially foreigners, remained a problem. The urgency of the new realities redirected most energies to coping with the immediate symptoms without addressing their causes from the past. In Botho Strauß's play *Schlußchor* (Closing Chorus, 1991) a historian and Anita, the daughter of a resistance fighter, discuss revisionist approaches to the Third Reich, yet the historian abruptly ends their conversation, saying "But, my God, who's interested in that now?" [Aber, mein Gott, wen interessiert das jetzt], when the news of the Wall being opened reaches them. Anita is left to wrestle with the German past both literally and metaphorically, as she tries to free an eagle, the German heraldic animal, from the zoo. The end of the play does not bode well for Germany's future: the eagle proves to be too tired to fly, so Anita tears it to pieces.

In *Wessis in Weimar* Hochhuth goes even further into the German past. He creates the image of a new German identity that encompasses former East and West German qualities in the plans of an actor who is self-referentially contemplating a theatrical scene with Klaus Kinkel, at the time the West German secretary of state, who had been the director of the West German central intelligence agency earlier in his career, and Markus Wolf, a high-ranking East German intelligence officer, in a play-within-the-play called *Wessis in Weimar*. As the actor realizes not only the similarity between Kinkel's and Wolf's backgrounds but also the fact that the two men never met, he resolves to play both characters as an incarnation of a German identity that includes a third historical personality, thus creating a foreboding sense of the potential military threat that may emanate from the new Germany: "I want to play both, Wolf and Kinkel. / Who else! / And best of all, Bismarck, too" [Ich will sie beide spielen, den Wolf und den Kinkel. / Wer sonst! / Und am besten auch Bismarck].

Among the immediate responses to German unification, those by playwrights focused on pointing out potential dangers that lie in not clearly addressing the issues of Germany's history. When the Berlin Wall fell, one of the hopes was that since the Cold War was over, literature could participate in a general endeavor to come to terms with the German past in order to make a truly fresh start. But the literary responses to the new political realities showed that the authors did not feel that such a fresh start took place; rather, their dramas presented the shock that normality seemed to have set in — a normality in which individuals experienced themselves as powerless and that seemed to have been made worse by the political dislocations of the 1990s.

*Changing of the guard* The theater of the 1980s was dominated by such directors as Peter Stein, Peter Zadek, and Dieter Dorn, all of whom remained influential in the 1990s. But after a period of stagnation in German drama in the 1980s that was followed by a financial crisis in the 1990s, particularly dire in the eastern part of Germany, a younger generation of theater directors in their late twenties to mid-thirties emerged that included Thomas Ostermeier, Sasha Waltz, Tom Kühnel, Robert Schuster, Andreas Kriegenburg, and Stefan Bachmann. In addition to classical plays and plays by established contemporary authors, such as Hein, Hochhuth, Kroetz, Strauß, Dorst, and Handke, the works of a new generation of playwrights gained visibility. While there were no major innovations, a number of the younger playwrights — including the Austrians Marlene Streeruwitz (b. 1950) and Werner Schwab (1958–1994), as well as the German Albert Ostermaier (b. 1967), all of whose debuts in the 1990s caused a stir — continued to explore the brutalization of the world, a project in the tradition of Heiner Müller, Thomas Bernhard, and Elfriede Jelinek. The shock that the new plays reflect was the shock at how brutal normality really had become.

Marlene Streeruwitz's plays are postmodernist patchworks in the feminist tradition. Scenes that portray brutal violence can be understood as an indictment of a hedonistic society that either turns a blind eye to violence or is voyeuristically attracted to it. While the titles of her plays suggest exoticism, the audience is confronted with familiar places into which violence intrudes. Her first play to be performed, *Waikiki Beach* (1992), is not set in Hawaii but in an old office building where an adulterous couple meets. Soon a gang attacks them; the man escapes, but the gang kills the woman. Standing by the woman's body, the man and the woman's husband later enter a pact in their roles as newspaperman and mayor, respectively, to exploit her death for political gain. What in a brief plot summary sounds like a simplistic plot with a political message, however, unfolds on the stage in a complex collage. Streeruwitz's plays include parallel scenes that quote from intertextual sources, such as other plays, movies, and poetry; for instance, the actors portraying the adulterous man and woman in *Waikiki Beach* take on the roles of Shakespeare's Antony and Cleopatra. Other collage effects include multimedia presentations, such as slide shows and sound effects. The author combines the theater of cruelty with black humor, and her plays are devoid of any utopian hope.

Like Streeruwitz's plays, Werner Schwab's dramas explore violence; and like her plays, which were successful on the stage, his were among the most performed plays at the time of his death. Schwab died young, and his alcohol abuse, which left unanswered the question whether his death was a suicide, adds an urgency to his plays. Schwab's texts always provoke — often starting with the title, which may include obscenities or startling punctuation, such as the double colon in *Faust::Mein Brustkorb:Mein Helm* (Faust::My Chest:My Helmet, 1994). The language of the plays reflects Schwab's affinity for poststructuralist theories informed by Jacques Lacan's postulation that it is language that "speaks" the individual.

Schwab's adaptation of Arthur Schnitzler's *Der Reigen* as DER REIZENDE REIGEN *nach dem Reigen des* REIZENDEN HERRN ARTHUR SCHNITZLER (THE PROVOKING RONDO after the Rondo by the PROVOKING MISTER ARTHUR SCHNITZLER, *reizend* can also mean "charming") premiered posthumously, after copyright problems, in 1995 and was published in 1996. The play is remarkable for how topical Schnitzler's exposure of promiscuity still was and for how Schwab updated the play with a language that "speaks" the characters and with the presentation of sexuality. Of these, Schwab's use of language was the most significant innovation. The complicated and stilted speech of the characters reflects their complicated and stifled lives. People never speak as individuals but as though they are defined by the exterior of their actions; they say sentences such as "although you never wanted to have a friendly exchange of language during my cutting of your hair" [wo Sie doch noch nie eine freundliche Sprachvertauschung haben wollten unter meinem Schneiden der Haare] instead of saying that the man never flirted with the hairdresser while she cut his hair. Schwab plays with language to the point that it appears nonsensical, as when

the husband says to the secretary he has just hired: "And your joblessness is really pleased to be working for me until it has lost its lessness"
[Und es freut Ihre Arbeitslosigkeit also wirklich, daß sie bei mir arbeiten darf, bis sie die Losigkeit verloren hat].

The structure of Schwab's play follows the promiscuous rondo of
one sexual partner to the next, in which one partner in each scene remains on stage for the following scene. Consequently, each character
appears in two of the ten scenes, and the play begins and ends with the
scenes in which the prostitute appears. The characters are updated from
Schnitzler's play but remain essentially the same; for example, "das süße
Mädel" (the sweet thing) has been replaced by the secretary. Schwab's
play, however, no longer comes across as a *danse macabre* — although
promiscuity is always close to death in the age of AIDS. Rather than
Schnitzler's indignation over moral decay, Schwab presents a peepshow
of sexual behaviors that have become normal but do not lead to happiness; rather, they reveal the extent to which humans have become alienated from each other and themselves. His use of language, which
flows well and is at times funny, brings out this sense of alienation. So
does his idea of how to portray the sexual act, which is left out in
Schnitzler's *Reigen*, on stage in a way that signifies the meaninglessness
and mechanization of modern sexuality. The stage directions specify
that "all male characters have detachable sexual organs. All female characters have replaceable vaginas" [Alle männliche Figuren haben ab-
schraubbare Geschlechtsteile. Alle weibliche Figuren haben aus-
tauschbare Muttern]. The ironic result is that sexual contact is possible
without any other physical contact. Usually, the male character hands
his "plastic cock" [Plastikschwanz] to the female character, and sexual
intercourse and orgasm take place as the two characters remain detached from each other. Their lives have become devoid of what makes
human beings human.

Albert Ostermaier's *Zuckersüß & Leichenbitter — oder: vom kaffee-
satz im zucker-stück* (Sweet as Sugar and Bitter as Death — or: about
the coffee grounds in the lump of sugar, 1995) also shows language
taking over people's lives. The title implies multiple puns; for instance,
*Leichenbitter* does suggest the contrast to sweet, but it is also the old-
fashioned German word for a person who invites guests to a funeral.
Moreover, one of the play's characters is named Leichenbitter, and he
has the proverbial *Leichenbittermiene* (mournful expression); he might
be the devil, the stage directions suggest. The main character is a
"lump of sugar" [Zuckerstück], hence the subtitle's allusion to a
"theater play of sugar" [zucker-stück]. In fact, the play is an extended
and rarely interrupted monologue in which the sugar lump faces a man
who sits in a dreary pub and is about to put the lump of sugar into his
coffee. To stay alive, the lump of sugar starts its breathless monologue,

which is printed without punctuation and with consistent lower-case spelling: "you do drink your coffee black right pal . . . i know pal youve certainly never laid eyes on a lump of sugar like me that even talks" [du trinkst deinen kaffee doch schwarz oder kumpel . . . ich weiss kumpel so'n zuckerstück wie ich das dazu noch spricht ist dir sicherlich noch nie unter die augen gekommen].

The lump of sugar pulls out all stops to keep the man's attention; it tells stories and a bad joke. But the question is: whose voice is speaking and what is it saying? The lump of sugar is identified as a voice; it is speech that flows from offstage and can be construed as the man's thoughts, yet it also seems to be influenced by the other character, Leichenbitter, who is always present, observing the man. The stage directions at one point identify the sugar lump's monologue as the man's "obsessive talking" [obsessiven Sprechen], but it is not his own voice. When the man briefly regains his own voice, Leichenbitter "immediately attempts to bury him under his spell again" [versucht, ihn sofort wieder in seinem Bann zu begraben]. The man becomes entranced by the voice, and finally Leichenbitter steps to the man's table, takes the lump of sugar, and eats it. Leichenbitter continues in the sugar lump's voice and laughs as the man drops dead; in his own voice, Leichenbitter cynically comments: "An unexpected death: Too much sugar in his dreams. That's bitter. Sleep sweetly (you two)" [Ein unerwarteter Tod: Zuviel Zucker in den Träumen. Das ist bitter. Schlaf(t) süss]. About to leave the pub in triumph, he freezes in horror as the jukebox begins to speak with the same words as the lump of sugar: "you do drink your coffee black right pal."

This reversal points to a cycle of dread, as Leichenbitter, who may be the devil just as the pub may represent hell, realizes that language determines even his identity. As a result, in this and other plays of the 1990s, the characters appear to enact linguistic roles forced on them by a brutalized world. While the language of these plays is one further element with which the characters are controlled, most prose and lyrical explorations of the decade were not as radical; they tended to look at language, if not as a means for controlling reality, then at least as a means for approaching the new realities.

## Modernist and Postmodernist Prose between National and World Literature

The decades before the 1990s saw the emergence of new literary discourses, such as feminist and minority literatures; they also saw the renewal of poetic forms, such as the historical novel. The innovations and renewals were accompanied by redefinitions of aesthetics, controversial and preliminary as the case might be, for instance, for a feminist aesthetics. The 1990s continued these discourses, forms, and aesthetic theories. As categories used to organize a literary history, they intersect with other categories to form the overall picture. Another important literary category centers on themes or subject matters that contribute to the identity of a text or group of texts. Such a thematic approach highlights the strengths of contemporary German literature, both with reference to specifically German issues (the Nazi legacy, the German division, and the new European realities) and to global themes shared by many national literatures (language and power, low-key apocalypses and epiphanies, and traditions of storytelling).

*German issues*  The German issues have a focus: memory. German history at times becomes the direct subject matter of a text; at other times, historical memories, such as of the Holocaust, are implicit and provide a subtext that generates an underlying sense of dread. Whether dealt with explicitly or implicitly, harm to mind and body, often epitomized in sexual suffering, is at the core of these texts. This issue ties in with larger and older ones. A heightened interest in the body was associated with Modernism. Postmodernism, however, radicalized the images of the body to include openly sadistic and masochistic visions. While this radicalization of tradition seems to favor dark visions, an abrupt turn toward the comical is close at hand. In the interplay of remembrance and invention, personal histories and retrospectives evolve into fictional interpretations of a world that is often defined by the postmodernist understanding of an expanded now. Therefore, the three most significant German issues are directed toward the past (the Nazi legacy and the German division) and toward the present (the new European realities) in such a way that they at times are telescoped together.

The interaction of these issues can be illustrated with the idiosyncratic blend of a melancholy tone with fact and fiction that allows Winfried Georg Sebald (b. 1944) to take a unique approach to memory in his prose texts. Historical memory in general dominated in *Schwindel.Gefühle* (Vertigo, 1990), which includes one narrative on Stendhal and another on Kafka. But Sebald focused his exploration of memory on the impact of German history in the stories of four men whose lives were shaped by the Third Reich and the Holocaust in *Die Ausgewanderten* (The Emigrants, 1992), and he expanded his approach to include encounters that are simultaneously more personal and more universal in *Die Ringe des Saturn* (The Rings of Saturn, 1995). The documentary quality is underscored by the pictures that all three novels incorporate. These pictures, however, are not referred to in the text; rather they generate their own "text." Integrated in the typographic flow, they enhance the exactitude of the prose and exaggerate the recreation of reality so that the boundary between fact and fiction becomes elusive and so that history, as told in Sebald's prose, seems to take on allegorical meaning.

One of the quotations prefaced to *Die Ringe des Saturn* is taken from the *Brockhaus,* a popular encyclopedia, and describes the rings of the planet Saturn as "fragments of a former moon that was too close to the planet and was destroyed by its tidal effect" [Bruchstücke eines früheren Mondes, der, dem Planeten zu nahe, von dessen Gezeitenwirkung zerstört wurde]. In the interaction with Sebald's writing, this motto suggests that natural history, the political history of humanity, and the life experience of individual humans are allegorical of each other. Sebald, furthermore, fictionalized his role of author as the narrator who is walking on foot through the English county of Suffolk. The narrator's chance encounters with and planned visits to the English landscape and its inhabitants imply a web of meaning, though a melancholy one.

In one encounter, Sebald talks with a gardener, who remembers airplanes taking off for the bombing raids on Germany during the Second World War. In the gardener's imagination the picture of German cities in ruins took hold to such an extent that he expected aerial raids to have also captured German literary imagination, but he observed: "To my astonishment, however, I soon found the search for such accounts invariably fruitless" [Zu meinem Erstaunen freilich mußte ich bald feststellen, daß die Suche nach solchen Berichten stets ergebnislos verlief]. The gardener's observation points to a disconnection between the different ways in which people attempt to understand the meaning of life and how they remember it. In his scholarly writing as a professor of German, Sebald used this observation to question whether the relatively minor role that the description of aerial bombings played in German postwar literature constituted a blind spot and, ultimately, an unwillingness to engage the complete spectrum of German history. The question addresses an important issue, specifically, which literary themes become dominant for the literature of a country. The absence of an overt treatment of a topic, however, does not necessarily mean that the topic is being ignored; for example, much post-Holocaust literature only barely, if at all, mentions the Holocaust, but that literature would remain largely unintelligible if the connection to events that remain unsaid were not made. In this instance, absence is a function of a presence that embedded itself in the literary remembrance of the Nazi legacy.

*The Nazi legacy* — The Holocaust is a defining moment in the history of Western civilization. While it engages the imagination of international literature, which is appalled by or attracted to the fascist mystique, it is a German legacy demanding to be addressed. Literary contributions to this process typically center on one of two aspects: the Third Reich or daily fascism.

Directly addressing the Third Reich means writing about experiences that took place during the Nazi regime, including how the lives of ordinary people were affected, as is portrayed in Günter Grass's *Die Blechtrommel*, and how the lives of persecuted people were destroyed, as reflected in the poetry by Paul Celan. Building on this longstanding literary tradition, German fiction of the 1990s ranged from realistic texts to postmodern speculations. Among the primarily realistic texts are *Die Bestandsaufnahme* (Taking Stock, 1995), by Gila Lustiger (b. 1963), which includes starkly realistic scenes describing the murder of the Jewish people; *Meine Sehnsucht ist das Leben* (My Yearning Is for Life, 1996), by Manfred Flügge (b. 1946), which recounts the antifascist resistance activities by a group called the Red Chapel; and the autobiographical trilogy by Ludwig Harig.

Harig's trilogy begins with his father's life in *Ordnung ist das ganze Leben* (Orderliness Is Everything, 1986) and extends to his own experiences growing up during the Third Reich in *Weh dem, der aus der Reihe tanzt* (Woe Be to Him Who Steps out of Line, 1990) and readjusting to life after the war in *Wer mit den Wölfen heult, wird Wolf* (To Howl with the Wolves Is to Join the Pack, 1996). The honesty with which the author approaches his own and his country's past becomes part of the text's structure, in which the process of remembering is refracted by the relativity of facts and their interpretation. In *Weh dem, der aus der Reihe tanzt* the author-narrator's new classmate René, who is different because he is rich and his father is French, is the target of the other classmates' cruelties. This episode has etched itself into the narrator's mind because he felt powerless; however, the narrator admits that later research proves that he — to protect himself from feeling guilty — mistook René for the boy whom they tortured.

One of the most acclaimed of the novels that use a postmodern imagination to gain a new perspective on Nazism is *Flughunde* (The Karnau Tapes, 1995), by Marcel Beyer (b. 1965). The novel is told mostly in the alternating monologues of Hermann Karnau and Helga, the eldest daughter of Joseph Goebbels, the Nazi minister of propaganda. About two-thirds of the way into the novel, a neutral narrator's seven-page report evokes the elusiveness of activities during the Third Reich: a formerly unknown "sound archive" [Schallarchiv] is discovered in Dresden in July 1992. A complex system of subterranean rooms includes a recording studio that is equipped with surgical instruments; the fact that tunnels connect the sound archive to the city's orphanage is ominous, especially since some blood traces are just a few weeks old. One person identified in the files of the sound archive is Karnau, who, when he is interviewed, reveals technical knowledge that exceeds his lowly official function as a guard: he is a sound specialist, whose study of acoustics represents the inhuman experiments of Nazi "science." His statement that the work in the archive ended before the Second World War sounds dubious, and the next morning he has disappeared.

The enormity of this inhumanity is exemplified in the fate of the Goebbels family. The history of the Third Reich has not only produced images of horror but also remarkably intense sound bites, not the least of which was Goebbels's infamous question whether his mass audience wanted total war. In a world composed of signs, Marcel Beyer tries to reconstruct the history of Nazi Germany as a history of sound, an acoustic nightmare. He does so through the invention of Karnau (the name of an actual guard in the *Führer*'s bunker in Berlin) as a man obsessed with sounds. This obsession makes Karnau a collaborator with the Nazis, since his research can be used for their purposes. He also takes care of the Goebbels children on occasion, and Helga tells about their first meeting at the time of her youngest sister's birth. Their last encounter takes place without Karnau; only one of his ubiquitous recording machines is present. He cannot or will not remember that he made the recording, and he resists recognizing what was recorded: the chilling irony of the poisoned Goebbels children slowly dying as total silence at the end of a total and cacophonic war. "The breathing of six children's lungs in transposed rhythms. The sound decreases in intensity and volume. In the end, nothing more can be heard. There is absolute silence although the needle continues to run along the groove" [Das Atmen von sechs Kinderlungen in versetztem Rhythmus. Es läßt an Intensität und Lautstärke nach. Schließlich ist gar nichts mehr zu hören. Es herrscht absolute Stille, obwohl die Nadel noch immer in der Rille liegt].

The passage illustrates the progression of dehumanization in terms of a slow dismembering of the human body. Karnau does not hear the children breathing in the recording; he hears their lungs — and not even the lungs are important to him, but the sounds they make. His entire sound archive is a monstrosity, because it lacks any trace of humanity. He senses this dilemma, and his search to preserve human sounds may ultimately express his yearning for the complete human being. But his recordings are sounds without bodies. That is the acoustic history of Nazism: human beings made incomplete by an inauthentic language of hatred that is no longer connected with human beings and that cannot reach human beings.

Daily fascism refers to the view that underlying authoritarian structures were not removed after Nazism was defeated; therefore, fascism remained alive and well — although often only in secret. Consequently, the goal of addressing daily fascism in literature had less to do with keeping a historical wound open than with pointing to the necessity of healing that wound. A broad range of literary texts addressed daily fascism, especially the father books of the late 1970s and early 1980s and feminist texts, such as the *Todesarten* project of Ingeborg Bachmann. The novels of the 1990s radicalized the generational conflict in the dreamlike reality of *Die schöne Frau* (The Beautiful Woman, 1994), by Judith Kuckart (b. 1959), and the melancholy matter-of-factness of the international bestseller *Der Vorleser* (The Reader, 1995), by Bernhard Schlink (b. 1944).

Schlink's short novel presents a story about German youth that connects the Nazi legacy with the present. Although told in a realistic manner, the novel is a metaphor for the coming-to-terms process that will necessarily remain unfinished. When the narrator, Michael Berg, has to admit to himself the truth about the story that involves him and the former concentration-camp guard, Hanna Schmitz, he implies the truth about all political attempts at laying the issue of the Nazi legacy to rest: "I made my peace with it. And it has still returned" [Ich habe meinen Frieden mit ihr gemacht. Und sie ist zurückgekommen]. Their sexual encounter is a metaphor of the innocence and vulnerability of the young generation and the secrets and guilt of the old, as well as the silences between the two generations. Fifteen-year-old Michael has fallen in love with thirty-six-year-old Hanna, of whom he knows little more than that she works as a streetcar conductor. His reading literature to her soon becomes an integral part of their meetings.

Hanna leaves town abruptly, and Michael does not see her again until years later when he is a law student. As part of a seminar Michael is observing a trial and thus finds out that Hanna was involved in the deaths of concentration-camp prisoners. He knows her secret: she is illiterate; therefore, she could not have written the reports that are used to convict her. Fiercely proud, however, she never reveals that she is unable to read and is sentenced to life imprisonment. Eighteen years later she receives a pardon. Michael, who has been sending her tapes with his readings of books — with which she has taught herself to read and write — helps her to prepare for life as a free woman, but Hanna commits suicide the day before her release. Visiting her cell, Michael finds out that she was reading literature on concentration camps; therefore, her suicide appears to be an acceptance of her guilt. Another ten years later, the relationship with Hanna still haunts him: What would have been the right thing for him to do — not to have loved her? To have saved her by telling the court that she could not read? The fact that Michael's life is unhappy and without commitment because he does not have the answers points beyond an individual's confusion to become an image of the discrepancy between large amounts of objective information (Hanna's books on the Holocaust) and the lack of personal communication between the two generations.

The side of the victim in the victim-victimizer dichotomy was addressed in a more radical way during the 1990s than it was previously. This holds especially true of texts by younger Jewish authors, such as Maxim Biller's collection of stories *Wenn ich einmal reich und tot bin* (When I Am Rich and Dead, 1990) and the novels *Suche nach M.* (Searching for M., 1997), by Doron Rabinovici (b. 1961), and *Der Musterjude* (The Model Jew, 1997), by Rafael Seligmann. The protagonists of these works are children of Holocaust survivors; these young adults live in a world that has become increasingly schizophrenic beneath the cloud of the unanswered question of how victims and victimizers relate to each other. The melancholy helplessness of Michael in *Der Vorleser* is a reflection of how difficult it is to deal with an issue that is often considered taboo. The other side of helplessness is aggressiveness: Biller mixes sex and violence in his stories, while Rabinovici's novel is as much a post-Holocaust novel as it is crime fiction. Rabinovici allegorizes guilt in the figure of Dani Morgenthau, who cannot help but take on the personality and suffering of anybody who carries guilt. This bizarre messiah has an alter ego in Arieh, who can, by sheer force of intuition, find those who are guilty.

Seligmann's *Der Musterjude* centers on the taboo of anti-Semitism itself by narrating a fictitious journalistic scandal that rocks Germany. Forty-year-old Moische Bernstein becomes, for a short time, a star among journalists with his articles claiming that the twentieth century was the century of Hitler: "Adolf Hitler was the only German revolutionary. He democratized the society of Germany and unified Europe. . . . he is the midwife for the birth of the Jewish state" [Adolf Hitler war der einzige deutsche Revolutionär. Er hat die Gesellschaft Deutschlands demokratisiert und Europa vereint. . . . er ist der Geburtshelfer des Judenstaates]. Such statements are untenable; they not only confuse means and ends but also mistake one historical phenomenon (Nazism) as the narrow-mindedly monocausal explanation of complex developments (postwar democracy). The ironic twist of Seligmann's story does not consist in the fact that Bernstein can make these statements without being accused of being apologetic for Nazism because he is a Jew (and that Seligmann could have his Bernstein make these statements for the same reason). The twist also does not consist in the fact that the German public in the novel gobbles up these statements, since there still is a strong undercurrent of anti-Semitism. The true irony lies in the fact that it all is a media ploy for higher sales of the journal and that, where there might have been a chance of taking the slow process of coming to terms a step further, the novel has Bernstein struggle with the problem of coming up with the next outrageous claim that will guarantee even higher sales. In the end, nothing has really changed.

Ingeborg Bachmann's prose of the 1960s and early 1970s exemplifies texts that, even though they do not name fascism as their subtext, cannot be understood without it. A large number of texts of the 1990s — from Elfriede Jelinek's and Christoph Ransmayr's apocalypses to the epiphanies of Patrick Roth (b. 1953) — belong in the this category. Jelinek's *Die Kinder der Toten* (The Children of the Dead, 1995) continues the feminist tradition, combining it with strong images of brutality. Set in a seemingly idyllic Alpine village, the novel follows the grotesque story of three undead characters whose bizarre afterlife of vampirism and cannibalism is as unfulfilling as their previous lives. All of this is symbolic of the brutal undercurrents of Austrian involvement with National Socialism, which was hidden under the image of Austria as Nazi Germany's first victim in 1938. In the epilogue, reports on disturbing discoveries of human hair and long-dead bodies — all allusions to the Holocaust — in the process of excavations after mudslides are met with the public's usual denial: "That's just not possible" [Das gibt es doch einfach nicht].

*The German division*

The German division is paradigmatic of the fissures of the twentieth century. While it is not necessarily a predominant subject in German literature, it is a central German issue. Furthermore, the unification and the broader context of the fall of Communism were historic events of sweeping significance. The end of the Cold War had an immediate effect on German culture. Literature once again had to reexamine its relationship with reality and political power. This examination involved the questions of some authors' collaboration with the infamous East German secret police and of literature's role between affirmation and emancipation. The claim after 1989 and in light of the expanding new media was that German literature could again become what it was supposed to be: literature. But this did not mean that literature withdrew from reality to focus on itself. In fact, as an immediate response to the fall of the Berlin Wall there was a surge in autobiographical and essayistic writing.

The discussion of literature's role also raised the question of what literature is allowed to do: can it address any issue, or are some issues, such as sex and violence, taboo? Or perhaps only specific ideological and political manifestations of violence are taboo — for example, anti-Semitism and terrorism? The core of the political issue is a human issue. The border between East and West all too often ran through families. The division cut deeply into personal histories and strongly affected an individual's sense of identity and belonging. For the period up to the late 1960s, the human dimensions of the German political division found their definitive treatment in Uwe Johnson's *Jahrestage*.

A sense of identity and belonging is crucial during the process of growing up. Childhood's archetypal condition, innocence, is changed in various ways by initiation processes, which oscillate between freedom, such as gaining independence from parents, and new obligations — the subject matter of the Bildungsroman. A number of prose texts of the 1990s dealt with these subjects. Growing up in West Germany in the 1950s is the focus of the narrative *Der Sonntag, an dem ich Weltmeister wurde* (The Sunday I Became a World Champion, 1994), by F. C. Delius; in the 1960s in the novel *Beat* (1995), by Woomy Schmidt (b. 1945), and Schlink's *Der Vorleser*; and in the 1970s in the novel *Wäldernacht* (Night of the Forests, 1994), by Ralf Rothmann (b. 1953), and *Erste Liebe Deutscher Herbst* (First Love German Autumn, 1997), by Michael Wildenhain (b. 1958). Schmidt's and Rothmann's novels incorporate elements of popular culture. Schmidt's novel is as upbeat as the music of the Beatles, which gives the novel its title.

Rothmann's darker novel includes elements of crime fiction. *Wäldernacht* depicts, in flashback episodes, events in the childhood of the forty-year-old narrator, a struggling artist. Returning to his provincial hometown as an artist-in-residence, the narrator meets his childhood friends, including Rocko, who is the narrator's rougher alter ego and who ends his criminal career in a shoot-out with the police. While the lives of the main characters are told in their everyday banality, the tone is as melancholy as the observations are precise because none of the troubled childhoods have turned into decent adulthoods. Rocko is dead, and the others seem caught in unhappy lives. Significantly, the novel ends with the image of a roller coaster that the narrator watches. Symbolic of his uncompleted life, the description of the roller coaster's cars ends in mid-sentence: "cars, which slowly . . . work their way up and, for a moment, seem to disappear in the late light, in the reflecting glow, in order to then" [Wagen, die sich langsam . . . hinaufmühen und momentlang zu verschwinden scheinen im späten Licht, im Gegenglanz, um dann].

Growing up in East Germany is at the center of the collected stories *Verfrühte Tierliebe* (Premature Love for Animals, 1995), by Katja Lange-Müller (b. 1951), and *Von allem Anfang an* (From the Very Start, 1997), by Christoph Hein. With these works Lange-Müller established herself, and Hein reestablished himself, as major writers of German prose. Both authors bring observed and experienced reality to life in their stories. Lange-Müller's typical narrative tone is a casual colloquialness that has the coolness and detachment of city slang; at the same time, it communicates the narrator's vulnerability as a girl or young woman in the late 1960s and early 1970s. This combination is encapsulated in the phrase "Kokelfeuer meiner Phantasie," which roughly translates as "playful fire of my imagination." The verb *kokeln* (to play with fire), however, not only evokes a playfulness but also exhibits the colloquial tone that provides depth for narrating the narrator's embarrassments and humiliations; for example, she has a schoolgirl crush on a dubious biologist in the first of the two stories, and she ends up covered with insects during an excursion. Hein achieves depth in a different way: his autobiographical narrator tells the events from the perspective of a boy during the 1950s; he does so with the adult author's suppleness but without losing the tone of innocence and surprise.

Life in the GDR was defined by the collectivist ideology that was enforced through the surveillance network of the secret police. For the younger generation of authors, this situation meant that they had to deal with generational problems in a continuation of the tradition of the father books — for example, in *Stille Zeile sechs* (Silent Row Six, 1991), by Monika Maron, and *Spiegelland* (Mirror Land, 1992), by Kurt Drawert (b. 1956). For the older generation, an observation by Günter de Bruyn in *Vierzig Jahre* (Forty Years, 1996), the second volume of his autobiography, illustrates one difficulty of assessing the GDR in the context of twentieth-century German history: "When I was fearing for my self-determination and self-respect in Ulbricht's state, the comparison was still close at hand with Hitler's even more unfree state, which, by a hair, had almost cost me my life" [Als ich in Ulbrichts Staat um Selbstbestimmung und Selbstachtung bangte, war zum Vergleich noch der unfreiere Hitlers nahe, der mich um ein Haar Kopf und Kragen gekostet hätte]. One's sense of identity and belonging was fundamentally undermined by a lack of trust. The extent of people's involvement with the secret police emerged only after access was gained to its files, which were used by some authors to document the repression they had been made to suffer — for instance, in *Deckname "Lyrik"* (Code Name "Poetry," 1990), by Reiner Kunze, and *Der Zorn des Schlafes* (The Wrath of Sleep, 1990), by Erich Loest.

Hans Joachim Schädlich edited a documentary anthology, *Aktenkundig* (On Record, 1992); however, his short story "Die Sache mit B." (The Case of B., 1992) brings the issue to a head in an autobiographically informed plot in which the phrase "Big brother is watching you" takes on a new meaning. B., the narrator's older brother, watches him grow up and gives brotherly support and advice on such matters as learning math and building a snowman. But later the big brother, now an agent of Big Brother — the secret police — is still watching the narrator: this time to spy on him and his potentially subversive activities as a writer. Only after the fall of the Wall does the author-narrator find out the truth. The breach of trust is so enormous that the narrator's life is yanked out of context. The story's unemotional tone is akin to that of Albert Camus's literary existentialism: people are isolated from each other and face decisions that are impossible to make, yet life goes on. But Schädlich's narrator cannot recover any sense of happiness, not even in his attempts at telling the story — unlike Sisyphus, who, according to Camus's Modernist myth, finds happiness because he is active, regardless of his activity's futility. After the narrator confronts his brother, he does not know what to do next; he cannot even fully rely on his narrative abilities because reality is elusive: "I can recount the case of B. only incompletely. And there is not even an end to the tale" [Ich kann die Sache mit B. nur unvollständig erzählen. Ein Ende hat die Erzählung auch nicht]. This admission points to the private dimensions of political problems.

Wolfgang Hilbig, a major writer and former laborer, began publishing in 1978 with prose and poems that evoked a lack of humanity. His texts were immediately suspicious to the East German authorities, and his troubles included imprisonment. His novel *"Ich"* ("Me," 1993) displays Hilbig's typical style in a Kafkaesque analysis of fleeting reality and identity. The narrator — only known by his code-name "Cambert" — spies for the Stasi on a writer with code name "Reader," who turns out to be a Stasi informant himself. Cambert shares with Hilbig his profession as a writer and a similar biographical background (Hilbig, however, was not a Stasi informant). Since Cambert is an unsuccessful writer, the Stasi is his audience, and his reports are his literature. He fears that his work concerning "Reader" is not important, so he starts spying on his own account, unwittingly botches another Stasi project, and is transferred from Berlin back to small-town Saxony.

Cambert feels removed from his life before the time he started working for the Stasi; he remembers that time as though it were covered by a "net of language, which I actually could refer to as an impenetrable tissue of simulation" [Netz von Sprache, das ich tatsächlich als ein undurchdringliches Gewebe von Simulation bezeichnen konnte]. Most of Cambert's existence has the appearance of a simulation, and he experiences his identity as "hollow and imaginary" [hohl und phantastisch]. External reality has the same qualities; it is evoked in timeless or archaic terms, such as Cambert's perception of Berlin from his underground perspective: "The city above my head was like an enormous generator whose never-ending vibration was barely noticeable in all the stone. . . . And everything we were able to learn and comprehend . . . was the realization that we had to come to an end — but not so the urban Moloch Berlin. [Die Stadt über mir war wie ein ungeheurer Generator, dessen unablässige Vibration kaum merklich in allem Gestein war. . . . Und alles, was wir lernen und begreifen konnten, . . . war die Erkenntnis, daß wir enden mußten, — nicht aber der urbane Moloch Berlin].

Dealing with the past of the GDR also gave rise to comic literature, such as Thomas Brussig's (b. 1965) novels *Helden wie wir* (Heroes Like Us, 1995) and *Am kürzeren Ende der Sonnenallee* (At the Short End of Sun Avenue, 1999). *Helden wie wir* presents East German history in satirical exaggeration. In a boastful speech, Klaus Uhltzscht claims to deserve two Nobel Prizes, one in literature (for his yet unwritten autobiography) and one for peace — and that is just on the novel's first page. The second page states why he earned the Nobel Peace Prize: "The way I managed that thing with the Berlin Wall" [Wie ich das mit der Berliner Mauer hingekriegt habe]. The full account of how his gigantic erection enabled him to open the Wall is related almost three hundred pages later, after he has told the story of his life.

*New European realities*   The end of the Cold War brought not only unification to Germany but also self-determination and independence to the former Soviet-bloc countries. What began with so much hope at the end of the 1980s and the beginning of the 1990s had, by the end of the decade, turned out to be a profound social and political upheaval. Elements of continuity and discontinuity are emphasized in the German perspective that combined the three significant stages in twentieth-century German history: Nazism, division (East Germany), and unification.

In the novel *Abschied von den Feinden* (Farewell to the Enemies, 1995), by Reinhard Jirgl (b. 1953), two brothers, born in East Germany soon after the war, are taken away from their mother because their father, a former Nazi, left for the West. One brother also goes to West Germany, while the other joins the East German secret police. At the end, one brother is murdered by the other. The fall of the Berlin Wall was a superficial change; beneath the surface the same old hatred and meaninglessness are untouched, although they are more diffuse since the Cold War enmities, which used to provide a focus, are gone. The author's Avant-Gardist affinities, from Dada to Arno Schmidt, are evident in his idiosyncratic spelling and punctuation. The novel's last two sentences, for example, include *1* for the indefinite article and *u:* for the conjunction *and* as an expression of opposites (in contrast to + which is used in dream passages): "There, in this slowly fading place, he, incommensurate with-himself a: his pictures, would remain 1 blind point, 1 spot" [Dort, in diesem langsam erbleichenden Ort, würde er, unvereinbar mit-sich u: seinen Bildern, 1 blinder Punkt sein, 1 Fleck].

Stefan Heym's short story that gave the collection *Auf Sand gebaut* (Built on Sand, 1990) its title also includes Nazi legacy, GDR history, and New German realities. An older East German couple lives in a house that they bought before unification. After unification the son of

the deceased previous owner drops by to inspect the house. A caricature of a slimy capitalist, he tells the couple that his father was never
properly compensated by the GDR authorities after they took possession of the property, implying that he has a legal claim on the house.
The visitor from the West leaves, only to allow the next visitor to compound the uncertainties. After her grandfather's death, a young woman
from Israel inherited the house, which had been taken without com-
pensation from its rightful owner by a Nazi, the father of the West
German capitalist. What began for the East German couple as a new
and exhilarating pursuit of monetary happiness, where "property ownership is under protection of the state, always and everywhere" [Besitz
steht unter staatlichen Schutz, immer und überall], has degenerated
into a confusing state of uncertainty. Heym's story articulates the feeling of the former East German population of being overrun and left
out by Western interests in restructuring the East German economy:
"But where does that leave *us* then?" [Aber wo stehen *wir* dann?], asks
the wife in "Auf Sand gebaut."

History is always present, even in texts that emphasize the new realities. Landolf Scherzer (b. 1941) and Ingo Schulze (b. 1962) found
these realities in small-town eastern Germany. Scherzer continued the
tradition of critical journalism in his collection of reports *Der Zweite*
(The Second, 1997), and Schulze tells of people's fears and hopes in
*Simple Storys* (1998) with great virtuosity so that the individual narrative episodes form a novel. Another obvious aspect of new German reality was the Berlin Republic. The unification, in conjunction with the
decision to move the federal government to Berlin, gave Germany a
"big city" again. In a country in which only Hamburg, Munich, and
Cologne have populations exceeding one million, Berlin is conspicuous
with over 3.5 million inhabitants. Moreover, because of major construction work, the Berlin of the 1990s was poised to emerge as
Europe's most modern city at the beginning of the twenty-first century.
Novels set in Berlin include *Ausdeutschen* (To Out-German, 1994), by
Andreas Neumeister (b. 1959); *In Berlin* (1994), by Irina Liebmann
(b. 1943 in Russia); and *Nox* (Night, 1995), by Thomas Hettche
(b. 1964).

Hettche's *Nox* is a novel of the city and of the human body; more
precisely, it is a novel of the city as body, since body imagery, such as
"wound" [Wunde] and "scar" [Narbe], is used to describe the condition of the city. The living bodies of people and of the city interact with
each other, as well as, paradoxically, with the dead body of the narrator.
While slowly decomposing, the narrator follows the sexual encounters
of the young woman who murdered him at the beginning of the novel.
This surrealistic construction makes it possible for the narrator to be
omniscient without being old-fashioned. The night to which the novel's

title refers is a special one: the night the Berlin Wall is opened. Highly charged with political implications, highly provocative with its violent sadomasochistic sexuality, and highly literary with texts by Kafka, Benn, Grass, and others as its subtext, *Nox* was just as highly controversial.

Intertextuality plays an important role in *Nox*. The dog in Nox is reminiscent of the dog in Grass's *Hundejahre;* another parallel can be established between Tulla in *Hundejahre* and the woman in *Nox* because of each woman's relationship to the dog in the respective novels. In both novels, the female character regresses to an animal-like state of existence; Tulla emerges from the doghouse after seven days, and the woman in *Nox* forgets her name and starts out through the city on her quest for identity. More than merely the rebirth of a nation and its capital city, the rebirth of humankind is suggested by the emerging sense of self that distinguishes humans from animals. In *Nox* the dog, which is not so much an animal as a mythical being like the She-Rat in Grass's *Die Rättin*, retells the myth of the original male-female human being, whose separation into two halves caused an existential wound and the yearning of each half for the other. In the novel's setting, the legend of the androgynous being is also a metaphor for the political wound of the Iron Curtain. The end of *Nox* ambiguously suggests the woman's success in finding her identity: before they part, she tells the narrator her name, but the reader does not learn what it is.

Literary explorations of the issue of identity that go beyond a narrowly German perspective may be instructive, for instance, in texts by Austrian, Swiss, and multicultural writers. Austrian writers, such as Robert Menasse (b. 1954), had their own perspective on the fall of the Iron Curtain as the borders between Czechoslovakia and Austria are opened in *Schubumkehr* (Thrust Reversal, 1995). Elfriede Jelinek and Gerhard Roth worked on unmasking an undercurrent of dreadful and political madness that they saw running through everyday life in Austria. A series of seven books that Roth published between 1980 and 1991 were grouped together as *Die Archive des Schweigens* (The Archives of Silence), but other novels of his, such as *Der See* (The Lake, 1995), share the same theme. An atmosphere of criminality encircles the Neusiedler Lake: the protagonist Paul Eck is addicted to pills, and his father was at one time involved in illegal arms sales. When he comes to the lake looking for his father, who has disappeared, Paul is a suspect. The remains of an old war plane in the underbrush and the chapter "Der vergessene Friedhof" (The Forgotten Cemetery), about the Jewish cemetery, evoke a pervasive sense of guilt that points back to National Socialism. At the end, Paul's father is found dead. Some threads of the plot are resolved, but others are left dangling; it is unclear how many of the events were Paul's hallucination.

The youngest generation of authors to emerge in the 1990s is represented by Kathrin Röggla (b. 1971) of Austria and Zoë Jenny (b. 1974) of Switzerland. Their texts expressed a new feeling for the world, a feeling that reacted against the counterculture generation turning into parents and that embraced contemporary conditions without illusion, although often with a sense of irony. Jenny's short novel *Das Blütenstaubzimmer* (The Pollen Room, 1997) shows the narrator Jo struggling to find her own identity and sense of belonging between, on the one hand, her divorced parents' patterns of love and self-realization, which have degenerated into a cold narcissism, and, on the other hand, the artificial contemporary world of techno parties and drugs like Ecstasy. The realistic narrative is focused on Jo's visit to and return from southern Europe, where her mother has been living for twelve years. Röggla's short novel *Abrauschen* (Taking Off, 1997) is similarly set in the hectic mobility of modern Europe but is completely different in style. The narrator moves with a six-year-old boy from Berlin to Salzburg, lives there in a tiny apartment, and moves back to Berlin. The narrator and the boy live on different time scales: while only a few months seem to elapse, the boy grows up to be a computer hacker. The discrepancy, however, could be a projection by the narrator or the textual process itself, which generates its own reality by combining fragments into collages. This process is grounded in the narrator's biography: "in reality my parents never existed, but school did exist, and school never finished with me" [in wirklichkeit hat es meine eltern auch nie gegeben, aber die schule, die gab es, die schule hat nie schluß gemacht mit mir].

*Multicultural authors* — Writers from ethnic backgrounds other than the dominant one are almost necessarily aware of language in a way that differs from the experiences of those who grow up with a language and culture that appears congruent with reality. In the 1990s multicultural German-language texts continued to reflect the endeavor to cope with new experiences that necessitate a new language.

*The realistic mode of guest-worker prose* — To a large extent, life in Germany for these authors was a "guest worker's" existence, and the themes of culture clash and treatment of the foreigner based on prejudice and exploitation were central to the first phase of migrant literature. While the second phase brought about a stronger emphasis on language, the original existential and political motivation for writing remained. Renan Demirkan (b. 1955 in Turkey) expresses in *Schwarzer Tee mit drei Stück Zucker* (Black Tea with Three Lumps of Sugar, 1991) the search for a new identity that transcends the limitations of both cultures involved: "for the girls the boundaries between 'us' and the 'others' . . . had become blurred within only two years" [für die Mädchen hatte sich innerhalb von nur zwei Jahren die Grenze zwischen "wir" und den "anderen" . . . verwischt]. Emine Sevgi Özdamar (b. 1946 in Turkey) recalls in *Die Brücke vom goldenen Horn* (The Bridge of the Golden Horn, 1998) her first encounters with German, including her and two other girls' attempts at shopping: "To describe eggs, we turned our backs to the shop assistant, wagged our rear ends, and said: 'Gak, gak, gak'" [Um Eier zu beschreiben, drehten wir unsere Rücken zu der Verkäuferin, wackelten mit unseren Hintern und sagten: "Gak gak gak"].

The two novels by Demirkan and Özdamar minimize psychological explanations; rather, they confront the experiences of young Turkish women at a descriptive level. In Demirkan's novel, a woman is waiting for the doctors to perform a Caesarian section on her; while she waits, her thoughts drift to memories ranging from the Turkish village where her grandparents live to her own life in Germany. In Özdamar's novel the narrator travels between Turkey and Europe, especially Berlin, during the 1960s. Both novels are effective because of their juxtaposition of the two worlds. Life's changes and challenges are presented in an often episodic manner. At a surface level, this suggests the characters' detachment from their own identities.

The treatment of multicultural experience presents an opportunity for cultures to learn about each other. Such a mutually enlightening and beneficial encounter is presented as a utopian goal in some texts, for example, when in Demirkan's novel the woman waiting to give birth talks to her unborn daughter about a new religion: "Then we will wake up with the Christian urge to do things, live the intelligent Jewish wisdom in the loving and relaxed manner of the Muslim, and fall asleep at night in Buddha's lap in hope of rebirth" [Dann werden wir mit dem christlichen Tatendrang aufwachen, in liebevoller, moslemisch gelassener Art die klugen jüdischen Weisheiten leben und abends mit der Hoffnung auf Wiedergeburt in Buddhas Schoß einschlafen]. But some — and sometimes the same — texts repeat ethnic and national stereotypes; for instance, in Demirkan's novel the only really decent nurse is not German but Dutch, and Özdamar ends her novel with her protagonist leaving Turkey after her mother encouraged her by saying: "Flee, and live your life. Go, fly" [Flieh und leb dein Leben. Geh, flieg]. Although stereotypes allow for easy misunderstandings, in literary works they appear as attitudes that should be overcome.

In the 1990s the predominantly realistic mode of the first phase of multicultural literature gave way to the predominantly aesthetic mode of the second phase, whose linguistic play was better equipped to imagine an overcoming of stereotypes. Özdamar explores the mode of imagination when her protagonist experiences falling in love with a young man in Paris in terms of a doubling of each of them as a result of seeing herself and the young man in the mirrors at Versailles. In other texts, the option of a new life or identity is clearly a function of language; for example, the title of one of Özdamar's books stands for her experiences: *Das Leben ist eine Karawanserei / hat zwei Türen / aus der einen kam ich rein / aus der anderen ging ich raus* (Life is a Caravansary / Has Two Doors / Out of One I came in / Out of the Other I Went Out, 1992).

*Linguistic play in minority prose* 
While their biographies connect Demirkan and Özdamar with the large Turkish segment in Germany, writers of other ethnic, national, and social backgrounds share the emphasis on the culture clash and liberation through language. Yoko Tawada (b. 1960 in Japan) and Libuše Moníková (1945–1998, born in Czechoslovakia) exemplify this point. When Tawada approaches Germany geographically in her autobiographical report *Wo Europa anfängt* (Where Europe Begins, 1991) on the Trans-Siberian Railroad, she also approaches the German language. She first wrote in Japanese and had her texts translated into German but then began writing in German. In her essay "Von der Muttersprache zur Sprachmutter" (From Mother Tongue to the Mother of Language) in *Talisman* (1996), Tawada describes what she felt when she learned the German word *Bleistift* for pencil and observes that the object called *Bleistift* in German and the one called *Enpitsu* in Japanese are the same; nevertheless, the strength of her emotional response surprised her. Using the German word caused her to feel shame: "It was comparable with the feeling that overcame me when I had to address my married acquaintance by her new last name" [Es war vergleichbar mit dem Gefühl, das auf mich zukam, als ich meine verheiratete Bekannte mit ihrem neuen Familennamen ansprechen mußte]. As a result, she realizes that the relationship between her and all objects is a linguistic one. The typewriter — according to the gender system of the German language, the only feminine item on Tawada's desk — becomes a "mother of language" for the author by giving her the gift of a new language. Tawada experiences the foreign language as liberation: while her native language seems to have stapled meanings and thoughts to words, the foreign language removes these staples.

In Moníková's short novel *Verklärte Nacht* (Transfigured Night, 1996), the experience with language is taken one step further when the narrator returns from Germany to Prague for a visit and realizes: "Back then I didn't think about names . . . even uncertainty felt familiar. Now I am no longer sure of any word" [Früher habe ich über Namen nicht nachgedacht . . . noch die Unklarheit war vertraut. Jetzt bin ich mir keines Wortes sicher]. Earlier, in working on her first publication, *Eine Schädigung* (A Damage, 1981), Moníková reportedly achieved a creative breakthrough only after she started to write in German. In the novel *Pavane für eine verstorbene Infantin* (Pavan for a Dead Infanta, 1983), Moníková explores the social and personal damages that result from being a woman and a foreigner; her themes are loss and pain. Her novel *Treibeis* (Drift Ice, 1992) presents these themes in conjunction with the loss of Prague and impossible love. In her last novel, *Verklärte Nacht*, Moníková has returned to Prague, and love, however fragile, is a possibility again.

Moníková's writing is characterized by diverse observations and thoughts, as well as by a strong intertextuality with citations from, allusions to, and discussions of other works of literature and art. Kafka is a constant presence in her novels; in *Verklärte Nacht*, the Kafkaesque threat of loss and pain is evoked when the narrator speculates about the location of "Joseph K.'s deserted rock quarry" [der verlassene Steinbruch von Joseph K.]. While the protagonist feels this sense of loss, she is also a strong woman, especially as she transcends the realistic frame of the story through an identification of her name, Leonora Marty, with that of Emilia Marty, one of the many names used by the woman who attained almost eternal youth, because her father made her drink a magic potion more than three hundred years earlier. The novel presents the Greek legend as having inspired the music of a Czech composer, which, in turn, is used by the protagonist's dance company, with Leonora in the title role. The protagonist further extends her existence three thousand years into the past to the realm of ancient myth when she has a fever dream of Egypt, in which she sees herself being mummified. Moníková makes the dehumanizing aspect of such a mythical existence visible as a life without love; with "terror and trembles" [Entsetzen und Schauer], a male partner experiences the woman as "cold as a corpse" [kalt wie ein Leichnam].

Leonora experiences love, in all its fragility, as an option of breaking through frozen gender relationships — metaphorically. Literally, she becomes ill after she and Thomas, her new German acquaintance, fall into a frozen river; he nurses her back to health with tenderness and understanding, at the same time intruding into her life. The encounter with the option of love brings complex dichotomies into play that are much like the teeming chaos that, according to Friedrich Schlegel (1772–1829), is at the core of romantic irony. The associative web of *Verklärte Nacht* — jumping from visits to the police museum to the use of dolphins by the Soviet navy — reveals domination as fundamental to gender, national, and political relationships.

These relationships are destabilized in the encounter of Leonora and Thomas in Prague; their history is identified as "a history of mutual answers between Czechs and Germans without either side having ever asked a question" [eine Geschichte der gegenseitigen Antworten zwischen Tschechen und Deutschen, ohne daß eine Seite jemals gefragt hätte]. Thomas appears in Leonora's life without her asking. Their encounter is more than a meeting between woman and man; it is an illustration of the human conflict between being sensitive without being weak and of being strong without being destructive. As a dominating character, Leonora has taken on qualities that are associated with men; likewise, Thomas displays nurturing qualities that are associated with women. Furthermore, she has a strong sense of national pride, while his attitude to Germany is influenced by the Nazi legacy and by some of his family roots being Czech. Both live a life that is international: she is the star of an international dance company, and he works for the European Academy of Music Theater with offices in Bayreuth, Tallinn, and Prague. The novel ends in an androgynous image of love's totalizing power and its fragility: "This night is a long illness, a fever, a delirium; the worst thing that can happen is to get well. . . . We don't know which body part belongs to whom; there are no parts. We fall asleep in this way" [Diese Nacht ist eine lange Krankheit, Fieber, Delir; das schlimmste, was passieren kann, gesund zu werden. . . . Wir wissen nicht, wem welcher Körperteil gehört, es gibt keine Teile. So schlafen wir ein].

*Global themes*

Since global themes are manifest in German issues, the previously discussed texts participate in world literature. Other texts have a wider focus, placing German issues in a broader context or embracing international themes, modes, or interests. German literature of the 1990s shared a strong historical interest with international literature. In the 1980s, a postmodernist interest in history for its own sake contributed to a revival of the German historical novel. In contrast to the historical canvas that Modernism used to paint a picture of its time, the postmodern approach to the past meant understanding one's historical roots and historical position in terms of an expanded now.

Related to history, considered as a journey in time, is the travel motif, which was popular in the 1990s. Other motifs that gained importance in international and in German literature included those derived from the tension among language, sexuality, and politics. Possibilities and limitations of language were expressed in motifs of writing and reading, as well as of the media, including the movie as a modern image of the discrepancy between imitation and real life. Sexuality as a motif varied from true love to sadomasochistic images of the human body, which, in turn, was presented as the motif of the battlefield where politics intrudes into people's private lives. Three important global aspects for German literature in the 1990s were language and power, apocalypses and epiphanies, and traditional themes of storytelling.

*Language and power*     Individual identities can be understood as negotiated in discourses, such as those on politics, sexuality, and language. These discourses are about power in social relationships; they defined the bourgeois consciousness at its various stages and were transformed again by the new conditions of life in the postmodern world. This involves not only literature *about* power but also literature *as* power. The debate over the extent to which authors should participate in public discourse is as old as censorship; speeches, open letters, essays, and other public utterances have always been part of literary history. In the 1990s a number of authors, such as Botho Strauß, Peter Handke, and Martin Walser, caused controversies with their publicly voiced opinions.

Literary works also caused major controversies. Prominent examples are Christa Wolf's short narrative *Was bleibt* and Günter Grass's massive novel *Ein weites Feld* (Too Far Afield, 1995). Rather than being just about power, these works are examples of the interrelationship of literature and power. Literature as a social institution is not only about freedom of expression in terms of civil liberties but also about who is free to express his or her opinion in the sense of economic feasibility. *Was bleibt*, an account of her being under Stasi surveillance, embroiled Wolf in a controversy over her privileges under the GDR, her own early and short-lived collaboration with the Stasi, and the relationship between writers and political power in general. This controversy can be seen in regard to the newly emerging book market of the united Germany. If Wolf and other former East German authors were discredited, their texts would be at a competitive disadvantage.

The title of Grass's novel is a quote from *Effi Briest* (1894–1895), by the German Realist writer Theodor Fontane (1819–1898). The protagonist of *Ein weites Feld*, the East German Theo Wuttke, is nicknamed "Fonty" because of his similarity to Fontane; he is Fontane's alter ego living one hundred years later. Fonty's shadow is Hoftaller, the reincarnation of the eternal spy from Schädlich's *Tallhover*. The controversy over the novel was about the power of literature: whoever tells the story determines what happened, and whoever determines what happened in the past probably determines the future. Grass was one of the most outspoken opponents of a quick unification of Germany, and *Ein weites Feld* was written in opposition to the general consensus that unification was a good decision. Many critics condemned it as merely a vehicle for Grass's arguments against German unification.

Rather than censoring the book, however, the harsh criticism functioned as advertising in a mass-media-driven book market that considers literature a commodity: within a month, Grass's novel sold almost 200,000 copies.

At the literary level, the theme of power was pervasive throughout the three German issues of Nazi legacy, division, and new realities. In addition to treating the theme of power in terms of German issues, however, literature by German-language authors included settings that are not specific to Germany or to Europe. International or nonspecific settings were often used to explore gender issues and the Third World.

The poetic archaeology of power, begun by Wolf in *Kassandra*, again defines the origins of gender relationships in her novel *Medea*. The new novel consists of a multiperspective ensemble of eleven chapter-length monologues spoken by six characters, or "voices" [Stimmen], as *Medea's* subtitle indicates. The classical myth of Medea is deconstructed piece by piece, and a new image of Medea as the peaceful and understanding woman is constructed. In Wolf's rewriting of the myth every negative quality or action that the classical myth attributed to Medea — from killing her own brother so that she can escape with her lover Jason to murdering Jason's new bride and her own children out of jealousy — is presented as a fabrication to discredit Medea and save face for patriarchy. Medea, like Kassandra, is a woman who has become a threat to the powers that be not just because of her independence but because she understands the foundations of the political system. While *Kassandra* can be seen as an ideal biography of a woman within a repressive system that she slowly begins to understand, *Medea* can be seen as an ideal biography of an outsider, who brings with her a mistrust of power that Kassandra had yet to develop.

No simplistic analogy, however, especially in terms of a roman à clef, should be suggested between Wolf's novels and the contemporary political situation. What is at issue is finding the origins of the political domination and repression that Wolf perceived as running through the last three thousand years of human history. If the post-Cold War situation appeared similar to the one evoked in *Medea*, it is not by analogy but because actual political decisions reflected in classical myths are at the beginning of the complex social development that led to contemporary society. Wolf's reconstruction of the myth presupposes the reader's knowledge of the classical myth that is being deconstructed to appreciate the enormity of the mythological lies that are used to bury the truth.

This enormity is evoked as the novel opens, when Medea slips away from a banquet into the labyrinthine cellar of the royal palace in Corinth. The society of Corinth tries to keep its power struggles secret, such as the politically motivated sacrifice of the young princess Iphinoe, whose remains Medea discovers in the cellar: "since then I have not been able to think of anything but this skull of a small child, these delicate shoulder blades, this fragile spine, oh" [kann seitdem an nichts anderes denken als an diesen schmalen kindlichen Totenschädel, diese feinknochigen Schulterblätter, diese zerbrechliche Wirbelsäule, ach].

As Medea proves to be strong-willed and independent-minded, she becomes a victim of power politics. She had left her native Kolchis because she had no ties to it after its matriarchal structures became only memories. She has grown apart from Jason, so his finding a new love does not upset her. At the end of the novel Medea will leave but knows that she will remain homeless: "Is a world conceivable, a time, into which I would fit. No one here whom I could ask. That is the answer" [Ist eine Welt zu denken, eine Zeit, in die ich passen würde. Niemand da, den ich fragen könnte. Das ist die Antwort]. Wolf's plea for addressing specific questions of power in specific historical contexts has become more intense with the darkness of the novel's end. *Medea* does not contain utopian elements, as *Kassandra* did; instead, *Medea*, despite its smooth, melodic prose and its origin in classical mythology, is about crass reality.

The same focus on crass reality is shared by Erich Hackl's short Third-World novel *Sara und Simón* (1995); the novel's style is a stark, almost documentary, realism — a trademark of Hackl (b. 1954 in Austria). On a scale of literary engagement with the Third World, *Sara und Simón* occupies a place at one end. On the opposite end are novels in which the Third World provides the setting for a plot that is carried primarily by characters from the First World — for example, *Bleeding Heart* (1993), by Ludwig Fels (b. 1946), and *Infanta* (1989) and *Der Sandmann* (1992), by Bodo Kirchhoff. Toward the end of the scale where Hackl's novel is located, there are novels that more openly address issues of colonialism and power. The individual treatments vary from specific aspects, such as connecting the colonial gaze with Nazi ethnography in *Himmelfarb* (1993), by Michael Krüger, to broad historical approaches, such as those by Hubert Fichte and Hans Christoph Buch, who concluded his Haiti trilogy with *Rede des toten Kolumbus am Tag des Jüngsten Gerichtes* (Speech Delivered by the Dead Columbus on Judgment Day, 1992). The latter work begins with the postcolonial confession of colonial guilt: "My name is Christopher Columbus, and I am the perpetrator who returns to the scene of his crime" [Mein Name ist Christoph Columbus, und ich bin der Täter, der an den Tatort zurückkehrt].

While most of these novels derive their conflicts from the encounter of First and Third Worlds, Hackl's *Sara und Simón* is about a conflict in a Third-World country that is carried solely by characters from within that country — and that is universal. The plot is simple and chilling. Based on a true story, it recounts the life of Sara, a political activist against the Uruguayan junta. She disappears into the torture chambers of the military prisons only days after giving birth to Simón, who is adopted by a well-meaning couple. Sara survives imprisonment and, years later, locates Simón, who has no recollection of her and fearfully clings to his identity as the couple's son. The novel ends without resolution, just as the real-life story. Uruguay's military rule can be seen as an extension of, or a successor to, colonial repression, because the former colonial powers collaborated with many juntas of the Third World; at the same time, the focus on one individual fate puts a human face on the universal issue of power and its abuses.

*Apocalypses and epiphanies*   Apocalyptic visions still played an important role in the 1990s; end-of-the-world scenarios, however, were increasingly supplemented by quests to reach a state of enlightened spirituality. The 1990s were interested in the same issues that the 1980s were, with one difference: the 1990s added spirituality. In German literature the apocalypses were mainly low-key but remained as dark as before; in addition, the hymnal tone, which was revived by Peter Handke and Botho Strauß in the 1980s, was continued in the 1990s with a growing number of literary visions and even epiphanies. Using fantastic and science-fiction scenarios, epiphanies in the 1990s did not remain vague, merely relying on the hymnal tone of revelation as texts by Handke and Strauß often did; rather, they suggested more concrete insights. Although mutually exclusive, literary apocalypses and epiphanies respond to the same fundamental problem — the survival of humankind — and often deal with the theme of power. Apocalypses shock the reader and, beyond the shock, mobilize an attitude that might save the world; in contrast, literary epiphanies suggest such an attitude or the process by which this attitude may be attained.

The wide spectrum of literary apocalyptic visions included texts that crossed over into a complex interaction with other topics — for example, gender issues, as in texts by Jelinek and Herta Müller, and the general theme of power, as in *Morbus Kitahara* (The Dog King, 1995), by Christoph Ransmayr. *Morbus Kitahara* presupposes political developments similar to those of the Second World War, but it relates an alternate history. It is the late 1960s; the war is still going on against Japan (it will, however, soon be ended with the explosion of an atomic bomb over Nagoya) but has been over in Europe since the mid-1940s. Germany and Austria are still under strict military rule by the Allies; they are governed according to "Stellamour's Law" [Stellamours Gesetz], the fictitious equivalent of the Morgenthau Plan, which had proposed returning Germany to an agricultural economy. The two countries are, however, in an anarchic condition with decentralized local authorities and marauding gangs in the mountains because the army has withdrawn to the lowlands. The alternate postwar reality has an oddly totalitarian character; it evokes an alpine version of scenarios familiar to audiences from postapocalyptic movies, such as *Mad Max* (1979).

The fictitious setting of Moor reflects, in a distorted way, the actual landscape of the Nazi concentration camp Mauthausen, so that the alternate history corresponds to an alternate geography. The army decides to turn the entire area of Moor into a training ground; when the village is evacuated, the three main characters, Ambras, Bering, and Lily, go to Brazil, where Ambras and Bering kill each other in the surreal finale of a story that choreographs an increasing brutalization of characters who cannot escape the detrimental effects of their environment. Each has a biography that inescapably draws him or her to violence. Ambras is director of a granite quarry and the most powerful man in the village, but he used to be one of the victims, forced into labor during the war. Bering's fascination with weapons qualifies him to become Ambras's bodyguard. Lily, a smuggler, has an elusiveness about her that is outside the law but that oscillates between victim and victimizer. Ransmayr's distortions of historical reality and extensions of geography situate the dilemma within the individual whose social embedding makes it impossible to cope with problems, such as violence, that come with a long past. As a result, these problems will continue wherever these individuals go.

Other stories of catastrophes build more strongly on fantasy elements, having a menacing other world intrude on the world of normality. For example, in *Der dreibeinige Doktor* (The Three-Legged Doctor, 1993), by Uwe Bremer (b. 1940), voodoo finds its way to central Europe. E. Y. Meyer's stories in *Wintergeschichten* (Stories of Winter, 1995), like the author's earlier works, evoke the destruction of the world in order to rebuild it in the work of art. The two connected stories, which begin and conclude the collection, structurally provide *Wintergeschichten* with a framework, while the experience of disorientation that the stories relate does not allow for closure. A nonrealistic trip takes a young man from central Europe to Siberia within hours in the first story, "Eine Reise nach Sibirien" (A Journey to Siberia), and leaves him with a feeling of complete alienation; the concluding story returns a young man — presumably the same one — to "Eine Mondstadt" (A Moon City). The fantastic trip into the vastness of Siberia in the first story is matched in the last one by the memory of a fantastic trip to the past and future of the world, from before the Ice Age to the nuclear destruction of the world, which extends the meaning of the story into the political realm.

In contrast to apocalyptic endgame scenarios, an epiphanic vision emerged in the narrative discourse on catastrophes. This may well be the most significant literary development of the 1990s because it concerned the theoretical distinction between Modernism and postmodernism. On the one hand, epiphanic texts regained a sense of center; Patrick Roth specifically used the term *Mitte* to indicate the destination of his protagonists' quest. If that new center was to be understood in absolute terms, then the Modernist search for a new myth and a new style had returned. On the other hand, the prerequisites for the search were altered as a reflection of the changed world, where several "local" centers can coexist. This view was indebted to a postmodern understanding of plurality, because both plurality and epiphanies suggest a coherent worldview, but neither makes a claim for the absolute truth.

In the 1990s Botho Strauß and Peter Handke continued to explore the epiphanic options in essayistic fictions, such as *Wohnen.Däm-mern.Lügen* (Living. Dozing. Telling Lies, 1994) and *Mein Jahr in der Niemandsbucht*, respectively. These texts are characterized by a tone that is hymnal, suggesting elements of praise and transcendence. In a secular world neither Strauß nor Handke sing praises to God, but their hymnal texts sometimes evoke a joyful sense of an insight that goes beyond empirical reality. Such an insight does not have to be metaphysical; it is an epiphany in the sense that something has been understood that was not understood before. A number of authors contributed a wide range of epiphanic fictions, including Robert Schneider (b. 1961 in Austria) with *Schlafes Bruder* (Sleep's Brother, 1992), Peter Weber (b. 1968 in Switzerland) with *Der Wettermacher* (The Weathermaster, 1993) and *Silber und Salbader* (Silver and Windbag, 1999), and Urs Widmer with *Im Kongo* (In the Congo, 1996).

Schneider's *Schlafes Bruder* is carried by the force of the protagonist's epiphany and resulting exceptional life. Set in the poverty and narrow-mindedness of an Austrian village of the early nineteenth century, the novel is the story of Johannes Elias Alder, who soars above his circumstances. He is a musical genius; although he cannot even read music, "nature became music" [Die Natur wurde Musik] when he plays the organ. From the first epiphany, on top of a smooth rock in the mountain creek where Alder hears the sound of the universe — including the heartbeat of the yet unborn girl with whom he will fall in love — to the last epiphany that the genius receives shortly before his death, which he causes by refusing to sleep, there is no doubt that Alder's suffering is not catastrophic but part of a metaphysical plan. For a last time, Alder listens to the silent music of his own body and psyche: "It had not been ordained that he hear more, for God had finished with him" [Mehr zu hören, wurde ihm nicht bestimmt, denn Gott war fertig mit ihm].

In Weber's *Der Wettermacher*, the protagonist August Abraham Abderhalden, who cannot talk, also soars above the circumstances of his human condition. Instead of being part of a grandiose plan as was Schneider's Alder, Abderhalden transcends into the mythical by becoming Weathermaster on his twentieth birthday: he "makes time stand still, stands the world on its head, and looks for and finds love between home and the railway station" [die Zeit zum Stillstehen bringt, der Welt den Kopf verdreht, zwischen Haus und Bahnhof seine Liebe sucht und findet]. While the style of *Wettermacher* has a lyrical and evocative quality, Urs Widmer's style is realistic, even though his short novel is fantastic.

*Im Kongo* combines Widmer's interests in grotesque and magical elements with his preference for adventure stories, in this case influenced by *Heart of Darkness* (1899), by Joseph Conrad (1857–1924). Three time periods — the present time, when the narrator Kuno is in the Congo; the period a year earlier when Kuno worked as a nurse in a retirement home; and memories of Kuno's childhood — interweave to combine two themes: Switzerland's role during the Second World War (it turns out that Kuno's father, a patient in the retirement home, was a high-ranking officer in the Swiss spy network against Nazi Germany) and Kuno's trip to self-discovery, which takes him from the realization that his father is a hero to reclaiming the girl he loved as a young man. Since she has lived all these years in the Congo with Kuno's childhood friend, who was sent to Africa to run a brewery, Kuno's self-discovery takes place on a trip to Africa. The exotic mix of magic encountered in Africa, including Kuno's turning black, is as entertaining as it may be problematic in the context of postcolonial discourses (because it suggests that white men make better black men). Nevertheless, Kuno arrives at the goal of his trip: he finds an identity with which he is happy.

*Patrick Roth's*
**Corpus Christi**
Among the fictions that explore epiphanies, the novels by Patrick Roth are particularly noteworthy, because they emphasize, more than the epiphanic texts of other authors, the "work" character of epiphanies. At the center of each novel is its protagonist's struggle to gain an insight into the human condition that provides him self-knowledge and peace of mind. The struggle, however, is fought by an ordinary human being; most importantly, the protagonist's success is the result of hard work (in terms of an intense psychological self-analysis), not of divine revelation, stroke of genius, or magic. While the spiritual aspect remains crucial, the experience of an epiphany is secularized. As a result, not only Roth's trilogy of "Bible thrillers" — *Riverside* (1990), *Johnny Shines* (1993), and *Corpus Christi* (1996) — but also his autobiographical narrative *Meine Reise zu Chaplin* (My Journey

to Chaplin, 1997) are epiphanic texts. The language of his trilogy is influenced by biblical language; however, it is archaic and modern at the same time because it always emphasizes the struggle to achieve crucial insights.

In *Johnny Shines*, Johnny remembers when he, as a young naive boy, wanted to communicate with Jesus. Young Johnny closed his eyes and sealed his ears with the wax from the big candle in his father's church, into which he had sneaked at night: " — when suddenly I felt His touch: His hand brushed mine. With a licking, a breathing, a heat-hastened stroke, it brushed. Passed by. Two hands had touched" [— da strich, da, schien mir, hauchte, leckte, heißfahrend rasch, Seine Hand: an meine Hand. Vorbei. Das Sich-Berühren zweier Hände]. What he had not noticed, because he blocked out sight and sound, was that he knocked over the candle and set the building ablaze. The "hand of Christ" that Johnny feels is the fire that he caused; metaphorically, it is the fire that burns inside him: the need for understanding the world (or at least parts of it). Yet that understanding does not come easily by blocking one's senses; it comes as the result of hard work that requires a tremendous amount of psychological energy.

In *Corpus Christi* the spiritual search is augmented by the literal search for the body of Jesus, which has disappeared three days after his burial. This is the point at which Roth's narrative begins: one of Christ's disciples — Judas Thomas, the author's adaptation of the biblical Thomas, who in the novel also bears the name of his long-dead twin brother, Judas (who is not the Judas who betrayed Christ) — resolves to find his master's body. The official version that the embarrassed authorities tell is that the body was stolen. Judas Thomas hears about a young woman, Tirza, who was arrested when she was discovered in the empty tomb. Judas Thomas waits for Tirza outside the prison, but she does not come out. In the meanwhile, Jesus appeared to the other disciples, they claim; Judas Thomas does not believe them. While he waits outside the prison for Tirza again, he talks to the guards about her, but nobody knows her. On the third day, while he is waiting for Tirza, the body of Jesus is found and a public cremation is announced. That day Judas Thomas suffers a fever attack. What follows constitutes the main part of *Corpus Christi*: the encounter between Judas Thomas and Tirza. But when Judas Thomas abruptly awakens toward the end of the narrative, he no longer knows whether he actually met Tirza or whether it was a dream — but that is not important, because their encounter is psychologically real.

The encounter begins with a surreal escape of Judas Thomas and Tirza through the narrow labyrinthine streets leading to the temple. There an intense dialogue ensues that pushes Judas Thomas to the limits of what he allows himself to think. Several stories are woven into the dialogue: Judas Thomas's childhood memories about his dead twin brother Judas; the story of a guard and his two sons, of whom one, Boas, sacrifices his life for his father's sake; and Tirza's story. The stories emphasize that humanity needs to overcome thinking in terms of opposites that are considered hostile to each other. Indeed, in his endeavor to find the truth about the body of Jesus, Judas Thomas is driven by his desire to know "what is and what is not" [was ist und was nicht]. Tirza tries to teach him that, while thinking in such dichotomies is important, it is only the first step; she encourages Judas Thomas to take the next step toward the union of opposites. She does so because that is her story. She tells Judas Thomas that after she was first beaten to death and then raped, she fell into a nothingness that was devoid of time and space. She was awakened from this state by Jesus, who commanded her to watch over him. By the time she found Jesus, he was on the cross. She hid in the tomb where he was to be laid to rest; there she watched over him, not to "follow" him "in death" [nachsterben] but to "bear his death" [sein Sterben auszuhalten]. In the tomb she was suddenly panicked, but then felt his body, immediately calmed down, and drifted into an epiphanic nightmare about being murdered with a knife. Tirza confronted her own demons in her nightmare, which was transformed into a vision of light so bright that it made the human experience of light seem like darkness. In the new light Tirza saw opposites in union, specifically, "haters and those hated, murderers and those murdered" [Hasser und Gehaßte, Mörder und Gemordete]. Her experience of the resurrection followed. It was an "embrace" [Umarmung], "for he has embraced those who have been divided" [Denn er hat die Getrennten umarmt].

Judas Thomas wakes with a start, not knowing whether his encounter with Tirza was real. Driven by what turns out to be his desire to embrace his own opposites, he attends the cremation of the body of Jesus. He jumps into the fire to see if it is really Jesus, but it is not; it is another body being burned by the authorities in an effort to calm the public about the mysterious disappearance of Jesus's body. Looking at the body, Judas Thomas is looking at his own face — that is, the face of his twin brother, who was considered dead all these years but who had grown up as Boas, the guard's foundling son. This surprise encounter relieves Judas Thomas's doubts about his own biography, and the experience of knowing who he is — the Other and yet himself — sets him free.

Patrick Roth explores the dynamic of identity formation by confronting the Other as a necessary part of oneself. Roth's narratives work through the stages of separation of self and Other (evoked in cultural archetypes of good and evil, such as Jesus and Judas) and the subsequent conscious reunion of the opposites. In the spiritual search for

God, humanity finds its own spirituality, but only by accepting the hard truth of being one's own worst enemy. Such an acceptance is possible as the result of a dialogic process between good and evil, which, in turn, makes it possible for human beings finally to engage in meaningful dialogue with each other. Roth understood this process as a potential for saving civilization from the destruction that other narratives evoke in apocalyptic visions. Also, in contrast to assuming a catastrophe as a prerequisite for creating the new human being, postmodernist epiphanies emphasized the need to avoid catastrophe — or, rather, they operated with the knowledge that the catastrophe had already happened. Like many other texts within the German tradition, Roth's writing was influenced by an awareness of the Holocaust. In Roth's case it is not first-hand knowledge, but his approach was tied to growing up in the 1960s, when German society was shocked by the Auschwitz trials, which for Roth epitomized the conflict of good and evil within humanity. Roth's narrative project attempts to bring this conflict to an epiphany — the conflict's positive resolution.

*Traditions of storytelling*       A story is the re-creation of an action (a sequence of events) that is driven by a central conflict. One literary device that is important in holding a reader's interest is suspense. It works by raising questions, while delaying their answers. As a result, the reader keeps reading to find the answers to such questions as: Who did it? What could possibly happen next? Literature that capitalizes on these aspects of the story is likely to entertain. Common prejudice has it that German literature prefers traditions other than storytelling, but while lyrical, essayistic, and documentary traditions were, indeed, strong in twentieth-century German literature, storytelling was never abandoned.

The main contention has to do with the quality of the stories. It has been argued that post-1945 German literature — especially in contrast to contemporary international literature and to prewar German writers, such as Thomas Mann and Franz Kafka — did not produce texts in the storytelling tradition that matched the quality of German texts written in other traditions. This observation was partially true, for instance, for the 1960s and 1970s, when the traditional notions of narrator and narration were declared obsolete; this was, however, not only a German but also an international phenomenon. Since then, the resurgence of the high-quality literary story continued through the 1990s. In fact, the traditional genre of the tightly structured and symbolically focused short narrative, the novella, is defined in part by its suspenseful characteristic — the unheard-of incident at the novella's center. The renewed interest in storytelling can also be seen in the growing number of authors who rediscovered the novella. Uwe Timm and Norbert Gstrein

(b. 1961 in Austria) added the genre identification *Novelle* to their longer prose texts *Die Entdeckung der Currywurst* (The Discovery of the Curried Sausage, 1993) and *O₂* (1993), respectively.

German literature successfully participated in the traditional themes of storytelling: history, travel, mythology, and mystery. History was at the core of the new historical novel. The travel motif was common to most novels written within the Third-World discourse. Classical mythology, especially important for GDR literature, was generally embraced by German writers. Even mysteries, while usually relegated to the realm of popular fiction, had a longstanding tradition with literary detective stories, such as *Der Richter und sein Henker* (The Judge and His Executioner, 1952), by Friedrich Dürrenmatt.

The treatment of classical mythology provides good examples of storytelling that not only are defined by dark catastrophic visions, such as Wolf's *Medea* and Ransmayr's *Die letzte Welt*, but that are characterized, if not by an epiphanic, at least by a playful mode of rewriting and inventing mythology. The most successful novels in the latter category include *Ein Gott der Frechheit* (A God of Mischief, 1994), by Sten Nadolny, and the first two volumes of the planned Odyssey trilogy by Michael Köhlmeier (b. 1949 in Austria): *Telemach* (1995) and *Kalypso* (1997). These works also illustrate the two principal approaches to incorporating classical mythology into an expanded now. While Nadolny's novel transposes the classical Greek gods into the modern world, Köhlmeier's novels take place in the mythical past — although it is, at the same time, the present.

Nadolny presented *Ein Gott der Frechheit* as an attempt at "freely continuing to spin the yarn of Greek mythology beyond the traditional stories" [griechische Mythologie jenseits der tradierten Geschichten frei weiterzuspinnen]. The main plot revolves around the premise that the Greek gods are retired and live unrecognized among humans, with two exceptions. Hephaestus, the god of fire and metalworking, is the tyrannical force behind the world's industrialization; and Hermes, the god of merchants and thieves, has been chained to a rock for two thousand years and now, as Hephaestus needs him to be an entertainer for a worldwide media company, is released. Hermes' return to the world after a long absence gives rise to humor when he encounters objects that are unfamiliar to him; he perceives a telephone receiver as a "white bone" [weißer Knochen] and a cigar as a "thick, brown phallus" [dickbrauner Phallus]. Hephaestus has grown disillusioned with his immortality and become suicidal; therefore, he plans to destroy the world, because that is the only way for a god to die: "as long as people are alive, the gods cannot die even if they want to" [solange Menschen leben, können Götter nicht sterben, nicht einmal wenn sie wollen]. With the help of his fellow gods, however, Hermes prevents Hephaestus from carrying out his plan. Most crucial is Apollo, who brings the news that a meteor is about to destroy the world in the near future anyway, so Hephaestus does not need do it.

At this point, the proximity of Nadolny's novel to epiphanic texts shows in its emphasis on connectedness and diffusion. Hephaestus was able to take over the world because he upset the balance by keeping Hermes from bringing disorder to the world. As a result, the world had become subject to technocratic orderliness — in other words, it had become inhuman. When Hermes returns, a balance can be achieved again, because he represents the element that was missing from a world in which everything is connected. Furthermore, the novel diffuses the practice of thinking in dichotomies. Beginning as opposites, Apollo and Hermes are successful in averting the destruction of the earth because each recognizes himself in the other. Known for stealing in regard to love, Hermes has become monogamous. Finally, the god of truth, Apollo, saves the world because he tells a lie, as he admits when he is asked how he was able to acquire the information about the meteor: "I invented it" [Ich habe sie erfunden]. The gods respond with laughter, the world has another chance, and the novel ends with this utopian hope. The novel functions on various levels, including as a fantasy of an East German woman, Helga, who imagines herself as Helle, daughter of Hephaestus and lover of Hermes. In the novel's expanded present, the gods stand for — as did those of ancient mythology — human properties, which in the 1990s included democratic values.

Similarly, Köhlmeier's Odyssey project is a rewriting of the classical myth as an endorsement of nonviolence and an indictment of war and heroism. In *Telemach* Athena's classical program of educating Odysseus's son to be a hero fails; instead, the goddess realizes that Telemachus "had at last remained true to his own will" [zuletzt aber in seinem eigenen Willen geblieben war]. Telemachus appears as a postmodern redefinition of a passive Odysseus: "It even resulted in a small achievement, although an improvised one, molded from your hesitation, your passivity, your suffering" [Ist sogar ein kleines Vollbrachtsein daraus geworden, wenn auch ein improvisiertes, ein aus deinem Zaudern, deiner Tatenlosigkeit, deinem Erleiden gefügtes]. The pastiche character of Köhlmeier's novels is more strongly emphasized than it is in Nadolny's. *Telemach* and *Kalypso* present a rewriting of classical mythology and, at the same time, are modern stories.

In Köhlmeier's version, Kalypso takes care of Odysseus after she finds him shipwrecked and exhausted; at one point she needs a few things, so she takes a bus to the train station downtown, walks to the department store, and winds up at a bookstore, where she buys a "Calvin and Hobbes" comic book for Odysseus. The gods Athena and Hermes slip into the comic book's characters to spy on Kalypso and Odysseus, adding a strong element of travesty to the novel. While such elements of travesty and the description of the sexual encounter between Odysseus and Kalypso were used by critics to accuse Köhlmeier of lowering his novel to the standards of popular fiction, it was also suggested that the repressed guilt concerning Odysseus's involvement in the Trojan War that he confronts during his stay with Kalypso is a reflection of the repressed German and Austrian guilt over the Holocaust.

The detective story is another area in which storytelling is central. The genre is often considered a poor relation of the serious novel; nevertheless, in the 1990s mysteries of literary quality were written by Jakob Arjouni (pseudonym of Jakob Bothe, b. 1964) and Jürgen Benvenuti (b. 1972). Elements of the detective story were used by a number of authors to tell complex stories, as Ralf Rothmann did in *Wäldernacht. Der Opernball* (The Opera Ball, 1995), by Josef Haslinger (b. 1955), is an example of a political thriller with literary ambitions. The action component — a poison-gas attack by a right-wing terrorist group on the prestigious Vienna Opera Ball leaves hundreds of people dead — is combined with other elements. For example, everything is covered by the media, which probably had some indication of the imminent attack; this plot line yields the element of media critique. Furthermore, the novel is presented as one reporter's reconstruction of the event; he takes testimony from various people, and the novel presents it in documentary fashion. The terrorist attack underscores the challenges faced by a democracy.

Other novels took popular culture as their subject matter, examining postmodern theoretical discourses and the party scene of the late 1990s: *Tomboy* (1998), by Thomas Meinecke (b. 1955); *Gut laut* (Pretty Loud, 1998), by Andreas Neumeister; and *Rave* (1998), by Rainald Goetz. Explorations into popular culture and entertainment also included short narrative forms. *Rupert* (1996), by Matthias Matussek (b. 1954), is a collection of humorous short stories that are grouped as chapters of a novel about a New York City movie critic who seems to be a complete loser but in the end finds a way to be content with his life. Other authors who have written well-told short prose that entertains the reader with humor include Burkhard Spinnen (b. 1956), Kurt Aebli (b. 1955), and Michael Schulte (b. 1941). Schulte's *Zitroneneis* (Lemon Ice Cream, 1996) contains a story in which a man tells his wife and children that they cannot come home to him from their vacation in Colorado because their house is encircled by 5,000 Comanches. His wife finally tells him that she is going to hire a helicopter to fly over the house and check out his story about the Comanches; he hears the Indians packing, and as suddenly as they had appeared, they are gone. The man has thirty hours to hire 5,000 extras dressed as Indians before his wife's helicopter shows up. He concludes the story: "I dial a number in Hollywood."

## New Poetic Languages for New Realities

At the end of the 1990s, poetry had a resurgence in popularity. "Poetry slams" in the hip-hop scene were fashionable. Hip-hop poetry, by poets, such as Bastian Böttcher (b. 1974), came across as a perfectly tuned sound machine that generated alliterating and homophonic strings of words, combined in the staccato rhythm of an easily flowing syntax. The subject matter was everyday life, often presented with an ironic twist. And in hip-hip tradition the individual poem was often integrated with music into a "number." But also less obviously commercial poetry was successful, and major newspapers regularly printed poems. Poetry's focus on experiences may help to explain why interest in poems underwent a revival in the 1990s: more than epic prose, poetry can immediately access and express experiences with the new realities; furthermore, poetry allows a highly self-conscious approach toward language. An important contributing factor was the renewed insistence on formal mastery in the poetry of the 1980s; therefore, when the political landscape changed at the turn of the decade, poets had a language and poetic devices at their disposal with which they could explore the new landscape of post-Cold War Europe.

As new as the situation after the demise of Communism seemed to be, it was a continuation of the postindustrial information age that defined Western capitalism. This fact led to a common point of departure for poems: they were based on a sense of being part of an artificial world from which the poet kept a distance. The distance could be expressed in various ways, ranging from indifference to biting irony or sorrow. The poetic detachment was keenly felt in the way in which experiences were communicated in the poems as though traditional topoi and language were exhausted. An awareness of the historical situation's precariousness predominated: nature in its endangered condition played only a minor role in German poetry of the 1990s, and language had to adjust to the new realities.

*Testing language and assessing new realities* The title of Durs Grünbein's collection of poems *Falten und Fallen* (1994) was identified by the author as a phrase describing the human brain; *Falten* can mean "folding" or "wrinkles," and *Fallen* "falling" and "traps." "Aus einem alten Fahrtenbuch" (From an Old Logbook), a prose text included in *Falten und Fallen*, identifies the function of language toward reality as an armored vehicle in which the poet sits, safely surrounded by "steel plates . . ., a stable grammar" [stählernen Platten . . ., stabile Grammatik]. Yet language is more than necessary protection against the "slaughter" [Gemetzel] of reality; it is "also a well-tempered piano" [auch ein wohltemperiertes Klavier], whose scope Grünbein's works demonstrate with virtuosity. Language will itself adjust to deal with what happens when "this terribly cerebral landscape ruptures" [diese fürchterlich zerebrale Landschaft zerreißt].

The searching for a new language was particularly pressing after Europe's political map was redrawn. Nevertheless, while politics was reflected in poetry by such authors as Durs Grünbein and Jürgen Bekker, most poets focused on existential dimensions of the new realities as change challenged the traditional ways and as technological advances redefined fundamental aspects of life, such as humanity's relationship with nature. Technology entered poetry to the extent that it replaced nature as a source of imagery.

The stereotypical experience of fast-paced life at the end of the twentieth century, the ubiquitous glowing light of electronic displays, became a poetic image. A poem in *Your Passport is Not Guilty* (1997, *guilty* is a pun on the German word *gültig*, meaning "valid"), by Brigitte Oleschinski (b. 1955), begins: "Toward morning it // must have been like the easing up of a current, nose and chin / a sleeping reef before the pale, digitally illuminated brow" [Gegen Morgen hin muß es // wie des Nachlassen einer Strömung gewesen sein, Nase und Kinn / ein schlafendes Riff vor der fahlen Leuchtziffernstirn]. The title is a syntactic part of the body of the poem, a radicalization of regular enjambment, which is also typical of the poems in Oleschinski's collection.

Poems by Barbara Köhler (b. 1959) show a similar linguistic displacement of nature in favor of technology. In her *Deutsches Roulette* (German Roulette, 1991), "Ortung" (Locating) is an antinature poem, because it evokes nature only in relation to civilization and as an image of loss: "the treeless streets refer / to a sky of rejected hope" [die baumleeren straßen verweisen / auf einen himmel verworfener hoffnung]. Köhler's next collection, *Blue Box* (1995), intensifies this approach. The title poem begins: "Why so sad Just now we were talking / The crammed-down lessons: expect nothing / . . . These are words / is all" [Woher so traurig Grade noch sprachen wir / Die eingebläute Lehre: nichts erwarten / . . . Das sind Worte / ist alles]. The poem is made up of language fragments that record a relationship. The "Blue Box" might be a language recorder for life just as a black box is a flight recorder for an airplane. Words are just "instruments in our language" (Instrumente in unserer Sprache), according to a quote from Ludwig Wittgenstein's *The Blue Book* (1958) that Köhler uses as a motto for her collection. The arbitrariness of the words and the human emotions whose fragments are recorded seem without context in the poem —

the absence of a specific context is, indeed, considered the defining quality of the postmodern technological age, in which videos and computer graphics combine and recombine elements and contexts.

The postmodern condition as life at the top of the garbage pile of cultural traditions, which are all available at the same time and continue to be recycled in memory loops, is suggested in the title of a collection of poems by Ulrike Draesner (b. 1962), *gedächtnisschleifen* (memory loops, 1995). Durs Grünbein's *Schädelbasislektion* (Skull Basic Lesson, 1991) and *Falten und Fallen* demonstrate that, like other contemporary poets, Grünbein had the entire literary tradition at his disposal; he brought together traditions that were considered mutually exclusive. His recourse, for instance, to both Rainer Maria Rilke and Gottfried Benn was significant because, like Rilke's Malte and Orpheus, writers of the 1990s had to learn to see things; and like Benn's lyrical ego, they had to deal with destroyed and destructive language (hence Grünbein's metaphor of the armored vehicle in the war zone of reality) to find their own new language that is appropriate for the new realities. The first thirty-nine thirteen-line poems in *Falten und Fallen* are each a "Variation auf kein Thema" (Variation on No Theme); they present observations of the "fissure / Between names and things" [Riß / Zwischen Namen und Dingen] in the contemporary world, in which "everything is coded" [alles codiert], even love, and in which daily routines have become oppressive: "Seen from the perspective / of a leg of a chair every table is a coffin" [Aus der Sicht / Eines Stuhlbeins ist jeder Tisch ein Sarg].

Other poets, such as Barbara Köhler and Thomas Kling, were more radical, especially in the way they fragmented and juxtaposed language. In the tradition of Friedericke Mayröcker and Oskar Pastior, Kling wrote experimental poetry that he published in the collections *brennstabn* (burnin rods, 1991), *nacht.sicht.gerät* (night.vision.instrument, 1993), and *morsch* (brittle, 1996). The collection *Fernhandel* (Foreign Trade, 1999) also included less radical texts. Kling's poems are based on intertextuality, with a great number of quotations and allusions; and their typographical appearance and fragmented words are immediately striking. For example, Kling consistently uses the spelling *di* for the definitive article *die;* separates words at line breaks in unorthodox ways, such as *wr* and *akk* for *Wrack* (in this instance even leaving out the hyphen); and runs other words together, such as "wasfürntempo" for "was für ein tempo" (not slow either) in "Russischer Digest 1" (Russian Digest 1, 1993): "escalator rolling down russia / a wreck burst o / pen in places visible clear- / ly intelligible leningrad airport not far from the runways rus- / sia down the land down the escalator & / notsloweither" [rolltreppe russland runter, / in teile zerborstenes wr / akk, gut sichtbar deutlich ver- / nehmbar lenin-

grad airport unweit der landebahnen russ- / land landunter, rolltreppe
runter u. / in wasfürntempo]. The surface of the poem comes across
like the fragmented and disparate sense impressions that make up the
normal experience of individuals, but beneath the surface an intelligible
image emerges. The deconstruction of linguistic form, then, suggests a
new language that, unfamiliar as it seems, corresponds to the world to
which it refers.

The more fragmented the poems are, as in *Blue Box* or
*nacht.sicht.gerät*, the more they are mimetic of the 1990s artificial life
worlds. The complexity that these poems represent is increased in other
poems that include marginal notes or appended annotations to interact
with the poem's "main" text. *Rauschstudie Vater + Sohn* (Study of Intoxication Father + Son, 1994) and *Treibender Kopf* (Floating Head,
1997), by Dieter M. Gräf (b. 1960), include poems that unfold a fuller
meaning in the interaction with the annotations. "Todt-Front, dahinter
das Meer" (Death-Front, behind it the Sea) in *Treibender Kopf* begins
as follows: "menacing Atlantic forces like, / caged in behind the crys-
tallized surf, / . . . / the never-crystallizing surf, the ocean" [bedrohli-
che atlantische Mächte wie die / hinter die erstarrt Brandung gesperrte
/ . . . / nie erstarrende Brandung, das Meer]. The annotation opens up
an intertextual meaning by giving two quotes from studies on an archaeology of bunkers (such as the Nazi bunkers at the Atlantic) and on
the fear of death. This intertextual interplay is even stronger in *Tropen*
(Tropes, 1998), by Raoul Schrott (b. 1964), because the "secondary"
text is on the page facing the poem's "main" text. The collection's first
poem is apparently about a sparrow that "hit the window like a bolt /
snapped from a latch" [an die scheibe schlug wie ein bügel / der aus
seinem schloß schnappt]. The poem's title, "Physikalische Optik I,"
would remain enigmatic, were it not for the marginal note on the facing page: it suggests that the poem is not just about a bird but also
about subatomic physics, because it cites the nuclear physicist Niels
Bohr as saying that to describe atomic phenomenon, "language can be
only used as in poetry" [kann die Sprache nur wie in der Poesie ver-
wendet werden]. These poems aim at linguistic innovation, but rather
than creating a new language itself, they aim at making accessible new
layers of linguistic meaning by opening up ways to include various
sources, especially from literary and cultural traditions.

Instead of emphasizing the need for a new language, other poets
preferred to use the suppleness of existing language to approach the
new realities. Continuing his tone of radical subjectivity, Uwe Kolbe
redefined his position in response to the fall of the Berlin Wall. While
*Vaterlandkanal* (Fatherland Canal, 1990) marked a transitional phase,
the following collections of poetry, *Nicht wirklich platonisch* (Not
Really Platonic, 1994) and *Vineta* (1998), combined Kolbe's interest

in poetic traditions with a more prosaic tone. In his 1994 collection this combination is illustrated by the last haiku of "Drei Japaner in Italien" (Three Japanese in Italy), which also defines the plural experiences of the lyrical subjectivity: "Civilization / is varied. Only the brute / yearns for the One thing" [Zivilisation / ist Vielfalt. Nur der Barbar / sehnt sich nach Einem]. The 1994 and 1998 collections are thematically related by the motif of Vineta, a mythical sunken city and also the name of a street near Kolbe's old neighborhood in eastern Berlin. Kolbe uses rhyme and free verse; his tone results from the productive interaction between his reserved and at times even sarcastic melancholy attitude toward life and a playful certainty of his poetic virtuosity.

The young trailblazers of the 1960s and 1970s stood for major poetic developments: Günter Kunert for the subjective "little however" voice in opposition to the collective ideology of the GDR, Hans Magnus Enzensberger for political poetry, and Jürgen Becker for experimental "texts" beyond traditional genre boundaries. In the 1990s they had become the older generation of poets; they remained true to themselves in some respects; however, except for an occasional reference to war, neither Kunert's nor Enzensberger's poetry collections contain directly political poems. Kunert's *Mein Golem* (My Golem, 1996) explores the author's relationships with other poets, such as Goethe, but it still reveals Kunert's bleak disillusionment with utopias. Significantly, the collection ends with a number of elegies, the ninth one mourning "Snow White, raped, beaten to death, / forever untouchable" [Schneewittchen, vergewaltigt, erschlagen, / auf ewig unberührbar]. In the title poem Kunert evokes a folklore motif from his Jewish roots, the man-made being who destroyed his creator. Such a threatening aspect of poetry — which, as the poet's creation, is his golem — suggests deeper, possibly political, layers of meaning. The poem "Poetologie letzter Hand" (Authorized Poetology) challenges the readers to look for those layers: "At the bottom of the poems / rests all that is unsayable. / Forced to the surface / it dissolves / into vocabulary" [Auf dem Grund der Gedichte / ruht alles Unsagbare. / An die Oberfläche gezwungen / löst es sich auf / in Vokabular]. The collection *Nacht Vorstellung* (Night Performance, 1999) continues in this tone: it ends with the warning that the "known world," for which Kunert uses the Latin *terra cognita*, has gone mad and is about to invade everybody's home.

In contrast to his earlier highly political poetry, Hans Magnus Enzensberger continued to relax his approach, as was already evident in "Der fliegende Robert" (Flying Robert) in *Die Furie des Verschwindens* (The Fury of Disappearance, 1980), in which Robert opens his umbrella and flies away into the air, disregarding the accusations of escapism. Enzensberger did not embrace escapism but remained a political author who, however, was aware of the hastiness of many judgments. Fittingly, Robert is also the name of the young protagonist who disappears for a while in Enzensberger's novel *Wo warst du, Robert?* (Where Were You, Robert? 1998), in which the potentially escapist fantasy element of time travel is used as an educational trip through history. In a similar vein, Enzensberger wonders in his collection of poetry *Zukunftsmusik* (Future Music, 1991) whether "even the end of the world / is perhaps / only temporary" [Auch das Ende der Welt / ist vielleicht / nur ein Provisorium]. The poems in *Kiosk* (1995) are also of a calmer quality. Enzensberger's tone varies in this collection between playfully poignant and playfully resigned. "Enttäuscht" (Disappointed) starts out in a resigned tone, presenting a litany of what people are disappointed in, from Mother to Communism; however, Enzensberger still concludes: "It is thus miraculous that we have, all our lives, always anew, / believed in the good of man — and anyway" [Wunderbar also, daß wir zeitlebens, immer von neuem, / geglaubt haben an das Gute im Menschen — und überhaupt]. The modest hope expressed by Enzensberger corresponds to the development of twentieth-century political visions from grand utopias — which reached their last climax in the 1960s counterculture, in which Enzensberger participated — to political projects whose scope, in response to the disillusionment with the grand utopias, had been scaled down to more modest and private dimensions.

Although born in what would become West Germany, Jürgen Bekker spent his childhood years in Thuringia, which became part of the GDR after the war. The year before the Berlin Wall came down, Becker published *Das Gedicht von der wiedervereinigten Landschaft*, whose allusion to political reunification was meant ironically. The collection *Foxtrott im Erfurter Stadion* (Fox Trot in Erfurt Stadium, 1993) contains poems that comment on Becker's visits to childhood places. Mostly melancholy, the encounters are always qualified by memories of political history; it was the Second World War that caused Becker's long absence from these places in Thuringia. In the poem "Reisefilm; Ausschnitte" (Travelogue; Film Clips) he mentions the tanks he sees standing near a train station, and the reference to "something paralyzing . . . in the air" [Lähmendes . . . in der Luft] evokes a sense of dread that originates in the memory of the wartime air raids. The lyrical subjectivity seems refracted and unsentimental because of the fundamental uncertainty of the speaker in the same poem, which begins: "Out of sequence, or did memory deliver / the wrong dates? Everything happens so fast" [Verdrehte Reihenfolgen, oder gab das Gedächtnis / die falschen Daten heraus? Es geht alles so schnell]. Compared to the political writers Kunert and Enzensberger, it is interesting that Becker in *Foxtrott im Erfurter Stadion* and *Journal der Wiederholungen* (A Journal of Repetitions, 1999) — with its direct references to the Nazi army, the

East German army, and escape attempts from East Germany — dealt most directly with political history and contemporary reality. Becker explored the same subject in his first novel *Aus der Geschichte der Trennungen* (From the History of Separations, 1999).

*Epigrammatic poetry* In the process of finding new languages for new realities, poets tested a variety of tones and registers. A lighter, more playful and poignant tone was used by authors ranging from hip-hop poets to those whose work usually has a more serious tone. Such lightness became more popular in the 1990s, although it had a long tradition in German poetry — from classical epigrammatic poetry to the openly political poems of Heinrich Heine and Bertolt Brecht, as well as the nonsense texts of Christian Morgenstern. It was practiced after the Second World War by writers such as Peter Rühmkorf (b. 1929) and Robert Gernhardt (b. 1937). Gernhardt's verses were especially popular, although they were often not recognized as his (for example, when the comedian Otto Waalkes used Gernhardt's material). Gernhardt's *Lichte Gedichte* (Light Poems, 1997) includes a turn to the serious subject matter of the author's bypass surgery, while retaining the typically ironic tone: "Yet the heart of a poet / pains at the diagnosis / that it suffers from 'manager's disease'" [Doch das Herz eines Dichters / schmerzt beim Befund, / es leide an der "Managerkrankheit"].

During the 1990s resurgence of public interest in poetry, a number of poets adapted this tradition to their individual styles. The resulting poetry was lighter not in the sense of being lower in literary quality but in the sense of a stronger emphasis on entertainment through tersely formulated, witty, and poignant insights. These poems can be seen as the equivalent of the well-told entertaining story that reemerged in German prose. At their best these poems had "bite." Older poetic devices, if used well, no longer appeared old-fashioned or stale but contributed to the effectiveness of the epigrammatic poem with snappy rhyme and flowing meter that increased the poem's momentum, as in Gernhardt's "Writing about love — you cannot. / Either you love or you do not" [Über Liebe kann man nicht schreiben. / Man liebt oder läßt es bleiben]. Free-verse forms equally heightened the impact of epigrammatic poems by emphasizing specific elements through the arrangement of the lines on the page. The traditions of epigrammatic poetry and aphoristic prose blended in the prosy tone of many poems.

Epigrammatic poems brought a new tone of cheerfulness and boldness to German poetry of the 1990s. In the title poem of *Die Lust der Frauen auf Seite 13* (Women's Pleasure on Page 13, 1994), Dagmar Leupold (b. 1955) reverses the centuries-old roles of voyeurism, claiming that postmodernity is the time for women to look at men as sexual objects. Other poems integrate images of the human body into shocking visions, which Albert Ostermaier defines as a program for poetry in his poem "Ratschlag für einen jungen Dichter" (Advice for a Young Poet) in *herz.vers.sagen* (heart.fail.ure, 1995, the title is a pun on the German word for "heart failure," which, as punctuated by the poet, literally reads "heart.verse.speak"): "to be a poet you've got to know how to / kill people squeeze heads in the vice of / lines" [als dichter musst du wissen wie / man leute killt köpfe zwischen / zeilen klemmt]. In "kissing disease" in Ostermaier's collection *Heartcore* (1999) "kisses are pricks with needles" [küsse sind nadelstiche] that leave tattoos on the speaker's tongue. Durs Grünbein's playful use of black humor in *Den Teuren Toten* (For Our Dear Dead, 1994) is also a case in point. In this collection, he describes grotesque deaths using poetic language in the tradition of Charles Baudelaire's *Les Fleurs du Mal* and Gottfried Benn's *Morgue*. In *Nach den Satiren* (After the Satires, 1999), Grünbein continues this approach in poems about history, including the Roman past, and about an archangel who suffers from Alzheimer's disease. Finally, epigrams can make openly political statements. For instance, in *Landverlust* (Loss of Land, 1993) and *Ankunft Konjunktiv* (Arrival Subjunctive, 1997), Franz Hodjak formulates general doubts, such as "glorious it is and honorable / to die / for a great cause — // this ought to be said for once / from personal experience" [ruhmvoll ist es und ehrenhaft / für eine große sache / zu sterben — // das soll mal einer sagen / aus eigner erfahrung], and specific experiences that derive from the conflict between two cultures that ethnic Germans, such as Hodjak, felt after coming to Germany.

*Multicultural poetry*    Encounters between cultures encourage a new language to express these experiences. The second phase of multicultural poetry, which occurred in the 1990s, is characterized by an emphasis on language and on universal themes, such as love; at the same time, the texts reflected each author's specific experience of being marginalized as the Other, the foreigner, the stranger.

The poetry of Zehra Çirak expresses a multicultural identity, an identity that is neither Turkish nor German but transcends both. Çirak asserts herself with idiosyncratic word choices that some might consider linguistic mistakes. Words that are not in the *Duden* (the standard German dictionary), however, may well be in what Çirak calls the "Ichden." Playing with the fact that *du* (the first syllable in *Duden*) also means "you," Çirak coins this neologism by substituting the German word for *Ich*, meaning "I," to express the right to her own language. Çirak thinks about various grammatical rules in her poem "Duden Ichden," published in her *Vogel auf dem Rücken des Elefanten* (Bird on the

Back of the Elephant, 1991), and concludes with her dream "of having to make .the spelling / for the whole area / run like blockwork" [der Aufgabe die Rechtschreibung / im gesamten Raum / einheitlich zu riegeln]. The form of the poem executes the dreams about language and identity that it expresses. The task would consist in ensuring that the spelling is done according to rules (like clockwork). The German verb is *regeln* (to regulate), not the verb *riegeln* (to block), which Çirak chooses to illustrate her insistence on "the wrong letter in my word" [der falsche Buchstabe in meinem Wort]. The difference between the *Duden* and the "Ichden" is not a question of good or bad language but a measure of linguistic freedom.

Works by authors who are legal aliens in Germany represent perhaps the most visible multicultural literature; however, other minorities, from the gay community to ethnic Germans living outside Germany, contributed to the dynamism between otherness and freedom that is different from mainstream literature. An additional dimension was added by those writers who grew up with German as their mother tongue and were legally German but were still perceived by common prejudice as different or foreign. A case in point is the Afro-German writer May Ayim (1960–1996), whose first publications appeared under her foster family's name, Opitz; after getting in touch with her roots in Africa, she adopted her father's name, Ayim, in 1992.

Like other authors with multicultural identities, Ayim defines *Heimat* (home or homeland) in nonterritorial terms as a temporal and existential experience as "today / the space between / yesterday and tomorrow" [heute / der raum zwischen / gestern und morgen] in the poem "auskunft" (information) in *nachtgesang* (night song, 1997). The poems in this collection address one of Ayim's central issues: racism. In "die farbe der macht" (the color of power) she defines racism as "the pale face / of violence" [das bleiche Gesichte / der Gewalt] that began to show itself more and more in Germany as violence against foreigners increased in the 1990s. Thus, the ugly specter of colonialism that allowed a tiny ruling class from the colonial powers to oppress native majorities in Asia, Africa, and the Americas still determined the way people treat each other. Consequently, the poem concludes, "the color of power / decides / for or against life" [die farbe der macht / entscheidet / für oder gegen das Leben]. In her first poetry collection, *blues in schwarz weiss* (blues in black and white, 1995), the title poem equates the development of history with the "rhythm of racism sexism and anti-Semitism" [rhythmus von rassismus sexismus und antisemitismus]. The poem's conclusion anticipates a radical confrontation in a world after the Cold War, in which the conflict is between the rich and powerful (who are identified as "white") and the poor: "1/3 of humanity celebrates in white / 2/3 of humanity does not go along" [1/3 der menschheit feiert in weiß / 2/3 der menschheit macht nicht mit].

Many of Ayim's poems have short lines, which give particular emphasis to the evocative quality of individual words or phrases in contrast to the poems' consciously colloquial tone. This contrast underscores the urgency of the subject matter: the dream of a life without oppression and the fear that this dream, like that of Martin Luther King Jr., will be reduced to "a three-liner in a history book" [dreizeiler in einem geschichtsbuch] and thus be wrongly portrayed as a thing of the past. For that reason, Ayim was politically active. In the poem "grenzenlos und unverschämt" (boundless and impertinent), which gave its title to her 1997 book, Ayim asserts both her blackness and her Germanness as who and what she is, and promises to continue to push the limits in solidarity with her sisters and brothers in spirit because that is where "our / FREEDOM / begins" [unsere / FREIHEIT / beginnt]. Thus, in the assertion of her identity and the political solidarity with others, Ayim also asserts a fundamental freedom.

Any claim to freedom implies the poetic freedom to explore other topics and not be restricted to the theme of the otherness of life in a foreign country. The most universal human attempt at overcoming otherness — and, hence, the ultimate experience of otherness — is love. Ayim wrote love poems; Çirak is known for her love poems; and other multicultural writers have written love poetry as well. For example, Zafer Şenocak observes in "Lu," published in his *Fernwehanstalten* (Wanderlust Companies, 1994, the title is a pun on *Fernsehanstalten*, or broadcasting companies): "I never got bored / because I loved this way and that / I never knew the emptiness / that comes when someone moves out" [ich langweilte mich nie / denn ich liebte so und anders / ich kannte nie die Leere / die entsteht wenn jemand auszieht]. While this observation might gain an additional dimension through the knowledge that Şenocak at one point moved from Turkey to Berlin, it stands on its own as a statement about how the poem's speaker experiences the difficulties of love. Speaking from a different social background, Cyrus Atabay — one of the modern precursors of German-language migrant literature's first phase — explored his own multicultural roots but also transcended the specific for the universal; "Ergänzungen" (Additions) in his *Die Wege des Leichtsinns* (Paths of Levity, 1994) call to mind the three teachings of Creation: "Decorum, usefulness, and love" [Das Angemessene, den Nutzen und die Liebe].

*Revisiting nature*  The images of nature in German poetry changed to the extent that nature hardly signified any deeper meaning for German poetry of the 1990s. Earlier, nature had implied a metaphysical connection between humanity and the transcendent, and it could be understood as an imitation of nature. Such an understanding of nature, while still sought after in the early twentieth century, became increasingly obsolete in the second half of the century. German poetry of the 1990s preferred to express experience that takes place in artificial — political, urban, interpersonal — places, but not in nature. Still, there were poems about nature, and nature continued to provide images that were used in poems, even though they no longer imitated nature.

Nature was often seen with a sense of sorrow because it was endangered by the sprawl of artificial worlds. This attitude is expressed in a haiku by Michael Donhauser (b. 1956 in Liechtenstein) in his collection *Das neue Leben* (The New Life, 1994): "Urban Sprawl: Forests / yellow autumn and dahlias / then a freight depot" [Zersiedlung: Wälder / gelber Herbst und Dahlien / dann ein Frachtbahnhof]. But then, as Karl Krolow reminds the readers of his poem "Das tödliche Blau" (Deadly Blue, 1995) about the poisonous monkshood plant, nature was toxic long before humankind made it so.

Donhauser's poems in *Von den Dingen* (About Things, 1993) mark one extreme approach toward revisiting nature: putting nature into the center of linguistic examination. For example, in a five-page prose poem, "Der Pfirsich," the peach is celebrated as an event taking form: "Concentrated within a peach. / Collected as a fruit: force" [Konzentriert in einem Pfirsich. / Gesammelt die Wucht, zu einer Frucht]. The peach is evoked as being in motion — a dance, akin to language itself. Every aspect of the fruit is mentioned: its aroma, its juice, its shape, and its parts. Donhauser's thing poems dynamically revolve around an object, such as a peach, in order to evoke the object's wholeness by suggesting all its detailed properties. It seems, however, as though Donhauser's collection of poetry is like a museum of natural sciences; it preserves the wholeness of nature that has been destroyed in the real world. Donhauser's attempt to reinstate nature in its old right as an absolute was not only restricted to poetry but was also an exception in German poetry of the 1990s.

The opposite extreme — assuming nature to be the result of a projection of and an interaction with the human mind — is exemplified in *natur-gedichte* (nature-poems, 1996), by Franz Josef Czernin (b. 1952 in Austria). Czernin sees his lyrical production as an encyclopedic work in progress, which he calls "*kunst des dichtens*" (art of poeisis). For him, the two possibilities of language — reference to the outside world and self-reference — are necessarily interrelated, a position on which he elaborates in a poetological essay, "Eine kleine Vor- oder Nachschule zur Ästhetik, auch der natur-gedichte" (A Short Pre- or Post-School for Aesthetics, including nature-poems), which is included in *natur-gedichte*. Czernin constructs nature from language, stipulating "that

humans appear and their heads . . . as a summit" [dass Menschen er-
scheinen und ihre Köpfe . . . als ein Gipfel]. What is more, not only
humans form landscapes; so does language: "conversations themselves
have summits, feet of mountains or valley-bottoms" [Gespräche selbst
auch Gipfel, Füsse von Bergen oder Tal-sohlen haben].

Czernin presents his argument with the support of his metaphoric
use of language, which derives from etymological connections. The
German word *Hang* — central element in his argument — means either "slope" or "preference"; an approximation in English would be
*incline* and *inclination*. Because *Hang* always means both incline and
inclination, talking about an inclination also suggests an incline, thus
generating a landscape; vice versa, describing an incline suggests an inclination, thus tying a physical phenomenon to a mental state. Since the
two codes of landscape and the mind are always contained in *natur-
gedichte*, all of the poems can be read in two different ways that necessarily imply each other.

In between the two radical poetic approaches to nature in *Von den
Dingen* and *natur-gedichte*, a spectrum of poems addressed nature in
interaction with human beings in modes ranging from the nature-
magical to the secular. Sarah Kirsch retained her prominence with her
collections *Erlkönigs Tochter* (Erlking's Daughter, 1992) and *Bodenlos*
(Bottomless, 1996). Kirsch continued to write poems that are informed
by a critical *Naturmagie*. Like her earlier poetry, *Erlkönigs Tochter* has a
solemn, wintry mood, and animals, especially cats, play an important
role. In addition to elements of sorrow, there is also humor that draws
animals and humans closer together. "Was ich in Norwegen lernte"
(What I Learned in Norway) compares the fur of animals with human
hair, stating that humans have the more hair the further north they live,
and the poems concludes: "In Tromsø / I dined with / A bear and
could / Walk around unclothed" [In Tromsø / Dinierte ich mit einem
/ Bären und konnte / Kleiderlos gehen].

In her 1996 collection Kirsch intensified her nature imagery by intertwining it with imagery that centers on the properties of a house. In
"Espresso" the speaker returns home after an absence of two months
and finds that "nothing / Is in place. Where is / Orion the halfmoon
the owl?" [und nichts / Ist in Ordnung. Wo denn / Orion der Halb-
mond die Eule?]. The chaos of nature appears as a reflection of human
confusion so that the poem expresses a sense of a general uneasiness of
being in the world. The world is metaphorically equated with a house
that does not quite offer its inhabitant a sense of being at home. Although this imagery can be seen as nature's resilience, it is more likely a
significant shift: from nature imagery that serves as an orientation for
human life to imagery of man-made objects for expressing humanity's
relationship with nature. Images in other poems back up this shift to

understanding nature in terms of the human world, including technology, by identifying an artificial source of natural phenomena: "Snow storms / From the door of opened refrigerator" [Schneegestöber / Aus der Tür offenen Kühlschranks].

*Silvatica* (1997) was the first collection of poetry that Helga M. Novak (b. 1935) published after the fall of the Berlin Wall. The poems in her *Märkische Feemorgana* (Marshland Fairy Mirage, 1989), with their evocation of prehistoric landscapes mostly devoid of human beings, express the poet's search for herself. In the 1997 collection humanity is back in every poem, beginning with "Geisterheere" (Army of Ghosts): "and silvatica is still alive as wild wumman" [und silvatica lebt noch als wilde wibe]. The meaning of *Silvatica* is fluid. The word refers to the goddess of the trees and forest; the Greek goddess of the hunt, Artemis, is mentioned in the next line as also being alive. Furthermore, the realm of Germanic myth is evoked in the poem with a reference to Dietrich von Bern, and the old form *wibe* for *Weib* (hence the old form *wumman* in English) alludes to the Germanic folktales of the wild or green man, whose mate is the "wilde wibe." The poems can be read as personal love poems in metaphorical guise so that their mythical dimensions never degenerate into an irrational mysticism — because love (like nature) is no longer unproblematic: "The hunt will begin again and again / for love has no off-season" [die Jagd wird aufgehn immer wieder / denn Liebe hat keine Schonzeit].

While Ulla Hahn rejected new poetic forms in her 1981 programmatic poem "Ars poetica," the poem of the same title in her *Epikurs Garten* (Epicurus's Garden, 1995) uses such new forms. In three unrhymed stanzas with predominantly long lines, Hahn asserts that objects exist before language: "die / Rose is a rose est una rosa / and would smell sweet without any name" [die / Rose is a rose est una rosa / und würde ohne jeden Namen duften]. The poem "Fortschritt" (Progress), in which she regrets the disappearance of the sonnet, is itself not a sonnet. The title poem contains the same traditional and apparently superficial images, ironies, and self-doubts about nature as the collection's other poems. It is a key to the other poems. In turn, the collection's motto, quoted from Nietzsche, helps to unlock "Epikurs Garten" by associating the garden with interpersonal connections rather than just with physical reality: "A small garden, figs, little cheeses, and then three or four good friends — that was Epicurus's abundance" [Ein Gärtchen, Feigen, kleine Käse und dazu drei oder vier gute Freunde, — das war die Üppigkeit Epikurs]. In "Epikurs Garten" the speaker talks to a man, presumably Epicurus, who passes on teachings about life itself being its own meaning and about human interconnectedness with nature: "Without knowledge of nature one cannot enjoy / any pleasure completely" [Ohne Wissen von der Natur kann man keine Freude / vollkommen genießen]. But nothing in the poem is quite what it appears to be. Similes play an important role; for instance, Epicurus "wished me joy / the way one says Hello" [wünschte mir Freude / wie man Guten Tag sagt]. This opens up the next level of the poem's meaning: that people should live in the city the way they live in the garden. It is a subtle poem that almost hides its double-coding as a poem about the city and nature. The garden is everywhere, because it is a way of belonging, not a specific space. Therefore, after bidding farewell to the poem's speaker, Epicurus "disappeared / at the corner of Madison and 78th where they have the classic hamburgers" [verschwand / Madison Ecke 78th wo es die klassischen hamburger gibt]. Nature and city may be real, but only belonging is true, the poem suggests.

*At the end of time* While death is beyond human knowledge, it is experienced in relation to life, and death comes in many forms: violently and prematurely or naturally, as an existential wound or with a sense of closure. A Yiddish poem, *Dos lied vunem ojsgehargetn jidischn volk* (The Song of the Famished Jewish People), was hailed as one of the most important publications of 1994, although it had been translated before. Written by the Polish Jew Jizchak Katzenelson at the time of the Holocaust, it is about the suffering and death of the Jewish people. The author himself died in Auschwitz a few weeks after he completed his poem in 1944. Fifty years later Wolf Biermann presented a new translation into German, which was published in a bilingual edition. In texts about the Holocaust, death — because here it is a crime against humanity — takes on a political and moral dimension that involves a sense of resistance rather than a coming to terms with dying as part of the human condition. Yet even in the latter sense, death not only implies the anthropological phenomenon of aging as a natural process, as it did in the poems of Krolow and Jandl, who died at the end of the decade; death can also involve a confrontation with a fate that is perceived both as premature and unavoidable, for example, in AIDS literature.

Karl Krolow reflected on beginnings and ends as patterns of human existence. In his collection *Ich höre mich sagen* (I Hear Myself Say, 1992), a poem ends: "we are being tested by dying" [wir werden geprüft vom Sterben]; it is, however, a test that is confined to empirical reality. In his collection *Die zweite Zeit* (The Second Time, 1995), the poem "Anfang und Ende vom Satz" (Beginning and End of the Sentence) soon extends from language to life, and other poems address different phenomena, such as love, health, and beliefs. Nevertheless, Krolow's short, formally perfect, usually rhymed poems are not bitter in tone; rather, they are unsentimental in assessing the process of his own aging. Some of his poems do contain biting resignation: "Exit" evokes "the laşt, fatal therapy" [der letzten, tödlichen Therapie] of loneliness with medical machinery. Language and life are tied together because "a sentence is mortal" [Ein Satz ist sterblich], Krolow writes in another poem. But there is also a tone of equally unsentimental resilience that encompasses the private and the political; the poet participates in assessing the new political realities; and the private and political realms come together in "Wir leben schneller" (We Live Faster), which paints a sarcastic picture of life in the electronic age with "war and sex as moving pictures" [Krieg und Koitus als laufende Bilder]. But the poem ends with hope: ". . . in the shadow / impatience, after the wrong diagnoses, / and a new sense / for utopias" [. . . im Schatten / die Ungeduld, nach den falschen Diagnosen, / und ein neuer Sinn / für Utopie].

In poems mostly written between 1992 and 1996 and published in *peter und die kuh* (peter and the cow, 1996), Ernst Jandl revisits his childhood and addresses his experience with aging; he does both in terse language that is less bitter than biting. Several poems are also written in Austrian dialect with a High German version included, such as the four-liner in which he settles the scores with his family, which the title calls, in English, a "four-headed monster": "my father — a wimp / my mother — a cow / my brother — a moron / only me — a genius" [da fooda — a lodsch / di muada — a drompä / da bruada — a bleampä / nur iii — a schenii]. While Jandl's poems acknowledge the toll that time takes, they also affirm a nonmetaphysical and ironic attitude that life needs to be lived in this world, the price of which is mortality: "forever lives / he who has / never lived" [ewig lebt / wer nie / gelebt hat].

Friedericke Mayröcker responded to the thoughts of her ailing friend Jandl with poems that give comfort and are derived from concrete situations, such as the opening lines of "für Ernst Jandl" (1990): "right now I'm tied to the bottle he says / I'll call you when the infusion's done he says" [ich hänge jetzt an der Flasche sagt er / rufe dich an wenn die Infusion vorüber ist sagt er]. Mayröcker's collections of poems *Das besessene Alter* (Possessed Old Age, 1992) and *Notizen auf einem Kamel* (Notes Taken on a Camel's Back, 1996) include but do not focus on the process of aging, which is usually observed as an experience that other people, such as her mother, undergo. Rather, Mayröcker continues to explore the options of language in metaphors and abrupt shifts and empty spaces within a poem. Mayröcker's poetic procedure attempts to avoid the control of meaning from the outside so that meaning might emerge on its own from within the poem. The seven-line poem "Anrichteschrank, Stilleben am Morgen" (Sideboard, Still Life in the Morning, 1996) illustrates this procedure: "NOT / THE SEASON FOR BUDDING . . originally red, threaded with / kitchen yellow : curly tangerine hair, and / flyblue and lilac green the wondrous world" [UN= / ZEITIGKEIT VON KNOSPE . . von roter Herkunft küchengelb / verflochten : krauses Mandarinen Haar, und / fliegenblau und fliedergrün die wunderbare Welt].

The image of death also changed in an age of AIDS, a disease that affected an increasing number of young people. After Mario Wirz (b. 1956) was diagnosed as HIV-positive in 1985, he made his fear of dying and his hunger for life the subject matter of his literary works encompassing prose texts, such as *Biographie eines lebendigen Tages* (Biography of a Lively Day, 1994), and poetry, such as the collections *Ich rufe die Wölfe* (Calling the Wolves, 1993) and *Das Herz dieser Stunde* (The Heart of This Hour, 1997). His poems are an example of a relatively quiet AIDS discourse, which had a flamboyant exponent in the filmmaker Rosa von Praunheim (pseudonym of Holger Mischwitzky, b. 1942), with whom Wirz on occasion collaborated. Wirz articulates his angers, frustrations, and fears, but above all an intensified awareness of existence, as expressed in the four-line poem "Schatz" (Treasure) in his 1993 collection: "I bend down / in the crowd / pick up an hour / that someone has lost" [Ich bücke mich / inmitten der Menge / hebe eine Stunde auf, / die jemand verloren hat]. His 1997 collection, which reflects his treatment for cancer, transcends the empirical reality of the stay in the hospital not by ignoring but by including it in images that are double-coded as referring to this world and a wishful one. Wirz's angel, "terrible and without mercy" [schrecklich und ohne Erbarmen], is both reminiscent of Rilke's angel and a reference to medical personnel. Quite matter-of-factly Wirz states that he has not mastered the "art of dying" [die Kunst des Sterbens] and that "existence is my calling" [Dasein ist meine Berufung]. Thus, the confrontation with individual death is perhaps at times melancholy, but it may become what literature is all about: an examination and celebration of life.

# Works Consulted

## 1. Literary Histories, Encyclopedias, etc.

Arnold, Heinz Ludwig, ed. *Kritisches Lexikon zur deutschsprachigen Gegenwartsliteratur*. Munich: edition text + kritik, 1994.

Bahr, Ehrhard. *Geschichte der deutschen Literatur: Kontinuität und Veränderung*, vol. 3. Tübingen: Francke, 1988 [=UTB 1465].

Balzer, Bernd, and Volker Mertens, eds. *Deutsche Literatur in Schlaglichtern*. Mannheim: Meyers Lexikonverlag, 1990.

Best, Otto F. *Handbuch literarischer Fachbegriffe: Definitionen und Beispiele*, revised ed. Frankfurt am Main: Fischer, 1987.

——, and Hans-Jürgen Schmitt, eds. *Die deutsche Literatur in Text und Darstellung*, vols. 13–16. Stuttgart: Reclam, 1974–1977.

Braak, Ivo. *Gattungsgeschichte deutschsprachiger Dichtung in Stichworten*, vols. Ib and IIc. Kiel: Ferdinand Hirt, 1975, 1981.

Brauneck, Manfred, ed. *Autorenlexikon deutschsprachiger Literatur des 20. Jahrhunderts*, revised ed. Reinbek: Rowohlt, 1995.

Einsiedel, Wolfgang von, et al., eds. *Kindlers Literatur Lexikon*, paperback ed. Munich: Deutscher Taschenbuch Verlag, 1974.

Emmerich, Wolfgang. *Kleine Literaturgeschichte der DDR*, revised ed. Leipzig: Gustav Kiepenheuer, 1997.

Fleming, William. *Arts & Ideas*, 9th ed. Fort Worth: Harcourt Brace, 1995.

Fowler, Roger, ed. *A Dictionary of Modern Critical Terms*, rev. ed. London: Routledge & Kegan Paul, 1987.

Glaser, Horst Albert, ed. *Deutsche Literatur: Eine Sozialgeschichte*, vols. 8 and 9. Reinbek: Rowohlt, 1982, 1983.

Hage, Volker, et al., eds. *Deutsche Literatur: Jahresüberblick*. Stuttgart: Reclam, 1981–1998.

Hardin, James, ed. *Dictionary of Literary Biography*, vols. 56, 66, 69, 75, 85, 118, 124. Detroit: Gale Research, 1987–1992.

Haus der Geschichte der Bundesrepublik Deutschland, ed. *Erlebnis Geschichte: Das Buch zur Ausstellung*. n.p.: Lübbe, n.d.

Jacobsen, Wolfgang, Anton Kaes, and Hans Helmut Prinzler, eds. *Geschichte des deutschen Films*. Stuttgart: Metzler, 1993.

Jung, Kurt M. *Weltgeschichte in einem Griff: Von der Urzeit bis zur Gegenwart.* Berlin: Safari, 1979.

Kunisch, Hermann, ed. *Handbuch der deutschen Gegenwartsliteratur.* Munich: Nymphenburger, 1965.

Magill, Frank N., ed. *Masterplots,* revised second ed. Pasadena: Salem Press, 1996.

Pleticha, Heinrich. *Deutsche Geschichte,* vols. 10–12. Gütersloh: Bertelsmann, 1984.

Saalfeld, Lerke von, Dietrich Kreidt, and Friedrich Rothe. *Geschichte der deutschen Literatur: Von den Anfängen bis zur Gegenwart.* Munich: Droemer Knaur, 1989.

Salzer, Anselm, et al., eds. *Illustrierte Geschichte der deutschen Literatur.* Cologne: Naumann & Göbel, n.d.

Schlosser, Horst Dieter. *dtv-Atlas zur deutschen Literatur.* Munich: Deutscher Taschenbuch Verlag, 1983.

Schnell, Ralf. *Geschichte der deutschsprachigen Literatur seit* 1945. Stuttgart: Metzler, 1993.

Schütz, Erhard, Jochen Vogt, et al. *Einführung in die deutsche Literatur des 20. Jahrhunderts.* Opladen: Westdeutscher Verlag, 1977.

Willhardt, Mark, and Alan Michael Parker. *Who's Who in Twentieth-Century World Poetry.* London and New York: Routledge, 2000.

Wilpert, Gero von. *Sachwörterbuch der Literatur,* 5th ed. Stuttgart: Kröner, 1969.

## 2. Monographs and Articles

Adorno, Theodor W. *Ästhetische Theorie.* Frankfurt am Main: Suhrkamp, 1977.

Ackermann, Irmgard. *Fremde AugenBlicke: Mehrkulturelle Literatur in Deutschland.* Bonn: Inter Nationes, 1996.

Arnold, Heinz Ludwig, ed. *Hans Henny Jahnn,* revised ed. Munich: edition text + kritik, 1980.

Balzer, Bernd. "Heinrich Bölls Werke: Anarchie und Zärtlichkeit," in *Heinrich Böll: Werke,* vol. 1, ed. Balzer. Cologne, Kiepenheuer & Witsch, 1977, 9–128.

Baumer, Franklin L. *Modern European Thought: Continuity and Change, 1600–1950.* New York: Macmillan, 1977.

Bennett, Benjamin. *Hugo von Hofmannsthal: The Theater of Consciousness.* Cambridge: Cambridge UP, 1988.

Berendt, Hans. *Rainer Maria Rilkes Neue Gedichte: Versuch einer Deutung.* Bonn: Bouvier, 1957.

Berman, Morris. *Coming to Our Senses: Body and Spirit in the Hidden History of the West*. New York: Simon & Schuster, 1989.

Blume, Bernhard. *Existenz und Dichtung. Essays und Aufsätze*. Frankfurt am Main: Insel, 1980.

Blumenberg, Hans. "Geld oder Leben. Eine metaphorologische Studie zur Konsistenz der Philosophie Georg Simmels," in *Ästhetik und Soziologie um die Jahrhundertwende: Georg Simmel*, ed. Hannes Böhringer and Karlfried Gründer. Frankfurt am Main: Vittorio Klostermann, 1976, 121–134.

Bradbury, Malcolm, and James McFarlane. *Modernism 1890–1930*. Harmondsworth, England: Penguin, 1976.

Bradley, Brigitte L. *R. M. Rilkes Neue Gedichte: Ihr zyklisches Gefüge*. Bern: Francke, 1967.

——. *Rainer Maria Rilkes "Der Neuen Gedichte anderer Teil": Entwicklungsstufen seiner Pariser Lyrik*. Bern: Francke, 1976.

Brauneck, Manfred. *Theater im 20. Jahrhundert: Programmschriften, Stilperioden, Reformmodelle*, revised ed. Reinbek: Rowohlt, 1986.

Brenneke, Reinhard. *Militanter Modernismus: Vergleichende Studien zum Frühwerk Ernst Jüngers*. Stuttgart: M&P, 1992.

Breuer, Stefan. *Ästhetischer Fundamentalismus: Stefan George und der deutsche Antimodernismus*. Darmstadt: Wissenschaftliche Buchgesellschaft, 1995.

Briggs, John, and F. David Peat. *Turbulent Mirror: An Illustrated Guide to Chaos Theory and the Science of Wholeness*. Grand Rapids: Harper & Row, 1989.

Brinkmann, Richard. "Hofmannsthal und die Sprache." *DVJS* 35 (1961): 69–95.

Bürger, Peter. *Theory of the Avant-Garde*. Minneapolis: U of Minnesota P, 1984.

——. *Prosa der Moderne*. Frankfurt am Main: Suhrkamp, 1988.

Burgess, Anthony. *99 Novels: The Best in English since 1939*. New York: Summit, 1984.

Calinescu, Matei. *Five Faces of Modernity: Modernism, Avant-Garde, Decadence, Kitsch, Postmodernism*. Durham, N.C.: Duke UP, 1987.

Del Caro, Adrian. *Hugo von Hofmannsthal: Poets and the Language of Life*. Baton Rouge: Louisiana State UP, 1993.

Demetz, Peter. *After the Fires. Recent Writing in the Germanies, Austria, and Switzerland*. New York: Harcourt Brace Jovanovich, 1986.

——. *Worte in Freiheit: Der italienische Futurismus und die deutsche literarische Avantgarde (1912–1934)*. Munich: Piper, 1990.

Denkler, Horst, and Karl Prümm, eds. *Die Deutsche Literatur im Dritten Reich: Themen — Traditionen — Wirkungen*. Stuttgart: Reclam, 1976.

Doležel, Lubomír. "Intensional Function, Invisible Worlds, and Franz Kafka." *Style* 17.2 (Spring 1983): 120–141.

Doppler, Alfred. "Die poetische Verfahrensweise in Rilkes *Neuen Gedichten*." *Studi Germanici* 14.2–3 (1976): 175–195.

Durzak, Manfred, ed. *Die deutsche Exilliteratur 1933–1945.* Stuttgart: Reclam, 1973.

——. *Zwischen Symbolismus und Expressionismus: Stefan George.* Stuttgart: Kohlhammer, 1974.

Ebert, Roger. "Ebert's Top Picks." (Universal Press) *The Bakersfield Californian* 1 Jan. 1999: E6, E18.

Eksteins, Modris. *Rites of Spring: The Great War and the Birth of the Modern Age.* Boston: Houghton Mifflin, 1989.

Esslin, Martin. *Das Theater des Absurden.* Reinbek: Rowohlt, 1965.

Faulkner, Peter. *Modernism.* London: Methuen, 1977.

Felstiner, John. *Paul Celan: Poet, Survivor, Jew.* New Haven: Yale UP, 1995.

Frisby, David. *Sociological Impressionism: A Reassessment of Georg Simmel's Social Theory.* London: Heinemann, 1981.

Fokkema, Douwe W. *Literary History, Modernism, and Postmodernism.* Amsterdam: Benjamins, 1984.

Freedman, Ralph. *The Lyrical Novel: Studies in Hermann Hesse, André Gide, and Virginia Woolf.* Princeton: Princeton UP, 1963.

Garten, H. F. *Modern German Drama.* Fair Lawn, N.J.: Essential, 1959.

Gay, Peter. *Die Republik der Außenseiter: Geist und Kultur in der Weimarer Zeit 1918–1933,* revised ed. Frankfurt am Main: Fischer, 1987.

Gleick, James. *Chaos: The Making of a Science.* New York: Viking, 1987.

Glenn, Jerry. *Paul Celan.* New York: Twayne, 1973.

Gnüg, Hiltrud, and Renate Möhrmann, eds. *Frauen Literatur Geschichte: Schreibende Frauen vom Mittelalter bis zur Gegenwart,* paperback ed. Frankfurt am Main: Suhrkamp, 1989.

Grimm, Reinhold, and Jost Hermand, eds. *Faschismus und Avantgarde.* Königstein: Athenäum, 1980.

Habermas, Jürgen. *Der Philosophische Diskurs der Moderne.* Frankfurt am Main: Suhrkamp, 1985.

Hähnel, Klaus-Dieter. *Rainer Maria Rilke: Werk — Literaturgeschichte — Kunstanschauung.* Berlin: Aufbau, 1984.

Hardt, Manfred. *Geschichte der italienischen Literatur.* Düsseldorf and Zurich: Artemis & Winkler, 1996.

Harvey, David. *The Condition of Postmodernity: An Enquiry into the Origins of Cultural Change.* Oxford: Blackwell, 1989.

Hayles, N. Katherine. *Chaos Bound: Orderly Disorder in Contemporary Literature and Science*. Ithaca, N.Y.: Cornell UP, 1990.

Heintz, Günter, ed. *Deutsche Arbeiterdichtung 1910–1933*. Stuttgart: Reclam, 1974.

Herf, Jeffrey. *Reactionary Modernism: Technology, Culture, and Politics in Weimar and the Third Reich*. Cambridge: Cambridge UP, 1984.

Hillebrand, Bruno. *Nietzsche und die deutsche Literatur*, 2 vols. Tübingen: dtv, 1978.

——. *Ästhetik des Nihilismus: Von der Romantik zum Modernismus*. Stuttgart: J. B. Metzler, 1991.

Hirsch, David H. *The Deconstruction of Literature: Criticism after Auschwitz*. Hanover, N.H.: UP of New England, 1991.

Horkheimer, Max, and Theodor W. Adorno. *Dialektik der Aufklärung: Philosophische Fragmente*, paperback ed. Frankfurt am Main: Fischer, 1979.

Huelsenbeck, Richard, ed. *The Dada Almanac*, trans. Malcolm Green. London: Atlas, 1993.

Jayne, Richard. *The Symbolism of Space and Motion in the Works of Rainer Maria Rilke*. Frankfurt am Main: Athenäum, 1972.

Jens, Walter. *Statt einer Literaturgeschichte*. Pfullingen: Neske, 1978.

Jurgensen, Manfred. *Frauenliteratur: Autorinnen — Perspektiven — Konzepte*. Munich: Deutscher Taschenbuch Verlag, 1983.

Kaufmann, Walter. *Nietzsche. Philosoph — Psychologe — Antichrist*. Darmstadt: Wissenschaftliche Buchgesellschaft, 1982.

Keilson-Lauritz, Marita. *Von der Liebe die Freundschaft heißt: Zur Homoerotik im Werk Stefan Georges*. Berlin: Verlag rosa Winkel, 1987.

Kellert, Stephen H. *In the Wake of Chaos: Unpredictable Order in Dynamical Systems*. Chicago: U of Chicago P, 1993.

Kern, Stephen. *The Culture of Time and Space 1880–1918*. London: Weidenfeld & Nicolson, 1983.

Kesting, Marianne. *Das epische Theater*, 7th ed. Stuttgart: Kohlhammer, 1978.

Ketelsen, Uwe-K. *Völkisch-nationale und nationalsozialistische Literatur in Deutschland 1890–1945*. Stuttgart: Metzler, 1976.

Kobel, Erwin. *Hugo von Hofmannsthal*. Berlin: De Gruyter, 1970.

Koch, Hans-Albrecht. *Hugo von Hofmannsthal*. Darmstadt: Wissenschaftliche Buchgesellschaft, 1989.

Koslowski, Peter. *Der Mythos der Moderne: Die dichterische Philosophie Ernst Jüngers*. Munich: Fink, 1991.

Kurzweil, Edith. *Briefe aus Wien: Jüdisches Leben vor der Deportation*. Vienna: Turia + Kant, 1999.

Lepenies, Wolf. *Die drei Kulturen: Soziologie zwischen Literatur und Wissenschaft*. Munich: Hanser, 1985.

Lodge, David. *The Art of Fiction: Illustrated from Classic and Modern Texts*. New York: Penguin, 1993.

Loewy, Ernst: *Literatur unterm Hakenkreuz: Das Dritte Reich und seine Dichtung*, revised ed. Frankfurt am Main: Europäische Verlagsanstalt, 1977.

Mandel, Siegfried. *Rainer Maria Rilke: The Poetic Instinct*. Carbondale: Southern Illinois UP, 1965.

Mason, Eudo C. "Rilkes Humor," in *Deutsche Weltliteratur. Von Goethe bis Ingeborg Bachmann*, ed. Klaus W. Jonas. Tübingen: Niemeyer, 1972, 216–215.

Mauser, Wolfram. *Hugo von Hofmannsthal. Konfliktbewältigung und Werkstruktur: Eine psychosoziale Interpretation*. Munich: Fink, 1977.

Mayer, Hans, ed. *Über Peter Huchel*. Frankfurt am Main: Suhrkamp, 1973.

Mayer, Mathias. *Hugo von Hofmannsthal*. Stuttgart: Metzler, 1993.

McGowan, John. *Postmodernism and Its Critics*. Ithaca, N.Y.: Cornell UP, 1991.

McHale, Brian. *Postmodernist Fiction*. New York: Methuen, 1987.

Meyer, Hermann. "Rilkes Sachlichkeit," in *Deutsche Weltliteratur. Von Goethe bis Ingeborg Bachmann*, ed. Klaus W. Jonas. Tübingen: Niemeyer, 1972, 203–216.

Meyer, Martin. *Ernst Jünger*. Munich: Hanser, 1990.

Midgley, David. *The German Novel in the Twentieth Century: Beyond Realism*. Edinburgh: Edinburgh UP / New York: St. Martin's, 1993.

Mitchell, Breon. *James Joyce and the German Novel 1922–1933*. Athens: Ohio UP, 1976.

Mitscherlich, Alexander. *Auf dem Weg zur vaterlosen Gesellschaft: Ideen zur Sozialpsychologie*, new ed. Munich: Piper, 1973.

Oppert, Kurt. "Das Dinggedicht. Eine Kunstform bei Mörike, Meyer und Rilke." *Deutsche Vierteljahrschrift für Literaturwissenschaft und Geisteswissenschaft* 4.4 (1926): 746–783.

Paulson, William R. *The Noise of Culture: Literary Texts in a World of Information*. Ithaca: Cornell UP, 1988.

Pike, Burton. *Robert Musil: An Introduction to His Work*. Ithaca, N.Y.: Cornell UP, 1961.

Piscator, Erwin. *Das politsche Theater*, revised ed. Reinbek: Rowohlt, 1979.

Plumpe, Gerhard. *Epochen moderner Literatur: Ein systemtheoretischer Entwurf*. Opladen: Westdeutscher Verlag, 1995.

Prang, Helmut. "Der moderne Dichter und das arme Wort." *Germanisch-Romanische Monatsschrift* 7 (1957): 130–145.

Puknus, Heinz. *Neue Literatur der Frauen: Deutschsprachige Autorinnen der Gegenwart.* Munich: Beck, 1980.

Pütz, Peter. *Friedrich Nietzsche.* Stuttgart: Metzler, 1974.

Richter, Hans. *Dada: Art and Anti-Art.* New York: Thames & Hudson, 1997.

Ritchie, J. M. *German Literature under National Socialism.* London: Croom Helm, 1983.

Roemer, Michael. *Telling Stories: Postmodernism and the Invalidation of Traditional Narrative.* Lanham, Md.: Rowman & Littlefield, 1995.

Roth-Bodmer, Eugen. *Schlüssel zu Nietzsche's Zarathustra.* Männedorf: Self-publication, 1975.

Rudolph, Hermann. *Kulturkritik und konservative Revolution.* Tübingen: Niemeyer, 1971.

Schäfer, Hans Dieter. *Das gespaltene Bewußtsein: Über deutsche Kultur und Lebenswirklichkeit 1933–1945,* revised ed. Frankfurt am Main: Ullstein, 1983.

Schlechta, Karl. *Nietzsche Chronik: Daten zu Leben und zu Werk.* Munich: Hanser, 1975.

Schwalbe, Jürgen. *Sprache und Gebärde im Werk Hugo von Hofmannsthals.* Freiburg: Scharz, 1971.

Schwarz, Egon. "Rainer Maria Rilke unter dem Nationalsozialismus," in *Rilke heute: Beziehungen und Wirkungen,* ed. Ingeborg H. Solbrig and Joachim Storck. Frankfurt am Main: Suhrkamp, 1975, 287–313.

——. *Poetry and Politics in the Works of Rainer Maria Rilke.* New York: Ungar, 1981.

Serke, Jürgen. *Frauen schreiben: Ein neues Kapitel deutschsprachiger Literatur.* Frankfurt am Main: Fischer, 1982.

Sichelschmidt, Gustav. *Liebe, Mord und Abenteuer: Eine Geschichte der deutschen Unterhaltungsliteratur.* Berlin: Haude & Spener, 1969.

Sokel, Walter H. *The Writer in Extremis: Expressionism in Twentieth-Century German Literature.* Stanford, CA: Stanford UP, 1959.

Solbrig, Ingeborg H. and Joachim Storck, ed. *Rilke heute: Beziehungen und Wirkungen.* Frankfurt am Main: Suhrkamp, 1975.

Sontag, Susan. *Under the Sign of Saturn.* New York: Vintage, 1981.

Stanley, Patricia H. *Wolfgang Hildesheimer and His Critics.* Columbia, S.C.: Camden House, 1993.

Stern, J. P. *Ernst Jünger: A Writer of Our Time.* Cambridge: Bowes & Bowes, 1953.

Stoehr, Ingo R. *Beyond the Zeus Principle: Two Hundred Years of Love and Politics in the Novel.* Bern: Peter Lang, 1993.

——. "The Dynamic Oscillation of Narrative and Thematic Consciousness in Uwe Johnson's *Jahrestage*-Complex." *Internationales Uwe-Johnson-Forum* 6 (1997): 31–72.

——. "The Recovering Patriarch: A Literary Type of the 1980s in Novels by Struck, Wolf, and Frischmuth," in *Barbara Frischmuth in Contemporary Context,* ed. Renate Posthofen. Riverside, CA: Ariadne Press, 1999, 224–241.

Suhr, Heidrun. "Ausländerliteratur: Minority Literature in the Federal Republic of Germany." *New German Critique* 46 (Winter 1989): 71–103.

Szondi, Peter. *Theorie des modernen Dramas (1880–1950),* revised ed. Frankfurt: Suhrkamp am Main, 1981.

Tarot, Rolf. *Hugo von Hofmannsthal: Daseinsformen und dichterische Struktur.* Tübingen: Niemeyer, 1970.

Wehdeking, Volker. *Die deutsche Einheit und die Schriftsteller: Literarische Verarbeitung der Wende 1989.* Stuttgart: Kohlhammer, 1995.

Welsch, Wolfgang. *Unsere postmoderne Moderne.* Weinheim: VCH, Acta Humaniora, 1987.

Wittstock, Uwe. *Leselust: Wie unterhaltsam ist die neue deutsche Literatur?* Munich: Luchterhand, 1995.

Worbs, Michael. *Nervenkunst: Literatur und Psychoanalyse im Wien der Jahrhundertwende.* 1983. Frankfurt: Athenäum, 1988.

Wulf, Josef. *Literatur und Dichtung im Dritten Reich: Eine Dokumentation.* Gütersloh: Mohn, 1963.

Wunberg, Gotthart. *Der frühe Hofmannsthal: Schizophrenie als dichterische Struktur.* Stuttgart: Kohlhammer, 1965.

Ziolkowski, Theodore. *The Novels of Hermann Hesse: A Study in Theme and Structure.* Princeton: Princeton UP, 1965.

——. *Strukturen des modernen Romans: Deutsche Beispiele und europäische Zusammenhänge.* Munich: List, 1972.

# Index

absolute prose. *See* autonomous prose

absurd, 50, 52, 54, 72, 80–81, 82, 86, 162, 249, 281, 329. *See also* theater, of the absurd

abuse: addiction, 417; child, 288; domestic, 296. *See also* violence

Achleitner, Friedrich, 304

Adenauer, Konrad, 230, 255, 330

Adorno, Theodor, 202, 231, 272, 340

Aebli, Kurt, 471

Aestheticism, 8, 11, 13, 16, 25, 54, 57, 59, 65, 68, 69, 83, 89, 92, 96, 98, 100–101, 105, 169, 193, 282, 306, 334; definition of, 19–21; styles of, 21–25, 29, 30, 38. *See also* decadence; Impressionism; *Jugendstil;* Symbolism

affirmation, 83, 122, 123, 151, 153, 225, 349, 351, 365, 414, 447. *See also* escapism

Afro-German writing, 480–81

aggressiveness, 45, 84, 86, 99, 233, 236, 261, 269, 300, 302, 315, 348, 350, 379, 416, 423, 429, 446

aging. *See* old age

agitprop, 131–32, 237

Aichinger, Ilse, 245, 270, 280

AIDS, 388, 439, 485, 487

air raid, 228, 239, 264, 282, 442, 477

alienation, 5, 7, 36, 39, 44, 51, 56, 57, 60, 61, 75, 76, 79, 100, 102, 144, 216, 249, 262, 273, 298, 321, 337, 340, 386, 400, 416, 439, 463

alienation effect. *See* defamiliarization effect

Altenberg, Peter, 22, 23, 26

ambiguity, 6, 19, 26, 30, 38, 62, 70, 125, 127, 151–52, 153, 161, 165, 175, 214, 226, 240, 300, 317, 318, 353, 370, 382, 427, 428–29, 453

Americanism, 147, 382. *See also* Westernization

Anacker, Heinrich, 165, 175–76

Andersch, Alfred, 244, 250, 252, 387; works by: *Der Vater eines Mörders* (The Father of a Murderer), 399

Anderson, Sascha, 429

Andres, Stefan, 153, 238; works by: *Die Versuchung des Synesius* (The Temptation of Synesius), 406, 407; "El Greco malt den Großinquisitor" (El Greco Paints the Grand Inquisitor), 152

Andrian, Leopold von, 26

androgyny, 46, 110, 200, 362, 377, 414–15, 453, 457

angel, 101–2, 184, 302, 310, 400–401, 479, 487

angst. *See* fear

*Ankunftsliteratur,* 295, 309–11

antiauthoritarian impulse, 331, 337, 404

antibourgeois attitude, 14, 19, 29, 63, 104, 218, 225, 331, 349

antifascism, 152–53, 155, 156–57, 212, 216, 229, 234–35, 236, 264, 279, 310

antihistory. *See* historical novel, new historical novel

anti-illusion, 47–48, 50, 127. *See also* theater, of anti-illusion

antimodernity, 4, 14, 144, 166–68, 189, 202, 218

anti-Semitism, 9, 13, 17, 18, 27, 58, 92, 141, 144, 148, 209, 269, 394–95, 434–35, 446, 447, 480

anxiety. *See* fear

Apitz, Bruno, works by: "Esther," 160; *Nackt unter Wölfen* (Naked Among Wolves), 279–80

APO (Außerparlamentarische Opposition), 293, 343

apocalypse, 65, 66, 67–68, 142, 226, 227, 282, 353, 383, 388, 392, 404, 408, 447, 462–64. *See also* endgame; nuclear catastrophe

apotheosis. *See* epiphany

Apollonian principle, 11, 58, 114

Aragon, Louis, 88

*Arbeiterdichtung,* 14–16, 17, 69, 120, 168

archetype, 76, 110, 220–21, 340, 401, 448, 467
Arendt, Erich, 345, 351; works by: *Ägäis*, 297; *entgrenzen* (delimit), 352
Arjouni, Jakob, 471
Arnim, Bettina von, 353
Arp, Hans, 85, 263; works by: "Dada-Sprüche" (Dada Sayings), 265
*Art Nouveau. See Jugendstil*
Artaud, Antonin, 328
artificiality, 6, 20, 32–33, 35, 69, 472, 475, 482, 484
Artmann, H. C., 304; works by: *med ana schwoazzn dintn* (with black ink), 304
Aschenbeck, Udo, 418
Astel, Arnfried, 348
Atabay, Cyrus, works by: *Die Wege des Leichtsinns* (Paths of Levity), 481; *Einige Schatten* (Several Shadows), 420; "Ergänzungen" (Additions), 481
atomic bomb, 118, 145, 255, 265, 326, 462. *See also* nuclear catastrophe
*Aufbau* literature, 237–38
Auschwitz, 212, 231, 292, 296, 328–29
Ausländer, Rose, 296–97, 347–48, 419, 423; works by: *Blinder Sommer* (Blind Summer), 297; "Gib auf" (Give Up), 422; *Ich spiele noch* (I'm Still Playing), 422; *Ich zähl die Sterne meiner Worte* (I Count the Stars of My Words), 422
Austen, Jane, 23
Austria, 13, 14, 25, 51, 53, 91, 98, 141, 163, 196–197, 198, 203, 212, 230, 254, 265, 268, 374, 394–395, 401, 420, 447
Austro-Hungarian Empire. *See* Austria
authenticity, 15, 89, 90, 97, 98, 119, 122, 125, 150, 168, 191, 262, 279, 310, 326, 347, 348, 349, 351, 354, 356, 360–64, 365, 371, 400, 405, 407, 411, 413, 421, 444. *See also* human touch
authoritarianism, 42, 48, 62, 92, 138, 165, 173, 281, 318–19, 344, 347, 362, 372, 391, 399, 405

authors of foreign roots, 416, 420–22, 454–58. *See also* minority; multiculturalism
autobiography (and autobiographical elements), 16, 45, 62, 108, 157, 159, 287, 310, 347, 348, 350, 360, 371, 374, 375, 399, 400, 401, 414, 443, 447, 449, 465
autonomous prose, 71–73
autonomy, xii, 20, 55–56, 69–70, 299, 306, 334, 338–39, 380
Avant-Garde, 8, 38, 41, 69, 99, 149, 193, 219, 227, 295, 303, 306, 336, 430, 451; definition of: 54–57. *See also* Dada; theater; epic theater; Expressionism; Surrealism
Ayim, May, works by: "auskunft" (information), 480; *blues in schwarz weiss* (blues in black and white), 480–81; "die farbe der macht" (the color of power), 480; *nachtgesang* (night song), 480; "grenzenlos und unverschämt" (boundless and impertinent), 481

Baader, Andreas, 343
Baader, Johannes, 84, 86–87, 88
Bachmann, Ingeborg, 217, 231, 250, 261, 266, 268–69, 280, 298, 354, 447; works by: "Alle Tage" (Every Day), 269; *Anrufung des großen Bären* (Conjuration of the Great Bear), 268; *Der Fall Franza. Requiem für Fanny Goldmann* (The Case of Franza, Requiem for Fanny Goldmann), 355; *Die gestundete Zeit* (On Borrowed Time), 268; *Malina*, 355–58; *Todesarten* (Ways of Dying), 355, 445
Bachmann, Stefan, 437
Bacmeister, Ernst, works by: *Siegfried*, 180
Bahr, Hermann, 25–26
Bairl, Helmut, works by: *Die Feststellung* (The Determination), 275; *Frau Flinz*, 275
Ball, Hugo, 84–86; works by: "Karavane" (Caravan), 85, 88
Balla, Giacomo, 56
Ball-Hennings, Emmy, 85

Döring, Stefan, 429
Dorn, Dieter, 437
Dörrie, Doris, works by: *Liebe Schmerz und das ganze verdammte Zeug* (Love Pain and the Whole Damn Business), 418; "Männer" (Men), 418
Dorst, Tankred, 378, 437; works by: *Auf dem Chimborazo* (On Top of the Chimborazo, with Ursula Ehler), 379; *Dorothea Merz* (with Ursula Ehler), 379; *Merlin* (with Ursula Ehler), 393; *Toller*, 327, 379
Dostoevski, Feodor M., 73
Draesner, Ulrike, works by: *gedächtnisschleifen* (memory loops), 474
drama: action drama, 179, 181–82, 183; classical tragedy, 127; crisis of classicist drama, 28, 30, 74, 131, 133; didactic plays, 135–36, 276, 277; documentary, 132; historical drama, 179–81, 187; monodrama, 75, 76, 77, 82, 131, 249; one-act play, 28, 131; production play, 277–78, 279; *Stationendrama*, 75; *Thingspiel*, 179, 182–84; tragicomedy, 209; *Volksstück*, 194–96, 324, 325, 378–79; well-made play, 30–31, 131. *See also* dialogue
Drawert, Kurt, works by: *Spiegelland* (Mirror Land), 449
dread. *See* fear
dream, 3, 26, 28–29, 31, 32, 44, 46–47, 48, 58, 61, 62, 71, 81, 100, 106, 108, 111, 113, 187, 189, 198, 239, 249, 270–71, 283, 309, 366, 394, 397, 410–11, 422, 440, 457, 466–67, 480, 481
Drewitz, Ingeborg, works by: *Gestern war heute* (Yesterday was Today), 358, 360, 372
Droste-Hülshoff, Annette von, 353
Duchamp, Marcel, 85, 88
Dujardin, Edouard, 27
Dürrenmatt, Friedrich, 50, 82, 261, 270, 272, 274, 387; works by: *Achterloo*, 391; *Der Besuch der alten Dame* (The Visit), 275; *Der Richter und sein Henker* (The Judge and His Executioner), 469; *Die Ehen des*

*Herrn Mississippi* (The Marriage of Mr. Mississippi), 275; *Die Physiker* (The Physicists), 275, 319–20; *Romulus der Große* (Romulus the Great), 250; "Theaterprobleme" (Problems with the Theater), 275
Dutschke, Rudi, 293
Dwinger, Edwin Erich, 186; works by: *Die letzten Reiter* (The Last Riders), 257

East German secret police. *See* Stasi
East-West conflict. *See* Cold War
Ebert, Friedrich, 52–53, 95
ecology, 424. *See also* nature
economic miracle, 254, 269, 285, 292, 313
Ehler, Ursula, 379, 393
Eich, Günter, 213, 214, 216, 258, 261, 268, 269, 302; works by: *Abgelegene Gehöfte* (Remote Farms), 243; *Botschaften des Regens* (Messages of the Rain), 263–64; "Die Häherfeder" (The Jay's Feather), 217; "Inventur" (Inventory), 243, 428; "Latrine," 243; *Maulwürfe* (Moles), 296; "Timetable," 296; *Träume* (Dreams), 264, 270–71
Einstein, Albert, 4
Einstein, Carl, 71–72, 74; works by: *Bebuquin*, 72
el libro libre, 164
Eliot, T. S., 34, 98
emancipatory (function of) literature, 151, 182, 206, 346, 349, 359, 360, 447. *See also* littérature engagée; operative literature; subversiveness
endgame, 349, 386, 388, 395, 425. *See also* apocalypse
Endler, Adolf, 299; works by: *In diesem besseren Land* (In this Better Country, with Karl Mickel), 299; *Schlichtenflotz*, 398
Engelke, Gerrit, 15, 69
Enlightenment, xiv, 8, 97, 112, 119, 123–24, 127, 129, 145, 202, 252, 280, 333, 339, 340, 408, 410
Ensslin, Gudrun, 343, 371